MASS MEDIA LAW

MASS MEDIA LAW

Third Edition

Don R. Pember
University of Washington, Seattle

wcb

Wm. C. Brown Publishers
Dubuque, Iowa

Book Team
Judith A. Clayton *Senior Developmental Editor*
Kevin Pruessner *Designer*
Kevin Campbell *Production Editor*

Wm. C. Brown *Chairman of the Board*
Mark C. Falb *President and Chief Executive Officer*

wcb

Wm. C. Brown Publishers, College Division
Lawrence E. Cremer *President*
James L. Romig *Vice-President, Product Development*
David Wm. Smith *Vice-President, Marketing*
David A. Corona *Vice-President, Production and Design*
E. F. Jogerst *Vice-President, Cost Analyst*
Marcia H. Stout *Marketing Manager*
Linda M. Galarowicz *Director of Marketing Research*
Marilyn A. Phelps *Manager of Design*
William A. Moss *Production Editorial Manager*
Mary M. Heller *Visual Research Manager*
Mavis M. Oeth *Permissions Editor*

CONTENTS

3 LIBEL 98

4 INVASION OF PRIVACY 186

5 ACCESS TO INFORMATION 238

6 PROTECTION OF NEWS SOURCES AND CONTEMPT OF COURT 283

7 FREE PRESS AND FAIR TRIAL 328

11 BROADCAST REGULATION 495

12 REGULATION OF THE MEDIA AS A BUSINESS 562

PREFACE

Each year in every area of mass media law the volume of cases and statutes and executive orders seems to grow and grow. Making sense out of this new law, sorting out the important rulings and decisions from those which are meaningful only to the litigants involved, adding this new material to an already large body of law—these were the challenges of putting together the third edition of *Mass Media Law*. As a media law teacher, I—like all other teachers—go through this process of updating my material every time I teach the media law course. Still, putting new material in a book has an aura of finality about it that makes it a bit more difficult than simply adding some new cases to a lecture.

Courts rarely cooperate with authors or teachers. The Supreme Court of the United States was supposed to resolve the issue of whether the home videotape recording of television programs was a fair use under United States copyright laws. But in July 1983, as final revisions of the manuscript were being made, the high Court asked the parties to reargue the case, and postponed a ruling until 1984, too late to be included in this edition.

Still, this new edition includes scores of new court rulings, many of them important reinforcements for existing law; some are predictors of changes we will soon see in the law, and others are good examples of established legal precedents. I have attempted to strengthen almost every chapter in the book. A slight reorganization of the text preceded the work on the chapters. The chapter entitled "Gathering News and Information" in the second edition of this book has been broken into two new chapters. Both of these chapters, "Access to Information" and "Protection of News Sources and Contempt of Court," have been moved to the middle of the book, after the introductory chapter on the legal system and chapters on freedom of the press, libel, and invasion of privacy.

Chapter 2, "Freedom of the Press," includes new material on so-called First Amendment theories, on book banning, and on new rules regarding permissible time, place, and manner limits. Chapter 3 on "Libel" has been fine-tuned to make it as complete and understandable as possible. A considerable amount of new material has been added to chapter 4 on "Invasion of Privacy," including a section on the right of publicity and whether or not such a right may be passed on to an heir. In the new chapter on "Access to Information," chapter 5, much more material has been included about the federal Freedom of Information Act, and the summaries of state open meeting and open records statutes have been enlarged. The new chapter 6 on "Protection of News Sources and Contempt of Court" ties these two areas of the law together more tightly. The chapter reflects the growing First Amendment source-identity protection being fashioned by many state and lower federal courts. In chapter 7 on "Free Press and Fair Trial" a great deal of new material has been added on the growing problem of closed courtrooms. Chapter 8, "Obscenity" attempts to outline the permissible limits of the growing number of public nuisance and zoning laws being used in an attempt to control the sale, distribution, exhibition of obscene material. As the nation's new copyright statute has gotten older, court decisions have helped clarify its meaning, and many of these decisions are cited in chapter 9. Chapter 10 on "Regulation of Advertising" and chapter 11 on "Broadcast Regulation" both attempt to outline the emerging trends toward deregulation. Current proposals for drastically changing the law in both these areas (but especially broadcasting) are discussed, as is the rationale for these proposals. The existing law is completely outlined as well. The final chapter in the book, "Regulation of the Media as a Business,'" includes new material on joint-operating agreements, reflecting decisions in the recent Seattle case and the U.S. Supreme Court's recent ruling on a Minnesota use-tax law.

The third edition has some other new features as well. There is an outline at the beginning of each chapter listing the major sections in the chapter. These outlines are also included in the table of contents. There are short summaries within the chapters which attempt to highlight the major points from sections of the chapter. This edition also contains a glossary of some common legal terms, and the words contained in the glossary appear in boldface type when they are introduced in the text.

As with earlier editions, the book contains a strong bias. I believe fervently that freedom of expression is probably the single most important human right we enjoy today. I also believe that censorship is anathema to both the democratic form of government and the full development of the human spirit. The book undoubtedly reflects this point of view. But I also believe that journalists are members of the human community and must behave like responsible members of any community. While the book attempts to outline the outer limits of legal behavior, there is also material in the text which suggests that responsible behavior often falls far short of these limits. Each journalist must decide what is and what is not responsible behavior within the limits of the law. This is not a proper task for either the government or for a journalistic association.

As always, many persons are both directly and indirectly responsible for the production of this edition of *Mass Media Law*. Users of the text have provided valuable suggestions, a great many of which have been incorporated into this edition. I would also like to thank Richard Hixson, Rutgers University; W. R. Steng, Oklahoma State University; Allan Larson, Clarion State College; Sherilyn Bennion, Humboldt State University; and Bill Chamberlin, University of North Carolina, for the valuable help they gave me in preparing this revision. My teaching colleagues at the University of Washington, Roger Simpson and Gerald Baldasty, have also provided great help. Jeremy Cohen of the University of Oregon faculty has given me insights in many areas. The publishing team at Wm. C. Brown, most notably Judith Clayton, Kevin Campbell, and Bea Rockstroh, have been very helpful. In the end, the greatest support came from the Pember family, Diann, Alison, and Brian. The third edition of this book is dedicated to these three persons for their help, understanding, and patience.

MASS MEDIA LAW

1 THE AMERICAN LEGAL SYSTEM

Probably no nation is more closely tied to the law than the American Republic. From the 1770s, when in the midst of a war of revolution we attempted to legally justify our separation from the motherland to the 1980s, when citizens of the nation attempt to resolve weighty moral, political, social, and environmental problems through the judicial process, and during the more than two hundred years between, the American people have showed a remarkable faith in the law. One could write a surprisingly accurate history of this nation using reports of court decisions as the only source. Beginning with the sedition cases in the late 1790s which reflected the political turmoil of that era, one could chart the history of the United States from adolescence to maturity. As the frontier expanded in the nineteenth century, citizens used the courts to argue land claims and boundary problems. Civil rights litigation in both the midnineteenth and midtwentieth centuries reflects a people attempting to cope with racial and ethnic diversity. Industrialization brought labor unions, workmen's compensation laws, and child labor laws, all of which resulted in controversies that found their way into the courts. As mass production developed and large manufacturers began to create most of the consumer goods used, judges and juries had to cope with new laws on product safety, honesty in advertising, and consumer complaints.

Americans have protested nearly every war the nation has fought—including the Revolutionary War. The record of these protests is contained in scores of court decisions. And as some young people refuse to register under the selective service laws of the 1980s, their protests will be recorded in judicial records when prosecutions occur. Prohibition and the crime of the twenties and the economic woes of the thirties both left residue in the law. In the United States, as in most other societies, law is a basic part of existence, as necessary for the survival of civilization as are economic systems, political systems, cultural achievement, and the family.

This chapter has two purposes: to acquaint readers with the law and to present a brief outline of the legal system in the United States. Students who study mass media law frequently face the serious difficulty of studying a special area of law without having an understanding of the law and the court system in general, a situation somewhat like a medical student studying neurosurgery before taking work in anatomy, basic medicine, and surgical techniques. While this chapter is not designed to be a comprehensive course in law and the judicial system—such material can better be studied in depth in an undergraduate political science course—it does provide sufficient introduction to understand the remaining eleven chapters of the book.

The chapter opens with a discussion of the law, giving consideration to the five most important sources of the law in the United States, and moves on to the judicial system including both the federal and state court systems. A summary of judicial review and a brief outline of how both criminal and civil lawsuits are started and proceed through the courts are included in the discussion of the judicial system.

SOURCES OF THE LAW

There are almost as many definitions of law as there are people who study the law. Some people say that law is any social norm or any organized or ritualized method of settling disputes. Most writers on the subject insist that it is a bit more complex, that some system of sanctions is required before law exists. John Austin, a nineteenth-century English jurist, defined law as definite rules of human conduct with appropriate sanctions for their enforcement. He added that both the rules and the sanctions must be prescribed by duly constituted human authority. Roscoe Pound, an American legal scholar, has suggested that law is really social engineering—the attempt to order the way people behave. For the purposes of this book it is probably more helpful to consider the law to be a set of rules which attempt to guide human conduct and a set of sanctions which are applied when those rules are violated.

Scholars still debate the genesis of "the law." A question that is more meaningful and easier to answer is, What is the source of American law? There are really five major sources of the law in the United States: the Constitution, the common law, the law of equity, the statutory laws, and the rulings of various executive and administrative bodies and agencies. Historically we can trace American law to Great Britain. As colonizers of much of the North American continent, the British supplied Americans with an outline for both a legal system and a judicial system. In fact, because of the many similarities between British and American law, many people consider the Anglo-American legal system to be a single entity. Today in the United States our federal Constitution is the supreme law of the land. Yet when each of these five sources of law is considered separately, it is more useful to begin with the earliest source of Anglo-American law, the common law.

The Common Law

The **common law,** which developed in England during the two hundred years after the Norman Conquest in the eleventh century, is one of the great legacies of the British people to colonial America. During those two centuries the crude mosaic of Anglo-Saxon customs was replaced by a single system of law worked out by jurists and judges. The system of law became common throughout England; it became the common law. It was also called the common law to distinguish it from the ecclesiastical (church) law prevalent at the time. Initially, the customs of the people were used by the king's courts as the foundation of the law, disputes were resolved according to community custom, and governmental sanction was applied to enforce the resolution. As such, the common law was, and still is, considered "discovered law." It is law that has always existed, much like air and water. When a problem arises, the court's task is to find or discover the proper solution, to seek the common custom of the people. The judge doesn't create the law; he merely finds it, much like a miner finds gold or silver.

This, at least, is the theory of the common law. Perhaps at one point judges themselves believed that they were merely discovering the law when they handed down decisions. As legal problems became more complex and as the law began to be professionally administered (the first lawyers appeared during this era and eventually professional judges), it became clear that the common law reflected not so much the custom of the land as the custom of the court—or more properly, the custom of the judges. While judges continued to look to the past to discover how other courts had decided, given similar facts (precedent is discussed in a moment), many times judges were forced to create the law themselves.

This common law system was the perfect system for the American colonies. Like most Anglo-Saxon institutions, it was a very pragmatic system aimed at settling real problems, not at expounding abstract and intellectually satisfying theories. The common law is an inductive system of law in which a legal rule is arrived at after consideration of a great number of specific instances of cases. (In a deductive system the rules are expounded first and then the court decides the legal situation under the existing rule.) Colonial America was a land of new problems for British and other settlers. The old law frequently did not work. But the common law easily accommodated the new environment. The ability of the common law to adapt to change is directly responsible for its longevity.

Fundamental to the common law is the concept that judges should look to the past and follow earlier court precedents. The Latin expression for the concept is this: *Stare decisis et non quieta movere* ("to stand by past decisions and not disturb things at rest"). **Stare decisis** is the key phrase: let the decision stand. A judge should resolve current problems in the same manner as similar problems were resolved in the past. When Barry Goldwater sued publisher Ralph Ginzburg for publishing charges that the conservative Republican senator was mentally ill, was paranoid, the judge most certainly looked to past decisions to discover whether in previous cases such a charge had been considered defamatory or libelous. There are ample precedents for ruling that a published charge that a person is mentally ill is libelous, and Senator Goldwater won his lawsuit (*Goldwater v. Ginzburg,* 1969).

The Role of Precedent

At first glance one would think that under a system which continually looks to the past the law can never change. What if the first few rulings in a line of cases were bad decisions? Are we saddled with bad law forever? Fortunately, the law does not operate quite in this way. While following **precedent** is the desired state of affairs (many people say that certainty in the law is more important than justice), it is not always the proper way to proceed. To protect the integrity of the common law, judges have developed several means of coping with bad law and with new situations in which the application of old law would result in injustice.

Imagine for a moment that the newspaper in your hometown publishes a picture and story about a twelve-year-old girl who gave birth to a seven-pound son in a local hospital. The mother and father do not like the publicity and sue the newspaper for invasion of privacy. The attorney for the parents finds a precedent (*Barber* v. *Time,* 1942) in which a Missouri court ruled that to photograph a patient in a hospital room against her will and then to publish that picture in a news magazine is an invasion of privacy.

Now does the existence of this precedent mean that the young couple will automatically win their lawsuit? that the court will follow the decision? No, it does not. For one thing, there may be other cases in which courts have ruled that publishing such a picture is not an invasion of privacy. In fact in 1956 in the case of *Meetze* v. *AP,* a South Carolina court made just such a ruling. But for the moment assume that *Barber* v. *Time* is the only precedent. Is the court bound by this precedent? No. The court has several options concerning the 1942 decision.

First, it can *accept* the precedent as law and rule that the newspaper has invaded the privacy of the couple by publishing the picture and story about the birth of their child. Second, the court can *modify* or change the 1942 precedent by arguing that *Barber* v. *Time* was decided more than forty years ago when people were more sensitive about going to a hospital, since a stay in a hospital was often considered to reflect badly on a patient, but that hospitalization is no longer a sensitive matter to most people. Therefore, a rule of law restricting the publication of a picture of a hospital patient is unrealistic, unless the picture is in bad taste or needlessly embarrasses the patient. Then its publication is an invasion of privacy. If not, the publication of such a picture is permissible. In our imaginary case, then, the decision turns on what kind of picture and story the newspaper published: a pleasant picture which flattered the couple? or one that mocked and embarrassed them? If the court rules in this manner, it *modifies* the 1942 precedent, making it correspond to what the judge perceives to be contemporary life.

As a third option the court can argue that *Barber* v. *Time* provides an important precedent for a plaintiff hospitalized because of disease—as Dorothy Barber was. But that in the case before the court the plaintiff was hospitalized to give birth to a baby, a different situation: Giving birth is a voluntary status; catching a disease is not. Consequently the *Barber* v. *Time* precedent does not apply. This practice is called *distinguishing the precedent from the current case,* a very common action.

Finally, the court can *overrule* the precedent. In 1941 the United States Supreme Court overruled a decision made by the Supreme Court in 1918 regarding the right of a judge to use what is called the summary contempt power (*Toledo Newspaper Co.* v. *U.S.,* 1918). This is the power of a judge to charge someone with being in contempt of court, to find him guilty of contempt, and then to punish him for the contempt—all without a jury trial. In *Nye* v. *U.S.* (1941) the high Court said that in 1918 it had been improperly informed as to the intent of a measure passed by Congress in 1831 which authorized the use of the summary power by federal judges. The 1918 ruling was therefore bad, was wrong, and was reversed. (Fuller explanation of summary contempt as it applies to the mass media is given in chapter 6.) The only courts that can overrule the 1942 decision by the Missouri Supreme Court in *Barber* v. *Time* are the Missouri Supreme Court and the United States Supreme Court. Judges in other states can just ignore the *Barber* v. *Time* precedent if they believe it to be a poor decision.

Obviously the preceding discussion oversimplifies the judicial process. Rarely is a court confronted with but a single precedent. And numerous other factors must be taken into account in addition to past case law. In fact, many people talk about the "hunch theory" of jurisprudence which suggests that judges decide a case on the basis of their instincts and then seek to find rational reasons to explain the decision. The imaginary invasion-of-privacy case just discussed demonstrates that the common law can have vitality, that despite the rule of precedent a judge is rarely bound tightly by the past. There is a saying, Every age should be the mistress of its own law. This saying applies to the common law as well as to all other aspects of the legal system.

It must be clear at this point that the common law is not specifically written down someplace for all to see and use. It is instead contained in the hundreds of thousands of decisions handed down by courts over the centuries. Many attempts have been made to summarize the law. Sir Edward Coke compiled and analyzed the precedents of common law in the early seventeenth century. Sir William Blackstone later expanded Coke's work in the monumental *Commentaries on the Law of England*. More recently, in such works as the massive *Restatement of Torts* the task was again undertaken, but on a narrower scale. Despite these compilations, in the eyes of some European attorneys the common law remains "the law nobody knows" because it is not spelled out neatly in a statute book or administrative edict.

Courts began to keep records of their decisions centuries ago. In the thirteenth century unofficial reports of cases began to appear in Year Books, but they were records of court proceedings in which procedural points were clarified for the benefit of legal practitioners, rather than collections of court decisions. The modern concept of fully reporting the written decisions of all courts probably began in 1785 with the publication of the first British Term Reports.

While scholars and lawyers still uncover the common law using the case-by-case method, it is fairly easy today to locate the appropriate cases through a simple system of citation. The cases of a single court (such as the United States Supreme Court or the federal district courts) are collected in a single **case reporter** (such as the *United States Reports* or the *Federal Supplement*). The cases are collected chronologically and fill many volumes. Each case collected has its individual **citation** which reflects the name of the reporter in which the case can be found, the volume of that reporter, and the page on which the case begins (fig. 1.1). For example, the citation for the decision in

Figure 1.1 Reading a case citation

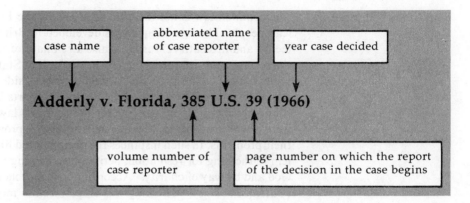

Adderly v. Florida (a freedom-of-speech case) is 385 U.S. 39 (1966). The letters in the middle (U.S.) indicate that the case is in the *United States Reports,* the official government reporter for cases decided by the Supreme Court of the United States. The number 385 refers to the specific volume of the *United States Reports* in which the case is found. The last number (39) gives the page on which the case appears. Finally, 1966 provides the year in which the case was decided. So, *Adderly* v. *Florida* can be found on page 39 of volume 385 of the *United States Reports.*

If you have the correct citation, you can easily find any case you seek. Locating all citations of the cases apropos to a particular problem—such as a libel suit—is a different matter and is a technique taught in law schools. A great many legal encyclopedias, digests, compilations of the common law, books, and articles are used by lawyers to track down the names and citations of the appropriate cases.

There is no better way to sum up the common law than to quote Oliver Wendell Holmes (*The Common Law,* published in 1881):

> The life of the law has not been logic; it has been experience. The felt necessities of the time, the prevalent moral and political theories, intuitions of public policy, avowed or unconscious, even the prejudices which judges share with their fellow-men, have had a good deal more to do than syllogism in determining the rules by which men should be governed. The law embodies the story of a nation's development through many centuries, and it cannot be dealt with as if it contained only the axioms and corollaries of a book of mathematics. In order to know what it is, we must know what it has been, and what it tends to become. . . . The very considerations which judges most rarely mention, and always with an apology, are the secret root from which the law draws all the juices of life. I mean, of course, considerations of what is expedient for the community concerned.

The Law of Equity

The common law is not the only legal legacy the British provided the American people. The law of **equity,** as developed in Britain beginning in the fourteenth and fifteenth centuries, is also a remnant of our British heritage and is the second basic source of the law in the United States. Equity was originally a supplement to the common law and developed side by side with the common law. During the 1300s and 1400s the king's courts became rigid and narrow. Many persons seeking relief under the common law for very real grievances were often turned away because the law did not provide a suitable remedy for their problems. In such instances the disappointed litigant could take his problem to the king for resolution, petitioning the king to "do right for the love of God and by way of charity." According to legal scholar Henry Abraham (*The Judicial Process*), "The king was empowered to mold the law for the sake of 'justice,' to grant the relief prayed for as an act of grace." Soon the chancellor, the king's right-hand man, set up a special office or court to settle the kinds of problems which the king's common law courts could not resolve. At the outset of the hearing the aggrieved party had to establish that he had no adequate remedy under the common law and that he needed a special court to hear his case. The office of the chancellor soon became known as the Court of Chancery. Decisions were made on the basis of conscience or fairness or "equity."

British common law and equity law were American law until the Revolution in 1776. After independence was won, the basic principles of common law in existence before the War of Revolution were kept because the cases remained acceptable precedent. After some hesitation, equity was accepted in much the same way. While present-day United States courts can consider decisions made in British courts after the Revolution, they are not bound by these decisions. For example, when the law of privacy is discussed, it will be seen that the decisions of British courts were often cited by American judges in the early development of privacy law, but were rarely fully accepted.

Initially there was a separate **court of equity, or chancery,** in Great Britain. But today in Great Britain and the United States, the same court hears cases both in equity and under the common law. Depending upon the kind of judicial relief sought by the plaintiff, the judge applies either the common law or the rules of equity.

The rules and procedures under equity are far more flexible than those under the common law. Equity really begins where the common law leaves off. Equity suits are never tried before a jury. Rulings come in the form of **judicial decrees,** not in judgments of yes or no. Decisions in equity are (and were) discretionary on the part of judges. And despite the fact that precedents are also relied upon in the law of equity, judges are free to do what they think is right and fair in a specific case.

Equity provides another advantage for troubled litigants—the restraining order. A judge sitting in equity can order preventive measures as well as remedial ones. Individuals who can demonstrate that they are in peril, or about to suffer a serious irremediable wrong, can usually gain a legal writ such as an injunction or a restraining order to stop someone from doing something. Generally a court issues a temporary restraining order until it can hear arguments from both parties in the dispute and decide whether an injunction should be made permanent.

In 1971 the federal government asked the federal courts to restrain the *New York Times* and the *Washington Post* from publishing what have now become known as the Pentagon Papers (this case is discussed in greater detail in chapter 2). This case is a good example of equity law in action. The government argued that if the purloined documents were published by the two newspapers the nation would suffer irremediable damage; that foreign governments would be reluctant to entrust the United States with their secrets if those secrets might someday be published in the public press; that the enemy would gain valuable defense secrets. The federal government argued further that it would do little good to punish the newspapers after the material had been published since there would be no way to repair the damage. The federal district court temporarily restrained both newspapers from publishing the material while the case was argued—all the way to the Supreme Court of the United States. After two weeks of hearings the high Court finally ruled that publication could continue, that the government failed to prove that the nation would be damaged (*New York Times Co.* v. *U.S.,* 1971).

Prior to the Revolution, Americans were also bound by laws made by their colonial legislatures as well as by the British Parliament. Following independence, the British statutes passed by Parliament were no longer applicable in the United States; instead the residents of the new nation were bound by the laws of their own local, federal, and state legislatures. Legislation is therefore the third great source of United States law.

Statutory Law

Today there are legislative bodies of all shapes and sizes. The common traits they share are that they are popularly elected and that they have the authority to pass laws. In the beginning of our nation, legislation, or statutory law, really did not play a very significant role in the legal system. Certainly many laws were passed, but the bulk of our legal rules were developed from the common law and from equity law. After 1825 statutory law began to play an important role in our legal system, and it was between 1850 and 1900 that a greater percentage of law began to come from legislative acts than from common law court decisions. Today, most American law comes from various legislatures: Congress, state legislatures, city councils, county boards of supervisors, township boards, and so forth. In fact, legislative action produces the greatest volume of American law in the 1980s.

Several important characteristics of statutory law can best be understood by contrasting them with common law. First, **statutes** tend to deal with problems affecting society or large groups of people, in contrast to common law, which usually deals with smaller, individual problems. (Some common law rulings affect large groups of persons, but this occurrence is rare.) It should also be noted in this connection the importance of not confusing common law with constitutional law. Certainly when judges interpret the Constitution they make policy which affects us all. However, it should be kept in mind that the Constitution is a legislative document voted upon by the people and is not "discovered law" or "judge-made law."

Second, statutory law can anticipate problems, and common law cannot. For example, a state legislature can pass a statute which prohibits publication of the school records of a student without prior consent of the student. Under the common law the problem cannot be resolved until a student's record has been published in a newspaper or broadcast on television and the student brings action against the medium to recover damages for the injury incurred.

Third, the criminal laws in the United States are all statutory laws—common law crimes no longer exist in this country and have not since 1812. Common law rules are not precise enough to provide the kind of notice needed to protect a criminal defendant's right to due process of law.

Fourth, statutory law is collected in codes and law books, instead of in reports as in the common law. When a proposal or bill is adopted by the legislative branch and approved by the executive branch, it becomes law and is integrated into the proper section of a municipal code, a state code, or whatever. However, this does not mean that some very important statutory law cannot be found in the case reporters.

Passage of a law is rarely the final word on the subject. Courts become involved in the process of determining what that law means. While a properly constructed statute sometimes needs little interpretation by the courts, judges are frequently called upon to rule upon the exact meaning of ambiguous phrases and words. The resulting process is called **statutory construction** and is a very important part of the law. Even the simplest kind of statement often needs interpretation. For example, a prohibition stating "it is illegal to distribute an obscene newspaper" is filled with ambiguity. What does *distribution* mean? Can an obscene newspaper be sent through the mail? distributed from house to house? passed out on street corners? Are all of these actions prohibited? What constitutes a newspaper? Is any printed matter a newspaper? Is any printed matter published regularly a newspaper? Are mimeographed sheets and photocopied newsletters considered newspapers? Of course, implicit is the classic question with which courts have wrestled in this country for nearly a century, What is obscenity?

Usually a legislature tries to leave some kind of trail to help a judge find out what the law means. For when judges rule on the meaning of a statute, they are supposed to determine what the legislature meant when it passed the law (the legislative intent), not what they think it should mean. Minutes of committee hearings in which the law was discussed, legislative staff reports, and reports of debate on the floor can all be used to help a judge determine the legislative intent. Therefore when lawyers deal with statutes, they frequently are forced to search the case reporters to find out how the courts interpreted a law in which they are interested.

Constitutional Law
Great Britain does not have a written **constitution.** The United States does have a written constitution, and it is an important source of our law. In fact, there are many constitutions in this country: the federal Constitution, state constitutions, city charters, and so forth. All of these documents accomplish the same ends. First, they provide the plan for the organization of the government. Next, they outline the duties, responsibilities, and powers of the various elements of government. Finally, they usually guarantee certain basic rights to the people, such as freedom of speech and freedom to peaceably assemble.

Legislative bodies may enact statutes rather easily by a majority vote. It is far more difficult to adopt or change a constitution. State constitutions are approved or changed by a direct vote of the people. It is even more difficult to change the federal Constitution. An amendment may be proposed by a vote of two-thirds of the members of both the United States House of Representatives and the Senate. Alternatively, two-thirds of the state legislatures can call for a constitutional convention for proposing amendments. Once proposed, the amendments must be approved either by three-fourths of the state legislatures or by three-fourths of the constitutional conventions called in all the states. Congress decides upon which method of ratification or approval is to be used. Because the people have an unusually direct voice in the approval and change of a constitution, constitutions are considered the most important source of United States law.

One Supreme Court justice described a constitution as a kind of yardstick against which all the other actions of government must be measured to determine whether the actions are permissible. The United States Constitution is the supreme law of the land. Any law or other constitution which conflicts with the United States Constitution is unenforceable. A state constitution plays the same role for a state: a statute passed by the Michigan legislature and signed by the governor of that state is clearly unenforceable if it conflicts with the Michigan constitution. And so it goes for all levels of constitutions.

While constitutions tend to be short and infrequently amended, the process of determining what specific areas of these documents mean and whether a specific law or government action violates a certain constitutional provision is a laborious one, usually taking hours and hours and days and days of court time. Consequently, with the exception of the bare-bone documents themselves, the case reporters are once again the repository for the constitutional law which governs the United States.

Twenty-six amendments are appended to the United States Constitution. The first ten of these are known as the Bill of Rights and provide a guarantee of certain basic human rights to all citizens. Included are freedom of speech and freedom of the press, rights you will come to understand more fully in future chapters.

Administrative Rules

By the latter part of the nineteenth century in the United States, not only had the simple idyllic life of the eighteenth century slipped away, but also the job of governing had become much more complex. Congress was being asked to resolve questions going far beyond such simple matters as budgets, wars, treaties, and the like. Technology created new kinds of problems for the Congress to resolve. Many such issues were complex and required specialized knowledge and expertise which the Congress lacked and could not easily acquire, had it wanted to. Federal agencies were therefore created to deal with these problems.

For example, the flow of natural gas through long pipelines which traversed the nation created numerous disputes. Since questions concerning use of these pipelines fell within the commerce power of the Congress, that deliberative body was given the task of resolving this complex issue. But pipeline regulation involved serious technical matters and competent regulation required a high level of expertise. To deal with these problems, Congress created the first **administrative agency,** the Interstate Commerce Commission (ICC). This agency was established by legislation and funded by Congress. Its members were appointed by the president and approved by the Congress. Each member served a fixed term in office. The agency was independent of the Congress, the president, and the courts. Its task was (and is) to regulate commerce between the states, a matter which concerned pipelines, shipping, and transportation. The members of the board presumably were somewhat expert in the area before appointment and of course became more so during the course of their term.

Today hundreds of such agencies exist at both federal and state levels. Each agency undertakes to deal with a specific set of problems which are too technical or too large for the legislative branch to handle. Typical is the Federal Communications Commission (FCC) which was created by Congress in 1934. Its task is to regulate broadcasting in the United States, a job which Congress has really never attempted. Its members must be citizens of the United States and are appointed by the president. The single stipulation is that at any one time no more than three of the five individuals on the commission can be from the same political party. The Senate must confirm the appointments.

Congress sketched the broad framework for the regulation of broadcasting in the Federal Communications Act of 1934, and this act is used by the agency as its basic regulatory guidelines. The agency also creates much law itself in administration of the 1934 Act. In interpreting provisions, handing down rulings, developing specific guidelines, and the like, the FCC has developed a sizable body of regulations which bind broadcasters. For example, the Federal Communications Act of 1934 states that broadcasters must operate in the public interest, convenience, or necessity. The FCC holds that one aspect of operation in the public interest is to air all sides of a controversial issue to make certain that the audience has access to the full range of opinion on the topic. This general rule gradually emerged during the past forty years as the Fairness Doctrine, a full-blown set of rules created by the FCC which carry the force of law. Broadcasters who fail to live up to these rules can be fined or (rarely) have their license to broadcast taken away.

Persons dissatisfied with rulings by the FCC can go to court and seek a reversal of the commission action. But courts are strictly limited in their power when reviewing decisions by administrative agencies, and can overturn a commission ruling or any other action by an administrative agency in only these limited circumstances: (1) if the original act which established the commission is unconstitutional, (2) if the commission exceeds its authority, (3) if the commission violates its own rules, or (4) if there is no evidentiary basis whatsoever to support the ruling. The reason for these limitations is simple: These agencies were created to bring expert knowledge to bear on complex problems, and the entire purpose for their creation would be defeated if judges with no special expertise in a given area can reverse an agency ruling merely because they have a different solution to a problem.

The case reporters contain some law created by the administrative agencies, but the reports which each of these agencies themselves publish contain much more such law. These reports are also arranged on a case-by-case basis in chronological order. A citation system similar to that used for the case reporters is used in these reports.

As the problems which governments must deal with become more complicated and more numerous, administrative agencies seem to proliferate, and more and more of our law comes from such agencies.

There are other sources of American law. Executives—a governor, a president, a mayor—have the power to make law in some circumstances through executive order. The five sources just discussed—common law, law of equity, statutory law, Constitutional law, and rules and regulations by administrative agencies—are the most important, however, and are of most concern in this book. First Amendment problems fall under the purview of constitutional law. Libel and invasion of privacy are matters generally dealt with by the common law and the law of equity. Obscenity laws in this country are statutory provisions (although this fact is frequently obscured by the hundreds of court cases in which judges attempt to define the meaning of obscenity). And of course the regulation of broadcasting and advertising falls primarily under the jurisdiction of administrative agencies.

While this section provides a basic outline of the law and is not comprehensive, the information is sufficient to make upcoming material on mass media law understandable.

Summary

There are five important sources of American law. The common law is the oldest source of our law, having developed in England more than six hundred years ago. The law became common throughout Great Britain and reflected the customs of the people. It was easily transported to the New World, and its pragmatic philosophy was highly useful on the rapidly developing North American continent. Fundamental to the common law is the concept that judges should look to the past and follow earlier court rulings called precedents. *Stare decisis:* "let the decision stand" is a key concept. But judges have developed the means to change or adapt the common law by modifying, distinguishing, or overruling precedent case law. The common law is not written down in a law book, but is collected in volumes which contain the reports of legal decisions. Each case is given its own legal identity through a system of numbered citations.

Equity law, the second source of American law, developed because in some instances the common law was simply too rigid to fairly resolve the real grievances of British subjects. The rules and procedures of equity are far more flexible than those of the common law and permit a judge (equity cases are never heard before a jury) to fashion a solution to unique or unusual problems. A court is permitted under equity law to restrain an individual or a corporation or even a government from taking an action. Under the common law a court can only attempt to compensate the injured party for the damage which results from the action.

Today the greatest volume of American law is generated by Congress, legislatures, city and county councils, and myriad other legislative bodies. This legislation is called statutory law and is the third important source of American law. All criminal laws are statutes. Also, statutes usually deal with problems which affect great numbers of people, and statutes can anticipate problems, whereas the common law cannot. All statutes are collected in codes or statute books. Courts become involved in the development of statutes when they are called upon to interpret the meaning of the words and phrases contained in a statute. Most American law is generated by legislative bodies.

Constitutions, the fourth source of our law, take precedence over all other American law. The United States Constitution is the supreme law of the land. Other laws, whether they spring from common law, equity, legislative bodies, or administrative agencies, cannot conflict with the provisions of the Constitution. Courts are often called upon to interpret the meaning of the provisions of our constitutions (one federal and fifty state constitutions) and through this process can often make these seemingly rigid legal prescriptions adaptable to contemporary problems.

There are thousands of administrative agencies, boards, and commissions in the nation which produce rules and regulations. This administrative law, the fifth source of American law, usually deals with technical and complicated matters requiring levels of expertise which normally members of traditional legislative bodies do not possess. Members of these agencies and commissions are usually appointed by presidents or by governors or mayors, and the agencies are supervised and funded by legislative bodies. Their tasks are narrowly defined, and their rulings, while they carry the force of law, can always be appealed.

THE JUDICIAL
SYSTEM

This section gives an introduction to the court system in the United States. Since the judicial branch of our three-part government is the field upon which most of the battles involving communications law are fought, an understanding of the judicial system is essential.

It is technically improper to talk about the American judicial system. There are fifty-one different judicial systems in the United States, one for the federal government and one for each of the fifty states. While each of these systems is somewhat different from all the others, the similarities among the fifty-one systems are much more important than the differences. Each of the systems is divided into two distinct sets of courts, trial courts and appellate courts. Each judicial system is established by a constitution, federal or state. In each system the courts act as the third branch of a common triumvirate of government: a legislative branch which makes the law, an executive branch which enforces the law, and a judicial branch which interprets the law.

Facts versus the Law

Common to all judicial systems is the distinction between trial courts and appellate courts, and it is important to understand this distinction. Each level of court has its own function: basically, **trial courts** are fact-finding courts and **appellate courts** are law-reviewing courts. Trial courts are the courts of first instance, the place where nearly all cases begin. Juries sit in trial courts, but never in appellate courts. Trial courts are empowered to consider both the facts and the law in a case. Appellate courts consider only the law. The difference between facts and law is significant. The facts are what happened. The law is what should be done about the facts.

The difference between facts and law can be emphasized by looking at an imaginary libel suit that might result when the *River City Sentinel* publishes a story about costs at the Sandridge Hospital.

Ineffective Medications Given to Ill, Injured
SANDRIDGE HOSPITAL OVERCHARGING PATIENTS ON PHARMACY COSTS

Scores of patients at the Sandridge Hospital have been given ineffective medications, a three-week investigation at the hospital has revealed. In addition, many of those patients were overcharged for the medicine they received.

The *Sentinel* has learned that many of the prescription drugs sold to patients at the hospital had been kept beyond the manufacturer's recommended storage period.

Many drugs stored in the pharmacy (as late as Friday) had expiration dates as old as six months ago. Drug manufacturers have told the *Sentinel* that medication used beyond the expiration date, which is stamped clearly on most packages, may not have the potency or curative effects that fresher pharmaceuticals have.

Hospital spokesmen deny giving patients any of the expired drugs, but sources at the hospital say it is impossible for administrators to guarantee that none of the dated drugs were sold to patients.

In addition, the investigation by the *Sentinel* revealed that patients who were sold medications manufactured by Chaos Pharmaceuticals were charged on the basis of 1982 price lists despite the fact that the company lowered prices significantly in 1983.

The Sandridge Hospital sued the newspaper for libel. When the case got to court, the first thing that had to be done was to establish what the facts were—what happened. Both the hospital and the newspaper presented evidence, witnesses, and arguments to support its version of the facts. Several issues had to be resolved. In addition to the general questions of whether the story had been published and whether the hospital had been identified in the story, the hospital had to supply evidence that its reputation had been injured, that its good name had been damaged, and that the newspaper staff had been negligent. The newspaper relied on the truth as its defense. It presented evidence to document its charges that the hospital overcharged patients, that the medications were stale, that expired medicine is less effective than fresh medicine, and that patients did receive the stale medicine.

All this testimony and evidence establishes the factual record—what actually took place at the hospital. When there is conflicting evidence, the jury decides whom to believe (in the absence of a jury, the judge makes the decision). Suppose that the evidence presented by the newspaper convinced the jury that the hospital did possess expired drugs, that patients were charged 1982 prices for some medications, and that most authorities do regard expired medication to be less beneficial than fresher drugs. Given the factual record of the case, what is the law? Had the newspaper really proved its charges against the hospital? Had it proved the truth? A simple explanation is that in order to successfully use the defense of truth (defense of truth is discussed further in chapter 3) the newspaper must prove the substance of its charges, the heart of its allegations. In this case, a judge would probably rule that the newspaper had not proved the substance of its charges: there was no evidence that any patients had been given expired medication. Therefore, the hospital wins the suit. If the newspaper is unhappy with the verdict, it can appeal.

In an appeal, the appellate court does not reconsider the factual record. No more testimony is taken. No more witnesses are called. The factual record established by the jury at the trial stands and cannot be reconsidered. What the appellate court can do is to decide whether the law has been applied properly in light of the facts. It is possible that in this case the appellate court would rule that in establishing that the drugs were stored in the hospital pharmacy the newspaper has in fact established the substance of its charge: that it is inconceivable that patients had not received the expired medicine and that the trial judge erred in applying the law. Perhaps the judge erred in allowing certain testimony into evidence, or he refused to allow a certain witness to testify. Nevertheless, in reaching an opinion the appellate court considers only the law; the factual record established at the trial stands.

What if new evidence is found or a previously unknown witness comes forth to testify? If the appellate court believes that the new evidence is important, it can order a new trial. However, the court itself does not hear the evidence. These facts are given at a new trial.

The important differences between trial and appellate courts have now been pointed out. Other differences will undoubtedly emerge as the specific structure of each court system is discussed.

In the discussion that follows, the federal court system and its methods of operating are considered first, and then some general observations about state court systems are given, based on the discussion of the federal system.

The Federal Court System

The Congress has the authority to abolish every federal court in the land save the Supreme Court of the United States. The United States Constitution calls for but a single federal court, the Supreme Court. Article III, Section 1 states: "The judicial power of the United States shall be vested in one Supreme Court." The Constitution also gives Congress the right to establish inferior courts if it deems these courts to be necessary. And Congress has, of course, established a fairly complex system of courts to complement the Supreme Court.

The jurisdiction of the federal courts is also outlined in Article III of the Constitution. The jurisdiction of a court is its legal right to exercise its authority. Briefly, federal courts can hear the following cases:

1. Cases that arise under the United States Constitution, United States law, and United States treaties
2. Cases that involve ambassadors and ministers, duly accredited, of a foreign country
3. Cases that involve admiralty and maritime law
4. Cases that involve controversies when the United States is a party to the suit
5. Cases that involve controversies between two or more states
6. Cases that involve controversies between a state and a citizen of another state (we must remember that the Eleventh Amendment to the Constitution states that a state must give its permission before it can be sued)
7. Cases that involve a controversy between citizens of different states

While special federal courts have jurisdiction which goes beyond this broad outline, these are the circumstances in which a federal court may normally exercise its authority. Of the seven categories of cases just listed, categories one and seven account for most of the cases getting to federal court. For example, disputes which involve violations of the myriad federal laws and disputes which involve constitutional rights such as the First Amendment are heard in federal courts. Also, disputes between citizens of different states—what is known as a diversity of citizenship matter—are heard in federal courts. It is very common, for example, for libel suits and invasion of privacy suits against publishing companies to start in federal courts rather than in state courts. If a citizen of Arizona should be libeled by *Time* magazine, the case would very likely be tried in a federal court in the state of Arizona, rather than in a state court. The magazine would look at the tribunal as a more neutral court. But the federal court would still follow Arizona law when hearing the case.

The Supreme Court

The Supreme Court of the United States is the oldest federal court, having been in operation since 1789. The Constitution does not establish the number of justices who will sit on the high Court. That task is left to the Congress. In 1789 the Congress passed the first judiciary act and established the membership of the high Court at six: a chief justice and five associate justices. This number was increased to seven in 1807, to nine in 1837, and to ten in 1863. The Supreme Court had ten members until 1866 when Congress ruled that only seven justices would sit on the high tribunal. Since 1869 the Supreme Court has had eight associate justices and the Chief Justice of the United States. (Note the title: not Chief Justice of the Supreme Court, but the Chief Justice of the United States.)

No attempt to change the size of the Court has occurred since the 1930s when President Franklin Roosevelt, unhappy about the manner in which it treated some of his New Deal legislation, proposed enlarging the Court. Publicly, Roosevelt argued that serving on the Court was arduous and that the work load for the older judges had become onerous. He sought the power to appoint one new justice for every justice over seventy years of age, to a limit of fifteen justices on the high Court. The public response to the president's plan was strongly negative, and the measure never came to a vote in the Senate. But the president won in the end when James McReynolds, one of the Court's staunchest New Deal foes, retired and Roosevelt was able to appoint a jurist more of his own philosophical bent as a replacement. In addition, following the announcement of the president's judiciary plan, the high Court handed down a ruling which seemed to indicate that one of the formerly anti-New Deal justices (Owen Roberts) had changed his position regarding the president's social and economic programs. Despite a political defeat, Roosevelt got his legislation, and in the end he appointed nine men to the high Court, more than any president except Washington.

The Supreme Court exercises both original and appellate jurisdictions. Under its **original jurisdiction,** which is established in the Constitution, the Supreme Court is the first court to hear a case and acts much like a trial court in ascertaining facts and deciding law. But original jurisdiction is rarely exercised. Legal scholar Henry Abraham reports in *The Judicial Process* that between 1789 and 1979, the high Court rendered decisions under the original jurisdiction clause of the Constitution in only one hundred forty-eight cases. Because the high Court is strictly limited by the Constitution to exercise its original jurisdiction in a few specific instances, and because Congress has given the lower federal courts concurrent jurisdiction with the Supreme Court in those specific instances, few persons begin their lawsuits at the Supreme Court.

The primary task of the Supreme Court is as an appellate tribunal, hearing cases already decided by lower federal courts and state courts of last resort. The appellate jurisdiction of the Supreme Court is established by the Congress, not by the Constitution. A case will come before the Supreme Court of the United States for review in one of two principal ways; on a direct appeal or by way of a writ of certiorari. The certification process is a third way for a case to get to the high Court, but this process is rarely used today. In fact, according to Abraham the Court hears more cases via its original jurisdiction than through certification. A case may be certified for review when a lower federal court, such as a court of appeal, seeks instructions from the Supreme Court on a legal question. For example, in 1963 the Court of Appeals in the Fifth Circuit certified a question to the Supreme Court about its power to hold Mississippi Governor Ross Barnett in contempt of court. The lower court wanted to know whether its contempt citation against Barnett and Lt. Governor Paul Johnson, Jr., required a trial by jury. The high Court said no (*U.S.* v. *Barnett*).

In some instances a litigant has a right, guaranteed by federal statute, to carry an appeal to the Supreme Court. This is called a **direct appeal.** In what kinds of instances? Here are three examples.

1. A federal court of appeals has ruled that a state statute violates the United States Constitution or conflicts with a federal law. The state has a right to appeal this decision to the Supreme Court.
2. A federal court declares an act of Congress to be unconstitutional. The United States government has a right to appeal this ruling to the United States Supreme Court.
3. A state court rules that a state law violates the United States Constitution. The state has a right to appeal that decision to the United States Supreme Court.

On the basis of what has been said so far, it appears that the Supreme Court must hear a case that comes to it on direct appeal. This is not true. Since 1928 the Supreme Court has had the right to reject such an appeal "for want of a substantial federal question." About 90 percent of the cases that come before the high Court through the direct appeal process are rejected. So despite the fact that a litigant may appear to have a statutory right to appeal a decision by a lower court to the Supreme Court, the high Court has the power to reject the appeal if the members of the tribunal do not feel that significant legal issues have been presented in the lawsuit.

The much more common way for a case to reach the nation's high Court is via a **writ of certiorari.** No one has the right to such a writ. It is a discretionary order issued by the Court when it feels that an important legal question has been raised. Litigants using both the federal court system and the various state court systems can seek a writ of certiorari. The most important requirement which must be met before the Court will even consider issuing a writ is that a petitioner exhaust all other legal remedies. While there are a few exceptions, this generally means that if a case begins in a federal district court, the trial level court, the **petitioner** must first seek a review by a United States Court of Appeals before bidding for a writ of certiorari. The writ can be sought if the Court of Appeals refuses to hear the case or sustains the verdict against the petitioner. All other legal remedies have then been exhausted. In state court systems every legal appeal possible must be made within the state before seeking a review by the United States Supreme Court. This usually means going through a trial court, an intermediate appeals court, and finally the state supreme court.

When the Supreme Court grants a writ of certiorari, it is ordering the lower court to send the records to the high Court for review. Each request for a writ is considered by the entire nine-member Court, and an affirmative vote of four justices is required before the writ can be granted. The high Court rejects most of the petitions it receives. Again, work load is the key factor.

Certain important issues must be decided each term, and the justices do not have the time to consider thoroughly most cases for which an appeal is sought. Term after term, suggestions to reduce the Court's work load are made. Chief Justice Burger has on several occasions argued that a second high court, a court just below the Supreme Court, is needed to screen out less important cases. Theoretically, the Supreme Court would then have more time to deliberate on really important matters, while the second-level court would arbitrate less cosmic problems.

But such plans have got a cool reception from attorneys, Congress, and the public. All citizens believe that they should have the right to appeal to the Supreme Court: even if the appeal will probably be rejected, and even if the Court may never hear the case, the right to make the appeal should remain.

Hearing a Case

While the operation of state and federal appellate courts vary from state to state and court to court, these courts have a good deal in common in the way in which they hear and decide a case. So by examining how the Supreme Court operates, we can also learn quite a bit about how other appellate courts operate.

The first thing the Court does is to decide whether it will hear a case, either on appeal or via a writ of certiorari. Once a case is accepted, the attorneys for both sides have the greatest burden of work during the next few months. Oral argument on the case is scheduled, and both sides are expected to submit **legal briefs**—their legal arguments—for the Court to study before the hearing. The greatest burden at this point is on the party seeking appeal since he or she must provide the Court with a complete record of the lower court proceedings in the case. Included are trial transcripts, lower-court rulings, and all sorts of other materials.

Arguing a matter all the way to the Supreme Court takes a long time, often as long as five years—sometimes longer—from initiation of the suit until the Court gives its ruling. James Hill brought suit in New York in 1953 against Time, Inc., for invasion of privacy. The United States Supreme Court made the final ruling in the case in 1967 (*Time v. Hill,* 1967). Even at that the matter would not have ended had Hill decided to go back to trial, which the Supreme Court said he must if he wanted to collect damages. He chose not to.

After the nine justices study the briefs (or at least the summaries provided by their law clerks), the **oral argument** is held. For a generation schooled on Perry Mason and Owen Marshall, oral argument before the Supreme Court (or indeed before any court) must certainly seem strange. For one thing, the attorneys are strictly limited as to how much they may say. Each side is given a brief amount of time, often no more than an hour or ninety minutes, to

The Bibliography at the end of each chapter supplies additional information about the sources and legal cases cited in the text. An explanation of how to locate a given case using its citation is provided on pages 8–9.

present its arguments. In important cases "friends of the court" (**amici curiae**) are allowed to present briefs and to participate for thirty minutes in the oral arguments. For example, the American Civil Liberties Union often seeks the friend status in important civil rights cases.

Deciding a Case

After the oral argument, which of course is given in open court with visitors welcome, is over, the members of the high Court move behind closed doors to undertake their deliberations. No one is allowed in the discussion room except members of the Court itself—no clerks, no bailiffs, no secretaries. The discussion, which often is held several days after the arguments are completed, is opened by the Chief Justice. Discussion time is limited, and by being the first speaker the Chief Justice is in a position to set the agenda, so to speak, for each case—to raise what he thinks are the key issues. Next to speak is the justice with the most seniority, and after him or her, the next most senior justice. The Court usually has an average of seventy-five items or cases to dispose of during one conference or discussion day; consequently brevity is valued. Each justice has just a few moments to state his thoughts on the matter. After discussion, a tentative vote is taken and recorded by each justice in a small, hinged, lockable docket book. In the voting procedure the junior justice votes first; the Chief Justice, last.

Under the United States legal system, which is based so heavily upon the concept of court participation in developing and interpreting the law, a simple yes-or-no answer to any legal question is hardly sufficient. More important than the vote, for the law if not for the **litigant,** are the reasons for the decision. Therefore the Supreme Court and all courts which deal with questions of law prepare what are called opinions in which the reasons, or rationale, for the decision are given. One of the justices voting in the majority is asked to write what is called the **Court's opinion.** If the Chief Justice is in the majority, he or she selects the author of the opinion. If he or she is not, the senior associate justice in the majority makes the assignment. Either the Chief Justice or the senior associate justice can write the opinion.

Opinion writing is a difficult task. Getting five or six or seven people to agree to yes or no is one thing; getting them to agree upon why they say yes or no is something else. The **opinion** must therefore be carefully constructed. After it is drafted, it is circulated among all Court members, who make suggestions or even draft their own opinions. The opinion writer incorporates as many of these ideas as possible into the opinion to retain its majority backing. While all this is done in secret, historians have learned that rarely do court opinions reflect solely the work of the writer. They are more often a conglomeration of paragraphs and pages and sentences from the opinions of several justices.

A justice in agreement with the majority who cannot be convinced to join in backing the Court's opinion has the option of writing what is called a

concurring opinion. This means that the justice agrees with the outcome of the decision, but does so for different reasons than those of the majority.

Justices who disagree with the majority can also write an opinion, either individually or as a group, called a **dissenting opinion.** Dissenting opinions are very important. Sometimes, after the Court has made a decision, it becomes clear that the decision was not the proper one. The issue is often litigated again by other parties who use the arguments in the dissenting opinion as the basis for a legal claim. If enough time passes, if the composition of the Court changes sufficiently, or if the Court members change their minds, the high Court can swing to the views of the original dissenters. This is what happened in the case of *Nye* v. *U.S.* (noted earlier) when the high Court repudiated a stand it had taken in 1918 and supported instead the opinion of Justice Oliver Wendell Holmes, who had vigorously dissented in the earlier decision.

Finally, it is possible for a justice to concur with the majority in part and to dissent in part as well. That is, the justice may agree with some of the things the majority says, but disagree with other aspects of the ruling. This kind of stand by a justice, as well as an ordinary concurrence, frequently fractures the Court in such a way that in a six-to-three ruling only three persons subscribe to the Court's opinion, two others concur, the sixth concurs in part and dissents in part, and three others dissent. Such splits by the members of the Court have seemingly become more common in recent years. In several key mass media law decisions (*Gannett* v. *DePasquale,* 1979 and *Island Trees* v. *Pico,* 1982, for example) such disarray has left substantial confusion among persons vitally interested in the issues.

The Supreme Court can dispose of a case in two other ways. A **per curiam** ("by the court") **opinion** can be prepared. This is an unsigned opinion drafted by one or more members of the majority and published as the Court's opinion. Per curiam opinions are not common, but neither are they rare.

Finally, the high Court can dispose of a case with a **memorandum order**— that is, it just announces the vote without giving an opinion. Or the order cites an earlier Supreme Court decision as the reason for affirming or reversing a lower court ruling. This device is quite common today as the work load of the high Court increases. In cases with little legal importance and in cases in which the issues were really resolved earlier, the Court saves a good deal of time by just announcing its decision.

One final matter in regard to voting remains for consideration: What happens in case of a tie vote? When all nine members of the Court are present, a tie vote is technically impossible. However, if there is a vacancy on the Court, only eight justices hear a case. Even when the Court is full, a particular justice may disqualify himself from hearing a case. When a vote ends in a tie the decision of the lower court is affirmed. No opinion is written. It is almost as if the Supreme Court had never heard the case.

During the circulation of an opinion justices have the opportunity to change sides, to change their vote. The number and membership in the majority may shift. It is not impossible for the majority to become the minority if one of the dissenters writes a particularly powerful dissent which attracts support from members originally opposed to his opinion. This event is probably very rare. Nevertheless, a vote of the Court is not final until it is announced on decision day, or opinion day. The authors of the various opinions—court opinions, concurrences, and dissents—publicly read or summarize their views. Printed copies of these documents are handed out to the parties involved and to the press.

Are lower courts bound to follow United States Supreme Court decisions? The answer to that is yes and no. Since the Supreme Court is the supervisor of the federal courts, lower federal courts are bound closely by the high Court rulings. Still, occasionally lower federal courts are reluctant to follow the lead of the high Court.

The Supreme Court is not empowered to make a final judgment when it reviews a state court decision. All it can do, as Henry Abraham writes in *The Judicial Process,* is "to decide the federal issue and remand it to the state court below for final judgment 'not inconsistent with this opinion.' " However, new issues can be raised at the lower level by the state courts, and the opportunity to evade the ruling of the Supreme Court always exists. One study undertaken by the *Harvard Law Review* showed that of one hundred seventy-five cases remanded to state courts between 1941 and 1951, twenty-two of the litigants who won at the high Court level ultimately lost in the state courts following the high Court ruling. As pointed out earlier, because courts operate on a case-by-case basis the opportunity for defiance beyond the instant case is real.

Finally, courts have no real way to enforce decisions and must depend upon other government agencies for enforcement of its rulings. The job normally falls to the executive branch. If perchance the president decides not to enforce a Supreme Court ruling, no legal force exists to compel him to do so. If former President Nixon, for example, had chosen to refuse to turn over the infamous Watergate tapes after the Court ruled against his arguments of executive privilege, no other agency could have forced him to give up those tapes.

At the same time, there is one force that usually works to see that court decisions are carried out: it is that vague force called public opinion or what political scientists call "legitimacy." People believe in the judicial process: they have faith that what the courts do is probably right. This does not mean that they always agree with court decisions, but they do agree that the proper way to settle disputes is through the judicial process. Jurists help engender this spirit or philosophy by acting in a temperate manner. The Supreme Court, for example, has developed means which permit it to avoid having to answer highly controversial questions in which an unpopular decision could weaken its perceived "legitimacy." The justices might call the dispute "a political question," a **nonjusticiable matter,** or they may refuse to hear a case on other grounds. When the members of the Court sense that the public is ready to accept a ruling, they may take on a controversial issue. School desegregation is a good example. In 1954 the Supreme Court ruled in *Brown* v. *Board of Education* that segregated public schools violated the United States Constitution. The foundation for this ruling had been laid by a decade of less momentous desegregation decisions and executive actions. By 1954 the nation was prepared for the ruling, and it was generally accepted, even in most parts of the South. The legitimacy of a court's decisions, then, often rests upon prudent use of the judicial power.

Other Federal Courts

The United States Supreme Court is the most visible, perhaps the most glamorous (if that word is appropriate), of the federal courts. But it is not the only federal court nor even the busiest. There are two lower echelons of federal courts, plus various special courts, within the federal system. These special courts, such as the Court of Military Appeals, Court of Claims, Customs Court, and so forth, were created by the Congress to handle special kinds of problems.

Most business in the federal system begins and ends in a district court. This court was created by Congress by the Federal Judiciary Act of 1789, and today in the United States there are nearly one hundred such courts staffed by 515 judges. Every state has at least one United States district court. Some states are divided into two districts: an eastern and western district or a northern and southern district. Individual districts often have more than one judge, sometimes many more than one. The Southern District of New York (a veritable hotbed of litigation), for example, has twenty-seven judges at work full time. Other metropolitan areas frequently have six or eight district judges.

When there is a jury trial, the case is heard in a district court. It has been estimated that about half the cases in United States district courts are heard by a jury.

At the intermediate level in the federal judiciary are the twelve United States courts of appeal. These courts were also created by the Federal Judiciary Act of 1789. Until 1948 these courts were called circuit courts of appeal, a reflection of the early years of the republic when the justices of the Supreme Court "rode the circuit" and presided at the courts-of-appeal hearings. While the title Circuit Courts of Appeal is gone, the nation is still divided into "circuits," each of which is served by one court of appeal.

First Circuit: Maine, Massachusetts, New Hampshire, Rhode Island, and Puerto Rico
Second Circuit: Connecticut, New York, and Vermont
Third Circuit: Delaware, New Jersey, Pennsylvania, and Virgin Islands

Fourth Circuit: Maryland, North Carolina, South Carolina, Virginia,
    and West Virginia
Fifth Circuit: Texas, Mississippi, and Louisiana
Sixth Circuit: Kentucky, Michigan, Ohio, and Tennessee
Seventh Circuit: Illinois, Indiana, and Wisconsin
Eighth Circuit: Arkansas, Iowa, Minnesota, Missouri, Nebraska, North
    Dakota, and South Dakota
Ninth Circuit: Alaska, Arizona, California, Hawaii, Idaho, Montana,
    Nevada, Oregon, Washington, Guam, and Northern Mariana Islands
Tenth Circuit: Colorado, Kansas, New Mexico, Utah, Oklahoma, and
    Wyoming
Eleventh Circuit: Alabama, Florida, Georgia, and the Canal Zone

The twelfth circuit is unnumbered and is known as the Court of Appeals for the District of Columbia.

The courts of appeal are appellate courts, which means that they hear appeals from lower courts and other agencies exclusively. These courts are the last stop for nine out of ten cases in the federal system. Each circuit has nine or more judges. While all judges can hear a single case—**sitting en banc** it is called—more commonly three judges hear a case. It is possible for two judges to hear a case, but this is unusual. In a case of great importance all the judges hear the case, as in the Pentagon Papers case, when in both the Second Circuit Court and the District of Columbia Circuit Court, all members of the court heard the appeals from the two district courts.

Federal Judges

All federal judges are appointed by the president and must be confirmed by the Senate. The appointment is for life. The only way a federal judge can be removed is by impeachment. Nine federal judges have been impeached. Four were found guilty by the Senate, and the other five were acquitted. Impeachment and trial is a long process and one rarely undertaken.

Political affiliation plays a distinct part in the appointment of federal judges. Democratic presidents usually appoint Democratic judges, and Republican presidents appoint Republican judges. Nevertheless, it is expected that nominees to the federal bench be competent jurists. This is especially true for appointees to the courts of appeal and to the Supreme Court. The Senate must confirm all appointments to the federal courts, a normally perfunctory act in the case of lower court judges. More careful scrutiny is given nominees to the appellate courts. The Senate has rejected twenty-one men nominated for the Supreme Court either by adverse vote or by delaying the vote so long that the appointment was withdrawn by the president, or the president left office and the new chief executive nominated a different individual.

American presidents have used various schemes to select justices to the Supreme Court, but normally most presidents ask the American Bar Association to approve a list of potential nominees. In selecting a justice to the high Court the president obviously seeks a person who reflects some of his personal philosophy. Because so many different kinds of issues confront the Court, to find someone who is both "right" on all the issues and professionally competent is virtually impossible. A potential nominee may have the same philosophy on law-and-order issues, but take a stance opposite the president on labor matters and antitrust law.

While district judges must live in the community in which they work and are therefore clearly sensitive to some public pressure, judges of the courts of appeal and the justices of the Supreme Court are quite isolated from public pressure. Hence, philosophy can change when an individual reaches the Court; judges and justices mature or change in many directions. Liberal President John Kennedy named Justice Byron White to the Supreme Court, but Justice White more often than not takes the conservative position in recent years. On the other hand conservative President Dwight Eisenhower appointed former Chief Justice Earl Warren and Justice William Brennan, two of the Court's most outstanding liberals in the last half of the twentieth century. It is difficult to predict just which way an appointee will move after reelection or reappointment is no longer a factor.

The State Court System   The constitution of every one of the fifty states either establishes a court system in that state or authorizes the legislature to do so. The court system in each of the fifty states is somewhat different from the court system in all the other states. There are, however, more similarities among than differences between the fifty states.

The **trial courts** (or court) are the base of each judicial system. At the lowest level are usually what are called courts of limited jurisdiction. Some of these courts have special functions, like a traffic court which is set up to hear cases involving violations of the motor vehicle code. Some of these courts are limited to hearing cases of relative unimportance, such as trials of persons charged with misdemeanors or minor crimes or civil suits where the damages sought fall below $1,000. The court may be a municipal court set up to hear cases involving violations of the city code. Whatever the court, the judges in these courts have limited jurisdiction and deal with a limited category of problems.

Above the lower level courts normally exist trial courts of general jurisdiction similar to the federal district courts. These courts are sometimes county courts and sometimes state courts, but whichever they are, they handle nearly all criminal and civil matters. They are primarily courts of original jurisdiction; that is, they are the first court to hear a case. However, on occasion they act as a kind of appellate court when the decisions of the courts of limited jurisdiction are challenged. When that happens, the case is retried in the trial court—the court does not simply review the law. This proceeding is called hearing a case de novo.

A **jury** is most likely to be found in the trial court of general jurisdiction. It is also the court in which most civil suits for libel and invasion of privacy are commenced (provided the state court has jurisdiction), in which prosecution for violating state obscenity laws starts, and in which many other media-related matters begin.

Above this court may be one or two levels of appellate courts. Every state has a supreme court, although some states do not call it that. In New York, for example, it is called the Court of Appeals, but it is the high court in the state, the court of last resort. Formerly a supreme court was the only appellate court in most states. As legal business increased and the number of appeals mounted, the need for an intermediate appellate court became evident. Therefore, in about one-half of the states there is an intermediate court, usually called the court of appeals. This is the court where most appeals end. In some states it is a single court with three or more judges. More often numerous divisions within the appellate court serve various geographic regions, each division having three or more judges. Since every litigant is normally guaranteed at least one appeal, this intermediate court takes much of the pressure off the high court of the state. Rarely do individuals appeal beyond the intermediate level.

State courts of appeal tend to operate in much the same fashion as the United States courts of appeal, with cases being heard by small groups of judges, usually three at a time.

Cases not involving federal questions go no further than the high court in a state, usually called the supreme court. This court—usually a seven- or nine-member body—is the final authority regarding the construction of state laws and interpretation of the state constitution. Not even the Supreme Court of the United States can tell a state supreme court what that state's constitution means. For example, in 1976 the United States Supreme Court ruled that the protection of the First Amendment did not include the right to distribute materials, demonstrate, or solicit petition signatures at privately owned shopping centers (*Hudgens* v. *NLRB*—this case is discussed fully on page 94). In 1980, however, the Supreme Court refused to overturn a decision by the California Supreme Court which declared that students had the right under the California constitution to solicit signatures for a pro-Israeli petition at a private shopping center in Cambell, California. Justice William Rehnquist wrote for the unanimous United States Supreme Court that perhaps the free-speech guarantee in the California constitution is broader than the First Amendment. In any case, the California high court was the final authority on the state's constitution (*Pruneyard Shopping Center* v. *Robins*).

State supreme court judges—like most state judges—are usually elected. Normally the process is nonpartisan, but because they are elected and must stand for reelection periodically, state court judges are generally a bit more politically motivated than their federal counterparts. In some states the judges or justices are appointed, and a few states have experimented with a system which both appoints and elects. Under this scheme, called the **Missouri Plan,** the state's high court judges (and sometimes all judges) are appointed to the bench by the governor from a list supplied by a nonpartisan judicial commission. After a one-year term the judge must stand before the people during a general election and win popular support. The voter's ballot asks "Shall Judge Smith be retained in office?" If Judge Smith wins support, his next term is usually a long one, up to twelve years. If support is not forthcoming, a new person is selected to fill the seat for one year, and at the end of the term the judge must seek voter approval.

The advantages of the Missouri Plan are appointment of a qualified person initially and eventual citizen participation in the selection process.

Judicial Review

One of the most important powers of courts and at one time one of the most controversial is the power of **judicial review**—that is, the right of any court to declare any law or official governmental action invalid because it violates a constitutional provision. We usually think of this in terms of the United States Constitution. However, a state court can declare an act of its legislature to be invalid because the act conflicts with a provision of the state constitution. Theoretically, any court can exercise this power. The Circuit Court of Lapeer County, Michigan, can rule that the Environmental Protection Act of 1972 is unconstitutional because it deprives citizens of their property without due process of law, something guaranteed by the Fifth Amendment to the federal Constitution. But this action isn't likely to happen, because a higher court would quickly overturn such a ruling. In fact, it is rather unusual for any court—even the United States Supreme Court—to invalidate a state or federal law on grounds that it violates the Constitution. Only about one hundred twenty-two federal statutes have been overturned by the courts in the nearly two-hundred-year history of the United States. During the same period about nine hundred fifty state laws and state constitutional provisions have been declared invalid. Judicial review is therefore not a power which the courts use excessively. In fact, a judicial maxim states: When a court has a choice of two or more ways in which to interpret a statute, the court should always interpret the statute in such a way that it is constitutional.

Judicial review is extremely important when matters concerning regulations of the mass media are considered. Because the First Amendment prohibits laws which abridge freedom of the press and freedom of speech, each new measure passed by the Congress, by state legislatures, and even by city councils and township boards must be measured by the yardstick of the First Amendment. Courts have the right, in fact have the duty, to nullify laws and executive actions and administrative rulings which do not meet the standards of the First Amendment. While many lawyers and legal scholars rarely consider constitutional principles in their work and rarely seek judicial review of a statute, attorneys who represent newspapers, magazines, broadcasting stations, and motion-picture theaters constantly deal with constitutional issues, primarily those of the First Amendment. The remainder of this book will illustrate the obvious fact that judicial review, a concept at the very heart of American democracy, plays an important role in maintaining the freedom of the American press, even though the power is not included in the Constitution.

Lawsuits

The final topic which needs to be understood before mass media law itself is considered is what happens in a lawsuit. The brief discussion of the process which follows is simplified as much as possible. Many good books on the subject are available for persons interested in going further into the intricacies of lawsuits (some are listed in the Bibliography at the end of the chapter).

The party who commences a civil action is called the **plaintiff,** the person who brings the suit. The party against whom the suit is brought is called the **defendant.** In a libel suit the person who has been libeled is the plaintiff, and is the one who starts the suit against the defendant—the newspaper, the magazine, the television station, or whatever. To file a civil suit is a fairly simple process. A civil suit is usually a dispute between two private parties. The government offers its good offices—the courts—to settle the matter. A government can bring a civil suit such as an antitrust action against someone, and an individual can bring a civil action against the government. But normally a civil suit is between private parties. (In a criminal action, the government always initiates the action.)

To start a civil suit the plaintiff first picks the proper court, one which has jurisdiction in the case. Then the plaintiff presents the charges in the form of a **civil complaint.** The plaintiff also summons the defendant to appear in court to answer the charges. If the defendant chooses not to answer the charges, he or she normally loses the suit by default. After the complaint is filed, a hearing is scheduled. Then the plaintiff prepares a more detailed set of charges and arguments called **pleadings,** a very formal, written statement of the charge and the remedy sought. Usually the remedy involves money damages.

The defendant then prepares his or her own set of pleadings which constitute an answer to the plaintiff's charges. If there is little disagreement at this point about the facts—what happened—and that a wrong has been committed, the plaintiff and the defendant might settle their differences out of court. The defendant might say, "I guess I did libel you in this article, and I really don't have a very good defense. You asked for $15,000 in damages, would you settle for $7,500 and keep this out of court?" The plaintiff might very well answer yes, because a court trial is costly and takes a long time, and the plaintiff can also end up losing the case. Smart lawyers try to keep their clients out of court if possible and settle matters in somebody's office.

If there is disagreement, the case is likely to continue. A common move for the defendant to make at this point is to file a motion to dismiss, or a **demurrer.** In such a motion the defendant says this to the court: "I admit that

I did everything the plaintiff says I did. On June 5, 1982, I did publish an article in which he was called a socialist. But Your Honor, it is not libelous to call someone a socialist." The plea made then is that even if everything the plaintiff asserts is true the plaintiff is not legally wronged. The law cannot help the plaintiff. The court might grant the motion, in which case the plaintiff can appeal. Or the court might refuse to grant the motion, in which case the defendant can appeal. If the motion to dismiss is ultimately rejected by all the courts up and down the line, a trial is then held. It is fair play for the defendant at that time to begin argument of the facts, in other words, to deny that his newspaper published the article containing the alleged libel.

Before the trial is held, the judge may schedule a conference between both parties in an effort to settle the matter before starting the formal hearing or at least to narrow the issues so that the trial can be shorter and less costly. If this move fails, the trial goes forward. If the facts are agreed upon by both sides and the question is merely one of law, a judge without a jury hears the case. There are no witnesses and no testimony, only legal arguments before the court. If the facts are disputed, the case can be tried before either a jury or, again, only a judge. Note that both sides must waive the right to a jury trial. In this event, the judge becomes both the fact finder and the lawgiver. Now, suppose that the case is heard by a jury. After all the testimony is given, all the evidence is presented, and all the arguments are made, the judge instructs the jury in the law. Instructions are often long and complex, despite attempts by judges to simplify them. **Judicial instructions** guide the jury in determining guilt or innocence if certain facts are found to be true. The judge will say that if the jury finds that X is true and Y is true and Z is true, then it must find for the plaintiff, but if the jury finds that X is not true, but that R is true, then it must find for the defendant.

After deliberation the jury presents its **verdict,** the action by the jury. The judge then announces the **judgment of the court.** This is the decision of the court. The judge is not always bound by the jury verdict. If he or she feels that the jury verdict is unfair or unreasonable, the judge can reverse it and rule for the other party. Needless to say this happens rarely.

If either party is unhappy with the decision, an appeal can be taken. At that time the legal designations change. The person seeking the appeal becomes the appellant. The other party becomes the **appellee** or **respondent.** The name of the party initiating the action is listed first in the name of the case. For example: Smith sues Jones for libel. The case name is *Smith* v. *Jones.* Jones loses and takes an appeal. At that point Jones becomes the party initiating the action and the case becomes *Jones* v. *Smith.* This change in designations often confuses novices in their attempt to trace a case from trial to final appeal. If Jones wins the appeal and Smith decides to appeal to a higher court, the case again becomes *Smith* v. *Jones.*

The end result of a successful civil suit is usually awarding of money **damages.** Sometimes the amount of damages is guided by the law, as in a suit for infringement of copyright in which the law provides that a losing defendant pay the plaintiff the amount of money he might have made if the infringement had not occurred, or at least a set number of dollars. But most of the time the damages are determined by how much the plaintiff seeks, how much the plaintiff can prove he or she lost, and how much the jury thinks the plaintiff deserves. It is not a very scientific means of determining the dollar amount. In chapter 3 in the discussion of libel damages we will see that considerable hocus-pocus is involved.

A **criminal suit** is like a civil suit in many ways. The procedures are more formal, are more elaborate, and involve the machinery of the state to a greater extent.

The state brings the charges, usually through the county or state prosecutor. The defendant can be apprehended either before or after the charges are brought. In the federal system persons must be indicted by a **grand jury,** a panel of twenty-one citizens, before they can be charged with a serious crime. But most states do not use grand juries in that fashion, and the law provides that it is sufficient that the prosecutor issue an **information,** a formal accusation. After being charged, the defendant is arraigned. An **arraignment** is the formal reading of the charge. It is at the arraignment that the defendant makes a formal plea of guilty or not guilty. If the plea is guilty, the judge then gives the verdict of the court and passes sentence, but usually not immediately, for presentencing reports and other procedures must be undertaken.

If the plea is not guilty, a trial is then scheduled. Some state judicial systems have an intermediate step called a preliminary hearing or preliminary examination. The preliminary hearing is held in a court below the trial court, such as a municipal court, and the state has the responsibility of presenting enough evidence to convince the court—only a judge—that a crime has been committed and that there is sufficient evidence to believe that the defendant might possibly be involved.

In both a civil suit and a criminal case, the result of the trial is not enforced until the final appeal is exhausted. That is, a money judgment is not paid in civil suits until defendants exhaust all of their appeals. The same is true in a criminal case. Imprisonment or payment of a fine is not required until the final appeal. However, if the defendant is dangerous or if there is some question that the defendant might not surrender when the final appeal is completed, bail can be required. Bail is money given to the court to ensure appearance in court.

Summary

There are fifty-one different judicial systems in the nation: one federal system and one for each of the fifty states. Courts within each of these systems are divided into two general classes, trial courts and appellate courts. In any lawsuit both the facts and the law must be considered. The facts or the factual record is an account of what happened to prompt the dispute. The law is what should be done to resolve the dispute. Trial courts determine the facts in the case; then the judge applies the law. Appellate courts, using the factual record established by the trial court, determine whether the law was properly applied by the lower court and whether proper judicial procedures were followed. Trial courts exercise original jurisdiction almost exclusively; that is, they are the first courts to hear a case. Trial courts have very little discretion over which cases they will and will not hear. Appellate courts exercise appellate jurisdiction almost exclusively; that is, they review the work done by the lower courts when decisions are appealed. While the intermediate appellate courts (i.e., courts of appeal; the appellate division) have limited discretion in the selection of cases, the high courts (supreme courts) in the states and the nation generally have the power to select the cases they wish to review.

Federal courts include the Supreme Court of the United States, the courts of appeal, the United States district courts, and several specialized tribunals. These courts have jurisdiction in all cases that involve the United States Constitution, United States law, and United States treaties; disputes between citizens of different states; and in several less important instances. In each state there are trial-level courts and a court of last resort, usually called the supreme court. In about half of the states there are intermediate appellate courts as well. State courts generally have jurisdiction in all disputes between citizens of their state which involve the state constitution or state law.

Judicial review is the power of a court to declare a statute, regulation, or executive action to be a violation of the Constitution and invalid. Because the First Amendment to the United States Constitution guarantees the rights of freedom of speech and freedom of the press, all government actions which relate to the communication of ideas and information face potential scrutiny by the courts to determine their validity.

There are two basic kinds of lawsuits, civil suits and criminal suits. A civil suit is normally a dispute between two private parties in which the government offers its good offices (the courts) to resolve the dispute. The person who initiates the civil suit is called the plaintiff; the person at whom the suit is aimed is called the defendant. A plaintiff who wins a civil suit is normally awarded money damages.

A criminal case is normally an action in which the state brings charges against a private individual, who is called the defendant. A defendant who loses a criminal case can be assessed a fine, jailed, or in extreme cases executed. A jury can be used in both civil and criminal cases. The jury becomes the fact finder and renders a verdict in a case. But the judge issues the judgment of the court, and does not always have to follow the jury verdict. Either party can appeal the decision of a trial court in a civil suit. While both parties can appeal a ruling in a criminal case, it is rare for the state to attempt to overturn a judgment of innocence by an appeal.

As stated at the outset, this chapter is designed to provide a glimpse, only a glimpse, of both our legal system and our judicial system. The discussion is in no way comprehensive, but it provides enough information to make the remaining eleven chapters meaningful. The chapter is not intended to be a substitute for a good political science course in the legal process. Students of communications law are at a distinct disadvantage if they do not have some grasp of how the systems work and what their origins are.

The United States legal and judicial systems are old and tradition bound. But they have worked fairly well for these last two hundred years. In the final analysis the job of both the law and the men and women who administer it is to balance the competing interests of society. How this balancing act is undertaken comprises the remainder of this book. The process is not always easy, but it is usually interesting.

BIBLIOGRAPHY

Here is a list of some of the sources that have been helpful in the preparation of chapter 1.

Books

Abraham, Henry. *The Judicial Process.* 4th ed. New York: Oxford University Press, 1980.

_____. *The Judiciary: The Supreme Court in the Governmental Process.* 3d ed. Boston: Allyn & Bacon, 1973.

American Law Institute. *Restatement of the Law of Torts.* St. Paul, Minn.: American Law Institute, 1939.

Blackstone, William. *Commentaries on the Laws of England.* Edited by St. George Tucker. Philadelphia: W. Y. Birch & Abraham Small, 1803.

Franklin, Marc A. *The Dynamics of American Law.* Mineola, N. Y.: Foundation Press, 1968.

Holmes, Oliver W. *The Common Law.* Boston: Little, Brown & Co., 1881.

Pound, Roscoe. *The Development of the Constitutional Guarantees of Liberty.* New Haven: Yale University Press, 1957.

Roche, John P. *Courts and Rights.* 2d ed. New York: Random House, 1966.

Cases

Barber v. *Time*, 159 S.W.2d 291 (1942).
Branzburg v. *Hayes*, 408 U.S. 665 (1972).
Gannett v. *DePasquale*, 99 S.Ct. 2898 (1979).
Goldwater v. *Ginzburg*, 414 F.2d 324 (1969).
Hudgens v. *NLRB*, 424 U.S. 507 (1976).
Island Trees v. *Pico*, 102 S.Ct. 2799 (1982).
New York Times Co. v. *U.S.*, 403 U.S. 713 (1971).
Nye v. *U.S.*, 313 U.S. 33 (1941).
Pruneyard Shopping Center v. *Robins*, 447 U.S. 74 (1980).
Time v. *Hill*, 385 U.S. 374 (1967).
Toledo Newspaper Co. v. *U.S.*, 242 U.S. 402 (1918).
U.S. v. *Barnett*, 376 U.S. 681 (1964).

2 FREEDOM OF THE PRESS

When a man reaches the final years of his life, he often ponders how people will remember him. What aspects of his character and his contributions to society will people cherish? What will be quickly forgotten? So too is it with nations. Historians outline the important contributions made by ancient Greece and Rome, by Imperial Spain, and by the British Empire. What will historians consider the outstanding contributions of America and Americans? William O. Douglas, former associate justice of the Supreme Court of the United States, suggests that United States technology will not be the most memorable aspect of the nation's life. Instead, it will be our experiment with freedom of expression, an experiment shared with other Western democracies. Freedom of speech and freedom of the press—they are the achievements people will look upon with awe in eons to come.

No one knows whether Justice Douglas will be right. Clearly the attempt by Western democracies during the past three centuries to construct societies based upon the freedom to speak, the freedom to publish, and the freedom to criticize the government is a remarkable effort. Perhaps even more remarkable is that the experiment has worked so well. The guarantee of freedom of expression can be found in the constitution of nearly every nation. Only in a few countries such as the United States, however, are the people and the government dedicated to making the ideal come true.

The purpose of this chapter is to sketch a broad outline of the meaning of freedom of the press in the United States today. Freedom of the press is an element in all aspects of mass media—libel, invasion of privacy, obscenity, regulation of broadcasting, and so forth. Indeed, in any area in which the law touches mass media the First Amendment is a material consideration. At the same time, broader general principles defining freedom of expression have been fashioned by the courts in the past half-century. It is these broader principles that we will focus upon in chapter 2.

HISTORICAL DEVELOPMENT

Before freedom of the press can be defined, however, a brief look at the roots of the idea, roots which wind through many centuries, is necessary. Freedom of the press is not, and was not, exclusively an American idea. We did not invent the concept—in fact, no one invented it. Like Topsy, it just grew from crude beginnings which can be traced back to Plato and Socrates. The concept developed more fully during the past four hundred years. The modern history of freedom of the press really began in England during the sixteenth and seventeenth centuries as printing developed and grew. Today the most indelible embodiment of the concept is the First Amendment to the United States Constitution, forged in the last half of the eighteenth century by the men who built upon their memory of earlier experiences. To understand the meaning of freedom of the press and freedom of speech, it is necessary to understand the meaning of censorship, for viewed from a negative position freedom of expression can be simply defined as the absence of censorship. To understand censorship it is necessary to look first at the experience of the British who fought to be free from the yoke of censorship more than four centuries ago.

Freedom of the Press in England

When William Caxton set up the first British printing press in Westminster in 1476 his printing pursuits were restricted only by his imagination and ability. There were no laws governing what he could or could not print—he was completely free. For five centuries Englishmen and Americans have attempted to regain the freedom that Caxton enjoyed, for shortly after he started publishing, the British Crown began the control and regulation of printing presses in England. Printing developed during a period of great religious struggle in Europe, and it soon became an important tool in that struggle. Printing presses made communication with hundreds of persons fairly easy and in doing so gave considerable power to small groups or individuals who owned and/or could use a printing press.

The British government soon realized that unrestricted publication and printing could seriously dilute its own power. Information is a powerful tool in any society, and the individual or individuals who control the flow and content of the information received by a people exercise considerable control over those people. The printing press broke the Crown's monopoly of the flow of information, and therefore control of printing was essential.

In his study of censorship of the British press during the three hundred years between establishment of printing in England and the American Revolution, Frederick Siebert (*Freedom of the Press in England*) lists several means used by the Crown to limit or restrict the press. Criticism of the government or of the king or of the great men of the realm was called "sedition" or **seditious libel** and was considered a serious crime. Whether the criticism was truthful was immaterial. In fact, for many years British courts considered truthful criticism of the government more harmful than untruthful criticism since untruthful criticism was easier to deny. Truthful criticism could more easily stir the people to dissatisfaction and anger.

In England, the press was licensed as well until the 1690s. **Licensing** meant prior censorship, since all printers were forced to get prior approval to publish from the Crown or the Church. **Bonding** ensured that printers followed the rules. Printers were required to put up large sums of money before they were allowed to print. If they violated the law or failed to assist the government in enforcing the law, they forfeited the money and were out of business until they raised another **bond.** The British government granted patents and monopolies to certain printers in exchange for their cooperation in publishing only acceptable material and for their assistance in locating printers who broke the law by printing without permission or printing seditious material. For their help these printers were granted exclusive rights to publish various categories of books such as spellers, Bibles, and grammar books.

These restraints were just some of the means used by the British between 1476 and 1776 to control printing. While most authorities considered British press control quite effective, this control did not go unchallenged. Men of ideas—writers, philosophers, even statesmen—argued for the rights of free British subjects to enjoy freedom of expression: the right to print without prior restraint and the right to criticize the government and the Church without punishment. Some notions regarding freedom of expression emerged from that amorphous doctrine referred to as "the natural rights philosophy." This philosophy, which developed in Europe in the late seventeenth and early eighteenth centuries, asserts that man is a rational, thinking creature and by virtue of the laws of nature may claim certain rights against the state such as the freedom of expression. The growth of democratic government also spurred men to challenge government censorship, for they strongly believed that democracy would surely fail without guarantees of freedom of expression. The flow of information within the society was the essential lubricant of the democratic process. So a mixture of philosophy and pragmatism fueled the protests against government control of the press.

The men who drafted the United States Constitution were well acquainted with these ideas as well as with British censorship and control of the press. In addition, the founding fathers could draw upon first-hand experience of British control of the press in the American colonies.

Freedom of the Press in Colonial America

There were laws in the United States restricting freedom of the press for almost thirty years before the first newspaper was published. As early as 1662 statutes in Massachusetts made it a crime to publish anything without first getting prior approval from the government, twenty-eight years before Benjamin Harris published the first—and last—edition of *Publick Occurrences*. The second and all subsequent issues of the paper were banned because Harris failed to get permission to publish the first edition, which contained material construed to be criticism of British policy in the colonies, as well as a report that scandalized the Massachusetts clergy because it said the French king took immoral liberties with a married woman (not his wife).

Despite this inauspicious beginning, American colonists had a much easier time getting their views into print (and staying out of jail) than their counterparts in England. There was censorship, but American juries were reluctant to convict printers prosecuted by the British colonial authorities. The colonial governments were less efficient than the government in England. Also, the British had only limited control over the administration of government in many of the colonies.

The British attempted to use sedition laws to control the press in America, but did not attempt to organize guilds or printing monopolies. Licensing, which died in England in 1695, continued until the 1720s in the colonies. In 1723 the government of Massachusetts forbade printer James Franklin to publish the *New England Courant* or any similar newspaper or pamphlet without government supervision. Franklin, who was Benjamin Franklin's older brother, angered officials by charging in his newspaper that the colonial government was ineffective in protecting coastal communities from raids by bands of pirates. This restraint was the dying gasp of licensing in America.

The few taxes on the press were legitimate taxes levied to raise revenues, not to censor the press. The taxes were generally ignored by publishers and printers. The most widely known tax, the Stamp Act of 1765, succeeded only in increasing disgust toward and hatred of Parliament and the king. The stamps were poorly distributed, not being available in many communities. Newspaper publishers, who were supposed to buy the stamps and affix one to each copy of papers printed and sold, devised a multitude of schemes to avoid the tax. Some publishers removed the nameplate (the name of the paper) from the first page and declared they no longer published newspapers, but pamphlets, which were not subject to the tax. Others defied the law with little fear of retribution.

Government censorship of the press was widely publicized throughout the colonies for the first time when John Peter Zenger was tried for seditious libel in 1735. However this was not the first time the Crown had attempted to use sedition law to silence the American press. Professor Harold L. Nelson reports that at least four sedition cases were tried prior to the Zenger trial (*American Journal of Legal History,* 1959).

The Zenger trial has attained an important place in American political mythology in the two hundred fifty years since it concluded. Unfortunately, the importance of both the man and the trial have been exaggerated with the passage of time. This is not to say that what John Peter Zenger and his attorneys accomplished was unimportant. But it was the recalcitrant jury of American yeomen which really deserves an accolade. The trial should probably stand as a monument to the jury system if it is to be remembered at all.

John Peter Zenger was an immigrant printer who was prosecuted because the newspaper he published, the *New York Weekly Journal,* contained statements which were critical of both Governor William Cosby and the state government. The *Journal* was sponsored by Lewis Morris and James Alexander, political opponents of the unpopular state governor. Morris was a wealthy politician who had his envious eye on the money which could be made from land speculation by the man who sat in the governor's mansion.

The first edition of the *New York Weekly Journal* appeared on November 5, 1733. The attacks on Cosby in subsequent editions were relentless, and in November 1734 Zenger found himself in jail, accused of printing and publishing seditious libels which "tended to raise factions and tumults in New York, inflaming the minds of the people against the government, and disturbing the peace." Since Zenger was one of only two printers in the colony (the other printed a progovernment newspaper), Morris and Alexander had to get him out of jail if they were to continue publication of the *Journal*.

A court-appointed attorney, John Chambers, prepared to defend Zenger as the trial opened in August 1735. He was ably assisted by Andrew Hamilton, a fifty-nine-year-old Scots attorney and a renowned criminal lawyer whose interest in the case led him to come from Philadelphia to participate in the defense. There was little dispute that Zenger had published what eighteenth-century law defined as seditious libels against the governor and the government. For this he should have been convicted under British law. But Zenger's attorneys appealed to the conscience of the jury and argued that the law was wrong. No man should be imprisoned or fined for publishing criticism of the government that was truthful and fair. The jury agreed and found the German printer not guilty. In doing so the jurymen ignored the law; it was a simple case of what is called "a jury revolt."

There are three important facts to remember about the case. First, the law of seditious libel did not change because of the jury verdict. Following the Zenger case it was still considered a crime to criticize the government in New York. Second, because of the jury verdict, British prosecutors had second thoughts about the usefulness of sedition laws as means to silence opposition to the government. We can find no records of sedition trials in the colonial courts following the *Zenger* case. Finally, the trial of John Peter Zenger was widely publicized both in this country and in England and became a rallying point for foes of government censorship of the press. James Alexander published an account of the trial which was widely circulated. It was through such publicity that the case began to take on its stature as an event somewhat larger than life.

After Zenger's trial, government strategy changed. Rather than haul printers and editors before juries often hostile to the State, the government hauled printers and editors before legislatures and state assemblies which were usually hostile to journalists. The charge was not sedition, but breach of parliamentary privilege, or contempt of the assembly. There was no distinct separation of powers then, and the legislative body could order the printer to appear, question him, convict him, and penalize him. The same kinds of criticism which previously provoked a sedition trial now resulted in a trial before a colonial assembly. Only the basis of the charge was changed. In a contempt hearing the printer was accused of questioning the authority of the assembly, detracting from its honour, affronting its dignity, or impeaching its behavior, rather than of arousing general dissatisfaction among the people. Professor Nelson estimates that probably a large number of persons were brought before legislatures on such charges, but much more research is needed before all that happened during that period is known. We do know that repression of this kind was powerful and quite common. The press was as free as the colonial legislatures and assemblies permitted it to be.

Does this mean that freedom of the press was limited in the United States colonies? Yes. But all freedom was limited, if not by the government then by the community. The belief of many persons that freedom was a hallmark of society in colonial America ignores history. Political scientist John Roche (*Shadow and Substance*) writes persuasively that in colonial America the people and their representatives simply did not understand that freedom of thought and expression means freedom for the other fellow also, particularly for the fellow with hated ideas. Roche points out that colonial America was an open society dotted with closed enclaves—villages and towns and cities— in which citizens generally shared similar beliefs about religion and government and so forth. Citizens could hold any belief they chose and could espouse that belief, but personal safety depended upon the people in a community agreeing with a speaker or writer. If they didn't, the speaker then kept quiet or moved to another enclave where the people shared his ideas. While there was much diversity of thought in the colonies, there was often little diversity of belief within towns and cities, according to Roche.

The propaganda war which preceded the Revolution is a classic example of the situation. In Boston, the Patriots argued vigorously for the right to print what they wanted in their newspapers, even criticism of the government. Freedom of expression was their right, a God-given right, a natural right, a right of all British subjects. Many persons, however, did not favor revolution or even separation from England. Yet it was extremely difficult to publish such pro-British sentiments in many American cities after 1770. Printers who published such ideas in newspapers and handbills did so at their peril in many instances. In cities like Boston the printers were attacked, their shops were wrecked, and their papers were destroyed. Freedom of the press was a concept with limited utility in many communities for colonists who opposed revolution once the Patriots had moved the populace to their side. In other cities where the pro-British citizens held the upper hand, colonists seeking independence published in fear for their safety.

The plight of the pro-British printer in Boston in the 1770s was not a unique chapter in American history. Such community censorship still exists today in all parts of the nation. Ask the druggist who seeks to sell *Playboy* or *Penthouse* magazine in his suburban pharmacy. Ask the small-town theater owner who wants to show a rather explicit R-rated film. Ask the small-town newspaper editor who seeks to publish the names of local men who have been arrested for soliciting an act of prostitution. Ask the television station manager who seeks to telecast a controversial documentary on abortion. The cure for these ills is education and maturity. An educated person understands that a free society cannot long tolerate even the informal suppression of freedom of expression. A tolerance of censorship can develop which makes a people an easy prey for dictatorship. A mature citizen understands that the right to disagree about ideas and values and religious beliefs is the essence of a democracy. And no individual's freedom is secure unless the freedom of all is ensured.

Summary

Freedom of the press is a part of the great Anglo-American legal tradition, but it is a right that has been won only through many hard-fought battles. The British discovered the power of the press in the early sixteenth century and devised numerous schemes to restrict publication. Criticism of the government, called seditious libel, was outlawed. Licensing or prior censorship was also common. In addition, the Crown used an elaborate system of patents and monopolies for many years to control printing in England.

While under British law for more than one hundred years, American colonists enjoyed somewhat more freedom of expression than did their counterparts in England. Censorship laws existed before the first printing press arrived in North America, but they were enforced erratically or not at all. Licensing ended in the United States colonies in the 1720s. There were several trials for sedition in the colonies, but the acquittal of John Peter Zenger in 1735 by a recalcitrant jury ended that threat. Colonial legislatures and assemblies then attempted to punish dissident printers by using their contempt power. By the time the American colonists began to build their own governments in the 1770s and 1780s, they had the history of a three-hundred-year struggle for freedom of expression upon which to build.

THE FIRST AMENDMENT

In 1781, even before the end of the Revolutionary War, the new nation adopted its first constitution, the Articles of Confederation. The Articles provided for a loose-knit confederation of the thirteen colonies, or states, in which the central or federal government had little power. The Articles of Confederation did not contain a guarantee of freedom of expression. In fact, it had no bill of rights of any kind. The men who drafted this constitution did not believe such guarantees were necessary. Under these articles states were the most powerful political entities; the national government had few prerogatives. Guarantees of freedom of expression were already a part of the constitutions of most of the thirteen states. The citizens of Virginia, for example, had adopted a new constitution which contained a declaration of rights in June 1776, five years before the Articles of Confederation were written. Freedom of the press was guaranteed as a part of that declaration of rights. Other states soon followed Virginia's lead.

But the system of government created by the Articles of Confederation did not work very well. In the hot summer of 1787 each of the thirteen states sent a handful of their best men to Philadelphia to revise or amend the Articles, to make fundamental changes in the structure of the government.

The New Constitution

It was a remarkable group of men; perhaps no such group has gathered before or since. The members were merchants and planters and professional men, and none were full-time politicians. As a group these men were by fact or inclination members of the economic, social, and intellectual aristocracy of their respective states. These men shared a common education centered around history, political philosophy, and science. Some of them spent months preparing for the meeting—studying the governments of past nations. While some members came to modify the Articles of Confederation, many others knew from the start that a new constitution was needed. In the end that is what they produced, a new governmental charter. The charter was far different from the Articles in that it gave vast powers to a central government. The states remained supreme in some matters, but in other matters they were forced to relinquish their sovereignty to the new federal government.

No official record of the convention was kept. The delegates deliberated behind closed doors as they drafted the new charter. However, some personal records remain. We do know, for example, that inclusion of a bill of rights in the new charter was not discussed until the last days of the convention. The Constitution was drafted in such a way as not to infringe upon state bills of rights. When the meeting was in its final week, George Mason of Virginia indicated his desire that "the plan be prefaced with a Bill of Rights. . . . It would give great quiet to the people," he said, "and with the aid of the state declarations, a bill might be prepared in a few hours." Few joined Mason's call. Only one delegate, Roger Sherman of Connecticut, spoke against the suggestion. He said he favored protecting the rights of the people when it was necessary, but in this case there was no need. "The state declarations of rights are not repealed by this Constitution; and being in force are sufficient." He said that where the rights of the people are involved Congress could be trusted to preserve the rights. The states, voting as units, unanimously opposed Mason's plan. While the Virginian later attempted to add a bill of rights in a piecemeal fashion, the Constitution emerged from the convention and was placed before the people for ratification without a bill of rights.

The new Constitution was not without opposition. The struggle for its adoption was hard fought. The failure to include a bill of rights in the document was a telling complaint raised against the new constitution. Even Thomas Jefferson, who was in France, lamented the lack of a guarantee of political rights in the charter in a letter he wrote to his friend James Madison. When the states finally voted on the new constitution, it was approved, but only after supporters in several states had promised to petition the first Congress to add a bill of rights.

James Madison was elected from Virginia to the House of Representatives, defeating James Monroe for the House seat only after promising his constituents to work in the first Congress toward adoption of a declaration of human rights. When Congress convened, Madison worked to keep his promise. He first proposed that the new legislature incorporate a bill of rights into the body of the Constitution, but the idea was later dropped. That the Congress would adopt the declaration was not a foregone conclusion. There was much opposition, but after several months, twelve amendments were finally approved by both houses and sent to the states for ratification. Madison's original amendment dealing with freedom of expression states: "The people shall not be deprived or abridged of their right to speak, to write or to publish their sentiments and freedom of the press, as one of the great bulwarks of liberty, shall be inviolable." Congressional committees changed the wording several times, and the section guaranteeing freedom of expression was merged with the amendment guaranteeing freedom of religion and freedom of assembly. The final version is the version we know today:

> Congress shall make no law respecting an establishment of religion, or prohibiting the free exercise thereon; or abridging the freedom of speech, or of the press; or the right of the people peaceably to assemble, and to petition the Government for a redress of grievance.

The concept of the "first freedom" has been discussed often. Historical myth tells us that because the amendment occurs first in the Bill of Rights it was considered the most important right. In fact, in the Bill of Rights presented to the states for ratification the amendment was listed third. Amendments one and two were defeated and did not become part of the Constitution. The original First Amendment called for a fixed schedule that apportioned seats in the House of Representatives on a ratio many persons thought unfair. The Second Amendment prohibited senators and representatives from altering their salaries until after a subsequent election of representatives. Both amendments were rejected, and amendment three became the First Amendment.

Passage of the last ten amendments did not occur without struggle. Not until two years after being transmitted to the states for approval did a sufficient number of states adopt the amendments for them to become part of the Constitution. Connecticut, Georgia, and Massachusetts did not ratify the Bill of Rights until 1941, a kind of token gesture on the one hundred fiftieth anniversary of its constitutional adoption. In 1791 approval by these states was not needed since only three-fourths of the former colonies needed to agree to the measures.

Freedom of Expression in the Eighteenth Century

What did the First Amendment mean to the people who supported its ratification in 1790? This is not an idle question. The Bill of Rights was, after all, approved by a vote of the people in the several states. By their votes of approval they enacted their definitions of such rights as freedom of the press into the supreme law of the land. Technically, the definition of freedom of the press approved by the nation when the First Amendment was ratified in 1791 is what is guaranteed today. To enlarge or narrow that definition requires another vote of the people, a constitutional amendment.

But most people today consider this notion so much legalistic poppycock. The nation has changed dramatically in two hundred years. Television, radio, and film did not exist in 1790, for example. Does this mean that the guarantees of the First Amendment should not apply to these mass media? Of course not. Our Constitution has lasted for two hundred years because it has been somewhat elastic. The United States Supreme Court, our final arbiter on the meaning of the Constitution, has helped adapt the document to changing times.

Still, it is important that we respect the document that was adopted almost two hundred years ago. If we stray too far from its original meaning, the document may become meaningless; there will be no rules of government. Anarchy will be but a step away.

So what did the First Amendment mean in 1790? One theory, held by most scholars until about twenty years ago, is that freedom of expression included the right to be free from **prior restraint** (prior censorship) and the right to criticize the government without fear of punishment. Freedom from prior restraint was supposedly guaranteed to all British subjects, as well as American subjects, even before the Revolution. Sir William Blackstone, a British legal scholar, published a major four-volume summary of the common law between 1765 and 1769. In this summary, *Commentaries on the Law of England,* Blackstone defined freedom of expression as "laying no previous restraints upon publication." Today we call that no prior censorship.

In addition to prohibiting prior censorship, the First Amendment also precludes punishment of persons who criticize the government, according to many American legal scholars. After all, they argue, one of the reasons for the Revolution was to rid the nation of the hated British sedition law. The First Amendment surely must guarantee unrestricted political discussion.

This view has been challenged, most notably by scholar Leonard Levy in a book entitled *Legacy of Suppression.* Levy argues with considerable supporting evidence that the common definition of freedom of the press in 1790 included only freedom from prior censorship. The crime of seditious libel remained intact following the adoption of the First Amendment. It was only challenged in the late 1790s during the fierce debates over the constitutionality of the alien and sedition laws, he argues. (These laws are discussed on pages 53–55.)

It must be recognized that any attempt to discern what a concept meant almost two hundred years ago is not without problems. The written residue of the period reveals only a partial story. Undoubtedly, in 1790 the First Amendment's guarantee of freedom of expression meant different things to different people. In fact, one can speculate that the inherent vagueness in the constitutional guarantee enhanced its chances of being adopted. The First Amendment could mean almost anything a citizen wanted it to mean. A more specific definition might have prompted heated debate and endangered passage of the First Amendment. This is not to say that there was no definition of freedom of expression in 1790. On the contrary, there were probably many definitions. There was probably little consensus on the exact meaning of the concept, even among the congressmen who drafted the First Amendment.

Freedom of Expression Today

If we are not certain what the First Amendment meant in 1790, do we know what it means today? More or less. The First Amendment means today what the Supreme Court of the United States says it means. Certainly many people often disagree with the definition of freedom of expression rendered by the High Court. But from the standpoint of the law—and that is what this book is about—the Supreme Court defines the meaning of the First Amendment to the Constitution.

The Supreme Court is a collection of nine justices, not a single individual. Consequently, at any given time there can be nine different definitions of freedom of expression. This has never happened, at least, not on important issues. What has happened is that groups of justices have subscribed to various theoretical positions regarding the meaning of the First Amendment. These theories of the meaning of the First Amendment help justices shape their vote on a question regarding freedom of expression. These theories have changed during the past fifty years, the point at which the First Amendment first came under serious scrutiny by the Supreme Court. It is rare that the justices themselves develop such theories. Most theories are proposed by persons outside the court: legal scholars, lower court judges, even philosophers. At some point a jurist finds a comfortable theory and uses it to assist in interpreting the First Amendment.

Legal theories are sometimes like amorphous wraiths—difficult to handle. Judge Learned Hand, a distinguished American jurist, referred to the propagation of legal theory as "shoveling smoke." With such cautions in mind we will attempt to identify five important First Amendment theories or strategies which have been used or are used today to help judges develop a practical definition of freedom of expression.

Absolutist Theory: The First Amendment declares that "no law" shall abridge the freedom of speech or of the press. "No law" means *no law.* Speech and press are absolutely protected from interference by the government. There are no exceptions. This is what was intended by the men who drafted the First Amendment.

No more than two Supreme Court justices—Hugo Black and William Douglas—have subscribed to this position. Critics of the absolutist theory argue that the key words in the First Amendment are "freedom of speech and press," not "no law." The freedom to speak and publish was not an absolute freedom in 1790; limits to this freedom were accepted by the people. What the amendment means, then, is that "no law" may abridge the limited protection given to the rights to speak and publish. If speech and press were to be protected absolutely, the First Amendment would have been written this way: "Congress shall pass no law abridging speech and press." The absolutist theory has received little public support because it lacks the recognition that other important human rights often conflict with freedom of speech and press.

Ad hoc balancing theory: Freedom of speech and press are one of a number of important human rights we value in this nation. These rights often conflict. When conflict occurs, it is the responsibility of the court to balance the freedom of expression with other values. For example, the government must maintain the military to protect the people from aggression. To function, the military must maintain security about many of its weapons, plans, and movements. Imagine that the press seeks to publish information about a secret weapon system. The right to freedom of expression must be balanced with the need for secrecy in the military.

This theory is called *ad hoc* balancing because the scales are erected anew in every case; the meaning of the freedom of expression is determined solely on a case by case basis. Freedom of the press might outweigh the need for the government to keep secret the design of its new rifle, but the need for secrecy about a new fighter plane might take precedence over freedom of expression.

Ad hoc balancing is really not a theory; it is a strategy. Developing a definition of freedom of expression on a case-by-case basis leads to uncertainty. Under *ad hoc* balancing we will never know what the First Amendment means except as it relates to a specific, narrow problem (e.g., the right to publish information about a new army rifle). If citizens cannot reasonably predict whether a particular kind of expression might be protected or prohibited, they will have the tendency to play it safe and keep silent. This will limit the rights of expression of all persons. Also, *ad hoc* balancing relies too heavily in its final determination on the personal biases of the judge or justices who decide a case.

Preferred position balancing theory: Freedom of expression is the foundation of the United States system of government. Without our ability to speak and publish freely, all other rights have little meaning. Of what value is the right to be free from illegal police searches if complaints about the police after such searches have been made cannot be published? Because it is so important, freedom of expression must be given a preferred status when balanced against other rights. Operationally this means that whenever balancing between freedom of expression and some other interest takes place a court will presume that the limitation upon freedom of speech or freedom of the press is illegal. It is the responsibility of the persons who seek to block the speech or publication to convince a court that their interests should be given preference. For example, imagine that the Navy seeks to block the publication of information about a new fighter plane. The Navy must prove to the court that the publication of this material will be harmful to the national interests. Those who seek to publish the material are not obliged to convince the court that publication of the matter will be harmless or that the people have a right to see this information. The burden of proof falls on the Navy.

Today, courts use this theory more than any other. While it retains some of the negative features of *ad hoc* balancing, by tilting the scales in favor of freedom of expression it adds somewhat more certainty to our definition of freedom of expression. By basing this balancing strategy upon a philosophical foundation (the maintenance of all rights is dependent upon free exercise of speech and press) it becomes easier to build a case in favor of the broad interpretation of freedom of expression under the First Amendment.

Meiklejohnian theory: Philosopher Alexander Meiklejohn presented the legal community with a rather complex set of ideas about freedom of expression in the late 1940s *(Free Speech and Its Relation to Self-Government).* Meiklejohn looked at the First Amendment in a pragmatic manner and argued that freedom of expression is worth little as an abstract concept; that its primary value is as a means to an end. That end is successful self-government. Freedom of speech and press are protected in the Constitution so that our system of democracy can function, and that is the only reason they are protected. Expression which relates to the self-governing process must be protected absolutely by the First Amendment. There can be no government interference with such expression. Expression that does not relate to the self-governing process is not protected absolutely by the First Amendment. The value or worth of such speech must be balanced by the courts against other rights and values.

Critics of this theory argue in a telling fashion that it is not always clear whether expression pertains to self-government (public speech) or to other interests (private speech). While not providing the specific definition sought by critics, Meiklejohn argued that a broad range of speech is essential to successful self-government. He included speech-related education (history, political science, geography, etc.), science, literature, and many other topics. This theory has been subscribed to by some members of the Supreme Court of the United States, most notably Justice William Brennan. American libel law was radically changed when Brennan led the Supreme Court to give First Amendment protection only to libels published about government officials and others who attempt to lead public policy, a purely Meiklejohnian approach to the problem.

Access theory: In the mid-1960s some legal scholars suggested that the First Amendment includes the right of the people to gain access to the mass media to publish or present their own views and ideas. Development of this theory was prompted by economic trends in the nation which showed a rapidly diminishing number of newspapers. Surely the First Amendment means more than simply the right of rich publishers to print their views. The First Amendment gives the average citizen the right to speak and publish freely. To make this right mean something, newspapers should be forced to open up their news columns to persons with ideas and views different from their own.

The Supreme Court unanimously rejected this notion in 1974 in *Miami Herald* v. *Tornillo.* Chief Justice Warren Burger, writing for the Court, said that the choice of material to go into a newspaper, and the decisions made as to limitations on the size of the paper and to content and treatment of public issues and public officials are decisions that must be made by the editors. The First Amendment does not give the government the right to force a newspaper to publish the views or ideas of a citizen. The *Tornillo* case sounded the legal death knell for this access theory for print media. See *South Wind Motel* v. *Lashutka* (1983) for an example of how courts have rejected the access theory since the *Tornillo* ruling.

However, the access theory remains a potent justification for the regulation of broadcasting. The Federal Communication Commission has justified its regulation of the content of broadcasting on the theory that the airwaves belong to the people, and that all persons really have a right to see and hear programs which reflect a diverse range of ideas. As Justice White said in the famous case of *Red Lion Broadcasting* v. *FCC* (1969), "It is the right of the public to receive suitable access to social, political, esthetic, moral, and other ideas and experiences, which is crucial here." Using this argument as a foundation the government has justified the application of the Fairness Doctrine and other rules which can force broadcasters to carry certain kinds of programming. As we will note in chapter 11, this philosophy of broadcast regulation is being undercut today by many factors.

The five theories or strategies just outlined guide jurists across the nation as they attempt to fathom the meaning of these seemingly simple thirteen words: "Congress shall make no law abridging freedom of speech or of the press." In the remainder of this book we will attempt to tell you what the courts—using these theories—say the First Amendment means. It is appropriate that we begin that discussion now.

Summary

The nation's first constitution, the Articles of Confederation, did not contain a guarantee of freedom of speech and press, but nearly all state constitutions provided for a guarantee of such rights. Citizens insisted that a written declaration of rights be included in the Constitution of 1787, and a guarantee of freedom of expression was a part of the Bill of Rights that was added to the national charter in 1791.

There is a debate within the legal-historical community over the meaning of the First Amendment when it was drafted and approved in the late eighteenth century. Some persons argue that it was intended to block both prior censorship and prosecution for seditious libel. Others argue that it prohibits only prior censorship. We will probably never know what the guarantee of freedom of expression meant to the persons who drafted it, but it is a good bet that citizens had a wide variety of interpretations of the First Amendment when they voted to approve it.

The meaning of the First Amendment today is largely determined through interpretation by the Supreme Court of the United States. Jurists use legal theories to guide them in determining the meaning of the Constitutional guarantee that "Congress shall make no law abridging freedom of speech or of the press." Five such theories are (1) absolutist theory, (2) *ad hoc* balancing theory, (3) preferred position balancing theory, (4) Meiklejohnian theory, and (5) public access theory. Theories two, three, and four have the most supporters on the Supreme Court, and all the theories have assisted members of the high Court to shape the meaning of the First Amendment.

SEDITIOUS LIBEL AND THE RIGHT TO CRITICIZE THE GOVERNMENT

The First Amendment of the United States Constitution states:

> Congress shall make no law respecting an establishment of religion, or prohibiting the free exercise thereof; or abridging the freedom of speech, or of the press; or the right of the people peaceably to assemble, and to petition the Government for a redress of grievances.

The essence of a democracy is the participation by citizens in the process of government. At its most basic level this participation is selecting leaders for the nation, the state, and the various local governments through the electoral process. Popular participation also includes examination of government and public officials to determine their fitness for serving the people. Discussion, criticism, and suggestion all play a part in the orderly transition of governments and elected leaders. The right to speak and print, then, is inherent in a nation governed by popularly elected rulers.

Whether the rights of free expression as defined in 1790 included a broad right to criticize the government, this kind of political speech has emerged as a central element of our modern understanding of the First Amendment.

The right to discuss the government, the right to criticize the government, the right to oppose the government, the right to advocate the change of the government—all of these dimensions of free speech and free press are at the center of our political philosophy today. But this has not always been the case. Even today we are sometimes troubled when asked to decide just how far an individual can go in criticizing or opposing the government. Can the use of force or violence be advocated as a means of changing the government? Can a citizen use the essence of democracy, free expression, to advocate the violent abolition of democracy and the establishment of a repressive state in which the rights of free speech and free press would be denied? Americans familiar with the history of the past two hundred years know these are more than academic questions. Some of the fiercest First Amendment battles have been fought over exactly these issues. Indeed, the new nation was less than ten years old when its resolve regarding freedom of expression was first put to the test. The results of the test were not encouraging.

Alien and Sedition
Acts

In 1798 John Adams was in his third year as president. As Washington's successor he was also the head of the nation's first political party, the Federalist party. This was the party which favored a strong national government, the party that many believed was somewhat antidemocratic. Arrayed against the Federalists was the party of Thomas Jefferson, the Republican or Democratic-Republican or Jeffersonian party.

The young nation was experiencing difficulties with the French in 1798. Some Federalist politicians said that war was imminent. This event was unlikely, even though the impact of the democratic ideas generated by the French Revolution clearly stirred some segments of the American population. The Republican press used the Federalist fear of the French to make political hay. The Republican editors, many of whom were French sympathizers and some of whom were French aliens, rarely missed an opportunity to attack President Adams and other Federalist leaders. Opposition to the Federalist government and the Federalist president aligned the Republican journalists with the French in the eyes of some of the Federalist leaders. Remember that the newspapers of this era were tied closely to political parties and sought to interpret news and events in terms of political affairs. Editorial attacks were often vicious compared to the genteel press of the late twentieth century.

No one will ever know whether John Adams really feared war with France and sought to stifle dissent in order for the nation to present a united front to Europe, or whether the trouble with France was a convenient excuse to muzzle some of his political enemies. In either case Adams approved of the efforts of some extremists in the Federalist party to curb the power of the aliens, the Republicans, and the Republican press. In 1798 the Federalist Congress passed four laws known today as the **Alien and Sedition Acts of 1798.** The first three acts dealt with aliens: the period of residence for naturalization was extended from five to fourteen years, and the president was given the power to apprehend, restrain, and deport aliens whom he deemed to be dangerous. The sedition law was aimed directly at the Jeffersonian press. It forbade false, scandalous, and malicious publications against the United States government, the Congress, and the president. The new law also punished persons who sought to stir up sedition or urged resistance to federal laws. The punishment was a fine of as much as $2,000 and a jail term of not more than two years.

Truth was a defense in a prosecution brought under the new law, and the jury was given the power to determine whether the words were seditious. However, these safeguards proved ineffective. The courts insisted that the defendant had to prove that his statements or opinions were true. This was a reversal of the normal criminal law presumption of innocence in which the state must prove that the words are false and scandalous. Since the trials were normally held in communities dominated by Federalists, both the judge and jury were highly sensitive to criticism of the Federalist government.

The fifteen prosecutions under the law ranged from ludicrous to absurd. Speaking for the Republican party were five major newspapers in Philadelphia, Boston, New York, Richmond, and Baltimore. The editors of four of the five newspapers were prosecuted, as well as the editors of four lesser Republican newspapers. Even Congressmen did not escape. Matthew Lyon, a Republican member of Congress from Vermont, was prosecuted for publishing an article in which he asserted that under President Adams, "every consideration of the public welfare was swallowed upon in a continual grasp for power, in an unbounded thirst for ridiculous pomp, foolish adulation and selfish avarice." He also printed a letter written by a friend that suggested the president be committed to a madhouse. For these offenses against the government Congressman Lyon was fined $1,000 and spent four months in jail. While he was in jail he was reelected to Congress.

Far from striking down dissension, Adams succeeded only in generating dissension among many persons who were formerly his supporters. The constitutional issues raised by the law never reached the Supreme Court, although the validity of the measure was sustained by Federalist judges and by three Federalist Supreme Court justices hearing cases on the circuit. The people, however, acted as a kind of court and voted Adams out of office in 1800, replacing him with his Republican foe Thomas Jefferson. Other factors prompted public dissatisfaction with the Massachusetts nationalist to be sure, but unpopularity of the alien and sedition laws cannot be underestimated. The Sedition Act expired in 1801. Jefferson pardoned all persons convicted under it, and Congress eventually repaid most of the fines.

Several lessons emerge from the experience under that set of laws. Foremost is the proposition that the First Amendment does nothing, in and of itself, to guarantee freedom of expression. The people and the courts must support the proposition before it becomes workable. In 1798 the courts were staffed with Federalists who were basically sympathetic to the law, and juries sympathetic to the Federalist cause could also be drawn quite easily. In 1798 the defense of truth did not help much when it was framed in such a way as to force the defendant to prove the truth of his assertions.

We discovered that in 1798 there was little consensus on what freedom of the press really means. Some of the best writing ever on the topic was published during this period as the Republicans attempted to define free expression in a way which tolerated a broader range of governmental criticism. Tracts by men like Tunis Wortman, forgotten by most scholars for more than one hundred fifty years, have emerged in the second half of the twentieth century and offer legal scholars profound insight into how freedom of expression and stability of the government can be balanced.

Another lesson is that the nation's first peacetime sedition law left such a bad taste that another peacetime sedition law was not passed until the Smith Act of 1940.

Our brief consideration of this episode also shows that Americans (to their probable chagrin) were not really so different from their colonial forebearers on the issue of free expression, that an American president and a Congress could be as ignorant of the importance of freedom of speech as a British king and parliament.

The conflict between political criticism and freedom of expression was not dormant for the next one hundred fifteen years, but neither was it at the forefront of public discussion. Debate on freedom of expression arose again during the period in which abolitionist publishers worked to end slavery in the United States. Between 1830 and 1840 both the states and the members of the federal government made serious efforts to stop the circulation of abolitionist newspapers on the grounds that they tended to incite slave revolt. The legal moves were defeated in northern states, and the Congress, instead of bowing to President Andrew Jackson's request to ban these publications from the United States mail, insisted that local postmasters had to deliver all mail, even if it contained abolitionist sentiments. Informal pressure was far more effective in stifling publication and circulation of abolitionist newspapers. This was especially true in the South where community pressure was a far more effective censor, despite the existence of laws in a few states making circulation of some abolitionist tracts punishable by death. During the antebellum period freedom of expression in most of the South meant freedom to discuss or publish only the views with which a community did not disagree.

In the North the issue of liberty of the press received a substantial airing during debates over censorial statutes in many state legislatures. However, because slavery did not touch the lives of many Northerners, persons living north of the Mason-Dixon line found it easier to stand behind a more expansive definition of freedom of expression.

Freedom of expression was an issue during the Civil War also. Some newspapers were temporarily closed in the North. The government effectively screened most war news published in the press, and Lincoln showed little sensitivity to civil liberties on some occasions. Still, the war was a national crisis of unprecedented proportions, and one way or another most persons were intimately involved in the war. Freedom of the press paled somewhat when placed next to the life-and-death struggle many persons suffered.

The right to criticize the government did not again become a controversial issue in this nation until after the turn of the century when the political "isms" of the late 1800s (socialism, anarchism, syndicalism) fused with the war in Europe. The safety of the nation appeared to be at stake, and repression once again seemed to be the proper answer.

In the late nineteenth century hundreds of thousands of Americans began to realize that democracy and capitalism were not going to bring the prosperity promised by some obscure national compact. The right to pursue happiness did not assure that one would find it. The advancing rush of the new industrial society left many Americans behind, and they were unhappy. Some of the more dissatisfied persons wanted to do something about the situation and proposed new systems of government and advanced new economic theories. The specter of revolution arose in the minds of millions of Americans. Emma Goldman, Big Bill Haywood, and Daniel DeLeon represented salvation and hope to their tens of thousands of followers, but they represented a violent change in the comfortable status quo to many other thousands of Americans. Hadn't the radicals caused a riot in 1886 in Chicago? Hadn't they killed President McKinley in 1902? Hadn't they planted bombs along the West Coast and in the Northwest? Didn't they advocate general strikes? Didn't they want to take over the plants and factories and let the workers control production? With this threat lurking in the background, the United States found a real live bogeyman in 1917 when the nation went to war against the Hun—to win the war that would make the world safe for democracy.

Sedition in the Twentieth Century

The history of sedition law in the United States during and since World War I centers upon the struggle by courts at all levels to fashion some kind of test which permitted the government to protect itself from damaging criticism without stifling expression which is protected by the First Amendment. Beginning with cases which grew out of dissent against the war in Europe through cases in the early 1970s, federal courts, especially the Supreme Court, have made numerous attempts to develop a satisfactory test or formula. In the following section these attempts are outlined through a discussion of many of the major cases which raised this difficult problem. But before the cases can be discussed, it is necessary to look briefly at the period which many regard as the most repressive in the history of the nation, the World War I era.

World War I is probably the most unpopular war this nation fought until the Vietnam conflict of the sixties and seventies. The war was a replay of the imperial wars of the seventeenth and eighteenth centuries in Europe, except that it was fought with more deadly new weapons. Patriots were thrilled that the United States was finally asked to fight in the big leagues. Farmers and industrialists saw vast economic gains. The military believed that no more than six months or so were needed to clean up what many called at the outset "that lovely little war." So most of the ins liked the idea of going to war. But most of the outs hated it because they had to fight the war, because many were born in nations now our enemies, and because a war always signals the beginning of a period of internal political repression for the outs. When persons who opposed the war in an organized way spoke out against it, their opposition became just another excuse for suppression, fines, and jail.

Suppression of freedom of expression reached a higher level during World War I than at any other time in our history. Government prosecutions during the Vietnam War, for example, were minor compared to government action between 1918 and 1920. Vigilante groups were active as well, persecuting when the government failed to prosecute.

Two federal laws were passed to deal with persons who opposed the war and United States participation in it. In 1917 the **Espionage Act** was approved by the Congress and signed by President Woodrow Wilson. The measure dealt primarily with espionage problems, but some parts were aimed expressly at dissent and opposition to the war. The law provided that it was a crime to willfully convey a false report with the intent to interfere with the war effort. It was a crime to cause or attempt to cause insubordination, disloyalty, mutiny, or refusal of duty in the armed forces. It also was a crime to willfully obstruct the recruiting or enlistment service of the United States. Punishment was a fine of not more than $10,000 or a jail term of not more than twenty years. The law also provided that material which violated the law could not be mailed.

In 1918 the **Sedition Act,** an amendment to the Espionage Act, was passed, making it a crime to attempt to obstruct the recruiting service. It was criminal to utter or print or write or publish disloyal or profane language which was intended to cause contempt of or scorn for the federal government, or of the Constitution, or the flag, or of the uniform of the armed forces. Penalties for violation of the law were imprisonment for as long as twenty years and/ or a fine of $10,000. Approximately two thousand offenders were prosecuted under these espionage and sedition laws, and nearly nine hundred were convicted. Offenders who found themselves in the government's dragnet were usually aliens, radicals, publishers of foreign-language publications, and other persons who opposed the war.

In addition the United States Post Office Department censored thousands of newspapers, books, and pamphlets. Some publications lost their right to the government-subsidized second-class mailing rates and were forced to use the costly first-class rates or find other means of distribution. Entire issues of magazines were held up and never delivered, on the grounds that they violated the law (or what the postmaster general believed to be the law). Finally, the states were not content with allowing the federal government to deal with dissenters, and most adopted sedition statutes, laws against criminal syndicalism, laws which prohibited the display of a red flag or a black flag, and so forth.

While the Congress adopted measures making it a crime to oppose the government or to oppose the recruiting service, the courts were given the task of reconciling these laws with the guarantee of freedom of expression in the First Amendment. The courts, ultimately the Supreme Court, had to specifically define what kinds of words were protected by the First Amendment and what kinds of words were outside the range of protected speech. The United States had been in the war but a short time when the case that would become the Supreme Court's first opportunity to reconcile the First Amendment and outlaw political speech began.

The Philadelphia Socialist party authorized Charles Schenck, the general secretary of the organization, to publish 15,000 antiwar leaflets. They were distributed through the party's bookshop and mailed directly to young men who had been drafted. The publication urged the young inductees to join the Socialist party and work for the repeal of the selective service law, told the young men that the law was a violation of the Thirteenth Amendment which abolished slavery, and told the draftees that they were being discriminated against because certain young men (Quakers and clergymen) did not have to go to war. The pamphlet also described the war as a cold-blooded and ruthless adventure propagated in the interest of the chosen few of Wall Street. Schenck and other party members were arrested, tried, and convicted of violating the Espionage Act. The socialists appealed to the high Court, asserting that the law denied them the right of freedom of speech and freedom of the press. Justice Oliver Wendell Holmes wrote the opinion in this important case (*Schenck* v. *U.S.,* 1919). Holmes initially asserted that the main purpose of the First Amendment is to prevent prior censorship, although he conceded that the amendment might not be confined to that. In ordinary times, such pamphlets might have been harmless and considered protected speech. "But the character of every act depends upon the circumstances in which it is done. . . . The question in every case is whether the words used, are used in such circumstances and are of such a nature as to create a clear and present danger that they will bring about the substantive evils that Congress has a right to prevent. It is a question of proximity and degree."

Translated, this is what Holmes's proposition means. Congress has a right to outlaw certain kinds of conduct which can be harmful to society. Words, as in publications or public speeches, which can result in persons undertaking the illegal conduct can also be outlawed, and publishers or speakers can be punished without infringing upon First Amendment rights. How great must be the connection between the forbidden conduct and the words? Holmes said the words must create a "clear and present danger" that the illegal activity will result.

Needless to say, in Holmes's view the requisite clear and present danger of obstructing the recruiting service existed in the *Schenck* case, and the conviction was upheld. In two other Espionage Act cases also decided in the spring of 1919, Holmes wrote the opinion for the Court and used the clear and present danger test to affirm the convictions of Jacob Frohwerk, editor of a German-language newspaper (*Frohwerk* v. *U.S.,* 1919) and Eugene V. Debs, leader of the American Socialist party during World War I (*Debs* v. *U.S.,* 1919). The requisite clear and present danger existed in both cases, Holmes said.

Political liberals in the nation were left in considerable dismay upon reading Holmes's opinion in the *Schenck* case. The aging jurist was regarded as a great civil libertarian, but his formulation of the "clear and present danger test" allowed little room for what most American liberals regarded as protected expression. There is some evidence that Justice Holmes was sadly underprepared in First Amendment law when he wrote the opinion. An even more interesting theory has been proposed by University of Oregon scholar Jeremy Cohen who suggests that Holmes may not have viewed the legal controversy primarily as a First Amendment case. Cohen suggests that Holmes's long background as a state judge and other factors set his mind to view the dispute in the *Schenck* case with strong judicial deference to legislative policymaking. Should the legislature or the courts make policy on this issue? Holmes may have asked himself. One needs only to look at Holmes's writing and his previous court opinions to determine the answer to the question, writes Cohen. The courts should not interfere with legislature in such policy matters.

Holmes was sharply criticized by many civil libertarians following the *Schenck* ruling. Some suggest that he was re-educated in constitutional law by a few of his friends during the subsequent summer (*see* Ragan article, *Journal of American History,* in the Bibliography on page 96).

Regardless, in November 1919, when the Court decided its first appeal of a conviction under the Sedition Act, Holmes split with the majority and wrote a moving dissent in defense of freedom of expression.

In *Abrams* v. *U.S.* (1919) the high Court upheld the convictions of five young radicals who protested the movement of American troops into the Soviet Union and called for a general strike to stop the production of munitions and arms. In writing for the majority Justice John Clarke wrote that the leaflets published by the defendants "obviously intended to provoke and to encourage resistance to the United States in the war." Whether they intended to hurt the United States was not at issue. "Men must be held to have intended, and to be accountable for, the effects which their acts were likely to produce." As Professor Fred D. Ragan notes: "Thus Clarke employed criteria used by Holmes earlier in the year . . . to sustain the conviction."

Holmes, on the other hand, joined his colleague Louis Brandeis in the dissent. The jurist wrote that the ultimate good desired is better reached by free trade in ideas, that the best test of truth is the power of a thought to get accepted in the marketplace. "That, at any rate, is the theory of our Constitution," he wrote. Holmes then argued that nobody could seriously believe that the silly leaflet published by the five defendants would hinder the war effort. He turned his back on notions of probable or indirect interference with the prosecution of the war. To be guilty of resistance meant direct and immediate opposition to some effort by the United States to prosecute the war. There was no evidence of that here, Holmes concluded.

Holmes's change of heart did not spell the demise of the clear and present danger test. It was used in other sedition cases by the high Court. However the only instances in which a majority of the high Court subscribed to the test were to uphold convictions under various sedition laws. Holmes and Brandeis used the test often to argue that the requisite clear and present danger was missing, that the utterances or published materials were protected by the First Amendment. These arguments, it should be noted, were in dissenting opinions.

The Gitlow Ruling

The next sedition case of significance during the postwar era was *Gitlow* v. *New York* (1925). Many scholars argue that this decision by the Supreme Court ranks as one of the most important civil rights decisions of the twentieth century, despite the fact that defendant Benjamin Gitlow lost his First Amendment appeal. Gitlow and three other persons were arrested, tried, and convicted of publishing and distributing a pamphlet which, the state of New York argued, advocated the violent overthrow of the government—a violation of the New York Criminal Anarchy Law. The pamphlet, the *Left Wing Manifesto,* was a dreadfully dull thirty-four-page political tract on revolution and social and economic change. In his book *Free Speech in the United States,* Zechariah Chafee, a renowned legal scholar of Harvard University, accurately notes, "Any agitator who read these thirty-four pages to a mob would not stir them to violence, except possibly against himself. This manifesto would disperse them faster than the riot act." Nevertheless Gitlow was sentenced to ten years in prison. In his appeal to the high Court he argued that the state criminal anarchy statute violated his freedom of expression guaranteed by the United States Constitution. In making this plea, Gitlow was asking the Court to overturn a ninety-two-year-old precedent.

In 1833 the Supreme Court of the United States ruled that the Bill of Rights, the first ten amendments to the United States Constitution, were applicable only in protecting citizens from actions of the federal government (*Barron* v. *Baltimore,* 1833). Chief Justice John Marshall ruled that the people of the United States established the United States Constitution for their government, not for the government of the individual states. The limitations of power placed upon government by the Constitution applied only to the government of the United States. Applying this rule to the First Amendment meant that neither Congress nor the federal government could abridge freedom of the press, but that the government of New York or the government of Detroit could interfere with freedom of expression without violating the guarantees of the Constitution. The citizens of the individual states or cities could erect their own constitutional guarantees in state constitutions or city charters. Indeed, such provisions existed in many places.

As applied to the case of Benjamin Gitlow, then, it seemed unlikely that the First Amendment (which prohibited interference by the federal government with freedom of speech and press) could be erected as a barrier to protect the radical from prosecution by the state of New York. Yet this is exactly what the young socialist argued.

Gitlow's attorneys, especially Walter Heilprin Pollak, did not attack the rule directly; instead they went around it. Pollak constructed his argument upon the Fourteenth Amendment to the Constitution which was adopted in 1868, thirty-five years after the decision in *Barron* v. *Baltimore*. The attorney argued that there was general agreement that the First Amendment protected a citizen's right to liberty of expression. The Fourteenth Amendment says in part "no state shall deprive any person of life, liberty or property, without due process of law. . . ." Pollak asserted that included among the liberties guaranteed by the Fourteenth Amendment is liberty of the press as guaranteed by the First Amendment. Therefore, a state cannot deprive a citizen of the freedom of the press which is guaranteed by the First Amendment without violating the Fourteenth Amendment. By jailing Benjamin Gitlow for exercising his right of freedom of speech granted by the First Amendment, New York State denied him the liberty assured him by the Fourteenth Amendment. Simply, then, the First Amendment as applied through the Fourteenth Amendment prohibits states and cities and counties from denying an individual freedom of speech and press.

The high Court had heard this argument before, but apparently not as persuasively as Mr. Pollak presented it. In rather casual terms Justice Edward Sanford made a startlingly new constitutional pronouncement: "For present purposes we may and do assume that freedom of speech and of the press—which are protected by the First Amendment from abridgement by Congress—are among the fundamental personal rights and 'liberties' protected by the due process clause of the Fourteenth Amendment from impairment by the states."

Despite this important ruling, Gitlow lost his case. Justice Sanford said that the New York law was warranted and did not violate the First Amendment nor the Fourteenth Amendment. Sanford then went on to outline his own rather novel interpretation of Holmes's clear and present danger test. He said that in passing the Espionage Act, the Congress forbade certain deeds—interference with the recruiting service, for example. In such instances when the defendant is charged with using words to promote the forbidden deeds, the courts must decide whether the language used by the accused creates a clear and present danger for bringing about the forbidden deeds. In other words, does the defendant's pamphlet create the danger that persons will in fact interfere with the recruiting service?

However, in this case, Sanford said, the New York legislature outlawed certain words—that is, words advocating violent overthrow of the government are forbidden. The clear and present danger test does not apply, he said. The only issue the court has to decide is, Do the words in question, in this case the *Left Wing Manifesto,* fall within the class of forbidden words, words that advocate violent overthrow of the government? The court has no power to determine in such a case if in fact the defendant's pamphlet creates the danger of a violent revolt. It is sufficient that the state has outlawed such words. Only if the judgment of the legislature is completely without foundation can the court interfere. In this case the legislature's action is warranted: Gitlow's pamphlet falls within the category of proscribed words—ten years in jail!

Holmes and Brandeis vigorously dissented, arguing that it was absurd to think that Gitlow's small band of followers posed any danger at all to the government. "It is said that this manifesto was more than a theory," Holmes wrote, "that it was an incitement. Every idea is an incitement. . . . The only difference between the expression of an opinion and an incitement in the narrower sense is the speaker's enthusiasm for the result." The argument was to no avail. After three years in prison Gitlow was pardoned by Governor Alfred Smith.

The importance of the *Gitlow* case is that the high Court acknowledged that the Bill of Rights places limitations upon the actions of states and local government as well as upon the federal government. The *Gitlow* case states that freedom of speech is protected by the Fourteenth Amendment. In later cases the Court placed freedom of the press, freedom of religion, freedom from self-incrimination, and freedom from illegal search and seizure under the same protection. Today, virtually all of the rights outlined in the Bill of Rights are protected via the Fourteenth Amendment from interference by states and cities as well as by the federal government. The importance of the *Gitlow* case cannot be underestimated. It truly marked the beginning of attainment of a full measure of civil liberties for the citizens of the nation. It was the key which unlocked an important door.

Sedition in the Twenties

The Sanford interpretation of the clear and present danger test was next used two years later when the Supreme Court reviewed the prosecution by California of sixty-year-old philanthropist Anita Whitney for threatening the security of the state (*Whitney* v. *California,* 1927). Miss Whitney, the niece of

Justice Stephen J. Field who served on the Supreme Court from 1863 to 1897, joined the Socialist party in the early 1920s. At a convention in Chicago the chapter to which Miss Whitney belonged seceded from the Socialist party and formed the Communist Labor party. The Communist Labor party held a convention in Oakland to which Miss Whitney was a delegate. She worked hard as a delegate to ensure that the new party worked through political means to capture political power, but the majority of delegates voted instead for the party to dedicate itself to gaining power through revolution and general strikes in which the workers would seize power by violent means. After this convention Miss Whitney was not active in the party, but she was nevertheless arrested three weeks after the Oakland convention and charged with violating the California Criminal Syndicalism Act which prohibited advocacy of violence to change the control or ownership of industry or to bring about political change.

Following her conviction she appealed to the high Court, arguing that the law violated the guarantees of freedom of expression. Justice Edward Sanford, writing for the majority, again ruled that the clear and present danger test did not apply, that the California state legislature outlawed certain kinds of words which it deemed a danger to public peace and safety, and that the Court could not hold that the action was unreasonable or unwarranted. There was therefore no infringement upon the First Amendment.

This time Holmes and Brandeis concurred with the majority, but only, Brandeis said, because the constitutional issue of freedom of expression had not been raised sufficiently at the trial to make it an issue in the appeal. In his concurring opinion, Brandeis disagreed sharply with the majority regarding the limits of free expression. In doing so he added flesh and bones to Holmes's clear and present danger test. Looking to the *Schenck* decision, the justice noted that the Court had agreed that there must be a clear and imminent danger of a substantive evil which the state has the right to prevent before an interference with speech can be allowed. Then he went on to describe what he believed to be the requisite danger (*Whitney* v. *California*):

> To justify suppression of free speech there must be reasonable ground to fear that serious evil will result if free speech is practiced. There must be reasonable ground to believe that the danger apprehended is imminent. There must be reasonable ground to believe that the evil to be prevented is a serious one. Every denunciation of existing law tends in some measure to increase the probability that there will be violation of it. Condonation of a breach enhances the probability. Expressions of approval add to the probability. Propagation of the criminal state of mind by teaching syndicalism increases it. Advocacy of law-breaking heightens it further. But even advocacy of violation, however reprehensible morally, is not a justification for denying free speech where the advocacy falls short of incitement, and there is nothing to indicate that the advocacy would be immediately acted on. The wide difference between advocacy and incitement, between preparation and attempt, between assembling and conspiracy, must be

borne in mind. In order to support a finding of clear and present danger it must be shown either that immediate serious violence was to be expected or was advocated, or that the past conduct furnished reason to believe that such advocacy was then contemplated.

Brandeis concluded that if there is time to expose through discussion the falsehoods and fallacies, to avert the evil by the process of education, the remedy to be applied is more speech, not enforced silence.

This truly is a clear and present danger test that even the most zealous civil libertarian can live with. And this is the test that many mistakenly confuse with Holmes's original pronouncement. Unfortunately, this version of the clear and present danger test has never found its way into a majority opinion in a sedition case.

Before the last two important sedition cases decided during this century are discussed, it should be noted that in 1927 the Supreme Court first struck down a state sedition conviction because the defendant's federal constitutional rights had been violated (*Fiske* v. *Kansas,* 1927). In Kansas a man named Fiske was arrested, tried, and convicted of violating that state's criminal anarchy statute. He was an organizer for the International Workers of the World (IWW), a radical union group. The evidence the state used against him was the preamble to the IWW constitution which discussed in vague terms the struggle between workers and owners and the necessity for workers to take control of the machinery of production and to abolish the wage system. No mention was made of violence, but the state supreme court upheld the conviction on the grounds that despite the lack of specific reference to violence it was possible for the jury to read between the lines in light of the reputation of the IWW. The United States Supreme Court reversed the conviction because there was no evidence on the record to support the conviction. There was no suggestion in the testimony that Fiske used anything but lawful methods, and thus the conviction was "an arbitrary and unreasonable exercise of the police power of the state, unwarrantably infringing upon the liberty of the defendant." While this was a terribly small victory and no major liberal interpretation of the First Amendment was announced, as Zechariah Chafee (*Free Speech in the United States*) notes, "the Supreme Court for the first time made freedom of speech mean something."

The Smith Act

The Congress adopted the nation's first peacetime sedition law in 1798 and approved the second law in 1940 when it ratified the **Smith Act,** a measure making it a crime to advocate the violent overthrow of the government, to conspire to advocate the violent overthrow of the government, to organize a group which advocates the violent overthrow of the government, or to be a member of a group which advocates the violent overthrow of the government.

The Smith Act, which was aimed at the Communist party, was drafted by Congressman Howard Smith of Virginia and Congressman John McCormack of Massachusetts. It received little publicity, and many months elapsed before civil libertarians realized that the act had been passed. Among others Zechariah Chafee (*Free Speech in the United States*) writes, "Not until months later did I for one realize this statute contains the most drastic restriction on freedom of speech ever enacted in the United States during peace."

A small band of Trotskyites, members of the Socialist Workers party, were prosecuted and convicted under the Smith Act in 1943, but not until 1948 did a federal grand jury indict twelve of the nation's leading Communists for advocating the violent overthrow of the United States government. The trial began in January 1949 and lasted nine months. Eleven defendants (one became sick during the trial and was excused temporarily) were convicted, including Eugene V. Dennis, one of the party leaders in the United States. Trial judge Harold Medina told the jury that the statute did not prohibit discussing the propriety of overthrowing the government by force or violence, but "the teaching and advocacy of action for the accomplishment of that purpose by language reasonably and ordinarily calculated to incite persons to such action." In other words, the Smith Act prohibited the teaching or advocacy of action aimed at the violent overthrow of the government.

The convictions were appealed all the way to the Supreme Court, and in *Dennis* v. *U.S.* (1951) the high Court once again was called upon to outline the limitations which might be constitutionally applied against persons who oppose the government. In arguing that the Smith Act violated the guarantees of freedom of speech and press in the First Amendment, the defendants raised the almost thirty-year-old clear and present danger test as a barrier to the prosecution. The actions of this small band of Communists did not represent a clear and present danger to the nation, they argued. Chief Justice Fred Vinson wrote the opinion for the Supreme Court in the seven-to-two ruling that upheld the constitutionality of the federal sedition law. In considering the clear and present danger test, Vinson could have chosen to adopt the crabbed view of freedom of expression enunciated by Holmes in the *Schenck* case, or he could have followed Brandeis's more liberal exposition of the test from the *Whitney* decision. Vinson ended up creating a new test which fell politically somewhere between the tests outlined by Holmes in 1919 and Brandeis in 1927.

Vinson first insisted that the evil involved in the case (the evil which Congress has the right to prevent) was a substantial one, the overthrow of the government. That was the professed aim of the Communists, no doubt, but it was not very realistic. That does not matter, Vinson wrote, rejecting the contention that success or probability of success is the criterion, "Certainly an attempt to overthrow the Government by force, even though doomed from the outset because of inadequate numbers or power of the revolutionists, is a sufficient evil for Congress to prevent. The damage which such attempts create both physically and politically to a nation makes it impossible to measure the validity in terms of the probability of success, or the immediacy of a successful attempt." However, Vinson equated advocacy of overthrow with actual attempt at overthrow. It could be asked, How likely is it that the words spoken or written by the defendants would lead even to an attempted overthrow? Vinson's opinion was a far cry from Justice Brandeis's statement in *Whitney*. Recall Brandeis's words: "But even advocacy of violation (of the law), however reprehensible morally, is not a justification for denying free speech where the advocacy falls short of incitement and there is nothing to indicate that the advocacy would be immediately acted upon. The wide difference between advocacy and incitement, between preparation and attempt, between assembling and conspiracy, must be borne in mind."

Vinson outlined the test used by Judge Learned Hand when the Second United States Court of Appeals sustained the conviction of the eleven Communists. "In each case [courts] must ask whether the gravity of the 'evil,' discounted by improbability, justifies such invasion of free speech as is necessary to avoid the danger." Vinson said, "We adopt this statement of the rule."

The clear and probable danger test really says little more than the original Holmes clear and present danger test if Holmes's exposition in the *Debs, Frohwerk,* and *Schenck* cases are added. If the gravity of the evil is considered, Holmes said that the evil must be substantive or serious. Hand said that the probability of what might occur must be considered. What might occur? Might the overthrow succeed? Might the overthrow be attempted? Might the words lead someone to attempt an overthrow? What kind of danger are we trying to avoid? The issue is so unclear.

One could speculate that if the clear and present danger test as articulated by Justice Brandeis had been applied in this case the convictions would have gone out the window. The danger was not clear, nor was it present. However, in the atmosphere of 1951, such was not likely. We were in the midst of both a cold war with the Soviet Union and a hot war with the North Koreans and Communist Chinese, and as was said previously, the Supreme Court (all courts for that matter) is a political body at least to some extent.

Chief Justice Vinson made one additional important observation. Almost in passing, he noted that the Smith Act is aimed at advocacy, not at discussion.

After the government's success in the *Dennis* case, more prosecutions were initiated against Communists in the United States. Seven separate prosecutions were started in 1951, three in 1952, one in 1953, and five more during the next three years. One trial begun in late 1951 involved the top Communist leadership on the West Coast. At the trial after hearing both sides, Judge William C. Mathes told the jury that any advocacy dealing with the forcible overthrow of the government and presented with a specific intent to accomplish the overthrow is illegal under the Smith Act. This is about what Vinson said in the *Dennis* case. The defendants appealed their conviction, and six years later, in 1957, the Supreme Court voted five to two to reverse the convictions (*Yates* v. *U.S.,* 1957). On what grounds? Several factors influenced the reversal in *Yates* v. *U.S.,* but the basic reason is that Judge Mathes failed to distinguish between the advocacy of forcible overthrow as an abstract doctrine and the advocacy of action aimed at the forcible overthrow of the government. The Smith Act reaches only advocacy of action for the overthrow of government by force and violence, Justice John Marshall Harlan wrote for the court. "The essential distinction," Harlan notes, "is that those to whom the advocacy is addressed must be urged to do something now or in the future, rather than merely to believe in something." How specific must this advocacy of action be? It does not have to be immediate action; it can be action in the future. But it must be an urge to do something: form an army, blow up a bridge, prepare for sabotage, train for street fighting, and so forth.

The government was unprepared to meet this new burden of proof. Far more evidence is needed to prove that someone has urged people to do something than to prove that someone has merely urged them to believe something. All but one of the cases pending were dismissed. The defendants in the single case that was tried were set free on an evidentiary issue (*Bary* v. *U.S.,* 1957) and were never retried. In fact, there has not been a single successful prosecution for advocacy of violent overthrow since the *Yates* decision. One successful prosecution under the membership clause of the Smith Act has occurred, but it was in 1961 (*Scales* v. *U.S.,* 1961).

To his credit, Justice Harlan did not attempt to apply either the clear and present danger test or the clear and probable danger test. This consideration wasn't necessary since the constitutionality of the law is not the heart of the appeal in the *Yates* case as it is in *Dennis*.

Few sedition trials have occurred since 1957. In 1969, the Supreme Court once again looked at a state sedition law in *Brandenburg* v. *Ohio* (1969). In this case a Ku Klux Klan leader was prosecuted by the state of Ohio for advocating unlawful methods of terrorism and crime as a means of accomplishing industrial and political reform. The high Court voided his conviction on the grounds that the Ohio law failed to distinguish between the advocacy of ideas and the incitement to unlawful conduct. In its per curiam opinion the Court said, "The constitutional guarantees of free speech and free press do not permit a State to forbid or proscribe advocacy of the use of force or of law violation except where such advocacy is directed to inciting or producing imminent lawless action or is likely to incite or produce such actions." This opinion comes close to how Louis Brandeis outlined the clear and present danger test in 1927 in the *Whitney* case.

The famous Holmes test is not dead by any means. It still lives, for example, in criminal contempt law where the high Court has fashioned it into a workable test to protect both courts and defendants from the interference of the mass media in the judicial process. If it is not dead, the test is certainly lifeless with regard to sedition law, partly because sedition law is not nearly so robust as it was forty years ago. The Communists long since ceased to be a threat in this nation. In fact one author suggests that the party is currently alive only because it is subsidized by the United States government. Indeed, political scientist John Roche (*Shadow and Substance*) asserts that if the many undercover FBI agents who are members of the party were to withdraw their membership and stop paying dues the party would collapse.

More seriously, the federal government chose not to use sedition laws in prosecuting protestors and dissidents during the Vietnam War. Instead the government used rather exotic conspiracy laws and still enjoyed little success. The Smith Act is still on the books, and it probably could have been used against some antiwar leaders. But it was not. The law is not popular today. Sedition laws are not popular today. When people feel little direct threat to their well-being, they are willing to exercise a remarkable range of tolerance of unpopular ideas and suggestions. Unpopular or unorthodox speakers and writers are written off as kooks, which in many cases they are. However, should there occur another serious war, a deep depression which causes loss of confidence in the government, or other situation in which people feel threatened, what could happen is difficult to predict.

Summary

Within eight years of the passage of the First Amendment the nation adopted its first (and most wide-ranging) sedition laws, the Alien and Sedition Acts of 1798. Many leading political editors and politicians were prosecuted under the laws, which made it a crime to criticize both President John Adams and the national government. While the Supreme Court never did hear arguments regarding the constitutionality of the laws, several justices of the Supreme Court presided at sedition act trials and refused to sustain a constitutional objection to the laws. The public hated the measures. John Adams was voted out of office in 1800 and was replaced by his political opponent and target of the sedition laws, Thomas Jefferson. The laws left such a bad taste that the federal government did not pass another sedition law until World War I, one hundred seventeen years later.

Sedition prosecutions in the period of 1915–1925 were the most vicious in the nation's history as war protestors, socialists, anarchists, and other political dissidents became the target of government repression. It was during this era that the Supreme Court began to interpret the meaning of the First Amendment. In a series of rulings stemming from the World War I cases, the high Court fashioned what is known as the clear and present danger test to measure state and federal laws and protest and other expression against the

First Amendment. The test was rigid and was never used to overturn a lower-court conviction, although in 1927 Justice Louis D. Brandeis did fashion a broad and liberal interpretation of the clear and present danger test in his dissent in the case of *Whitney* v. *California.* In 1925 the high Court ruled that the guarantees of freedom of speech apply to actions taken by all governments, that freedom of speech under the First Amendment protects individuals from censorship by all levels of government, not just from actions by the federal government. This pronouncement in *Gitlow* v. *New York* opened the door to a much broader protection of freedom of expression in the nation.

The nation's most recent sedition law was adopted in 1940. The Smith Act, as it is known, prohibits the advocacy of the violent overthrow of the government. Following a series of trials and two Supreme Court rulings in the 1950s, the law has become a relatively benign prohibition. The high Court ruled in 1957 in *Yates* v. *U.S.* that to sustain a conviction under the Smith Act the government must prove that the defendants advocate specific violent or forcible action toward the overthrow of the government. The government found it impossible to do this in the 1950s, and the Smith Act has not been invoked to punish an act of expression for more than twenty-five years.

PRIOR RESTRAINT

The great compiler of the British law William Blackstone defined freedom of the press in the 1760s as freedom from "previous restraint," or **prior restraint.** Regardless of the difference of opinion on whether the First Amendment is intended to protect political criticism, most students of the constitutional period agree that the guarantees of freedom of speech and press were intended to bar the government from exercising prior restraint. Despite the weight of such authority, the media in the United States in the 1980s still faces instances of prepublication censorship. The issue is clearly not completely settled.

Prior censorship, or prior restraint, is probably the most insidious kind of government control. Speakers and publishers are stopped before they can speak or print. The people are not allowed to discover what was going to be said or published. We are denied the benefit of these ideas or suggestions or criticisms.

Prior censorship is difficult to define, as scores of laws and government actions hold the potential for a kind of prior restraint. In privacy law, for example, it is possible under some statutes to stop the publication of material which illegally appropriates a person's name or likeness. In extreme cases the press can be stopped from publishing information it has learned in a criminal case. The two instances just mentioned as well as others will be discussed fully in later, more appropriate sections of this book. The purpose of this section is to outline those kinds of prior restraint that seem to fall outside the boundaries of other chapters in the book. We will therefore discuss injunctions against public nuisances, laws which place limits on when and where materials may be distributed, cases involving national security matters, and other topics.

The Supreme Court did not consider the issue of prior restraint until more than a decade after it had decided its first major sedition case. In 1931 in *Near* v. *Minnesota* the high Court struck an important blow for freedom of expression.

Near v. *Minnesota* City and county officials in Minneapolis, Minnesota, brought a legal action against Jay M. Near and Howard Guilford, publishers of the *Saturday Press,* a small weekly newspaper. Near and Guilford were reformers whose purpose was to clean up city and county government in Minneapolis. In their attacks upon corruption in city government, they used language which was far from temperate and defamed some of the town's leading government officials. Near and Guilford charged that Jewish gangsters were in control of gambling, bootlegging, and racketeering in the city, and that city government and its law enforcement agencies did not perform their duties energetically. They repeated these charges over and over in a highly inflammatory manner.

Minnesota had a statute which empowered a court to declare any obscene, lewd, lascivious, malicious, scandalous, or defamatory publication a public nuisance. When such a publication was deemed a public nuisance, the court issued an injunction against future publication or distribution. Violation of the injunction resulted in punishment for contempt of court.

In 1927 County Attorney Floyd Olson initiated an action against the *Saturday Press.* A district court declared the newspaper a public nuisance and "perpetually enjoined" publication of the *Saturday Press.* The only way either Near or Guilford would be able to publish the newspaper again was to convince the court that their newspaper would remain free of objectionable material. In 1928 the Minnesota Supreme Court upheld the constitutionality of the law, declaring that under its broad police power the state can regulate public nuisances, including defamatory and scandalous newspapers.

The case then went to the United States Supreme Court which reversed the ruling by the state supreme court. The nuisance statute was declared unconstitutional. Chief Justice Charles Evans Hughes wrote the opinion for the Court in the five-to-four ruling, saying that the statute in question was not designed to redress wrongs to individuals attacked by the newspaper. Instead, the statute was directed at suppressing the *Saturday Press* once and for all. The object of the law, Hughes wrote, was not punishment but censorship—not only of a single issue, but also of all future issues—which is not consistent with the traditional concept of freedom of the press. That is, the statute constituted prior restraint, and prior restraint is clearly a violation of the First Amendment.

One maxim in the law holds that when a judge writes an opinion for a court he should stick to the problem at hand, that he should not wander off and talk about matters that do not really concern the issue before the court. Such remarks are considered **dicta,** or words that do not really apply to the case. These words, these dicta, are never really considered an important part of the ruling in the case. Chief Justice Hughes's opinion in *Near* v. *Minnesota* contains a good deal of dicta.

In this case Hughes wrote that the prior restraint of the *Saturday Press* was unconstitutional, but in some circumstances, he added, prior restraint might be permissible. In what kinds of circumstances? The government can constitutionally stop publication of obscenity, the government can stop publication of material which incites people to acts of violence, and it may prohibit publication of certain kinds of materials during wartime. Hughes admitted, on the other hand, defining freedom of the press as the only freedom from prior restraint is equally wrong, for in many cases punishment after publication imposes effective censorship upon the freedom of expression.

Near v. *Minnesota* stands for the proposition that under American law prior censorship is permitted only in very unusual circumstances; it is the exception, not the rule. Courts have reinforced this interpretation many times since 1931. Despite this considerable litigation, we still lack a complete understanding of the kinds of circumstances in which prior restraint might be acceptable under the First Amendment, as a series of recent cases (some of which are concerned with national security) illustrate.

Austin v. *Keefe*

A case that to some extent reinforced the *Near* ruling involved the attempt of a real estate broker to stop a neighborhood community action group from distributing pamphlets about him (*Organization for a Better Austin v. Keefe,* 1971). The Organization for a Better Austin was a community organization in the Austin suburb of Chicago. Its goal was to stabilize the population in the integrated community. Members were opposed to the tactics of certain real estate brokers who came into white neighborhoods, spread the word that blacks were moving in, bought up the white-owned homes cheaply in the ensuing panic, and then resold them at a good profit to blacks or other whites. The organization received pledges from most real estate firms in the area to stop these blockbusting tactics. But Jerome Keefe refused to make such an agreement. The community group then printed leaflets and flyers describing his activities and handed them out in Westchester, the community in which Keefe lived. Group members told the Westchester residents that Keefe was a "panic peddler" and said they would stop distributing the leaflets in Westchester as soon as Keefe agreed to stop his blockbusting real estate tactics. Keefe went to court and obtained an injunction which prohibited further distribution by the community club of pamphlets, leaflets, and literature of any kind in Westchester on the grounds that the material constituted an invasion of Keefe's privacy and caused him irreparable harm. The Organization for a Better Austin appealed the ruling to the United States Supreme Court. In May 1971 the high Court dissolved the injunction. Chief Justice Warren Burger wrote, "The injunction, so far as it imposes prior restraint on speech and publication, constitutes an impermissible restraint on First Amendment rights."

He said that the injunction, as in the *Near* case, did not seek to redress individual wrongs, but instead sought to suppress on the basis of one or two handbills the distribution of any kind of literature in a city of 18,000 inhabitants. Keefe argued that the purpose of the handbills was not to inform the community, but to force him to sign an agreement. The Chief Justice said this argument was immaterial and was not sufficient cause to remove the leaflets and flyers from the protection of the First Amendment. Justice Burger added (*Austin* v. *Keefe*):

> Petitioners [the community group] were engaged openly and vigorously in making the public aware of respondent's [Keefe's] real estate practices. Those practices were offensive to them, as the views and practices of the petitioners are no doubt offensive to others. But so long as the means are peaceful, the communication need not meet standards of acceptability.

The *Keefe* case did a good job of reinforcing the high Court's decision in *Near* v. *Minnesota*.

Pentagon Papers Case

While it is more famous, another 1971 decision is not as strong a statement in behalf of freedom of expression as either *Near* or *Keefe*. This is the famous Pentagon Papers decision (*New York Times Co.* v. *U.S.; U.S.* v. *Washington Post,* 1971). While the political implications of the ruling are very important, the ruling itself is legally quite unsatisfying.

The case began in the summer of 1971 when the *New York Times,* followed by the *Washington Post* and a handful of other newspapers, began publication of a series of articles based on a top-secret forty-seven-volume government study entitled "History of the United States Decision-Making Process on Vietnam Policy." The day after the initial article on the Pentagon Papers appeared, Attorney General John Mitchell asked the *New York Times* to stop publication of the material. When the *Times*'s publisher refused, the government went to court to get an injunction to force the newspaper to stop the series. A temporary restraining order was granted as the case wound its way to the Supreme Court. Such an order was also imposed upon the *Washington Post* after it began to publish reports based on the same material.

At first the government argued that the publication of this material violated federal espionage statutes. When that assertion did not satisfy the lower federal courts, the government argued that the president had inherent power under his constitutional mandate to conduct foreign affairs to protect the national security, which includes the right to classify documents secret and top secret. Publication of this material by the newspapers was unauthorized disclosure of such material and should be stopped. This argument did not satisfy the courts either, and by the time the case came before the Supreme Court the government argument was that publication of these papers might result in irreparable harm to the nation and its ability to conduct foreign affairs. The *Times* and the *Post* consistently made two arguments. First, they said that the classification system is a sham, that people in the government de-classify documents almost at will when they want to sway public opinion or influence a reporter's story. Second, the press also argued that an injunction against the continued publication of this material violated the First Amendment. Interestingly, the newspapers did not argue that under all circumstances prior restraint is in conflict with the First Amendment. Defense attorney Professor Alexander Bickel argued that under some circumstances prior restraint is acceptable, for example, when the publication of a document has a direct link with a grave event which is immediate and visible. Former Justice William O. Douglas noted that this is a strange argument for newspapers to make—and it is. Apparently both newspapers decided that a victory in that immediate case was far more important than to establish a definitive and long-lasting constitutional principle. They therefore concentrated on winning the case, acknowledging that in future cases prior restraint might be permissible.

On June 30 the high Court ruled six to three in favor of the *New York Times* and the *Washington Post*. The Court did not grant a permanent injunction against the publication of the Pentagon Papers, but the ruling was hardly the kind which strengthened the First Amendment. In a very short per curiam opinion the majority said that in a case involving the prior restraint of a publication the government bears a heavy burden to justify such a restraint. In this case the government failed to show the Court why such a restraint should be imposed upon the two newspapers. In other words, the government failed to justify its request for the permanent restraining order.

The decision in the case rested upon the preferred position First Amendment theory or doctrine (see page 49). The ban on publication was *presumed* to be an unconstitutional infringement upon the First Amendment. The government had to prove that the ban was needed to protect the nation in some manner. If such evidence could be adduced, the Court would strike the balance in favor of the government and uphold the ban on the publication of the articles. But in this case the government simply failed to show why its request for an injunction was vital to the national interest. Consequently the high Court denied the government's request for a ban on the publication of the Pentagon Papers on the grounds that such a prohibition was a violation of the First Amendment. Note: The court did not say that in all similar cases an injunction would violate the First Amendment. It did not even say that in this case an injunction was a violation of the First Amendment. It merely said that the government had not shown why the injunction was needed, why it was not a violation of the freedom of the press. Such a decision is not what one would call a ringing defense of the right of free expression.

In addition to the brief unsigned opinion from the majority, the Chief Justice and each of the eight associate justices wrote short individual opinions. They were not very instructive, but should be noted anyway.

Justices Black and Douglas clung to the absolutist theory and argued that they could conceive of no circumstance under which the government can properly interfere with freedom of expression. Debate on public questions must be open and robust, Justice Douglas wrote. Justice William Brennan echoed the Court's opinion: there was no proof that the publication of the papers would damage the national security or the nation. Justice Potter Stewart agreed and attacked the notion of classifying public documents and excessive secrecy in government. "For when everything is classified," he wrote, "then nothing is classified, and the system becomes one to be disregarded by the cynical or the careless, and to be manipulated by those intent on self-protection or self-promotion."

Justice Byron White supported the notion that the government lacked the evidence needed to sustain an injunction. But Justice White added that he believed the publication of the material would damage the national interest, and if the government chose to bring the newspapers back to court for criminal prosecution for violating an espionage statute, he could surely support a conviction. These last remarks are another example of dicta. The last member of the majority, Justice Thurgood Marshall, said he did not believe the president has the right to classify documents in the first place, that Congress has consistently rejected giving the executive this power, and that consequently the Court should not support such questionable authority.

All three of the dissenters, Chief Justice Warren Burger, Justice John M. Harlan, and Justice Harry Blackmun, complained that there had not been sufficient time to properly consider the case. The issues were too important for such a rush to judgment, Justice Burger said, noting his dissent was not based upon the merits of the case. Harlan and Blackmun did dissent on the merits. Harlan argued that foreign relations and national security are both concerns of other branches of the government, and the Court should accept the government's assertions in this case—even without evidence—that disclosure of the material in the Pentagon Papers would substantially harm the government. Justice Blackmun wanted to send the case back to the trial courts for fuller exposition of the facts and to allow the government more time to prepare its case.

What many people at first called the case of the century ended in a fizzle, at least with regard to developing First Amendment law. The press won the day; the Pentagon Papers were published. But thoughtful observers expressed concern over the ruling. A majority of the Court had not ruled that such prior restraint was unconstitutional—only that the government had failed to meet the heavy burden of showing such restraint was necessary in this case.

Progressive Magazine Case

The fragile nature of the Court's holding became clear in early 1979 when the government again went to court to block the publication of material it claimed could endanger the national security (*U.S.* v. *Progressive*, 1979). Freelance writer Howard Morland had prepared an article entitled "The H-Bomb

Secret: How We Got It, Why We're Telling It." The piece was scheduled to be published in the April edition of the *Progressive* magazine, a seventy-year-old political digest founded by Robert M. LaFollette as a voice of the progressive movement.

Morland had gathered the material for the article from unclassified sources. After completing an early draft of the piece, he sought technical criticism from various scholars. Somehow a copy found its way to officials in the federal government. With the cat out of the bag, *Progressive* editor Erwin Knoll sent a final draft to the government for prepublication comments on technical accuracy. The government said the piece was too accurate and moved into federal court to stop the magazine from publishing the story.

The defendants in the case argued that all the information in the article was in the public domain, that any citizen could have gotten the same material by going to the Department of Energy, federal libraries, and the like. Other nations already had this information or could easily get it. Experts testifying in behalf of the magazine argued that the article was a harmless exposition of some exotic nuclear technology.

The government disagreed. It said that while some of the material was in the public domain much of the data were not publicly available. Prosecutors and a battery of technical experts argued that the article contained a core of information that had never before been published. The United States also argued that it was immaterial where Morland had got his information and whether it had come from classified or public documents. Prosecutors argued that the nation's national security interest permitted the classification and censorship of even information originating in the public domain if, when such information is drawn together, synthesized, and collated, it acquires the character "of presenting immediate, direct and irreparable harm to the interests of the United States." The United States was arguing, then, that some material is automatically classified as soon as it is created if it has the potential to cause harm to the nation. The information in Morland's article met this description, prosecutors argued.

It fell to United States District Judge Robert Warren to evaluate the conflicting claims and reach a decision on the government's request to enjoin the publication of the piece. In a thoughtful opinion in which Warren attempted to sort out the issues in the case, he agreed with the government that there were concepts in the article not found in the public realm—concepts vital to the operation of a thermonuclear bomb. Was the piece a do-it-yourself-guide for a hydrogen bomb? No, Warren said, it was not. "A number of affidavits make quite clear that a sine qua non to thermonuclear capability is a large, sophisticated industrial capability coupled with a coterie of imaginative, resourceful scientists and technicians." But the article could provide some nations with a ticket to bypass blind alleys and help a medium-sized nation to move faster in developing a hydrogen bomb.

To the *Progressive*'s argument that the publication of the article would provide people with the information needed to make an informed decision on nuclear issues, Warren wrote, "This Court can find no plausible reason why the public needs to know the technical details about hydrogen bomb construction to carry on an informed debate on this issue."

Looking to the legal issues in the case Warren said he saw three differences between this case and the *Pentagon Papers* ruling of 1971. The Pentagon Papers themselves were a historical study; the Morland article was of immediate concern. In the *Pentagon Papers* case there had been no cogent national security reasons advanced by the government when it sought to enjoin the publication of the study. The national security interest is considerably more apparent in the *Progressive* case, Warren noted. Finally, the government lacked substantial legal authority to stop the publication of the Pentagon Papers. The laws raised by the government were vague, not at all appropriate. But Section 2274 of the Atomic Energy Act of 1954 is quite specific in prohibiting anyone from communicating or disclosing any restricted data to any persons "with reasons to believe such data will be utilized to injure the United States or to secure an advantage to any foreign nation." Section 2014 of the same act defined restricted data to include information on the design, manufacture, or utilization of atomic weapons.

Warren concluded that the government had met the heavy burden of showing justification for prior restraint. The judge added that he was not convinced that suppression of the objected-to technical portions of the article would impede the *Progressive* in its crusade to stimulate public debate on the issue of nuclear armament. "What is involved here," Warren concluded, "is information dealing with the most destructive weapon in the history of mankind, information of sufficient destructive potential to nullify the right to free speech and to endanger the right to life itself."

When the injunction was issued, the editors of the *Progressive* and their supporters inside and outside the press vowed to appeal the ruling—to the Supreme Court if necessary. Yet there was a distinct uneasiness among even many persons who sided with the publication. Judge Warren had done a professional job of distinguishing this case from the *Pentagon Papers* ruling. There were important differences. The membership on the high Court had changed as well. Black and Douglas, who both voted against the government in 1971, had left the Court, as had Harlan who voted with the government. Some newspapers, the *Washington Post* and the *New York Times*, for example, expressed the fear that a damaging precedent could emerge from the Supreme Court if the *Progressive* case ultimately reached the high tribunal.

Then in September of 1979, as the *Progressive* case began its slow ascent up the appellate ladder, a small newspaper in Madison, Wisconsin, published a story containing much of the same information in the Morland article.

When this occurred, the Department of Justice unhappily withdrew its suit against the *Progressive* (*U.S.* v. *Progressive*, 1979). The confrontation between the press and the government in the Supreme Court was averted. Many journalists expressed relief.

But the victory in the *Progressive* case was bittersweet at best. The publication of the article had been enjoined. A considerable body of legal opinion supported the notion that the injunction would have been sustained by the Supreme Court, rightly or wrongly. Prior restraint, which had seemed quite distant in the years succeeding *Near* v. *Minnesota* and in the afterglow of the press victory in the *Pentagon Papers* case, took on realistic and frightening new proportions.

In 1982 and 1983 the federal government made new attempts to restrict the flow of information relating to the national security. President Ronald Reagan issued an executive order in 1982 which revised the government's classification system and made it easier for persons in the defense department and other sensitive areas to keep material from public scrutiny. Reagan issued a second directive to tighten control over sensitive material in March 1983. (These orders are discussed in chapter 5, page 254.)

In another action Congress made it a crime for a journalist or anyone else to disclose or publish the names of United States government agents or intelligence sources who are working undercover. Under the statute it does not matter whether the names are obtained from either public or secret sources. In order to successfully prosecute the government must prove that the disclosure was made after the person charged had engaged in a "pattern of activities intended to identify and expose covert agents." The government would also have to show that the disclosure was made with reason to believe that it would harm United States intelligence efforts. A three-year jail term and/or a fine of $15,000 is the punishment for violating the statute.

"Fighting-Words" Doctrine

While national security issues are frequently the source of prior restraint problems, other issues can provoke authorities to the application of restraint. In 1942, in the case of *Chaplinsky* v. *New Hampshire*, the Supreme Court identified one category of speech in which the application of prior censorship is not necessarily a violation of the First Amendment. Justice Frank Murphy wrote:

> There are certain well-defined and narrowly limited classes of speech, the *prevention* [emphasis added] and punishment of which have never been thought to raise any constitutional problems. These include . . . fighting words—those which by their very utterance inflict injury or tend to incite an immediate breach of the peace. It has been well observed that such utterances are no essential part of any exposition of ideas, and are of such slight social value as a step to the truth that any benefit that may be derived from them is clearly outweighed by the social interest in order and morality.

In the *Chaplinsky* case a Jehovah's Witness, who sought to distribute pamphlets denouncing religion as a fraud in Rochester, New Hampshire, angered citizens. When warned by a law officer of the danger to his safety, the Witness called the marshal a "God-damned racketeer" and a "damned Facist." He was convicted of violating a state statute which forbid any person to "address any offensive, derisive, or annoying words, to any other person who is lawfully in any street or other public place, nor call him by any offensive or derisive name."

The prohibition of this kind of verbal assault is permissible so long as the statutes are carefully drawn and do not permit the application of the law to protected speech. Also, the "fighting words" must be used in a personal, face-to-face encounter—a true verbal assault. In 1972 the Supreme Court ruled that laws on the subject must be limited to words "that have a direct tendency to cause acts of violence by the person to whom, individually, the remark is addressed" (*Gooding* v. *Wilson*, 1972).

The 1977 confrontation in Skokie, Illinois, between Nazi protesters and city officials presents a contemporary example of a multitude of free-speech problems including the so-called fighting-words doctrine. In 1976 members of the National Socialist party said they planned to peacefully demonstrate in Skokie, a community with a large Jewish population, to protest the racial integration of nearby Chicago schools. The protest was prohibited by village officials who said the Nazis had failed to obtain $350,000 worth of liability and property damage insurance as required by a Skokie Park District ordinance.

After the Nazis announced that they planned to protest against the insurance ordinance, the village obtained a temporary restraining order blocking the demonstration and then adopted three new ordinances regarding public marches and protests. In addition to the insurance requirements, the village ruled that a member of a political party cannot march in a military-style uniform and ruled that it is not permissible to disseminate material intended to incite racial hatred. State and federal courts in Illinois invalidated all the ordinances, ruling that they were discriminatory or abridged constitutionally protected rights of free speech (*Collin* v. *Smith*, 1978; *Village of Skokie* v. *National Socialist Party*, 1978).

The Illinois Supreme Court, in refusing to enjoin the display of the swastika and other Nazi symbols, rejected the contention that such display constituted "fighting words" sufficient "to overcome the heavy presumption against the constitutional validity of a prior restraint" (*Village of Skokie* v. *National Socialist Party*, 1978). "Peaceful demonstrations cannot be totally precluded solely because that display [of the swastika] may provoke a violent reaction by those who view it. . . . A speaker who gives prior notice of his message has not compelled a confrontation with those who voluntarily listen."

In *Handbook of Free Speech and Free Press*, authors Jerome Barron and C. Thomas Dienes suggest two key questions in determining whether so-called fighting words might be suppressed. First, is there imminent danger of disorder? Second, does the speaker use provocative language which constitutes fighting words or which incites his audience to a clear and present danger of disorder? Both questions must be answered in the affirmative before the speech can reasonably be restrained.

Freedom of Expression in Schools

The prior restraint of speech and press in schools is also permissible in circumstances that run parallel to the fighting-words doctrine, but fall far short of its ultimate protection of free expression. The unequivocal regulation of expression in the schools—high schools, colleges, and universities—was the rule in this country until the 1960s.

In 1967 a federal district court in Alabama ruled that suspension from school of the editor of the Troy State College campus newspaper for publishing an editorial critical of state legislators was a violation of the student's First Amendment rights. The court ruled that the First Amendment provides protection for the expression of students and school children. School officials cannot infringe upon such rights unless the student publications or speeches "materially and substantially interfere with requirements of appropriate discipline in the operation of the school" (*Dickey* v. *Alabama*, 1967). In a subsequent case, *Tinker* v. *Des Moines School District* (1969), in which the expression at issue was the wearing of an armband as a symbolic protest, the United States Supreme Court accepted the rule as established in the *Dickey* case.

Yet recent cases have made it clear that prior restraint of student expression is clearly acceptable, provided there is sufficient reason to believe that disruption or other harm might result. In 1977 a federal appeals court in New York ruled that school officials can stop students from surveying their classmates' attitudes on certain sexual matters if the school officials showed they have a reasonable basis for believing the survey would cause significant psychological harm to some students. The court said both the distribution of the voluntary survey and the subsequent publication of an article in the high school newspaper on findings elicited by the survey could be stopped so long as school officials showed that *some* psychological experts predicted that *some* students would experience *some* level of stress from confronting *some* of the questions which were asked in the questionnaire. The court added that school officials might be legitimately concerned that the proposed interpretive article would draw misleading conclusions about the sexual behavior of the students at the school (*Trachtman* v. *Anker*, 1977).

The following year a federal district court in New York upheld the restraint by the principal of an entire edition of the Sewanhaka High School newspaper on the grounds that he (the principal) believed that two letters published in the paper might substantially disrupt school activities and might harm the personal reputation of a student. The principal said he feared that one letter, which was vulgar but clearly not obscene, might provoke a violent confrontation between members of the paper's staff and the lacrosse team. The second letter, which criticized the conduct of a student government leader, could have been libelous or a violation of the student's right to privacy, the principal said.

Later examination and investigation proved that the principal's fears were probably groundless, but the court ruled that the judiciary cannot be in the business of second guessing school authorities after the fact. The question to be asked was: Did school authorities demonstrate a substantial basis for their conclusion that harm might result? The principal apparently consulted with members of his staff as well as with students at the time he seized the copies of the newspaper and concluded that distribution of the edition could cause a substantial risk of disruption and harm. "It is not terribly important what can be proved about the truth or falsity of material after the fact," the court said. The crucial question is whether the principal made a reasonable determination based on the information he had at the time (*Frasca* v. *Andrews*, 1978).

School officials, then, are granted significantly more leeway in applying prior restraints than are civil authorities outside the educational setting. Some authorities believe that the decisions in both the *Trachtman* and *Frasca* cases substantially undercut what was seen as a broad protection for student expression following *Dickey* and *Tinker*. As courts consider more specific instances of school censorship, the broadly drawn rules of *Dickey* and *Tinker* will probably be tightened.

Book Banning

Another school censorship problem arose in the early 1980s and quickly became a serious legal issue. The banning of books in libraries—primarily school libraries—reached epidemic levels in 1981 and 1982. A survey by the American Library Association reported that the number of challenges to books in libraries tripled to nearly 1,000 during 1981. Conservative groups have been active in banning attempts, but other individuals not usually associated with this problem are active as well. Black parents in several areas, for example, urged a ban on Mark Twain's *The Adventures of Huckleberry Finn* because of what they felt was racist language. The most common reason would-be censors give to justify removing books from library shelves is that a book is unsuitable for minors because of its vulgarity or its description of sexual behavior, according to the *New York Times*. But these censors also condemn the depiction of unorthodox family arrangements; speculations about Christ; sexual explicitness, even in a biological context; unflattering portraits of American authority; criticisms of business and corporate practices; and radical political ideas.

Censorship activities have focused upon a wide variety of books, according to the survey sponsored by the Association of American Publishers, the American Library Association, and the Association for Supervision and Curriculum Development which was reported in the *New York Times*. Some of the books most commonly attacked by censors are:

Jaws by Peter Benchley
Several books by Judy Blume, a best-selling children's author
The Pill Versus the Springhill Mine Disaster and other novels by
    Richard Brautigan
Manchild in the Promised Land by Claude Brown
Kramer Versus Kramer by Avery Corman
Catch-22 by Joseph Heller
Sons by Evan Hunter
Valley Forge by MacKinlay Kantor
One Flew Over the Cuckoo's Nest by Ken Kesey
The Thorn Birds by Colleen McCullough
The Godfather by Mario Puzo
One Day in the Life of Ivan Denisovitch by Aleksander Solzhenitsyn
The American Heritage Dictionary
The Dictionary of American Slang
Trial of the Catonsville Nine by Daniel Berrigan
Our Bodies, Ourselves by the Boston Women's Health Book Collective
The Art of Loving by Erich Fromm
Boss: Richard J. Daley of Chicago by Mike Royko
The Electric Kool-Aid Acid Test by Tom Wolfe

Also included in the list of frequently censored books are *A Farewell to Arms, 1984, Brave New World, The Catcher in the Rye, The Merchant of Venice, The Grapes of Wrath, Huckleberry Finn,* and *Stuart Little*.

Most school boards were woefully unprepared for the pressure generated by parents and community groups to remove books from the shelves of libraries. While book banning has occurred as a periodic nuisance over the past two hundred years, the problem has rarely reached the courts. Consequently, little law exists on the subject to advise library supervisors or school boards. It took only a few years for a case to reach the Supreme Court of the United States during this round of book censorship.

Members of the Board of Education of the Island Trees School District in Eastern New York removed nine books from the high school library. Included among the banished books were *The Fixer* by Bernard Malamud, *Slaughterhouse Five* by Kurt Vonnegut, *The Naked Ape* by Desmond Morris, *Soul on Ice* by Eldridge Cleaver, and the *Best Short Stories by Negro Writers*. Student Council President Steven Pico and four other students challenged this action in the United States district court. They argued that their First Amendment rights to read these books had been violated. But United States District Judge George Pratt rejected these arguments and ruled that a school board has the right to remove books which are irrelevant, vulgar, and immoral and in bad taste. The First Amendment was not violated by such action, Pratt ruled, citing a seven-year-old Second United States Court of Appeals decision (*President's Council District 25* v. *Community School Board,* 1972). The judge's ruling came on the board of education's motion for summary judgment. No trial was ever held to establish the facts, including the school board's motives for removing these volumes (*Pico* v. *Island Trees,* 1979).

The Second United States Court of Appeals reversed Judge Pratt's order and ordered the district court to hold a trial. The court stood by its earlier decision that permitted school authorities to remove vulgar or immoral books from the school library. But Steven Pico and the other students should have been given a chance at trial to persuade the court that the school board's ostensible justification for removing the books (that they were in bad taste, vulgar, etc.) was merely a pretext for the suppression of freedom of speech. The board could not ban the books if their decision to remove them was based on their political or moral disagreement with the content of the works.

In March 1982 the Supreme Court heard arguments in the case and three months later handed down one of the least-satisfying rulings in many years. On the bottom line the high Court affirmed the court of appeals and returned the case to district court for trial. However the high Court was fractured into several groups, and seven different opinions were written.

The Court's opinion was written by Justice William Brennan. A school board cannot, under the First Amendment, remove books from a school library simply because it disapproves of the political ideas or philosophies expressed in the books, wrote Justice Brennan. Books may be removed if they are persuasively vulgar, or if they are educationally unsuitable. But the First Amendment guarantees to students a right to receive ideas, and the board of education cannot interfere with that right simply because it disagrees with those ideas. Brennan mustered the support of Justices Thurgood Marshall and John Stevens behind his opinion.

Justice Harry Blackmun concurred with all of Brennan's opinion except his reference to a "right to receive ideas," a controversial notion Brennan has promulgated in recent years. Blackmun said he based his opinion on a principle narrower and far more basic than the right to receive ideas. The state may not suppress exposure to ideas for the sole purpose of suppressing exposure to those ideas, he wrote. The fifth vote in the five-to-four decision came from Justice Byron White who seemed dismayed at Brennan's exploration of constitutional issues. A trial was needed, he said, to find out what motivated the removal of the books. When the facts are established, he wrote, the Court can develop constitutional law on the matter.

Chief Justice Warren Burger and Justices Lewis Powell, William Rehnquist, and Sandra O'Connor all dissented. All the dissenting opinions reflected the position that it was the responsibility of the school board, not of a federal court, to run the school. "The plurality [Brennan, Marshall, Blackmun, and Stevens] concludes that the Constitution requires school boards to justify to its teenage pupils the decision to remove a particular book from a school library," Burger wrote. Other dissenters echoed Burger's complaint.

The ruling was particularly unsatisfactory because the Court failed to provide any clear guidance on an issue which is plaguing scores of school libraries across the nation. The splits within the Court left even a careful reader of the decision with little certainty about how the Court would act in a subsequent case. Four justices said school boards cannot remove books from a library for political or moral reasons; four justices said school boards can remove books for any reason; and Justice White refused to say where he stands on the issue. "We should not decide constitutional questions until it is necessary to do so," he wrote. Even the language in the Court's opinion lacks clarity. Brennan said that a book can be removed from the shelves if it is "persuasively vulgar" or "educationally unsuitable." What do these terms mean? Until the high Court takes the opportunity to give a clearer answer in another case, school boards, librarians, teachers, parents, and students all face a period of uncertainty.

Summary

While virtually all American legal scholars agree that the adoption of the First Amendment in 1791 was designed to abolish prior restraint in this nation, prior censorship still exists by virtue of an opinion of the Supreme Court in 1931. In *Near* v. *Minnesota* Chief Justice Charles Evans Hughes ruled that while prior restraint is unacceptable in most instances there are times when it must be tolerated if the republic is to survive. The most vivid example cited by Hughes is the prior restraint of the publication of information that may assist the enemy during wartime. Hughes's "wartime" exception has been translated today to mean a "national security" exception, and in recent years in two important cases the press has been stopped from publishing material which courts believed to be too sensitive. While the Supreme Court finally permitted the *New York Times* and the *Washington Post* to publish the so-called Pentagon Papers, the newspapers were blocked for two weeks from printing the material. And in the end the high Court merely ruled that the government had failed to make its case, not that the newspapers had an absolute right to publish the material. The *Progressive* magazine was enjoined from publishing an article about the hydrogen bomb. Only the publication of the material by an underground newspaper in Wisconsin thwarted government efforts to permanently stop publication of the material.

Chief Justice Hughes said in 1931 that prior restraint is also permissible in instances in which a speaker or publisher is attempting to incite violence. The Supreme Court has developed a "fighting-words" doctrine which has been applied in several instances to block expression which might incite others to violence, although in recent cases involving a protest by members of the Nazi party in Illinois, both federal and state courts have ruled that members of an audience have an obligation to restrain themselves and expression cannot be prohibited merely because the speaker has chosen to appear before a volatile group.

Schools must live by the First Amendment. So long as expression does not substantially and materially interfere with the requirements of appropriate discipline in the operation of the schools, students may speak and publish freely, subject only to other community and state laws such as libel or invasion of privacy statutes. There is however a new threat to freedom of expression in the schools as a wave of book banning has hit school libraries. A plurality of the Supreme Court ruled in 1982 that the removal of books from the shelves of school libraries cannot be motivated because school members disagree with the political ideas or philosophies in the books. Books can be removed, however, if they are considered persuasively vulgar or educationally unsuitable. The Court was badly split in the decision and the ruling was murky. The issue remains in doubt.

TIME, PLACE, AND MANNER RESTRICTIONS

Justification of the previously noted instances of prior restraint—both inside and outside the schools—was based on the content of the article or the speech. That is, what was written or said provoked the prior censorship. Prior censorship can also be justified, however, on the basis of where or when a particular expression is scheduled to occur. In these instances the content of the publication or speech is not considered material in determining whether the prior restraint is justified or whether it is prohibited by the First Amendment. Such rules are called **time, place, and manner restrictions** and focus on when, where, or how the expression is to be made public. Sometimes these rules involve the need for licenses prior to the public distribution of printed matter; sometimes restrictions on door-to-door solicitation are concerned. In all cases, however, courts insist that such rules be applied without regard to the content of the publication or message. For example, when the city of Brentwood, Tennessee, adopted a rule which said that commercial handbills could not be delivered in any public place, but that newspapers, political, and religious material could be delivered in this manner, the Tennessee Supreme Court invalidated the ordinance because it was not content neutral (*H & L Messengers* v. *Brentwood*, 1979). Similarly, a federal district court in New Mexico ruled that an Alamogordo city ordinance which exempted religious and charitable organizations from a general ban on door-to-door solicitation was invalid because it allowed the city manager discretion in determining what is and what is not a religious cause. This is a content consideration (*Weissman* v. *Alamogordo*, 1979).

Consideration of such time, place, and manner rules by the Supreme Court dates to the 1930s.

Public Forums

The preeminent judicial ruling on the question of the validity of licensing laws is the case of *Lovell* v. *Griffin* decided by the nation's high Court in 1938. The city of Griffin, Georgia, had an ordinance which prohibited distribution of circulars, handbooks, advertising, and literature of any kind without first obtaining written permission from the city manager. Under the law, the city manager had considerable discretion as to whether he gave permission. Alma Lovell was a member of the Jehovah's Witnesses religious sect, an intense and ruggedly evangelical order which suffered severe persecutions in the first half of this century. But the Witnesses doggedly continued to spread the Word, passing out millions of leaflets and pamphlets and attempting to proselytize anyone who would listen. Laws like the distribution ordinance were common in many communities in the United States and were directed at stopping the distribution of material by groups such as the Witnesses.

Alma Lovell didn't even attempt to get a license before she circulated pamphlets, and she was arrested, convicted, and fined fifty dollars for violating the city ordinance. When she refused to pay the fine, she was sentenced to fifty days in jail. At the trial the Jehovah's Witnesses freely admitted the illegal distribution, but argued that the statute was invalid on its face because it violated the First Amendment guarantees of freedom of the press and freedom of religion.

On appeal the Supreme Court agreed that the law did indeed violate freedom of the press. Chief Justice Charles Evans Hughes wrote, "We think that the ordinance is invalid on its face" because it strikes at the very foundation of freedom of the press by subjecting it to license and censorship. The city argued that the First Amendment applies only to newspapers and regularly published materials like magazines. The high Court disagreed, ruling that the amendment applies to pamphlets and leaflets as well: "These indeed have been historic weapons in the defense of liberty, as the pamphlets of Thomas Paine and others in our own history abundantly attest. The press in its historic connotation comprehends every sort of publication which affords a vehicle of information and opinion."

Lawyers for Griffin also argued that the First Amendment was not applicable because the licensing law said nothing about publishing, but only concerned distribution. Again the high Court disagreed, noting that liberty of circulation is as essential to freedom of expression as liberty of publication. Chief Justice Hughes wrote, "Without the circulation, the publication would be of little value."

Nineteen months after the *Lovell* decision the Supreme Court decided a second distribution case, a case which involved licensing laws in four different cities. The four cases were decided as one (*Schneider* v. *New Jersey*, 1939). A Los Angeles ordinance prohibited the distribution of handbills on public streets on the grounds that distribution contributed to the litter problem. Ordinances in Milwaukee, Wisconsin, and Worcester, Massachusetts, were justified on the same basis—keeping the city streets clean.

An Irvington, New Jersey, law was far broader, prohibiting street distribution or house-to-house calls unless permission was first obtained from the local police chief. The police department asked distributors for considerable personal information and could reject applicants the law officers deemed not of good character. This action was ostensibly to protect the public against criminals.

Justice Owen Roberts delivered the opinion of the Court which struck down each of the four laws. Justice Roberts said that a city can enact regulations in the interest of public safety, health, and welfare, but not regulations which interfere with the liberty of the press or freedom of expression. He then gave some examples of what he meant, examples which have proved most helpful in framing such ordinances. Cities, he said, have the responsibility to keep the public streets open and available for the movement of people and property, and laws to regulate the conduct of those who would interfere with this legitimate public problem are constitutional (*Schneider* v. *New Jersey*, 1939):

> For example, a person could not exercise this liberty [of free expression] by taking his stand in the middle of a crowded street, contrary to traffic regulations, and maintain his position to the stoppage of all traffic; a group of distributors could not insist upon a constitutional right to form a cordon across the street and to allow no pedestrian to pass who did not accept a tendered leaflet; nor does the guarantee of freedom of speech or of the press deprive a municipality of power to enact regulations against throwing literature in the streets.

These kinds of activities, Roberts said, bear no relationship to the freedom to speak, write, print, or distribute information or opinion. The justice closed by saying that the high Court characterized freedom of speech and freedom of the press as fundamental personal rights and liberties: "The phrase is not an empty one and was not lightly used. . . . It stresses, as do many opinions of this Court, the importance of preventing the restriction of enjoyment of these liberties."

A somewhat different dimension of this same problem arose in a Connecticut case in which, again, members of Jehovah's Witnesses faced criminal prosecution under an ordinance which limited the solicitation of funds (*Cantwell* v. *Connecticut*, 1940). Jesse Cantwell and his two sons attempted to carry their religious message along the streets of a heavily Catholic neighborhood in New Haven, Connecticut. They were arrested for violating a state law which prohibited the solicitation of money by a religious group without first gaining approval from the local public official whose job it was to decide whether the religious cause in question was a "bona fide object of charity" and whether it conformed to "reasonable standards of efficiency and integrity." The Supreme Court tossed out the law as a violation of the First Amendment. For the unanimous Court, Justice Roberts wrote that the state could, in order to protect its citizens from fraudulent solicitations, require strangers in the community to establish identity and authority to act for the cause they purport to represent before permitting any solicitation in the community. And the state could pass rules setting reasonable regulatory limits on the time of day solicitations could be made (no solicitations before 9 A.M. or after 10 P.M., for example):

> But to condition the solicitation of aid for the perpetuation of religious views or systems upon a license, the grant of which rests in the exercise of a determination by state authority as to what is a religious cause, is to lay a forbidden burden upon the exercise of liberty protected by the Constitution.

Airports

Each of these three cases concerned restrictions of expression in the so-called public forum—public streets and parks. Other recent cases have focused on this same problem. Airports, for example, have become a popular place for solicitors for various religious and political causes. Milwaukee County was one of many governing bodies which tried to restrict such solicitation on the grounds that the passageways and corridors at General Billy Mitchell Field were too narrow and crowded to allow such activity. The United States District Court for Eastern Wisconsin ruled that the county airport is a public forum and that county rules which require prior permission before any solicitation can take place violate the First Amendment: "Crowded conditions may require restrictions to ensure the efficient operation of the airport," the court ruled. But such conditions did not justify sweeping rules which totally excluded solicitation by many persons and groups (*International Society for Krishna Consciousness* v. *Wolke*, 1978). Other courts have made similar rulings with regard to airport regulations.

State Fairs

In a similar manner the United States Supreme Court ruled that officials of the Minnesota State Fair can regulate solicitations on the fair grounds during the annual summer event. Anyone who seeks to sell or distribute merchandise or even hand out written material is required to work from booths rented for a small fee from fair officials. Booths are provided on a first-come, first-serve basis, and the rule applies to everyone—commercial, nonprofit, and charitable organizations—equally. The International Society for Krishna Consciousness challenged the rule, arguing it violated their religious freedom as well as their freedom of expression. Justice White and four other members of the high court disagreed.

White reiterated that in order for a time, place, and manner rule to be acceptable it must (1) be content neutral, (2) serve a significant governmental interest, and (3) leave ample alternative channels for the communication of the information. The Minnesota State Fair rules are content neutral; they apply to all equally. The state has a strong interest in maintaining the orderly movement of crowds at the fairgrounds. The grounds are small, only 125 acres; crowds are heavy, up to 160,000 persons on a weekend day. The fairgrounds are not like a public street, White said, which is always open and normally uncongested. Finally, the members of the Society for Krishna Consciousness can perform their ritualistic solicitation outside the fairgrounds. Members can mingle with the crowds on the grounds, talk with people, and propagate their views. They can even have a booth on the fairgrounds. There are alternative means to communicate their information. "The Minnesota State Fair is a limited public forum in that it exists to provide a means for a great number of exhibitors temporarily to present their products or views . . . to a large number of people in an efficient fashion," Justice White wrote. Considering these limits, the rules are reasonable (*Heffron* v. *International Society,* 1981).

Justice Brennan and three other members of the court agreed that rules which confined selling goods and literature and the solicitation of funds to the booths are permissible. They would have struck down, however, the portion of the rules which prohibit the distribution of literature on the grounds, arguing that this certainly does not exacerbate crowd-control problems.

News Racks and Billboards

Restrictions regarding the placement of news racks on city streets have also been scrutinized by the courts in recent years. So long as these rules do not discriminate unfairly against one particular publication or one kind of publication, rules which limit the number of racks on any one corner are generally considered permissible time, place, and manner restrictions. Glendale, California, for example, adopted an ordinance which said that no more than eight news racks could be on a public sidewalk in a space of 200 feet in any direction within the same block of the same street. In setting priorities to determine which publications could use the limited number of news racks, the city gave preference to "newspapers of general circulation for Los Angeles County." The county code defined a newspaper of general circulation as one with a subscription list of paying customers that has been published at least weekly within the district for at least three years. Also, according to the code, a newspaper of general circulation must have substantial distribution and contain at least 25 percent news in each edition. Papers not meeting this description were given a lower priority under the city ordinance. Because its paper did not contain at least 25 percent news, the Socialist Labor party challenged the ordinance as a violation of the First Amendment. The California Court of Appeals rejected the challenge. The court said:

> When the law, ordinance, or other rule is aimed directly at pure speech or content, it is examined for constitutionality by strait and narrow measures and almost no interference is allowed. On the other hand, when only the mechanical means or particular time or place of dissemination is involved, some reasonable limitation is recognized.

The court said sidewalk space is limited; the city has an obligation to allocate it. The ordinance was not intentionally aimed at the Socialist Labor party paper, but at any publication which did not contain 25 percent news. The preference for newspapers of general circulation is "simply a means of balancing the problem of public demand and its supply" (*Socialist Labor Party* v. *Glendale*, 1978).

A Texas civil court of appeals ruled that a city of Houston ordinance which made it unlawful for persons to sell newspapers from street corners to passing motorists was unconstitutional. The problem the ordinance sought to solve was a real one. There was considerable traffic congestion at downtown streets; the newspaper hawkers, often either quite young or quite old, stood on medians in the roadway to sell the newspapers to persons in automobiles stopped temporarily in traffic. This means of selling was dangerous to both motorists and to the salespersons. Still, the city ordinance went too far, the court said. "The city has banned newspaper sales by persons of all ages to occupants of all motor vehicles located on public property, including residential neighborhoods, regardless of the time of day or night, and regardless of whether the cars are moving, standing, parked or even not in the traffic lanes," the court noted. As such the law was too broad. While the city might fashion a ban on such selling on congested downtown streets during rush hours, the ordinance went too far and interfered with protected freedoms (*Houston Chronicle* v. *Houston,* 1981).

Several states and cities have attempted to regulate the placement of billboards, with mixed results. The problem in such regulation is coping with the rights of store owners to advertise their businesses. The dilemma is best illustrated by a 1981 United States Supreme Court ruling on a San Diego billboard ordinance. The ordinance prohibited all outdoor advertising except on-site commercial signs that promoted goods or services offered by businesses on the premises. That is, owners of hardware stores could erect signs on their property which advertised materials sold in the hardware store. Acknowledging that the ban was prompted by substantial state interests in the aesthetic quality of the city and in traffic safety, the Supreme Court nevertheless struck down the city law. The flaw in the ordinance was the broad exemption granted for on-site commercial speech. "Insofar as the city tolerates billboards at all,"

Justice White wrote in the plurality Court opinion, "it cannot choose to limit their content to commercial messages." The law is not content neutral; it reaches into the realm of protected speech, he wrote. To be constitutional, then, the ordinance must allow noncommercial (Save the Whales, Abortion Is a Crime, etc.) on-site billboards as well. A total ban on billboards, if properly justified, might also be acceptable (*Metromedia* v. *San Diego,* 1981; see also *Donnelly* v. *Campbell,* 1980; *Metromedia* v. *Baltimore,* 1982; and *Norton* v. *Arlington Heights,* 1982).

Other Public Forums   Public streets, airports, and state fairs are some of the public forums that have been discussed thus far in relation to permissible time, place, and manner rules. In the early 1980s federal courts were asked to examine two other communication forums and to determine (1) whether they were public forums and (2) whether decisions made regarding their use violated the First Amendment. The forums were mailboxes and public television stations.

For nearly fifty years the Congress has prohibited deposit of unstamped mailable matter in a letter box in front of someone's home. The rule was adopted in 1934 when the postal service was losing revenues because many organizations and businesses were hand delivering circulars, letters, bills, and other mailable material and depositing them in homeowners' mailboxes. The law is justified today by the government on three grounds.

1. The law protects postal revenues.
2. The law facilitates the efficient and secure delivery of the mail.
3. The law promotes a mail patron's privacy.

Number one has just been discussed. A mailbox filled with nonstamped junk can crowd out real mail, slowing the delivery of the mail. Thieves can use the delivery of circulars as a ruse to examine the contents of a mailbox and then steal checks and other valuable material. Finally, the mail received by an individual should be private, not exposed to other persons who are hand delivering circulars or other matter.

The postal regulation was challenged by the Council of Greenburgh Civic Association which delivered pamphlets and notices to local residents by placing them in mailboxes. The local postmaster ordered the practice stopped. The council said the postal regulation violated their rights under the First Amendment. The Supreme Court disagreed in a seven-to-two ruling. In his majority opinion Justice William Rehnquist rejected the notion that a mailbox is a public forum. He wrote that a mailbox was much like a military base, a jail or a prison, or the advertising space in a city transit system. "In all these cases, this Court recognizes that the First Amendment does not guarantee access to property simply because it is owned or controlled by the government," Rehnquist wrote. "It is a giant leap from the traditional 'soap box' to the letter box designated as an authorized depository of the United States mails, and we do not believe the First Amendment requires us to make that leap," he added.

Because the mailbox is not a public forum, there is no need to evaluate whether the statute is a reasonable time, place, and manner rule. However, Rehnquist added, there are ample reasons to support the law even if the mailbox were considered a public forum. He cited the government's justifications for the law (see one through three above). He also noted that there are numerous alternative means that the civic council could use to communicate information to residents. Justices Brennan and White said that they believed the mailbox to be (or at least is like) a public forum, but that the rules were reasonable. Marshall and Stevens dissented (*Postal Service* v. *Council,* 1981).

While a mailbox may not be a public forum, a federal district court in Texas ruled that a public television station is a public forum and cannot refuse to broadcast a controversial program. KUHT-TV, the public station licensed to the University of Houston, chose not to broadcast "Death of a Princess" in late 1980. The program is about a Saudi Arabian princess who had a non-sanctioned love affair with a young man and was subsequently executed. The Saudi government put pressure on the United States state department to block the showing of the film in the United States. The station managers of KUHT-TV said they did not want to show the program because it was offensive and in bad taste, and that it could interfere with the school's long friendship and contractual relationships with the Saudi Arabian government. Viewers protested, and when no relief was granted, a federal court suit was initiated to force KUHT-TV to show the film. The United States district court ruled that the station is a public forum and failure to broadcast the film was a prior restraint. "The people of this country have a First Amendment right to see and hear without having their sights and sounds subjected to the censorship of those wrapped in the cloak of the state. . . .," the court ruled (*Barnestone* v. *University of Houston,* 1981).

The district court ruling was appealed to the Fifth United States Court of Appeals. Another panel of Fifth Circuit judges had ruled three months earlier that the refusal of the Alabama Educational Television Commission to show "Death of a Princess" was not a prior restraint. In the Alabama case the judges ruled that a station's decision not to show the film was a programming decision and that, "it would demean the First Amendment to find that it required a public referendum on every programming decision made every day by every public television station solely because the station is owned and partially funded by the state government." Citing the *Postal Service* case (pages 90–91), the court said that a piece of property does not become a public forum just because it is owned or controlled by the government. "It is only when the government has created a public forum dedicated to public use that a right of access may obtain," the court added (*Muir* v. *Alabama Educational Television Commission,* 1981).

When *Barnestone* v. *University of Houston* reached the Fifth United States Court of Appeals, the decision was reversed because the panel of judges said they felt bound by the decision in the Alabama case. Shortly thereafter, however, it was announced that an en banc panel of the Fifth Circuit would rehear both the *Barnestone* case and the *Muir* case. The cases were reargued before all twenty-two judges in the circuit, and in October 1982 a majority ruled that public television stations are free—like commercial broadcasting stations—to make editorial judgments on the basis of content in selecting programs to broadcast. The court acknowledged that the First Amendment was designed to protect the press from government interference, not vice versa. Still, the court ruled, "The First Amendment does not preclude the government from exercising editorial control over its own medium of expression. To find that the government is without First Amendment protection is not to find that the government is prohibited from speaking or that private individuals have the right to limit or control the expression of the government. Even without First Amendment protection government may participate in the marketplace of ideas and contribute its own views to those of other speakers," the court added (*Muir* v. *Alabama Educational Television Commission,* 1982).

Private Forums

The cases just noted concern public forums. Courts have generally tolerated more restrictions upon expression exercised in private forums—shopping centers and private residences, for example. Residential distribution and solicitation have consistently been a vexing problem as the rights of freedom of expression are measured against the rights of privacy and private property.

Private Homes

In 1943 the Supreme Court faced an unusual ordinance adopted by the city of Struthers, Ohio, which totally prohibited door-to-door distribution of handbills, circulars, and other advertising materials.

The law also barred anyone from ringing doorbells to summon householders for the purpose of distributing literature or pamphlets. Justice Hugo Black wrote the opinion for the majority in the divided Court. He said the arrest of Thelma Martin, another Jehovah's Witness, for ringing doorbells in behalf of her religious cause was a violation of her First Amendment rights. Door-to-door distributors can be a nuisance and can even be a front for criminal activities, Justice Black acknowledged. Further, door-to-door distribution can surely be regulated, but it cannot be altogether banned. It is a valuable and useful means of the dissemination of ideas and is especially important to those groups which are too poorly financed to use other expensive means of communicating with the people. Black said a law which makes it an offense for a person to ring the doorbell of householders who have appropriately indicated that they are unwilling to be disturbed would be lawful and constitutional. However, the city of Struthers cannot by ordinance make this decision on behalf of all its citizens—especially when such a rule clearly interferes with the freedom of speech and of the press. "The right of freedom of speech and press has broad scope. The authors of the First Amendment knew that novel and unconventional ideas might disturb the complacent, but they chose to encourage a freedom which they believed essential if vigorous enlightenment was ever to triumph over slothful ignorance" (*Martin* v. *City of Struthers*, 1943).

Nearly ten years later, in 1951, the high Court was confronted with still another case of door-to-door solicitation. This case, however, concerned solicitation of subscriptions for nationally circulated magazines (*Breard* v. *Alexandria*, 1951). The Alexandria, Louisiana, ordinance in question prohibited door-to-door solicitation for sale of goods, wares, or merchandise without the prior consent or invitation of the homeowner. Jack H. Breard, who was employed by a Pennsylvania magazine subscription company, appealed his conviction all the way to the Supreme Court on the grounds that the law violated his First Amendment rights. This time the divided Court ruled against the solicitor, stating that the restriction was not a violation of the First Amendment.

Justice Stanley Reed distinguished the early cases from the *Breard* case by arguing that *Breard* was a case of door-to-door sale of wares, not of propagation of ideas or religious faith. "This kind of distribution is said to be protected because the mere fact that money is made out of the distribution does not bar the publications from First Amendment protection. We agree that the fact that periodicals are sold does not put them beyond the protection of the First Amendment. The selling, however, brings into the transaction a commercial feature," Reed wrote. He added that there are many other ways to sell magazines besides intruding upon the privacy of a householder through door-to-door techniques. Justices Black, Douglas, and Vinson disagreed with Justice Reed, arguing that the high Court turned its back on earlier free expression decisions. "The constitutional sanctuary for the press must necessarily include liberty to publish and circulate. In view of our economic system, it must also include freedom to solicit paying subscribers," Black wrote. The jurist added that homeowners could themselves place the solicitor on notice by using a sign that they do not wish to be disturbed.

The majority opinion in the *Breard* case which distinguishes commercial solicitation and distribution from noncommercial solicitation and distribution has been seriously undercut recently by the Supreme Court's rulings that commercial speech is also entitled to the protection of the First Amendment (these rulings are discussed in chapter 10). For example, the Third United States Court of Appeals recently invalidated a township ordinance which prohibited the distribution of advertising matter without first getting consent of the homeowner. *Ad World,* which publishes *Piggy Back,* a sixteen-page tabloid which is filled mostly with advertising, but which also carries a few community announcements and bits of consumer information, challenged the ordinance.

The court ruled, "The line between commercial and noncommercial speech cannot be drawn by some magic ratio of editorial to advertising content. The important question is whether the publication as a whole relates solely to the economic interests of the speaker and its audience." The court said that an ordinance aimed at "purely commercial advertising" might be constitutional, but only if the community can justify the need for such a law. Doylestown Township argued that the accumulation of free newspapers on a doorstep might tip off burglars that the homeowner is out of town. But the township offered no evidence to support this argument. Also the township failed to show why the homeowner should not be called upon to request that delivery be stopped if the delivery of *Piggy Back* was not desired (*Ad World* v. *Doylestown,* 1982).

Shopping Centers

The problem of dealing with distribution of materials at privately owned shopping centers has also been a troubling one. In 1968, in *Amalgamated Food Employees Local 590* v. *Logan Valley Plaza,* the Supreme Court ruled that the shopping center was the functional equivalent of a town's business district and permitted informational picketing by persons who had a grievance against one of the stores in the shopping center. Four years later in *Lloyd Corp.* v. *Tanner* (1972), the high Court ruled that a shopping center can prohibit the distribution of handbills on its property when the handbilling is unrelated to the shopping center operation. Protesters against nuclear power, for example, cannot use the shopping center as a forum. Persons protesting against the policies of one of the stores in the center, however, can use the center to distribute materials.

In 1976 the Supreme Court recognized the distinctions it had drawn between the rules in the *Logan Valley* case and the rules in the *Lloyd Center* case for what they were—restrictions based on content. The distribution of messages of one kind was permitted, while the distribution of messages about something else was banned. In *Hudgens* v. *NLRB* (1976), the high Court ruled that if in fact the shopping center is the functional equivalent of a municipal street, then restrictions based on content cannot stand. But rather than to open the shopping center to the distribution of all kinds of material, *Logan Valley* was overruled, and the high Court announced that "only when . . . property has taken all the attributes of a town" can property be treated as public. Distribution of materials at private shopping centers can be prohibited.

But just because the First Amendment does not include within its protection of freedom of expression the right to circulate material at a privately owned shopping center does not mean that such distribution might not be protected by legislation, or by state constitution. The California Constitution explicitly authorizes individuals to exercise their free speech rights on privately owned shopping center property. In 1980 the United States Supreme Court ruled that such a provision was valid and did not violate the property rights of the owners of the shopping center (*Pruneyard Shopping Center* v. *Robins,* 1980).

Finally, in an interesting decision which focused upon the mail rather than upon the mailbox, the Supreme Court ruled that the New York Public Service Commission could not restrict the content of inserts Consolidated Edison, a private utility company, put in billing envelopes. The utility company used the inserts to promote the value of nuclear power to its customers. The commission passed a regulation prohibiting utilities from using bill inserts to discuss political matters, including the desirability of future development of nuclear power. Justice Powell, who wrote the seven-to-one ruling, said the regulation was not content neutral. "The First Amendment means that government has no power to restrict expression because of its message, its ideas, its subject matter or content," he wrote. In addition, the state was hard pressed to outline a compelling or substantial state interest it was attempting to protect through such a regulation (*Consolidated Edison* v. *Public Service Commission,* 1980).

As noted previously, other examples of prior restraint can be found within the law. Films may be censored before they are shown, for example (see chapter 6). Under certain circumstances the press may be prohibited from publishing material which might prejudice a defendant's chance for a fair trial (see chapter 7). Such examples will be noted as other aspects of mass media law are discussed.

Summary

The prior restraint of expression is permissible under what are known as time, place, and manner regulations. That is, the government can impose reasonable regulations about when, where, and how individuals or groups may communicate with other persons. Time, place, and manner rules apply to both public forums (settings owned or controlled by a government such as a public street or an airport) and private forums (privately owned settings such as residences and shopping centers). In order to be constitutional time, place, and manner restraints must meet certain criteria:

1. The regulation must be content neutral; that is, application of the rule cannot depend upon the content of the communication.
2. The regulation must serve a substantial governmental interest, and the government must justify the rule by explicitly demonstrating this interest.
3. There cannot be total prohibition of the communication. The speakers or publishers must have reasonable alternative means of presenting their ideas or information to the public.
4. The rules cannot be broader than they need to be to serve the governmental interest. For example, the government cannot stop the distribution of literature on all public streets if it only seeks to stop the problem of congestion on public streets which carry heavy traffic.

BIBLIOGRAPHY

Here is a list of some of the sources that have been helpful in the preparation of chapter 2.

Books

Alexander, James. *A Brief Narrative on the Case and Trial of John Peter Zenger.* Edited by Stanley N. Katz. Cambridge, Mass.: Harvard University Press, 1963.

Barron, Jerome, and Dienes, C. Thomas. *Handbook of Free Speech and Free Press.* Boston: Little, Brown & Co., 1979.

Chafee, Zechariah. *Free Speech in the United States.* Cambridge: Harvard University Press, 1941.

Fellman, David. *The Limits of Freedom.* New Brunswick, N. J.: Rutgers University Press, 1959.

Gerald, J. Edward. *The Press and the Constitution.* Minneapolis, Minn.: University of Minnesota Press, 1948.

Jensen, Merrill. *The Articles of Confederation.* Madison, Wis.: University of Wisconsin Press, 1966.

_____. *The Making of the American Constitution.* New York: Van Nostrand Reinhold Co., 1964.

Levy, Leonard. *Freedom of Speech and Press in Early American History.* New York: Harper & Row, Harper Torchbooks, 1963.

Meiklejohn, Alexander. *Free Speech and Its Relation to Self-Government.* New York: Harper & Brothers, 1948.

Miller, John C. *Crisis in Freedom.* Boston: Little, Brown & Co., 1951.

Peterson, H. C., and Fite, Gilbert. *Opponents of War, 1917–1918.* Seattle: University of Washington Press, 1957.

Roche, John P. *Shadow and Substance.* New York: Macmillan Co., 1964.

Rutland, Robert. *The Birth of the Bill of Rights.* Chapel Hill: University of North Carolina Press, 1955.

Siebert, Frederick. *Freedom of the Press in England, 1476–1776.* Urbana: University of Illinois Press, 1952.

Smith, James Morton. *Freedom's Fetters.* Ithaca, N. Y.: Cornell University Press, 1956.

Articles

Nelson, Harold L. "Seditious Libel in Colonial America," 3 *American Journal of Legal History* 160, 1959.

Pember, Don R. "The Pentagon Papers Decision: More Questions Than Answers." 48 *Journalism Quarterly* 403, 1971.

_____. "The Smith Act as a Restraint on the Press." 10 *Journalism Monographs* 1, 1969.

Ragan, Fred D. "Justice Oliver Wendell Holmes, Jr., Zechariah Chafee, Jr., and the Clear and Present Danger Test for Free Speech: The First Year, 1919." 53 *Journal of American History* 24, 1971.

Cases

Abrams v. *U.S.,* 250 U.S. 616 (1919).

Ad World v. *Doylestown,* 672 F.2d 1136 (1982).

Amalgamated Food Employees Local 590 v. *Logan Valley Plaza,* 391 U.S. 308 (1968).

Barnestone v. *University of Houston,* 660 F.2d 137 (1981).

Barron v. *Baltimore,* 7 Pet. 243 (1833).

Bary v. *U.S.,* 248 F.2d 201 (1957).

Brandenburg v. Ohio, 395 U.S. 444 (1969).
Breard v. Alexandria, 341 U.S. 622 (1951).
Cantwell v. Connecticut, 310 U.S. 296 (1940).
Chaplinsky v. New Hampshire, 315 U.S. 568 (1942).
Collin v. Smith, 578 F.2d 1197, cert. den. 99 S.Ct. 291 (1978).
Consolidated Edison v. Public Service Commission, 447 U.S. 529 (1980).
Debs v. U.S., 249 U.S. 211 (1919).
Dennis v. U.S., 341 U.S. 494 (1951).
Dickey v. Alabama, 273 F. Supp. 613 (1967).
Donnelly v. Campbell, 639 F.2d 6 (1980).
Fiske v. Kansas, 274 U.S. 380 (1927).
Frasca v. Andrews, 463 F. Supp. 1043 (1978).
Frohwerk v. U.S., 249 U.S. 204 (1919).
Gitlow v. U.S., 268 U.S. 652 (1925).
Gooding v. Wilson, 405 U.S. 518 (1972).
H. & L. Messengers v. Brentwood, 577 S.W. 2d 444 (1979).
Heffron v. International Society, 101 S.Ct. 2559 (1981).
Houston Chronicle v. Houston, 630 S.W.2d 927 (1982).
Hudgens v. NLRB, 424 U.S. 507 (1976).
International Society for Krishna Consciousness v. Wolke, 453 F. Supp. 869 (1978).
Island Trees v. Pico, 102 S.Ct. 2799 (1982).
Lloyd Corp. v. Tanner, 407 U.S. 551 (1972).
Lovell v. Griffin, 303 U.S. 444 (1938).
Martin v. City of Struthers, 319 U.S. 141 (1943).
Metromedia v. Baltimore, 538 F. Supp. 1183 (1982).
Metromedia v. San Diego, 101 S.Ct. 2882 (1981).
Miami Herald v. Tornillo, 418 U.S. 241 (1974).
Muir v. Alabama Educational TV Commission, 656 F.2d 1012 (1981); 688 F.2d 1033 (1982).
Near v. Minnesota, 383 U.S. 697 (1931).
New York Times Company v. U.S.; U.S. v. Washington Post, 713 U.S. 403 (1971).
Norton v. Arlington Heights, 433 N.E.2d 198 (1982).
Organization for a Better Austin v. Keefe, 402 U.S. 415 (1971).
Pico v. Island Trees, 747 F.Supp. 387 (1979); revd. 638 F.2d 404 (1980).
President's Council District 25 v. Community School Board, 457 F.2d 566 (1972).
Pruneyard Shopping Center v. Robins, 447 U.S. 74 (1980).
Red Lion Broadcasting v. FCC, 395 U.S. 367 (1969).
Scales v. U.S., 367 U.S. 203 (1961).
Schenck v. U.S., 249 U.S. 47 (1919).
Schneider v. New Jersey, 308 U.S. 147 (1939).
Socialist Labor Party v. Glendale, 82 Cal. App.3d 722 (1978).
South Wind Motel v. Lashutka, 9 M.L.Rept. 1661 (1983).
Tinker v. Des Moines School District, 393 U.S. 503 (1969).
Trachtman v. Anker, 563 F.2d 512 (1977).
U.S. v. Progressive, 467 F. Supp. 990 (1979).
Village of Skokie v. National Socialist Party, 373 N.E.2d 21 (1978).
Weissman v. Alamogordo, 472 F. Supp. 425 (1979).
Whitney v. California, 274 U.S. 357 (1927).
Yates v. U.S., 354 U.S. 298 (1957).

3 LIBEL

Defamation, or **libel,** is probably the most common legal problem most journalists face in the 1980s. Not that there are a great many libel suits. There are not. Reporters and newspapers and broadcasting stations are rarely sued for libel. Still, the potential for libel exists with virtually every story that is published or broadcast. Consequently, libel is an ever-present, if not always obvious, danger in the newsroom.

Probably considerably more defamation is published and broadcast than editors like to imagine. Still, a lawsuit is rare. The chances of success in winning a libel suit are often very low. Many attorneys advise their clients that a lawsuit often only publicizes the original defamation far beyond the original audience. A defamatory falsehood published in a small gossip magazine or obscure newspaper column has a limited audience. A lawsuit based on such publication draws attention to the defamation, and many persons who did not originally see the story are drawn to it. Other lawyers argue that the truth rarely catches up with a lie, and it is best just to ignore the defamation because the public will soon forget it. Finally, while many defamatory statements may be partially false, they may be partially true as well. The injured person may be reluctant to admit that a portion of the defamation is true in order to prosecute the untrue portion in a lawsuit.

Hesitancy to sue, however, is sometimes offset by the possibility and hope of a large money judgment. Losing a major libel suit can be financially devastating to the mass media. In recent years record libel judgments have been entered against the press.

1. Carol Burnett was awarded $800,000 in **damages** in her successful lawsuit against the *National Enquirer.* The damage award was reduced to $200,000 on appeal.

2. Two San Francisco police officers successfully sued the *San Francisco Examiner* for $4.5 million for an article which suggested the officers attempted to frame a suspect. The judgment is under appeal.
3. The *Alton* (Ill.) *Telegraph* was forced into bankruptcy when it lost a $9.2 million libel judgment to a local contractor whom two of the newspaper's reporters accused of having ties to a savings and loan association which was alleged to have ties with organized crime. The paper ultimately settled the suit for $1.4 million.
4. Nearly $6 million in libel damages were awarded to Willow Cramlet in her suit against the producers of the "Phil Donahue Show."

The Libel Defense Resource Center reported in late July 1983 that damage awards averaged $8 million apiece in seven of eleven recent libel verdicts. While many if not most high awards are reduced or overturned on a post-trial motion or an appeal, some are not. A large media corporation like the *Washington Post* or Columbia Broadcasting System (CBS) can sustain the loss of a million-dollar libel judgment, but smaller publications or broadcasting stations cannot. A financial penalty of such proportions could kill the *Texas Observer* or *New Republic* or a small community paper. Even if the publication wins, victory can carry a high price tag. The cost of defending a suit, with attorney's fees averaging $1,000 a day, can be very expensive. Newspapers in Palm Beach, Florida, and Baton Rouge, Louisiana, recently reported litigation costs of $100,000 each for libel suits they won on appeal, according to Robert Picard in an article in *The Press* (March 1981). John Zollinger, publisher of the *New Mexico Independent,* lamented to Picard, "It's no joke anymore. . . . You win and you still pay."

Many lawyers, even those skilled in defending the press in libel actions, are still often troubled by the immense inconsistencies in libel law.

The roots of libel law are in the common law. In some states libel law is codified, and statutes have been approved by various state legislatures. Regardless, differences exist from state to state. Even within states many areas of the law remain unsettled. Libel attorney and author Paul Ashley wrote in his handbook *Say It Safely:*

> Significant segments of the law of libel are unique—dissimilar from legal rules with which lawyers and judges are most familiar. Libel cases are relatively few in number. Judges are not ordinarily experienced in the practical application of the esoteric concepts of privilege and fair comment essential to the preservation of freedom of speech and, in turn, of a free society. And so it is that here and there will be found maverick decisions which distort the law of libel.

No editor wants his newspaper to become the victim of one of these maverick decisions. The impetus toward self-censorship is strong.

Libel, therefore, remains a very important consideration for publishers and broadcasters. Despite the libel protections for the press which have evolved in the past few years through constitutional law, the threat of a libel suit still works against the kind of free and robust communication system envisioned by many philosophers of the First Amendment.

The law of defamation is ancient; its roots can be traced back several centuries. Initially the law was an attempt by government to establish a forum for persons involved in a dispute brought about by an insult or by what we today call a defamatory remark. One man called another a robber and a villain. The injured party sought to avenge his damaged reputation. A fight or duel of some kind was the only means of gaining vengeance before the development of libel law. It was obvious that fights and duels were not satisfactory ways to settle such disputes, so government offered its "good offices" to solve these problems. Slowly the law of defamation evolved.

Today, the process of going to court to avenge one's honor is highly institutionalized. In addition, some scholars in the field suggest that the purpose of the law has subtly changed as well. While protection of reputation still remains a primary objective of the law of defamation, the law is also seen as a means of gaining press accountability. Standards of responsible journalism and professional conduct are frequently applied to the press in determining liability, and in this way society and the government, via the court system, are taking a role in defining acceptable journalistic practices.

In other parts of the world different schemes are used to accomplish similar ends. In continental Europe libel suits are uncommon. When a newspaper defames a person, that person has the right—under law—to strike back, using the columns of the same newspaper, to tell his side of the story, so to speak, to blast the writer or the editor. This right is called the right of reply, and it exists in the United States in a far less advanced form, as is noted near the end of this chapter. Many people favor the notion, that is, letting the parties fight it out in print or by broadcast. They say it is far better to set out after the truth in this fashion than to rattle the chains on the courthouse door every time an insult is flung in the public press.

Over the centuries the law of defamation has become very complex and very confusing. Parts of the law, however, do not really concern journalists. In this chapter the discussion of the law of libel is generally confined to those areas of the law which are important to reporters, editors, and broadcasters, and some aspects of libel law are not included. For example, the law of defamation regarding private communications as opposed to public communications differs somewhat. What a newspaper can legally do is somewhat different from what an employer writing a job evaluation for an employee can legally do. Defamation contained in personal letters, credit reports, job evaluations—a whole range of relatively private communications—is treated somewhat differently in the eyes of the law. The focus of this chapter is defamation in the mass media, that is, public communication libel.

Additionally, it must be remembered that libel law is essentially state law. It is possible to describe the dimensions of the law in broad terms that transcend state boundaries, and that is what this chapter attempts to do. But important variations in the law from state to state exist as will be demonstrated later in this chapter in the discussion of fault requirements. It is important for students to focus on the specific elements of the law in their states after gaining an understanding of the general boundaries of the law.

Another complex problem in the law has to do with whether a communication is a libel (written defamation) or a **slander** (an oral defamation). The law in many states distinguishes between the two. The problem was simple one hundred years ago. Because of the state of technology, a public communication, one meant for a wide audience, was a printed communication— a newspaper, magazine, or handbill. Therefore a law which dealt with libel more harshly than with slander made sense: libel caused more severe damage. A libel lasted longer than a slander since a libel was printed, more people saw it, and it was generally considered to be planned defamation, not words accidentally spoken in the heat of argument. Film, radio, and television have made these distinctions meaningless. If a performer defames someone on "The Tonight Show," despite the fact that the defamation is not printed, the defamation still has immense impact and is heard by millions. A great many states continue to wrestle with the problem of whether defamatory radio and television broadcasts are libel or slander. We are going to take the position—supported by several authorities—that a published defamation, whether it is in a newspaper, on radio or television, in the movies, or what have you, is a libel. And libel rules apply.

The purpose of this chapter is to give journalists guidance and rules to apply in the process of gathering, writing, and publishing and broadcasting the news. People who want to learn to litigate a lawsuit should go to law school. This author's goal is to keep reporters and broadcasters out of libel suits or at least to keep them from losing a libel suit.

The chapter is divided into two basic parts. The first section deals with the nature of a defamation suit: definitions of libel, what a plaintiff must prove in a libel suit, words that tend to be defamatory, and so forth. The second section outlines the various defenses—legal excuses for publishing defamatory matter—for a libel suit.

ELEMENTS OF LIBEL

There are many definitions of defamation, and they are all about the same. A few typical definitions follow.

In their book *Libel* Phelps and Hamilton include this definition:

> Defamation is a communication which exposes a person to hatred, ridicule, or contempt, lowers him in the esteem of his fellows, causes him to be shunned, or injures him in his business or calling.

The legal encyclopedia *Corpus Juris* defines libelous words as follows:

. . . words which have a tendency to disgrace or degrade the person or hold him up to public hatred, contempt, ridicule or cause him to be shunned and avoided; the words must reflect on his integrity, his character, and his good name and standing in the community. . . . The imputation must be one which tends to affect the plaintiff in a class of society whose standard of opinion the court can recognize. It is not sufficient, standing alone, that the language is unpleasant and annoys and irks plaintiff and subjects him to jests or banter, so as to affect his feelings.

The new edition of the *Restatement of Torts* (2nd ed.), a compilation by the American Law Institute of what it thinks the common law says, defines libel this way:

. . . a communication which has the tendency to so harm the reputation of another as to lower him in the estimation of the community or to deter third persons from associating with him.

Here's a shorter definition: Defamation is any communication which holds a man up to contempt, hatred, ridicule, or scorn.

Each of the four preceding definitions reveals common and important elements of defamation.

1. Defamation is an action which damages the reputation of a person, but not necessarily the individual's character. Your character is what you are; your reputation is what people think you are. Reputation is what the law protects.

2. To be actionable defamation, the words must actually damage a reputation. There must be some harm done to the individual's reputation. Without proof of this harm the party who claims injury will not be able to recover damages for the injury.

3. At least a significant minority of the community must believe that the plaintiff's reputation has been damaged, but the minority must not be an unrepresentative minority. A Delaware superior court ruled that it was not defamatory for a television newscaster to refer to a convict as "an alleged FBI informant." The plaintiff complained that the statement hurt his reputation among his fellow prisoners at the state penitentiary. Conceding that the "informant" label might harm his prison reputation, the court ruled that "it is not one's reputation in a limited community in which attitudes and social values may depart substantially from those prevailing generally which an action for defamation is designed to protect." The public in general would not think any less of the plaintiff for being an informant for the FBI (*Saunders* v. *WHYY-TV,* 1978). To summarize this point: The defamation must lower a person's reputation in the eyes of a significant number of people, and unless unusual circumstances exist, these people must fairly reflect representative views.

Persons can be injured through a libel in numerous ways. The statement may simply hurt their reputation, or it may be that lowering their reputation deprives them of their right to enjoy social contacts, which is a fancy way of saying that their friends don't like them any more or their friends want to avoid them. A man or woman's ability to work or hold a job or make a living may be injured. A person need only be injured in *one* of these three ways to have a cause of action for libel. If plaintiffs can show actual harm in any one of these areas, chances are good they will recover some damages. That is one of the reasons libel law exists—to compensate the plaintiff for injury. There are other reasons. A libel suit can help vindicate the plaintiff, help restore the damaged reputation. A victorious plaintiff can point a finger at the newspaper or television station and say, "See, they were wrong, they lied, they made an error." A damage judgment is also considered punishment for the defendant. Hopefully, having to pay a sum of money will remind the editor or broadcaster to be more cautious in the future. It can stand also as an example to other journalists to avoid such behavior.

Any living person can bring a suit for civil libel. If a dead person is libeled, relatives cannot sue in the name of the deceased. However, as noted in the last section of this chapter, it is possible (but highly improbable) for the state to bring a criminal libel action against the publisher of a defamation against a person who has died. Note, however, that if a living person is defamed, brings suit, and then dies before the matter is settled by the court, it is possible in some states for relatives to continue to pursue the lawsuit (see *MacDonald* v. *Time,* 1983, for example). A business corporation can sue for libel, as can a nonprofit corporation, if it can show that it has lost public support and contributions because of the defamation. There is a division in judicial opinion about whether unincorporated associations like labor unions and political action groups can sue for libel. Some court rulings say no, others say yes. Find out what the law is in your state. Cities, counties, agencies of government, and governments in general cannot bring a civil libel suit. This question was decided years ago and is settled law (see *City of Chicago* v. *Tribune Co.,* 1923). Nevertheless, every now and then an angry public official brings an action against the media in the name of the city or state rather than sue as an individual. In 1979 the United States Department of Justice filed a lawsuit charging the city of Philadelphia, its mayor, Frank Rizzo, and various police officials with violating the civil rights of many citizens by pursuing policies of police abuse and brutality. After the *Washington Post* published an account of the lawsuit, the city of Philadelphia brought a libel action against the newspaper. The federal district court ruled that the city could not maintain an action for libel. "A governmental entity is incapable of being libeled," Judge Fullam ruled (*City of Philadelphia* v. *Washington Post,* 1979). Neither can relatives of defamed persons sue simply because they are relatives. If you call

John Smith a fraud, John's brother Homer cannot sue just because he is related to John.* It is a different story if Homer can show that the libel reflects on him. For example, if you call John Smith illegitimate, the charge reflects directly on his parents, and they can sue.

PROVING THE INITIAL ELEMENTS

In a libel suit, as in any kind of lawsuit, certain tasks fall to the plaintiff and certain tasks fall to the defendant. Since the plaintiff initiates the suit, he or she bears the burden of getting the case started. In a libel suit the plaintiff is charged with establishing four elements, and without proof of these elements the case will be dismissed even before it really starts. The four conditions which the plaintiff must prove are as follows:

1. That the libelous communication was published
2. That the plaintiff was identified in the communication
3. That the communication is defamatory in some way
4. That the libelous matter was published due to neglect or disregard or carelessness, that its publication is not the result simply of an honest error

The last element, known as the fault requirement, is probably applicable only to those libel suits brought against mass media defendants (see *Columbia Sussex* v. *Hay,* 1981, for example). The courts have not finally resolved this issue. Since this book is about mass media law, and we know that proof of fault is required before a plaintiff can win a libel action against a newspaper or magazine or broadcasting station, we will consider some evidence of fault to be a required part of the plaintiff's case.

The fault requirement is the most complicated of the four elements. The kind of fault which must be proved by the plaintiff, whether the defamation results from simple negligence by the reporter or from deliberate disregard of the plaintiff's reputation, depends upon who the plaintiff is and in which state the lawsuit is filed. Many persons consider the fault requirement to be a libel defense. But since the burden of proving fault rests with the plaintiff, it is more properly considered an element of the plaintiff's case than a part of the defendant's case. The defendant's obligations do not technically begin until the injured party has established publication, identification, defamation, and fault. The fault requirement and all its extraneous components are thoroughly discussed after the first three elements of the plaintiff's lawsuit are considered.

Publication

Before the law recognizes a statement or comment as a civil libel (**criminal libel** is different; see page 179), the statement must be published. In the eyes of the law, **publication** occurs when one person, in addition to the writer and

*John Smith, Jane Adams, Frank Jones, Professor LeBlanc, KLOP, the *River City Sentinel,* *Scam* magazine, and the like, are my fictional creations and are used to illustrate specific points I wish to make when actual case law either does not exist or is unknown to me.

the person who is defamed, sees or hears the material.* Think of the situation as a kind of triangle. The writer or broadcaster (ultimately the defendant) is at the first point, the subject of the defamatory statement (ultimately the plaintiff) is at the second point, and a third person is at the third point. All three are necessary for a libel suit. The issue of publication becomes a real problem in defamation via private communication. You send a nasty letter to someone and a secretary opens it first by mistake. Is that publication? You dictate a letter to your secretary. Is that publication? (In both instances the law answers with a resounding "it depends.") In defamation by the mass media, publication is virtually presumed, however. In fact, some cases are on record in which courts ruled that if a statement was published in a newspaper or broadcast over television it is presumed that a third party saw it or heard it (*Hornby* v. *Hunter*, 1964).

Technically, every republication of a libel is a new libel. Judge Leon Yankwich *(It's Libel or Contempt If You Print It)* wrote more than two decades ago:

> In brief, the person who repeats a libel assumes responsibility for the statement and vouches for its truth as though it had been of his own making or on his own information, no matter how emphatically the qualifying words show that the statement is made on the basis of a source other than the writer himself.

If the *River City Sentinel* is being sued for libel for calling John Smith a communist and the *Ames Daily Gazette* informs its readers about the suit and notes that the *Sentinel* called Smith a communist, the *Gazette* has republished the libel. A more common problem under republication has to do with one of the great myths of American journalism called attribution. A great many people erroneously presume that a publication is not responsible for a libelous statement so long as the statement is attributed to a third person. For example, it is clear that it is libelous for a newspaper to say that John Smith shot and killed his wife's lover. It is just as libelous, however, for a newscaster to report that "according to police Smith shot and killed his wife's lover," or that "Captain Jack Jones or Prosecutor Webley Webster said that Smith shot and killed his wife's lover." The attribution does not help. The newscaster has republished the libel, and the law treats the bearer of tales in the same manner that it treats the author of tales.

---

*This statement may confuse some people who see it as a contradiction of an earlier statement that to be defamatory something must lower an individual's reputation in the eyes of a significant minority of the community. It is not a contradiction. Publication is what is being discussed here: how many people must see something before the law considers it to have been published. The earlier remark refers to damage to an individual: how many people must think less of a person upon hearing or reading the statement. It is necessary for the plaintiff to convince the court that a significant number of people in the community think less of him because of the libelous remark, but it is not necessary that the plaintiff show that these people have actually seen the libelous remark, only that they would think less of him if they had seen it.

Because of the republication rule nearly everybody in the chain of production of a news story is liable in a lawsuit. The reporter is liable: he or she wrote the story and published it by giving it to the editor. (In fact, more and more reporters are being named defendants in libel suits.) The editor passes it along after checking it (another publication); the copy editor does the same. The story goes to the composing room, and the printers and the delivery boys—every one of them—are technically republishing the libelous remark. The law releases vendors of publications from liability unless it can be shown they had knowledge of the defamatory content. The other people at the newspaper really are not worth suing; they do not have any money to speak of. So the publication is sued.

Identification

The second element in a libel suit is **identification:** the injured party must be identified. All sorts of nasty things can be published about anonymous people, but as soon as someone is named, or identified in some other way, a libel suit can result. Not all readers have to recognize the person about whom you write. Not even the majority of readers need know to whom you refer. Some authorities say it is sufficient if only a single person can identify the subject of the story.*

A person can be identified in a number of ways. He can be named; the Knave of Hearts stole the tarts. A photograph without a name is considered identification. A person can be identified by his pen name, by his nickname, by his initials, and even by a pencil or pen drawing. Circumstances can sometimes point the finger at someone. Several years ago a New York gossip columnist wrote, "Palm Beach is buzzing with the story that one of the resort's richest men caught his blonde wife in a compromising spot the other day with a former FBI agent." A man named Frederick Hope sued the Hearst Corporation (for whom the columnist worked) for libel. Hope, who was a former member of the Federal Bureau of Investigation (FBI), convinced the jury that the article identified him. He had recently joined the county attorney's staff and had been given considerable local publicity. His background as a former FBI man was given special prominence. He was also able to show that he was the only former G-man who ran with Palm Beach high society. Hope claimed that many of his friends would put these two facts together and know that the columnist referred to him. Hope won a $58,000 judgment (*Hope v. Hearst Corp.*, 1961).

It is also possible to put two stories together to make an identification. Imagine that this story was broadcast on Monday: "A fugitive wanted by the FBI for bank robbery was injured today when the automobile in which he was

---

*This situation should not be confused with damage to the plaintiff. Only one person has to see a story for it to have been published. Some authorities (e.g., Phelps and Hamilton) also say that only one person has to identify the plaintiff. However, when a judge and jury consider whether the material is defamatory and damaging to the plaintiff, they must decide whether the statement can lower the plaintiff's reputation in the eyes of a significant minority of the community.

riding was struck by a train." No name appears here, so there is no problem. Tuesday's story appears to be safe as well: "John Smith who was severely injured yesterday when the automobile in which he was riding was struck by a train. . . ." Smith can put two stories together and claim that he has been identified as the fugitive and bank robber.

If a libelous statement does not explicitly identify the plaintiff, then the plaintiff must prove that the defamatory words refer to him. This is not usually an insurmountable burden, and reporters must be extremely careful when making identification in a news story, especially if business affiliations are included in a story. Comments about an executive of a corporation, the president, for example, may reflect on the prestige of the firm and give rise to cause of action by the corporation. The corporation must prove, however, that the comments about the management discredit the business in some way.

One of the most common problems in libel is careless identification which results in a case of mistaken identity. Years ago the *Washington Post* ran a story about a District of Columbia attorney named Harry Kennedy who was brought back from Detroit to face charges of forging a client's name. The attorney charged was Harry P. L. Kennedy, a man who used his middle initials when he gave his name. The *Post* left out the middle initials. Harry F. Kennedy, another District of Columbia attorney who did not use his middle initial in business, sued the newspaper and won a substantial judgment (*Washington Post* v. *Kennedy,* 1924). That was sloppy journalism.

Most journalists learn early that complete identification is required when an individual in a news story is discussed. The identification should include the name, John Smith; the address, 2185 Pine Street; the age, 34; and if possible the occupation, carpenter. This complete identification clearly separates this John Smith from any other John Smith in the area. Complete identification protected the now defunct *Washington Star* newspaper in a lawsuit brought by a man who was erroneously named a suspect in a shooting. When prominent physician Michael Halberstam was shot in the nation's capital, the *Star* reported that police had arrested a suspect named "Jerry Summerlin, 22, of the 5500 block of Dana Place N.W." This address is just a block from Dr. Halberstam's home in the District of Columbia. The *Star* also reported that the suspect had been hit by the victim's car and was in the District General Hospital. The assailant was really Bernard Welch, who refused to provide any identification to police. The court ruled that Summerlin had not been libeled because he had not been identified. Summerlin was not 22 years old, lived in Silver Springs, Maryland, and was not in the District General Hospital after the shooting. In fact the *Star* had got everything correct in its identification of the shooting suspect except the name. By adding the details of identification, the newspaper saved itself from a lawsuit (*Summerlin* v. *Washington Star,* 1981).

The number of suits which result from mistaken identity is high, and most are preventable. One thing a young reporter should learn immediately is to not take anyone's word for an identification. If the police tell you they have arrested John Smith of Pine Street, you should double-check their statement. Numerous means of checking are available: city directories, utility company records, and so forth. Newspapers, broadcasting stations, and magazines are sometimes held responsible even for errors which result from official blunders because they compound the error.

The most troublesome question regarding identification is group identification. Can the members of a group sue when the group as a whole is libeled? The answer to this question is not completely clear. If the group is massive, there can be no suit. A group of Michigan hunters sued CBS following the broadcast of "Guns of August," a program which was critical of hunting practices and which was filmed partly in Michigan. The Sixth United States Court of Appeals ruled that "vague, general references to a comparatively large group do not constitute actionable defamation" (*Michigan Conservation Clubs* v. *CBS,* 1981). In another recent suit, the New York Supreme Court ruled that several nonprofit Puerto Rican community organizations could not bring a libel action based on the remark "nine hundred-thousand Puerto Ricans live in New York and they're all on food stamps." The court ruled that such remarks aimed at ethnic or racial groups in general do not cause direct, focused harm to individual group members. (*Puerto Rican Legal Defense Fund* v. *Grace,* 1983). If the group is small—a three-man zoning board is corrupt— each member can sue. The group is small enough so that each member can be clearly identified. What about a middle-sized group? The *Restatement of Torts* (2nd ed.) says this:

> One who publishes defamatory matter concerning a group or class of persons is subject to liability to an individual member of it, but only if (A) the group or class is so small that the matter can reasonably be understood to refer to the individual or (B) the circumstances of publication reasonably give rise to the conclusion that there is particular reference to him.

According to the *Restatement,* publication of defamatory statements about groups having more than twenty-five members is safe. However, at least one case of a group with sixty members—the University of Oklahoma football team—suing because of derogatory statements is on record. The members of the team successfully sued *True* magazine after it charged that some members of the team used drugs (*Fawcett Publications* v. *Morris,* 1962). Other authorities put the number at one hundred. If the group is smaller, there can be trouble.

Circumstances and what is said play a big part in this question. Several years ago employees of Neiman-Marcus department store in Dallas sued the publisher of a book entitled *USA Confidential* for statements in the book about the store's sales staff and models. The author of the book charged that the models and salesgirls were call girls and that most of the salesmen in the menswear department were homosexual. Only nine models were employed in the store, and that suit was uncontested. The store had twenty-five menswear salesmen. The article said most were "fairies," and the court allowed recovery for several individual salesmen. However, there were more than three hundred salesgirls in the store, and the federal court said the group was too large. "No reasonable man would take the writer seriously and conclude from the publication a reference to any individual saleswomen," the judge ruled (*Neiman-Marcus* v. *Lait,* 1952).

Recent case law on the issue of group identification tends to support the notion that courts seem reluctant to find liability unless it is quite clear the specific plaintiff has been identified, as the following four cases show.

In Washington State, courts ruled that comments about the sale of Bicentennial junk, including bootleg products and counterfeit official seals by "local souvenir shops" were not specific enough to identify plaintiff Richard Sims, who operated a Bicentennial Shop at the Seattle Center (*Sims* v. *KIRO,* 1978).

The question in a Massachusetts newspaper, "Is it true that a Bellingham cop locked himself and a female companion in the back of a cruiser in a town sandpit and had to radio for help?" did not specifically identify any single member of the community's twenty-one-member police department (*Arcand* v. *Evening Call,* 1977).

A franchised Kentucky Fried Chicken dealer in Bowling Green, Kentucky, lost his suit against Colonel Harland Sanders after the colonel made disparaging remarks about the Kentucky fried chicken, mashed potatoes, and gravy. The state court ruled that there are more than five thousand outlets selling Kentucky Fried Chicken products around the world, and there was nothing in the article which identified the Bowling Green restaurant as the object of the remarks (*KFC of Bowling Green* v. *Sanders,* 1978).

Finally, a federal court ruled that a small group of editors and reporters for the Manchester *Union-Leader* newspaper could not maintain a lawsuit against the *Boston Globe* because of critical comments published in the *Globe* about the New Hampshire publication. The *Union-Leader,* which was published for many years by William Loeb, a very controversial figure in journalism, was described in a *Globe* editorial as "probably the worst newspaper in America." The *Globe* said that Loeb "runs a newspaper by paranoids for paranoids." Three editors and twenty-four other employees including some reporters brought suit against the *Globe,* but a United States district court in Massachusetts dismissed the action. "Defamation of a large group gives rise to no civil action on the part of an individual member of the group unless he can show special application of the defamatory matter to himself," the court ruled. Three hundred twenty-five persons were employed at the newspaper.

The group was too large. Admitting that the general references to the paper probably hurt the editors more than other employees because they were ostensibly responsible for what appeared in the *Union-Leader,* the court ruled that no special application or particular reference to these three persons could be inferred from the general criticism of the newspaper (*Loeb* v. *Globe Newspaper,* 1980).

Despite these victories by the press, caution is urged upon reporters who describe even a very large group in a defamatory manner. Caution is especially appropriate if only a small number of the defamed group live in the community. If the charge is made that all astrologers are frauds and there is but one astrologer in the community, the remark can be dangerous. The plaintiff could convince a sympathetic jury that he or she has been severely harmed by the remark. Saying "all" members of a group are corrupt is worse than saying "most" members are corrupt. Saying "most" is worse than saying "some," and saying "some" is worse than saying "one or two." This is a particularly unsettled area of the law, and the journalist must remember that ultimately the suit will be decided by a judge and jury who may neither look at the issue in the same manner as the journalist, nor be particularly sympathetic to the charges made by the journalist.

Defamation

The third element in the plaintiff's case are the words themselves. There are two kinds of defamatory words. The first kind consists of words which are libelous on their face, words which obviously can damage the reputation of any person. Words like *thief, cheat,* and *Communist*—there is no question that they are defamatory.

The second kind of words are innocent on their face and become defamatory only if the reader or viewer knows other facts. To say that Jane Adams had a baby appears safe enough. But if the reader knows that Ms. Adams is not married, then the words are libelous.

The distinction between these two kinds of words used to be more important than it is now. At one time plaintiffs had to prove they were specifically harmed by the words in the second category, sometimes called "libel per quod." Damage was presumed from the words in the first category, often called "libel per se." All libel plaintiffs must prove harm of some kind today. Yet in some states today the plaintiff suing for the so-called libel per quod must meet a more rigorous fault requirement than the plaintiff suing for libel per se. For example, in some jurisdictions the libel plaintiff suing on the basis of words that appear innocent on their face (libel per quod) must prove that the defendant was grossly negligent in publishing the statement, whereas the plaintiff suing for words which are plainly defamatory must show only simple **negligence.** (The meanings of the various fault requirements are discussed on pages 143–51.)

A description of the kinds of words that are libelous is codified (by statute) in most states. These laws are most general, however, describing kinds of words (words which hold someone up to ridicule, hatred, scorn, etc.), rather than specific words. Only by looking at the numerous court decisions in libel law can one get a fairly good picture of the specific kinds of words which can be libelous. Even then the process is imprecise.

There is another problem. The meanings people attach to words change over time. Socialists were once feared and hated, and the word was defamatory. It is doubtful that calling someone a Socialist today would be libelous. Labeling someone a communist was and is defamatory, except during the period between 1942 and 1945 when the Communists were our allies in World War II. The term *slacker* seems harmless enough today, but in World War I *slacker* had a derogatory meaning: the word described someone who sought to avoid military service.

At a libel trial a judge and a jury are supposed to consider words in light of their ordinary meaning unless the evidence is persuasive that the defendant meant something else when the statement was published. Some states, such as Illinois, have what is called an **innocent construction rule,** which means that if there is a way to read the supposedly libelous material in a nondefamatory way that is how it should be read. For example, in 1977 the Illinois State Appeals Court ruled that the term "political hack" can have a derogatory meaning, but when it is used in an editorial criticizing a circuit court clerk, the term is not intended to suggest such a meaning. The court ruled that when the entire article is read "the natural and obvious meaning" of the phrase is to describe someone whose job is based upon political selection and is not meant to suggest that the clerk is incompetent. The term is susceptible to an innocent construction and that was the construction the court presumed (*Cooper* v. *Rockford Newspapers,* 1977). Other states, however, do not have such a rule. In Oklahoma, for example, the courts take just the opposite tack and give the material the strictest possible reading. Hence, it is easier for a plaintiff to win a libel suit in Oklahoma than in Illinois.

As a general rule it is for the judge to decide whether an ambiguous statement can convey a defamatory meaning and for the jury to decide whether in fact the statement does convey that meaning. A judge can dismiss a suit without a trial if he or she believes the words cannot be considered defamatory. By letting a case go to the jury the judge is only ruling that a jury could find that the words are defamatory.

A person may be defamed in any number of ways. Simply saying that Robert Smith is the illegitimate child of John and Mary Smith is defamatory. The parents have been defamed. Implication can be used: John and Mary Smith have been married for six years and have a seven-year-old son named Robert. Some journalists think that if they do not spell a situation out, just drop subtle hints, they are on safe ground. In Massachusetts a libel case resulted when a newspaper reporter thought something was wrong and tried to say so subtly. Here is part of the story:

> The Veterans Hospital here suspected that 39-year-old George M. Perry of North Truro, whose death is being probed by federal and state authorities, was suffering from chronic arsenic poisoning.
>
> State police said the body of Perry, and of his brother, Arthur, who is buried near him, would probably be exhumed from St. Peter's Cemetery in Provincetown.
>
> George Perry died in the VA hospital last June 9, 48 hours after his tenth admission there. . . . His brother, who lived in Connecticut and spent two days here during George's funeral, died approximately a month later. About two months later, in September, George's mother-in-law, 74-year-old Mrs. Mary F. Mott, who had come to live with her daughter, died too. Her remains were cremated.

While the story lacked a good deal in journalistic clarity, an Ellery Queen or a Perry Mason is not needed to get the gist of what the reporter was saying. Mrs. Perry murdered her husband, her brother-in-law, and her mother. Lizzie Borden strikes again! The insinuations are that Arthur died after visiting the plaintiff's home and that the mother had "died too." Isn't it too bad that her remains were cremated. This story cost the Hearst Corporation, publishers of the *Boston Record,* $25,000 (*Perry v. Hearst Corp.,* 1964).

A libel suit cannot be based on an isolated phrase wrenched out of context. The article as a whole must be considered. A story about baseball's legendary base stealer Maury Wills might contain the sentence "Wills might be the best thief of all time," referring to his base-stealing ability. Wills cannot sue on the basis of that single sentence. The story itself makes it clear the kind of thievery the writer is discussing. Nevertheless, a libelous remark in a headline—even though it is cleared up in the story which follows—can be the basis for a libel suit.

Also, a headline cannot go beyond the story and say more than the story says. For example, a consulting engineer was asked to prepare plans and specifications for a sound system for a Louisiana state school for the blind. In a letter describing the engineer's report, a state official said that the proposal was good, but that the bid specifications "seem somewhat proprietary to certain manufacturers." Something which is proprietary is something associated with a specific manufacturer. In its story on the report the *New Orleans Times-Picayune* said that the specifications seemed proprietary according to state officials. The headline, however, said, "Bid Specs Reported Rigged." This statement went far beyond any charge in the state official's letter or story, and a $10,000 libel judgment was affirmed against the newspaper by the state court of appeals (*Forrest v. Lynch and Times-Picayune Co.,* 1977).

A federal court in Seattle ruled that reader habits can also be material in a libel case. Suit was brought against the *Seattle Post-Intelligencer* for a story it published about the redemption of a home mortgage by a local attorney. The headline and the first four or five paragraphs suggested that the attorney had done something illegal or unethical. The remainder of the story—which was about fifty paragraphs long and jumped from page to page after leaving the front page—explained that what the attorney had done was not illegal or unethical, that his actions were fair and aboveboard. The court admitted expert testimony on reader habits which indicated that people tend not to finish such long stories, that many people stop reading as soon as the story is continued on the inside pages of a newspaper. The plaintiff argued that in the minds of most readers the libelous opinion created by the first part of the story was not corrected since they did not finish the story. The jury awarded the attorney $100,000 in damages (*McNair* v. *Hearst Corp.,* 1974).

Factual statements can obviously be defamatory. What about an opinion? "I think Mayor Frank Jones is doing a rotten job of running this city." An opinion cannot be defamatory. In 1974, in a very important case, the Supreme Court of the United States ruled (*Gertz* v. *Welch,* 1974):

> Under the First Amendment there is no such thing as a false idea. However pernicious an opinion may seem, we depend for its correction not on the conscience of judges and juries but on the competition of other ideas.

The revised *Restatement of Torts* states that an opinion statement can be defamatory only if "it also expresses, or implies the assertion of a false and defamatory fact which is not known or assumed by both parties to the communication."

The next one hundred pages of this book could be a kind of Sears Roebuck catalog of defamatory words, but such an enumeration here is a waste of time. Instead, we will consider specific examples of the kinds of words which in the past were held to be defamatory. These examples should permit you to generalize about specific remarks. Simply ask this question when you evaluate whether something is defamatory: Will the people in the community think less of this person after I publish this story than they do before I publish it? If the answer is yes, then the statement, remark, or comment is probably defamatory.

Accusation of a Crime   Probably the category of words responsible more than any other for the greatest number of libel suits pertains to crime and criminal acts. Any imputation that a man or woman has done something illegal—from murder to jaywalking—is libelous. The statement can be a straightforward charge: John Smith is an arsonist or John Smith was convicted of arson. The imputation can be indirect: John Smith makes his living using matches and gasoline. The statement might note only that John Smith has spent much of his life in jail because fire fascinates him. A description might be used: John Smith went to the Fuddle Paint Company, poured gasoline on an outside wall, and then lit a match. Maybe John has a nickname—John the Torch. Each of these statements and many more which you can think of accomplish the same end: they defame poor John Smith.

It is also libelous to call John an "alleged arsonist," which points out another great myth of journalism. According to the dictionary, to allege means "to assert without proof." The police assert that John is an arsonist, and by calling him an alleged arsonist the journalist republishes the libel the police officer uttered. Republication of a libel is a new libel.

A serious problem faced by the reporter who writes or broadcasts about crime is lack of knowledge about the meaning of criminal terms. Not every killing is a homicide or murder. When John Smith kills his wife he might be acting in self-defense. Calling him a murderer creates a problem. Be certain the term used does not go beyond the action.

The *Calvin* (Okla.) *Chronicle* was angered when a federal district judge, fearful of the impact of intense prejudicial publicity, changed the venue for the trial of a state official. In an editorial the newspaper noted that "State Treasurer Leo Winters and all the other people are just as guilty in Guymon on the panhandle, Idabel in Southeastern Oklahoma, Bartlesville in the Northeast, Lawton in the Southwest, or right smack in downtown Oklahoma City." Winters sued for libel and the state supreme court ruled that the charge that he was guilty of a crime was libelous per se (*Winters* v. *Morgan,* 1978).

Sexual Slurs

It has been said that the United States is a nation overly concerned with sex. Sexual references, comments about sexual morality, sexual abnormality, and so forth, all constitute bases for libel suits. Supposedly, we are in the midst of a sexual revolution, but many people are not aware of the fact. For a woman to be sleeping with a man to whom she is not married may be perfectly normal in some parts of our society, but is still not acceptable behavior in other parts of our society. If such a charge were made against a woman, a libel suit would probably stand. Woman's virtue is strongly protected by our courts via the libel suit. Any charge made in any fashion that a woman may be unchaste or may not be virtuous is dealt with harshly by a court. Charges of rape come within this category as well.

Similarly, comments about sexual abnormality are dangerous. John is gay or John is queer, Jane is a lesbian, Frank is an exhibitionist: all are defamatory remarks. Caution must be exercised as well in stories about less exotic sexual concerns: calling a man impotent can be libelous. Charges of wife swapping and failure to fulfill "marital obligations" are also defamatory.

Much of a person's reputation is concerned with his personal habits. Is he honest, ethical, and kind? Does he pay his bills on time or is he a deadbeat? Is she clean, does she drink too much liquor, does she use dope, does she smoke pot? Statements regarding all such behavior have been and will continue to be the subject of libel suits. To call a man dishonest is defamatory. Likewise are charges that he is unkind to his children and unethical in the way he conducts his financial affairs. She drinks too much, she is a drunkard, she is always potted or smashed, she is an alcoholic, she is a member of Alcoholics Anonymous, she is on the juice, she was arrested for drunken driving: all of these charges are libelous. The same is true of statements regarding the use of drugs and marijuana. A good credit rating is very important today; therefore any charge that reflects on financial standing—the Smiths live beyond their means, they are broke, they don't pay their bills, they owe money all over town—is defamatory.

Reporters must be wary of many other aspects of personal characteristics. Imputation that a person has a certain kind of disease can be dangerous. What kinds of diseases? Not a cold or the flu: anyone can have these disorders. Syphilis, gonorrhea, and genital herpes—euphemistically called social diseases—suggest a kind of loose sexual behavior and uncleanliness frowned upon by many people. Diseases which cause a person to be shunned—contagious diseases such as smallpox, infectious hepatitis, or even the widely publicized A.I.D.S.—are examples.

In an interesting decision by a United States circuit court of appeals a former Philadelphia Eagles football player lost a libel suit based on the published erroneous assertion that he had contracted polycythemia vera, an abnormal cell condition which can precipitate dangerous clotting of blood. The court ruled that polycythemia vera is not a loathesome disease, not contagious, and not attributed in any way to socially repugnant conduct. As such, the charge was not defamatory (*Chuy* v. *Philadelphia Eagles,* 1979).

Mental illness is another dangerous area. To say that someone is crazy or insane or nuts is defamatory. We are becoming a bit more sophisticated in this area. While fifty years ago the charge that someone had a nervous breakdown was probably defamatory, today such a charge is probably safe unless the plaintiff can prove that the charge caused some special harm such as the loss of a job.

If a person professes to belong to a specific faith, a charge which reflects on her commitment to or acceptance by that faith can be defamatory. To say that a Catholic was denied the right of Holy Communion is a serious charge, for to most people it suggests some ghastly kind of behavior by the excommunicant. The same rule applies to political and patriotic affiliations. To charge that a person had been stripped of his citizenship is defamatory. Charging someone with being a traitor or a spy or with urging sedition or anarchy or revolution are all defamatory statements.

What about derogatory nationalistic references? John is a polack or a spic or a dago. These terms are probably not libelous. However, in some back-water regions of the United States to mistakenly identify a white person as being a black is still probably considered libelous. No suits of the opposite nature—a black suing for being called a white—are on record. A person's affiliations frequently suggest a good deal about the person. Consequently, persons can be defamed by merely naming them members of a certain group. Adams is a member of the Ku Klux Klan, the Nazi party, the Communist party, or any group currently thought to be repugnant.

It can be libelous to ridicule someone, to make him appear foolish. Ridicule is a difficult area to describe because not all ridicule is defamatory. Many humorous stories about people have been ruled to be safe. Newspapers are frequently the victims of false obituaries, and generally courts rule that such stories are not libelous to the person alleged to have died (*Cohen* v. *New York Times*, 1912). In one case the false obituary had the deceased lying in state in a saloon (*Cardiff* v. *Brooklyn Eagle*, 1948). Other humorous kinds of accounts are generally protected. However, the New York Supreme Court recently permitted a suit for the negligent infliction of emotional distress against the *New York Post* when the newspaper erroneously published a death notice for a person who had not died. See *Rubenstein* v. *New York Post*, 1983.

Ridicule which can be libelous is that which makes the plaintiff appear to be uncommonly foolish, which carries a kind of sting that hurts. Everyone must die, and therefore a false obituary really says nothing derogatory about the plaintiff. It is just a joke at his expense. But a story in a New England newspaper about a man so thrifty that he built his own casket and dug his own grave was ruled to be libelous ridicule. The story made the man appear to be foolish, weird, and unnatural. A fifty dollar judgment was awarded (*Powers* v. *Durgin-Snow Publishing Co.*, 1958). How can reporters tell the difference between the two kinds of stories? The distinction is often very difficult. Extreme care is needed to avoid problems.

Business Reputation

Thus far the kinds of charges that can injure almost all persons, hurt their reputation, cause them to lose friends, have been discussed. The law goes beyond these limits in protecting some individuals; it goes to the point of protecting both men and women in their business or occupation. Any comment which injures a person's ability to conduct a business or occupation successfully can be considered defamatory. For example, comments about business ethics can be defamatory. Sid, a butcher, sells tainted meat. Archie, a mechanic, overcharges his customers. Similarly, statements about competence to do a job can be defamatory. Milton lacks the skill to be an architect. Doris, a nurse, cannot tell a bedpan from a baby bottle. Comments about honesty, about the financial solvency of a businessman—anything which tends to impair an individual's means of making a livelihood or discredits him in his business or profession—can be the basis for a successful libel suit.

Because reputation is an essential element in the success of many professional persons, such a person is probably more easily defamed and more likely to sue than a typical working man or woman. In fact, Professor Marc Franklin of Stanford University recently reported, following his study of more than five hundred libel suits, that professional people were one of six groups of people responsible for two-thirds of all the libel suits filed in the United States. The other groups were business managers, government employees, law enforcement personnel, corporations, and public officials. Teachers, doctors, journalists, businessmen, lawyers, and many other persons are very easily defamed by comments about their business or occupation. Yet such persons are not above honest criticism; journalists should not totally abdicate their role as consumer protectors. James Southard, an antique automobile dealer and the creator of something called Classic Car Investments, sued *Forbes* magazine for what he said amounted to questioning his integrity as a businessman. *Forbes* did an article on the growing field of investment in classic cars which was critical of speculators and promoters. It discussed Southard's plan to develop an investment program in classic automobiles which he hoped to sell to doctors, lawyers, and corporations. The magazine quoted Southard as saying, "The value of those cars never goes down, so you're guaranteed to make money." Writer Alvin Butkus then noted, "If he made claims like that for stocks, Southard would be in the soup. But there is no Securities and Exchange Commission for classic cars." Southard said Butkus's statement implied he was unethical, that he had violated federal securities laws, that he was selling unregistered securities. The Fifth Circuit Court of Appeals disagreed and said that the meaning placed on the statement by Southard was farfetched. The article at worst, the court ruled, suggested that the plaintiff was puffing the value of an investment in classic cars to an extent beyond what was permitted in marketing of securities. "The fundamental message was caveat emptor [buyer beware] to potential customers of Southard and others in his business. . . . It lacks the element of personal disgrace necessary for defamation" (*Southard* v. *Forbes,* 1979).

The law also provides some other exceptions. For example, the law does not presume that people think that business or professional people are perfect. Therefore, to report that a professional person or a business person has made an error is not always defamatory. It depends upon how the statement is made. If the statement merely suggests that the individual made an isolated mistake—Dr. John Smith operated on Jane Adams yesterday to remove a sponge he failed to remove during an earlier operation on Ms. Adams—it is probably not libelous. However, if the published comment suggests a pattern of incompetence—this is the fifth time in the past two years Dr. Smith has had to operate a second time to remove a surgical tool left in a patient—the statement clearly is defamatory. Be careful in this area. Recourse to this rule is never an excuse for clumsy or careless journalism. This rule (called by some the **single-mistake rule**) is not constructed upon an unassailable foundation (see *Hentell* v. *Knopf,* 1982, for an example of how this rule can protect a libel defendant).

One other kind of "businessmen" can sue if they are improperly criticized: government officials and politicians. Charges of corruption, bribery, vote buying, gross dereliction of duty, and graft can all stand as the basis for a successful libel action. Accusing a judge of being biased and unfair, accusing the head of the street department of improperly maintaining the public roads, and accusing a public official of selling out to the mob are all defamatory charges. (As will be noted later, it is much harder for government officials to win a libel suit than it is for a private business person.)

While a person's general reputation is fairly nebulous, the individual's right to earn a living, practice a profession, successfully operate a business, and so forth, are quite specific. Courts are prone to protect such individuals from unwarranted attack. Journalists and broadcasters must exercise caution in dealing with such subjects lest they inadvertently damage that right.

About a Business

In addition to damaging a person, a defamatory statement can injure a business or corporation. A corporation can maintain a lawsuit when it believes its credit has been damaged or its reputation has been hurt. The same kinds of words that can defame an individual can also defame a corporation or business. Any assertion that the corporation has engaged in criminal activity, is dishonest, has ties to organized crime, lacks integrity, fails to pay its bills on time, and so forth, can be libelous. Corporations can be hurt in other ways as well.

An assertion that the corporation makes unsafe products—not that the products are unsafe, but that the corporation deliberately produces unsafe products to cut costs—can result in a libel suit. Statements which reflect on the company's labor policies—management runs a real sweatshop, takes advantage of its workers, violates labor laws—are libelous. Attacks on fiscal integrity (better not buy a car from Acme Motors because chances are good that the company won't be around next year to fix the car when it breaks down) are defamatory. An assertion that DooDad Industries does not maintain safe working conditions, or that the company makes illegal political contributions, or that it cheats its customers is libelous to that business.

Some authorities assert that making derogatory statements about persons who manage a business, who work at a business, or who are customers of a business can also be used as the basis for a defamation suit. The law is not settled in this area. Publishing nasty things about the president and vice-president of DooDad Industries will not give the corporation the right to sue unless it can be proved that such statements actually damaged the reputation of the company. Reporting that DooDad employees are "a bunch of louts" might also serve as the basis for a damage suit if the company can prove that the charge somehow reflects on the corporation's ability to hire the proper people.

There is little chance, however, that a corporation can sue merely because of actions or behavior of its customers. Several years ago Louis Stillman sued Paramount Pictures for the remark in the motion picture *Country Girl* that punch-drunk fighters frequented Stillman's Gym in New York City. Stillman argued that the remark reflected upon him and his business. The court disagreed (*Stillman* v. *Paramount Pictures,* 1957). Proprietors of public businesses have no control over the kinds of persons who use their establishments. Therefore, readers should not think anything less of Stillman because punch-drunk fighters might be training in his gym. Another example of the problem is a story saying that for the second time in two weeks a fight broke out at a local tavern last night. Again, the proprietor does not have much control over who drinks in his tavern and what happens when they drink. Any implication that the owner of the place encourages this kind of behavior, condones it, fails to call authorties after it starts, and so forth, will of course change the nature of the remark and can be libelous.

About a Product

Criticism of a product falls into a different legal category called "disparagement of property." While such criticism is often called **trade libel,** it is not really libel at all, but product disparagement. What is the difference? A plaintiff finds it significantly harder to win a trade libel case than to win a garden-variety libel suit. First, consider some examples of trade libel. Bango rifles fail to eject empty cartridges. Crumo bread gets stale in one day. DooDad motorcycles fail to stop within a safe distance. The remarks are aimed at the products, not at the companies. There is no implication that the manufacturer intentionally makes a bad product, tries to cheat customers, or conducts its business fraudulently. DooDad may make the best motorcycles it can make; they just turn out to be unsafe.

Since the company itself is not presumed to be hurt, the law raises some stiff barriers to a successful trade libel suit. First, the plaintiff, the manufacturer of the product, must prove that the statement is untrue. Proof is difficult, but not too difficult for the kinds of statements just given. If DooDad is able to demonstrate to the court that some of its motorcycles brake to a stop within a safe distance, the company then shows the falsity of the charge. It is much safer to refer to individual products. For example, rather than say that DooDad motorcycles do not stop safely, report that of the ten motorcycles tested none stopped safely, or that of the Bango rifles tested none ejected cartridges properly. The manufacturer will then have to refute this evidence, not merely find examples of the product which are in good working order.

Next, the plaintiff will have to show special damage—actual monetary loss because of the comments. Loss of orders attributable to the unfavorable report is such evidence, and testimony from potential customers who failed to purchase the maligned product because of the comment can be used to support the damage claim. Finally, the plaintiff has to prove that the false remarks were motivated by ill will, bad feeling, or gross carelessness. The plaintiff can prove this if he can show that the negative remarks were published "to get him" and that the writer doesn't like him. The plaintiff might also be able to prove that the writer was grossly negligent in checking the truth of the statement. Before the plaintiff can collect for trade libel, it must prove all three charges: falsity, damage, and malicious motives or extreme carelessness.

Evaluate the following three statements on the basis of the foregoing discussion of trade libel:

1. DooDad autos are superior to Acme cars.
2. Acme cars stop running after about one year.
3. Acme cars stop running after about one year because the company has a plan to force customers to buy a new car every year.

Is statement one libelous? It contains no libel, no disparagement, no anything. Nothing negative was said about Acme; only a positive statement about DooDad cars was made. Statement two? This statement is trade libel, an attack upon the product. Statement three? Here we have garden-variety libel. The comment states that Acme purposefully sells automobiles that break down after one year and reflects upon the integrity of the business itself.

Banks and Insurance Companies

One other point should be made before we leave this topic. In addition to the protections businesses and corporations have against libel, many states have laws which prohibit critical and untrue comments about banks, insurance companies, and other such organizations. What these laws are designed to do is to protect such organizations from attack upon their fiscal integrity to avoid turning customers against them and destroying them. After all, a bank has only its fiscal integrity and other people's money to sell.

Suits under such statutes are rare, but occasionally they do occur. And then the newspaper or broadcasting station soon discovers that the many protections the press enjoys in a libel suit often do not apply when a suit is brought under such a law. Check the insurance laws and the banking laws in your state. If such laws exist, find out how the courts interpreted the laws. This check might save a lot of grief some time in the future.

Summary

A plaintiff bears the initial burden of proof in a libel suit and must prove four conditions to a court:

1. That the libel was published
2. That the plaintiff was identified

3. That the words were defamatory
4. That the libelous matter was published because the defendant was irresponsible or careless

Publication can be established if the plaintiff can show that one additional person besides the plaintiff and the defendant has seen the material. An individual can be identified for purposes of a libel suit by a name, nickname, or photograph or even through a report of circumstances. Statements made about a very large group of people cannot be used as the basis for a libel suit by a single member of that group. However, if the group is smaller, all the members might be able to sue for comments made about the entire group. A statement is defamatory if it lowers the reputation of the injured party. The most common kinds of defamatory statements reflect such matters as suggestions of criminal behavior or sexual impropriety, comments about personal habits or characteristics, statements reflecting upon patriotism or political beliefs, and reports about competence and qualifications in an individual's occupation or business. Corporations and other businesses can be defamed; the manufacturer of a product which has been criticized can sue for product disparagement.

THE FAULT REQUIREMENT

The fault requirement, the fourth element in the plaintiff's case, is a relatively new element in libel litigation. Since the mid-1960s **public persons**—that is, persons in the public eye—have had to prove an element of fault when they sued mass media defendants. **Private persons** have had to prove fault since 1974.

The fault requirement has a kind of dual nature which makes it both indispensable to the plaintiff's libel case and a privilege used by the defense. In some regards it can be considered to fit naturally as a requisite which must be met by the plaintiff along with the demonstration of publication, identification, and defamation. Yet it is also a prerogative raised by defendants to protect themselves from a libel suit. In this regard it has many of the characteristics of a defense to libel. The dual nature of this requirement is recognized in this book by placing the discussion of fault including consideration of private and public persons and the meaning of fault between the outline of the plaintiff's case and the defenses to libel. It must be remembered that in proving fault by a defendant in a libel suit, that is, in proving that the newspaper or magazine was careless or reckless in allowing the libelous report to be published, both the plaintiff and the defendant have a role. The plaintiff must convince the judge and/or jury that the publication or broadcasting station was indeed at fault, that it was negligent or reckless. The defendant, on the other hand, must attempt to convince the court either that there was no negligence or that the highest possible level of negligence needs to be proved.

That is, the newspaper will argue that the plaintiff needs to prove that the publication of the story resulted from something more serious than simple carelessness—that it was published because of reckless disregard for the truth. The defendant wants to make the plaintiff's task as difficult as possible. Given this perspective, two sets of questions need to be considered. First, what is the fault requirement for private persons? What is the fault requirement for public persons? How does the law distinguish between private and public persons? Second, how have the courts defined the various levels of fault? And how can such fault be proved by plaintiffs?

Two generalizations are useful as guidelines in the understanding of fault.

1. Private persons who sue the media for defamation must at least prove that the material was published through negligence. **Negligence** is defined in the law as conduct which creates an unreasonable risk of harm. Another way of describing this concept is that something published negligently was published *without* the exercise of reasonable care by the defendant.

2. Public persons who sue the media for defamation because of the publication or broadcast of stories about their public conduct must normally prove that the defendant exhibited **actual malice** when the material was published. Actual malice is defined in the law as publishing the material with the knowledge that it is false, or publishing the material with a reckless disregard for the truth.

Both of these generalizations need important qualification and clarification, and that is the purpose of the bulk of this section.

Throughout almost its entire history the tort of libel has been governed by a standard called "strict liability." **Strict liability** means that if you harm someone you are responsible for that harm, regardless of how it happened to come about. You could have undertaken every possible effort to ensure that no harm would result from your action; nevertheless, if someone is hurt, the responsibility is yours. In the law of libel this meant that even though editors attempted to verify a story in every possible way, even though they exercised every caution normally exercised by careful journalists, even though there was no doubt at all in their mind that the story was accurate and truthful, if the story defamed someone the newspaper was liable for damages.

In 1964 the Supreme Court of the United States ruled that in libel law the doctrine of strict liability violated the First Amendment insofar as the defamatory statement concerned government officials and focused upon their official conduct. The dispute from which the ruling sprang was played against the vivid backdrop of the civil rights struggle in the South. In some ways the result of the lawsuit was a recognition by the Supreme Court that while for all practical purposes the law of **seditious libel** had become impotent by the last half of the twentieth century, government leaders could use civil libel actions to accomplish the goals of sedition law: to quiet criticism of the government.

In the early 1960s important segments of the American press took a strong stand in support of the passage and enforcement of civil rights laws. In Alabama five government officials attempted to retaliate against the press by filing a series of lawsuits against the *New York Times* for three million dollars.

The material upon which the suits were based was not even a news article; it was an editorial advertisement (an advertisement which promoted an idea rather than a product or commercial service). A civil rights group, the Committee to Defend Martin Luther King and the Struggle for Freedom in the South, had placed the advertisement. In the narrative part of the full-page advertisement charges were leveled at various Alabama government leaders. While it was basically true, the advertisement was nevertheless peppered with small factual errors. These errors proved to be the downfall of the *Times* in an Alabama state court where the newspaper lost the first suit brought by Montgomery, Alabama, Police Commissioner L. B. Sullivan. Sullivan won a $500,000 judgment—all that he asked for—and this ruling was affirmed by the state supreme court. One must remember that as much as anything the case against the *Times* allowed Alabamians to vent their pipes which had been filling with steam ever since that (according to prevailing Southern thought) "damned, liberal [radical, communist] New York scandal sheet" had taken a leadership role in seeking passage and enforcement of federal civil rights guidelines in the South. The political implications of this case are beyond the scope of this text, but should not be overlooked.

The *New York Times* appealed the decision to the Supreme Court of the United States and won a unanimous reversal of the judgment. In reversing the Alabama state courts in the case of *New York Times Co.* v. *Sullivan* (1964), the Supreme Court changed the law of libel forever.

Before the significance of the high Court's decision in this case is explained, it is important to explain why the Court made the ruling, or at least the reasons the justices gave for their decision, for this rationale remains today the basic foundation of the important First Amendment libel defense.

Only with the benefit of hindsight is it possible to get at what the Supreme Court said in the 1964 *Sullivan* ruling, and some points still remain less than crystal clear. Under the traditional law of libel the newspaper was in serious trouble. There had been publication and identification, and the words were clearly defamatory. The *Times* could not use truth as a defense; the publication contained numerous errors. Other libel defenses were equally inapplicable.

But Justice William Brennan and his eight colleagues on the high Court did not apply the traditional law of libel. Sullivan was not a typical plaintiff; he was a government officer. The defamation did not concern his private life; it focused on his role as police commissioner. The high Court ruled therefore that because of the nature of this suit, because of the immense First Amendment implications, plaintiff Sullivan was forced to carry an added burden of proof. He had to show that the publication of the advertisement was made with actual malice. Actual malice was defined as knowledge of falsity or reckless disregard of whether the story was truthful. Sullivan, then, had to show that the *New York Times* published the advertisement with knowledge that some of its charges were false, or that the newspaper exhibited reckless disregard as to whether the charges were true.

The Court's decision can be explained on three bases. First, this libel case was really a kind of seditious libel case. A government official was criticized for the manner in which he conducted his public office. He sued for civil libel and won. The *New York Times* was punished for criticizing the government. Punishment for criticism of government is the essence of sedition. It matters little that the punishment comes in the form of a money judgment that must be paid to the government official as opposed to a fine which must be paid into the public treasury. The results are the same; others will be more cautious in their comments about those who control the government. With the exception of the **Smith Act,** which is aimed at prohibiting the advocacy of action toward the violent overthrow of the government (see pages 64–67), sedition has been effectively abolished in this country. In *New York Times Co. v. Sullivan,* the Supreme Court simply made it much harder (but not impossible) for government officials to accomplish the goals of sedition law through civil libel suits.

The Court was also concerned that these kinds of lawsuits might have an impact upon debate about political issues. Quoting numerous earlier high Court opinions, Brennan wrote (*New York Times Co. v. Sullivan,* 1964):

> The general proposition that freedom of expression upon public questions is secured by the First Amendment has long been settled by our decisions. The constitutional safeguard, as we have said, "was fashioned to assure the unfettered interchange of ideas for the bringing about of political and social changes desired by our people. . . ." The maintenance of the opportunity for free political discussion to the end that government may be responsive to the will of the people and that changes may be obtained by lawful means, an opportunity essential to the security of the Republic. . . . "The First Amendment," said Judge Learned Hand, "presupposes that right conclusions are more likely to be gathered out of a multitude of tongues, than through any kind of authoritative selection."

Thus, Brennan wrote, this case is considered against the background of a profound national commitment to the principle that debate on public issues should be uninhibited, robust, and wide open.

Turning to the fact that there were errors in the publication, Brennan asserted, "Erroneous statement is inevitable in free debate, and it must be protected if the freedoms of expression are to have the 'breathing space' that they need . . . to survive." Whatever is added to the field of libel, the associate justice noted, is taken from the field of free debate. This concept—traditional concern with maintaining free debate—formed the philosophical basis for the decision.

Finally, as a public official, a government leader, Sullivan voluntarily took a position for which criticism was common, usual, and, indeed, expected. As a servant of the public one must expect to be criticized, sometimes quite strongly. In a way, he had asked for criticism. Also, as a public official and a politician he had easy access to the press to respond to criticism. Whereas a private person whose reputation has been damaged may have no recourse but to go to court to win vindication, Sullivan could give as good as he got. He could deny the charges in the public press; he could make countercharges. In short, he had access to an effective means of rebuilding his damaged reputation without relying upon a libel suit which, as we have noted, can have a serious impact upon the freedom of expression.

These reasons are the pillars upon which the *Sullivan* decision rested. In taking this stand the high Court followed a course of action which a handful of other states adopted years earlier. In 1908 the Kansas Supreme Court ruled that public officials and candidates for public office must carry a more rigorous burden of proof than private citizens to sustain a libel judgment in order to preserve the immense public benefit gained from free and robust debate (*Coleman* v. *MacLennan,* 1908). The *Sullivan* case amplified and extended this ruling to every state in the Union. Henceforth, public officials had to prove actual malice in order to sustain a civil libel suit.

In 1966 a federal court extended much of the reasoning of the *Sullivan* ruling to persons it called "public figures" in the case of *Pauling* v. *Globe-Democrat.* The plaintiff in this case was Linus Pauling, a Nobel Prize-winning physicist who was very active in the movement to ban atmospheric testing of nuclear weapons. Pauling had never held public office and could not in any sense be considered a public official. Yet in the libel suit which resulted when the *St. Louis Globe-Democrat* incorrectly published that the Nobel laureate had been convicted of contempt of Congress, the United States Eighth Court of Appeals ruled that as a "public figure" Pauling must prove that the story was published with actual malice (*Pauling* v. *Globe-Democrat,* 1966). The rationale?

> Professor Pauling, by his public statements and actions, was projecting himself into the arena of public controversy and into the very vortex of the discussion of a question of pressing public concern. He was attempting to influence the resolution of an issue which was important, which was of profound effect, which was public, and which was internationally controversial.

Conscious that important public debate frequently involves persons not in government, and that the threat of a libel suit could interfere with such debate, the Court ruled that the first Amendment protects this kind of discussion. One year later in *AP* v. *Walker* and *Curtis Publishing Co.* v. *Butts,* the Supreme Court accepted this argument and made the actual malice fault requirement applicable to public figures as well.

It was not until 1974 that the Supreme Court completed the development of the fault requirement. In a case which will be discussed often for other reasons, *Gertz* v. *Welch,* the high Court ruled that henceforth private persons would no longer be able to sue for libel unless they, too, were able to demonstrate that the media was in some way at fault in publishing the story. Justice Lewis Powell said that states must require that nonpublic persons prove that the defendant is, at the very least, negligent. States can, however, ask private persons to prove a greater degree of fault. That is, under the ruling in *Gertz,* states can insist that all libel plaintiffs—not just public officials and public figures—prove actual malice, or anything in between simple negligence and actual malice. Negligence is the minimum requirement, but state courts can ask for proof of a higher degree of fault.

Since 1974 the courts in most, if not all, states have decided upon which level of fault is applicable when a private person sues a media defendant for libel. The simple way to find whether your state has adopted a negligence requirement, a slightly higher level of fault such as gross negligence, or actual malice is to locate the most recent state supreme court libel rulings. Within the text of these cases will be found the level of fault applicable to private-persons plaintiffs in your jurisdiction.

Thus far we can summarize the fault requirement in this manner: When a newspaper, magazine, broadcasting station, or other kind of mass media defendant is sued for libel, the plaintiff must prove fault. A plaintiff who is considered a private person must prove at least that the defendant acted in a negligent manner in publishing the libel. That is, the defendant did not exercise reasonable care. In some states the private-person plaintiff is required to prove an even higher level of fault than negligence—that the publisher of the libel acted in a grossly negligent manner. In all states a plaintiff who is a public person must prove to the court that the publisher of the libel acted with actual malice; that is, the publisher had knowledge that the material was false and still published it, or the publisher acted in reckless disregard of the truth. Remember the standards of fault are incremental. Simple negligence is simple carelessness, fairly easy to prove. Gross negligence is acting in a very irresponsible manner and is somewhat more difficult to prove. Actual malice is knowing that information is false but still publishing it, or acting with little concern for determining what the truth may be. This is normally very difficult to prove. Please note that all these levels of fault are discussed in much greater detail on pages 143 through 151.

Let us now take up the important question of the differences between private persons and public persons as defined by the courts.

PRIVATE PERSONS VERSUS PUBLIC PERSONS

Whenever a court takes a common description and attempts to shape it into a legal concept, much confusion results. Such is the case with the private-person-versus-public-person dichotomy in the law of libel. A majority of the United States Supreme Court has seemingly settled upon a rationale which has been cited consistently over the past two or three years to justify the distinction the Court has drawn in applying the fault requirement differently to private persons than to public persons. The rationale has two parts. First, public persons are somewhat less vulnerable to injury from defamatory statements because they enjoy a much higher degree of access to the press to rebut or deny the libelous statements. The only recourse for a private person is a lawsuit; a public person can use the press to respond and deny the charges, to correct the errors. Hence, private persons need more protection; the press needs to be more careful when it writes about private persons.

Second, and probably more important, public persons are less deserving of protection than other persons because public persons have voluntarily exposed themselves to the increased risk of injury by moving into the public spotlight. Public persons do this by running for government office, attempting to lead public opinion upon important issues, or working publicly toward the resolution of important societal issues. The avowed goal of the Supreme Court is to protect the integrity of the debate which results when society attempts to resolve important issues; in order that such debate be open and free, the threat of libel actions must be minimized. Hence, because of the higher fault requirements, it is more difficult for a public person to win a libel suit (see *Gertz* v. *Welch,* 1974; *Time, Inc.* v. *Firestone,* 1976; *Wolston* v. *Reader's Digest,* 1979; and *Hutchinson* v. *Proxmire,* 1979).

Who is a private person? Who is a public person? Stating the rationale for distinguishing between plaintiffs who are private persons and plaintiffs who are public persons is far easier than outlining the legal distinction between these two kinds of plaintiffs. We must rely upon often incomplete or ambiguous criteria provided by the courts to define whether a particular person in a particular case is a private person or a public person. This latter point is very important. When you attempt to determine whether a plaintiff is a public or private person, always evaluate the plaintiff in relationship to the facts in the libel case. It is very likely that a person who might be considered a public person in one case would be considered a private person in another libel suit.

Who Is a Public Person?

The courts have classified public persons into these three categories:

1. Public officials
2. All-purpose public figures
3. Limited public figures

Public Officials   Two questions must be asked to determine whether a libel plaintiff should be considered a public official.

1. Who is this plaintiff? What kind of job does this person have?
2. What was the allegedly libelous story about?

Let us consider these questions separately.

A public official is someone who works for a government and draws a salary from the public payroll. Included are persons from the president of the United States to a patrolman on a beat. Yet not all persons who are government employees qualify as public officials under the law of libel. In 1966 when the Supreme Court was confronted with a lawsuit from a former director of a county ski area, Justice Brennan attempted to define those persons in government who would fall under the rubric public official. "It is clear," he wrote, "that the 'public official' designation applies at the very least to those among the hierarchy of government employees who have or appear to the public to have substantial responsibility for or control over the conduct of governmental affairs" (*Rosenblatt* v. *Baer,* 1966). Brennan added that the person must hold a position that invites public scrutiny of the person holding it, entirely apart from the scrutiny and discussion occasioned by the particular charges in the controversy.

This latter dimension is terribly important. The Supreme Court demonstrated this in 1979 when it refused to consider the research director of a public mental hospital to be a public official. There could be little doubt that Ronald Hutchinson was a well-paid public employee. In addition to his state salary he was the recipient of about a half-million dollars in public funds for his research on aggression in animals. Senator William Proxmire, who apparently thought the expenditure of public money on such research was wasteful and foolish, named the public agencies which funded the scientist's research recipients of one of his Golden Fleece awards for making a "monkey out of the American taxpayer." In the libel suit that followed the Supreme Court ruled that there was little public interest in Hutchinson's job before he was made the butt of Proxmire's joke. Chief Justice Burger said that those charged with defamation cannot by their own conduct create their own defense by making the plaintiff a public person (*Hutchinson* v. *Proxmire,* 1979). In other words, Hutchinson's position was not one that invited public scrutiny apart from the scrutiny and discussion caused by the defamatory charges.

State courts have not always followed this rule to the letter. In *Press* v. *Verran* (1978) the Tennessee Supreme Court ruled that a junior state social worker was a public official because her job carried with it "duties and responsibilities affecting the lives, liberty, money or property of a citizen or that may enhance or disrupt his enjoyment of life. . . ." The Washington Supreme Court in 1979 said that the administrator of a small county motor pool who worked without direct supervision, had two assistants, and could independently spend up to $500 of county money on open charge accounts at several local parts dealers was a public official. "The public quite naturally has a legitimate and continuing interest in how local tax revenues are spent by those county employees vested with the power to utilize the public purse," wrote Chief Justice Robert Utter for the court (*Clawson* v. *Longview Publishing Co.,* 1979). The defamation in this case was an allegation that the plaintiff had used small amounts of county funds to repair private vehicles. Similarly, police officers, who are relatively low-level government employees, have frequently been held to be public officials because they hold the power of life and death over the citizens in a community (see *Malerba* v. *Newsday,* 1978).

It is safe to conclude that any government employee who stands for election periodically is a public official in the eyes of the law. As just noted, appointed officials can also meet the established criteria. The appointed Attorney General of the United States is undoubtedly a public person; similarly, the appointed head of a large public utility qualifies. Since 1964 courts have held that judges, senators, state legislators, mayors, school board members, teachers, city tax assessors, and many others are public officials.

What about a consulting firm which advises a government on a controversial but important government policy question? The Iroquois Research Institute was hired by Fairfax County, Virginia, to evaluate the historical and archeological value of an island in the Potomac River on which the county hoped to construct water-intake facilities. Lowes Island was the subject of a great zoning controversy in the community, and when Iroquois reported that the work could be done without harming the island, the research institute became the focus of sharp criticism. The *Loudoun* (Va.) *Times Mirror* published a story which challenged the competence of Iroquois researchers, and a libel suit followed. The Fourth United States Court of Appeals ruled that the consulting firm could not be considered a public official in terms of the libel suit. The court said that the institute made no recommendations to the county, participated in no policy determinations, and exercised no discretion. In short, it had no control over the conduct of governmental affairs. "Its position was not of such apparent importance that the public has an independent interest in its qualifications," the court ruled. The court conceded in some instances a consultant employed by the government entity can be classified a public official, but not this time (*Artic* v. *Loudoun Times Mirror,* 1980). If this ruling is adopted throughout the nation, it will be highly unlikely, regardless of what the court said, that a consultant to a government could ever be considered a public official, unless the consultant exercises considerably more control over policymaking than is typical.

The context in which the defamation occurs is often important. A planner with a state geological survey office might not normally hold a position that invites public scrutiny. But if this person is appointed by the governor to conduct a study of the feasibility of constructing three nuclear power plants near the state capital, this special assignment brings with it closer public scrutiny. In such a case a person who was not a public official might suddenly become one in terms of libel law.

This leads to the second question in determining who is a public official in a libel suit: What is the nature of the supposedly libelous story?

Persons who work for the government in a position of authority may not be termed a public official for the purposes of a lawsuit if the allegedly libelous story does not pertain either (a) to the plaintiff's official conduct, the manner in which the official conducts the official public role or (b) to the plaintiff's general fitness to hold public office.

Stories which fall under category a are obvious. These stories focus upon how well or how badly public officials handle their job. Stories in category b are far more troublesome for journalists.

If the mayor is drunk when he attempts to preside at a meeting of the city council, his personal habits directly affect his fitness for office. But what if the mayor has a serious drinking problem that does not visibly affect his work? And what if a newspaper erroneously reports following the mayor's arrest for drunken driving that it was the third arrest for such an offense? Will the mayor be forced to prove actual malice in the libel suit that follows? This is a tough question. As a rule of thumb, the lower persons are on the scale of public officialdom the more their private life will be protected by the law. Because of the immense responsibilities, almost everything the president of the United States does reflects upon his fitness to hold the job. The private life of a United States senator is probably less open to public scrutiny than the private life of a president, but more investigation of the senator's private life will be permitted than of the life of an elected prosecutor of Clinton County, Michigan.

Public Figures

The concept of the public figure was introduced into libel law in the mid-1960s. However it was not until 1974 that the category was divided into two subcategories by the Supreme Court. Initially, in his opinion in *Gertz* v. *Welch* (1974), Justice Lewis Powell attempted to outline the essence of the public-figure category:

> Hypothetically, it may be possible for someone to become a public figure through no purposeful action of his own, but the instances of truly involuntary public figures must be exceedingly rare. For the most part those who attain this status have assumed roles of especial prominence in the affairs of society.

Powell then noted that there were two separate categories of persons who might be classified public figures:

> Some [persons] occupy positions of such persuasive power and influence that they are deemed public figures for all purposes. More commonly, those classed as public figures have thrust themselves to the forefront of particular public controversies in order to influence the resolution of the issues involved. In either event, they invite attention and comment.

While Justice Powell's dichotomy makes sense on paper, the courts have had a devil of a time identifying persons who fall into Justice Powell's all-purpose public figure category. Television personality Johnny Carson was considered a total public figure in a lawsuit (*Carson* v. *Allied News*, 1976); so was conservative writer and gadfly William F. Buckley (*Buckley* v. *Littel*, 1976). It has been speculated that Jacqueline Kennedy Onassis and Ralph Nader *might* be total public figures. In *Handbook of Free Speech and Free Press,* Barron and Dienes suggest: "It is almost as if the courts are saying that a plaintiff will have to be totally exposed to constant media attention in order to be classified as a total public figure." The two authors suggest the key to be instant national recognition and constant media exposure.

On a national level this definition of a public figure is probably true, but there is another way of looking at the problem. It is quite probable that there are persons in small communities who might have the status of a total public figure. Consider the woman who lives in a community of 6,500 persons. She was formerly the mayor, has served on the school board in the past, and has been a perennial choice for president of the Parent-Teacher Association. She is the president of the largest real estate company in town, is a director on the board of the local bank, and owns the local pharmacy and dry cleaners. She is active in numerous service clubs, is a leader in various civic projects, and is instantly recognizable on the street by virtually all of the town's residents. Her family founded the town one hundred fifty years earlier. If she is libeled in a community newspaper whose circulation remains almost exclusively in the community, it could be argued persuasively that this woman is a total public figure in the community. (See *Steere* v. *Cupp,* 1979, where the Kansas Supreme Court ruled such an individual was a total or all-purpose public figure.) And in 1982, the Montana Supreme Court ruled that investment and commodity adviser Larry Williams was an all-purpose public figure in his libel suit based on a Democratic Party press release which erroneously charged that he had been under federal indictment for political dirty tricks. The court listed the following activities by Williams which convinced the court that he was an all-purpose public figure: he published an investment advisory service; he wrote three books on stocks; he was the subject of an article in *Forbes* magazine and another article in the *Wall Street Journal;* he frequently gave speeches, and ran unsuccessfully for the United States Senate; he was chairman of the Republican Party in Montana; and he was an active member of the National

Taxpayers Union (*Williams* v. *Pasma*, 1982). As in the case of public officials, context can play an important role. The status of the plaintiff in the community in which the libel is circulated might arguably be a factor in the determination that an individual is a total public figure.

Regardless of these examples, few persons fall into the category of total public figure. Far more important for journalists is Justice Powell's second category, the limited public figure.

The Supreme Court has spent more time since 1974 on defining who is and who is not a limited public figure than on any other aspect of libel law. The high Court wrote opinions in four libel suits following the *Gertz* ruling in 1974, and in three of the four cases a central question was whether the plaintiff was a limited public figure (*Time, Inc.* v. *Firestone*, 1976; *Wolston* v. *Reader's Digest*, 1979; and *Hutchinson* v. *Proxmire*, 1979). The fourth case was *Herbert* v. *Lando* (1979) which focused upon the discovery procedures in a libel action. When the essential elements are extracted from *Gertz* and the three subsequent public figure cases, certain basic criteria in the definition of a limited public figure emerge.

In *Gertz* v. *Welch*, plaintiff Elmer Gertz was a well-known and widely respected Chicago attorney who had gained prominence in civil rights disputes in that city. He had written several books and articles and on many occasions served on commissions and committees in Chicago and Cook County. When a young man was slain by a Chicago police officer, Gertz agreed to represent the family in a civil action against the officer. The policeman had been tried and convicted of murder in the shooting, but Gertz played no role in that criminal action. His only role in the entire matter was as an attorney representing the family in the action for civil damages. He became the subject of a vicious attack by *American Opinion*, a magazine published by the John Birch Society, which accused him of being a communist fronter, a Leninist, and the architect of a frame-up against the police officer. It also charged that Gertz had a long police record.

In the libel suit that followed, the Supreme Court ruled that despite his prominence in the civil rights area Elmer Gertz was not a public figure for the purposes of this lawsuit. The words of Justice Powell stand as an important guideline (*Gertz* v. *Welch*, 1974):

> It is preferable to reduce the public figure question to a more meaningful context by looking to the nature and extent of an individual's participation in the particular controversy giving rise to the defamation.

The key phrase is "extent of an individual's participation in the particular controversy giving rise to the defamation." To be a limited public figure, the plaintiff must be shown to have played a prominent role in the particular controversy giving rise to the defamation, the controversy prompting publication of the defamatory statement or comment. Gertz would have been a limited public figure if the dispute in the case had involved civil rights in Chicago. He would have had to prove actual malice in such circumstances. But the particular controversy which gave rise to the article in *American Opinion* was the murder of the young man and the subsequent trial of the police officer. Gertz was not an important participant in that issue. He was simply acting as an attorney—which is his profession—in representing the family of the youth in a civil action. He was acting as a private individual and as such had only to prove simple negligence.*

Two years later the high Court ruled that a socially prominent Palm Beach woman was not a public figure with regard to the divorce action in which she was involved. The case, *Time, Inc.* v. *Firestone* (1976), resulted from a short notice published in *Time* magazine that Russell Firestone was granted a divorce from his wife on grounds of extreme cruelty and adultery. Firestone was in fact granted a divorce from his wife, but on grounds that neither member of the couple was "domesticated." Mary Alice Firestone sued *Time* for libel, claiming she had been called an adulteress. *Time* argued that her prominence in the Palm Beach community made her a public figure. On the record she clearly appeared to be a public figure, a leading member of the "Four Hundred of Palm Beach society," an "active member of the sporting set," a person whose activities attracted considerable public attention. She even maintained a clipping service to keep track of her publicity. The divorce case became a *cause célèbre* in the community, prompting forty-three articles in a Miami newspaper and forty-five stories in the Palm Beach newspapers. She held several press conferences during the course of the seventeen-month legal dispute. Nevertheless, the Supreme Court refused to acknowledge that Mary Alice Firestone was a public figure in the context of the divorce case, the subject of the *Time* article which was defamatory. Justice William Rehnquist wrote:

> Respondent did not assume any role of especial prominence in the affairs of society, other than perhaps Palm Beach society, and she did not thrust herself to the forefront of any particular public controversy in order to influence the resolution of the issues involved in it.

Time argued that because the trial was well publicized it must be considered a public controversy and Mary Alice Firestone a public person. "But in doing so," Justice Rehnquist wrote, "petitioner seeks to equate 'public controversy' with all controversies of interest to the public." The Justice said that a divorce proceeding is not the kind of public controversy referred to in *Gertz*. While there was public interest in the proceedings, the case was not an important public question.

*The case of *Gertz* v. *Welch,* which began in 1969, finally ended in the summer of 1982 when a $400,000 judgement against *American Opinion* was upheld by the Seventh United States Court of Appeals (*Gertz* v. *Welch,* 1982).

Rehnquist also pointed out that Mrs. Firestone was not a voluntary participant in the divorce proceeding. She was forced to go into public court to dissolve her marriage. Whether individuals have voluntarily thrust themselves into the public spotlight is probably not a controlling issue in most cases. But Justice Powell did write in the *Gertz* decision, "it may be possible for someone to become a public figure through no purposeful action of his own, but the instances of truly involuntary public figures must be exceedingly rare. For the most part those who attain this status have assumed roles of especial prominence in the *affairs of society* [author's emphasis]."

The meaning of *Gertz* and *Firestone* was reemphasized in 1979 in two rulings by the Supreme Court which clearly indicated that the high Court intended the limited-public-figure category to be narrow. In both cases, *Hutchinson* v. *Proxmire* and *Wolston* v. *Reader's Digest,* the Supreme Court reversed rulings by lower federal courts which had declared that the plaintiffs were in fact limited public figures.

The facts in the *Hutchinson* case were mentioned earlier. The plaintiff was the research director at a public mental hospital in Michigan. He was also the recipient of about $500,000 in federal grants to support his research on animal aggression. Believing that such research was unimportant, Senator William Proxmire bestowed his monthly Golden Fleece Award on several federal agencies which had funded Hutchinson's research for nearly seven years. In the process the Wisconsin lawmaker accused Hutchinson of putting the "bite" on the American taxpayer and making "a monkey" out of the American people. Hutchinson sued.

Chief Justice Burger refused to consider the plaintiff a public figure. He said there was no controversy about the research until Proxmire's defamatory comments about Dr. Hutchinson. The scientist did not thrust himself or his views into a public display or issue. In fact, Burger said, the defendants "have not identified such a particular controversy; at most they point to concern about general public expenditures." Hutchinson, the Chief Justice noted, at no time assumed any role of public prominence in the broad question of concern about expenditures. The researcher, then, had no part in the controversy that gave rise to the defamation, according to Burger. Simply taking public money to do research is not enough to make a person like Hutchinson into a public figure, the Court ruled. "If it were, everyone who received or benefited from the myriad public grants for research could be classified as a public figure. . . ."

Finally, the Chief Justice drew upon the basic rationale for the distinction between private and public persons and said that "we cannot agree that Hutchinson had such access to the media that he should be classified as a public figure." His access, Burger noted, was limited to responding to Proxmire's announcement of the Golden Fleece Award. The decision of the Court was eight to one in favor of Hutchinson, and the single dissenting vote by Justice Brennan was based solely on how the Court responded to another question, not to the public-figure issue.

The facts in the *Wolston* case are somewhat more complicated. Ilya Wolston was identified in a 1974 book, *KGB: The Secret World of Soviet Agents,* as a Soviet agent. His description as such stemmed from events which had taken place nearly twenty years earlier when a federal grand jury in New York State was investigating the activities of Soviet agents in the United States. Wolston's aunt and uncle, Myra and Joe Soble, were well-publicized American Communists who were arrested in January 1957 and charged with spying. Wolston himself was interviewed by the Federal Bureau of Investigation (FBI) and testified several times before the New York grand jury. In July 1958 he failed to respond to yet another grand jury subpoena. His failure to appear was publicized in the press. He said he had not testified because he was in a state of mental depression. Later he changed his mind and offered to give testimony. He subsequently pleaded guilty to a charge of contempt and was sentenced to three years probation. During the six weeks between the time he refused to testify and his sentencing, fifteen news stories were published about Ilya Wolston in New York and Washington newspapers. He was never indicted for espionage.

His libel suit was based on his misidentification in the *KGB* book published by *Reader's Digest.* The publication argued that because of his contempt conviction in 1958 Wolston was a limited public figure for purposes of a discussion of Soviet agents and espionage. Eight members of the Supreme Court disagreed. Justice William Rehnquist, writing for the majority, argued that Wolston did not "inject" himself into any controversy, that he was dragged into the controversy when the government pursued him during the investigation of Soviet agents. "The mere fact that petitioner voluntarily chose not to appear before the grand jury, knowing that his action might be attended by publicity, is not decisive on the status of public figure," Rehnquist said. The justice noted that Wolston played a minor role in whatever controversy there might have been over Soviet espionage, that he had never talked about this matter with the press. "We decline to hold that his mere citation for contempt rendered him a public figure for purposes of comment on the investigation of Soviet espionage."

Rehnquist stressed that Wolston had made no effort to influence the public on the resolution of any issue. The plaintiff did not in any way seek to arouse public sentiment in his favor or against the investigation. Quoting his own opinion in the *Firestone* (1976) case, Rehnquist wrote:

> While participants in some litigation may be legitimate "public figures," either generally or for the limited purpose of that litigation, the majority will more likely resemble respondent [Mary Firestone or Ilya Wolston], drawn into a public forum largely against their will in order to attempt to obtain the only redress available to them or to defend themselves against actions brought by the state or by others.

The question now is, what can we learn from the language in these Supreme Court rulings? Three basic points seem to emerge.

1. Limited public figures normally must voluntarily step into the public spotlight. The Court said it would be exceedingly rare for someone to be an involuntary public figure. Such instances as rising to deny charges made against you and going to court to end a marriage or to defend yourself from government charges do not represent voluntary behavior. They represent a response to the behavior of someone or something else.

2. A limited public figure is someone who plays a role in the resolution of an important public or social issue. A messy divorce, an investigation of aggression in animals, a charge of contempt for failure to testify before a grand jury are not the kinds of "affairs of society" which the Court considers to be important. One gets the impression that the justices are looking to the discussion of social issues (abortion, discrimination), economic issues (taxpayers' revolt, city budget), educational problems (busing, minimum competency requirements), governmental rulings (censorship, arms control), and the like, to find the kinds of persons they would consider limited public figures. A public controversy might be defined as a controversy in which the resolution of the issues will affect the general public or at least a wider group of persons than those individuals involved in the controversy.

3. There must have been some attempt by the plaintiff to influence public opinion in the resolution of these issues. This speaks to the basic point made by Justice Powell in the *Gertz* case—the nature and extent of the individual's participation in the particular controversy giving rise to the defamation. In *Hutchinson* the issue was wasteful expenditures, but Dr. Hutchinson had said little if anything about that before being libeled by Senator Proxmire. Similarly, Ilya Wolston had said nothing about the issue of Soviet agents in this country—which is what the defendant contended was the issue in *Wolston* v. *Reader's Digest* (1979).

Inherent in an attempt to influence the outcome of a public issue is the ability of the plaintiff to get access to the mass media. The plaintiff generally must have some means of speaking out on the issue or of responding to criticism. Also, the media cannot create the controversy by defaming the plaintiff and then argue that the role of the plaintiff is important to the resolution of the issue. These are the key points, then, in determining whether an individual is a limited public figure.

1. There must be an important public controversy.
2. The plaintiff must inject himself or herself voluntarily into the controversy.

3. The plaintiff must attempt to influence public opinion about the resolution of the issue, and have some access to the press to accomplish this feat.

Let us now look at how some lower courts have attempted to apply these criteria in recent cases. Here are some cases in which the court refused to declare the plaintiff a limited public figure.

Attorney William Denny worked for the Koehring Company of Wisconsin for fifteen years before he resigned in 1969 to go into private practice. In 1974 he became visibly involved in a campaign by dissident stockholders to oust the management of Koehring, whose stock had plummeted in price between 1969 and 1974 from $45 per share to $5 per share. *Business Week* erroneously reported that Denny had been fired from Koehring in its story on the stockholders' dispute. Denny sued for libel, and the Wisconsin Supreme Court ruled that he was not a public figure for purposes of the libel action because there was no public controversy. The court defined a public controversy as one which, when resolved, will have an impact upon more than the immediate participants in the controversy. This was a stockholders' fight; its outcome would have no impact upon the general public (*Denny* v. *Mertz,* 1980).

In a similar decision a United States district court in New York ruled that no public controversy existed in a lawsuit by a writer against an erotic magazine which had erroneously identified the picture of a woman in a sexual orgy as the writer. "A public controversy is a dispute that in fact has received public attention because its ramifications will be felt by persons who are not direct participants." The plaintiff was not a public figure in this case despite the fact she was a celebrated novelist (*Lerman* v. *Chuckleberry Publications,* 1981).

When KSL-TV broadcast a news segment on animal cruelty in 1974, the station identified W. Garth Seegmiller as a rancher who failed to take care of his horses. The station charged that a number of the animals were malnourished and two had died. The story contained several errors and Seegmiller sued. KSL argued that cruelty to animals was an important public issue. The Utah Supreme Court agreed with that argument, but declared that the plaintiff was not a voluntary participant in attempting to resolve the controversy. "On the contrary, he was plucked by the defendant from the anonymity of private life and thrust against his will into the limelight," the state's high court noted. Even if he had been guilty of a misdemeanor, the court ruled, that fact by itself would not be sufficient to compel the conclusion that he is a public figure" (*Seegmiller* v. *KSL-TV,* 1981).

A book-banning controversy arose at San Rafael High School in California when the members of an Elks lodge complained about a textbook being used in an American government class. The book was used in a unit on political philosophies and contained writings from the underground of the sixties, articles on revolution, drugs, and sex. The board of education held several public meetings to discuss the issue. Teacher Virginia Franklin, who taught the class, testified at the meetings, but took no other part in the dispute. The *Elks Magazine* published a story on the controversy, but erroneously reported that teacher Franklin had been fired from a previous job for "teaching the same sort of rot." In the libel suit that followed, the California court of appeals rejected the magazine's contention that Franklin was a public figure. Her only voluntary overt act had been to order several copies of the book for the class. Her testimony was mandated by the school district. "There is no showing that appellant (Franklin) ordered the book for the purpose of inciting controversy. She declares without contradiction that she did not anticipate controversy. It is not clear that, but for the vigorous reaction of Lodge 1108 [the Elks] there would ever have been a controversy," the court noted (*Franklin* v. *Lodge 1108,* 1979). (Please note that in other cases teachers have been declared to be public officials. See *Johnston* v. *Corinthian Television,* 1978, Oklahoma Supreme Court, for example.)

Finally, the Tenth United States Court of Appeals ruled in 1981 that the political aide for a United States Senate candidate was not a public figure in his libel action against then incumbent Senator Frank Moss. G. Andrew Lawrence worked for candidate Orrin Hatch in 1976 as a private consultant in political polling, strategy, voter targeting, volunteer organizations, advertising, fund raising, and speech writing. He came to Utah to work for Hatch in September 1976 after work in the early seventies on Vice-President Spiro Agnew's staff and for the General Services Administration (GSA). Charges of improper conduct were brought against Lawrence while he worked at GSA, but these charges were dropped after he resigned. He then became an independent political consultant.

During the 1976 campaign Frank Moss charged that Lawrence had been Spiro Agnew's "bagman," someone who "picked up the money Spiro Agnew would get." When Lawrence sued for libel, Moss contended that the political consultant was a public figure. The United States Court of Appeals (District of Columbia) said no. His participation in Hatch's political campaign may have made Lawrence newsworthy, but that fact did not transform him into a public figure. At no time did Lawrence thrust himself into public prominence in order to resolve important public controversies. He participated behind the scenes. The statements he made on public controversies were made in private for his employer, Orrin Hatch. It is the plaintiff's status that is the controlling factor, "not the nebulous interest of the public in a matter with which he is inconspicuously involved," the court ruled (*Lawrence* v. *Moss,* 1981).

More often than not, courts do find that libel plaintiffs are public figures. In fact, plaintiffs lose about 75 percent of the libel suits they bring against mass media defendants, according to Stanford law professor Marc Franklin. Here are some cases in which plaintiffs have been ruled to be public figures. Note the differences between these cases and the earlier examples.

An attorney who was a former state legislator and who was appointed the guardian of an estate that became the center of controversy was deemed to be a limited public figure by the Idaho Supreme Court. A trial judge ruled that the plaintiff's management of the estate had been negligent. Consequently, the state's high court ruled, Glenn Bandelin was "a pivotal figure in the controversy regarding the accounting of the estate that gave rise to the defamation. . . ." (*Bandelin* v. *Pietsch,* 1977).

A United States district court in the District of Columbia ruled that the question of protein supplements in the human diet was a question of public concern, and consequently the president of a firm selling such tablets was a limited public figure for the purposes of a libel suit against the *Washington Post.* An article in the newspaper identified the plaintiff as someone who was making lots of money selling the tablets to athletes. When the plaintiff promoted and sold the dietary supplements, he was voluntarily injecting himself into a public controversy, the court ruled (*Hoffman* v. *Washington Post,* 1977).

In 1980 the United States Court of Appeals in the District of Columbia ruled that Eric Waldbaum, former head of the nation's second largest consumer cooperative, was a public figure regarding a story about his dismissal as president of that organization. The court ruled that Waldbaum had played an active role in attempting to bring consumer-related issues before the public through the media and was a limited public figure in his role with the cooperative (*Waldbaum* v. *Fairchild Publications,* 1980). The Second United States Court of Appeals ruled in 1980 that John Yiamouyiannis, long an outspoken foe of the fluoridation of public water supplies, was a limited public figure in a lawsuit he brought against Consumers Union for criticizing him and his research on the subject (*Yiamouyiannis* v. *Consumers Union*, 1980).

Tex Maule, a sportswriter for *Sports Illustrated,* was deemed to be a public figure in his libel action against *New York* magazine. *New York* criticized Maule's workmanship, called him the worst writer on the magazine, and said the *Sports Illustrated* staff rewrote most of his stories. "The essential element underlying the category of 'public figure' is that the publicized person has taken an affirmative step to attract attention," the Appellate Division of the New York Supreme Court wrote. The court said Maule had done this through the publication of many books and articles in the sports field (*Maule* v. *New York Magazine,* 1980). Note that the criticism of Maule was aimed at his writing, the means by which he had attracted attention to himself.

Finally, in one of the most interesting cases in many years, the Sixth United States Court of Appeals ruled in 1981 that a woman who had become a public figure during a celebrated trial in 1931 was still a public figure in relationship to that event. Victoria Price Street was the chief witness against the so-called Scottsboro Boys in a sensational rape trial in Alabama. In a National Broadcasting Company (NBC) dramatization of the long legal struggle the viewer is left with the strong impression that Victoria Street falsely accused the young men of rape. NBC thought that Mrs. Street was dead. When she sued for libel, the television network argued that she was a limited public figure in connection with the Scottsboro Boys trial. The plaintiff conceded she may have been a public figure during the trial, but that was forty years ago. The court of appeals sided with the network, ruling that "once a person becomes a public figure in connection with a particular controversy, that person remains a public figure thereafter for purposes of later commentary or treatment of that controversy" (*Street* v. *NBC,* 1981). Mrs. Street appealed the decision to the Supreme Court of the United States, which accepted the case. But before arguments were heard NBC and Mrs. Street agreed upon an out-of-court settlement. Apparently NBC was fearful that it would lose the case in the Supreme Court.

The precedent of *Street* v. *NBC,* that a former public figure remains a public figure for purposes of commentary or retelling of the original controversy, is still law in the Sixth United States judicial circuit (Kentucky, Michigan, Ohio, and Tennessee). However, until other courts in other parts of the nation have accepted this precedent, it should not be considered a rule of law.

Corporations have been deemed to be limited public figures in some instances and not in other instances. In *Steaks Unlimited* v. *Deaner* (1980) the Third United States Court of Appeals ruled that a company accused of misrepresentation because it advertised low-priced inspected, ungraded, frozen, tenderized, boxed beef was a limited public figure in relation to the sale of the beef. The company voluntarily marketed the beef product in an unusual fashion which attracted great public interest. Similarly, a United States district court in Massachusetts ruled that when the Bose Corporation extensively advertised its unconventional Bose 901 stereophonic speakers it precipitated a public discussion of the relative merits of the speaker system. The *Consumer Reports* article which criticized the speakers did not create a controversy. Bose had done this by using a market strategy which emphasized the unconventional design of the speakers (*Bose* v. *Consumers Union,* 1981).

On the other hand, courts recently ruled that two corporations were not public figures in libel suits against publications which had made critical comments about their products. The *Boston Globe* published four articles critical of commercial fishing boats manufactured by the Bruno and Stillman Company. First United States Court of Appeals ruled that there had been no controversy or public discussion about the boats before the libelous stories were published. "The mere selling of products itself cannot easily be deemed a public controversy," the court said. The plaintiff was an involuntary participant in the boat controversy which had been created by the newspaper (*Bruno and Stillman* v. *Globe Newspapers,* 1980). And a United States district court in Virginia ruled that the General Products Corporation, a manufacturer and seller of air-insulated, triplewall stove chimneys, was not a public figure in a libel suit against the publisher of the *Better Homes and Gardens Home Plan Ideas Magazine.* The magazine published an article claiming the chimneys were not safe. The court ruled that there was no indication of any public controversy surrounding the use of triple-walled chimneys, that the plaintiff had not injected itself or been drawn into any such controversy, or that it did not engage in any media blitz to influence the public on a matter of public interest (*General Products* v. *Meredith Corp.,* 1981).

Is there an apparent difference between those businesses that were ruled to be public figures and those that were ruled to be private figures? Yes. Those firms that courts declared to be public figures had promoted a product in an unusual manner. They attempted to draw attention to themselves in an out-of-the-ordinary way. It is safe to assume that a business or corporation which conducts its operations in a relatively routine fashion will not be deemed to be a public figure.

An outline of these cases was presented to give you some insight into how the courts have applied the criteria established by the Supreme Court to determine whether a libel plaintiff is a limited public figure. The simplest way to determine whether a particular individual would be considered a public figure is to apply the test given us by Justice Powell. Determine the extent and the nature of the individual's participation in the controversy giving rise to the defamation. What is the controversy? How did the plaintiff get involved in the controversy? What was the plaintiff's role in the controversy? The answers to these questions will normally lead to the correct answer.

Summary

Under the fault requirement all persons who sue a mass medium for libel must prove that the defendant was somehow at fault in publishing the defamatory material; the publication (or broadcast) did not result from an innocent error. What the courts call a "public person" must normally prove that defendant acted with actual malice in publishing the libel; that is, the defendant knew the material was false but still published it, or exhibited reckless disregard for the truth. What the courts define as "private persons" must prove at least that the defendant acted negligently, that is, in such a way as to create an unreasonable risk of harm. The courts have ruled that there are three kinds of "public persons."

1. *Public officials:* Persons who work for a government in a position of authority, who have substantial control over the conduct of governmental affairs, and whose position in government invites independent public scrutiny beyond the general public interest in the qualifications and performance of all government employees. Libelous comments must focus upon the plaintiff's official conduct (the manner in which the plaintiff conducts his or her job) or upon the plaintiff's general fitness to hold public office.

2. *All-purpose public figures:* Persons who occupy persuasive power and influence in the nation or in a community, persons who are usually exposed to constant media attention.

3. *Limited public figures:* Persons who voluntarily inject themselves into an important public controversy in order to influence public opinion regarding the resolution of that controversy. The key elements are:

    a. Public controversy, the resolution of which must affect more persons than simply the participants. The outcome must have an impact upon people in a community.

    b. Plaintiffs who voluntarily thrust themselves into this controversy. An individual who has been drawn involuntarily into a controversy created by someone else (such as the press) is not a limited public figure.

    c. Plaintiffs who attempt to influence the outcome of the controversy, to shape public opinion on the subject. This implies that a plaintiff has some access to the mass media to participate in the public discussion surrounding the controversy.

THE MEANING OF FAULT

We have attempted to establish which persons must prove negligence and which persons must prove actual malice. It is now time to explore the meaning of those terms as they pertain to the fault requirement. What is negligence? What is actual malice?

Negligence

Negligence is a term that has been commonly used in tort law for centuries, but has only recently been applied to libel law. In simple terms, negligence implies the failure to exercise ordinary care. In deciding whether to adopt the negligence or the stricter actual malice fault requirements, state courts are providing their own definitions of the standard. Washington State adopted a "reasonable care" standard. Defendants are considered negligent if they do not exercise reasonable care in determining whether a statement is false or will create a false impression (*Taskett* v. *King Broadcasting,* 1976). The Tennessee Supreme Court has adopted a "reasonably prudent person test": What would a reasonably prudent person have done or not have done in the same circumstance? Would a reasonably prudent reporter have checked the truth of a story more fully? Would such a reporter have waited a day or so to get more information? Would a reasonably prudent reporter have worked harder in trying to reach the plaintiff before publishing the charges? (See *Memphis Publishing Co.* v. *Nichols,* 1978.) In Arizona, negligence has been defined as conduct which creates unreasonable risk of harm. "It is the failure to use that amount of care which a reasonably prudent person would use under like circumstances," the Arizona Supreme Court ruled (*Peagler* v. *Phoenix Newspapers,* 1976).

What kinds of measures are used to determine negligence? What is reasonable care? Courts are just beginning to struggle with these questions, and the answers are not coming easily. Given the breadth of journalism, few professional standards exist, as they do in law and medicine. Its few codes of ethics, promulgated by such groups as the American Society of Newspaper Editors and the Society of Professional Journalists, are vague and have no sanctions. At best, journalism can be called a craft, and its standards vary from medium to medium and among individual units within a medium. The *New York Times* probably has higher standards than most American newspapers. The television network news departments probably have higher standards than do news departments at most local stations. The situation is due partly to wealth and time. The richer media can afford to do more checking. A magazine editor has more time to check a story than a daily newspaper editor has. A television documentary team has more time to verify details than does the producer of the nightly news. The question becomes this: The standard of conduct will be that of reasonable care. But what is reasonable journalistic care? What standards do we use? Perhaps the courts will measure the conduct of media defendants against the conduct of other persons in the same medium—the stories of one magazine editor against those of another, the films of one television documentary team against those of another team. Courts will probably use expert testimony to evaluate some of these matters, but there is little agreement on matters in some areas. In law, for example, the lawyer is obligated to investigate if he thinks his client's claim in a lawsuit is fraudulent. Furthermore, the lawyer has the time to investigate. What about the editor who, the day before an election, gets a report—attested to by two independent sources—that a candidate for mayor has taken bribes? Does he publish the story? Should he check it further? What is the editor's obligation to the candidate? What is the editor's obligation to the public? to the voters? What is reasonable care?

While there have been numerous judicial decisions on the question, it is hard to see meaningful guidelines. The case law does, however, provide some examples. Courts have been reluctant to find negligence when a reporter bases a story on the report of a normally reliable "official" source. A Florida court of appeals ruled that a story based upon an inaccurate report from an immigration officer was not published negligently. The same officer had provided consistently accurate information in the past (*Karp* v. *Miami Herald,* 1978). In 1977 the Philadelphia Police Department arrested two brothers, John and Tyrone Mathis, for attempted bank robbery. The police supplied pictures of the suspects to the *Philadelphia Daily News,* but the photograph identified as John Mathis by the police was not the same John Mathis arrested in connection with the attempted bank robbery. The John Mathis incorrectly identified as an attempted bank robber sued for libel, but the United States District Court for Eastern Pennsylvania ruled that there was no evidence that the newspaper was negligent—the publication was an accurate report of an inaccurate government report (*Mathis* v. *Philadelphia Newspapers,* 1978).

The South Carolina Supreme Court ruled that the failure of a reporter to examine a public judicial record when writing about a criminal case could be negligence. The plaintiff in the case had been arrested with four other men and charged with pirating stereo audio tapes. Two months later four of the men arrested pleaded guilty to the charges, but the charges were dismissed against the plaintiff. The newspaper published a story saying that the plaintiff had also pleaded guilty to the charges. The reporter had gotten his information about the case in a telephone conversation with the prosecuting attorney. The attorney testified that he had given the reporter the correct information. Six days elapsed between the dismissal of charges and the erroneous story. The South Carolina high court concluded that the correct information was available to the reporter in the court records, and that he could have looked at this material before publishing the story. He instead chose to rely upon a telephone conversation and in doing so got the story fouled up. The jury could readily conclude that the reporter was negligent, the court ruled (*Jones* v. *Sun Publishing,* 1982).

The North Carolina Court of Appeals ruled that failure to retract a libelous statement is not evidence of fault of any kind (*Walters* v. *Sanford Herald,* 1976). But the Arizona Supreme Court ruled that it was reasonable to expect a reporter to attempt to verify charges made by two former employees of the Phoenix Better Business Bureau about a local automobile dealer. The former employees charged the businessman with misrepresentation in advertising. The reporter did not attempt to verify the statements by calling the Better Business Bureau to determine the truth of the charges. This was negligent conduct, the court ruled (*Peagler* v. *Phoenix Newspapers,* 1976).

The definition of the term *negligence* will undoubtedly vary from state to state and possibly from judge to judge within a state. It is going to be some time before any kind of broad, consistently applied guidelines emerge. The United States Supreme Court will be of little help in this case, as it appears to be the intention of the Court to leave the matter to the states.

While the uncertainty in this area of the law exists, reporters and editors need to put a premium on *reasonable caution.* Newspapers and broadcasting stations should attempt to develop their own standards of care, and these should be applied in publishing and broadcasting the news. The Tennessee Supreme Court noted in 1978 that the negligence standard was *not* a "journalistic malpractice test" (*Memphis Publishing Co.* v. *Nichols,* 1978). Liability will be based upon a departure from supposed standards of care set by publishers themselves. Reporters need to become better bookkeepers and undertake to keep records on how and when they investigate the veracity of libelous charges. The key term is "good faith effort." So long as the press makes a good faith effort to establish the truth or falsity of libelous charges, it does not appear that negligence will be a serious problem.

As noted previously, other states have chosen to adopt other standards. The gross irresponsibility or gross negligence standard of New York falls somewhere between simple negligence and actual malice, which will be discussed shortly. Courts in New York have defined gross irresponsibility as acting with a degree of awareness of the probable falsity of the published statements (*Chapadeau* v. *Utica Observer-Dispatch, Inc.,* 1975). That is, the reporter or editor or broadcaster probably had some degree of knowledge that the material which was going to be published or broadcast was false. This would be harder for a plaintiff to prove, obviously, than that the defendant did not exercise reasonable care.

Actual Malice

Defining actual malice is somewhat easier than defining who is and who is not a public figure or public official. In *New York Times Co.* v. *Sullivan* (1964) Justice Brennan defined actual malice as "knowledge of falsity or reckless disregard of whether the material was false or not." The two parts of this definition should be considered separately.

Knowledge of Falsity

"Knowledge of falsity" is a fancy way of saying "lie." If the defendant lied, and the plaintiff can prove it, actual malice has then been shown. But plaintiffs are rarely in a position to show that the defendant lied. Furthermore, not many defendants, at least not many mass media defendants, lie. However, this did occur on one occasion. In 1969 Barry Goldwater was able to convince a federal court that Ralph Ginzburg published knowing falsehoods about him during the 1964 presidential campaign in a "psychobiography" carried in Ginzburg's *Fact* magazine. Ginzburg sent questionnaires to hundreds of psychiatrists asking them to analyze Goldwater's mental condition. Ginzburg published only those responses that agreed with the magazine's predisposition that Goldwater was mentally ill and changed the responses on other questionnaires to reflect this point of view. Proof of this conduct plus evidence of other kinds of similar practices led the court of appeals to conclude that Ginzburg had published the defamatory material with knowledge of its falsity (*Goldwater* v. *Ginzburg,* 1969; see also *Morgan* v. *Dun & Bradstreet, Inc.,* 1970).

A few months after the initial decision in the *Sullivan* case, the Supreme Court defined reckless disregard in a **criminal libel** action (*Garrison* v. *Louisiana,* 1964) as "a high degree of awareness of probable falsity" of the material or statements. In 1968, in *St. Amant* v. *Thompson,* the high Court said that before a court can conclude that reckless disregard for the truth exists "there must be sufficient evidence to permit the conclusion that the defendant in fact entertained serious doubts as to the truth of his publication." Failure to investigate in and of itself is not sufficient evidence to prove actual malice, wrote Justice White.

Both are good definitions of reckless disregard for the truth, but they are not much help to the working journalist who needs a more practical measure of reckless disregard. The Supreme Court has to an extent provided that as well. Look at *New York Times Co.* v. *Sullivan,* for example. All that was required to check the truth of the charges made in the advertisement that ultimately became the basis for the libel suit was for someone to compare the assertions in the advertisement with clippings in the newspaper's files, a simple matter. Yet the Court in that case did not indicate that such a check was really called for. There was no reason for the advertising staff to doubt the veracity of the claims in the document. The newspaper had every reason to believe that the charges contained in the advertisement were true.

A better practical definition of reckless disregard evolved from the cases of *Curtis Publishing Co.* v. *Butts* and *AP* v. *Walker* (1967). In developing the criteria that follow, Justice Harlan said he was attempting to determine whether the plaintiffs in these cases had seriously departed from the standards of responsible reporting. He did not call his opinion a definition of reckless disregard. Some of the other members of the Court did, however, refer to these standards as a measure of reckless disregard, and so have many lower federal and state courts.

These two appeals came before the Supreme Court at about the same time and were joined and decided as one case. In the first case Wally Butts, the athletic director at the University of Georgia, brought suit against the *Saturday Evening Post* for an article it published which alleged that Butts and University of Alabama football coach Paul "Bear" Bryant had conspired prior to the annual Georgia-Alabama football game to "fix" the contest. The *Post* obtained its information from a man who said that while making a telephone call he had been accidentally plugged into a phone conversation between Butts and Bryant. George Burnett, who had a criminal record, told the *Post* editors that he had taken careful notes. The story was based on these notes.

In the other case Major General (retired) Edwin Walker, a political conservative and segregationist from Texas, brought suit against the Associated Press (AP) and a score of publications and broadcasting stations for publishing the charge that he led a mob of white citizens against federal marshals who were attempting to preserve order at the University of Mississippi during the crisis over the enrollment of James Meredith. The AP report, which was wrong, was filed by a young AP correspondent on the scene.

The court ruled that in the *Butts* case the *Post* had exhibited highly unreasonable conduct in publishing the story, but that in the *Walker* case no such evidence was present. Again, it is important to note that while Justice John Marshall Harlan did not call the conduct reckless disregard at the time, most authorities accept these cases as good indicators of what the court means by reckless disregard. Look at the details of each case.

In the *Butts* case the story was not what would be called a hot news item. It was published months after the game occurred. The magazine had ample time to check the report. The source of the story was not a trained reporter, but a layman who happened to be on probation on a bad-check charge. The *Post* made no attempt to investigate the story further, to screen game films to see if either team made changes in accord with what Bryant and Butts supposedly discussed. Many persons were supposedly with Burnett when he magically overheard this conversation and none were questioned by the *Post*. The magazine did little, then, to check the story, despite evidence presented at the trial that one or two of the editors acknowledged that Burnett's story needed careful examination.

In the *Walker* case different circumstances were present. It was a hot story, one that had to get out on the wires right away. It was prepared in the "heat of battle" by a young, but trained, reporter who in the past had given every indication of being trustworthy. All but one of the dispatches from the correspondent said the same thing: Walker led the mob. So there was internal consistency. Finally, when General Walker's previous actions and statements are considered, the story that he led a mob at Ole Miss was not terribly out of line with his prior behavior. There was nothing to cause AP to suspect that the story was wrong as, for example, would be a report that the Archbishop of New York led a mob down Fifth Avenue. A red light should signal those kinds of instances which should suggest further checking because the story doesn't sound very likely.

When all this is sorted out, three key factors emerge.

1. Was the publication of the story urgent? Was it a hot news item? Or was there sufficient time to check the facts in the story fully?
2. How reliable was the source of the story? Should the reporter have trusted the news source? Was the source a trained journalist? Should the editor have trusted the reporter?
3. Was the story probable? Or was the story so unlikely that it cried out for further examination?

These factors make up a fairly good operational definition of reckless disregard and are the kinds of considerations a court might take a close look at in determining the reasonableness of the conduct of an editor or a broadcaster.

By combining the two conceptual definitions from *Garrison* and *St. Amant* and the practical guidelines from *Butts* and *Walker,* you should have a pretty good idea of the meaning of actual malice. The standard from *St. Amant,* the requirement of evidence that the defendant in fact entertained serious doubts as to the truth of the material, is a significant burden for the plaintiff to overcome. In addition, in bringing forward evidence to prove to the jury that the defendant did "entertain serious doubts," the plaintiff must meet a rigorous burden of proof. The normal evidentiary test in civil suits—the plaintiff must prove with a preponderance of evidence—has been abandoned in cases involving the *Times* rule. Instead the plaintiff must prove with "convincing clarity," must bring forth "clear and convincing evidence," that there was reckless disregard. If there is doubt in a juror's mind, the vote must be for the defendant. This standard strengthens the *Times* rule additionally.

Lower courts have had some of the same kinds of difficulties applying the actual-malice guidelines as they have had in applying the limited-public-figure guidelines. But standards do exist—even though contradictory decisions, especially from state courts, are not uncommon. It is obvious, for example, that reckless disregard for the truth is not the same thing as a sloppy journalistic error. When the *St. Louis Globe-Democrat* inadvertently attributed a city alderwoman's admission that she had had two abortions to another alderwoman who was a strong opponent of abortion, the Missouri Supreme Court ruled the error negligent, but not actual malice. The reporter gave the correct facts to a rewrite man over the telephone, but somehow the rewrite man, who was working on a close deadline, botched the facts. The emphasis placed on the close deadline by the Missouri court reflects Justice Harlan's opinions in the *Butts* and *Walker* cases (*Glover* v. *Herald Co.,* 1977). Other courts have focused upon these dimensions as well.

A New Mexico radio station broadcast false charges against a deputy sheriff which it had gained from interviews with confidential informants. The state's court of appeals ruled that the failure to investigate these charges before broadcasting them did not itself demonstrate actual malice (*Ammerman* v. *Hubbard,* 1977). Quoting the *Restatement of Torts* (2nd ed.) the court said:

> Availability of sufficient time and opportunity to investigate the truth of the statement is a significant factor in determining whether the publisher was negligent, and it may have some relevance in determining whether the publisher acted with reckless disregard as to truth or falsity.

When an Oklahoma newspaper published a libelous letter to the editor without checking the truth of serious charges made against a candidate for sheriff, the state's high court ruled that the total failure to make inquiry into the truth of *inherently improbable statements* could be evidence of reckless disregard for the truth (*Weaver* v. *Pryor-Jeffersonian,* 1977). This of course was another of the guidelines used by Justice Harlan in *Butts* and *Walker.* Similarly, the South Carolina Supreme Court ruled that malice was evident when a newspaper published charges that a stockholder in a large land development was being manipulated by his brother, whom the newspaper described as a "con man." In ruling for the plaintiff in the case, the court emphasized that the story was not a hot news item, and that despite obvious reasons to investigate the charges, the paper did little checking into the matter before publication (*Stevens* v. *Sun Publishing Co.,* 1978).

However, other courts have emphasized that, by itself, the failure to investigate a story is not evidence of actual malice. Other parts of the record in the case must also be considered. The Vermont Supreme Court ruled in 1977 that failure to properly investigate a contradicted story in itself did not establish reckless disregard for the truth (*Columbo* v. *Times-Argus Association,* 1977). And the New York Supreme Court said that a reporter's failure to check the newspaper's clipping file before writing an article in which he falsely stated that a former judge had been convicted of perjury is not evidence of actual malice. It was a serious oversight, the court ruled, but did not demonstrate that the journalist entertained serious doubts as to the truth or falsity of the charge (*Dilorenzo* v. *New York Times,* 1979).

What happens when the plaintiff in a lawsuit denies the truth of the libelous allegations before they are printed, but the newspaper publishes the story anyway? Is this actual malice? A United States district court in Tennessee ruled that it is not. Trucker Aubrey Roberts called the *Tennessean* newspaper and told reporter Albert Cason that he had been harrassed by a Tennessee highway patrolman. Roberts said he had made some unflattering comments about the patrolman over his citizens-band radio. This apparently angered Trooper Mike Dover. Roberts claimed Dover buzzed his truck in his highway patrol helicopter. The truck Roberts was driving was pulled over, and the trucker was put into the backseat of a patrol car which had arrived to assist Dover. Roberts reported the patrolmen rolled up all the windows in the car and turned on the car heater full blast. It was a very hot day. After a short time in the steamy patrol car, Roberts was released. Reporter Cason said he believed Roberts's story because the trucker was so upset, and because it would be very hard for someone to make up such a farfetched story. But Cason held the story until he talked to Dover. Dover denied most of the story, insisting that Roberts had been stopped for speeding, but he could not explain why the trucker was not ticketed if he had been speeding. The story was published as Roberts had told it to the reporter.

Dover sued for libel. The police officer, who admittedly was a public official, argued that because he had told the reporter that the story was not true, but the story was published anyway, publication was evidence of actual malice. Reporters and editors at the newspaper knew the story was false and still published it. The court disagreed. Dover's denial of the charges, standing alone, was not sufficient to sustain the inference that the reporter knew the charges were false. "To require that a reporter withhold such a story or face potential liability for defamation because a police officer denies a citizen's allegations of misconduct is exactly the type of self-censorship the *New York Times* rule was intended to avoid," the court noted. Police are always likely to have different stories from citizens in these kinds of cases. It is true that the reporter might have done other things to more fully check the story. "Indeed, such efforts might have resulted in a better news story. However, it cannot be said on this record that any failure of Cason or the *Tennessean* to make such further prior investigation constitutes proof sufficient to present to a jury a question on actual malice," the court concluded (*Roberts* v. *Dover,* 1981).

These contradictory rulings are not presented simply to confuse the issue of actual malice. They demonstrate that any determination of whether reckless disregard for the truth is apparent is a fairly complex matter, and that the courts will consider a variety of circumstances and conditions in any given case. They also show, however, that the guidelines from the *Butts* and *Walker* cases are important: That deadline pressure will be considered, that the credibility of the source is material, and that whether the libelous charges appeared probable or outrageous will all be considered in determining the need for investigation. These are useful guidelines for the media.

The fault requirement has done much in the past two decades to ease the burden of libel suits. This is especially true with regard to publication about persons in government and persons who attempt to lead or shape public opinion. The presumed function of the press, after all, is to educate and inform the public on such issues. Freedom to undertake this role is important, and simple relief from the threat of libel action will enhance the undertaking.

Since 1964 public officials have been asked to prove actual malice when suing for libel. Three years later so-called public figures were asked to meet the same standard. In 1974 the Supreme Court limited to a certain extent those persons falling into the public figure realm, but insisted that private persons who sue the media must also prove at least simple negligence to sustain their suits. States are free to place a higher level of fault upon private persons, and a handful have done so. Negligence has been defined as the lack of ordinary or reasonable care; actual malice means publishing material with the knowledge that it is false or with reckless disregard of whether it is truthful. As we have seen, all of these concepts are what might be called "terms of art," subject to the nuances and differences in meaning which judges across the land might apply.

Summary

In a lawsuit against a mass medium, a private person must prove that the defendant was at least negligent in publishing the defamatory matter. Negligence has been defined as the failure to exercise reasonable care, or as acting in such a way as to create a substantial risk of harm. In some states, in some cases private persons will be required to prove more than simple negligence. They may be required to prove gross negligence which is a standard which implies a greater degree of carelessness on the part of the defendant. An individual who has been declared to be a public person for the purposes of a libel suit must prove actual malice. Actual malice is defined as knowledge of falsity or reckless disregard of the truth. Transmitting a story with the knowledge of its falsity means that the publishers of the story knew it was not true, but still communicated it to the public. To prove reckless disregard for the truth the plaintiff must show that the publisher of the defamation had a "high degree of awareness of the probable falsity of the material" when it was published or that the publisher in fact "entertained serious doubts about the truth of the material" before it was published. The courts have established a set of three criteria which are used to help determine whether material was published with reckless disregard of the truth. The jurists tend to look at these factors:

1. Whether there was time to investigate the story, or whether the material had to be published quickly
2. Whether the source of the information appeared to be reliable and trustworthy
3. Whether the story itself sounded probable or farfetched

If the item was hot news, if the source was a trained journalist, and if the information in the story sounded probable, there can be no finding of reckless disregard. However, if there was plenty of time to investigate, or the source of the material was questionable, or if the information in the story sounded completely improbable, courts are more likely to permit a finding of reckless disregard for the truth.

SUMMARY JUDGMENT

No attempt is made in this book to teach anyone how to try a libel suit; students need to go to law school to find that out. But even journalists should know about one procedural matter in a libel suit. This is called "a motion for **summary judgment.**" After plaintiffs have made all their allegations in a lawsuit, but before the actual trial has begun, defendants can ask the court for a summary judgment. The United States Court of Appeals for the District of

Columbia described a summary judgment in this way (*Nader* v. *deToledano,* 1979):

> . . . a summary judgment should be granted if (1) taking all reasonable inferences in the light most favorable to the nonmoving party [the plaintiff in this case], (2) a reasonable juror, acting reasonably, could not find for the nonmoving party, (3) under the appropriate burden of proof.

This is a good outline, but by using an example we can assist in translating it for nonlawyers. John Smith is sued by Jane Adams for libel. After Ms. Adams has presented all her allegations and arguments to the court, and after the court gives her the benefit of the doubt in any instance which might be questionable, if the judge believes that a juror could not possibly rule in her favor, the judge can grant a summary judgment for the defendant. The defendant would win without going to trial.

The summary judgment has proved especially useful in libel suits since 1964 when the Supreme Court raised the constitutionally mandated "actual malice" fault requirement for public persons. Whether or not there was actual malice in a case was considered a "constitutional fact" that could be determined by a judge. This was not necessarily a jury question. Therefore, if the plaintiff in the lawsuit could bring forth no evidence at all of actual malice, the judge could dismiss the suit on a motion for summary judgment. As more and more persons fell under the rubric of public person and more and more cases hinged upon the finding of actual malice, motions for summary judgments became commonplace in libel suits. And they were granted with some regularity. This worked out well for the press; a costly trial was avoided in a lawsuit that the newspaper or broadcasting station would have ultimately won anyway. In fact, because of the importance placed upon freedom of expression, the summary judgment seemingly became the rule in a libel suit. Judge Skelly Wright of the Court of Appeals in Washington, D.C., wrote in 1970 that "unless the court finds, on the basis of pretrial affadavits, depositions, or other documentary evidence that the plaintiff can prove actual malice in the *Times* [*New York Times* v. *Sullivan*] sense, it should grant summary judgment for the judgment for the defendant" (*Wasserman* v. *Time, Inc.,* 1970).

Granting summary judgments to libel defendants is somewhat controversial. Warren Burger, the Chief Justice of the United States, has attempted to discourage lower courts from granting summary judgments in cases in which actual malice is a question. In a footnote to his opinion in *Hutchinson* v. *Proxmire* the Chief Justice noted that "proof of actual malice calls a defendant's state of mind into question . . . and does not lend itself to summary disposition." Burger raised an issue that many persons—especially plaintiffs' attorneys—think is real and important. Can a court adequately determine a defendant's state of mind—whether the person in fact entertained serious doubts as to the truth of the material—without a trial in which the adversary process can be conducted to hopefully unearth material facts? While footnotes in Supreme Court opinions are not to be taken lightly, lower courts seem to be largely ignoring the Chief Justice's suggestion. It is still quite possible for a libel defendant to win a summary judgment when there is no genuine issue about any material fact in the case, and when the law is clearly on the side of the defendant.

Now it is time to turn to the subject of the defenses to libel suits. A libel defense can be defined as a legally acceptable reason for publishing something which is defamatory. There are many different kinds of defenses, some very old and some relatively new. The libel defenses considered here are truth, privileged communication, fair comment, consent, and right of reply. The applicability of each defense in a particular case is determined by the facts in the case—what the story is about, how the information was gained, the manner in which it was published. Before looking at the substantive defenses, it is appropriate to consider the one remedy offering a defendant complete immunity in a libel action—the statute of limitations.

STATUTE OF LIMITATIONS

For nearly all crimes and most civil actions there is a **statute of limitations.** Courts do not like stale legal claims. They have plenty of fresh ones to keep them busy. Prosecution for most crimes except homicide and kidnapping must be started within a specified period of time. For example, in many states if prosecution is not started within seven years after an armed robbery is committed, the robber cannot be brought to trial. He or she is home free. (However, the robber can still be prosecuted for failing to pay income tax on money taken from a bank, but that is another story.)

The duration of the statute of limitations differs from state to state, varying from one to five years. In most states the duration is one or two years. What this means is that a libel suit must be started within one or two years following publication of the offending material. The date of publication on a newspaper determines when the duration of the statute begins. In television and radio the statute of limitation begins on the day the program is telecast or broadcast. Magazines pose a somewhat different problem. The publication date on the magazine rarely coincides with the date the publication is actually distributed. Magazines dated November are usually distributed in October, sometimes even in late September. Courts have ruled that the statute of limitations begins on the date that a magazine is distributed to a substantial portion of the public. *Time* magazine was sued in New Jersey, which has a one-year statute of limitations, for an article published in an issue dated February 18, 1980. The suit was filed on February 17, 1981. But the magazine proved that a substantial portion of the magazine had been distributed to subscribers and newsstands before February 17, 1980. The United States district court ruled that the statute of limitations had expired by February 17, 1981 (*MacDonald* v. *Time,* 1981). In a similar suit Don Wildmon failed in his attempt to sue *Hustler* magazine for an article published in the November 1978 issue. Wildmon filed his suit on October 9, 1979, but the magazine proved that the November 1978 issue of *Hustler* went on sale on October 3, 1978, and subscriber copies were mailed one to two weeks earlier. The United States district court dismissed the suit because the one-year statute of limitations in Mississippi had expired (*Wildmon* v. *Hustler,* 1980).

The libel republication rule can be a factor in considering the statute of limitations. In many states buying a back issue of a publication is considered new publication, and the statute of limitations starts over. More and more jurisdictions have rejected this rule and substituted the single publication rule. This rule states that the entire edition of a newspaper or magazine is a single publication and that isolated sales in the months or years to come do not constitute republication. Therefore the statute of limitations starts on the day the edition hit the newsstands and ends one or two or three years later. The statute cannot be reactivated by a later sale. About one-half of the states have this progressive rule. Find out if your state does.

Summary

A libel suit must be started before the statute of limitations expires. Each state determines how long this period will be. In most states it is one, two, or three years. A libel suit started after the expiration of the statute of limitations will be dismissed.

TRUTH

Truth is a complete defense in a libel suit. If a statement can be proved to be true, a plaintiff cannot collect libel damages because the statement was published. It is true that in a handful of states the law says that only truthful statements published for justifiable ends or with good motives are protected. As we have noted, appellate courts are overturning these laws as being in violation of the First Amendment. Such a law was declared null and void in Illinois, for example, in 1969 (*Farnsworth* v. *Tribune Co.*).

The words may be defamatory, they may harm the reputation of the plaintiff, but injured parties will lose their case if the statement is true. Sounds nice, doesn't it? But hold on a minute. In a libel suit the law presumes that the libelous statement is false, that it is not true. It is up to defendants to convince the jury that what they have published is the truth. Truth of the statement is not something that the plaintiff must refute.* If the plaintiff can

*The Sixth United States Court of Appeals ruled in *Wilson* v. *Scripps-Howard* in 1981 that "falsity is an element of fault under the First Amendment that should be proved and not presumed." Because the plaintiff bears the burden of proof of fault, the plaintiff must also prove the falsity of the article, the court said. Before the United States Supreme Court could hear arguments in the case, a settlement between the parties was reached. This controversial rule can be said to apply only in the Sixth Circuit (Ohio, Michigan, Tennessee, and Kentucky), and it is not considered a firm rule in those states.

demonstrate there was a libel, there was publication, there was identification, and there was negligence, the defendant has to prove the truth of the statement. And that is not always easy to do. What is provable in court is often far less than what a reporter knows to be true. Judge Leon Yankwich (*It's Libel or Contempt If You Print It*) once wrote, "Libel lurks in vague general charges and inferences. Easy to make, they are the most difficult to prove." A specific charge—John stole a car—is often far easier to prove than a general statement—John is a thief. The problem of proving the truth is more complex than this, however.

Many people who are willing to tell a reporter something in confidence are frequently reluctant to repeat the charge in public. They may fear for their safety or their job. Often to reveal the truth publicly may compromise their reputation. Some people make bad courtroom witnesses. People with criminal records or other stains upon their past are often easily impeached as witnesses by clever attorneys for the plaintiff. Sometimes witnesses cannot be found; they have left the community or have died. What the reporter has seen and heard himself is usually persuasive testimony. But remember, the plaintiff may tell the jury a different story, and the case can come down to which party is the more credible witness. Libel defendants therefore do not often rely on truth. Many other better defenses, defenses easier to use in court, are available. Nevertheless it is important to know the dimensions of this defense.

To prove the truth, the evidence presented in court must be as broad as the libelous charge. The proof must be direct and explicit; it must go to the whole charge. If there is conflicting evidence, the judge or the jury (whichever is the fact finder) decides who is telling the truth. If the *River City Sentinel* publishes that John Smith operates a fraudulent business, proving that Smith once cheated a customer will likely not convince a court of the truth of the libelous charge. The published charge suggests a pattern of cheating or continuous cheating. Similarly, if a broadcaster asserts that Mayor Smith is a wife beater, evidence that he once slapped her in a fit of rage probably will not establish the truth of the assertion.

You are not required to prove every word of the defamatory charge, just the main charge, the part that carries the sting or the gist of the libel. John Smith is a violent man, you report. He likes to beat people, to hit them with clubs and chains and rocks. It will not damage your argument if you cannot prove that Smith hit people with rocks so long as you can prove that he hit them with chains and clubs.

What the court is looking for is substantial truth. For example, a Michigan newspaper published that a land developer had been "Charged in Shopping Mall Fraud." The story said Harlan Orr had been charged with fifteen counts of fraud, outlined what it called his "phony shopping mall investment scheme," and referred to his behavior as an "alleged swindle." Orr sued for libel. He admitted that the basic facts of the story were true: he had been charged with five counts of the sale of unregistered stock, with eight counts of failure to disclose information, and two acts of deceit. Orr had told potential investors in his scheme that J.C. Penney Company had already leased space in his proposed shopping center. That was not true. What Orr objected to was the use of the words "fraud," "swindle," and "phony" scheme. The United States Court of Appeals for the Sixth Circuit overturned a jury verdict in behalf of Orr and ruled that the article was substantially true. The word *fraud* is an accurate and appropriate description of a violation of the Michigan security laws, the court said. The word *swindle* is a common colloquialism for the term *defraud*. The J.C. Penney scheme was "phony." The court admitted that the words in the story could mean more; they could mean a "flimflam." But they could be used also to mean what Orr had done (*Orr* v. *Argus Press,* 1978).

Extraneous errors will not destroy the defense. The *Ashtabula Telegraph* reported that George C. Horvath had been arrested with several other persons in a drug raid. The reporter talked with various police agencies in gathering information on the story and learned that Horvath was supposedly funneling the money earned from the sale of the drugs back into his businesses, Horvath Service and All-Seasons Nursery. But in fact his father, George J. Horvath, owned the businesses. George C. had worked at the businesses and was even perceived by some to be the owner. George J. Horvath sued for libel. The newspaper relied on the defense of truth. George J. Horvath said that there were falsehoods in the story, that George C. did not own the businesses, and that the business was named All-Seasons Archery, not All-Seasons Nursery. Everything else was true. The Ohio court of appeals ruled that the gist of the article was true and that the two minor errors did not distract from the story. The article was true under the law (*Horvath* v. *Ashtabula Telegraph,* 1982).

How does the court evaluate whether the defendant successfully proved the truth of the charge? The jury does this with guidance from the judge. The judge will probably give the jury a test to use in evaluating the evidence against a defamatory charge. One of the commonly used tests comes from a 1934 New York case, *Fleckstein* v. *Friedman.* Defendant Benny Friedman, a former all-star professional football player, charged that some of the players in the National Football League were sadists and bullies. Friedman named names in his *Collier's* magazine story, and one of the players identified, William Fleckstein, sued.

In attempting to prove the truth of the charge, Friedman demonstrated some of the tactics used by these rough players. In instructing the jury in this case, the judge said:

> . . . a workable test of truth is whether the libel as published would have a different effect on the mind of the reader from that which the pleaded truth would have produced. When truth is so near to the facts as published that fine and shaded distinctions must be drawn and words pressed out of their ordinary usage to sustain a charge of libel, no legal harm has been done.

In simpler terms this is what the court said: After reading the article, readers were left with a certain opinion of William Fleckstein, a negative opinion since he was called a bully and a sadist in the story. Now, if persons who had not seen the story had a similar opinion of Fleckstein after seeing the evidence Friedman presented in court, Friedman then succeeded in proving his charges. The point here is a lot simpler than it sounds, but it is something which should be understood. The proof must be as broad as the charge; the evidence presented in court must leave the reader with the same impression of the plaintiff as did the defamatory charge.

One more point should be stressed about truth. Correctly quoting someone or accurately reporting what someone else has told you does not constitute proof of the truth of the charge. Imagine that John Smith tells a reporter that the police chief changes arrest records of certain prisoners to simplify their getting bail and winning acquittal. This charge, attributed to John Smith, is contained in the reporter's story which is subsequently published. The police chief sues for libel. It is not sufficient for the reporter to prove merely that the statement in her story was an accurate copy of what Smith said. Even if the reporter's story contained an exact duplicate of Smith's charge, truth can be sustained only by proving the substance of the charge, that the police chief has altered arrest records. A newspaper or broadcasting station is responsible for proving the truth of a libelous charge, not merely of the accuracy of the quote in the story. Accuracy, then, is not always the same thing as truth.

Summary

Anything that can be proved to be true may be published or broadcast without fear of a successful defamation suit, but the defendant must be able to prove what is asserted in the libelous publication. It is often difficult to satisfactorily prove a charge in a court of law. The evidence presented in court must be as broad as the libelous charge. The defendant must prove the gist or the substance of the defamation. Minor errors which do not relate to the basic substance of the libel will not destroy the defense of truth.

PRIVILEGED COMMUNICATIONS

Traditionally in the United States we value robust debate as a means of discovering those elusive truths which we continually pursue. The law takes pains to protect this debate, making sure that speakers are not unduly punished for speaking their minds. Article 1, Section 6, of the federal Constitution provides that members of the Congress are immune from suits based on their remarks on the floor of either house. This is called a privilege. The statement in question is referred to as a privileged communication.

Absolute Privilege

Today, privilege attaches to a wide variety of communications and speakers. Anyone speaking in a legislative forum, congressmen, senators, state representatives, city councilpersons, and so forth, enjoys this privilege. Even the statements of witnesses at legislative hearings are privileged. But the comments must be made in the legislative forum. The Supreme Court ruled in 1979 that while a speech by a senator on the floor of the Senate would be wholly immune from a libel action, newsletters and press releases about the speech issued by the senator's office would not be protected by the privilege. Only that speech which is "essential to the deliberations of the Senate" is protected, and neither newsletters to constituents nor press releases are parts of the deliberative process (*Hutchinson* v. *Proxmire,* 1979).

Similarly, the privilege attaches to communications made in judicial forums—courtrooms, grand jury rooms, and so forth. Judges, lawyers, witnesses, defendants, plaintiffs, and all other persons are protected so long as the remark is uttered during the official portions of the hearing or the trial. Finally, persons who work in the administrative and executive branches of government enjoy privilege as well. Presidents, mayors, governors, department heads—official communications or official statements by these kinds of persons are privileged. In 1959 in *Barr* v. *Mateo* the Supreme Court suggested that the privilege applies to any publication by government officials which is in line with the discharge of their official duty. This case involved a press release from a department head explaining why two federal employees had been fired. "A publicly expressed statement of the position of the agency head," the Court ruled, "announcing personnel action which he planned to take in reference to the charges so widely disseminated to the public was an appropriate exercise of the discretion which an officer of that rank must possess if the public service is to function effectively."

More recently the Court of Appeals in New York State ruled that a press release issued by an assistant attorney general concerning the investigation of possible fraudulent activities by fund raisers was protected from a lawsuit by privilege. The court said that since the attorney general as an executive official enjoys absolute privilege while exercising the functions of his office the same privilege applies to his subordinates who exercise delegated powers (*Gautsche* v. *New York,* 1979). The difference in the treatment of the assistant attorney general by the New York court and Senator Proxmire by the United States Supreme Court over essentially the same item—a press release—stems from the different roots of the privilege. Congressional privilege stems directly from the United States Constitution and is limited by the constitutional language. The privilege applied to the state attorney general stems from the common law. Also, the functions of the two offices are different. Senators are supposed to deliberate and make legislative policy. Reporting to the public on the results of an official investigation is one of the governmental functions of an attorney general.

The privilege just discussed is an **absolute privilege.** The speaker cannot be sued for defamation on the basis of such a remark.

A similar kind of a privilege applies also to certain kinds of private communications. Discussions between an employer and an employee are privileged; the report of a credit rating is privileged; a personnel recommendation by an employer about an employee is privileged. These kinds of private communications remain privileged so long as they are not disseminated beyond the sphere of those who need to know.

Qualified Privilege

What is called **qualified privilege** goes far beyond the absolute immunity granted to speakers at public and official meetings and the conditional immunity applied to certain types of private communication. The press is granted a qualified or conditional privilege to report what happens at official governmental meetings and other meetings open to the public. This is how the privilege is outlined in the second edition of the *Restatement of Torts:*

> The publication of defamatory matter concerning another in a report of any official proceeding or any meeting open to the public which deals with matters of public concern is conditionally privileged if the report is accurate and complete, or a fair abridgement of what has occurred.

This means that a libel suit premised upon such a publication will not stand. While technically the press has no special privileges in the law of defamation, in actual operation of the law this privilege is invoked so infrequently on behalf of anyone other than the press that it is generally regarded to be a privilege of the press. In fact, this privilege is sometimes called the privilege of the reporter, as opposed to the absolute immunity noted earlier which is referred to as the privilege of the participant.

There is much to discuss about this privilege. Perhaps the most important point which needs to be made is that it is a *conditional* privilege. That is, the privilege of the reporter works as a defense in a libel suit only if certain conditions are met. First, the privilege applies only to reports of certain kinds of meetings, generally meetings of governmental bodies, public meetings on issues of public importance, and other public proceedings. Second, the privilege applies only to reports which are a fair and accurate or truthful summary of what occurred at the meeting. Third, publication of a report cannot be motivated by malicious feelings such as ill will. However, if the meeting is the kind covered by the privilege, if the report is a fair and true summary of what took place at the meeting, and if there is no malice in the report, the conditional privilege then provides absolute protection for the press. It will totally defeat a libel suit.

The defendant bears the burden of proving that the privilege applies to the libelous material. The court determines whether the particular occasion (meeting or proceeding) is privileged. The jury determines whether the defendant's story is a fair and accurate report. Each of these elements needs closer scrutiny. Let us, therefore, focus now on meetings and proceedings said to be privileged.

The privilege applies at the very least to reports of all official proceedings of a governmental agency. Some authorities contend that it also applies to all public meetings at which matters of public concern are discussed (more on this in a moment). The qualified privilege applies to official proceedings of the legislative branch of government, to the judicial branch, and to the executive branch. Let's look at each briefly.

Legislatures

Quite obviously, the privilege applies to meetings of organizations like Congress, state legislatures, city councils, county councils, and so forth. The privilege also applies to the reports of meetings of committees of such organizations, as well as to stories about petitions, complaints, and other communications received by these bodies. The only requirement which must be met in regard to this aspect of the privilege is that the official body, such as a city council, must officially receive the complaint or petition before the privilege applies. If the Citizens for Cleaner Streets bring a petition charging the street superintendent with incompetence and various and sundry blunders in his job to a city council meeting, publication of these charges is privileged as soon as the city council officially accepts the petition. Nothing has to be done with the document. It must merely be accepted.

The privilege likely applies to stories about the news conferences of members of a legislative body following a session, to stories about what was said during a closed meeting by the body, and to what was said during an informal gathering of legislators before or after the regular session. If what is said or what occurs during these kinds of events is of great public interest and there is a compelling public need to know, the privilege then likely applies.

The Courts

The privilege of the reporter also applies to actions which take place in judicial forums: testimony of witnesses, arguments of attorneys, pronouncements of judges, and so forth. Stories about trials, decisions, jury verdicts, court opinions, judicial orders and decrees, and grand jury indictments are all protected by the privilege.

Probably the most serious problem a reporter on the court beat has to face is what to do when a lawsuit is initially filed. Under our legal system a lawsuit is started when a person files a complaint with a court clerk and serves a summons on the defendant. The complaint is filled with charges, most of which are usually libelous. Can a reporter use that complaint as the basis for a story?

The states are divided on this question. In some states a complaint is not considered privileged until a judge takes some kind of action on the lawsuit. This action may only be the scheduling of an appearance by the litigants, or it may be more. But a judge must get involved in the matter before the complaint becomes a privileged document. In other states the complaint becomes privileged as soon as it has been filed with the court clerk and a summons has been issued. It is important for you to determine which rule governs civil complaints in your state. The simplest way to do this is to look for opinions on this question in cases decided by your state high court.

Stories about those parts of the judicial process which are closed to public view are not protected by the privilege. Frequently, court sessions for juveniles and divorce proceedings are closed in order to further a public policy. The legislature or the courts feel obligated to discourage publicity about what occurs during such hearings. A few years ago the *New York Daily News* published a series of articles about a sensational divorce case, one in which the wife accused the husband of keeping a harem of women in a private plane which he used for business (and pleasure?) trips. When the husband sued the newspaper for libel, the *Daily News* argued that it had taken its report directly from court records and trial testimony.

In New York, however, divorce proceedings are closed to the public. The state's high court ruled that the legislature deemed it to be in the public interest to close divorce proceedings to public scrutiny (*Shiles* v. *News Syndicate Co.,* 1970):

> Since, then, such matrimonial actions were and are not proceedings which the public had the right to hear and see, it follows—and it has been consistently held—that the privilege generally accorded to reports of judicial proceedings is unavailable to reports of matrimonial actions.

Government Executives and Administrators

Reports of the statements and proceedings conducted by mayors, department heads, and other persons in the administrative and executive branches of government are generally privileged. The best guideline is that the privilege is confined to stories about actions or statements which are official in nature, the kinds of things which are substantially "acts of state." By law administrators are required to prepare certain reports and to hold certain hearings, and the privilege certainly covers stories on these activities. Although not required by law, other actions are unmistakably part of the job. Reports on these affairs are undoubtedly protected as well. The California Supreme Court, for example, recently ruled that a report on organized crime prepared for the state attorney general by a special commission was a privileged document once it was released to the press and public (*Kilgore* v. *Younger,* 1982).

Reports of police activities also fall under the heading of executive actions, but the privilege is applied sparingly here. It is fairly well settled that a report that a person has been arrested and charged with a crime is privileged. The arrest and charge is a public kind of event. All the additional information the police and prosecutor are wont to give the press—how the crime was committed, statements by witnesses, circumstances surrounding the arrest—is clearly not protected by the privilege. The police really go beyond their authority in making such statements and frequently defame the suspect in the process. There is some indication that the privilege is expanding in this area, however. *Time* magazine published an article which described an individual as a "capo [chief] in his Mafia family." The story summarized information from Federal Bureau of Investigation investigatory documents which *Time* had obtained legally. The Third United States Court of Appeals ruled this information is protected by a qualified privilege (*Medico* v. *Time,* 1981).

Other Public Concerns   The privilege of the reporter is not confined only to those instances of reporting official government proceedings. For example, an Idaho court ruled that the privilege applied to a story about a meeting called by citizens to protest the actions of a judge. It clearly was not an official meeting, but concerned important public business, the conduct of a public official. The court said, "There is a general doctrine that what is said at a public meeting, at which any person of the community or communities involved might have attended and heard and seen for himself, is conditionally privileged for publication" (*Borg* v. *Boas,* 1956).

The *Restatement of Torts* (2d ed.) says that reports of what occurs at meetings open to the public at which matters of public concern are discussed are privileged. Paul Ashley, libel authority and author of *Say It Safely* (1976), wrote that the privilege probably applies to a public meeting even though admission is charged, so long as everyone is free to pay the price. "By supplying them with information about public events," Ashley writes, "the publisher is acting as the 'eyes and ears' of people who did not attend."

In such a circumstance, the report of a public meeting, the key element undoubtedly is the subject of debate. Was it of public concern? Was it of limited public concern? Was it a purely private matter? Using the standard of public concern, we can look at some kinds of nonofficial public meetings and try to determine whether the privilege applies.

1. Meeting of local Rotary Club: probably of private concern; not privileged
2. Meeting of board of directors of United Fund: of public concern; privileged

3. Meetings of local bar association or medical society: of limited public concern; privileged
4. Meeting of stockholders of General Motors Company: about private business and of private concern; not privileged
5. Meeting of county Democratic party: of public concern; privileged

At this point how far the privilege will extend in protecting nonofficial public meetings cannot be said. Traditionally each state handles this problem differently, and therefore you should seek guidance from local statutes and court decisions. The privilege is clearly extended to gatherings outside the official governmental sphere.

Neutral Reportage

The privilege has grown in another direction in some parts of the country with the development of what many libel authorities call the defense of **"neutral reportage."** One thing which must be remembered about neutral reportage is that it is by no means accepted as a legitimate defense in all states, or even in most states.

The neutral reportage privilege developed most directly from an interesting suit in New York State concerning the annual Audubon Society Christmas bird count. The *New York Times* printed charges made by an official of the Audubon Society that any scientist who argues that the continued use of the pesticide DDT has not taken a serious toll of bird life is "someone who is being paid to lie about it or is parroting something he knows little about." The implication was, of course, that certain scientists were being paid by the pesticide industry to lie about the impact of the chemicals on wildlife. The *Times* story included the names of several scientists given to the reporter by Robert Arbib, the official at the Audubon Society. Some of these scientists sued for libel, but the Second Circuit Court of Appeals ruled the story published by the *Times* containing the libelous charges was privileged, even though reporter John Devlin might have believed the charges made by Arbib were false when he published them. The court called the privilege "neutral reportage" and described it in the following manner (*Edwards* v. *National Audubon Society,* 1977):

> When a responsible prominent organization like the National Audubon Society makes serious charges against a public figure, the First Amendment protects the accurate and disinterested reporting of those charges, regardless of the reporter's private views regarding their validity. What is newsworthy about such accusations is that they were made. . . . The public interest in being fully informed about controversies that often rage around sensitive issues demands that the press be afforded the freedom to report such charges without assuming responsibility for them. We must provide immunity from defamation where the journalist believes, reasonably and in good faith, that his report accurately conveys the charges made.

In simple terms the neutral reportage rule may be stated this way: publication of an accurate account of information about a public figure from a reliable source by a reporter who doubts the truth of the assertions is still privileged. When charges are made by responsible agencies or persons, the public should hear these charges, even when the journalist doubts their veracity. It is newsworthy that the charges have been made; that fact alone might add materially to the public debate on the issue.

As applied in a handful of courts since the *Edwards* case the neutral reportage privilege seems to have four distinct requirements:

1. The story must be newsworthy; it must be of public interest.
2. The individual who has been libeled must be a public figure.
3. The reporter must accurately report the libelous charges *and* present all sides of the controversy.
4. The publication must play the role of an impartial transmitter of information and not espouse the libelous charges.

A United States district court recently denied the application of the neutral reportage privilege in a libel suit because the target of the charges was not a public figure (*Dresbach* v. *Doubleday,* 1982). The Second United States Court of Appeals ruled the neutral reportage inapplicable in a case in which the defendant publication not only inaccurately reported the charges against the public figure, but also vigorously supported these charges in a personal attack upon the plaintiff. Obviously, the reportage ceased to be neutral (*Cianci* v. *New Times,* 1980).

Neutral reportage remains a limited privilege. Some courts, such as the Third United States Court of Appeals, have rejected the privilege (*Dickey* v. *CBS,* 1978; *Postill* v. *Booth Newspapers,* 1982). Other courts have accepted it (see, for example, *Orr* v. *Lynch,* 1978; *Krauss* v. *Champaign News Gazette,* 1978; *Wade* v. *Stocks,* 1981; and *El Amin* v. *Miami Herald,* 1983). Probably the Supreme Court of the United States will be asked to decide upon the viability of the defense. Until such a definitive ruling, neutral reportage remains a creative effort in a few jurisdictions to expand the range of permissible reporting.

Abuse of Privilege

Whether qualified privilege applies to a particular story is only part of the problem. There is also the question of whether the privilege was abused.

A jury might find that abuse occurred in one of two ways: (1) the publisher used the privilege as a shield in order to attack the plaintiff or (2) the story was not really a fair and accurate account of what took place at the meeting, was not a fair summary of the court's ruling, or did not give a fair and accurate account of the conclusion of the official report.

The purpose of the privilege is to foster public understanding of what is happening, to allow wide public exposure of what takes place at a public meeting, in a public trial, or at a public session of the legislature. If fostering public understanding was not the primary purpose of the publication, if the publisher or broadcaster instead sought to harm the person defamed at the hearing or trial or in the report, and if publication was motivated by ill will and not by serving the public good, the privilege was then abused. Once the defendant has successfully convinced the court that the privilege should apply, it is up to the plaintiff to show its abuse. This is not an easy task, but it can be done. By showing previous ill will on the part of the publisher, the plaintiff might be able to establish an "evil" state of mind and convince a jury that publication was made to hurt him, not to inform the public. There are other ways as well.

The privilege can also be destroyed if the story in question is not a fair and accurate or true report of what took place. *Fair* means balanced. If at a public meeting speakers both attack and defend John Smith, the story should reflect both the attack and the defense. A story which just focuses on the charges is not fair, and the privilege will have been abused. Similarly, if the story concerns a continuing kind of an affair, a legislative hearing, a trial, and so forth, in which testimony is given for several days, the press is obligated to publish stories about each day's events if the privilege is to be used. There has to be balance. If a story about a civil suit based upon the charges listed in the complaint is prepared, it is important to get the defendant's response as well. Balance is the key.

An accurate or true report means just that: it should honestly reflect what took place or what was said. An attorney named Frank Marcone was indicted in Pennsylvania for giving money to other persons to invest in drug trafficking, such as buying marijuana. The indictment was later dismissed. *Penthouse* magazine published a story in which it said that Marcone had "contributed down payments of up to $25,000 on grass transactions. Charges against him were dropped because he cooperated with further investigations." *Penthouse* argued this was a privileged story since it relied upon the grand jury indictment, a privileged document. But an indictment is an allegation or charge that someone has done something. *Penthouse* reported that Marcone had in fact provided money for drug purchases. The story was not a fair and accurate report of the indictment. The magazine could have said Marcone had been indicted for providing money to purchase drugs or that there were allegations that he had provided money to purchase drugs. The story as published went beyond the official document (*Marcone* v. *Penthouse,* 1982). As with truth, little errors will not destroy the privilege. So long as the error has nothing to do with the basic defamation, there is no problem. It must be remembered that the story must be substantially true. If it is an untruthful report, the privilege is lost.

The story must also be in the form of a report. If defendants fail to make it clear that they are reporting something that was said at a public meeting or repeating something that is contained in the public record, the privilege is lost. The law says the reader should be aware that the story is a report of what happened at a public meeting or at an official hearing or is taken from the official record. These facts should be noted in the lead and in the headline if possible.

At City Council Session
MAYOR BLASTS CONTRACTOR WITH CHARGES OF FRAUD

Mayor John Smith during a city council meeting today charged the Acme Construction Co. with fraudulent dealings.

Finally, the privilege protects only that part of a story based on an official proceeding or a public record or report. Anything added to the story from outside these sources will not be protected by the qualified privilege.

The privilege of the reporter is a very important defense and protects the press in a large percentage of the stories which are printed or telecast. Privilege is much easier to use than truth since all the defendant must prove is that the event, meeting, or report was in fact a privileged occasion and the story was a fair and true report.

Summary

The publication of defamatory material in a report of a public meeting, legislative proceeding, legal proceeding, or in a story which reflects the content of an official government report is conditionally privileged. The privilege extends to the meetings of all public bodies, to all aspects of the legal process, to reports and statements issued by members of the executive branch of government, and even to nonofficial meetings of the public in which matters of public concern are discussed. Such reports cannot be the basis for a successful libel suit as long as these requirements are met:

1. The report presents a fair (balanced) and accurate (truthful) account of what took place at the meeting or what is contained in the record.
2. The report is not motivated by ill will toward the person who is libeled.

FAIR COMMENT

Fair comment is another kind of privilege. It permits the journalist to express defamatory opinions on matters of public interest. The key words are *opinions* and *public interest.* Once again the law allows the press valuable protection when it concerns itself with matters of importance to readers and viewers. By its very nature an opinion is not subject to proof or to test by evidence. An opinion is a subjective statement which reflects the speaker's tastes, values, or sensitivities. As such, the defense of truth is worthless. The privilege of the reporter which has just been discussed is often limited in its application by the kinds of proceedings and reports to which it is applicable.

The roots of fair comment are deep. British courts long ago recognized the need for some means of permitting critical views and opinions to be aired. Lord Ellenborough summed up the basis of the defense of fair comment in the early nineteenth century (*Tabart* v. *Tipper,* 1808):

> Liberty of criticism must be allowed, or we should have neither purity of taste nor of morals. Fair discussion is essentially necessary to the truth of history and the advancement of science. That publication, therefore, I should never consider as a libel which has for its object not to injure the reputation of any individual, but to correct misrepresentations of fact, to refute sophistical reasoning, to expose a vicious taste in literature or to censure what is hostile to morality.

More recently the Supreme Court has noted that the privilege of fair comment rests within the First Amendment as well. Writing in *Gertz* v. *Welch* Justice Powell noted:

> We begin with the common ground. Under the First Amendment there is no such thing as a false idea. However pernicious an opinion may seem, we depend for its correction not on the conscience of judges and juries, but on the competition of other ideas.

On the same day the *Gertz* ruling was handed down, the Supreme Court ruled that the naming of some postal workers "scabs" during a labor dispute was protected. The expression of such an opinion, even in the most perjorative terms, the court said, is protected (*Old Dominion Branch No. 496, National Association of Letter Carriers* v. *Austin,* 1974). Opinion, then, will be protected. But the application of the fair comment privilege is somewhat more complicated than that. A discussion of the requirements of the fair comment defense follows.

Legitimate Public Interest

The first requirement is that the comment must concern something of legitimate public interest. The courts have granted a wide range of topics that are fair game for comment. Educational, charitable, and religious institutions are eligible for comment, as are quasi-public organizations such as bar associations, medical societies, and other professional groups. Manufacturers who place products on the market must expect criticism; businesses which cater to the public such as restaurants, theaters, and galleries are subject to the same treatment. Any solicitation for public support such as an advertisement is fair game, as are artistic and creative efforts such as movies, plays, operas, books, paintings, recitals, comic strips, and television and radio programs. The work of journalists and broadcasters may be commented upon. The performances of those who seek to entertain the public—actors, musicians, athletes, and the like—are also considered legitimate targets for fair comment. In the 1930s a football coach sued a newspaper for its criticism of his team and his coaching abilities. The court found little sympathy for the plaintiff (*Hoeppner* v. *Dunkirk Printing Co.,* 1930):

> When the plaintiff assumed the position of . . . coach to the football team of the Dunkirk High School, he was no exception to the habits and customs which have become a part of the game. His work and the play of his team were matters of keen public interest; victories would be heralded, defeats condemned. The same enthusiasm which welcomed the home-coming of the Roman conqueror now finds expression in the plaudits of the bleachers and the grandstand. The conquered now appear not in chains, but what may be far worse, amidst ridicule and derision—the boos of the crowd.

More recently, the Illinois court of appeals ruled that when the chairman of a university department described the scholarship of one of the faculty members in the department as "neither the quantity nor the quality of . . . work [which] justifies a grant of tenure" that it was a fair comment. It was an opinion on the man's public work. "Once published material is placed into the stream of ideas it cannot be defamation when that material is critiqued, be it by a reviewer or a superior" (*Byars* v. *Kolodziej,* 1977). A broad range of subjects, then, come under the purview of the privilege.

As a kind of a corollary to the rule that the comment must concern something of public interest, the comment must also focus upon the public aspects of the subject. That is, while Elvis Presley's performances may have been legitimate targets of criticism, his private life was not. Similarly, while a book might be the fair subject even of scathing critical analysis, fair comment is no license to undertake scathing criticism of the author or the author's life. A very old case makes the point best. The plaintiff was a lecturer and teacher named Oscar Lovell Triggs. After a series of lectures by Triggs in New York, the *New York Sun* editorially attacked Triggs's public performance and his public pronouncements. These were fair game. But the newspaper went further and criticized the plaintiff because he and his wife took a year to name their baby. This attack was upon his personal life and could not be excused as a fair comment (*Triggs* v. *Sun Printing and Publishing Association,* 1904). To quote Lord Ellenborough about another case (*Carr* v. *Hood,* 1808), "Every man who publishes a book commits himself to the judgment of the public and any one may comment upon his performance. If the commentator does not step aside from the work, . . . he exercises a fair and legitimate right."

Another requirement of the privilege is that the opinion expressed by writers or broadcasters be their true opinion. It does not have to be the right opinion or the majority opinion. The jury does not have to agree with the opinion of the defendant. It just must be the author's honest opinion. What happens when a newspaper or magazine quotes someone else's libelous opinion in its news columns? Can the publisher use the defense of fair comment to ward off a libel suit? A United States court of appeals ruled in 1964 that a libel defendant cannot. In that case *Look* magazine quoted the management of the San Franscisco Giants who made critical and libelous comments about baseball star Orlando Cepeda. The court ruled that fair comment did not apply because the opinions expressed in the article were not those of the writer of the article (*Cepeda* v. *Cowles Magazine & Broadcasting, Inc.,* 1964). That ruling is probably out-of-date. For example, we can look to a recent ruling by the Oklahoma Supreme Court. When George Miskovsky was running for the United States Senate in Oklahoma in 1978, he raised the issue of the sexual preferences of one of his opponents, Governor David Boren. Boren denied all charges, and the press throughout the state came down hard on Miskovsky for making "cesspool allegations." In both stories and editorials the *Daily Oklahoman* quoted many of the critical comments made by radio stations and newspapers against Miskovsky. He sued the *Oklahoman* for libel and won a one-million-dollar judgment from a jury. But the Oklahoma Supreme Court overturned the verdict, declaring that all the libelous comments in the newspaper were opinions and hence were protected by fair comment (*Miskovsky* v. *Oklahoma Publishing,* 1982). Undoubtedly the United States Supreme Court ruling in 1974 which placed opinion statements squarely under the protection of the First Amendment has forced courts to change the rule enunciated in the *Cepeda* case just cited.

Offensive Hyperbole

The opinion does not need to be temperate. As a federal court once noted, an opinion can be good, bad, or indifferent, immature, premature, or ill-founded. A newspaper in Alaska once called the late Drew Pearson "the garbage man of the Fourth Estate." The court permitted this comment (*Pearson* v. *Fairbanks Publishing Co., 1966*). Decades ago the *Des Moines Leader* published this review of a vocal trio, the Cherry Sisters (*Cherry* v. *Des Moines Leader,* 1901):

> Effie is an old jade of 50 summers, Jessie is a frisky filly of 40, and Addie, the flower of the family, a capering monstrosity of 35. Their long skinny arms, equipped with talons at the extremities, swung mechanically, and anon waved frantically at the suffering audience. The mouths of their rancid features opened like caverns, and sounds like the wailing of damned souls issued therefrom. They pranced around the stage with a motion that suggested a cross between the danse du'ventre and fox trot—strange creatures with painted faces and hideous mien. Effie is spavined, Addie is stringhalt, and Jessie, the only one who showed her stockings, has legs with calves as classic in their outlines as the curves of a broom handle.

This review was considered fair comment.

Rex Reed referred to musician-composer Jerry Orbach as a "tone-deaf mediocrity" and a "nonprofessional embarrassment." The court ruled this was a fair comment. "No doubt, the writer's review was exaggerated. However, the law of libel is not concerned with questions of exaggeration, taste, or propriety in the use of language," the New York Supreme Court noted (*Orbach* v. *New York News*, 1978). The *Barre* (Vt.) *Times Argus* was sued for libel when it quoted one political candidate who called his opponent "a horses's ass, a jerk, an idiot and paranoid." The Vermont Supreme Court ruled that the words may be insulting, abusive, unpleasant, and objectionable, but they are opinions protected by the First Amendment (*Blovin* v. *Anton*, 1981).

Finally, the Louisiana Supreme Court refused to permit recovery for libel when a devastating review of a prominent restaurant was published in the *New Orleans States Item*. Reviewer Richard Collin began his review of the Maison De Mashburn, "T'aint Creole, t'aint Cajun, t'aint French, t'aint country American, t'aint good." He said the food was hidden under a melange of "hideous sauces" and called the menu a "travesty of pretentious amateurism." He described the oysters as "a ghastly concoction," the poached trout "trout a la green plague," and said that "most of the food tastes as if the conceptions were wrong to begin with." And there was more. But the review was an opinion, the court said, and the restaurant was a public commercial establishment (*Mashburn* v. *Collin*, 1977). It was fair comment.

Factual Basis

In 1974 the U.S. Supreme Court ruled that defamatory opinion statements are protected by the First Amendment. In the last ten years many courts have had to wrestle with the question of what is a statement of opinion and what is not. In August 1983 the U.S. Court of Appeals for the District of Columbia noted, as many courts have, that the constitutional protection mandated by the *Gertz* ruling only protects what it called "pure opinion." Pure opinion statements, the court said, are incapable of being judged true or false. Such statements include expressions of personal taste, literary criticism, political views, and many aesthetic judgments. Also included are what the court described as "loosely defineable, variously interpretable, generally derogatory remarks that are often flung about in colloquial argument or debate, terms such as toady, facist, cuckoo, and the like." Finally, hyperbole and metaphorical and figurative speech is generally considered pure opinion (*Ollman* v. *Evans*, 1983).

But other kinds of opinion statements reflect a judgment or evaluation of a person or a work that is based on facts. These kind of "hybrid opinion" statements normally can be tested for their truthfulness. The opinion "Frank is an incompetent mechanic" lends itself to testing based on facts about Frank's work. This second kind of opinion statement is protected only if the factual basis is accurately presented with the opinion, or the facts are widely known in the community.

The question of facts is complicated. The *Restatement of Torts* (2d ed.), section 566, outlines three kinds of situations in which these hybrid opinions might be published. In the first instance the person who makes the comments states the facts upon which the opinion is based right in the article. To wit:

> In 1975 Mayor Robert Allen bought six road graders for the city, none of which were needed or used. Two years later he spent $500,000 of the people's money upon an auditorium which stands vacant 350 nights a year. Last year he sent four of his staff to Europe to study how mass transit is operated there, and three of the cities his staff visited have no mass transit system. Mayor Allen has been squandering taxpayers' money for too long; he is wasteful and pays little heed to need for fiscal caution.

The opinion—that Allen has been squandering taxpayers' money—was supported by the factual statements in the first part of the story.

But the facts do not have to be actually outlined so long as both parties to the communication—the writer and the readers, for example—know the facts or can assume their existence. This is the second kind of situation. The *Wilmington* (Del.) *News-Journal* in an editorial about a local public official who had just pled guilty to a charge of official misconduct added this sentence: "Other men in quite recent local memory abused their offices and forfeited their right to them: former County Director Melvin A. Slawik. . . ." Slawik had pled guilty three years earlier to a charge of obstruction of justice. He sued the newspaper for libel, but the Delaware Supreme Court ruled the phrase "abused their offices" was an opinion protected by fair comment. What about facts to support the opinion? The court ruled that since Slawik's departure from office had received intensive publicity when it occurred the facts upon which the newspaper's opinion were based were well-known in the community (*Slawik* v. *News-Journal*, 1981).

The third situation noted by the *Restatement* is different. In this case the opinion appears to be based upon facts regarding the plaintiff or the plaintiff's conduct, but the facts are not stated. The "factual understanding" upon which the negative opinion is based cannot be presumed to exist between the writer and her audience or the broadcaster and his viewers. In such an instance, when the facts are not well known and the defendant fails to state them in the critical story or broadcast, the defense of fair comment will likely not work. Why? It is argued that in such a case the reader or viewer is left with an impression that the writer or broadcaster knows something bad about the plaintiff—something which has not been stated. This suggestion of negative facts is defamatory; it is defamation.

For example, the *New York Times* published a story in 1978 about entertainer Phoebe Snow. Quoting singer-writer Janis Ian, the author of the story described Ms. Snow in this way: "She is also paranoid. . . . Her record company and her manager all screwed her at once." Phoebe Snow's manager sued for defamation. The court acknowledged that the statement that Phoebe Snow was "screwed" by her manager was an opinion, a rather colorful way of saying that he treated Ms. Snow unfairly. That is fine. But the facts upon which this conclusion was drawn were not stated in the article, nor could it be assumed that all readers knew what the writer was referring to. Saying that she had been "screwed" by her manager implied the existence of negative, defamatory facts, the court ruled. "If the author represents that he has private, firsthand knowledge which substantiates the opinions he expresses, the expression of opinion becomes as damaging as an assertion of fact," the court ruled (*Rand* v. *New York Times,* 1978).

The New Mexico court of appeals reached the same opinion in a 1981 ruling involving a weekly newspaper. The weekly, in its criticism of a competing newspaper, reported that the competitor "actually printed a piece by rabid environmentalist Jack Kutz, who used to send us letters so violent we turned them over to the police." Kutz sued for libel. The court ruled that the phrase "rabid environmentalist" was protected opinion, but the reference to violent letters implied that the newspaper's editors had private, negative defamatory facts about Kutz to support the opinion that he was a rabid environmentalist. None of this information was in the article to allow readers to make up their minds about Kutz. The court of appeals sent the case back for trial (*Kutz* v. *Independent Publishing,* 1981).

Finally, as for the privilege of the reporter, the comment of the writer cannot be motivated by ill will. It cannot be published solely to hurt someone. It may in fact hurt someone: Critics have closed Broadway shows, ended politicians' careers, torpedoed advertising campaigns. The harm is not important. What is important is whether the comment was made for the purpose of hurting someone, not for the purpose of enlightening the public, educating readers and viewers, or warning consumers or theatergoers.

Fair comment is a valuable privilege, and writers and broadcasters must be most cautious when ascertaining the facts. The comment may be fair, but if the subject of the criticism can sustain a libel suit because the facts are untrue, the defense helps very little.

Summary

Under the First Amendment there is no such thing as a false idea. Defamatory opinions may be published or broadcast about matters of public interest. There is no need for these opinions to be temperate; they may be abusive and distasteful so long as they only reflect upon the public life of the individual who has been defamed. There must be some basis in fact for these opinions. These facts should be truthfully outlined in the publication which contains the criticism, or they should be very well-known by the members of a community. In this way the public has the ability to develop its own opinion about the individual or the issue. If the facts are not stated or are not well-known, the defense of fair comment will not work. The court will presume that the defendant harbored negative and defamatory information about the subject of the critical opinion, and this suggestion to the readers or listeners is defamatory.

CONSENT

There are two additional libel defenses. Both defenses have been used on occasion to successfully ward off a libel suit, but their foundations are tenuous. They have been accepted in some courts, and rejected in other courts. Reliance upon either of them as the only defense is therefore not advised. However, both make excellent backup defenses, to be used with privilege or fair comment. The two defenses are **consent** and **right of reply.**

As one authority notes, an otherwise actionable defamation may be privileged if the plaintiff consented to its publication. Imagine that Frank Jones, a reporter for the *River City Sentinel,* hears rumors that John Smith is a leader of organized crime. Jones visits Smith and tells him that he has heard these rumors. Then Jones asks Smith if he cares if the rumors are published in the newspaper. Smith says it is OK with him, and Jones writes and publishes the story. In this instance Smith consented to publication of the defamation.

Now, this event is not too likely to happen, is it? Cases of consent are extremely rare. Courts insist that the plaintiff either know or have a good reason to know the full extent of the defamatory statement in advance of its publication before consent can be said to exist.

At least one authority (Phelps and Hamilton) has suggested that while the kind of direct consent just noted is difficult to obtain, indirect consent is a viable defense. Indirect consent means that individuals were informed of the defamatory charges against them and were asked to comment upon the charges. The logic behind this defense is that if the newspaper publishes the response to the charges it must publish the charges as well.

For example, let us look at Smith and Jones again. Frank Jones tells John Smith that the police have called Smith "a big-time gangster." Jones says he is going to print the charge, and then asks Smith, "Would you care to comment on the charge?" Smith denies the charge and claims that he is a legitimate businessman. He calls the man who made the charge a liar. Again, the logic of the defense suggests that if Smith's denial is printed the charge which he denies must also be printed.

This reasoning may be logical, but few courts have accepted it. On record are one or two cases in which this kind of indirect consent by itself worked to defeat a libel suit (*Pulverman v. A. S. Abell Co.,* 1956). A very imaginative judge is needed to accept these arguments.

This does not mean, however, that it is not good policy to get a comment from the defamed party before the story is published. The facts may be wrong, and the subject of the story can then point out errors and save the newspaper from a suit. Even if the story is not incorrect, the reporter's attempt to get both sides of the story, to discover the truth, will impress a jury if a suit does result. His efforts will demonstrate that he was not malicious in printing the story, that he honestly sought the truth, and that the plaintiff was given a chance to explain the charges. This policy is far more effective than giving the plaintiff the chance to reply after he has been defamed. At that point, the offer looks like an afterthought. Similarly, even if the subject of the story cannot be reached, it is good policy for the journalist to tell readers that he tried to contact the person or that the person refused to comment. A reporter can have no worse experience than to testify in a libel suit that he made no attempt to contact the plaintiff before printing the story. "You mean you didn't even try to find out from the plaintiff whether the charges were true or not? You didn't have the decency to make a simple phone call?" the plaintiff's attorney will ask as the jury sits up attentively.

Indirect consent can help in a defense, but it is rare indeed for it to defeat a libel suit when standing by itself. As with other defenses, publication of materials for malicious reasons, and not for public enlightenment, can invalidate the protection.

RIGHT OF REPLY

Right of reply is a better defense than consent, is used more often, and is somewhat more substantial. The basis of right of reply is simple: The one who has been libeled may answer in kind. John Smith calls Steve Wilson a cheat, a fraud, and a common thief. Wilson has the right to answer Smith in kind. He can defame Smith in response.

The right of reply is based on the broader concept of self-defense; in fact, it is often referred to as *the* self-defense. As in self-defense, right of reply does have limitations. If a woman walks down the street and someone begins to pepper her with a peashooter, she has the right to stop her assailant, to protect herself. She does not have the right to pull out a .44-magnum pistol and pump three or four slugs into her attacker. Her defense then far exceeds the threat of the original attack. The same is true in a libel case. If a woman has been defamed, she may respond in kind. She may defame her attacker, but her reply cannot exceed the provocation: she cannot hit back harder than she was hit.

In a famous lawsuit two American journalists assailed one another in print. Newsman Quentin Reynolds suggested that columnist Westbrook Pegler had once called a third journalist, Heywood Broun, a liar. This bothered Broun, Reynolds wrote, to the extent that he could not sleep. Broun became ill and finally died. Pegler was incensed by this comment, claiming it charged him with moral homicide. So he attacked Reynolds, calling him sloppy, a sycophant, a coward, a slob, and a four-flusher. Pegler accused Reynolds of public nudism, of being a war profiteer, and of being an absentee war correspondent. Pegler also attacked the deceased Broun, calling him a liar and someone who made his living by controversy.

In the libel suit that followed Pegler raised the defense of right of reply. The court agreed that Pegler's comments about Broun bore a resemblance to a reply, but that the columnist had gone too far in his attack on Quentin Reynolds. This portion of the article had no conceivable relationship to a reply. Reynolds was awarded $175,000 from Pegler, the *New York Journal-American,* and the Hearst Corporation (*Reynolds* v. *Pegler,* 1955).

The right of reply works. Where does the press fit in? Many authorities argue that the press has the right to carry the reply and remain immune from suit. In several cases it was held that where the plaintiff's charge was made in a newspaper the newspaper was privileged to carry the defendant's reply (*Fowler* v. *New York Herald,* 1918). Otherwise the right of reply is of no avail to the defendant; no one would be able to see or read the reply if he were denied use of the press. Similarly, it was held that the reply can even be carried in a newspaper or a medium different from the medium used for the attack.

In *Cases and Materials on Torts,* law professor Harry Kalven writes:

> The boundaries of this privilege are not clearly established and it gives rise to questions amusingly reminiscent of those raised in connection with self-defense: How vigorous must the plaintiff's original aggression have been? Must the original attack itself have been defamatory? What if it [the original attack] is true or privileged? How much verbal force can the defendant use in reply? Can he defend third parties?

Questions like these continue to reduce the true effectiveness of the defense of right of reply. Most authorities agree that the original attack must be defamatory in order to defend a defamatory reply, and many authorities argue that the defendant can in fact defend third parties in a reply. There are so few reported cases in which this defense either stood or fell on its own accord that its substance as a defense remains quite tenuous. It is useful as a second defense, to back up either the privilege of the reporter or of fair comment, perhaps. Beyond this use its value is limited, at least at this point. Malicious motive can also invalidate this defense.

DAMAGES

If the court gets to the point in a libel suit of assessing **damages,** it is obvious that the plaintiff has met all requirements, including proving fault, and that none of the defenses just outlined have worked. How damages are assessed is not an essential piece of information for a journalist to carry; yet some feeling for the subject is useful. Libel law operates with four kinds of damages today. In each instance, before any damages can be awarded, the plaintiff must prove one thing or another to the court.

Actual Damages

In present-day law the basic element in damages is what are called **actual damages,** or damages for actual injury. Plaintiffs have to convince the jury that they have suffered actual harm. What kind of harm? Not physical harm, obviously. The best definition of actual damages (as they are now defined) comes from the *Gertz* case. Justice Powell wrote that actual injury is not limited to out-of-pocket loss or money loss, which is how many authorities defined actual damages prior to this decision. Powell said, "Indeed, the more customary types of actual harm inflicted by defamatory falsehood include impairment of reputation and standing in the community, personal humiliation, and mental anguish and suffering." This statement is a very broad definition of actual damage. How can someone prove that he has suffered mental anguish? What is evidence of personal humiliation? These are very hard questions to answer. Libel damages have never been precise, and the new formulation does not promise additional precision. The plaintiff will have to bring evidence of some kind, and as in the past, the jury will be the key factor in making the determination of how much harm and how much damage.

Special Damages

Special damages are specific items of pecuniary loss caused by published defamatory statements. Special damages must be established in precise terms, much more precise terms than those for the actual damages just outlined. If a plaintiff can prove he lost $23,567.19 because of the libel, that amount is then what he can ask for and what he will likely get if he can convince the jury of his case. Special damages represent a specific monetary, and only monetary, loss as the result of the libel. Most plaintiffs do not seek special damages. However, in some cases special damages are all that can be sought. In trade libel, for example, the only award a plaintiff can get is special damages.

Presumed Damages

Presumed damages are damages that a plaintiff can get without proof of injury or harm. The only way a plaintiff may be awarded presumed or general damages is if actual malice, knowledge of falsity, or reckless disregard of the truth is proved.

Punitive Damages

Lawyers used to call **punitive damages,** or exemplary damages, the "smart money." Punitive damage awards are usually very large. The other kinds of damages just discussed are designed to compensate the plaintiff for injury. Punitive damages are designed to punish defendants for their misconduct and to warn other persons not to act in a similar manner. The only way plaintiffs can win punitive damages is if they can prove actual malice—knowledge of falsity or reckless disregard for the truth.

Punitive damages are the most onerous aspect of any libel suit, and many persons think they are grossly unfair. Consequently some state courts have abolished punitive damages—regardless of a showing of actual malice. Massachusetts (see *Stone* v. *Essex County Newspapers,* 1975) and Washington (*Taskett* v. *King Broadcasting,* 1976) are two such states.

One point should be made clear about damages. When defenses were discussed earlier, it was pointed out that only public officials and public figures (and in some states private persons involved in matters of general concern) have to prove actual malice to win their case. But all plaintiffs can attempt to prove actual malice in the hope of getting punitive and presumed damages, and it is only if they meet this burden that they can collect the smart money.

Retraction Statutes

The phrase "I demand a retraction" is common in the folklore of libel. What is a **retraction?** A retraction is both an apology and an effort to set the record straight. Let us say you blow one as an editor. You report that Jane Adams was arrested for shoplifting, and you are wrong. In your retraction you first tell readers or viewers that Jane Adams was not arrested for shoplifting, that you made a mistake. Then you might also apologize for the embarrassment caused Ms. Adams. You might even say some nice things about her. At common law a prompt and honest retraction is usually relevant to the questions of whether the article was published with malice and whether the plaintiff's reputation was actually harmed. After all, you are attempting to reconstruct that part of her reputation which you tore down just the day before. She might have difficulty proving actual harm.

A good example of correction, or retraction, occurred about five years ago and involved of all things *Playboy's Book of Wines*. The slick-paper wine book erroneously charged on page 63 that a leading Italian winery, Bolla Vineyards, doctored its wine. As one writer noted, "All hell broke loose" when the American distributor of Bolla wines saw the reference. Playboy Press reached an agreement with the vintners in which it called back all five thousand copies of the book already distributed, sliced the two offending pages out of those copies and replaced them with two new pages containing flattering references to Bolla, stopped publication of the book until corrections could be made, and issued multiple apologies. These were extreme measures, but they prevented a lawsuit.

In the several states which have retraction statutes, a plaintiff must give the publisher an opportunity to retract the libel before a suit may be started. If the publisher promptly honors the request for a retraction and retracts the libelous material in a place in the newspaper as prominent as the place in which the libel originally appeared, the impact will reduce and in some instances cancel any damage judgment the plaintiff might later seek in a lawsuit. Failure to seek a retraction limits the plaintiff's right to bring a lawsuit against the publisher. About thirty-five states have retraction laws of one kind or another.

In an unusual case the Montana Supreme Court recently declared that state's retraction statute was unconstitutional. The court ruled that the state constitution guarantees that the state courts shall be open to every person who seeks a remedy for any injury to person, property, or character. The court ruled that a retraction is not a remedy in the terms intended in the constitution. Consequently, the state's statute, under which persons who fail to seek a retraction are not permitted to sue for libel, denied citizens the remedy promised by the state constitution (*Madison* v. *Yunker,* 1978).

Retraction laws make good sense. It is the truth we seek, after all; a successful libel suit results in lining the plaintiff's pocket, but it is not very effective in correcting the errors in people's minds resulting from publication of the defamation.

Summary

To collect damages in a libel suit plaintiffs must demonstrate to the court that there was actual harm to their reputation. These are called *actual damages.* If plaintiffs can demonstrate specific items of monetary loss, *special damages* may be awarded. If actual malice can be proved, plaintiffs can seek to have *punitive damages* awarded. In nearly thirty-five states a timely retraction of the libel can reduce damages significantly and even lessen the likelihood of a libel suit. These rules are governed by state laws called *retraction statutes.*

CRIMINAL LIBEL

Since this book is for persons in the media or persons who plan to work in the media, there is really little reason to spend time discussing criminal libel. But it is there and is difficult to ignore. So here are a few well-chosen words on the subject.

The bulk of this chapter deals with civil libel—one person suing another for defamation. In most states, however, libel can be a crime as well. That is, there are criminal libel statutes, laws which make certain kinds of defamation a crime. For the most part these laws go unused today. They are relics of the past. In some states, in the South especially, recent instances of criminal libel prosecution have occurred. In the 1980s most states are not very interested in taking on someone else's troubles and suing for libel. A prosecutor has very little to gain from such an action. In fact, he would probably be roundly criticized for instituting criminal libel charges. In an age when people are mugged, robbed, raped, and murdered with alarming frequency, damage to an individual's reputation, or even to the reputation of a large number of persons, somehow does not seem too serious. Moreover, individuals who have been harmed already have recourse—a civil suit. Several years ago in New York a judge stated this proposition very well (*People* v. *Quill,* 1958):

> The theory, in simplest terms, is that when an individual is libeled, he has an adequate remedy in a civil suit for damages. The public suffers no injury. Vindication for the individual and adequate compensation for the injury done him may be obtained as well in the civil courts. Thus the rule has always been that

the remedy of criminal prosecution should only be sought where the wrong is of so flagrant a character as to make a criminal prosecution necessary on public grounds.

Despite the fact that they are not used, criminal libel statutes remain on the books in most states. In Louisiana the law is defined in this manner:

Defamation is the malicious publication or expression in any manner, to any one other than the party defamed, of anything which tends:

(1) To expose any person to hatred, contempt, ridicule or to deprive him of the benefit of public confidence or social intercourse; or

(2) To expose the memory of one deceased to hatred, contempt or ridicule; or

(3) To impair any person, corporation or association of persons in his or their business occupations.

Whoever commits the crime of defamation shall be fined not more than $3,000 or imprisoned for not more than one year or both.

As you can see, the crime of defamation is very similar to the tort of defamation: a person can get into trouble in both instances by doing about the same thing. It can be seen from the statute quoted that it is possible to criminally libel a dead person. Since the deceased cannot sue to protect his own good name, it only makes sense to allow the state to intercede. Criminal libel differs from civil libel in several other ways as well.

First, in a few states criminal libel is tied to causing or potentially causing a breach of the peace. This charge used to be quite common. If a publication, speech, or handbill so provoked the readers or listeners that violence became possible or did in fact occur, criminal libel charges might result. In 1966 the United States Supreme Court undermined most of the "breach of the peace" statutes as well as the actions of those states that brought criminal libel actions under the common law. The case was *Ashton* v. *Kentucky* and involved a mining dispute in Hayard, Kentucky. An agitator was arrested for circulating a pamphlet which contained articles attacking the chief of police, the sheriff, and a newspaper editor, among others. At the criminal libel trial the judge defined the offense as "any writing calculated to create a disturbance of the peace, corrupt public morals or lead to any act, which when done, is indictable."

The Supreme Court reversed the conviction. Writing for a unanimous court Justice William O. Douglas said the crime as defined by the trial court is too general and indefinite. It left the standard of responsibility—whether something is illegal or not—wide open to the discretion of the judge. Also, Douglas noted, the crime is determined not by the character of the man's words, not by what he says or writes, but rather by the boiling point of those who listen to him or read his pamphlet. The law makes a man a criminal simply because his neighbors have no self-control and cannot refrain from violence.

This decision was an important factor, but only one factor, in the passing of "breach of the peace" as an aspect of criminal libel. It is extremely rare for such a case to occur today.

It is also possible to criminally libel a large group or race of people. The Supreme Court upheld such a law in 1952, a law which made it a crime to libel any race, color, creed, or religion. The case originated in Illinois where a white racist named Joseph Beauharnais distributed insulting literature at a time when blacks were attempting to integrate the white Chicago suburb of Cicero. Beauharnais's words were strong at a time when police and other officials had their hands full keeping the peace. He was arrested, tried, and fined $200 for his pamphleteering.

He argued that his conviction violated the First Amendment. In a five-to-four vote, the Court upheld the conviction on the grounds that libelous utterances are not within the protection of the First Amendment. Justice Felix Frankfurter wrote that if an utterance directed at an individual may be the object of criminal penalties the high Court could not then deny the right of a state to make such utterances aimed at a well-defined group criminal as well (*Beauharnais* v. *Illinois,* 1952).

The rationale for this decision was eroded if not completely undercut by the *New York Times* decision: Libelous utterances are protected by the First Amendment in an increasing number of instances. There is serious doubt in the minds of most press-law scholars whether the *Beauharnais* ruling remains viable today. It is very likely, given the opportunity, that the Supreme Court would overturn that decision.

The high Court has heard one criminal libel case since the *Sullivan* ruling. The high Court ruled in *Garrison* v. *Louisiana* (1964) that when the defamation of a public official is the basis for a criminal libel suit the state has to prove actual malice on the part of the defendant, that is, knowledge of falsity or reckless disregard for the truth or falsity of the matter. Justice Brennan wrote that the reasons which persuaded the Court to rule that the First Amendment protected criticism of public officials in a civil libel suit applies with equal force in a criminal libel suit. "The constitutional guarantees of freedom of expression compel application of the same standard to the criminal remedy," he added. However, the question of what the Court would do with a group libel suit of the kind it faced in 1952 is still not answered.

Criminal libel is not a real problem for journalists and broadcasters. Within the few criminal libel cases on record since World War II, cases in which the media were the defendants can be counted on one hand. Normally the action is brought against the writer of the article or the speaker of the words, not against the medium publishing the comments.

As was noted at the beginning of this chapter, libel is probably the most common legal problem most journalists and broadcasters face today. Unlike difficulties with courts and problems in getting information from the government, which occur infrequently, libel is something the press lives with day in and day out. Virtually every story contains the potential for a libel suit.

The press is much better protected today than it was thirteen years ago before the *New York Times* decision. The *Sullivan* ruling has helped the press in many ways. In the past plaintiffs with only the remote possibility of victory were lured to court by the possibility of a large windfall judgment. Recent cases have made the smart money tougher to get. Also, infusion of good, solid First Amendment idealism and logic into the law has made judges at all levels far more sensitive to the needs of the press. These events have been very helpful. While "freedom of the press" may be legally vague, a judge or jury who thinks about the First Amendment is likely to be more receptive to the arguments of the defense.

BIBLIOGRAPHY

Here is a list of some of the sources that have been helpful in the preparation of chapter 3.

Books

American Law Institute. *Restatement of the Law of Torts.* 2d ed. Philadelphia: American Law Institute, 1975.

Ashley, Paul. *Say It Safely.* 5th ed. Seattle: University of Washington Press, 1976.

Gregory, Charles O., and Kalven, Harry, Jr. *Cases and Materials on Torts.* 2d ed. Boston: Little, Brown & Co., 1969.

Hansen, Arthur. *Libel and Related Torts.* New York: Publishers Association Foundation, 1969.

Phelps, Robert, and Hamilton, Douglas. *Libel.* New York: Macmillan Co., 1966.

Prosser, William L. *Handbook of the Law of Torts.* St. Paul, Minn.: West Publishing Co., 1963.

Thomas, Ella C. *The Law of Libel and Slander.* Dobbs Ferry, N.Y.: Oceana Publications, 1963.

Yankwich, Leon R. *It's Libel or Contempt If You Print It.* Los Angeles: Parker & Sons Publications, 1950.

Articles

Anderson, David A. "Libel and Press Self-Censorship," 53 *Texas Law Review* 422, 1975.

"Defamation Law in the Wake of *Gertz* v. *Welch, Inc.,*" 69 *Northwestern University Law Review* 960, 1975.

Frakt, Arthur N. "Evolving Law of Defamation: *New York Times Co.* v. *Sullivan* to *Gertz* v. *Welch, Inc.,* and Beyond," 6 *Rutgers Camden Law Journal* 471, 1975.

"Torts: Libel," 41 *Brooklyn Law Review* 389, 1974.

Cases

Ammerman v. *Hubbard,* 572 P.2d 1258 (1977).

Arcand v. *Evening Call,* 567 F.2d 1163 (1977).

Artic v. *Loudoun Times Mirror,* 624 F.2d 518 (1980).

Ashton v. *Kentucky,* 384 U.S. 195 (1966).

Bandelin v. *Pietsch,* 563 P.2d 395 (1977).

Barr v. *Mateo*, 353 U.S. 171 (1959).
Beauharnais v. *Illinois*, 343 U.S. 250 (1952).
Blovin v. *Anton*, 431 A.2d 489 (1981).
Borg v. *Boas*, 231 F.2d 788 (1956).
Bose v. *Consumers Union*, 508 F. Supp. 1249 (1981).
Bruno and Stillman v. *Globe Newspapers*, 633 F.2d 583 (1980).
Buckley v. *Littel*, 539 F.2d 882 (1976).
Byars v. *Kolodziej*, 363 N.E.2d 628 (1977).
Cardiff v. *Brooklyn Eagle*, 75 N.Y.S.2d 222 (1948).
Carr v. *Hood*, 1 Camp. 355 (1808).
Carson v. *Allied News*, 529 F.2d 206 (1976).
Cepeda v. *Cowles Magazine & Broadcasting, Inc.*, 328 F.2d 869 (1964).
Chapadeau v. *Utica Observer-Dispatch, Inc.*, 341 N.E.2d 569 (1975).
Cherry v. *Des Moines Leader*, 86 N.W. 323 (1901).
Chuy v. *Philadelphia Eagles*, 595 F.2d 1265 (1979).
Cianci v. *New Times*, 639 F.2d 54 (1980).
City of Chicago v. *Tribune Co.*, 139 N.E.2d 86 (1923).
City of Philadelphia v. *Washington Post*, 482 F. Supp. 897 (1979).
Clawson v. *Longview Publishing Co.*, 589 P.2d 1223 (1979).
Cohen v. *New York Times*, 138 N.Y.S. 206 (1912).
Coleman v. *MacLennan*, 98 P.2d 281 (1908).
Columbia Sussex v. *Hay*, 627 S.W.2d 270 (1981).
Columbo v. *Times-Argus Association*, 380 A.2d 80 (1977).
Cooper v. *Rockford Newspapers*, 365 N.E.2d 746 (1977).
Curtis Publishing Co. v. *Butts* and *AP* v. *Walker*, 388 U.S. 130 (1967).
Denny v. *Mertz*, 318 N.W.2d 141 (1980).
Dickey v. *CBS*, 583 F.2d 1221 (1978).
Dilorenzo v. *New York Times*, 4 M.L. Rept. 2230 (1979).
Dresbach v. *Doubleday*, 8 M.L. Rept. 1793 (1982).
Edwards v. *National Audubon Society*, 556 F.2d 113 (1977).
El Amin v. *Miami Herald*, 9 M.L. Rept. 1079 (1983).
Farnsworth v. *Tribune Co.*, 253 N.E.2d 408 (1969).
Fawcett Publications v. *Morris*, 377 P.2d 42 (1962).
Fleckstein v. *Friedman*, 195 N.E. 537 (1934).
Forrest v. *Lynch and Times-Picayune Co.*, 347 So.2d 1255 (1977).
Fowler v. *New York Herald*, 172 N.Y.S. 423 (1918).
Franklin v. *Lodge 1108*, 97 Cal. App.3d 915 (1979).
Garrison v. *Louisiana*, 379 U.S. 64 (1964).
Gautsche v. *New York*, 415 N.Y.S.2d 280 (1979).
General Products v. *Meredith Corp.*, 526 F. Supp. 546 (1981).
Gertz v. *Welch*, 94 S.Ct. 2997 (1974).
Glover v. *Herald Co.*, 549 S.W.2d 858 (1977).
Goldwater v. *Ginzburg*, 414 F.2d 324 (1969).
Hentell v. *Knopf*, 8 M.L. Rept. 1908 (1982).
Herbert v. *Lando*, 441 U.S. 153 (1979).
Hoeppner v. *Dunkirk Printing Co.*, 172 N.E. 139 (1930).
Hoffman v. *Washington Post*, 433 F. Supp. 600 (1977).
Hope v. *Hearst Corp.*, 294 F.2d 681 (1961).
Hornby v. *Hunter*, 385 S.W.2d 473 (1964).
Horvath v. *Ashtabula Telegraph*, 8 M.L. Rept. 1657 (1982).
Hutchinson v. *Proxmire*, 99 S. Ct. 2675 (1979).
Johnston v. *Corinthian Television*, 583 P.2d 1101 (1978).

Jones v. *Sun Publishing*, 292 S.E.2d 23 (1982).
Karp v. *Miami Herald*, 359 So.2d 580 (1978).
KFC of Bowling Green v. *Sanders*, 563 S.W.2d 8 (1978).
Kilgore v. *Younger*, 180 Cal. Rptr. 657 (1982).
Krauss v. *Champaign News Gazette*, 375 N.E.2d 1362 (1978).
Kutz v. *Independent Publishing*, 638 P.2d 1088 (1981).
Lawrence v. *Moss*, 639 F.2d 635 (1981).
Lerman v. *Chuckleberry Publications*, 521 F. Supp. 228 (1981).
Loeb v. *Globe Newspaper*, 489 F. Supp. 481 (1980).
MacDonald v. *Time*, 7 M.L. Rept. 1981 (1981).
MacDonald v. *Time*, 554 F. Supp. 1053 (1983).
McNair v. *Hearst Corp.*, 494 F.2d 1309 (1974).
Madison v. *Yunker*, 589 P.2d 126 (1978).
Malerba v. *Newsday*, 406 N.Y.S.2d 552 (1978).
Marcone v. *Penthouse*, 533 F. Supp. 353 (1982).
Mashburn v. *Collin*, 355 So.2d 879 (1977).
Mathis v. *Philadelphia Newspapers*, 455 F. Supp. 406 (1978).
Maule v. *New York Magazine*, 429 N.Y.S.2d 891 (1980).
Medico v. *Time*, 634 F.2d 134 (1981).
Memphis Publishing Co. v. *Nichols*, 569 S.W.2d 412 (1978).
Michigan Conservation Clubs v. *CBS*, 665 F.2d 110 (1981).
Miskovsky v. *Oklahoma Publishing*, 7 M.L. Rept. 2607 (1982).
Morgan v. *Dun & Bradstreet, Inc.*, 421 F.2d 1241 (1970).
Myers v. *Boston Magazine*, 403 N.E.2d 376 (1980).
Nader v. *deToledano*, 408 A.2d 31 (1979).
Neiman-Marcus v. *Lait*, 13 F.R.D. 311 (1952).
New York Times Co. v. *Sullivan*, 376 U.S. 254 (1964).
Old Dominion Branch No. 496, National Association of Letter Carriers v. *Austin*, 94 S.Ct. 2770 (1974).
Ollman v. *Evans*, 9 M.L. Rept. 1969 (1983).
Orbach v. *New York News*, 3 M.L. Rept. 2229 (1978).
Orr v. *Argus Press*, 586 F.2d 1108 (1978).
Pauling v. *Globe-Democrat*, 362 F.2d 188 (1966).
Peagler v. *Phoenix Newspapers*, 547 P.2d 1074 (1976).
Pearson v. *Fairbanks Publishing Co.*, 413 P.2d 711 (1966).
People v. *Quill*, 177 N.Y.S.2d 380 (1958).
Perry v. *Hearst Corp.*, 334 F.2d 800 (1964).
Postill v. *Booth Newspapers*, 325 N.W.2d 511 (1982).
Powers v. *Durgin-Snow Publishing Co.*, 144 A.2d 294 (1958).
Press v. *Verran*, 589 S.W.2d 435 (1978).
Puerto Rican Legal Defense Fund v. *Grace*, 9 M.L. Rept. 1514 (1983).
Pulverman v. *A. S. Abell Co.*, 228 F.2d 797 (1956).
Rand v. *New York Times*, 4 M.L. Rept. 1556 (1978).
Reynolds v. *Pegler*, 223 F.2d 429 (1955).
Roberts v. *Dover*, 525 F. Supp. 987 (1981).
Rosenblatt v. *Baer*, 383 U.S. 75 (1966).
Rubenstein v. *New York Post*, 9 M.L. Rept. 1581 (1983).
St. Amant v. *Thompson*, 390 U.S. 727 (1968).
Saunders v. *WHYY-TV*, 382 A.2d 257 (1978).
Seegmiller v. *KSL-TV*, 626 P.2d 968 (1981).

Shiles v. *News Syndicate Co.*, 261 N.E.2d 251 (1970).

Sims v. *KIRO*, 580 P.2d 642 (1978).

Slawik v. *News-Journal*, 428 A.2d 15 (1981).

Southard v. *Forbes*, 588 F.2d 140 (1979).

Steaks Unlimited v. *Deaner*, 623 F.2d 624 (1980).

Steere v. *Cupp*, 602 P.2d 1267 (1979).

Stevens v. *Sun Publishing Co.*, 240 S.E.2d 812 (1978).

Stillman v. *Paramount Pictures*, 147 N.E.2d 741 (1957).

Stone v. *Essex County Newspapers*, 330 N.E.2d 161 (1975).

Street v. *NBC*, 645 F.2d 1227 (1981).

Summerlin v. *Washington Star*, 7 M.L. Rept. 2460 (1981).

Tabart v. *Tipper*, 1 Camp. 350 (1808).

Taskett v. *King Broadcasting*, 546 P.2d 81 (1976).

Time, Inc. v. *Firestone*, 96 S.Ct. 958 (1976).

Triggs v. *Sun Printing and Publishing Association*, 71 N.E. 739 (1904).

Wade v. *Stocks*, 7 M.L. Rept. 2200 (1981).

Waldbaum v. *Fairchild Publications*, 627 F.2d 1287 (1980).

Walters v. *Sanford Herald*, 228 S.E.2d 766 (1976).

Washington Post v. *Kennedy*, 3 F.2d 207 (1924).

Wasserman v. *Time, Inc.*, 424 F.2d 920 (1970).

Weaver v. *Pryor-Jeffersonian*, 569 P.2d 967 (1977).

Wildmon v. *Hustler*, 508 F. Supp. 87 (1980).

Williams v. *Pasma*, 9 M.L. Rept. 1004 (1982).

Wilson v. *Scripps-Howard*, 642 F.2d 371 (1981).

Winters v. *Morgan*, 576 P.2d 1152 (1978).

Wolston v. *Reader's Digest*, 99 S.Ct. 2701 (1979).

Yiamouyiannis v. *Consumers Union*, 619 F.2d 932 (1980).

4 <u>INVASION OF PRIVACY</u>

Privacy: How much do we have? Every person seems to give up a little more privacy as each year passes. Each of us gives up considerable privacy to fully participate in our buy now–pay later, opinion-research-oriented, fully insured, credit-card, big-government, security-conscious society. There are people who have withdrawn from this kind of society to live in a cabin in a remote wilderness. But most modern Americans refuse to give up the comforts that modern life provides.

Privacy is a very difficult concept to define. It has many meanings. One individual may say that he believes in the right of privacy, but also believes that the police have the right to wiretap telephone conversations. A shopkeeper may assert that she stands behind the right of privacy, but is reluctant to give up the television cameras which scan every nook and cranny of the shop in an effort to discourage shoplifting. The government is supposed to help citizens protect their privacy; yet governments at all levels seriously invade our privacy by gathering massive amounts of data on private citizens for a variety of reasons, good and bad.

In 1888 in *Treatise on the Law of Torts* Thomas M. Cooley defined privacy as "the right to be let alone." More recently privacy was defined as the right of individuals to control information about themselves. The right of privacy was first proposed as a narrow legal right in 1890. However, as Professor Edward J. Bloustein writes in "Privacy as an Aspect of Human Dignity," "What began at the turn of the century as a limited private right to prevent undue and unreasonable publicity concerning private lives has now developed into an extraordinarily broad constitutional right, the limits of which are still not clear."

Today **invasion of privacy** encompasses a wide range of behavior which includes wiretapping, illegal surveillance, misuse of information by retail credit agencies, use of two-way mirrors in department store dressing rooms, and collection of private information by researchers, banks, and government agencies. The mass media are also frequently accused of invasion of privacy. This chapter is about invasion of privacy by the press, by radio and television, and by the motion-picture industry.

The chapter opens with a brief history of the law of privacy. Then each of the four ways in which the media can run afoul of the law for invasion of privacy is discussed and the defenses for each kind of invasion of privacy are outlined. It is important to remember this point. Invasion of privacy by the media really involves four distinct legal wrongs: (1) **appropriation** of an individual's name or likeness for commercial purposes without first getting consent, (2) **intrusion** upon a person's solitude, (3) **publication of private information** about a person, and (4) publication of false information about a person, or putting someone in a **false light.** Each area has defenses which the press may erect in an effort to ward off a plaintiff's lawsuit. The defenses that work for one kind of invasion of privacy suit are generally not effective in defending another kind of suit for invasion of privacy. The defense of newsworthiness, for example, can be used to stop a suit for the publication of private information, but the defense will not work in a suit based upon appropriation of a likeness or name. It is best to think of invasion of privacy as four separate legal problems, each with its own defenses.

Despite its apparent similarity to libel, the law of privacy is far less mature than its older tort cousin. In fact, from the standpoint of the centuries-old common law system, privacy is downright modern. Unlike most other areas of the law, we can say specifically that a legal remedy for invasion of privacy was first advocated less than one hundred years ago.

The concept of privacy is old, but the law of privacy is young, growing out of the dramatically changing social conditions of the late nineteenth century, the era which spawned present-day urban United States. The Industrial Revolution brought crowded cities and reduced space to a premium, and at the same time the American press changed profoundly. In the fight for circulation the mass press of the big cities undertook new schemes to attract readers. It is perhaps an understatement to note that this was not journalism's finest hour.

While privacy was something which people enjoyed and sought, it was not something with which our legal system could cope. There was no legal right to privacy, no law which guaranteed the right to be left alone. In 1890 two young lawyers proposed in the *Harvard Law Review* ("The Right to Privacy") that such a law should exist. One of the pair, the prominent Boston attorney Samuel D. Warren, was annoyed at what he described as the gossipy, snoopy Boston press which frequently focused on the social activities of the Warren family. Warren sought the aid of his former law partner, former Harvard Law School classmate and close friend, Louis D. Brandeis, in preparing a plea for the legal recognition of the right to be let alone.

The pair argued, "Instantaneous photographs and newspaper enterprise have invaded the sacred precincts of private and domestic life; and numerous mechanical devices threaten to make good the prediction that 'what is whispered in the closet shall be proclaimed from the house-tops.' " Warren and Brandeis said they were offended by the gossip in the press, which they said had overstepped in every direction the obvious bounds of propriety and decency:

> To satisfy a prurient taste the details of sexual relations are spread broadcast in the columns of the daily papers. To occupy the indolent, column upon column is filled with idle gossip, which can only be procured by intrusion upon the domestic circle. . . .
>
> The common law has always recognized a man's house as his castle, impregnable, often, even to its own officers engaged in the execution of its commands. Shall the courts thus close the front entrance to constituted authority, and open wide the back door to idle or prurient curiosity?

To stop this illicit behavior the two young lawyers proposed that the courts recognize the legal right of privacy; that is, citizens should be able to go to court to stop such unwarranted intrusions and also secure money damages for the hardship they suffered from such prying and publication of private material about them.

To a modern observer, the Boston press does not appear to be nearly so scandalous as the charges Warren and Brandeis suggested. One gets the distinct impression that Mr. Warren was an overly sensitive individual.

The article also appears to have been Warren's idea. He sought help from Brandeis, who was indeed a legal scholar. Brandeis later went on to have a distinguished career as a jurist. Finally, despite the eloquence of their plea, the Warren and Brandeis proposal fell on somewhat deaf ears. Thirteen years passed before any state recognized the legal right of privacy. In 1903 New York passed a privacy statute which guaranteed its citizens protection from invasion of their privacy, but the statute contained a far different concept of privacy than that proposed in 1890. What the New York law did was prohibit commercial exploitation of the name or picture of any citizen.

From these rather humble beginnings more than ninety years ago, privacy law has grown until today it is an important segment of our legal rights. It has also become a serious problem for the mass media. The courts or the legislatures in virtually all the states have recognized the legal claim of invasion of privacy. But the recognition of a right merely states a legal conclusion. It does not, by itself, provide a full set of legal principles which can be used to grant relief to a plaintiff. The law has grown over the past ninety-plus years by fits and starts. It has a somewhat ragged profile. Some parts of the right to privacy bear little resemblance at all to the plan proposed by Warren and Brandeis in 1890. In fact "the right to privacy" today contains dimensions which have little to do with what we traditionally think of as privacy. As noted previously, invasion of privacy today encompasses not just one, but four, legal wrongs. They are different and should be thought of as separate wrongs. Let us briefly summarize these four wrongs and then study each of them in depth.

The first kind of invasion of privacy is called appropriation and is defined as taking a person's name, picture, photograph, or likeness and using it without his permission for commercial gain. This is technically the only right of privacy which is guaranteed in some of the states which have privacy statutes. The laws are limited to outlawing this one kind of behavior. But as a matter of fact, judicial construction of these laws has allowed them to encompass many of the other aspects of invasion of privacy as well.

Intrusion is the second type of invasion of privacy, an area of the law growing rapidly today, and is what most people think of when invasion of privacy is mentioned. Intrusion upon the solitude and into the private life of a person is prohibited.

The law prohibits publication of private information—truthful private information—about a person. What is truthful private information? Gossip, substance of private conversations, and details of a private tragedy or illness have all been used as the basis of a suit.

Finally, the publication of any false information about a person can result in a privacy suit, whether the material is defamatory or not. The fourth area of the law is an outgrowth of the first, the appropriation area. Maybe both should be in a single category, but they are probably easier to understand when they are considered separately.

Some people have said that a law of privacy is really not needed. Several years ago law professor Frederick Davis ("What Do We Mean by Right to Privacy?") wrote, "Indeed, one can logically argue that the concept of a right of privacy was never required in the first place, and that its whole history is an illustration of how well-meaning but impatient academicians can upset the normal development of the law by pushing it too hard."

One can make a persuasive argument that Davis is right. The appropriation area of the law really deals with a property right and would probably fit more comfortably as part of the law of literary property, product disparagement, trademark protection, and the like. Intrusion is really more akin to the law of trespass. False information is very close to defamation. Publication of private information—the only truly unique aspect of the law—has enjoyed such limited success that it might be abandoned altogether with little loss. Control of this kind of behavior might better be left to public opinion and the conscience of reporters and editors, as Professor Zechariah Chafee once suggested.

Regardless of whether it is legally logical, the law of privacy does exist; it is a part of our legal system. Persons in the media must be constantly aware of it. The number of privacy suits seems to increase a little each year. A considerable number of cases are settled in favor of the plaintiff. For better understanding of the law, each of the four types or kinds of invasion of privacy is discussed at length in the pages that follow.

APPROPRIATION

Appropriation is the oldest and in many ways the least ambiguous of the four types of invasion of privacy. Two of the earliest cases remain good examples of this area of the law.

1. In 1902 young Abigail Roberson of Albany, New York, awoke one morning to find her picture all over town on posters advertising Franklin Mills Flour. Twenty-five thousand copies of the advertisement were placed in stores, warehouses, saloons, and other public buildings. Abigail said she felt embarrassed and humiliated, that she suffered greatly from this commercial ex-

ploitation, and she therefore sued for invasion of privacy. But she lost her case, and the state's high court ruled (*Roberson* v. *Rochester Folding Box Co.,* 1902):

> . . . an examination of the authorities leads us to the conclusion that the so-called "right of privacy" has not yet found an abiding place in our jurisprudence, and, as we view it, the doctrine cannot now be incorporated without doing violence to settled principles of law by which the profession and the public have long been guided.

Following this decision a great controversy arose in New York, led by the press, much of which expressed outrage at the way the court had treated Abigail. The controversy settled on the state legislature which during the following year, 1903, adopted the nation's first privacy law. The statute was very narrow: that is, it prohibited a very specific kind of conduct. Use of an individual's name or likeness without his consent for advertising or trade purposes was made a minor crime. In addition to the criminal penalty, the statute allowed the injured party to seek both an injunction to stop the use of the name or picture and money damages. This was the first privacy statute.

2. Two years later Georgia became the first state to recognize the right of privacy through the common law. Paolo Pavesich, an Atlanta artist, discovered that a life insurance company had used his photograph in newspaper advertisements. Pavesich's photograph was used in a before-and-after advertisement to illustrate a contented, successful man who had bought sufficient life insurance. A testimonial statement was also ascribed to the artist. He sued for $25,000 and won his case before the Georgia Supreme Court which ruled (*Pavesich* v. *New England Mutual Life Insurance Co.,* 1905):

> . . . the form and features of the plaintiff are his own. The defendant insurance company and its agents had no more authority to display them in public for the purpose of advertising the business . . . than they would have had to compel the plaintiff to place himself upon exhibition for this purpose.

Before the ramifications of this aspect of the law are discussed, let us ask the question, For what are plaintiffs compensated in an invasion of privacy suit? What is their damage? In a libel case the reputation is damaged, a fairly invisible injury. But in a privacy suit the damage is even more invisible: the damage is the humiliation, embarrassment, and general bother that an ordinary person might experience from invasion of privacy. In other words, the damage is personal. The right of privacy is a personal right.

Use of Name or Likeness

Everybody knows what a name is, and it is therefore unnecessary to dwell on that term. It should be noted, however, that stage names, pen names, pseudonyms, and so forth, count the same as real names in the eyes of the law. If the name of rock star Elton John is used in an advertisement for dental floss without his permission, the suit cannot be defended on the basis that since Elton John's real name is Reginald Kenneth Dwight his "name" was not appropriated illegally. It should also be noted that the law of privacy protects only people's names. Company names, trade names, and corporate names are not protected. Only people enjoy the right of privacy. Businesses, corporations, schools, and other "things" are not protected under the law. However, the use of a trade name like Kodak or Crest can create other serious legal problems.

What is a likeness? Obviously a photograph, a painting, and a sketch—anything that suggests to readers and viewers that the plaintiff is pictured—are likenesses. Federal courts in New York State ruled recently that a sketch of a black man sitting in the corner of a boxing ring was, for purposes of an invasion-of-privacy suit, the "likeness" of former heavyweight champion Muhammed Ali. The boxer looked a little like Ali, and the photograph was accompanied by a verse which referred to the boxer as "the Greatest" (*Ali* v. *Playgirl,* 1978). ABC Records lost the right-to-privacy suit brought by classical guitarist Jean Pierre Jumez over an album cover. As part of a promotional scheme to attract the attention of young people, ABC packaged Jumez's record in an album which depicted a bearded man playing a guitar. The hairy-legged individual, whose face was obscured, was dressed in a tuxedo jacket, but wore no pants. Jumez contended record buyers would think the picture was of him. "Any sufficiently clear representation of a living person is violative of the [New York] statute if it is used for commercial purposes without the subject's consent," the court ruled. Since the face of the man was obscured, record buyers could not tell whether the picture was of Jumez or not. But since the artist's name was on the album cover, people might surely believe Jumez was the individual in the picture (*Jumez* v. *ABC Records,* 1978).

What are advertising and trade purposes? While minor differences exist among the states—especially among the states with statutes—a general guideline can be set down: advertising or trade purposes are commercial uses; that is, someone makes money from the use. Here are examples of the kinds of actions which clearly are commercial use:

1. Use of a person's name or photograph in an *advertisement* on television, on radio, in newspapers, in magazines, on posters, on billboards, and so forth
2. Display of a person's photograph in the window of a photographer's shop to show potential customers the quality of work done by the studio
3. A testimonial falsely suggesting that an individual eats the cereal or drives the automobile in question

In Utah recently a broadcaster announced the name of a person on the "Dialing for Dollars" television feature. The individual sued, arguing that the program was simply an advertising device used by the station to attract viewers, and that since no consent was given for the use of the name over the air the use was an invasion of privacy. The Utah Supreme Court agreed with the plaintiff, declaring that the name had been used to promote a commodity—the television station (*Jeppson* v. *United Television,* 1978).

What about this argument? A newspaper runs a photograph of John Smith on the front page after his car rolled over several times during a high-speed police pursuit. Smith sues for invasion of privacy, arguing that his picture on the front page of the newspaper attracted readers to the paper, resulted in the sale of newspapers, and therefore was used for commercial or trade purposes. Despite the arguments of many persons—even today—courts have consistently rejected this claim.

This plea was first made in 1907 by a New Yorker who objected to having his picture appear on the front page of the *New York World.* The state supreme court rejected the argument, noting that surely the intent of the state legislature was not to prohibit a newspaper or magazine from publishing a person's name or picture in a single issue without his consent (*Moser* v. *Press Publishing Co.,* 1908). Two years later another New York court reiterated this stand, ruling that advertising and trade purposes referred to commercial use, not to the dissemination of information (*Jeffries* v. *New York Evening Journal,* 1910). The United States Supreme Court has ruled that the fact that newspapers and books and magazines are sold for profit does not deny them the protection of liberty of expression (*Time, Inc.* v. *Hill,* 1967).

Anyone who has worked in journalism for very long knows that material created for promotional or trade purposes is often published or broadcast under the guise of news or information. A newspaper, for example, may publish what appears to be a newsworthy column on new products. In reality the material is an advertisement for these new products. In these instances the courts will rule that the publication was made to further a trade purpose, and an invasion of privacy suit will often stand. But the courts scrutinize these cases quite closely and offer considerable leeway to the press. For example, *Seventeen* magazine features what it calls its "make-over" section each month. Teenage girls are given clothing, cosmetics, and considerable advice to use to try to improve their appearance. The article accompanying the before-and-after pictures discusses the make over and the brand names of products are prominently mentioned. The teenagers are paid and are supposed to sign permission forms, but one young woman inadvertently did not sign a model release. She sued and argued that her name and likeness had been appropriated for trade purposes. She lost. A court ruled that the article about grooming, makeup, and clothing was newsworthy to the teenage audience at which it was aimed. Mention of the brand names of products was incidental to the article and pictures (*Lopez* v. *Triangle Communications,* 1979). In a recent suit against *Family Circle* magazine a plaintiff contended that the publication by the magazine of a letter she had written to the authors was an advertisement for the authors' book. The book, *Your Baby's Sex: Now You Can Choose It,* was published in 1970 by Dodd, Mead & Company. The plaintiff successfully used the techniques suggested in the book and wrote an unsolicited laudatory letter to the authors. A revised edition of the book was to be published, and many of the unsolicited letters received by the authors were to be included in a chapter in the revision. *Family Circle* paid Dodd, Mead & Company $2,500 for the right to publish some of the material from the revised book—including plaintiff's letter—in an edition of the magazine. When this occurred, the plaintiff sued, arguing that the article was simply a promotion for the book, an advertisement in disguise. This was use of her name for a trade purpose she said. The Appellate Division of the New York Supreme Court disagreed, noting that *Family Circle* had paid for the right to publish the material, that Dodd, Mead & Company had not paid out one cent. Conceding that the article might have incidental promotional value for the book, this incidental value was not sufficient to create a trade purpose (*Heller* v. *Family Circle,* 1981).

The law of privacy, like all law, contains narrow exceptions to general rules, and what follows is one of them. Despite what has just been said, there is a category of advertisements in which use of a person's name or picture without consent is not an invasion of privacy. These are advertisements for media—newspapers, television, and magazines—which are otherwise protected by freedom of expression. The use of a person's name or picture in such an advertisement will not result in liability provided that the picture or name had been used earlier in a news or information story. Here is an example from a real case.

The controversy which sparked this rule involved actress Shirley Booth. She was photographed in Jamaica, and the picture was published in a feature story in *Holiday* magazine. *Holiday* then used the same picture to advertise the magazine itself. The full-page advertisement told readers that the picture was typical of the material appearing in *Holiday* magazine and urged people to advertise in the periodical or subscribe to *Holiday.* Ms. Booth did not object to her photograph in the feature story, only to its use in the subsequent advertisement. The courts, however, refused to call the use an invasion of privacy. The New York Supreme Court ruled that the strength of a free press depends upon economic support from advertisers and subscribers, and hence a publication or broadcasting station must promote itself. Since the picture in this case was first used in an information story, its subsequent use in a promotion for the magazine was really only "incidental" to its original use and was merely to show the quality and content of the magazine. The picture was not used to sell spaghetti or used cars. Hence the use did not constitute an invasion of privacy (*Booth* v. *Curtis Publishing Co.,* 1962).

In advertisements promoting itself a newspaper can republish stories and photographs which contain the names and pictures of people—private citizens as well as celebrities. A television station can put together a montage of news clips from stories it has broadcast and use the montage as a promotion. The advertisements must be for the medium itself—"self-ads" as they are sometimes called. A commercial firm cannot republish a news story in its advertising without liability. If there was a fire at the Acme Furniture Store, and the local newspaper wrote a long story about it which contained the names of firemen, employees, witnesses, and so forth, Acme could not republish this story in its Fire Sale advertisements unless it first deleted the names of the persons mentioned and covered up the faces of any persons identifiable in the photographs. The exception to the general rule applies only to advertisements for the mass media which contain pictures or names previously used in informational or news stories.

How far can a medium go in republishing or broadcasting stories and photographs for promotional purposes? While there are obviously limits, the courts have granted considerable leeway. Former professional quarterback Joe Namath sued *Sports Illustrated* when the magazine used a 1969 Super Bowl photograph of Namath (which it had previously published) to promote subscriptions to the magazine. This was an incidental republication of the picture, the court ruled (*Namath* v. *Sports Illustrated,* 1976). But performer Cher won a lawsuit against *Forum* magazine when it used her picture to promote an edition of the magazine. The promotional advertisements stated that Cher endorsed the magazine, which was not true. A United States district court in California ruled that the use of the performer's name and picture went much farther than establishing the news content and the quality of the periodical. The advertising was not merely incidental to the original publication. Complicating the case was the fact that *Forum* had illegally obtained the interview with Cher, but that was not a material factor in the court's ruling (*Cher* v. *Forum International,* 1982).

Consent as a Defense

The law prohibits only the unauthorized use of a name or picture. In those states that have privacy statutes, the law specifically requires that the consent be a written authorization from the subject. In the remainder of the states the law is more ambiguous on the question. Nevertheless, defendants are forced to prove they do have written consent if and when a lawsuit arises. Therefore, it only makes sense to obtain written consent. An example of a standard consent or release form appears on page 198.

The problems which can arise from the defense of consent are numerous, and in each case they are more severe when written consent has not been obtained. For example, it is always possible for the person to withdraw consent after it has been given. Columbia Broadcasting System prepared a fictional television drama about the kidnapping of Jackie Gleason. Gleason played himself in the story, and an actor played the part of Gleason's manager. The manager's real name was used in the script. Suddenly the manager decided after the program was filmed that he did not want his name included in the program. Despite the fact that he had worked on the play for many weeks, planning and writing, a New York court said that inclusion of the plaintiff's name in the film against his will constituted an invasion of privacy (*Durgom* v. *CBS*, 1961). While this suit falls under category four of invasion of privacy, the rules are the same for both appropriation and falsehood. Columbia Broadcasting was therefore forced to write the plaintiff out of the script and reshoot part of the production.

Had the network gained written consent from the subject, and had it paid the plaintiff for using his name in the play, he would have found it much harder—if not impossible—to revoke consent at the last minute. Written consent has a distinct advantage. The safest rule is to always get written consent. Photographers especially are advised to carry copies of a standard release form in their gadget bags so that when that once-in-a-lifetime picture comes along, the one they are certain to sell for $10,000, they can obtain written consent from the subject on the spot.

There are times when even written consent does not work as a defense, and the media must be aware of such situations.

1. Consent given today may not be valid ten years hence, especially if it is gratuitous oral consent. In Louisiana a man named Cole McAndrews gave permission to the owner of a health spa to use his before-and-after pictures in advertisements for the gym. But the owner, Alvin Roy, waited ten years to use the photographs, and in the interim McAndrews's life had changed considerably. He sued Roy, who argued that it was McAndrews's responsibility to revoke the consent if he no longer wanted the pictures used. But a Louisiana court of appeals agreed instead with the plaintiff. Judge Robert D. Jones wrote (*McAndrews* v. *Roy*, 1961):

> We are of the opinion that it would be placing an unreasonable burden on the plaintiff to hold he was under duty to revoke a gratuitous authorization given many years before. As the defendant was the only person to profit from the use of the pictures then, under all the circumstances, it seems reasonable that he should have sought renewal of the permission to use the old pictures.

Reauthorization is needed when a name or photograph is used many years after consent was first given. A professional actor in New York gave the manufacturer of artificial Christmas trees permission to use his picture in a commercial for one year. When the commercial was used after one year, he sued for appropriation, and the New York high court sustained his privacy suit against the challenge by the defendant that only an action for breach of contract should be permitted (*Welch* v. *Mr. Christmas Tree*, 1982).

2. Some persons cannot give consent. A teenage girl is perfect to appear in an Acme Shampoo advertising campaign. She agrees to pose and signs a release authorizing use of her picture in the advertisements. The pictures are great, the advertisements are great, everything is great—until notice arrives

that the model is suing for invasion of privacy! But she signed the permission form. Right. But she was only sixteen years old, and under the law minors cannot give consent. Parental consent is required in such instances. If parents or guardians do give consent for the use of a minor's name or picture, under the common law in many states it is possible for the minors to revoke that consent when they reach the legal age. When Brooke Shields was ten years old, a photographer was given permission by Brooke's mother to use a picture he had taken of the child model. The Appellate Division of the New York Supreme Court ruled that Brooke could revoke that consent when she became an adult (*Shields* v. *Gross,* 1982). But the state's high court reversed this ruling. The Court of Appeals said it recognized that such a revocation was possible under the common law, but the New York state privacy statute specifically permits parents to give written consent on behalf of a minor child. The statute, the court said, derogates, or rejects, the common law rule. Brooke Shields had no recourse, since her mother had previously given written permission for the use of the photograph (*Shields* v. *Gross,* 1983).

Other people are unable to give consent as well. Columbia Broadcasting System (CBS) was sued on behalf of David Delan by his guardian for including the young man in its film "Any Place But Here," a documentary about mental illness. Delan had been hospitalized for more than five years as a psychotic at the Creedmor State Hospital in New York. He was legally incompetent to sign a consent form, and the network failed to gain a signed release from a physician. A psychologist gave CBS permission to film David, but the New York state law specifically requires the signature of a medical doctor on the release agreement before patients in the state's mental hospitals can be photographed or interviewed (*Delan* v. *CBS,* 1981). CBS ultimately prevailed in the case when the Appellate Division of the New York Supreme Court ruled that the broadcast was not made for advertising or trade purposes, and therefore consent from David Delan was not required (*Delan* v. *CBS,* 1983). But the point made by the trial court is well taken. Persons who are unable to give consent because for one reason or another they are wards of the state are risky subjects for publications or broadcasts which are made for advertising or trade purposes.

It is important to know that the person from whom consent is obtained is legally able to give consent.

3. Finally, consent to use a photograph of a person in an advertisement or on a poster cannot be used as a defense if the photograph is materially altered or changed. Several years ago a well-known and well-paid New York fashion model posed for pictures to be used in an advertising campaign for a

bookstore. After the photography session, model Mary Jane Russell signed this standard release form:

> The undersigned hereby irrevocably consents to the unrestricted use by Richard Avedon [the photographer], advertisers, customers, successors, and assigns, of my name, portrait, or picture for advertising purposes or purposes of trade, and I waive the right to inspect or approve such completed portraits, pictures, or advertising matter used in connection therewith.

It sounds as though she signed her life away, and with regard to the pictures Avedon took she did. However, the bookstore sold one of the photographs to a maker of bed sheets. The bedding manufacturer had a reputation for running sleazy advertising and consequently had trouble getting first-class models to pose for advertising pictures. The manufacturer substantially retouched the Avedon photographs, changing the context. Mary Jane Russell sued for invasion of privacy, but the manufacturer answered her by telling the court that the model had given irrevocable consent for anyone to use those pictures, that she had waived her right to inspect the completed pictures and the advertising, and so forth.

The court agreed that Mary Jane had given up her right of privacy with regard to the pictures Avedon took. But the picture used by the sheet maker in its advertising was not the same picture taken by Avedon. It had been altered. And Mary Jane won her case. Justice Matthew Levy of the New York Supreme Court wrote (*Russell* v. *Marboro Books*, 1959):

> If the picture were altered sufficiently in situation, emphasis, background, or context, I should think that it would no longer be the same portrait, but a different one. And as to the changed picture, I would hold that the original written consent would not apply and that liability would arrive when the content of the picture has been so changed that it is substantially unlike the original.

What is substantial alteration? It probably means something other than minor retouching, but how much retouching is permissible before a privacy suit can accrue is difficult to say. This is one of the few cases on this legal point. Persons who want to retouch a photograph should be careful, even when they have written consent. They might change the picture sufficiently so that the consent would not apply.

The reference to altering the context of a picture arose recently in New York when a model sued and won after her seminude photograph was used to advertise an allegedly obscene movie. She had signed a release permitting the use of her photograph for "any purpose whatsoever," but the New York Supreme Court ruled that "any purpose whatsoever" does not include a "degrading use" (*Dittner* v. *Troma*, 1980).

Right of Publicity   In 1953, a distinguished American jurist, Jerome Frank, noted in an appropriation case that some plaintiffs might indeed be embarrassed and humiliated to see their name or face used to promote cornflakes or shampoo. Yet other plaintiffs, Frank argued, were not upset because they were humiliated; they were angry because they had not been paid for the commercial exploitation of their name or likeness (*Haelan Laboratories, Inc., v. Topps Chewing Gum*, 1953). Judge Frank identified what he called the "right of publicity," the right of persons to control the commercial exploitation of their name or likeness. The logic behind this assertion is that persons have a property right in their name just as they can have a property right in a book or a piece of land.

The relative youth and somewhat ambiguous state of the law of privacy resulted in most courts ignoring Judge Frank's ideas for many years. However, recently several jurisdictions have accepted the idea of this property right ancillary to the right of privacy.

Right of publicity cases generally involve persons who have developed a significant property right in their names through their exploits. Athletes, entertainers, writers, and other celebrities have all argued that the use of their name without consent and without compensation deprived them of rightful income. In cases in 1967 and 1970 courts ruled that several professional athletes like Arnold Palmer and Jack Nicklaus have the right to enjoy the fruits of their own industry free from unjustified interference, and that celebrities have a legitimate proprietary interest in their public personality. These cases involved the use of the athletes' names and pictures in board games without compensation or permission (*Palmer v. Schonhorn Enterprises*, 1967, and *Uhlaender v. Henricksen*, 1970). A judge noted that the celebrity's "identity, embodied in his name, likeness, statistics and other personal characteristics, is the fruit of his labors and a type of property." However, in New Jersey a court said that even noncelebrities enjoy a property right in their identity when it ruled that a real estate company could not use a family's name and picture in its advertisements without permission (*Canessa v. J. I. Kislak*, 1967). "However little or much plaintiff's likeness and name may be worth," the judge wrote, "defendant, who has appropriated them for his commercial benefit, should be made to pay for what he has taken. . . ."

Some courts have simply refused to recognize the claims of the right of publicity. When comedian Pat Paulsen announced his candidacy for president in 1968, unauthorized campaign posters of the comedian were published. Paulsen sued, claiming appropriation of his likeness (*Paulsen v. Personality Posters*, 1968). But the court refused to compensate the entertainer, arguing that by declaring for president, even in jest, he had lost his right to privacy regarding his picture (see also *Man v. Warner Brothers*, 1970).

In its only ruling on the subject, the Supreme Court of the United States left many observers bewildered when it ruled that it is a violation of the right to publicity for a television station to broadcast news film of an entertainer's entire performance (*Zacchini* v. *Scripps-Howard Broadcasting Co.,* 1977). In a case which clearly proves the old judicial maxim that hard cases make bad law, the high Court overturned a decision by the Ohio Supreme Court and ruled that Hugo Zacchini, "The Human Cannonball," had indeed been harmed by the broadcast. The case was a hard one for at least two reasons. Zacchini's performance—being shot out of a cannon into a net—took only about fifteen seconds and consequently fit neatly into a small segment on a thirty-minute newscast. Obviously such is not the case with most performers. Also, Zacchini had specifically asked the television station employees not to film the act, which was playing at a local county fair. A cameraman filmed it anyway. Zacchini argued that the television broadcast hurt his ability to make a living. Why should people pay to get into the fair to see his act if they had seen it on the television news? Justice Byron White and four other members of the high Court agreed. The broadcast of the film of Zacchini's *entire* performance posed a substantial threat to the economic value of that performance, Justice White wrote. It went to the heart of his ability to earn a living as an entertainer, he added. Yet the ruling raised more questions than it answered. In previous right-of-publicity cases the defendant had gained monetarily by exploiting the plaintiff's name or likeness. Yet in this case the television station made no monetary gain from showing the short film of Zacchini being shot from a cannon. The cannon shot was a news item, like an automobile accident or a street parade.

White made the point that the station televised the *entire act.* But what does this mean? Zacchini took several minutes to do his act—adjusting the net, preparing to get into the cannon, building the suspense. The film lasted but fifteen seconds and included only the actual cannon shot. Would a newspaper be prohibited from publishing a detailed word description of the feats of Zacchini? If Zacchini were seriously injured in performing this stunt, could the accident be safely filmed? The dissenters in the case argued strongly— but to little avail—that the important question to be decided was not whether Zacchini's *entire act* was broadcast, but the purpose for which the film was used. Had the station filmed the shot, promoted it, built a show around it, and got advertisers to pay money to sponsor it? Such action would clearly be exploitation of Zacchini. But this was a routine newscast, Justice Powell noted. There was no violation of any right.

The Zacchini case will probably have little impact upon the emerging— and often confusing—right of publicity. White's ruling was based largely on the fact that the television station telecast the *entire act.* Since few performers have such abbreviated acts, there seems to be few persons who could use the ruling as a precedent in a similar suit.

While the right to privacy is a personal right and in nearly all states (Georgia is one exception) ends upon the death of the individual, the right of publicity—based upon a theory of property rights—does not necessarily terminate upon death. In some instances it may be passed on to benefit the heirs like any other part of the estate. But this aspect of the law is currently in a state of hopeless confusion because of contradictory court rulings and the unwillingness of the Supreme Court of the United States to settle the question. In about one-half of the reported decisions regarding the survivability of the right of publicity, the courts have ruled that the right can survive the death of well-known or prominent figures. This rule normally applies, however, only if the well-known individuals attempted to exploit that right during their lifetime. That is, if the performers sold the right to use their name in advertising or on T-shirts or in some other way, their heirs have the exclusive right to do the same thing. Here are some cases which demonstrate this rule.

The estate of Agatha Christie attempted to stop the presentation of the film *Agatha* on the grounds that it violated the writer's right of publicity, a right which had been passed on to the estate when Mrs. Christie died. The court agreed that Mrs. Christie had recognized the extrinsic commercial value of her name while she lived and attempted to exploit this value through various contracts with publishing companies. Hence, the right could be assigned to her estate like any other piece of property (*Hicks* v. *Casablanca Records et al.,* 1978). Because the film was obviously fictitious, however, the court ruled that the right of publicity had not been violated, and the estate lost the suit.

The heirs of actor Bela Lugosi were not successful when they attempted to stop Universal Studios from exploiting the Count Dracula characterization created by Lugosi when he worked for the motion-picture company. The court ruled that because during his lifetime Bela Lugosi had not tried to exploit his name and likeness for commercial purposes he had not created a property right which could then be assigned to an heir upon his death. The estate did not enjoy the exclusive right of publicity to the image created by the horror film actor (*Lugosi* v. *Universal,* 1979).

The limitations upon the use of material about an individual who did exploit the right to publicity prior to death are not total by any means. Marilyn Monroe was astute enough to take full advantage of the publicity value of her name and likeness while she was alive. Yet the New York Supreme Court ruled in 1979 that despite her right to publicity which she passed on to heirs a publishing company could not be stopped from printing and distributing an illustrated biography of the blond motion-picture star (*Frosch* v. *Grossett & Dunlap,* 1979).

Other courts have rejected this argument, stating the right to publicity dies with the death of the performer or celebrity who exploited it while alive. The confusion between these two rules has created a serious legal mess regarding the right of publicity, the late Elvis Presley, and the state of Tennessee.

We will briefly recount this conundrum to document the sorry state of legal clarity in this area.

In 1978 the Second United States Court of Appeals (whose jurisdiction is Connecticut, New York, and Vermont) ruled that because Elvis Presley had exploited his name and likeness in many ways while he was alive this property right could be assigned to his heirs and that a company called Pro Arts could not sell posters of Presley memorializing his death (*Factors, Etc.* v. *Pro Arts, Inc.*, 1978). But two years later the Sixth United States Court of Appeals (whose jurisdiction is Kentucky, Michigan, Ohio, and *Tennessee*) ruled in just the opposite manner in a suit brought by Presley's heirs against a Memphis company which was selling eight-inch pewter replicas of a Presley statue for twenty-five dollars each. The court said the right of publicity should not be given the status of a "devisable right," even where a person has exploited that right during life (*Memphis Development Company* v. *Factors, Etc.*, 1980). Pro Arts petitioned the Second United States Court of Appeals for a rehearing on the basis of the *Memphis Development* decision, and in June 1981, the court reversed itself and said Presley's right of publicity died when he died. Why did the court reverse itself? In deciding whether Elvis Presley's right of publicity could be passed on to his heirs both United States courts of appeal were attempting to determine the applicable *state* law in this instance. It was Tennessee law that counted, since that was where Presley lived and where Factors, Etc., the company licensed to control publicity about the performer, was incorporated. Tennessee is included within the jurisdiction of the Sixth United States Court of Appeals; hence it is the court which can most authoritatively expound Tennessee law. Judges in the Second United States Court ruled that they must defer to the judgment of the Sixth United States Court of Appeals. Hence, the 1978 decision was reversed (*Factors, Etc.* v. *Pro Arts*, 1981). (See also *Groucho Marx Productions* v. *Day and Night Co.*, 1982.)

Complicating this matter even more are two Tennessee state court decisions: one which said that the right of publicity may be passed on to heirs in Tennessee (*Commerce Union Bank* v. *Coors*, 1981), and one which ruled that the right of publicity may not be passed on to survivors (*Lancaster* v. *Factors*, 1982). The Supreme Court of the United States was asked to try to resolve some of the legal questions, but refused to review the *Factors, Etc.* v. *Pro Arts* decision.

The Georgia Supreme Court seemingly confused the issue even more when it recently ruled that the right of publicity survives death, regardless of whether individuals exploited it during their lifetime. The case involved attempts by the Martin Luther King Center to stop another firm from marketing a plastic bust of the Reverend Dr. King. In this case the court said that Dr. King probably did not exploit his likeness during his lifetime because it would have impaired his ministry, but that this fact should not stop his estate from protecting his memory from exploitation after death (*The Martin Luther King Center* v. *American Heritage Products*, 1982).

While the question of the survivability of the right of publicity is a confusing matter, it is not an unimportant question. As one legal scholar recently noted, from the time that "George Washington slept here" until today, this kind of exploitation has undoubtedly become a part of the national system of advertising and promotion. Resolution of this issue is sorely needed, and the sooner the better.

Summary

Appropriation of a person's name or likeness without permission for commercial or trade purposes is an invasion of privacy. Use of an individual's photograph, a sketch of the person, a nickname, or stage name are all considered use of a name or likeness. However, the publication of news and information in magazines, books, newspapers, and news broadcasts is not considered a trade purpose, even though the mass medium may make a profit from such publication. Consequently, persons who are named or pictured in news stories or other such material cannot sue for appropriation. Also, a news medium may republish or rebroadcast news items or photographs already carried as news stories in advertising for the mass medium to establish the quality or kind of material carried by the medium.

Anyone who seeks to use the name or likeness of an individual for commercial or trade purposes should gain written consent from that person. Even written consent may be invalid as a defense in an invasion of privacy suit if the consent was given many years before publication, if the person from whom the consent was gained cannot legally give consent, or if the photograph or other material that is used is substantially altered.

Courts have also recognized what is known as the right to publicity. Right to publicity actions are most often instituted by well-known persons who believe the unauthorized use of their name or likeness has deprived them of an opportunity to reap financial gain by selling this right to the user. The United States Supreme Court has ruled that it is a violation of the right to publicity for a television news station to broadcast an entertainer's complete act without permission, even if this is done in the context of a news broadcast. In some states the right to publicity can be passed on to heirs like any other piece of property, which means that a performer's estate can control the use of his or her name and likeness after the performer's death.

INTRUSION

The intrusion category is what a lot of people think of when they hear the phrase "right to privacy." Wiretapping, using cameras with telephoto lenses, peeping-Tom actions, bugging rooms, using supersensitive microphones and hidden transmitters are the kinds of behavior that many people—especially people outside the press—associate with violations of the right to privacy. This kind of behavior does occur, people are caught, and lawsuits do result. Until recently such suits were simply not brought against mass-media defendants. Even now such litigation is relatively rare.

The press does not often go in for this kind of snooping or at least does not get caught frequently. Probably, the earliest known intrusion case involving the press occurred in 1926 when a reporter for the *Washington* (D.C.) *Herald* stole a picture from the home of Mrs. Louise Peed, who had nearly died from asphyxiation when a gas jet was carelessly left open in the home of a friend she was visiting. The court held the newspaper responsible because it had published the plaintiff's picture, not because it had stolen the picture (*Peed v. Washington Times Co.,* 1927). A similar suit in Los Angeles a few years later failed altogether (*Metter v. Los Angeles Examiner,* 1939).

The *Peed* case points out a very important aspect of intrusion in invasion of privacy. In appropriation cases and in cases based upon publication of private information or publication of falsehoods, the legal wrong occurs when the picture or story is published. It must be published. A photographer who takes a picture of a skier, enlarges it to eight-by-ten inches, and hangs it on his kitchen wall has not invaded the skier's privacy. If he were to publish the picture in an advertisement, for example, appropriation, an illegal invasion of privacy, then occurs. If a newspaper reporter uncovers private information about a teacher's life but keeps the information to himself, no invasion of privacy occurs. Only when he publishes this information might a lawsuit succeed.

In intrusion, however, the legal wrong is committed as soon as the intrusion takes place, whether the fruits of the intrusion are published. If your home is bugged, someone intrudes upon your privacy. Invasion of privacy occurred regardless of whether the content of the overheard conversations are published. If a reporter breaks into a private office and copies information from a private file, his act would probably be considered an invasion of privacy, an intrusion.

Intrusion cases are not too common. Those that have occurred seem to fall into a handful of categories. Here are some examples of the kinds of intrusion problems faced by the mass media.

Publication of Material Obtained Through Intrusion

In two cases in the late sixties federal courts in Washington, D.C., established the principle that a news medium which publishes material obtained via intrusion by someone not connected with the medium cannot be held liable for the intrusion. In the two instances, the late newspaper columnist Drew Pearson obtained documents from private files of the Liberty Lobby, a right-wing, public-interest group in Washington, and from the files of former Connecticut Senator Thomas Dodd. Employees of both Dodd and Liberty Lobby took the files from the private offices, made copies of them (which were given to Pearson), and then returned the purloined files. In both cases the court ruled that the publishers could not be held responsible for the actions of the intruders (*Liberty Lobby v. Pearson,* 1968; *Pearson v. Dodd,* 1969).

Judge J. Skelly Wright wrote in the *Dodd* case:

> If we were to hold appellants liable for invasion of privacy on these facts, we would establish the proposition that one who receives information from an intruder, knowing it has been obtained by improper intrusion, is guilty of a tort. In an untried and developing area of tort law, we are not prepared to go so far, . . .

This principle was supported in 1978 by a Maryland circuit court when several former and current members of the University of Maryland basketball team sued the *Baltimore Evening Star* for publishing an article which revealed portions of their academic record. Somebody gave the newspaper the information. There was no evidence presented that the reporters had either personally inspected the records or asked someone else to do it. Consequently, no suit could be maintained by the athletes on the intrusion theory (*Bilney* v. *Evening Star,* 1979).

Possessing Stolen Property

There is, however, another aspect of intrusion which can result in a problem for a journalist. If a reporter has original files that belong to someone else, a suit based on the doctrine of conversion could possibly be maintained. Conversion means to unlawfully convert someone else's property for your own use. This is property law and would be applicable only if journalists have the actual files—someone else's property—in their possession. In both the *Dodd* and *Liberty Lobby* cases just noted the plaintiffs attempted to sue for conversion, but columnist Pearson did not have the original files, only copies of those files. Hence, no conversion had occurred.

In California the publisher and a reporter of the *Los Angeles Free Press* were found guilty of possession of stolen goods after they bought a list of names of undercover narcotic agents stolen from the attorney general's office. Art Kunkin and Robert Applebaum were freed upon appeal to the state's high court, but only because there was insufficient evidence to prove that they had known the list was stolen when they purchased it (*People* v. *Kunkin,* 1973). If the state could have adduced any evidence at all that the pair had knowledge that the list was stolen, the conviction would have stood. As it was, the thief was a former employee of the attorney general's office, and Kunkin and Applebaum said they thought he still worked for the attorney general. The thief also asked that they return the list to him after it was copied, presumably to return it to the proper file, the two journalists said.

This whole area of the law is gray. Of course, if employees of the publication are the intruders, liability might result, depending upon whether they acted on their own or at the employer's suggestion. In any case, intruders are always liable if they are caught, regardless of what use is made of the purloined material.

Journalists should ask tough questions of their sources of documents and files. Did you steal it? Did you copy it illegally? If a jury can be convinced that the journalist knew it was obtained illegally, or should have known it was obtained illegally (secret files, for example, can normally only be obtained illegally), a suit based on property law, not on privacy, might then in fact hold up.

News Gathering

While reporters may not engage in stealing or breaking and entering, they may undertake other kinds of intrusions. These intrusions are harder to define, and generally involve the use of snooper aids, that is, hidden cameras, telephoto lens, and hidden microphones.

No broad, general proposition can be stated here, and we must rely instead upon examples. Hopefully, as more and more cases are litigated, the gaps will be filled and a rule formulated. Reporters have the right to photograph persons in public places, even when they do not know they are being photographed. These people are present in a public, not a private, place and are visible to anyone passing by. A recent ruling by the Eighth United States Circuit Court of Appeals supports this proposition. An attorney who was jailed for drunken driving became angry when jailed and began hitting and banging on the cell door, hollering and cursing, and calling police officers names. The sounds were recorded by a television reporter, who played them during a newscast. The attorney sued for invasion of privacy, but the appellate court ruled that there was no zone of privacy in a jail cell. The court ruled that the reporter "could not be prevented from reporting the statements he could so easily overhear aurally; use of a device to record them cannot create a claim for privacy when one would not otherwise exist." The court noted that undoubtedly the plaintiff had not made his boisterous outbursts with any expectation of privacy at all (*Holman* v. *Central Arkansas Broadcasting*, 1979).

On record is a case in which harassment, not invasion of privacy, was charged. In another state the case might have been a privacy case, but New York does not recognize this kind of invasion of privacy. The photographer was Ron Galella, whose whole life seemed to revolve around taking pictures of Jacqueline Kennedy Onassis. He went everywhere she went, blocked her path, made a general nuisance of himself. When he was not around Mrs. Onassis, he followed the Kennedy children. In one instance his penchant for getting close almost resulted in a serious accident for young John Kennedy when the horse he was riding bolted after being frightened by Galella. The Secret Service, which guards the Kennedy children and Mrs. Onassis, went to court to stop Galella. A federal court enjoined the photographer from coming within twenty-four feet of Mrs. Onassis and within thirty feet of the children, from blocking their movement in any way, from doing anything which might put them in danger or might harass, alarm, or frighten them, and from entering the children's play area at school (*Galella* v. *Onassis,* 1973). In 1982 a United

States district court in New York found Galella in contempt of court for violating this order on twelve separate occasions. The photographer faced a severe fine and possible imprisonment (*Galella* v. *Onassis, 1982*).

The lawsuit against Galella was based on harassment. Could an invasion of privacy suit for intrusion have worked as well for Mrs. Onassis? No. Taking pictures on a public street or in a public schoolyard is not considered an intrusion. In an intrusion suit the courts will ask, Was there any expectation of privacy or solitude for the plaintiff when the photograph was taken? There can be none in a public setting. What can be seen on a public street or in a public park is open to public scrutiny. A pharmacist in Seattle, Washington, sued KING-TV for invasion of privacy after the television station photographed the interior of his pharmacy through the front window. The druggist had been charged with cheating the state out of Medicaid funds. He refused to talk with reporters after the charges were made, so the KING-TV camera operator placed the camera against the outside of the store's front window and photographed the druggist as he talked on the telephone. The filming was done from the exterior of the building, from a place open to the public. The court ruled that an intrusion must be something which the general public would not be free to view. In this case any passerby could have seen what was recorded on film by the KING-TV camera operator. There was no unwarranted intrusion (*Marks* v. *King Broadcasting, 1980*).

There are some instances when an invasion of privacy suit based upon photography may very well stand. For example, imagine that a homeowner has a fenced-in yard with a pool. The pool area is hidden from public view by a fence and foliage. Surely someone at pool side would enjoy the expectation of privacy. But a photographer climbs a nearby hill and using a supertelephoto lens takes photographs of persons swimming in the pool. This action could very likely be considered an intrusion. Or imagine that a photographer films the interior of a home through a crack in the draperies while standing on private property surrounding the home. This is a scene that a passerby would not see. This, too, is fertile ground for an intrusion suit. Many problems also surround the use of hidden cameras and recording devices, as the next series of cases readily demonstrates.

A disabled veteran and journeyman plumber named A. A. Dietemann practiced healing using clay, minerals, and herbs. Dietemann practiced his strange version of medicine in his home. It was there that two *Life* magazine reporters who had agreed to work with Los Angeles law enforcement people visited the healer. Jackie Metcalf and William Ray pretended they were married, and Ms. Metcalf complained of a lump in her breast. Dietemann diagnosed the ailment as due to rancid butter she had eaten eleven years, nine months, seven days previously. While the "doctor" examined Ms. Metcalf, Ray photographed him with a secret camera. The conversation between the reporters (who did not reveal that they were reporters) and the healer was also broadcast via a hidden microphone to investigators waiting in a car outside.

Dietemann was arrested weeks later and charged with practicing medicine without a license. *Life* photographers took more pictures at the time of the arrest, and in an article on medical quackery included those pictures with pictures taken by the hidden camera. Dietemann sued for invasion of privacy. *Life* magazine said the pictures were informational and newsworthy and were protected. The court agreed that the pictures were indeed newsworthy, but ruled that they had been obtained by intruding upon Dietemann's privacy. The magazine had the right to publish the pictures; the publication did not constitute an invasion of privacy. It was the use of the secret camera and microphone which turned the relatively routine news-gathering venture into an illegal intrusion into Dietemann's privacy. Judge Shirley Hufstedler wrote (*Dietemann* v. *Time, Inc.,* 1971):

> One who invites another into his home or office takes a risk that the visitor may not be what he seems, and that the visitor may repeat all he hears and observes when he leaves. But he does not and should not be required to take the risk that what is heard and seen will be transmitted by photography or recording, or in our modern world, in full living color and hi-fi to the public at large or any segment of it that the visitor might select.

Recognizing that news gathering is an integral part of news dissemination, Judge Hufstedler said she still did not believe there was a need to use mechanical devices in gathering information:

> The First Amendment is not a license to trespass, to steal, or to intrude by electronic means into the precincts of another's home or office. It does not become such a license simply because the person subjected to the intrusion is reasonably suspected of committing a crime.

The magazine protested, saying the story was simply an example of good investigative reporting. Judge Hufstedler was unimpressed:

> Investigative reporting is an ancient art; its successful practice long antecedes the invention of miniature cameras and electronic devices. The First Amendment has never been construed to accord newsmen immunity from torts or crimes committed during the course of news gathering.

The facts in the *Dietemann* case are significant. The reporters were in the plaintiff's home, posing as persons other than reporters, taking secret pictures and making a clandestine recording of the conversation. Cases since 1971 have demonstrated the importance of the nature of the intrusion in the *Dietemann* case.

In 1975 Arlyn Cassidy and several other Chicago police officers were acting as undercover agents, investigating massage parlors in the city. The owner of one massage parlor where police previously had made arrests believed he was being harassed by the lawmen and invited a television news camera crew to come in and secretly film an encounter between an undercover agent and a model at the parlor. The camera was set up behind a two-way mirror and was filming when officer Cassidy came in, paid thirty dollars for deluxe lingerie modeling, and subsequently arrested the girl for solicitation. Three other agents came into the room at about the same time the television news crew burst through another door, filming as they left the building. The officers sued the station for intrusion, using the *Dietemann* case as precedent.

But the Illinois appellate court ruled in favor of the journalists, distinguishing the *Dietemann* case in two important ways. First, Cassidy and the other plaintiffs were public officers acting in the line of duty as the filming took place. Second, the film crew was not in a private home, but in a public business. "In our opinion," the court ruled, "no right of privacy against intrusion can be said to exist with reference to the gathering and dissemination of news concerning discharge of public duties" (*Cassidy* v. *ABC,* 1978).

In 1979 a Kentucky circuit court ruled that it was not an intrusion when a young woman, at the instigation of a newspaper, secretly recorded a conversation she had with an attorney. Kristie Frazier met with attorney John T. McCall after she was indicted on a drug charge. According to Ms. Frazier, the attorney said he would guarantee that he could get her "off the hook" if she could come up with $10,000. He said he would return $9,000 if he failed to have her set free. Setting a fee in a criminal case in such a manner is considered unethical conduct for an attorney.

Ms. Frazier, who apparently was no stranger to legal problems, recognized the unusual fee arrangement and went to the offices of the *Louisville Courier-Journal.* Reporters were interested in Ms. Frazier's allegations against McCall, but were unwilling to take her word for what had been said in the private conversation. They gave her a small tape recorder and told her to propose a second meeting with McCall—to try to trap him into repeating what he had said earlier. McCall repeated his proposal, Ms. Frazier recorded it secretly, and the *Courier-Journal* published the transcript. McCall sued for intrusion, but lost.

The court distinguished *Dietemann* by noting that Frazier—who may or may not have been an agent of the newspaper—was in McCall's office at his invitation. There was no intrusion into McCall's private affairs because they were also the affairs of Ms. Frazier. "A lawyer, an officer of the court, discussing in a public court with a potential client, is not in seclusion within the meaning of the law," the court ruled. "Human dignity demands the rights of privacy be enforced, but when the rights of privacy encroach upon the most sacred trust the public possesses, namely, the judicial system, then those rights must give way," the judge added (*McCall* v. *Courier-Journal*, 1979). The trial court ruling for the newspaper was upheld in March 1980 by the Kentucky court of appeals.

Cassidy and *McCall* have chipped away at some of the fears the press had after the *Dietemann* case. The California case must be viewed as a fairly narrow ruling. Remember, the intrusion in *Dietemann* took place in the plaintiff's home, and Anglo-American courts have protected a citizen's home from government intrusions for centuries. ("A man's home is his castle," ruled Lord Chief Justice Sir Edward Coke in the early seventeenth century.) Remember also that the reporters carried hidden electronic devices into the plaintiff's home. The courts have suggested that different rules apply in public places and in business offices, especially when public officers (such as police officers and attorneys who are considered officers of the court) are being scrutinized in the performance of their duty. Some persons have expressed concern that an intrusion may occur if a reporter poses as someone other than a reporter to gain a story. That is not likely; the fact that reporters posed as patients in the *Dietemann* case does not appear to be a material consideration. This conclusion is strengthened by the decision in *Rifkin* v. *Esquire,* 1982, when a United States district court in California ruled that no invasion of privacy took place when reporters posed as a friend of the plaintiff, Stan Rifkin, in order to get information about Rifkin from his friends and neighbors. The court said this did not constitute an intrusion upon plaintiff Rifkin's solitude.

Because intrusion is such a new area of the law, no good defenses have been developed. A heavy burden rests upon the plaintiff to prove that the behavior by the reporter or cameraman was in fact an intrusion, an invasion of privacy. If invasion of privacy can be established, there are no good "legal excuses" with which to defend this behavior. In addition to the legal problems involved, members of the press themselves have begun to raise ethical questions about such behavior. Defending illegal behavior on the grounds that it is in the public interest is an excuse which the American people seemed to reject when the members of the Nixon White House used it in 1973 and 1974. There are few causes that are "good enough" to justify illegal intrusion upon the privacy of others. Intrusion as an aspect of invasion of privacy should really not be a problem to journalists who conduct their business in an ethical fashion. Still, the paucity of good guidelines at this time can be somewhat frightening. Until there is more law to guide the press, journalists are advised to be guided by the common sense, conscience, and integrity one normally expects from responsible adults.

Trespass

An invasion of privacy suit for intrusion is one legal problem facing a reporter who pursues the news a bit too aggressively. Other intrusion-like situations must be understood. **Trespass,** the failure to respect authorized police barricades, and the failure to obey the lawful order of a police officer can pose other, equally serious problems for journalists. In the past ten years numerous reporters and news organizations have been convicted for failing to respect property lines. This line of trespass cases began in Florida in 1976. A photographer and a reporter were invited by police and fire officials into a house that had been gutted by fire. The owner of the house, who was not on the premises at the time of the fire, later brought suit for trespass against the journalists. The journalists were exonerated in this instance, but only because the homeowner had not objected at the time the newspaper people entered the home. The Florida Supreme Court said it was common custom for the press to inspect private premises after a serious fire or a crime and that this common custom constituted a kind of indirect consent to the trespass. But it was clear from the court's opinion that had the homeowner been at the scene of the fire and objected to the reporter and photographer coming on the property, common custom or not, the journalists would have been guilty of trespass (*Florida Publishing Co.* v. *Fletcher,* 1976).

As if to emphasize what could have happened to the reporters in Florida, a state court in New York sustained a trespass action against a broadcasting film crew stemming from an incident at an exclusive New York City restaurant. The news crew had been sent to visit various restaurants cited by local authorities for health code violations. The crew entered the restaurant with its cameras rolling and floodlights on. Although the proprietor of the restaurant commanded the reporters to leave, the journalists stayed with the cameras and continued to film until they were physically escorted from the premises. In the meantime, customers ducked under tables, and some fled without paying their bills.

The broadcasting company, CBS, attempted to defend its action by using the First Amendment as a shield to protect itself from the trespass suit. The court disagreed. "Clearly, the First Amendment is not a shibboleth before which all other rights must succumb," the judge ruled (*Le Mistral, Inc.* v. *CBS,* 1978):

> This Court recognizes that the exercise of the right of free speech and free press demands and even mandates the observance of the co-equal duty not to abuse such right, but to utilize it with right reason and dignity. Vain lip service to "duties" in a vacuous reality wherein "rights" exist, sovereign and independent of any balancing moral or social factor, creates a semantical mockery of the very foundation of our laws and legal system.

In a subsequent trespass action which mirrored the facts in *Fletcher,* the New York Supreme Court in Monroe County followed the *Le Mistral* precedent closely. A Humane Society investigator obtained a search warrant to enter a home whose occupants had been the object of numerous complaints of cruelty to animals. The investigator invited reporters and film crews from three television stations to accompany him in this foray. The journalists went inside the home despite the protests of one of the occupants, filmed the interior of the home, and then broadcast the news story. In a lawsuit that followed, the television stations attempted to raise the defense of "implied consent through custom and usage" accepted by the Florida courts in the *Fletcher* case, but the New York court disagreed vigorously.

The so-called implied consent to enter a private home is a custom created by the press itself, the judge noted. "This is a boot-strapping argument," he said, which does not eliminate the trespass in this case. News people do not stand in any favored position with regard to trespass, the judge said. "If the news media were to succeed in compelling an uninvited and nonpermitted entry into one's private home whenever it chose to do so, this would be nothing less than a general warrant equivalent to the writs of assistance which were so odious to the American colonists," he added (*Anderson* v. *WROC-TV*, 1981).

Reporters in Oklahoma were found guilty of criminal trespass when they followed protestors into restricted areas during demonstrations at a nuclear facility. The Oklahoma Court of Criminal Appeals ruled that journalists enjoyed reasonable access to the events taking place in areas set aside by authorities for the press and for legal protests and did not need to trespass to get the story (*Stahl* v. *Oklahoma*, 1983).

The trespass problem is likely to be more common in the future and could become even more difficult to resolve. A Colorado district court judge recently noted that in the past the press has been afforded considerable First Amendment protection when disseminating the news, but very limited (if any) protection when gathering the news. But the judge asked, when a television reporter is standing in a field, instantly reporting a story with an electronic "instant cam" or "live-action cam" is that gathering or disseminating the news? The court suggested that charges of trespass should stand only if reporters were aware that they were committing a trespass, and if the plaintiff suffered damage as a result of the trespass (*Allen* v. *Combined Communications*, 1981).

But a charge of trespass is not the only problem that faces a reporter in news gathering. The New Jersey Supreme Court recently upheld the disorderly person conviction of a press photographer who was charged with impeding a police officer in the performance of his duty at the scene of a serious traffic accident. The photographer was standing near the wreckage when the state trooper, who feared a fire might begin and who also wanted to preserve the accident scene for investigation, ordered the area cleared of spectators. The news photographer moved back five feet, but when he refused to move any farther, he was arrested.

The journalist Harvey J. Lashinsky argued that the state's disorderly person statute was inapplicable to him because he was a member of the press. The state's high court disagreed, noting that "the constitutional prerogatives of the press must yield under appropriate circumstances to other important and legitimate interests." Acknowledging that the press does play a special role in society, the court nevertheless said that the photographer clearly impeded the officer by refusing his request to leave the area. While the officer was arguing with the journalist, he could have been giving assistance to the accident victims and beginning the investigation of the crash (*State* v. *Lashinsky,* 1979).

The brief discussion of these cases makes it clear that the courts will insist that reporters obey the law like all other citizens; their status as members of the press which is granted protection under the First Amendment is generally immaterial when they are called upon to account for their behavior while gathering news for publication and broadcast.

Summary

Intruding upon an individual's solitude is an invasion of privacy. While the press is not often the subject of intrusion privacy suits, cases have occurred more often in recent years. An invasion of privacy takes place as soon as the intrusion has been made. Publication of the fruits of the intrusion is irrelevant in such cases. Journalists will not normally be held responsible for intrusion if they publish material which other persons have obtained through an intrusion. However, the journalist may be charged with the possession of stolen goods if in fact the material was stolen and the news person is aware of that fact.

Courts will not permit a successful intrusion suit based upon the recording of events which take place in public places. The court will only permit a suit if the plaintiff in the case can prove that at the time the intrusion was made there was an "expectation of solitude"; that is, the plaintiff was in a place where he or she could expect to be alone. Courts are sensitive about protecting the privacy of a home and are likely to rule it is an intrusion to secretly film or record what occurs there. Courts are less sensitive about protecting what takes place in a business office.

In addition to the danger of intrusion suits, reporters are expected to obey other laws as they gather news. Unauthorized crossing of property lines can result in a criminal or civil trespass suit. Failure to obey the order of a police officer can result in a charge of disorderly conduct. The responsibility of gathering the news does not place journalists above the law.

The most controversial aspect of the right of privacy in the current decade is that aspect of the law which penalizes the publication of private information about a person. The *Restatement of the Law of Torts* defines this section of the law this way:

> One who gives publicity to a matter concerning the private life of another is subject to liability to the other for invasion of his privacy, if the matter publicized is of a kind that
> a. would be highly offensive to a reasonable person, and
> b. is not of legitimate concern to the public.

This, of course, is the kind of privacy protection that Warren and Brandeis sought in 1890. Strangely, as we will see shortly, American courts have been most reluctant to curb this kind of journalism, for it touches at the very foundation of our long-held notions about freedom of the press. This aspect is what makes invasion of privacy controversial, for even today many commentators argue that the press goes too far sometimes in publicizing the lives of persons who attempt to stay out of the public spotlight. They would limit the protection of the press to that coverage which deals with "governing affairs," or information citizens need to vote and discuss public issues.

The courts have been reluctant to prescribe this limitation. Starting in 1895 American judges have granted the press a broad protection to publish whatever it wants about people—within very broad boundaries—so long as there is some evidence of public interest in the topic. There is probably a good explanation for this attitude of the courts. Truth is not a defense in a suit brought for the publication of private information. If the material is of an intimate nature, its truth or nontruth is immaterial. This fact is difficult for many persons to accept, including judges who have for centuries ruled that truth is a good, solid defense in a libel suit. By creating a liability for the publication of truthful material, one opens all sorts of doors, doors which are then difficult to close. If the journalist can be held responsible for publishing truthful, intimate reports, the historian can then be held liable as well. Indeed, there are some scholars who question the validity of this category of invasion of privacy on the grounds that it is unconstitutional to punish someone for publishing a truthful statement. Clearly, the language of the Supreme Court in numerous libel suits, beginning with *New York Times* v. *Sullivan* in 1964, makes dubious the notion of imposing liability for the publication of truthful comments. In a 1975 privacy ruling, *Cox* v. *Cohn*, the high Court ruled that it is not possible for a person to recover damages when the press merely publicizes truthful comments that are already a part of the public record. (The *Cox* case, which will be discussed in detail later, concerned the publication of the name of a rape victim.) But the Court chose not to rule at that time on whether the publication of all truthful statements, no matter how offensive they might be, will be protected by the First Amendment.

Most courts use a two-step evaluation in considering whether this kind of invasion of privacy has occurred. This method also lends itself to presentation of a simple explanation of the law. First, the determination must be made that private facts about a person's life have indeed been publicized, which requires examination of two concepts: publicity and private facts. If there has been *no* publicity about private facts, there has been *no* invasion of privacy. If there *has been* publicity about private facts, a second evaluation must be made. The questions asked are (1) would this publicity be highly offensive to a reasonable person? and (2) was the matter published of legitimate public concern? In this second stage, a kind of balancing process normally results, with the importance to the public of the revelation of the private material being weighed against how offensive the publication is to the plaintiff. While guidelines do exist, the balancing process often tends to be quite subjective, and matters of personal taste and sensitivity frequently play a role in the outcome. Reporters should spend time in considering how to present important but sensitive material in the least offensive manner.

This category of right to privacy can be best understood by considering each of the two elements of the law individually.

Publicity

The words *publicity* and *publication* mean different things in privacy law than they do in libel law. In defamation, *publication* means to communicate the material to a single third party. The word *publicity* in privacy law implies far more. It means that the material is communicated to the public at large or to a great number of people, making it certain that the facts will shortly become public knowledge. Needless to say this kind of publicity can usually be presumed when a story is published in a newspaper or broadcast over radio and television.

Private Facts

Before there can be an invasion of privacy, it must be demonstrated that the material publicized was indeed private. What happens in public is considered public information. A fan at a Pittsburgh Steeler football game urged a news photographer to take his picture. The photographer did, but when the photograph was published in *Sports Illustrated*, the fan sued for invasion of privacy, arguing that the photograph revealed that his trousers were unzipped and that this was quite embarrassing. The District Court for Eastern Pennsylvania ruled against the plaintiff, primarily because the picture was taken in a public place with the defendant's knowledge and encouragement. It was not private information (*Neff* v. *Time, Inc.,* 1976). Similarly, the United States Court of Appeals (D.C. circuit) refused to find liability for the broadcast of news film which showed two men on a public street being escorted by police officers. Plaintiff Darryl Harrison argued that the pictures were embarrassing because they portrayed him as being a criminal. But the court ruled that an action for invasion of privacy cannot be maintained for pictures of events which take place in public view. The photographer in this case was standing on a public sidewalk while he took the pictures (*Harrison* v. *Washington Post,* 1978). The Massachusetts court of appeals ruled that no privacy exists when a person is standing in a line at a government building. The plaintiff in the case was photographed while standing in a line of persons waiting to collect unemployment benefits at the state employment security office. "The appearance of a person in a public place necessarily involves doffing the cloak of privacy which the law protects," the court ruled (*Cefalu* v. *Globe Newspaper,* 1979; see also *Arrington* v. *New York Times,* 1982). In the past, courts have ruled as nonactionable pictures of women exercising in a public gymnasium (*Sweenek* v. *Pathé News,* 1936), the details of a divorce case that were revealed in public court (*Berg* v. *Minneapolis Star & Tribune,* 1948), and photographs of the victim of a tragic accident (*Kelley* v. *Post Publishing Co.,* 1951). In each instance the fact that the events occurred in public was material in determining that there had been no invasion of privacy.

In 1975 the United States Supreme Court ruled that the broadcast or publication of the name of a rape victim that was included in the public record during a criminal trial could not be considered an invasion of privacy. At that time, at least four states had statutes making the publication of such information an invasion of privacy. The rationale for such laws was generally accepted: nonpublication would save victims from embarrassment and might, in turn, encourage more women to report such incidents. Decreased reporting of names might therefore result in more prosecutions of rapists. There had been at least two decisions prior to the 1975 ruling upholding these laws (see, for example, *Nappier* v. *Jefferson Standard Life Insurance Co.,* 1963). When an Atlanta, Georgia, television station broadcast the name of a young woman who had been raped and murdered, her parents sued. In *Cox Broadcasting Co.* v. *Cohn* (1975), the United States Supreme Court overturned the Georgia state court ruling and held that the press cannot be held liable for invasion of privacy for reporting information already part of the public record. Justice Byron White noted that most persons depend upon the mass media for information about the operations of the government via public meetings and the public record. Judicial proceedings are an important part of our governmental system and are something in which the public has always expressed a great interest. By making judicial records and proceedings public, the state of Georgia must have concluded that the public interest was being served (*Cox Broadcasting Co.* v. *Cohn,* 1975):

> We are reluctant to embark on a course that would make public records generally available to the media but forbid their publication if offensive to the sensibilities of the supposed reasonable man. Such a rule would make it very difficult for the press to inform their readers about the public business and yet stay within the law. The rule would invite timidity and self-censorship and very likely lead to the suppression of many items that would otherwise be put into print and that should be made available to the public.

Quoting the latest revision of the *Restatement of Torts* (2nd ed.), which attempts to summarize the law of torts, the Court said, "There is no liability when the defendant merely gives further publicity to information about the plaintiff which is already public. Thus there is no liability for giving publicity to facts about the plaintiff's life which are matters of public record."

Since 1975 the impact of the decision in *Cox* v. *Cohn* has been felt nationwide. A 1982 New Jersey ruling is a good example. When the victim of a sexual assault in Willingboro, New Jersey, reported the crime, she asked police to keep her name and address confidential. The hospital at which she was treated routinely gave out her name, and a reporter for the *Burlington County Times* followed the story up by talking with a police officer who was investigating the case. Three stories were published about the incident, and in each the plaintiff was identified. Details of the attack were not included, however. In her invasion of privacy suit the plaintiff argued that this case was different from *Cox* v. *Cohn* where the reporter got the information from an official court record. This story was obtained orally from a police officer. But the New Jersey Superior Court rejected the plaintiff's argument. "The fact that the story was derived directly from a person in charge of the investigation and not from a written record of such investigation . . . does not distinguish [this case from] *Cox* in the opinion of the court." The police officer was an official source, the court ruled. This was a matter of great public interest (*Griffith* v. *Rancocas Valley Hospital et al.,* 1982).

Despite the legal resolution of this issue in *Cox* v. *Cohn,* the publication of the name of a rape victim remains a controversial social question. Many persons ask that newspapers and broadcasting stations think about all the harm that can result from such identification and balance that with the limited public good that derives from such publication or broadcast.

The single danger journalists face with regard to the public record question is that they must be certain that the document quoted is a public record and the meeting reported is a public meeting. Several years ago in Florida the *Tampa Tribune* published what really amounted only to a legal notice that a woman named Virginia Patterson had been committed to a state hospital as a narcotic addict. When Ms. Patterson sued for invasion of privacy, the newspaper argued that it obtained the information from the court progress docket, which is a public record. The paper was unaware that the legislature had passed a law specifically restricting the inspection of the records of narcotic commitment proceedings. Such records are not public records. The newspaper asked how was it to know that this part of the progress docket was not a public record, since the court clerk had not stopped the reporter from looking at it. This argument was unpersuasive. The Florida Supreme Court said it was the responsibility of the newspaper to know the law and not to compound the error of the court clerk (*Patterson* v. *Tribune Co.,* 1962). Reporters should make certain they are quoting a public record. Asking the court clerk or person at the desk is not always the best way to find out. Most newspapers retain or have access to legal counsel. If there is a question, call the lawyer.

Offensive Material

When the determination has been made that private facts about a person's life have been published, a court must then ask two subsequent questions:

1. Would the publication of the material offend a reasonable person?
2. Was the published material of legitimate public concern?

Frequently courts are faced with the real dilemma that while revelation of the material was extremely offensive and embarrassing its publication, however, was of great importance for the public. Except in extremely unusual circumstances the press will win such decisions. The judiciary places great weight upon the role of the press as an agent to inform and enlighten the public upon matters of interest and importance. Judges have ruled time and again that it is the responsibility of the press to bring such "newsworthy" information to the people. And courts have been hesitant to define narrow limits upon what the public needs to know or upon the kinds of information in which the people have a genuine interest. And remember, the publication of the material must be offensive to a reasonable person. The feelings of a hypersensitive person or someone who is especially sensitive do not count. Peggy Jo Fry sued the *Ionia* (Mich.) *Sentinel-Standard* for invasion of privacy when it reported that her husband and another woman had died in a fire which destroyed a cottage near Lake Michigan. The story mentioned that Ted Fry had been seen with Rita Hill at a tavern prior to the fire and related details about Fry's wife and children. The court ruled that these details were simply not highly offensive to a reasonable person (*Fry v. Ionia Sentinel-Standard*, 1980). Generally, if journalists stick to their job—reporting what is newsworthy—there is little to worry about. But privacy is an emotional subject. There are times when the revelation of details is highly offensive, and even seemingly newsworthy reports lose their immunity from a successful invasion of privacy suit.

Several years ago a woman with a rather unusual disorder—she ate constantly, but still lost weight—was admitted to a hospital. The press was tipped off and descended upon her room, pushed past the closed door, and took pictures against the patient's will. *Time* magazine ran a story about the patient, Dorothy Barber, whom in inimitable "*Time* style" it called "the starving glutton." Mrs. Barber sued and won her case. The judge said the hospital is one place people should be able to go for privacy (*Barber v. Time, Inc.*, 1942). More than the privacy of the hospital visit influenced the ruling, because there are several decisions in which persons in hospitals have been considered to be the subject of legitimate concern and did not therefore enjoy the right to privacy. The material about the unusual disorder was surely offensive, almost mocking. The disorder was not contagious, and the implications for the general public were minimal. The *Time* story seemed to focus upon Mrs. Barber almost as if she were a freak and in doing so was highly offensive to any reasonable person.

A Georgia housewife took her two sons to the county fair and finally succumbed to their pressure to be taken through the fun house. As she left the building an air jet blew Mrs. Flora Bell Graham's dress up over her head, and she was exposed from the waist down except for her underclothing. As fate would have it, a local photographer was nearby and captured the moment on film. The picture was featured in the Sunday edition of the local newspaper as a publicity piece for the fair. Mrs. Graham sued. By logical analysis one could suggest that she should not have won. The event took place in public. Many people saw her. She could not be readily identified in the picture because her dress was over her head. Persons who knew the children, who were also in the picture, could make the connection between mother and children. Regardless, Mrs. Graham did win (*Daily Times-Democrat* v. *Graham,* 1962). She suffered an immense amount of embarrassment from the most intimate kind of revelation, and the public value of the photograph was extremely low.

Most recently a Mississippi court ruled that it was an invasion of privacy to publish an admittedly sympathetic story about mental retardation which named four children as victims of the impairment. The story focused upon special education classes at a local school. The story attempted to demonstrate both the problems faced by children who suffer from such difficulties and the steps taken by a school district to help these children overcome such problems. But the court ruled the publication was still an invasion of privacy. "It is difficult to conceive that any information can be more delicate or private in nature than the fact that a child has limited mental capabilities or is in any sense mentally retarded," the court ruled (*Deaton* v. *Delta Democrat Publishing Co.,* 1976).

Legitimate Public Concern

While the three cases cited do not stand alone they are unusual. Far more often courts rule that public concern over the issues involved outweighs any embarrassment to plaintiffs. Several factors have been cited in weighing the public concern or interest in a particular matter.

In determining whether something is of public concern, courts have focused upon such factors as what the story is about, who the story is about, when the incidents described in the story took place, and sometimes where they took place.

Factual stories, reports or broadcasts which have great public interest, have generally been protected in invasion of privacy suits. The courts have been really quite liberal in defining public interest not as something people should read about, but as something they do read about, something in which people are interested.

A twelve-year-old girl who gave birth to a baby (*Meetze* v. *AP*, 1956), the suffocation of two children in an old refrigerator (*Costlow* v. *Cuismano,* 1970), the sterilization of an eighteen-year-old girl (*Howard* v. *Des Moines Register,* 1979), the death of a young man from a drug overdose (*Beresky* v. *Teschner,* 1978), the activities of a bodysurfer (*Virgil* v. *Time,* 1975), and other subjects have all been ruled to be of legitimate concern and interest to the public. The courts have been most generous to the press in their understanding of American reading and viewing habits. In a 1975 ruling in California the Ninth United States Court of Appeals noted that "in determining what is a matter of legitimate public interest, account must be taken of the customs and conventions of the community; and in the last analysis what is proper becomes a matter of community mores" (*Virgil* v. *Time,* 1975). Thirty-five years earlier another federal judge noted that the public enjoyed reading about the problems, misfortunes, and troubles of their neighbors and other members of the community. "When such are the mores of the community, it would be unwise for a court to bar their expression in the newspapers, books, and magazines of the day," Judge Charles Clark wrote (*Sidis* v. *F-R Publishing Co.,* 1940).

Even the way a story is presented is normally not a factor: sensationalism and sensational treatment generally do not remove the protection of newsworthiness. Concerning the story of the suffocation of the two young children, the parents found the sensational treatment of the story as objectionable as the story itself. However, the court ruled that the manner in which the article was written was not relevant to whether the article was protected by the constitutional guarantees of free speech and free press—which, by the way, it was. In another case a Boston newspaper published a horrible picture of an automobile accident in which the bloodied and battered body of one of the victims was clearly visible and identifiable, and the court rejected the plaintiff's claim. The Massachusetts Supreme Court noted, "Many things which are distressing or may be lacking in propriety or good taste are not actionable" (*Kelley* v. *Post Publishing Co.,* 1951).

What the story is about, then, is an important aspect of determining whether it is newsworthy. American readers, viewers, and listeners are believed to have a wide range of interests which often focus on grotesque events and the tragedy, unhappiness, and misfortune of other persons.

Who the story is about is also taken into account in determining whether the material is of legitimate public concern. As in the law of libel, stories about public officials and persons who thrust themselves into the public eye are looked at much differently than are stories about private persons. A story that Mayor John Smith has a serious drinking problem would not be considered an invasion of privacy; the same story about barber Bill Brown might in fact be an invasion of privacy. How far can the press go in publishing details of the private life of so-called public persons? That is a difficult question to answer.

Certainly the status of the individual is important. Probably few details of the life of a president are considered private in terms of the law, but a circuit judge in a rural county, also an elected official, would probably enjoy considerably more privacy. In an interesting case in California, federal courts were asked to determine how far the press can go in looking into the private life of a public person.

The story focused upon Mike Virgil, widely regarded in southern California as one of the best bodysurfers along the Pacific Coast. *Sports Illustrated* decided to publish a feature on bodysurfing, and writer Curry Kirkpatrick chose to emphasize the prowess of Virgil. Virgil was known for his almost total disregard for personal safety and talked freely with the writer about his private life, as well as about his surfing. He told Kirkpatrick that he was reckless in private as well and described several incidents to demonstrate this attitude. These incidents included putting out a burning cigarette with his mouth, burning a hole in his wrist with a cigarette, diving headfirst down a flight of stairs, and eating live insects. But after the interview Virgil had second thoughts about the story and asked *Sports Illustrated* not to include the material about his private life. The magazine published the story as Kirkpatrick had written it, and Virgil sued. The Ninth Circuit Court of Appeals ruled that the line between private and public information "is to be drawn when the publicity ceases to be the giving of information to which the public is entitled, and becomes a morbid and sensational prying into private lives *for its own sake* [emphasis added]." In applying this standard to the Virgil case, the United States district court ruled that "any reasonable person reading the article would conclude that the personal facts concerning the individual were revealed in a legitimate journalistic attempt to explain his extremely daring and dangerous style of bodysurfing" (*Virgil* v. *Time*, 1976). Judge Thompson ruled that no one could reasonably conclude that these personal facts were included for any inherent morbid, sensational, or curiosity appeal they might have. If *Sports Illustrated* had published these personal details about Virgil without any other information, it might have been an invasion of privacy. But in the context of the story about his public life as a surfer, the publication was not an invasion of privacy.

Iowa courts recently used the same sort of standard when ruling that a story about a girl who had been sterilized when she was eighteen years old was not an invasion of privacy. The story focused upon the unusual activities at a county juvenile home. As an example of what occurred there, the *Des Moines Register* recounted the story of a girl who was sterilized against her will because a psychiatrist reported to officials that she was "impulsive" and "hair-triggered" and would probably have sexual problems in the future. The girl's name was used, but was not prominent in the story. The court ruled that the paper had not pried into the girl's life simply to shock or outrage the community. The facts were presented to demonstrate to the community the kind of activities taking place at the home. As such, the material was of legitimate public concern (*Howard* v. *Des Moines Register,* 1979). But was it necessary to use the victim's name in this story? Was it not possible for the newspaper to present this story to readers without identifying an unfortunate victim of this county home? The Iowa high court ruled it was legitimate to conclude that the name was an essential ingredient in the story (*Howard* v. *Des Moines Register,* 1979):

> In the sense of serving an appropriate news function, the disclosure [of the name] contributed constructively to the impact of the article. It offered a personalized frame of reference to which the reader could relate, fostering perception and understanding. Moreover, it lent specificity and credibility to the report. In this way the disclosure served as an effective means of accomplishing the intended news function. . . . Moreover, at a time when it was important to separate fact from rumor, the specificity of the report would strengthen the accuracy of the public perception of the merits of the controversy.

The Tenth United States Court of Appeals used this same argument to refute charges of invasion of privacy brought by a physician against the periodical *Medical Economics.* The story in the magazine was entitled "Who Let This Doctor in the O.R.? The Story of a Fatal Breakdown in Medical Policing," and described several patients of an anesthesiologist who suffered fatal or severely disabling injuries in the operating room. The article focused upon the lack of self-policing by physicians and the lack of disciplinary action by hospitals. To document these allegations the author of the story discussed the plaintiff anesthesiologist's psychiatric and related personal problems. Her picture and name were included in the story. While the plaintiff conceded the story was newsworthy, she argued that the publication of her photograph, name, and private facts revealing her psychiatric and marital histories added nothing to the story and were an invasion of privacy. The court disagreed, stating that the inclusion of the name and photograph strengthened the impact and credibility of the article. "They obviate any impression that the problems raised in the article are remote or hypothetical, thus providing an aura of immediacy and even urgency that might not exist had plaintiff's name and photograph been suppressed," the court said. The plaintiff's psychiatric and marital problems were connected to the newsworthy topic by the rational inference that her personal problems were the underlying causes of the acts of alleged malpractice (*Gilbert* v. *Medical Economics,* 1981).

What courts often look for in these kind of cases, then, is a nexus between the admittedly private and embarrassing information and the newsworthy subject of the story. How far the press can go in reporting the private life of public persons, then, depends not only upon what was said—how private the information is—but also upon why the material was used. When an individual's public life is explained, many parts of that person's private life are of legitimate public concern.

Since 1929 American courts have also recognized what might be called the "involuntary public figure" in privacy law. The Kentucky Supreme Court first noted such a person and gave this definition of the status (*Jones* v. *Herald Post Co.,* 1929):

> The right of privacy is the right to live one's life in seclusion, without being subjected to unwarranted and undesired publicity. In short, it is the right to be let alone. . . . There are times, however, when one, whether willing or not, becomes an actor in an occurrence of public or general interest. When this takes place he emerges from his seclusion, and it is not an invasion of his right of privacy to publish his photograph with an account of such occurrence.

The court later noted that private citizens can become "innocent actors in great tragedies in which the public has a deep concern." The scope, therefore, of the rubric involuntary public figure is wide. In Kansas City not too long ago a young man was arrested by police outside the local courthouse on suspicion of burglary. Local television news cameramen filmed the arrest, and it was broadcast on televison that night. The young man, however, had been released by police who admitted they arrested the wrong man. An invasion of privacy suit followed, but the courts rejected it, stating that the plaintiff must show a serious, unreasonable, unwarranted, and offensive invasion of private affairs before recovery can be allowed (*Williams* v. *KCMO Broadcasting Co.,* 1971):

> In the case at bar, plaintiff was involved in a noteworthy event about which the public had a right to be informed and which the defendant [television station KCMO] had a right to publicize. This is true even though his involvement therein was purely involuntary and against his will.

An Illinois appeals court ruled in 1978 that a story which reported the death of a boy from an apparent drug overdose and then went on to outline details of the youth's life was not an invasion of privacy. The subject was of legitimate concern; in addition, the youth became an involuntary public figure by his actions within the drug culture in the community. "It is not necessary for an individual to actively seek publicity in order to be found in the public eye," the court ruled (*Beresky* v. *Teschner,* 1978).

There has been speculation that, given the opportunity, the United States Supreme Court would reject the so-called involuntary-public-figure rule in privacy law. The rationale behind this speculation rests upon the language of recent Supreme Court rulings in libel (*Firestone* v. *Time* and *Wolston* v. *Reader's Digest* among others). In those decisions members of the high Court ruled that public figures in libel law must actively thrust themselves into the forefront of a public issue. They must voluntarily choose to be public figures by attempting to lead public opinion. But while libel law and invasion of privacy are similar in many respects, the argument that the Supreme Court will ultimately apply the same rules in privacy invasion should be largely ignored. There is a fundamental difference of crucial importance between a suit for libel and one for the publication of private facts. In the libel case the published material is false; in the privacy suit the material is truthful. This difference is critical. It is more likely that the Supreme Court would lessen the restrictions upon the publication of truthful material, as it did in the *Cox* case. The involuntary-public-figure rule has been a part of privacy law for more than fifty years, and it is unlikely the high Court would abandon it.

Persons who are thrust, even unwillingly thrust, into the public spotlight lose some of the protection of their right of privacy. How much privacy is lost? Probably only the privacy which protects that part of their life which has come into focus because of the event or incident. This line is not easy to draw. Imagine that John Smith, publisher of *The Daily Sentinel,* is arrested for violating the state unfair labor practices act. Under the guise of his status as an involuntary public figure how far into his life can the press go? Can it report his extramarital affairs? that he has a gun fetish? that he cheats at cards? All these questions are hard to answer. Probably the answers depend upon the status of the person involved, the magnitude of the event, the scope of public interest, and the connection or nexus between these private personal matters and the newsworthy aspects of the story.

Sometimes the people who are close to public figures also lose some of their privacy. In 1971 in Pennsylvania the state high court ruled that the *Saturday Evening Post* was not liable for the publication of the names of the children of an entertainer in a story relating that the entertainer, Lillian Corabi, was accused of masterminding a complex burglary (*Corabi* v. *Curtis Publishing Co.,* 1971). The court said that "Tiger Lil" Corabi was a public figure and that anyone could legitimately publish her biography without consent and could include the names of the members of her family.

When a white Southern civil rights leader published his autobiography, it was not an invasion of privacy to include information about his brother's wife, according to a United States district court. In *Brother to a Dragonfly* author Will D. Campbell portrayed his life and his relationship to his deceased brother Joe whom he regarded as a major inspiration in his life. Joe was a pharmacist who became addicted to drugs. This resulted in a dramatic change in his personality, and at times he seriously abused his wife, Carlyne, who was also mentioned several times in the book. She sued for invasion of privacy. "The fact that she [the plaintiff] was the wife of a close and influential family member of the author justifies her inclusion in the book," the United States district court ruled. "Joe's problems with drugs and the profound effect that had on the author justifies the extent of her inclusion" (*Campbell* v. *Seabury Press,* 1979).

Recounting the Past   A great number of privacy suits have resulted from both published and broadcast stories about people who were formerly in the public eye. In these cases the plaintiffs have consistently argued that the passing of time dims the public spotlight, and a person stripped of privacy because of great notoriety regains the protection of privacy after several years. Courts have not accepted this argument very often. The general rule is that once a person becomes a public figure he pretty much remains a public figure, despite attempts to avoid publicity. Two kinds of stories fall into this category: (1) stories that merely recount a past event (fourteen years ago today Walter Denton jumped off the Golden Gate Bridge and survived) and do not tell readers what the subject of the story does today, and (2) stories that recount a past occurrence and attempt to focus as well on what the participant does today (fourteen years ago Walter Denton jumped off the Golden Gate Bridge and survived and today he is principal of Madison High School).

Stories that fall in the first category are protected in almost every instance. In 1975 the Kansas Supreme Court, for example, ruled it was not an invasion of privacy when a newspaper republished in a "Looking Backward Column" a story that a police officer had been suspended and then fired in 1964 after a complaint from a citizen. The court said that "official misconduct is newsworthy when it occurs, and remains so for so long as anyone thinks it worth retelling." The court added, "Once these facts entered the public domain, they remained there . . . plaintiff could not draw himself like a snail into his shell" (*Rawlins* v. *The Hutchinson Publishing Co.,* 1975). Such decisions are the rule.

The second kind of story can be a problem. While courts have gone on record permitting the where-are-they-now kind of story, judges have nevertheless indicated that stories aimed at humiliating or purposely embarrassing a person because of his past conduct might not be tolerated under all circumstances (see *Kent* v. *Pittsburgh Press,* 1972; *Sidis* v. *F-R Publishing Co.,* 1940; *Bernstein* v. *NBC,* 1955). A real risk is run in broadcasting a story about a local banker which mentions that twenty years ago he was arrested for car theft. However, if the banker is running for public office, the situation is different. Also, a story saying that here is a man who was down and out twenty years ago, but now see what he has accomplished, would probably pass muster. However, it would be best to first get the banker's approval. Stories which for no good reason purposely dig into a person's past in search of indiscretions are the ones likely to cause problems.

Stories which relate past events are some of the most difficult to evaluate in terms of public interest and public concern. For a time California courts were not satisfied with the tests just outlined. They asked an additional question when confronted with an article or broadcast which told about the prior events in a person's life: Is there any social utility or social value in retelling this story? This question emerged from an unusual case prompted by the publication in the *Reader's Digest* of a story about a man who had been convicted for hijacking a truck. The story focused upon the national epidemic of hijacking, and the incident about Marvin Briscoe was only a detail in the clearly newsworthy story. But the magazine did not reveal that Briscoe had committed this offense eleven years before the publication of the article. Briscoe claimed he had served his time in jail and had led an exemplary life since he was freed from prison. This story revealed to friends, neighbors, and family a portion of his life he had hidden.

The story was obviously a part of the public record. But the California Supreme Court questioned the value in retelling it in the magazine. The state had rehabilitated this man; he was living a productive life; retelling this old story negated the state's effort in rehabilitating Briscoe. The privacy suit was sent back for trial, but before proceedings could get underway, the *Reader's Digest* had the case removed to a federal district court and a federal judge granted a motion for summary judgment for the magazine (*Briscoe* v. *Reader's Digest Association,* 1971).

California followed this "social utility" rule for nearly ten years. The United States Supreme Court ruling in *Cox* v. *Cohn* which said that the press is free to publish what is contained in court records clearly undercut the California state court rule. The clear implication of the *Cox* ruling was that the high Court put no time limit upon when the press can relate the content of the court records: today, tomorrow, or in five years. The social utility rule was also too broad. It affected historians, museums (cannot display old newspapers), and many other persons in the mass media. In 1980 the California Supreme Court did everything but throw out the test when it ruled that in the future it would apply the social utility rule only in those cases in which the facts precisely mirrored the *Briscoe* case; that is, the state's work in rehabilitating a former criminal was harmed by the publication of the individual's past criminal record (*Forsher* v. *Bugliosi,* 1980).

The publication of private facts generates many lawsuits, but few are successful. The key to avoiding successful litigation in this area is for the news person to stick to reporting the news. It is when the journalist makes a foray into nonnewsworthy private lives of average persons in order to titillate or amuse readers or viewers that this area of invasion of privacy can prove extremely troublesome.

Summary

It is an invasion of privacy to publicize private information about another person's life if the publication of this information would be embarrassing to a reasonable person and the information is not of legitimate public interest or concern. Publicize means to communicate the information to a large number of people. There is no liability for giving further publicity to information that is already considered public. The press is free, for example, to report even embarrassing and sensitive matters contained in public records. The information which is publicized must be considered offensive to a reasonable person; the law does not protect hypersensitive individuals.

Courts use many strategies to determine whether information has legitimate public concern. Stories which have great interest have legitimate public concern. Stories about both voluntary and involuntary public figures are normally considered of legitimate public concern. When private information is published or broadcast, it is important that there is a connection between the revelation of the embarrassing private information and the newsworthy aspects of the story. Embarrassing details about a person's private life cannot be publicized simply to amuse or titillate audiences. News stories which recount past events—including embarrassing details of an individual's life—are normally protected from successful privacy suits. However, courts will normally insist upon a good reason for attempting to relate these embarrassing past events to an individual's current life or work.

FALSE LIGHT
PRIVACY

The fourth category of invasion of privacy looks, at first glance, as if it has little to do with what we traditionally think of as privacy. It has nothing to do with digging into a person's past, taking pictures with a telephoto lens, or using someone's picture to advertise toothpaste. What this category of invasion of privacy bans is the publication of false information about a person. The law states that it is an invasion of privacy to publish material which puts an individual in a false light. There are two qualifications to this rule. First, the published false information must be highly offensive to a reasonable person. Second, it must be shown that the publisher knew the information was false when it was published, or acted with reckless disregard for the truth or falsity of the information. (This is the actual malice rule from libel law.) This is the youngest area of the law of privacy. Its boundaries remain somewhat obscure. Yet today a remarkably large number of these false light actions are filed, and a substantial number of those filed are successful.

False light cases come in a wide variety of shapes and colors. Some involve blatant fictionalization of otherwise true stories; others result from simple errors in news stories, much like the problems which cause a libel suit. And that raises this question: How does a false light suit differ from a libel suit? There are two primary distinctions.

1. In order to maintain a libel action plaintiffs must prove that the material has damaged their reputation, that it is in fact defamatory. In false light cases the plaintiff must only show that the published material is considered highly offensive by a reasonable person.

2. In libel law only plaintiffs who are classed as public officials and public figures have to show that the defamatory material was published with knowledge of its falsity or with reckless disregard of the truth. Any plaintiff who sues for false light based on a story about a subject of general or public interest must prove knowledge of falsity or reckless disregard of the truth. The First Amendment protection in libel has been applied in false light invasion of privacy suits as well.

Many persons have speculated that because the Supreme Court of the United States has limited the scope of the First Amendment protection in libel suits to specific categories of people—public officials and public figures—that it is likely that these libel rules would be applied to privacy as well. That has not happened yet, even though the Supreme Court had an opportunity to do that in 1974 (*Cantrell* v. *Forest City Publishing Co.*). As of now, we must presume that any story which deals with a subject of public interest is protected by this First Amendment malice standard from false light invasion of privacy suits, regardless of whether the people discussed in the story are public persons or private persons.

Let us look at some typical examples of false light invasion of privacy suits to try to develop guidelines on this subject.

Fictionalization

Radio and television writers who dramatize true stories are commonly the victims of false light suits. A few years ago the National Broadcasting Company dramatized the heroism of a naval officer who, as a passenger on a flight from Honolulu to California, was responsible for saving many lives when the plane crash-landed at sea. The drama stuck to the hard facts of the story, but of course dialogue between passengers and crew was added. In addition, the naval officer was somewhat humanized: he smoked a cigarette and prayed before the crash. The court which heard the officer's privacy suit ruled that these embellishments constituted fictionalization and resulted in an invasion of privacy (*Strickler* v. *NBC*, 1958).

Newspapers and magazine writers have been caught when they dramatized true stories in the same manner by adding dialogue, changing the scene slightly, and so forth. A writer for a Philadelphia newspaper uncovered an interesting divorce suit involving a teenage couple. The boy married the girl only to spite her parents who did not like him. The newspaper story described the couple as they secretly planned the marriage, as they walked to the justice of the peace, and so forth. Dialogue between the couple was invented. A suit resulted, and the newspaper lost the case because the story was written "in a style used almost exclusively by writers of fiction" (*Acquino* v. *Bulletin Co.*, 1959). Note, the court did not say that the story was fiction, because it was not. The basic facts were true, but were presented in a fictional style.

Such opinions are not always the rule. Other courts in other cases have said that minor fictionalization, the creation of dialogue, does not constitute invasion of privacy in an otherwise true story (*Carlisle* v. *Fawcett Publishing Co., 1962*). The foregoing examples point up the confused state of the law in this area noted earlier.

The style of the fiction writer—putting heavy emphasis on descriptive detail, using dialogue, narrating the story from the subject's, rather than the writer's, point of view—is used increasingly today by some journalists. Writers such as Gay Talese, Tom Wolfe, Jimmy Breslin, Joan Didion, and Norman Mailer are leading the way in the exploration of stylized nonfiction writing, often called New Journalism. Nonfiction novels like Truman Capote's *In Cold Blood* and Joseph Wambaugh's *The Onion Field* demonstrate the journalistic power of this style. Yet, these writers clearly open themselves to lawsuits unless extreme care is taken.

The simplest way to avoid a suit for false light, if the truth is embellished in any way, is to change the names of the characters in the story. This strategy will work in every case except in those stories which are about a specific person. It does not make much sense to do a character sketch about Mick Jagger if you must refer to him throughout the piece as John Smith because parts of the story are embellished or fictionalized.

On the opposite side of the fictionalization coin is the problem of using the name of a real person in what is clearly a work of fiction.

What happens when a novel is about a fictional character named Judy Splinters and a real Judy Splinters exists? Can the real Ms. Splinters sue for invasion of privacy? The first point to remember is that the little notice in the front of the book—all characters in this book are fictional and any resemblance to persons living or dead is purely coincidental—does not help much. It is impossible to escape liability by merely saying you are not liable. If a man commits an illegal act, he is responsible for his action, regardless of the notices he may have published. If someone trips on a broken piece of cement in a sidewalk, it matters not that the owner of the property has a sign on his lawn declaring that he takes good care of his property and that he is not responsible for the injuries to other persons.

Does Judy Splinters have a case? If only her name is used, she does not. The names of many people get into works of fiction. Such occurrences are coincidental. Liability does not accrue unless Judy can convince a jury that in fact she is the character in the book. She can do this by showing that more than her name is used, that other aspects of her identity are used as well.

For example, the author and publisher of a book entitled *Match Set* was sued by a woman who had the same name as the central character in the novel. Both women were named Melanie Geisler. The character in the novel is a female transsexual tennis player who is induced to participate in tennis fraud.

The plaintiff in the case worked for a small publishing company for six months and was acquainted with the defendant author who also worked at the same company for a short time. The plaintiff and the fictional Melanie Geisler share many physical characteristics. The real Melanie Geisler argued that the similarity of names and physical descriptions, coupled with the fact that she and the author were acquainted for a short time, led many persons to believe the book is about her. The Second United States Court of Appeals ruled that a reasonable person could come to such a conclusion, rejected the defendant's motion for dismissal, and sent the case back for trial (*Geisler* v. *Petrocelli,* 1980). Some authors can face a problem even if the plaintiff does not have the same name as a character in the novel. In a Florida case a novelist knowingly used a real person with whom she was acquainted as the basis for a character in a book. She was sued for invasion of privacy and lost the case. The court ruled that because the character described in the novel was so unusual many persons in the community recognized her even though the name had been changed (*Cason* v. *Baskin,* 1947).

Finally, what about novels like E. L. Doctorow's *Ragtime* in which famous people play an incidental part in a fictional story? The courts in at least one jurisdiction, New York, have ruled that such incidental use of the name and character of real notable people is not an invasion of privacy so long as it is evident to readers that the book is a work of fiction, and that individuals named are included simply to add color to the book (*Hicks* v. *Casablanca,* 1978).

False Statements

Today most false light cases do not involve blatant fictionalization. They instead result from news and feature stories which are either intentionally or unintentionally embellished. Typical of the first sort of case is one in which a writer for a national newspaper told his readers that a mystery surrounded the suicide death of a mother. The woman killed herself after murdering her children, and the writer said police, family, and friends were baffled because she had been a happy, normal woman. Her husband sued, charging false light. He was able to show that the woman had a history of psychiatric care and mental illness. She was quite despondent before the incident, and her death was really not a mystery at all. The court ruled that the publication had put the woman in a false light (*Varnish* v. *Best Medium,* 1968).

Photographs are a more common source of false light cases than are stories. The late, great *Saturday Evening Post* seemed to have a penchant for false light cases, most of which involved photographs. Years ago the magazine published a picture of a little girl who was brushed by a speeding car in an intersection and lay crying in the street. The girl was the victim of a motorist who ignored a red traffic light, but in the magazine the editors implied that she caused the accident herself by darting into the street between parked cars.

The editors simply needed a picture to illustrate a story on pedestrian carelessness and plucked this one out of the files. The picture was totally unrelated to the story except that both were about people being hit by cars.

Eleanor Sue Leverton sued the *Post* and won. Judge Herbert F. Goodrich ruled that the picture was clearly newsworthy in connection with Eleanor's original accident (*Leverton* v. *Curtis Publishing Co.,* 1951):

> . . . but the sum total of all this is that this particular plaintiff, the legitimate subject for publicity for one particular accident, now becomes a pictorial, frightful example of pedestrian carelessness. This, we think, exceeds the bounds of privilege.

Just before the *Post* succumbed, it faced another suit for the same action. This time the magazine used a picture taken at a gambling club in the Bahamas to illustrate a story about organized crime infiltrating the casinos on the islands. The caption said: "High rollers at Monte Carlo [the name of the club] have dropped as much as $20,000 in a single night. The U. S. Department of Justice estimates that the Casino grosses $20 million a year, and that one-third is skimmed off for American Mafia families." Included in the picture was one James Holmes, neither a high roller nor a Mafioso. He sued, claiming that the photograph and article put him in a false light (*Holmes* v. *Curtis Publishing Co.,* 1969).

Sometimes an error simply occurs, and there is nothing anyone can do about it. One simple precaution can be taken to avoid false light suits: refrain from using unrelated pictures to illustrate news stories. When the annual Christmas story warning readers to be wary of shoplifters in department stores is prepared, control the impulse to pull from the files a picture of people shopping and run it as artwork with the story. When a story warning older men to be wary of overexertion as they shovel the first snow lest they fall victim to a heart attack is published, do not use a file picture of a sixty-year-old man clearing his driveway. In both cases the juxtaposition of the story and the photograph implies a relationship which is not necessarily true.

Highly Offensive Material

Before a plaintiff can win a false light case, the court must be convinced that the material which is false is highly offensive to a reasonable person. While there are on record a handful of cases where nonoffensive material was the basis for a successful false light suit (see *Molony* v. *Boy Comics Publishers,* 1946), these cases are old and should not be regarded as authoritative today. Typical of modern decisions is the case of *Cibenko* v. *Worth Publishers*. The plaintiff is a New York–New Jersey Port Authority police officer whose photograph appeared in a college sociology text. In a section of the book entitled "Selecting the Criminals" the picture depicts a white police officer (Cibenko) in a public place apparently prodding a sleeping black with his nightstick. The caption for the picture states:

> The social status of the offender seems to be the most significant determinant of whether a person will be arrested and convicted for an offense and of the kind of penalty that will be applied. In this picture a police officer is preventing a black male from falling asleep in a public place. Would the officer be likely to do the same if the "offender" were a well-dressed, middle-aged white person?

Officer Cibenko claimed the photograph and caption made him appear to be a racist, and this was false. A United States district court in New Jersey disagreed and ruled that there was no offensive meaning attached to the photograph and caption, especially not a highly offensive meaning (*Cibenko v. Worth Publishers*, 1981).

The Fault Requirement

Since 1967 most plaintiffs in false light suits have been required to carry a fault requirement much like the one applied in libel cases. In order to win a right-to-privacy case based upon the publication of a false report, plaintiffs must show that the material was published with knowledge that it was false or with reckless disregard for the truth or falsity of the matter.

The case in which this fault requirement was applied to invasion of privacy was the first mass media–invasion of privacy suit ever heard by the United States Supreme Court. In the early 1950s the James Hill family were held captive in their home for nearly twenty-four hours by three escaped convicts. The fugitives were captured by police shortly after leaving the Hill home. The incident became a widely publicized story. A novel, *The Desperate Hours,* was written about a similar incident, as was a play and a motion-picture script. *Life* magazine published a feature story about the drama, stating that the play was a reenactment of the ordeal suffered by the James Hill family. The actors were even taken to the home in which the Hills had lived (but now vacant) and were photographed at the scene of the original captivity.

James Hill sued for invasion of privacy. He complained that the magazine used his family's name for trade purposes, and that the story put the family in a false light. *The Desperate Hours* did follow the basic outline of the Hill family ordeal, but contained many differences. The fictional Hilliard family, for example, suffered far more physical and verbal indignities at the hands of the convicts than did the Hill family.

The family won money damages in the New York state courts, but the Supreme Court of the United States vacated the lower court rulings and sent the case back for yet another trial. The Hill family gave up at this point, and no subsequent trial was held.

Justice William Brennan, in a five-to-four ruling, declared that the family's name and photographs had not been used for trade purposes. Brennan reminded all concerned that informative material published in newspapers and magazines is not published for purposes of trade (see pages 193–94), even though these publications generally are considered profit-making businesses.

Turning to the false light action, Brennan applied the same First Amendment standards he had developed in the *New York Times* v. *Sullivan* libel suit to this category of invasion of privacy litigation. "We hold that the constitutional protections for speech and press preclude the application of the New York [privacy] statute to redress false reports of matters of public interest in the absence of proof that the defendant published the report with knowledge of its falsity or in reckless disregard of the truth," he wrote. The standard applies to *all plaintiffs* who sue for false light based on stories or reports of matters of public interest. As noted previously, some persons have speculated that this rule will be narrowed and that only persons classed as public figures or public officials will be asked to prove knowledge of falsity or reckless disregard in false light cases in the future. Private persons may have to prove only negligence (see *Cantrell* v. *ABC,* 1981). But there is no evidence that the Supreme Court intends to do this. At present we must presume that all plaintiffs bear the heavier burden.

A plaintiff who is asked to prove knowledge of falsity or reckless disregard in a false light privacy suit bears the same burden as the libel plaintiff. Knowledge of falsity and reckless disregard are defined in the same fashion, and at times libel rulings are used as precedents in false light cases. Three false light cases demonstrate this.

1. In 1967 a bridge across the Ohio River between West Virginia and Ohio collapsed, killing forty-three people. Reporter Joe Eszterhas wrote a feature story about the family of one of the victims for the *Cleveland Plain-Dealer.* A year later Eszterhas revisited the scene of the tragedy and wrote a story about how the family managed without their husband and father. The story contained several inaccuracies about the family's poverty and other matters. In addition Eszterhas implied that he had seen and talked to the widow, described her, and told readers she said she refused money from people in town and was reluctant to talk about the tragedy. In fact, the woman was not at home when the reporter made his second visit, and he did not see her. The Supreme Court said that evidence of these "calculated falsehoods" was sufficient proof of actual malice (*Cantrell* v. *Forest City Publishing Co.,* 1974). The reporter must have known, Justice Stewart wrote, that a number of statements in his story were untrue.

2. Sixty-seven-year-old James Kent was released from prison after twenty-seven years of incarceration on a murder charge. He had won a new trial, and the state chose not to reprosecute. Therefore, in the eyes of the law, Kent was innocent of the murder he had been charged with. A story in the *Pittsburgh Press* on prison reform made a single-sentence reference to Kent as a man who had taken a life. He sued for publication of a false report, arguing that had the reporter checked with the prison officials he would have discovered the facts—that Kent's conviction for murder had been overturned. The

federal district court said that the story was not reckless disregard for the truth, it was not malice (*Kent v. Pittsburgh Press*, 1972):

> Obviously if Grochot [the reporter] had checked the court records relating to Kent, he could have discovered the reason for his release. Obviously too, however, he had no reason in the circumstances to entertain any doubts, quite apart from serious doubts, as to the matter of Kent's release.

3. In a case mentioned earlier, a young mother killed her three children and then took her own life. In the *National Enquirer* story about the incident the victim was pictured as "the happiest mother" with no apparent reason to commit suicide. The newspaper published what it called a "cryptic" suicide note giving no hint as to the reason for the murder-suicide. The victim's husband, Melvin Varnish, sued the weekly newspaper for publishing a false report. He proved that the reporter had access to records which indicated that Mrs. Varnish was depressed and despondent before the incident. He also proved that the reporter had a copy of the entire suicide note, of which the paper published only a portion, and that the entire note clearly explained the reasons for the murder-suicide. The federal court of appeals ruled that this evidence was sufficient to support a finding of reckless disregard for the truth (*Varnish v. Best Medium*, 1968).

Summary

It is an invasion of privacy to publish false information which places an individual into what is called a false light. However, this false information must be considered offensive to a reasonable person. Also, if the story is about a subject of public interest, the plaintiff must prove that the information was published with knowledge of its falsity or with reckless disregard for the truth.

One common victim of false light privacy suits is any drama which adds fictional material to an otherwise true story. The use of fictional rather than real names in such a drama will normally preclude a successful invasion of privacy suit. The coincidental use of a real name in a novel or stage play will not stand as a cause of action for invasion of privacy. Most false light cases, however, result from the publication of false information about a person in a news or feature story. Pictures of persons who are not involved in the stories they are used to illustrate frequently provoke false light privacy suits.

To succeed in a false light case the plaintiff must demonstrate to the court that the publication of the false material offends a reasonable person. Also, in stories about matters of public interest the plaintiff must show that the material was published with knowledge that it was false or with reckless disregard of the truth.

Before the discussion of the right of privacy comes to an end, we need to recall a few points. First, remember that only people have the right of privacy. Corporations, businesses, and governments do not enjoy the legal right of privacy as such. Second, unlike libel, the law of privacy does provide that the plaintiff may seek an injunction to stop an invasion of privacy. This action is in addition to the right to seek money damages. However, it is difficult for a plaintiff to get an injunction. Courts are very hesitant to enjoin tortious conduct unless the plaintiff can show that the action will cause irreparable injury and that the tortious conduct will likely be continued. Such was the case in the *Galella-Onassis* suit. A plaintiff is far more likely to get an injunction in either an intrusion or an appropriation case than in a private-facts or false light suit. Normally courts refuse to grant injunctions, because they believe an adequate legal remedy is available, or because they believe that the injunction could constitute prior censorship in violation of the First Amendment. The plaintiff bears an immense burden in convincing a court that prior restraint is called for. While it is possible to get an injunction, it is difficult.

Third, it is impossible to civilly libel a dead person, but a few state privacy statutes make it possible for an heir to maintain an action for invasion of privacy.

Although privacy law is not as well charted as libel law, and although there are fewer privacy cases, suits for invasion of privacy are a growing menace to journalists. If journalists stick to the job of responsibly reporting the news, they may rest assured that the chance for a successful privacy suit is slim.

BIBLIOGRAPHY

Here is a list of some of the sources that have been helpful in the preparation of chapter 4.

Books

Pember, Don R. *Privacy and the Press.* Seattle: University of Washington Press, 1972.

Articles

Bloustein, Edward J. "Privacy as an Aspect of Human Dignity: An Answer to Dean Prosser." 39 *New York University Law Review* 962, 1964.

Davis, Frederick. "What Do We Mean by Right to Privacy?" 4 *South Dakota Law Review* 1, 1959.

Levine, Marla E. "The Right of Publicity as a Means of Protecting Performers' Style." 14 *Loyola of Los Angeles Law Review* 129, 1980.

Pember, Don R. "The Burgeoning Scope of Access Privacy and the Portent for a Free Press." 64 *Iowa Law Review* 1155, 1979.

Pember, Don R., and Teeter, Dwight L. "Privacy and the Press Since *Time, Inc.* v. *Hill.*" 50 *Washington Law Review* 57, 1974.

Prosser, William L. "Privacy." 48 *California Law Review* 383, 1960.

Sims, Andrew B. "Right of Publicity: Survivability Reconsidered." 49 *Fordham Law Review* 453, 1981.

Cases   *Acquino* v. *Bulletin Co.*, 190 Pa. Super. 528 (1959).
Ali v. *Playgirl*, 447 F. Supp. 723 (1978).
Allen v. *Combined Communications*, 7 M.L. Rept. 2417 (1981).
Anderson v. *WROC-TV*, 441 N.Y.S.2d 815 (1981).
Arrington v. *New York Times*, 55 N.Y.2d 433 (1982).
Barber v. *Time, Inc.*, 159 S.W.2d 291 (1942).
Beresky v. *Teschner*, 381 N.E.2d 979 (1978).
Berg v. *Minneapolis Star & Tribune*, 79 F. Supp. 957 (1948).
Bernstein v. *NBC*, 232 F.2d 369 (1955).
Bilney v. *Evening Star*, 406 A.2d 652 (1979).
Booth v. *Curtis Publishing Co.*, 11 N.Y.2d 907 (1962).
Briscoe v. *Reader's Digest Association*, 483 P.2d 34 (1971).
Campbell v. *Seabury Press*, 614 F.2d 395 (1979).
Canessa v. *J. I. Kislak*, 235 A.2d 62 (1967).
Cantrell v. *ABC*, 529 F. Supp. 746 (1981).
Cantrell v. *Forest City Publishing Co.*, 95 S.Ct. 465 (1974).
Carlisle v. *Fawcett Publishing Co.*, 210 Cal. App.2d 733 (1962).
Cason v. *Baskin*, 159 Fla. 131 (1947).
Cassidy v. *ABC*, 377 N.E.2d 126 (1978).
Cefalu v. *Globe Newspaper*, 391 N.E.2d 935 (1979).
Cher v. *Forum International*, 7 M.L. Rept. 2593 (1982).
Cibenko v. *Worth Publishers*, 510 F. Supp. 761 (1981).
Commerce Union Bank v. *Coors*, 7 M.L. Rept. 2204 (1981).
Corabi v. *Curtis Publishing Co.*, 273 A.2d 899 (1971).
Costlow v. *Cuismano*, 311 N.Y.S.2d 92 (1970).
Cox Broadcasting Co. v. *Cohn*, 95 S.Ct. 1029 (1975).
Daily Times-Democrat v. *Graham*, 162 So.2d 474 (1962).
Deaton v. *Delta Democrat Publishing Co.*, 326 So.2d 471 (1976).
Delan v. *CBS*, 7 M.L. Rept. 2453 (1981); 9 M.L. Rept. 1130 (1983).
Dietemann v. *Time, Inc.*, 499 F.2d 245 (1971).
Dittner v. *Troma*, 6 M.L. Rept. 1991 (1980).
Durgom v. *CBS*, 214 N.Y.S.2d 752 (1961).
Factors, Etc. v. *Pro Arts, Inc.*, 579 F.2d 215 (1978); 652 F.2d 278 (1981).
Florida Publishing Co. v. *Fletcher*, 340 So.2d 914 (1976).
Forsher v. *Bugliosi*, 608 P.2d 716 (1980).
Frosch v. *Grossett & Dunlap*, 427 N.Y.S.2d 828 (1979).
Fry v. *Ionia Sentinel-Standard*, 300 N.W.2d 687 (1980).
Galella v. *Onassis*, 487 F.2d 986 (1973); 533 F. Supp. 1076 (1982).
Geisler v. *Petrocelli*, 616 F.2d 636 (1980).
Gilbert v. *Medical Economics*, 665 F.2d 305 (1981).
Griffith v. *Rancocas Valley Hospital*, 8 M.L. Rept. 1760 (1982).
Haelan Laboratories, Inc. v. *Topps Chewing Gum*, 202 F.2d 866 (1953).
Harrison v. *Washington Post*, 391 A.2d 781 (1978).
Heller v. *Family Circle*, 445 N.Y.S.2d 513 (1981).
Hicks v. *Casablanca Records et al.*, 464 F. Supp. 426 (1978).
Holman v. *Central Arkansas Broadcasting*, 610 F.2d 542 (1979).
Holmes v. *Curtis Publishing Co.*, 303 F. Supp. 522 (1969).
Howard v. *Des Moines Register*, 283 N.W.2d 789 (1979).
Jeffries v. *New York Evening Journal*, 124 N.Y.S. 780 (1910).
Jeppson v. *United Television*, 580 P.2d 1087 (1978).
Jones v. *Herald Post Co.*, 18 S.W.2d 972 (1929).

Jumez v. *ABC Records*, 3 M.L. Rept. 2324 (1978).
Kelley v. *Post Publishing Co.*, 327 Mass. 275 (1951).
Kent v. *Pittsburgh Press*, 349 F. Supp. 622 (1972).
Lancaster v. *Factors*, 9 M.L. Rept. 1109 (1982).
Le Mistral, Inc. v. *CBS*, 402 N.Y.S.2d 815 (1978).
Leverton v. *Curtis Publishing Co.*, 192 F.2d 974 (1951).
Liberty Lobby v. *Pearson*, 390 F.2d 489 (1968).
Lopez v. *Triangle Communications*, 421 N.Y.S.2d 57 (1979).
Lugosi v. *Universal*, 160 Cal. App.3d 323 (1979).
McAndrews v. *Roy*, 131 So.2d 256 (1961).
McCall v. *Courier-Journal*, 4 M.L. Rept. 2337 (1979), affd. 6 M.L. Rept. 1112
    (1980).
Man v. *Warner Brothers*, 317 F. Supp. 50 (1970).
Marks v. *King Broadcasting*, 618 P.2d 572 (1980).
The Martin Luther King Center v. *American Heritage Products*, 296 S.E.2d 697
    (1982).
Meetze v. *AP*, 95 S.E.2d 606 (1956).
Memphis Development Company v. *Factors, Etc.*, 616 F.2d 956 (1980).
Metter v. *Los Angeles Examiner*, 95 P.2d 491 (1939).
Molony v. *Boy Comics Publishers*, 65 N.Y.S.2d 173 (1946).
Moser v. *Press Publishing Co.*, 109 N.Y.S. 963 (1908).
Namath v. *Sports Illustrated*, 39 N.Y.2d 897 (1976).
Nappier v. *Jefferson Standard Life Insurance Co.*, 322 F.2d 502 (1963).
Neff v. *Time, Inc.*, 406 F. Supp. 858 (1976).
New Mexico v. *McCormack*, No. CR-81-215 (N. M.Dist. Ct., Eddy County, 1982).
Palmer v. *Schonhorn Enterprises, Inc.*, 232 A.2d 458 (1967).
Patterson v. *Tribune Co.*, 146 So.2d 623 (1962).
Paulsen v. *Personality Posters*, 299 N.Y.S.2d 501 (1968).
Pavesich v. *New England Mutual Life Insurance Co.*, 122 Ga. 190 (1905).
Pearson v. *Dodd*, 410 F.2d 701 (1969).
Peed v. *Washington Times Co.*, 55 Wash. L. Rept. 182 (1927).
People v. *Kunkin*, 100 Cal. Rptr. 845 (1972), revd. 107 Cal. Rptr. 184 (1973).
Rawlins v. *The Hutchinson Publishing Co.*, 543 P.2d 288 (1975).
Rifkin v. *Esquire*, 8 M.L. Rept. 1384 (1982).
Roberson v. *Rochester Folding Box Co.*, 171 N.Y. 538 (1902).
Russell v. *Marboro Books*, 183 N.Y.S.2d 8 (1959).
Shields v. *Gross*, 8 M.L. Rept. 1928 (1982); 9 M.L. Rept. 1466 (1983).
Sidis v. *F-R Publishing Co.*, 113 F.2d 806 (1940).
Stahl v. *Oklahoma*, 9 M.L. Rept. 1945 (1983).
State v. *Lashinsky*, 404 A.2d 1121 (1979).
Strickler v. *NBC*, 167 F. Supp. 68 (1958).
Sweenek v. *Pathé News*, 16 F. Supp. 746 (1936).
Time, Inc. v. *Hill*, 385 U.S. 374 (1967).
Uhlaender v. *Henricksen*, 159 F. Supp. 1277 (1970).
Varnish v. *Best Medium*, 405 F.2d 608 (1968).
Virgil v. *Time, Inc.*, 527 F.2d 1122 (1975), 424 F. Supp. 1286 (1976).
Welch v. *Mr. Christmas Tree*, 8 M.L. Rept. 2366 (1982).
Williams v. *KCMO Broadcasting Co.*, 472 S.W.2d 1 (1971).
Zacchini v. *Scripps-Howard Broadcasting Co.*, 433 U.S. 562 (1977).

5 ACCESS TO INFORMATION

One of the truly revolutionary changes in American journalism in the past two hundred years has been the fundamental shift in emphasis in the American press from journals of opinion, commentary, and some small bits of "intelligence" to the predominance of publications which offer readers a steady diet of news and information. The "news" paper as we know it simply did not exist in the era of the founding of the republic. And the significant legal battles which faced the eighteenth-century editor developed over the right to criticize, ridicule, and even libel the government and government officials. Sedition law was the primary legal problem faced by leading journalists who used their newspapers and pamphlets to form and lead political opinion.

To the editor of the 1980s the law of sedition is about as relevant as a hand-operated printing press. News and information are today the lifeblood of most newspapers, many magazines, and significant sections of the radio and television industry. Gathering and publishing news about government and government officials has become the central task of many journalists.

Most journalists consider the press in the United States to be the eyes and ears of the people with regard to their government, a function often referred to as "a watchdog role." It is the responsibility of the press to inform the people about their government—whether it is operating efficiently, whether it is living up to its constitutional requirements, whether it is treating its citizens fairly, whether its officials are acting responsibly and honestly. This interest in reporting on the activities of government has grown markedly since the 1930s, most particularly since the social and political upheavals of the late sixties and early seventies. Paradoxically, as the journalist's appetite for reporting news of government has grown, so too has grown the societal interest in government secrecy and the right to privacy. The modern reporter who seeks to scrutinize the operation of government at any level is frequently faced with legal impediments which stem from the countervailing interests in secrecy and privacy.

Government secrecy is not a new idea, but it has blossomed with new vigor since World War II. Secrecy results from many conditions. The cold war of the fifties provoked government to actions inconsistent with an open, democratic society. In the name of national security thousands and thousands of documents are classified as confidential or secret. In 1977 *Science* magazine reported that nearly 14,000 persons in the federal government had the power to classify material. More than 4 million documents were classified each year, and the Departments of Defense, State, and Energy and the Central Intelligence Agency were the most prolific classifiers. Scientific data which relate in obscure ways to sophisticated weapon systems, military plans and procedures, maps, photographs, documents and papers relating to foreign policy and strategic materials—all are sifted, stamped, and filed away beyond the view of the press or the public. While the veil obscuring government operations was lifted somewhat while Jimmy Carter was president, Ronald Reagan, via executive order, tightened the curtain around the operation of the executive branch of the federal government. (See page 254.)

The tremendous growth of bureaucracy at all levels of government has also resulted in cutting off public access to many governmental processes and operations. In his classic analysis of bureaucracy as a form of social organization, Max Weber argued that preoccupation with secrecy is an inherent characteristic of administrative organizations. Weber asserted that this preoccupation is based partially on the functional need to keep certain phases of administrative operation a secret to maintain a competitive edge over rival administrative units. Weber also noted that it is not uncommon that this secrecy is transformed into an obsession, that is, an action began simply as a means to achieve organizational objectives often becomes an end in itself.

The ineptness, dishonesty, and stupidity of some government officials are also conditions which provoke secrecy in government. An inefficient, unethical, or dishonest government official can find the cloak of secrecy a convenient means of covering up misfeasance or malfeasance in office.

The emergence of the right to privacy as an obstacle to gathering news and information about government is an even more recent phenomenon. Citizens of the United States have used the law of privacy as a means of redressing excesses by the press and others for nearly eight decades (this dimension of privacy is fully explored in chapter 4). As our government at all levels has become more entwined in our personal lives through massive programs of public assistance, education, financial aid, and health care, the amount of information the government possesses about individual citizens has dramatically increased. Similarly, as the scope of government regulation of business, industry, financial institutions, transportation, and other activities has enlarged, government knowledge about confidential business practices, manufacturing processes, and related matters has grown as well. And as this storehouse of information about both people and institutions has grown, government has more often raised the right of privacy of these citizens or institutions as a barrier to the scrutiny of its own operations.

The purpose of this chapter is to explore the problems of gathering news and information in a society which manifests a growing interest in secrecy and privacy, but which at the same time gives at least lip service to a growing interest in watching government more closely than ever. The chapter has five main sections:

1. The right to gather information from government which is implied or may be inferred from the common law and the First Amendment to the United States Constitution
2. Federal open records and open meetings laws
3. State open records and open meetings laws

4. Federal and state statutes which specifically preclude public access to information held by the government
5. Public and press access to evidence that is presented in a court of law

While this chapter is generally comprehensive in coverage of the federal statutes and guidelines, only an overview of state law is offered. But this does not mean that state law is not important. For most reporters state laws governing access to records and meetings are more important than federal laws, because local journalists spend more time reporting on local and state governments. To be a successful reporter a journalist must have a good working knowledge of state laws governing access to information. This knowledge is as much a part of the reporter's trade as a pencil or a notebook. A reporter without full knowledge of state laws governing access to information will simply not get all the information and news to which the public is entitled. We will all be losers. Information about state laws can be obtained from teachers and professors, from press organizations within the state (such as the Society of Professional Journalists and Women in Communication, Inc.), from attorneys who represent newspapers and broadcasting stations, and from the statutes and court decisions themselves.

NEWS GATHERING, THE COMMON LAW, AND THE CONSTITUTION

Persons unacquainted with the legal problems involved in news gathering are usually startled to discover that there is no clear common law right to gather news or information. Despite the tradition of open government both in this country and in Great Britain, the common law provides only bare access to government documents and to meetings of public agencies. In Great Britain, where the common law developed, complete and total access to Parliament, for example, was not guaranteed until 1874, and even then the House of Commons could exclude the public by a majority vote. Initially the public was excluded because members of Parliament feared reprisal from the Crown for statements made during floor debate. Later this fear subsided, but secret meetings continued in order to prevent voters from finding out that many members of the legislative body were not faithful in keeping promises to constituents.

Secrecy in England had a direct impact upon how colonial legislatures conducted their business. The Constitutional Convention of 1787 in Philadelphia was conducted in secret. The public and the press had almost immediate access to sessions in the United States House of Representatives, but it was not until 1794 that spectators and reporters were allowed into the Senate chamber. While today access is guaranteed to nearly all sessions of Congress, much (maybe even most) congressional business is conducted by committees which frequently meet in secret.

Common law precedents exist which open certain public records to inspection by members of the public, but distinct limitations have been placed upon this common law right. For example, under the common law a person seeking access to a record must have an "interest" in that record. And most often this interest must relate to some kind of litigation in which the person who seeks the record is a participant. Also, only those records "required to be kept" by state law are subject to even such limited disclosure under the common law. Many important records kept by the government are not "required to be kept" by law. Hence, the common law must be found wanting as an aid in the process of news gathering.

The Constitution and News Gathering

The United States Constitution is another source of the law in this nation. Does this document provide any assistance to the citizen who seeks to scrutinize government records or attend meetings of government bodies? Surprisingly, perhaps, the First Amendment plays a rather insignificant role in defining the rights of citizens and journalists in the news-gathering process. The amendment was drafted in an age when news gathering was not a primary function of the press. The congressional records of the drafting and adoption of the First Amendment fail to support the notion that the protection of the news-gathering process was to be included within the scope of freedom of the press. The adoption of antecedents to the First Amendment, such as the free speech provisions of the Virginia Declaration of Rights, and the letters and publications of men like Adams, Madison, and Jefferson are also found wanting in support of this idea. On August 15, 1789, during the House debate on the adoption of the First Amendment, James Madison, its principal author in the Congress, stated that if freedom of expression means nothing more than that "the people have a right to express and communicate their sentiments and wishes, we have provided for it already" in what was to become the First Amendment. "The right of freedom of speech is secured; the liberty of free press is expressly declared to be beyond the reach of this government; the people may therefore publicly address their representatives, may privately address them, or declare sentiments by petition to the whole body," Madison added. While not terribly illuminating, one is hard pressed to find within this description of the First Amendment guarantee of freedom of expression expansive notions about the right to gather news and information. The First Amendment was seen as a means by which the public could confront its government, not necessarily report on its activities.

A peripheral dimension of the relationship between the First Amendment and information gathering was raised by Justice Potter Stewart in 1974 when he asserted in a speech at Yale University that the free-press clause of the First Amendment was intended as a protection of the "publishing business"; the press as an "institution outside of Government" designed to act as a check upon the three official branches of government. The general right of freedom of expression which all members of the society share was guaranteed under the free-speech clause of the First Amendment according to Stewart.

It is tempting for the press to applaud the remarks of Justice Stewart. If Stewart is right and the free-press clause was designed to give the press, as an institution, special protection in its function as a watchdog, then freedom of the press must include the right of the press to scrutinize very closely the government it is supposed to watch. Such scrutiny would surely include the right to an almost unimpeded access to information about the government.

But Stewart offers no proof to support his contention that those who drafted the Bill of Rights intended to distinguish between the rights guaranteed under the freedom-of-speech clause and the rights protected under the free-press provision. There simply is no historical evidence to support this notion. A close study of the records of the period suggests if anything that the words *speech* and *press* were used almost interchangeably and were intended only to distinguish between those who sought to disseminate their ideas by print and those who sought to disseminate their ideas orally. Indeed, one is hard pressed to describe the printed press of the 1780s as a "publishing business" or an "organized private business," terms used by Justice Stewart in his argument.

The United States Constitution is a living document, and as Justice Oliver Wendell Holmes reminded us, each age should be the mistress of its own law. Courts are not precluded today from finding a right to gather news under the First Amendment even if such a right was not thought to exist in 1791. Yet jurists have been remarkably hesitant to rule that the First Amendment guarantees much more than the right to publish and disseminate the news. There are a few cases in which courts have said that freedom of the press implies the right to gather news and information. For example, in 1950 in Rhode Island a federal district judge ruled that when public records are restricted from examination and publication "the attempt to prohibit their publication is an abridgement of the freedom of the speech and press" (*Providence Journal Co.* et al. v. *McCoy* et al., 1950). The case involved two newspapers seeking to examine tax cancellation and abatement records. The Pawtucket city council gave permission to one newspaper (the paper which supported the city government in power), but refused to give similar access to an opposition newspaper. In addition to ruling that denial of access was an abridgement of freedom of the press, the federal court ruled this kind of action to be a denial of equal protection of the law. The court of appeals upheld the lower court ruling, but solely on the grounds of equal protection. The lower court ruling that denial of access is a violation of the First Amendment is therefore of limited value. Yet this case stands as one of the very few times when a court of any kind ruled that freedom of the press is somehow diminished when access to information is denied.

There are obvious reasons why courts might be reluctant to interpret the First Amendment as permitting a broad right of access to meetings and public records. The consequences of establishing such a principle, it is thought, would be to arm the press with a key which it would use to unlock *all* doors and thereby gain access to material restricted for the welfare and protection of society. This is a very weak argument and is based on the notion that the press is totally irresponsible and that the law is the only factor keeping newspapers and broadcasting stations from destroying this country.

There is another argument for the judiciary's unwillingness to establish a constitutional right of access.

"The reluctance of the courts to recognize distinctly a news-gathering right in the press," writes Lynn C. Malmgren in the *Villanova Law Review* (1974), "stems from a valid concern with the administrative problems and from the logical necessity of making the determination of what constitutes the press for the purposes of constitutional protection." If the right of the press to gather news is merely the same as the right of the public to gather news, the commentator adds, then the press may go only where the public may go. But if the press has a special right, reporters would have access to many more areas than does the public. The problem then is this: Who is a reporter? or What is the press? As will be noted in chapter 6 in the discussion of the shield law controversy, there is a long tradition that freedom of the press protects everyone, that the provisions of the First Amendment apply equally to a citizen who publishes a mimeographed newsletter and to the publisher of the *New York Times*. If the courts declare that the press has the constitutional right of access, they must either also delineate what comprises "the press" or be prepared to face the potential onslaught of all the citizenry seeking access to records and meetings. The courts have found it far easier just to refuse to acknowledge that the First Amendment protects the right to gather the news.

The Supreme Court of the United States has considered the First Amendment and the right to gather news in several different contexts. In 1964 the high Court ruled that the constitutional right to speak and publish does not carry with it the unrestrained right to gather information. This ruling came in an unusual case concerning the right of a United States citizen to travel to Cuba in violation of a state department ban on such travel (*Zemel* v. *Rusk,* 1964). This ruling was regarded as the law until the 1970s.

Beginning in 1972 in a series of cases involving specific news-gathering problems, the Court attempted to shape the albeit narrow boundaries of the constitutional right to gather news and information.

In *Branzburg* v. *Hayes* in 1972 the high Court suggested for the first time that the United States Constitution provides at least a limited right to gather news and information. The case involved the assertions by a trio of journalists that reporters enjoyed the right under the First Amendment to refuse to reveal to a grand jury the names of confidential news sources, since such a revelation would interfere with their ability to gather news from other confidential sources (this case is discussed more on pages 288–91). Justice Byron White, who wrote the Court's opinion for the four-man plurality, disagreed with the reporters' arguments. But, he added, "Nor is it suggested that news gathering does not qualify for First Amendment protection; without some protection for seeking out the news, freedom of the press could be eviscerated." White could find no connection, however, between news gathering and the reporters' reluctance to reveal the names of confidential news sources. Two years later the high Court considered the right to gather news in federal and state prisons.

Access to Prisons

In *Pell* v. *Procunier* (1974) reporters in California attempted to interview specific inmates at California prisons. In *Saxbe* v. *Washington Post* (1974) reporters from that newspaper sought to interview specific inmates at federal prisons at Lewisburg, Pennsylvania, and Danbury, Connecticut. In both instances the press was barred from conducting the interviews. The United States Bureau of Prisons rule, which is similar to the California regulation, states:

> Press representatives will not be permitted to interview individual inmates. This rule shall apply even where the inmate requests or seeks an interview.

At issue was not access to the prison system. The press could tour and photograph prison facilities, conduct brief conversations with randomly encountered inmates, and correspond with inmates through the mails. Outgoing correspondence from inmates was neither censored nor inspected, and incoming mail was inspected only for contraband and statements which might incite illegal action. In addition, the federal rules had been interpreted to permit journalists to conduct lengthy interviews with randomly selected groups of inmates. In fact, a reporter in the *Washington Post* case did go to Lewisburg and interview a group of prisoners.

The argument of the press in both cases was that to ban interviews with specific inmates abridged the First Amendment protection afforded the news-gathering activity of a free press.

The Supreme Court disagreed in a five-to-four decision in both cases. Justice Stewart's opinion was subscribed to by the chief justice, and Justices Blackmun, White, and Rehnquist. Justice Stewart wrote that the press already had substantial access to the prisons and that there was no evidence that prison officials were hiding things from reporters. Stewart rejected the notion that the First Amendment gave newsmen a special right of access to the prisons. "Newsmen have no constitutional right of access to prisons or their inmates beyond that afforded the general public," the justice wrote. Since members of the general public have no right to interview specific prisoners, the denial of this right to the press does not infringe upon the First Amendment.

The high Court did not disagree with the findings of the district court in the *Saxbe* case that face-to-face interviews with specific inmates are essential to accurate and effective reporting about prisoners and prisons. What the Court seemed to say was that while the First Amendment guarantees freedom of expression it does not guarantee effective and accurate reporting. In fact, about five months after the *Saxbe* and *Pell* decisions on November 2, in a speech at the Yale Law School Sesquicentennial Convocation, Justice Stewart made this exact point:

> The press is free to do battle against secrecy and deception in government. But the press cannot expect from the Constitution any guarantee that it will succeed. There is no constitutional right to have access to particular governmental information, or to require openness from the bureaucracy. The public's interest in knowing about its government is protected by the guarantee of a free press, but the protection is indirect. The Constitution itself is neither a Freedom of Information Act nor an Official Secrets Act. The Constitution, in other words, establishes the contest, not its resolution.

In 1978 the high Court split along similar lines on a case involving press access rights to a county jail. An inmate at the Santa Rita County, California, jail committed suicide in 1975. Following the death and a report by a psychiatrist that jail conditions were bad, KQED television in San Francisco sought permission to inspect and take pictures in the jail. Sheriff Houchins announced that the media could certainly participate in one of the six tours of the jail facility which were given to the public each year. However, the tours did not visit the disciplinary cells nor the portion of the jail in which the suicide had taken place. No cameras or tape recorders were allowed, but photographs of some parts of the jail were supplied by the sheriff's office.

Reporters at KQED took a jail tour, but were not happy at the limits placed upon them. Sheriff Houchins contended that unregulated visits through the jail by the press would infringe on the inmates right of privacy, could create jail celebrities out of inmates that would in turn cause problems for jailers, and disrupt jail operations. Houchins noted that reporters did have access to inmates—they could visit individual prisoners, could visit with inmates awaiting trial, could talk by telephone with inmates, could write letters to prisoners, and so forth. But KQED argued that it had a constitutionally protected right to gather news and challenged the limits (*Houchins* v. *KQED,* 1978).

Chief Justice Burger wrote the opinion for the court in the four-to-three decision in which neither Justice Blackmun nor Justice Marshall took part. "Neither the First Amendment nor the Fourteenth Amendment mandates a right of access to government information or sources of information within the government's control," Burger asserted. The chief justice seemed troubled by the argument of KQED that only through access to the jail could the press perform its public responsibility (*Houchins* v. *KQED,* 1978):

> Unarticulated but implicit in the assertion that the media access to jail is essential for an informed public debate on jail conditions is the assumption that the media personnel are the best qualified persons for the task of discovering malfeasance in public institutions. . . . The media are not a substitute for or an adjunct of government. . . . We must not confuse the role of the media with that of government. . . .

Looking back at the dictum in *Branzburg* that "news gathering is not without its First Amendment protections," Burger said this must be looked at in its context—forcing a reporter to disclose to a grand jury information received in confidence. "There is an undoubted right to gather news 'from any source within the law . . .' but that affords no basis for the claim that the First Amendment compels others—private persons or government—to supply information." Problems at the jail can be investigated by citizens' task forces or grand juries, Burger said, public bodies which can be coerced to disclose what they have discovered. There is no way to force a journalist who has been given special access to the jail to publish the information gained in such an inspection.

In the summer of 1980 the United States Supreme Court ruled that the First Amendment does provide the right for all citizens—press and public alike—to attend criminal trials (*Richmond Newspapers* v. *Virginia;* see pages 360–61 for a full discussion of this case). But the Court's opinion, written by Chief Justice Warren Burger, was less clear on the larger question of a First Amendment right to gather news. As scholar Thomas Emerson recently pointed out, "The decision can be viewed as a very narrow one, limited to a situation where the information sought historically has been available to the public and the press. . . ." In other words, the high Court ruled there is the right for the public to attend criminal trials and nothing more. Or the opinion can be read more expansively, as Emerson notes, "On the other hand, the Supreme Court held, for the first time, that the First Amendment does compel the government to furnish some information." This surely can be interpreted as a limited First Amendment right for the public and press to gather information.

The eight justices who took part in the seven-to-one decision in *Richmond Newspapers* v. *Virginia* wrote a total of seven opinions: the Court's opinion, five concurring opinions, and a dissent. The multiple opinions make it difficult to determine both the depth and breadth of the Court's devotion to a limited constitutional right to gather news and information. But at least two unambiguous points were made by the decision in this case. All seven justices in the majority agreed that the right to attend criminal trials is a right which belongs to both journalists and nonjournalists. There seems little support among the members of the high Court for a special right of access or a special news-gathering right for members of the press. Also, whatever right to gather the news that might exist within the First Amendment, it is not an absolute right. Chief Justice Burger made it clear that even the right to attend criminal trials is not absolute; in some cases some limits upon attendance could be constitutionally applied.

No clearly delineated right to gather news has emerged from court interpretations of the First Amendment during the past decade. Surely the Supreme Court is willing to protect the press as it endeavors to gather news and information from sources normally accessible to any citizen. And some members of the high Court have tentatively suggested that the press should have access to information beyond that which is provided to members of the general public. But this position has never been subscribed to by a majority of the members of the Supreme Court. Few judges anywhere are willing to accede to this notion. (But see *Westinghouse* v. *National Transportation Safety Board,* 1982, where a United States district judge ruled that journalists, but not the general public, should have access to the site of a plane crash because the press acts on behalf of the public in such cases.) Thoughtful persons have suggested that journalists should be satisfied with the right to gather news and information which is equal to that of citizens generally: If journalists are granted special rights, they might then be held accountable to fulfill special responsibilities. These persons add that the inherent strength in the constitutional guarantees of freedom of expression resides in the fact that these guarantees protect us all equally.

Summary

Access to information held by the government has been a problem faced by citizen and journalist alike for centuries. Changes in both the size and nature of government in recent years have exacerbated this age-old difficulty. The common law offers little assistance to persons attempting to inspect government records. The United States Constitution was drafted at a time when news gathering was not the central role of the press. There is little evidence to suggest that the right to gather news was intended to be guaranteed by the First Amendment. Federal courts have in recent years suggested that gathering news and information is entitled to some protection under the United States Constitution, but they have been stingy in granting such protection. The United States Supreme Court has limited the right of reporters to gather information at prisons and jails to the rights enjoyed by other citizens. And the high Court has also rejected the notion that the limited protection granted news gathering entitles journalists special rights to protect the identity of their confidential news sources. The Supreme Court did rule that all citizens have the right to attend criminal trials, and this ruling has been interpreted by some observers as suggesting that there is a First Amendment guarantee to gather news and information. The Supreme Court has also suggested, however, that any First Amendment right to gather news is a right enjoyed by all citizens, not just by the press, and that this right is not absolute.

FEDERAL STATUTES
AND NEWS
GATHERING

Neither the common law nor the Constitution has provided the clear and well-defined right of access to government information that most citizens believe is needed. Beginning in the early 1950s there have been concerted efforts by press and citizen lobbying groups to pass statutes which guarantee to public and press alike the right to inspect records and other information held by the government and to attend meetings held by public agencies. These laws exist in almost every state. In addition, there are federal open records and open meetings laws. Let us look at the federal legislation first.

The Freedom of
Information Act

Between 1789 and 1966 access to the records of the federal government was largely an unsettled question. Various housekeeping laws, administrative procedure statutes, had been passed by Congress, but none were aimed at providing the kind of access to government records that both the press and a large segment of the population believed necessary for the efficient operation of our democracy. Before 1966 the laws Congress passed were really laws authorizing information to be withheld, rather than laws forcing government agencies to open their files. Also, reporters could do little when requests for information were denied. In 1966 after many years of hearings and testimony and work, Congress adopted the **Freedom of Information Act** (FOIA) which was ostensibly designed to open up records and files long closed to public inspection.

One can write an open records law in two basic ways. The first way is to declare that all of the following kinds of records are to be open for public inspection and then list the kinds of records which are open. The second way is to proclaim that all government records are open for public inspection except the following kinds of records and then list the exceptions. Congress approved the second kind of law in 1966, and it went into effect in 1967. The law was substantially amended in 1974 and again in 1976.

The United States Freedom of Information Act gives any person access to all the records kept by all federal agencies, unless the information falls into one of nine categories of exempted material. An agency has been defined under the law as:

> . . . any executive department, military department, government corporation, government-controlled corporation or other establishment in the executive branch of government (including the Executive Office of the President), or any independent regulatory agency.

The laws govern records held by agencies in the executive branch of government and all the independent regulatory agencies like the Federal Trade Commission, the Federal Aviation Agency, and the Securities and Exchange Commission. The law does not cover records held by Congress or the federal courts.

What is a record? While Congress did not specify the physical characteristics of a record, records include not only documents written on paper, but also films, tapes, and probably even three-dimensional materials such as weapons which have been used as evidence in criminal cases. The Ninth United States Court of Appeals ruled in 1979 that computer tapes are records for the purposes of the law (*Long* v. *IRS*).

Few disagreements have arisen about the definition of either an agency or a record. But there has been considerable litigation about the nature of an "agency record." Courts have ruled that there must be a connection between the agency and the record before the FOIA is applicable. If the agency creates the record and possesses and controls the record, it is an agency record under the law. Mere possession of a record created by others does not bring the material under the FOIA. A transcript of a congressional hearing that was in the possession of the Central Intelligence Agency for thirty years is not an agency record, according to the United States Court of Appeals (D.C). The "record" had been created by Congress, which is not governed by the FOIA (*Goland* v. *CIA,* 1978). A report prepared by members of Ronald Reagan's staff prior to his inauguaration as president but possessed by a high official in the Department of Health and Human Services (HHS) is not an agency record, a United States district court recently ruled. "In this case, although copies of the report are physically located in HHS, the report was not generated by HHS, is not within the control of HHS, and indeed never entered the department's files or was ever used by the department for any purpose," Judge Gesell ruled (*Wolfe* v. *Department of Health and Human Services,* 1982).

What about records that were created by an agency, but are no longer possessed by the agency? The Reporter's Committee on Freedom of the Press raised this question before the Supreme Court of the United States in 1980. At issue were transcripts and summaries of telephone conversations made by Henry Kissinger while he was secretary of state. When Kissinger left his post in government, reporters asked the state department to see copies of these materials. The agency said it could not comply with the request because Kissinger had donated the material to the Library of Congress; the state department did not possess the records. The Reporter's Committee sued, arguing that these were agency records which should be disclosed by the Department of State under the FOIA. Justice William Rehnquist, who wrote the Supreme Court's opinion, ruled that it was unnecessary to decide whether these telephone notes were agency records since the covered agency—the Department of State—had not withheld the documents from the reporters. "The FOIA is directed only at requiring agencies to disclose those 'agency records' for which they have chosen to retain possession or control," Rehnquist added (*Kissinger* v. *Reporter's Committee,* 1980). While the facts in this case cloud the issue somewhat (were the telephone transcripts the personal property of Kissinger or something created by the agency?), the case strongly suggests that the Freedom of Information Act cannot be used to gain access to records no longer possessed by an agency.

One of the most vexing problems regarding the definition of agency records has to do with material created for an agency by a private consulting firm. Many persons argue that when the Congress amended the FOIA in 1974 it intended that the law cover all entities that "performed governmental functions and controlled information of public interest." This phrase was contained in a House of Representatives report (93rd Cong., 2d sess., H. Rept. 876) that focused on the amendment. This language surely would place many government consultants under the aegis of the FOIA, according to Anne Wright in an article in the *Georgetown Law Journal.* But the courts have not rigorously applied the law to consulting agencies, even though in some cases these firms do a tremendous amount of government work. Wright reports that in fiscal year 1979 the federal government spent $2.3 billion on consulting services. Seven federal agencies relied on consultants to meet more than 40 percent of their congressionally mandated reporting requirements, according to the legal scholar.

In 1980 the Supreme Court ruled that the FOIA does not normally apply to materials generated and retained by consulting firms. The National Institute of Arthritis, Metabolism, and Digestive Diseases (NIAMDD) hired private consultants to study the effectiveness of certain diabetes treatments. The consultants kept the raw data generated by the study, but NIAMDD had access to the data. The consultants concluded in their reports that the use of certain drugs in diabetes treatment increased the risk of heart disease. Access to the raw data was sought by persons outside government. The agency's refusal to grant access to the material was supported by the Supreme Court which ruled that data generated by a privately controlled organization which has received federal grants are not agency records. "We agree with the opinions of the courts below . . . that an agency must first either create or obtain a record as a prerequisite to it becoming an agency record within the meaning of the FOIA," wrote Justice Rehnquist for the majority of the Court (*Forsham* v. *Harris,* 1980).

Because of the importance to the news-gathering process of FOIA exemptions, of procedures for obtaining information under the FOIA, and of the potential for change in the Freedom of Information Act, all are treated here in separate sections although all are subordinate to the overall discussion of the Freedom of Information Act.

Before the FOIA becomes applicable, then, the information which is sought must be considered an agency record under the law. Agency records may be inspected and copied by the public, unless they fall into one of the nine categories of exempt material. Federal agencies are not required to withhold documents from disclosure even if they fall within an exemption to the FOIA (*Chrysler Corp.* v. *Brown,* 1979). They may choose to disclose this information. But if records or documents properly fall under one of the nine exemptions, access to this material may be properly denied under the law.

Let us look at each exemption separately, try to illuminate its meaning, and note any important court interpretations of the language in the law. The Freedom of Information Act exempts the following nine categories of materials from disclosure.

Exemption 1: Matters specifically authorized under criteria established by an executive order to be kept secret in the interest of national defense or foreign policy and in fact properly classified pursuant to such an executive order. This exemption deals with a wide range of materials, from the highest secrets of state to more or less mundane matters. The United States Court of Appeals (D.C.) recently ruled, for example, that the army's compilation of combat units operation readiness reports was properly classified as confidential and exempt from disclosure under the Freedom of Information Act (*Taylor* v. *Army,* 1982).

As adopted in 1966 this national security exemption stated, "matters specifically required by Executive order to be kept secret in the interest of the national defense or foreign policy" will not be open to inspection. The intent of the exemption was good, but in practice the exemption was badly abused, especially by the Nixon administration. In simple translation the exemption meant that any material classified confidential, secret, or top secret did not have to be revealed. In March 1973 when former President Nixon realized that testimony at the trial of Daniel Ellsberg in Los Angeles would reveal that White House security agents had rifled confidential files in the office of Ellsberg's psychiatrist, Nixon and his aides decided to cloak the raid in a national security label, classifying all information about the break-in and thereby ensuring that this information could not be revealed. This action was clearly a violation of the spirit, if not of the letter, of the FOIA.

Federal courts took the position that once information was classified the classification could not be challenged. In 1970 when scholars attempted to gain access to classified files on Operation Keelhaul, the forced repatriation of anti-Communist Russians after World War II, the Court of Appeals ruled that it did not have the authority to review an agency's decision to classify material (*Epstein* v. *Resor,* 1970). No justification for the classification was needed: all the agency need do was to go to court and assert that the material was confidential or secret. The United States Supreme Court took the same position three years later in *EPA* v. *Mink* (1973) when Congresswoman Patsy Mink sought classified documents from the Environmental Protection Agency that supposedly justified the decision to conduct a nuclear test on Amchitka Island, Alaska. Congresswoman Mink argued that the Court should review the documents in private and determine whether they were classified properly or whether the government was merely attempting to hide controversial material from the public. Justice White, and a majority of the high Court, disagreed, stating that in wording exemption one as it did Congress specifically precluded judicial inspection of the contents of classified documents:

> We do not believe that Exemption 1 permits compelled disclosure of documents . . . that were classified pursuant to this Executive Order. Nor does the exemption permit in camera [private or something that is done in the judge's chambers] inspection of such documents to sift out so-called "non-secret" components. Obviously, this test was not the only alternative available. But Congress chose to follow the Executive's determination in these matters and that choice must be honored.

Once a document is classified, the Court argued, no further inquiry can be made into its contents. By spring 1973 the time was ripe for amendment of the law. As one commentator said, "The Nixon administration was subjecting the national security label to abuse, the courts hesitated to expand their own scope of review, and the Supreme Court hinted in *Mink* that an appropriate solution would have to come from the legislative branch." The exemption was revised in 1974. Courts now have the power to inspect classified documents in private to determine whether they are classified properly. That is, the executive branch must establish criteria for classification (for example, it may declare that all material dealing with United States troop strength in Europe will be classified), and the court can then determine whether the classified documents meet the criteria set down by the government. The new law also permits a court to review decisions by government agencies to withhold requested material to determine whether decisions were properly arrived at or whether they are arbitrary and capricious.

It is important to note in respect to these changes that they are actions courts *can* take, not actions they *must* take. The Fourth Circuit Court of Appeals turned down a request that it privately examine specific secret materials to see whether the documents were classified properly. The court claimed it lacked the expertise to make such a judgment and told the complainant to file a complaint with the agency denying access originally (*Knopf* v. *Colby,* 1975).

In taking this tack the courts seemed to reflect the reluctance of Congress itself to view the FOIA as a means to reform the classification process or to bring about systematic review of individual decisions. The Senate-House conference committee report on the 1974 amendment, for example, noted:

> The executive departments responsible for national defense and foreign policy matters have unique insights into what adverse effects may occur as a result of public disclosure of a particular classified record. Accordingly, the conferees expect that federal courts . . . will accord substantial weight to an agency's affidavits concerning the details of the classified status of a disputed record.

Judicial reluctance to second-guess the executive branch on the classification of national security materials has become a much more serious problem since President Ronald Reagan sharply tightened the national security classification regulations. President Jimmy Carter had required government agencies to consider the public interest as well as the government interest before classifying any document. Under the Carter administration most documents automatically were declassified after six years unless the federal agency reviewed the material and requested reclassification for six more years. Also under President Carter, government agencies had to prove that "identifiable damage" to national security would result if the information were not classified.

President Reagan changed these policies in an executive order issued in April 1982 (Executive Order 12356). The order ended the explicit consideration of public interest before classification and directed officials to opt for the highest level of secrecy possible when classifying material. The order also permitted classification of materials if the agency could show "any damage" rather than "identifiable damage" to the national security. Material is no longer automatically declassified after six years. Reagan's executive order also permits the reclassification of material that has already been made public. These rules went into effect on August 1, 1982. Reagan added strong support for this executive order in March 1983 when he signed a directive ordering all federal employees with access to sensitive information to sign a nondisclosure agreement as a condition of gaining access to this information. The FBI was given enhanced authority to investigate so-called "leaks," and federal employees could be forced to take lie detector tests during investigations of these leaks, under provisions of the presidential directive.

Exemption 2: Matters related solely to the internal personnel rules and practices of an agency. This exemption covers what is known as "housekeeping" materials: vacation schedules, coffee-break rules, parking-lot assignments, and so forth. Little harm would result if these materials were made public; the exemption is offered simply to relieve the agencies of the burden of having to maintain such material in public files.

The most controversial aspect of exemption two is whether it applies to agency staff manuals. For example, a citizen recently sought access to a Bureau of Alcohol, Tobacco, and Firearms staff manual entitled *Surveillance of Premises, Vehicles, and Persons*. The Bureau released all but twenty pages of the manual which it said described internal personnel rules and practices of the agency. The United States Court of Appeals for the District of Columbia ruled in favor of the agency in the lawsuit that followed. The court noted that during the debate on the FOIA in Congress members spoke without contradiction that exemption two was designed to protect law enforcement investigatory manuals from disclosure (*Crooker* v. *Bureau*, 1981). Other federal courts agree (See *Hardy* v. *Bureau of Alcohol, Tobacco, and Firearms*, 1980).

Exemption 3: Matters specifically exempted from disclosure by statute (other than section 552b of this title) provided that such statute (a) requires that the matters be withheld from the public in such a manner as to leave no discretion on the issue, or (b) establishes particular criteria for withholding or refers to particular types of matters to be withheld. This exemption is designed to protect from disclosure information required or permitted to be kept secret by dozens of other federal laws. A wide range of records fall under this exemption including census bureau records, public utility information, trade secrets, patent applications, tax returns, bank records, veterans benefits, and documents held by both the Central Intelligence Agency and the National Security Agency.

Courts generally ask three questions when determining whether exemption three applies to a specific record or document.

1. Is there a specific statute that authorizes or requires the withholding of information?
2. Does the statute designate specific kinds of information or outline specific criteria for information which may be withheld?
3. Does the record or information which is sought fall within the categories of information which may be withheld?

If all three questions are answered yes, disclosure can be legally denied.

Exemption 4: Trade secrets and financial information obtained from any person and privileged or confidential. A trade secret has been defined as information used in business that is commercially valuable to the user, is secretly maintained, and is not generally known in the trade. The "financial information" exemption applies only to information supplied to the government by individuals or private business firms. It is this second section of the exemption that has undergone the most thorough judicial interpretation. The *Miami Herald* recently sought records from the Small Business Administration (SBA) regarding loans made to small contractors that had become delinquent. The SBA attempted to block the disclosure by citing exemption four. Courts have interpreted exemption four to apply only if the disclosure of the information will impair the government's ability to obtain information in the future, or cause substantial harm to the competitive position of the person from whom the information was obtained. The SBA failed to present any evidence that the delinquent borrowers would suffer competitive harm if this information was disclosed. In fact, there was no evidence presented that the borrowers were even in competition with anyone. A United States court of appeals ordered the material disclosed (*Miami Herald* v. *Small Business Administration,* 1982). The federal courts have applied the criteria outlined above in the *Miami Herald* case rigorously. To block disclosure the government must clearly demonstrate that the provider of the information will suffer considerably more than mere embarrassment or a small loss of business.

Exemption 5: Interagency and intraagency memorandums and letters which would not be available by law to a private party in litigation with the agency. This exemption is described in an FOI Service Center bulletin as designed to protect working papers, studies, and reports prepared within an agency or circulated among government personnel as the basis of a final agency decision. In addition, this exemption shields from disclosure communications between an agency and its attorney.

Two recent cases demonstrate the kinds of materials covered by exemption five. A request was made for material on the United States Air Force report on the use of herbicides in Vietnam. The government provided the final report prepared by the Air Force, but refused to give out portions of the first draft of the report which were never included in the final report. The court of appeals upheld the government's refusal. The court said (*Russell* v. *Air Force,* 1982):

> There are essentially three policy bases for this privilege. First, it protects creative debate and candid consideration of alternatives, within an agency, and thereby improves the quality of the agency policy decisions. Second, it protects the public from the confusion that would result from premature exposure to discussions occurring before the policies affecting it had actually been settled upon. And third, it protects the integrity of the decision-making process itself by confirming that "officials should be judged by what they decided, not for matters they considered before making up their minds."

The portions of the first draft of the report sought by the plaintiff in the case were considerations not decisions and part of the decision-making process, designed to be protected by this exemption.

However, in another instance, the same court ruled against the government when it attempted to use exemption five. In the late 1970s the United States attorney general set up a task force to investigate charges that a Federal Bureau of Investigation (FBI) informant inside the Ku Klux Klan had committed illegal acts while in the Klan, including shooting a civil rights worker. A 302-page report was produced, and *Playboy* magazine sought a copy of the document. The FBI resisted, citing several exemptions including exemption five. The court ruled that while some parts of the report (i.e., names and identifying data) were exempt from the law under other exemptions (exemption seven), the entire report was not protected under exemption five. This exemption is designed to protect the deliberative process, to protect opinions and recommendations from which government decisions are made, the court said. It does not protect purely factual material appearing in documents in a form that is totally severable without compromising the private remainder of the documents (*Playboy* v. *Justice Department,* 1982).

Exemption five is also called the "executive privilege exemption." **Executive privilege** is an old concept in the history of the republic. Since 1794 beginning with President George Washington, American chief executives have asserted that the president enjoys a common law privilege to keep presidential papers, records, and other documents secret. Washington asserted the privilege when Congress called for all papers and records in the possession of the president which would facilitate its investigation of the negotiation of the Jay Treaty, a controversial agreement with Great Britain. Washington refused to comply with the congressional demand, citing executive privilege. Andrew Jackson refused to give Congress information relating to a boundary dispute in Maine. Millard Fillmore refused a request from the Senate that he provide that body with information regarding negotiations with the Sandwich (Hawaiian) Islands.

In modern times, however, the heads of agencies within the executive branch have asserted that they also enjoy a kind of limited executive privilege. Exemption five covers the kinds of documents—working papers, memorandums, and so forth—traditionally claimed exempt from public scrutiny by executive privilege. The purpose of the exemption is to protect the confidentiality of the decision-making process. However, exemption five is often used as a shield to avoid disclosing all manner of material totally unrelated to decision making. Legal memorandums, correspondence, minutes and transcripts, staff analyses, interpretations and opinions, and recommendations of experts and consultants have all been at one time or another declared to fall within the boundaries of exemption five.

In 1974 in *U.S.* v. *Nixon*, the Supreme Court sharply limited the boundaries of the traditional executive privilege. In this case several of the famous White House tapes were subpoenaed by the special prosecutor for use in the criminal trial of some of the Nixon aides. The former president argued that the tapes were protected by executive privilege. He said that revelation of the material on the tapes would damage the integrity of the decision-making process, and that under our system of separation of powers the courts were precluded from reviewing his claim of privilege. He also argued that even if his claim of absolute executive privilege should fail the court should at least hold as a matter of constitutional law that his privilege superseded the subpoena.

However, in a unanimous opinion (eight-to-nothing since Justice Rehnquist did not participate in the decision) the Burger Court rejected the notion of absolute privilege in this case. The Court said that an absolute privilege can only be asserted when the material in question consists of military or diplomatic secrets. When other kinds of information are involved, privilege of the president must be balanced against other values, in this case, against the operation of the criminal justice system. The need for the privilege must be weighed against the need for the information. Courts will have to make these decisions from private examination of the materials in question.

How does this decision affect exemption five? Since exemption five is based on the notion of the executive privilege, and since the courts have said such an absolute privilege does not exist in the absence of military or diplomatic secrets, agencies which claim exemption five as reason to deny access will have to allow the courts to scrutinize the material in question and evaluate whether the need for secrecy outweighs the benefits of disclosure. The mechanical process of the past under which agencies could gain the exemption merely by asserting that the material in question fell under the purview of the fifth exemption is probably gone. Now, when they are challenged, agencies will have to prove to a judge that the material does in fact come within the fifth exemption. Disclosure of much such material withheld in the past should be ensured.

Exemption 6: Personnel and medical files and similar files the disclosure of which would constitute a clearly unwarranted invasion of privacy. This exemption is designed to shield from public view personal and private information held in government files about millions of Americans. There has been considerable litigation involving exemption six, and it is possible to outline a fairly authoritative interpretation of its meaning.

The exemption protects "personnel and medical and similar files." What are similar files? They are files which contain highly personal information, similar to the kind of personal information which can be found in medical and personnel files. In February 1981 the United States Court of Appeals (D.C.) suggested that "similar files" were files *like* medical and personnel files (*Washington Post* v. *State Department,* 1981). But fifteen months later the Supreme Court of the United States rejected that interpretation and said that that phrase "similar files" had a broad meaning and covered a wide range of different kinds of files. What is being protected from disclosure, Justice William Rehnquist wrote for the unanimous Court, is a kind of *information,* not a kind of *file.* An individual's medical and personnel files contain highly personal information about that individual. A file is a "similar file" if it contains the same kind of highly personal information (*State Department* v. *Washington Post,* 1982). Be careful here. Not every file that contains personal information will be considered a "similar file." "The test is not merely whether the information is in some sense personal, but whether it is of the same magnitude—as highly personal or as intimate in nature—as contained in personnel or medical records," according to the First United States Court of Appeals (*Kurzon* v. *Health and Human Services,* 1981; see also *Miami Herald* v. *Small Business Administration,* 1982).

Establishing that a file contains personal information is only the first step in the application of exemption six. The court must ask two additional questions:

1. Would the release of this information constitute an invasion of personal privacy?
2. If it will, is this invasion of privacy clearly unwarranted?

Whether an invasion of privacy is warranted or unwarranted will be determined largely by the public benefit which may be derived from the release of the information. In a 1976 decision the Supreme Court said that exemption six does not protect from disclosure every incidental invasion of privacy, but rather "only such disclosures as constitute clearly unwarranted invasions of personal privacy" (*Department of the Air Force* v. *Rose,* 1976). A United States district court in Washington, D.C., recently rejected a request by the *Congressional Quarterly* to gain access to navy department records that list the description, quantity, and price of prescription drugs ordered for members of Congress. The navy operates the Office of the Attending Physician to the United States Congress. Even though no names would be revealed through the release of the data, the court said this material—when put together with other information gathered in other places—would reveal considerable information about the personal health of members of Congress. This is intimate personal information and its release would be an invasion of privacy. The information is of almost no value to the public, the court concluded; hence it is a clearly unwarranted intrusion into the private lives of these legislators (*Arieff* v. *Department of the Navy,* 1982).

Exemption 7: Investigatory records compiled for law enforcement purposes, but only to the extent that the production of such records would (a) interfere with enforcement proceedings, (b) deprive a person of the right to a fair trial or an impartial adjudication, (c) constitute an unwarranted invasion of personal privacy, (d) disclose the identity of a confidential source and, in the case of a record compiled by a criminal law enforcement authority in the course of a criminal investigation or by an agency conducting a lawful national security intelligence investigation, confidential information furnished only by the confidential source, (e) disclose investigative techniques and procedures, or (f) endanger the life or physical safety of law enforcement personnel.

The release of certain documents could seriously harm ongoing criminal or civil investigations being conducted by federal agencies. This exemption is designed to block the release of these documents. At one time many federal agencies used this exemption in a loose fashion to improperly shield a wide range of information. Exemption seven was amended in 1974, and now the law requires the government to prove that documents it seeks to withhold were compiled for specific criminal, civil, or other law enforcement proceedings, and that disclosure would actually result in one of the six listed harms.

Courts follow a two-step approach in applying exemption seven.

1. Was the document an investigatory record compiled for law enforcement purposes?
2. If it was, would the release of the document have one of the six results specified in the exemption?

A recent court ruling demonstrates how this exemption is applied. The Office of Federal Contract Compliance of the labor department charged Rockwell International with maintaining discriminatory employment practices. A FOIA request was made to gain access to documents related to these charges, but the labor department refused, citing exemption seven. Were these documents investigatory records? A United States district court said yes; an investigation was underway into Rockwell employment practices. Were these documents compiled for law enforcement purposes? The review of these employment practices was undertaken to see whether Rockwell hiring practices violated federal law. Law enforcement purposes include activities directed toward enforcing the law, and include prevention as well as detection and punishment, the court said. Will the release of this information interfere with enforcement proceedings? Yes, the court concluded. Rockwell and the labor department were undertaking intensive conciliation meetings in an attempt to resolve this problem. Conciliation is a valuable dispute-resolution mechanism. The release of these documents could interfere with this process, the court said. It could also harm future efforts to gain compliance with antidiscrimination laws by making the conciliation process ineffective and making the government attempts to obtain voluntary compliance more difficult (*Brinkerhoff* v. *Montoya,* 1981; see also *Alirez* v. *NLRB,* 1982).

Summaries of investigatory records compiled for law enforcement purposes are also protected by exemption seven, according to a 1982 ruling by the Supreme Court of the United States. In 1969 the White House requested that the FBI summarize and transmit to the president information in its files concerning particular individuals who had criticized the administration. Howard Abramson sought to see these summaries in 1976. The FBI said the documents were shielded by exemption seven; these were investigatory records gathered for law-enforcement purposes. Abramson agreed that so long as the information was in the FBI files it was exempt from disclosure, but when it was taken out of the files, summarized, and sent to the White House, it was no longer an investigatory record compiled for law enforcement purposes. The high Court disagreed in a five-to-four ruling. "We hold that information initially contained in a record made for law-enforcement purposes continues to meet the threshold requirements of exemption seven where that recorded information is reproduced or summarized in a new document prepared for a non–law enforcement purpose," Justice Byron White wrote for the majority. He said there was no question that exemption seven would shield the data if the FBI had given verbatim records to the White House. Summarization of this data does not withdraw the material from the protection of exemption seven. In a sharp dissent Justice William Brennan accused the majority of rewriting the law and said the court was rejecting a logical and straightforward interpretation of the statute and replacing it with one less plausible (*FBI* v. *Abramson,* 1982).

Exemption 8: Matters contained in or related to examination, operating, or condition reports prepared by, on behalf of, or for the use of any agency responsible for the regulation and supervision of financial institutions. This is a little-used exemption that is designed to prevent the disclosure of sensitive financial reports or audits which, if made public, might undermine the public confidence in banks, trust companies, investment banking firms, and other financial institutions.

Exemption 9: Geological and geophysical information and data, including maps concerning wells. People who drill oil and gas wells provide considerable information about these wells to the government. This exemption prevents speculators and other drillers from gaining access to this valuable information.

Handling FOIA Requests

Government departments must answer requests for records and documents within ten days. If an appeal is filed after a denial, the agency has only twenty days to rule upon the appeal. Each agency must publish quarterly, or more frequently, an index of the documents and records it keeps. If an agency charges for searching out records or for duplicating them, it must have a uniform schedule of fees (everyone is charged the same amount) and the charges must be fair and reasonable.

The cost factor has been used by agencies in an attempt to thwart FOIA requests. Attempts have been made to place heavy financial burden on persons seeking information. When Philip and Sue Long sought certain records from the Internal Revenue Service (IRS), the agency said that identifying data would have to be edited from the records and that the Longs would be billed for the editing costs—some $160,000. The Ninth Circuit Court ruled against the taxing agency and said that while it was permissible to charge persons seeking records for the cost of searching out the documents or duplicating them the agency had to bear the costs of segregating the identifying data from the material that must be released under the law. As it turned out, the Longs wanted far fewer records than the IRS asserted, and the cost of editing was only a fraction of the initial estimate of $160,000 (*Long* v. *IRS,* 1979).

Agencies are required to report to Congress each year and must include in the report a list of the materials to which access was granted and to which access was denied and the costs incurred. If a citizen or a reporter has to go to court to get the agency to release materials and the agency loses the case, the agency may be assessed the cost of the complainant's legal fees and court costs. Finally, agency personnel are now personally responsible for granting or denying access, a requirement federal agencies object to strenuously. An employee of an agency who denies a request for information must be identified to the person who seeks the material, and if the access is denied in an arbitrary or capricious manner, the employee can be disciplined by the Civil Service Commission.

The Freedom of Information Act is not difficult to use. In an informative article in the *Columbia Journalism Review* ("The Revised F.O.I. Law and How to Use It"), longtime right-of-access proponent Sam Archibald offers some suggestions to journalists on making the law work.

1. Find out which agencies have the material in which you are interested. The *United States Government Manual* lists all federal agencies (Archibald writes), explains what they are supposed to do, and usually lists local addresses and telephone numbers.

2. Call or write the agency to get background information about the material and information in which you are interested.

3. When you have determined what records you seek, write an official request for the material. Address it to the head of the agency, describe as specifically as possible the material you seek, and state that the request is made under the Freedom of Information Act: 5 United States Code, Section 552 (see "Sample FOI Request Letter").

4. If your request is rejected, file an appeal with the head of the agency. Send along the copy of the rejection letter and make a strong argument why you think the material is not exempt.

5. If the appeal is rejected—and you really want to get the material— go to court. This final point, more than any other, needs to be emphasized. So long as government agencies are confident that the press and public will not bother with lawsuits, the tendency to withhold information will be reinforced. But strong sanctions can be applied against government officials who are found to have deliberately withheld material illegally. Sanctions can only be applied, however, after judicial determination of the matter. The application of this kind of pressure on a regular basis by the press and the public can have generally positive impact in the battle for open government.

Potential Changes in the Freedom of Information Act

President Ronald Reagan worked hard during his term in office to gain significant changes in the Freedom of Information Act, changes which would reduce the effectiveness of the law by tightening the restrictions on the release of information. Congress resisted these major changes. In May 1982 the Senate Judiciary Committee approved a package of rather modest changes in the law. Here are the most important of these proposed changes.

1. Agencies would be authorized to waive search and copying fees if the information is being requested by the news media, by nonprofit groups that intend to make the information public, or by scholars.

2. Exemption six would be enlarged to include "records or information concerning individuals, including compilations or lists of names and addresses that could be used for solicitation purposes, the release of which could reasonably be expected to be a clearly unwarranted invasion of personal privacy."

SAMPLE FOI REQUEST LETTER

Tele. No. (business hours)
Return Address
Date

Name of Public Body
Address

To the FOI Officer:

This request is made under the federal Freedom of Information Act, 5 U.S.C. 552.

Please send me copies of *(Here, clearly describe what you want. Include identifying material, such as names, places, and the period of time about which you are inquiring. If you wish, attach news clips, reports, and other documents describing the subject of your research.)*

As you know, the FOI Act provides that if portions of a document are exempt from release, the remainder must be segregated and disclosed. Therefore, I will expect you to send me all nonexempt portions of the records which I have requested, and ask that you justify any deletions by reference to specific exemptions of the FOI Act. I reserve the right to appeal your decision to withhold any materials.

I promise to pay reasonable search and duplication fees in connection with this request. However, if you estimate that the total fees will exceed $___ , please notify me so that I may authorize expenditure of a greater amount.

(Optional) I am prepared to pay reasonable search and duplication fees in connection with this request. However, the FOI Act provides for waiver or reduction of fees if disclosure could be considered as "primarily benefiting the general public." I am a journalist *(researcher, or scholar)* employed by *(name of news organization, book publishers, etc.)*, and intend to use the information I am requesting as the basis for a planned article *(broadcast, or book). (Add arguments here in support of fee waiver)*. Therefore, I ask that you waive all search and duplication fees. If you deny this request, however, and the fees will exceed $___ , please notify me of the charges before you fill my request so that I may decide whether to pay the fees or appeal your denial of my request for a waiver.

As I am making this request in the capacity of a journalist *(author, or scholar)* and this information is of timely value, I will appreciate your communicating with me by telephone, rather than by mail, if you have any questions regarding this request. Thank you for your assistance, and I will look forward to receiving your reply within 10 business days, as required by law.

(Signature)

Sample FOIA request letter, from *How to Use the FOI Act*, 2d ed., FOI Service Center Publication, Washington, D.C., 20005, 1980.

3. An exemption would be added barring the release of "technical data that may not be exported lawfully outside the United States without an approval, an authorization, or a license under the federal export laws."

4. The Secret Service would be given new powers to withhold information concerning its protective responsibilities.

These changes had not been adopted by the Congress by the fall of 1983.

Federal Open Meetings Law

In 1976 Congress passed and the president signed into law the Government in Sunshine Act, the **federal open meetings law.** The statute affects approximately fifty federal boards, commissions, and agencies "headed by a collegial body composed of two or more individual members, a majority of whom are appointed to such position by the president with the advice and consent of the Senate." These public bodies are required to conduct their business meetings in public. Notice of public meetings must be given one week in advance, and the agencies are required to keep careful records of what occurs at closed meetings. The law also prohibits informal communication between officials of an agency and representatives of companies and other interested persons with whom the agency does business unless this communication is recorded and made part of the public record.

Courts have strictly interpreted the requirement that the law only applies to bodies whose members are appointed by the president. In 1981 the United States Court of Appeals for the District of Columbia ruled that the Government in Sunshine Act did not govern meetings of the Chrysler Loan Guarantee Board, a body created by the Congress to oversee federal loan guarantees for the financially troubled automaker. Persons who serve on the board are not actually named by the president, but serve because they hold other federal offices (i.e., secretary of the treasury, comptroller general, chairman of the Federal Reserve). "If Congress had wanted to subject the board to the provisions of the Sunshine Act, it could have so provided when the board was established," the court noted (*Symons* v. *Chrysler Corporation Loan Guarantee Board,* 1981).

Even agencies or commissions which fall under the aegis of the law may meet behind closed doors. The 1976 law lists ten conditions or exemptions under which closed meetings might be held. The first nine of these exemptions mirror the exemptions in the Freedom of Information Act. The tenth exemption focuses upon situations in which the agency is participating in arbitration or is in the process of adjudicating or otherwise disposing of a case.

The Court of Appeals in Washington, D.C., recently ruled that agencies may not automatically hold budget deliberations behind closed doors. "The Sunshine Act contains no express exemption for budget deliberations as a whole. Specific items discussed at budget meetings might, however, be exempt and might justify closing portions of a commission meeting on an individual and particularized basis," Judge Skelly Wright ruled. In each case the agency must defend its closure of the meeting by demonstrating that the discussion would focus on material excluded from public disclosure by one of the ten exemptions (*Common Cause* v. *Nuclear Regulatory Commission,* 1982). The tenth exemption was recently used to block access to a meeting of the Nuclear Regulatory Commission. The NRC was discussing the reopening of the nuclear power plant at Three Mile Island in Pennsylvania. The federal district court ruled that this meeting would likely focus upon the final adjudication of the federal action involving the nuclear reactor and hence could be closed to press and public (*Philadelphia Newspapers* v. *Nuclear Regulatory Commission,* 1983).

There has been relatively little litigation under the Government in Sunshine Act, and reporters who work in Washington, D.C., report that compliance with the law is not good. The same problems existed in the early years of operation of the Freedom of Information Act. Constant pressure and frequent litigation against agencies which refused to comply with the FOIA finally made the law effective. The same pressure is needed to make the Government in Sunshine Act live up to its promise.

Summary

Statutes provide public access to both federal records and meetings held by federal agencies. The federal records law, the Freedom of Information Act, makes public all records held by agencies within the executive branch of government and the independent regulatory commissions. Courts have given a broad meaning to the term *record,* but have ruled that an agency must normally create and possess such a record before it becomes subject to the Freedom of Information Act. Nine categories of information are excluded from the provisions of the law. These include exemptions for national security, agency working papers, highly personal information, and law enforcement investigatory files. Agencies must publish indexes of the records they hold and must permit copying of these materials. It is important to follow specific procedures when making a Freedom of Information Act request to see certain records or documents.

The Government in Sunshine Act is the federal open meetings law. This law reaches about fifty agencies in the executive branch and the regulatory commissions. Members of these organizations are not permitted to hold secret meetings unless they will discuss material which falls into one of ten categories. These categories mirror the Freedom of Information Act exemptions, but also include a provision which permits closed-door meetings to discuss attempts to arbitrate or adjudicate certain cases or problems. This is a newer law and does not seem to work as well as does the Freedom of Information Act.

STATE LAWS ON RECORDS AND MEETINGS

It is not as easy to talk about access at the state level as it is at the federal level, for we are dealing with hundreds of different statutes. (Most states have multiple laws dealing with access to meetings, access to records, and other access situations.) We can at best make a few generalizations. Harold Cross made some of the most astute generalizations in 1953 in his pioneering book *The People's Right to Know.* Cross was really the first scholar to present a comprehensive report on access problems. In his book he listed four issues or questions common to every case of access.

1. Is the particular record or proceeding public? Many records and meetings kept or conducted by public officers in public offices are not really public at all. Much of the work of the police, though they are public officers and work in public buildings, is not open to public scrutiny.

2. Is public material public in the sense that records are open to public inspection and sessions are open to public attendance? Hearings in juvenile courts are considered public hearings for purposes of the law, but they are rarely open to the public.

3. Who can view the records and who can attend the meetings open to the public? Many records, for example, might be open to specific segments of the public, but not to all segments. Automobile accident reports by police departments are open to insurance company adjusters and lawyers, but such records are not usually open to the general public.

4. When records and meetings are open to the general public and the press, will the courts provide legal remedy for citizens and reporters if access is denied?

The last question is probably not as important today as it was when Cross wrote his book in 1953, for at that time access to many public records and meetings in the states was based on the common law. Today this fact is no longer true. Access to meetings and records is nearly always governed by statute, and these statutes usually, but not always, provide a remedy for citizens who are denied access. This provision is more widespread in open meeting laws, which tend to be more efficient in providing access, than in open records laws, which are still weak and vague in many jurisdictions.

State Open Meetings Laws

Virtually all states have some kind of constitutional or legislative provision regarding the need for open meetings. At least forty-seven states have specific statutes which mandate open meetings, and these laws range from good to awful. The need for **open meeting laws** is obvious. There never was a solid common law right to attend the meetings of public bodies, and as noted earlier, the constitutional provisions regarding freedom of expression have proved inadequate with regard to access.

Many states have good laws with strong sanctions to be used against public officials who fail to live up to the legislative mandate.

William R. Wright II, writing in a recent edition of the *Mississippi Law Review* ("Open Meeting Laws: An Analysis and a Proposal"), outlined the basic provisions of state open meeting laws. According to Wright, the most vital provision of such a law is a strong, clear statement by the legislature to open up the deliberations and actions of the government to the people. If a provision of the law is questioned in court, a strong legislative declaration in favor of open access can be used to persuade a judge that if a section of the law is vague it should be interpreted to grant access rather than to restrict access, since that is what the legislature wants.

In Washington the state's open meeting law begins as follows:

> The legislature finds and declares that all . . . public agencies of this state and subdivisions thereof exist to aid in the conduct of the people's business. It is the intent of this chapter that their actions be taken openly and that their deliberations be conducted openly.

State legislatures have usually written their open meeting laws in one of two ways. Some state legislatures have declared that all meetings will be open except specific meetings and then list the meetings to be open. Other states list the agencies which must hold open meetings. Generally excluded from the provisions of an open meeting law in either case are meetings of the legislature itself, of legislative committees, of parole and pardon boards, of law enforcement agencies, of military agencies like the national guard, of public hospital boards, and so forth.

Wright says that a good law should specifically define a meeting by giving the number of members of the board or commission who must be present to constitute a public meeting (a quorum? at least two? etc.), by stating that all deliberative stages of the decision-making process are considered meetings and must be open to the public, and by stating that social gatherings and chance encounters are not considered meetings and are therefore excluded from the provisions of the law. Some laws are not this specific and merely refer to all meetings, all regular or special meetings, all formal meetings, or whatever.

The exclusion of chance meetings and social gatherings is often troublesome to the press, especially in small towns. It is not uncommon that all members of the school board or the city council happen to have dinner at the same restaurant just before a meeting. If the dinner is obviously a ploy to avoid the law, a suit can be brought against the members. Often it is difficult to prove that the dinner is anything other than a chance encounter or a social gathering.

Most open meeting laws provide for closed or **executive sessions** in certain kinds of cases. Meetings at which personnel problems are discussed is an obvious example. A public airing of a teacher's personal problems could be an unwarranted invasion of privacy. The discussion of real estate transactions is another obvious example. When a school board considers buying a parcel of land for a new high school, premature public disclosure of this fact could cost the taxpayers money should the owner raise the price of the property or speculators buy it and force the school district to pay far more than it is worth. Meetings involving public safety are sometimes best conducted in private rather than in public. Virtually every open meeting law has the provision that no final action can be taken at an executive session, that the board or commission must reconvene in public before a final determination can be made on any issue.

Most open meeting statutes require not only that meetings be open to the public, but also that the public be notified of both regular and special meetings far enough in advance that they can attend if they wish. Time requirements vary, but normally a special meeting cannot be held without an announcement a day or two in advance.

The laws in more than one-half of the states provide procedures for enforcement. In other states complainants must muddle through on their own in the courts. In many states any action taken at a meeting which was not public, but should have been public, is null and void. The action must be taken again at a proper meeting. Most laws provide fines and short jail terms for public officers who knowingly violate the law, but prosecution is rare.

While a few laws date from the nineteenth century, the open meeting laws in most states are a relatively new phenomenon. Such laws, which owe their passage to strong, forceful pressure from the press, have developed largely since 1950. In 1959 only twenty states had such laws. Formation in the early 1970s of the public lobby Common Cause gave great impetus to the passage of open meeting laws. In 1972 and 1973, alone, nine states passed such statutes. But after it had evaluated all of the nation's open meeting laws in 1973, the organization concluded that many states had inadequate laws. Common Cause defined an adequate law as one which covers both the legislative and executive branches, permits executive sessions only in extremely limited circumstances, and also includes provisions which void actions taken at illegally closed sessions.

One commentator recently noted that the lack of effectiveness of these laws "means that the reporter's most marketable skill is still very much in demand for covering local government. His or her special talent has been to ferret news from unexpected or well-cultivated sources." There is much truth in this statement with regard to open meeting laws. Despite open meeting legislation, one informal remedy is still very effective: to subject the commission or board which decides to meet in secret to public embarrassment. Reporters should never voluntarily leave a meeting which they believe should be public. Rather, they should force public officials to escort them to an exit. Resistance is not advised, for criminal charges then might be levied against the reporter. If possible, a photographer should record the removal from the meeting. The photograph and the story can then be prominently featured on page one the next day. Public officials do not really like to meet in public, but they like even less to be pictured conducting "the public's business" behind closed doors. Voters begin to wonder what goes on in secret meetings.

State Open Records Laws

Every state in the union, except Mississippi, has some kind of **open records law.** The access laws either follow the federal formula—all records are open except the following—or list the kinds of records which the public does have a right to inspect. In a useful article in the *George Washington Law Review* attorneys Burt Braverman and Wesley Heppler ("A Practical Review of State Open Records Laws") outlined the basic dimensions of the state freedom of information laws.

Most state laws permit inspection of records by any person, but a few limit access to public records to citizens of the state. The reason persons want to see a record is normally considered immaterial when determining whether they can gain access to the record. The freedom of information laws provide access to records held by public agencies in the state, and normally these statutes provide a broad definition of these agencies. In Washingon, for example, an "agency" includes both state and local agencies. The law further states:

> State agency includes every state office, public official, department, division, bureau, board, commission, or other state agency. Local agency includes every county, city, city and county, school district, municipal corporation, district, political subdivision, or any board, commission or agency thereof, or other local public agency.

State access laws usually do not include the courts or legislature in the definition of agency.

Braverman and Heppler report that state laws follow either a liberal or conservative definition of a public record. *All records possessed by an agency* are deemed to be public records in those states with a liberal definition of a public record. But some state laws are more conservative and provide access only to those *records which are required to be kept by law.*

All state freedom of information laws provide exemptions to disclosure. Agencies *may* withhold material that falls under an exemption in some states; agencies *must* withhold this information in other states. Braverman and Heppler list the six most common substantive exemptions to the state open records laws as follows:

1. Information classified as confidential by state or federal law
2. Law enforcement and investigatory information
3. Trade secrets and commercial information
4. Preliminary departmental memoranda (working papers)
5. Personal privacy information
6. Information relating to litigation against a public body

The attorneys report that although state laws vary widely state courts have almost uniformly held that exemptions should be construed narrowly. That is, they should be read in such a way as to provide public access to the greatest amount of information. The federal Freedom of Information Act requires agencies to maintain an index of documents and records; not many state laws have the same requirement. But in every state except Indiana the right to inspect records includes the right to copy records. Procedures to gain access to state agency records follow the federal FOIA model. Two-thirds of the state statutes have provisions for judicial review of agency rulings where the state bears the burden to show that the record should remain undisclosed. But at least two states have tried to develop means which keep the question of access to records out of court.

Connecticut has established an independent commission to handle citizen appeals on denial of information requests. The three-member commission must meet within twenty days after receiving an appeal, hear the matter, and issue a ruling within fifteen days. The body can uphold the denial or make the agency provide access to the material. Either citizens or government agencies can appeal any decision by the commission to a court.

The New York State access law established a Committee on Public Access to Records. This committee has wide authority to issue regulations for the use of records and implementation of the new statute. There are seven members on the committee—three government officials and four persons appointed by the governor, two of whom must be from the media. The committee's function is different from the Connecticut commission which acts as a review board. In New York the committee advises agencies and local government on access questions through guidelines, opinions, and regulations. It is supposed to recommend changes in the law when problems arise. In addition, to make the new law work more efficiently the commission issues rules and guidelines: rules regarding the time and place records must be available, fees for copying, persons responsible for divulging records, and so forth. Finally, it is the job of the committee to ensure that the right of privacy of New York citizens is protected in connection with public access to the state's records. Some people criticize this last function, arguing that it makes little sense to make the same agency in charge of facilitating public access responsible for protecting the right of privacy.

This trend toward establishing public committees or commissions to handle access problems, to help interpret the law, and to issue guidelines is a very good one. It is far easier to complain to a commission when access is denied than to file a court suit. Committees like the New York Committee on Public Access to Records will make a state law far more meaningful and useful when a local government is dealt with. Access laws passed by states are often ignored at local levels because of ignorance or because citizens and press are unlikely to complain until a big issue arises. By providing guidelines and rules for local communities, a committee on public access immediately breathes life into an access law.

It is incumbent on all journalists and broadcasters to be as familiar as possible with the laws regarding access in their state. Knowledge of these kinds of laws is vital to efficient and complete reporting on government activities. Employees of public agencies are often as uninformed as average citizens about their responsibility to provide access to meetings, especially to records. Because of the normal adversary relationship between press and government, the natural tendency is to want to keep the reporter out of public documents and public meetings. Too often reporters are buffaloed by stubborn, uninformed, untruthful public employees who insist that they are not permitted by law to allow public inspection of certain records. If reporters know the law, they can recognize such bluffs on the spot and fulfill their responsibility to keep the public fully informed on the business and activities of government.

Summary

Nearly all the states have laws which govern access to public meetings and public records. Good state open meetings laws have strong legislative declarations in support of public meetings, specifically define a public meeting by listing the number of members who must gather to constitute a meeting, and declare void all actions taken during a meeting that was improperly closed to the public. Most laws provide for closed sessions to discuss such matters as personnel actions, real estate transactions, and litigation.

State public records laws tend to mirror the federal law. Both state and local agencies are governed by the laws which apply to most governmental bodies except the legislature and the courts. Most state laws govern all records kept by these agencies, but a few are applicable only to records that are required to be kept by law. Exemptions to state open records laws include material specifically excluded by other statutes, law enforcement investigatory information, working papers, and highly personal information. Most laws provide for access to the judicial system in case a request for data is rejected, but both New York and Connecticut have established commissions to act as arbiters in these matters.

LAWS WHICH RESTRICT ACCESS TO INFORMATION

Just as there are laws which provide for public access to government-held documents, there are laws which specifically preclude access to government-held information. There are provisions in scores of federal laws alone which limit the right of access. Tax statutes, espionage laws, legislation on atomic energy, and dozens of other kinds of laws are filled with limitations on the dissemination of information (e.g., personal information on taxes, national security questions, and matters relating to nuclear weapons). But in addition to these kinds of laws the federal government has adopted in the past decade at least three rather broad sets of regulations regarding information held by the government. All three were adopted in the name of protecting the right to privacy, a value which seems to have replaced national security as the most commonly asserted reason the government uses to keep things secret. While these regulations cannot here be considered in a comprehensive sense, persons who gather information for a living need to be aware of their implications.

General Education Provisions Act

An amendment to the General Education Provisions Act (1974) is aimed at increasing both the parental access to and the confidentiality of educational records. On the one hand, the law forces all federally funded schools and educational agencies to permit parents to inspect and review their children's educational records. On the other hand, the statute prohibits the distribution of personally identifiable information, excluding what is called directory data, to unauthorized persons without consent of the parents. The result is that student records or files must be kept confidential. This goal is hardly a hardship on the press in most instances. However, because of the stiff penalty in the law—possible loss to the school of federal funds—educators have occasionally overreacted and declared data that are actually unprotected by the statute to be confidential. In one absurd case a reporter-photographer indicated that school officials chased him off school property when he attempted to photograph children playing outside at recess. The officials cited the 1974 law as a reason that picture taking was no longer permitted on school property. Of course, instances like that are rare, and the significance of the law is its indication of the extreme interest in privacy today rather than its threat to the legitimate news-gathering tasks of the press.

The Federal Privacy Law

The **Privacy Act** of 1974 has two basic thrusts. First, it attempts to check the misuse of personal data obtained by the federal government, the quantity of which has, of course, reached staggering proportions. Second, the law is intended to provide access for individuals to records about themselves that are held by federal agencies. The first objective of the law could be the most troublesome to the press.

The act requires that each federal agency limit the collection of information to that which is relevant and necessary, to collect information directly from the subject concerned when possible, and to allow individuals to review and amend their personal records and information. Also, under the act agencies are forbidden from disclosing what is called "a personally identifiable record" without the written consent of the individual to whom the record pertains. Since this section of the law is seemingly contradictory to the spirit of the federal FOIA, Congress was forced to clarify the responsibilities of federal agencies with regard to the law. A provision was added to the Privacy Act that declares that records required to be disclosed under the FOIA are not subject to the provisions of the Privacy Act and consequently cannot be withheld from inspection. To the government official with control of information, however, neither the Privacy Act nor the FOIA is unambiguous.

The difficulty in resolving aspects of the Privacy Act and the Freedom of Information Act is graphically illustrated by a recent case decided by the United States Court of Appeals for the District of Columbia. Frank Greentree was indicted and convicted in federal court on drug charges. He filed a civil suit to block state prosecution based on the same events. Greentree sought information from both the Drug Enforcement Administration (DEA) and the United States Bureau of Customs to assist him in his civil action. When the agencies refused to give him the material he sought, he filed both a Freedom of Information Act request and a Privacy Act request to get the information. The documents sought by Greentree were contained in something called the Investigations Record System, and this system of records has been declared to be exempt from the access provisions of the Privacy Act. Hence it was unavailable to Greentree through the federal privacy law. Because the information could not be released under the Privacy Act, the government argued that it was also unavailable under FOIA exemption three. Remember exemption three: it provides that the Freedom of Information Act does not apply to matters "specifically exempt from disclosure by statute." The material Greentree sought was exempt from disclosure under the federal privacy statute; therefore, the government argued, it was also exempt from disclosure under exemption three of the Freedom of Information Act. In two previous appellate court rulings this government argument was sustained. (See *Terkel* v. *Kelly,* 7th Circuit, 1979, and *Painter* v. *Federal Bureau of Investigation,* 5th Circuit, 1980.) But in Greentree the United States Court of Appeals for the District of Columbia denied the validity of this argument and ruled against the government. Judge Wald said that throughout its consideration of the Privacy Act the Congress struggled to hold separate the Privacy Act and the FOIA. That effect was ultimately successful, he said. Judge Wald noted that section (b) (2) of the Privacy Act clearly states that "no agency shall disclose any record which is contained in a system of records . . . *unless disclosure of the record would be required under section 552 (The Freedom of Information Act) of this title* [author emphasis]." "We must conclude," Wald wrote, "that this section of the Privacy Act represents a congressional mandate that the Privacy Act *not* be used as a barrier to FOIA access." Congress could not have intended that a section of the Privacy Act could serve as a withholding statute under FOIA exemption three, the judge said. It is possible, he noted, that the information may not be available under exemption seven (the law enforcement exemption of the FOIA), but the government would have to prove that the material sought by Greentree was exempt from disclosure (*Greentree* v. *Customs Service,* 1982).

Discussion of the General Education Provisions Act and the Federal Privacy Law, pages 272–74, is adapted from Don R. Pember, "The Burgeoning Scope of 'Access Privacy' and the Portent for a Free Press," 64 *Iowa Law Review* 1155, 1979.

The Privacy Act imposes a cost on an agency if it releases a file that should remain private. To the bureaucrat, that presents a real dilemma, as was emphasized in the *Harvard Civil Rights/Civil Liberties Law Review* (1976):

> If government officials refuse to disclose the material, they risk being sued by the party who requested the file under the Freedom of Information Act. Under the FOIA the court may award to a successful plaintiff his costs and attorney's fees. If, on the other hand, agencies release material, they risk being sued under the Privacy Act by the person who is the subject of the file. In that case, the plaintiff might win by showing that the file was exempt from disclosure under FOIA. A successful Privacy Act plaintiff can collect not only his costs and attorney's fees, but also actual damage sustained because of disclosure.

Given this distinction between the statutes, it is easy to recognize that bureaucrats will choose to err on the side of caution—it is wiser to withhold the information and risk suit under the FOIA than possibly incur Privacy Act penalties.

Other conflicts exist in the administration of the two laws. Before passage of the Privacy Act, materials that were not required to be disclosed under the FOIA were nevertheless disclosable at the discretion of a government agency. Now, information falling under an FOIA exemption and thus not required to be disclosed will routinely be withheld out of fear of violating the Privacy Act.

Criminal History
Privacy Laws

In accordance with the broad scope of the Omnibus Crime Control and Safe Streets Act of 1968, the federal Law Enforcement Assistance Administration, an agency created by the Nixon administration to help local police forces fight crime, sought to develop a national computerized record-keeping system. The system that was established permits any police department in the nation to have access to the records of virtually all other police departments.

Congressional concern about the misuse of this record system led to limitations on access to the data. Police records have always contained a considerable amount of misinformation, information that is out of date, and information that is private. The centralized record-keeping system presents a problem referred to by some writers as the "dossier effect." The contrast between these computerized and centrally maintained records immediately accessible across the country and those police records of the past was sharp and immediately evident: fragmented, original-source records kept by a single police agency for a limited geographical area were not readily accessible because of their bulk and associated indexing problems. Hence, federal rules were adopted that require states, if they wish to participate in the national record-keeping system, to adopt rules that, among other things, limit the dissemination of some criminal history nonconviction data.

Discussion of Criminal History Privacy Laws, pages 274–76, is adapted from Pember, "Access Privacy and Free Press."

The *Code of Federal Regulations* ("Criminal Justice Information Systems") defines nonconviction data as follows:

> . . . arrest information without disposition if an interval of one year has elapsed from the date of arrest and no active prosecution of the charge is pending, or information disclosing that the police have elected not to refer a matter to a prosecutor, or that a prosecutor has elected not to commence criminal proceedings, or that proceedings have been indefinitely postponed, as well as all acquittals and all dismissals.

As a result of the state laws, press access to criminal history records kept by the police has been virtually eliminated unless data sought pertain to an incident for which a person is currently being processed by the criminal justice system, are conviction records, or are original records of entry, such as arrest records, that are maintained chronologically and are accessible only on that basis. Reporters can also obtain information about arrests not resulting in conviction, however, if they are aware of the specific dates of the arrests. The new laws have been in effect too short a time to determine whether they will substantially affect the press's ability to meet its societal responsibility to scrutinize and report on the criminal justice system. Nevertheless, potential problems are apparent. In commenting on the social desirability of press access to criminal records Higgins ("Press and Criminal Record Privacy") recently noted:

> On the one hand, the uncontrolled dissemination and publication of certain criminal history records can adversely affect the individual himself. On the other hand, the public and the press must have access to basic records of official action if they are to effectively scrutinize and evaluate the operations of the police, the prosecuting agencies, and the courts.

The ability to achieve that scrutiny is important. For example, it is possible to envision a situation in which a prosecutor is accused of favoring friends or certain ethnic or racial groups when deciding whether to prosecute arrested persons. Without access to arrest records that can be compared with prosecution records, such a charge would be difficult to investigate. Persons within the criminal justice system could gain access to the needed records, but history indicates that these people must be prodded before they take action. And, of course, prodding is the function of the press.

There is another related, more serious problem that should be of great concern to persons earnestly worried about invasions of privacy. If the press cannot obtain official criminal history records, which admittedly are sometimes incorrect, journalists will rely on their own record-keeping systems, which are much more frequently inaccurate. Newspapers and broadcasting stations usually build record systems—called morgues—by saving clippings from newspapers and film from newscasts. Errors in these original stories are seldom corrected. For example, suppose Jones was arrested in 1965 and charged with driving a stolen car. The local newspaper published incorrectly that he was arrested for car theft. Jones was never prosecuted. Fifteen years later he runs for the school board. The newspaper goes back into its own records—which it cannot verify with the police—and republishes its original error, that Jones was arrested for car theft. In such circumstances everyone—Jones, the press, the public—suffers.

To avoid such consequences, society would probably be served better if laws were passed that force law enforcement agencies to continually monitor, update, and correct their criminal records, but that nevertheless permitted public access to the records. Such laws could require, for instance, that when arrest data are released disposition data must accompany the arrest data. There is, of course, no guarantee that the press or other agencies would publish the complete story—the arrest and the dismissal, for example, or the arrest and the subsequent acquittal—but no system that depends on a human element is risk free. In the end, public access to complete and accurate information is much to be preferred to a growing dependence on "private" media data banks.

State Statutes Which Limit Access to Information

All states have statutes which limit access to information that would otherwise be available under a freedom of information law. Arizona, for example, has thirty-nine such laws. Some of these state statutes are aimed at blocking access to trade secrets; others limit access to information submitted to the state in compliance with environmental laws. The working papers of assessors, poll lists from prior elections, and reports from oil and gas companies are also frequently exempted from disclosure by a specific statute. State privacy laws are the most common kind of statutory limitation on the access to information.

In 1978 it was reported in *Access Reports* that forty-three of the fifty states had statutes which limited access to government-held information on right-to-privacy grounds. While these laws are not traditionally thought of in the same terms as the tort of privacy (see chapter 4), they nevertheless have a similar impact. Tort law discourages the publication of private information by penalizing the press through the assessment of money damages. These statutes permit the state to institute civil or criminal action against the press for the publication of so-called private information or simply to bar access to this material so that it cannot be published.

Newspapers in Alabama can no longer get information regarding births and deaths from county officials. Citing state laws and rulings by the public health board, county officers say only persons who have a "valid and tangible interest" in these materials can gain access to them. Otherwise, publication of such information can be an invasion of personal privacy (*Birmingham News v. Roper,* 1978). In Vermont the press had to go to court to force the release of information relating to pardons granted several persons by a former governor of the state. Lower courts had ruled that the disclosure of such material might constitute an unwarranted invasion of the privacy of the persons pardoned. Yet it was only through the release of this information that citizens could evaluate the governor's actions in granting these pardons. The state supreme court finally opened up the records (*Doe* v. *Salmon*, 1977).

These two rulings are symptomatic of a wide range of privacy problems which have begun to haunt persons interested in access to information. In recent years fear of losing privacy has provoked passage of laws which impede the public's right to information. The press has generally failed to bring the negative aspects of these new privacy laws to the attention of the public, and now we all must suffer what may be severe consequences. Invasion of privacy statutes and invasion of privacy exemptions are perhaps the most common impediments to full access to government-held information in the United States today.

Summary

All of the states and the federal government have laws which specifically exclude certain kinds of information from the public scrutiny. Some of these exclusions were noted in the discussion of exemption three of the Freedom of Information Act. Today, the right to privacy has been erected as a substantial barrier to access to information held by government agencies. The federal government has adopted a law protecting the privacy of student records. The Congress passed a federal privacy law, which often conflicts with the provisions of the Freedom of Information Act. The federal government has also insisted that states pass statutes which control access to criminal history records. Much privacy legislation has been passed by the states themselves, and today the right to privacy is being erected frequently to block access to public records.

**ACCESS TO
JUDICIAL RECORDS**

Courts generally govern the access to information gathered through the judicial system. While the press and public have had some difficulty in recent years in gaining access to pretrial hearings and in some instances even in gaining access to trials (see pages 352–63), it is a general rule that evidence introduced in a criminal or civil case is open to public inspection. It may be viewed, described, or photographed. But what if the evidence is a videotape of the defendant committing a criminal act, or an audiotape of the defendant proposing an illegal deal? Can these tapes be broadcast over radio and television?

This is a recent access problem for both courts and broadcast journalists. The seeming litany of government "sting" and "scam" undercover operations have provided ample opportunity for this issue to be litigated. Thus far the federal courts have not reached a consensus on the matter. In some instances courts have permitted this material to be copied and then broadcast or telecast. In other instances the courts have refused to allow such access to these materials.

The lack of resolution of this issue is at least partially the result of a decision by the Supreme Court of the United States. Tapes made by President Richard Nixon at the White House were used as evidence in many of the Watergate trials of the seventies. Broadcasters sought to make copies of these tapes and broadcast them. The high Court agreed that there is a generally recognized right to access to inspect the evidentiary record in a case, but this is not an absolute right. "The decision as to access is one best left to the sound discretion of the trial court, a discretion to be exercised in light of the relevant facts and circumstances of the particular case," the Court said (*Nixon* v. *Warner Communications,* 1978; see also *Nixon* v. *Carmen,* 1982).

Judges have been exercising their own discretion in these cases, and not surprisingly different judges have reached different conclusions. The courts have considered a variety of factors in reaching a decision on whether to permit the broadcast or telecast of these kinds of electronic recordings. Whether transcripts of the recordings have already been published is an important factor. Courts have also considered whether the broadcast or telecast of the material would enhance public understanding of an important historical or public occurrence. The rights of the defendant are also considered: Would the broadcast of this material prejudice the right to a fair trial? (See *U.S.* v. *Maddox,* 1982, where the court rejected a claim of potential prejudice, and *U.S.* v. *Bolen,* 1981, where the court denied broadcasters the right to telecast material because broadcast could interfere with the defendant's right to a fair trial.) It is often important whether the tapes which are sought have been introduced into evidence. When John Hinckley was tried for the attempted assassination of Ronald Reagan, the television networks sought to televise the videotaped deposition given by actress Jodie Foster in the case. The court refused the request, noting that the testimony was never admitted into evidence. It was simply a statement from a witness; it just happened to be videotaped. No right existed to videotape and telecast the testimony of other witnesses. The videotaped deposition would not be an exception to that rule (in re *Application of ABC,* 1982). The New Mexico Supreme Court recently denied the press the right to copy and broadcast recordings of wiretaps which resulted in criminal indictments but were never played in open court or received into evidence (*New Mexico* v. *Brennan,* 1982). Who has been videotaped is also an important consideration when a court examines a request to broadcast the material. Videotapes of defendants and undercover police agents are more likely to be released than recordings of innocent third parties. Jodie Foster was an "innocent witness" in the Hinckley case. She had been pulled into the case inadvertently. A United States district court in Minnesota rejected requests from broadcasters to air videotapes of a hostage recorded by her kidnapper. The court ruled that it would create serious hardship for the victim of the crime and would serve no proper purpose (in re *Application of KSTP,* 1980). A good way to outline the dimensions of this problem is to look at two different cases, one where access was granted and one where it was denied.

The government presented a considerable amount of evidence on both videotape and audiotape on Congressman John Jenrette and John Stowe in the Abscam trial. They were recordings of the defendants in the case making what the government alleged were illegal deals with undercover FBI agents. The networks sought to copy and broadcast these tapes. The United States district court refused the request, fearing that if the tapes were televised it would be difficult to later impanel an impartial jury should a retrial be ordered by a higher court. The United States Court of Appeals for the District of Columbia disagreed and promulgated this test:

> Access may be denied only if the district court, after considering the relevant facts and circumstances of the particular case, and after weighing the interests advanced by the parties in light of the public interest and the duty of courts, concludes that justice so requires. . . . The court's discretion must clearly be informed by this country's strong tradition of access to judicial proceedings. In balancing the competing interests the court must also give appropriate weight and consideration *to the presumption—however gauged—in favor of public access to judicial records* [author emphasis].

Several factors favored release of the tapes, the court concluded. They were admitted into evidence and played to a jury at a public trial. The tapes contained only admissible evidence. This was a trial where the defendant was a high public official charged with betraying the public trust. The court admitted a retrial *might* be a problem, but there was no evidence that if there was a retrial impartial jurors could not be found. What about protecting innocent third parties who were also pictured or heard in the tapes? There were only one or two instances of that, and the trial court can delete these sections, the court said. The tapes must be released (in re *Application of NBC,* 1981).

The Fifth United States Court of Appeals reached the opposite conclusion in another 1981 decision. The speaker of the Texas House of Representatives, two attorneys, and a labor leader were all indicted in an alleged bribery scheme. The speaker and the two attorneys were tried and acquitted. Broadcasters wanted to air audiotapes that had been made during the FBI sting operation which resulted in the indictments. These were discussions between the defendants and FBI undercover operatives that had been secretly recorded. The trial court refused on the grounds that the broadcast might make it difficult for the fourth defendant to have a trial by an impartial jury. The Fifth United States Court of Appeals supported this decision. The court noted that while there is a right in this country to inspect and copy judicial records and documents it is not an absolute right. The trial court may exercise considerable discretion in granting or refusing to grant access to material. Clearly the concern that the fourth defendant's trial might be prejudiced if the tapes were broadcast is a legitimate concern, the court said. It is not the job of the appellate courts to second-guess the trial courts on these matters. Finally, the court said it could not agree with decisions by the District of Columbia Court of Appeals and other courts that there exists a strong presumption in favor of access to this kind of evidence. The court said it could not find a basis for that presumption (*Belo Broadcasting* v. *Clark,* 1981).

The differences between these rulings represent to a certain extent the differences in the cases. The retrial was a distant possibility in the first case; the trial of the fourth defendant was about to take place in the second situation. But these rulings also represent differences in judicial philosophy. And so long as the Supreme Court is content to let the lower courts use their discretion in making these decisions, different rules will be applied in different parts of the nation.

By late 1982 there had been rulings favorable to access to the electronically recorded evidence by the Second United States Court of Appeals (*U.S.* v. *Myers,* 1980), the Third United States Court of Appeals (*U.S.* v. *Criden,* 1980), and the Court of Appeals in the District of Columbia (in re *Application of NBC,* 1981). In addition several United States district courts in the eleventh judicial circuit have ruled in favor of access (see *U.S.* v. *Maddox,* 1982, for example).

However, the Fifth United States Court of Appeals (*Belo Broadcasting* v. *Clark,* 1981), the Eighth United States Court of Appeals (in re *Application of the Kansas City Star,* 1981), and the Seventh United States Court of Appeals (in re *Application of Video-Indiana,* 1982) have rejected attempts by broadcasters to copy and air this kind of material. The Supreme Court might ultimately be required to resolve this question.

Gaining public access to government-held information has been a problem for about as long as democracy has existed as a form of government. With the development of a corps of professional information and news gatherers in this century, the problem has become more visible. Couple this fact with the enormous growth of government in the past half-century, and a problem of rather large proportions develops. Until the last twenty years most journalists depended upon friendship with sources, skill, and wile to get the news from governments. Many reporters argue that this is still the best way to find out what is going on. The law plays an ever-increasing role today in gathering news and information. Much of the process of getting the news and keeping it has been institutionalized by statute and court decisions. At the same time the law has raised serious impediments to information gathering which the press has thus far had difficulty in hurdling. Many of the most important press-government battles in the next decade will be fought over these issues, and at present the question of who will be the winner—the press, the government, or the public—is far from being answered.

BIBLIOGRAPHY

Here is a list of some of the sources that have been helpful in the preparation of chapter 5.

Books

Adams, John B. *State Open Meeting Laws: An Overview*. Columbia, Mo.: Freedom of Information Foundation, 1974.

Cross, Harold. *The People's Right to Know*. New York: Columbia University Press, 1953.

Gerth, H. H., and Mills, C. Wright, eds. *From Max Weber: Essays in Sociology*. New York: Oxford University Press, 1946.

How to Use the Federal FOI Act. 2d ed. Washington, D.C.: FOI Service Center, 1980.

Marwick, Christine M., ed. *Litigation Under the Amended Freedom of Information Act*. 2d ed. Washington, D. C.: American Civil Liberties Union and Freedom of Information Clearing House, 1976.

Padover, Saul, ed. *The Complete Madison*. New York: Harper & Row, 1953.

Rourke, Francis E. *Secrecy and Publicity*. Baltimore: Johns Hopkins University Press, 1961.

Articles

Archibald, Sam. "The Revised F.O.I. Law and How to Use It." July/August *Columbia Journalism Review* 54, (1977).

Braverman, Burt A., and Heppler, Wesley. "A Practical Review of State of Open Records Laws." 49 *George Washington Law Review* 721, 1981.

"Criminal Justice Information Systems." 28 *Code of Federal Regulations,* section 20.3(K).

"The Definition of 'Agency Records' Under the Freedom of Information Act." 31 *Stanford Law Review* 1093, 1979.

"The Freedom of Information Act's Privacy Exemption and the Privacy Act of 1974." 11 *Harvard Civil Rights/Civil Liberties Law Review* 596, 1976.

Higgins, Steven. "Press and Criminal Record Privacy." 20 *St. Louis University Law Journal* 509, 1977.

Malmgren, Lynn C. "First Amendment: Freedom of the Press to Gather News." 20 *Villanova Law Review* 189, 1974.

"National Security and the Public's Right to Know: A New Role for the Courts Under the FOIA." 123 *University of Pennsylvania Law Review* 1438, 1975.

Pember, Don R. "The Burgeoning Scope of 'Access Privacy' and the Portent for a Free Press." 64 *Iowa Law Review* 1155, 1979.

"The Rights of the Public and the Press to Gather Information." 87 *Harvard Law Review* 1505, 1974.

Scher, Jacob. "Access to Information: Recent Legal Problems." 37 *Journalism Quarterly* 41, 1960.

Wright, Anne H. "The Definition of 'Agency' Under the Freedom of Information Act as Applied to Federal Consultants and Grantees." 69 *Georgetown Law Journal* 1223, 1981.

Wright, William R. II. "Open Meeting Laws: An Analysis and a Proposal." 45 *Mississippi Law Review* 1151, 1974.

Cases

in re *Application of ABC,* 537 F. Supp. 1168 (1982).

Alirez v. *NLRB,* 676 F.2d 423 (1982).

Arieff v. *Department of the Navy,* 8 M.L. Rept. 1684 (1982).

Belo Broadcasting v. *Clark,* 654 F.2d 426 (1981).

Birmingham News v. *Roper,* 4 M.L. Rept. 1075 (1978).
Branzburg v. *Hayes,* 408 U.S. 655 (1972).
Brinkerhoff v. *Montoya,* 7 M.L. Rept. 2240 (1981).
Chrysler Corp. v. *Brown,* 99 S.Ct. 1705 (1979).
Common Cause v. *Nuclear Regulatory Commission,* 674 F.2d 921 (1982).
Crooker v. *Bureau,* 670 F.2d 1051 (1981).
Department of the Air Force v. *Rose,* 425 U.S. 352 (1976).
Doe v. *Salmon,* 378 A.2d 512 (1977).
EPA v. *Mink,* 401 U.S. 73 (1973).
Epstein v. *Resor,* 296 F. Supp. 214 (1969), affd. 421 F.2d 930 (1970).
FBI v. *Abramson,* 102 S.Ct. 2054 (1982).
Forsham v. *Harris,* 100 S.Ct. 978 (1980).
Goland v. *CIA,* 607 F.2d 339 (1978).
Greentree v. *Customs Service,* 674 F.2d 74 (1982).
Hardy v. *Bureau of Alcohol, Tobacco, and Firearms,* 631 F.2d 653 (1980).
Houchins v. *KQED,* 438 U.S. 1 (1978).
in re *Application of the Kansas City Star,* 666 F.2d 1168 (1981).
Kissinger v. *Reporter's Committee,* 100 S. Ct. 960 (1980).
Knopf v. *Colby,* 502 F.2d 136 (1975).
in re *Application of KSTP,* 504 F.Supp. 360 (1980).
Kurzon v. *Health and Human Services,* 649 F.2d 65 (1981).
Long v. *IRS,* 596 F.2d 362 (1979).
MacEwan v. *Holm,* 359 P.2d 413 (1961).
Miami Herald v. *Small Business Administration,* 670 F.2d 610 (1982).
in re *Application of NBC,* 653 F.2d 609 (1981).
New Mexico v. *Brennan,* 645 P.2d 982 (1982).
Nixon v. *Carmen,* 670 F.2d 346 (1982).
Nixon v. *Warner Communications,* 435 U.S. 591 (1978).
Painter v. *FBI,* 615 F.2d 689 (1980).
Pell v. *Procunier,* 94 S.Ct. 2800 (1974).
Philadelphia Newspapers v. *Nuclear Regulatory Commission,* 9 M.L. Rept. 1843 (1983).
Playboy v. *Justice Department,* 8 M.L. Rept. 901 (1982).
Providence Journal Co. et al. v. *McCoy, et al.,* 49 F. Supp. 186 (1950).
Richmond Newspapers v. *Virginia,* 100 S.Ct. 2814 (1980).
Russell v. *Air Force,* 682 F.2d 1045 (1982).
Saxbe v. *Washington Post,* 94 S.Ct. 2811 (1974).
State Department v. *Washington Post,* 102 S.Ct. 1957 (1982).
Symons v. *Chrysler Corporation Loan Guarantee Board,* 670 F.2d 238 (1981).
Taylor v. *Army,* 684 F.2d 99 (1982).
Terkel v. *Kelly,* 599 F.2d 214 (1979).
U.S. v. *Bolen,* 8 M.L. Rept. 1048 (1981).
U.S. v. *Criden,* 648 F.2d 814 (1980).
U.S. v. *Maddox,* 7 M.L. Rept. 2600 (1982).
U.S. v. *Myers,* 635 F.2d 945 (1980).
U.S. v. *Nixon,* 94 S. Ct. 3090 (1974).
in re *Application of Video-Indiana,* 672 F.2d 1289 (1982).
Westinghouse v. *National Transportation Safety Board,* 8 M.L. Rept. 1177 (1982).
Wolfe v. *Department of Health and Human Services,* 539 F. Supp. 276 (1982), aff'd. 9 M.L. Rept. 2024 (1983).
Zemel v. *Rusk,* 381 U.S. 1 (1964).

6 PROTECTION OF NEWS SOURCES AND CONTEMPT OF COURT

American journalists are no strangers to the confines of jail cells and prisons. In 1722 James Franklin, the less-publicized older brother of Benjamin Franklin, was jailed in a small cell for publishing a newspaper without the consent of the government of Massachusetts. He was the first of many American journalists to see the inside of a jail cell.

Today in the United States reporters are often jailed for disobeying court orders which instruct them to make public information they choose not to disclose. Journalists frequently want to keep the names of their news sources confidential. Some people tell things to reporters "off-the-record" with the expectation that this information will not be revealed. Often there is more to a story than fits in the newspaper or on the evening news. What remains is held in a reporter's notebook or a newspaper computer memory or a videotape cassette.

Most of us have little interest in what the journalist chooses not to reveal. For some, however, this information is valuable. A police agency might be interested in what a criminal suspect or a witness told a reporter off-the-record. A plaintiff in a libel suit might be interested in the name of the source of an allegedly libelous story. A prosecutor might be interested in film of a violent campus demonstration that was never aired on the evening news.

Reporters are often asked to reveal information they have gathered but chosen not to publish or broadcast. In many instances journalists comply with such requests. At times, however, they refuse. When this happens, the persons interested in getting this information often get a court order called a **subpoena** to force the journalist to reveal the name of the news source or to disclose the confidential information. Or government agents may get a warrant to search a newsroom or a reporter's home to find the information they want.

In our society the press is supposed to represent a neutral entity as it gathers and publishes news and information. When the government or anyone else intrudes into the newsroom or the reporter's notebook, it compromises this neutrality. A news source who normally trusts journalists may choose not to cooperate if government agents can learn his name by threatening the journalist with a court order. Television news crews will hardly be welcome at protest rallies if the demonstrators know that the government will use the film to identify and prosecute the protestors. The effectiveness of the reporter as an information gatherer may be seriously diminished if government agents or civil and criminal litigants can force journalists to reveal information they choose not to disclose. Society also may ultimately suffer because the flow of information to the public may be reduced.

This chapter is about the problems a reporter can face when government agents or other persons use the power of the judicial system to gain access to the news-gathering processes. We will study the problems of source confidentiality and newsroom searches. We will also look at recent judicial and legislative attempts to resolve these issues. Finally, we will examine the powerful weapon the government may employ to get its way in these disputes: the contempt power.

NEWS AND NEWS
SOURCES

If news and information are the lifeblood of the press, then news sources are one of the wells from which that lifeblood springs. Many journalists, especially those who consider themselves investigative journalists, are often no better than the sources they can cultivate. News sources come in all shapes and sizes. Frequently their willingness to cooperate with a reporter is dependent upon assurances from the journalist that their identity will not be revealed. Why would a news source wish to remain anonymous? There are undoubtedly many reasons. Often the source of a story about criminal activities has participated in criminal activities himself. He has no desire to publicize this fact. Frequently the source of a story about government mismanagement or dishonesty is an employee of that government agency, and revelation of her identity could result in the loss of her job for informing the press of the errors made by her superiors. Some persons simply do not want to get involved in all the hassle that frequently results when an explosive story is published; by remaining anonymous they can remain out of the limelight.

Journalists have probably always used confidential sources, but it is only in the past fifteen years that they have been frequently called upon to reveal the identity of their anonymous sources. In seemingly more and more instances today the journalist who has published or broadcast a story based upon information gained from an anonymous source is confronted with official inquiries from the government regarding the identity of that source. If the journalist is subpoenaed to testify before a grand jury or at a trial, the options open to the reporter are remarkably limited. He can tell the authorities what they wish to know, he can attempt to attack the validity of the subpoena and seek to have it quashed, or he can refuse to testify—and very likely be cited for **contempt of court** and be sent to jail.

Shielding the identity of news sources has recently become a more serious problem for journalists for numerous reasons. The agitation, and ultimately the violence, of the civil-rights movement of the sixties and the antiwar movement of the seventies led to an increase in government investigations of events which the press deemed newsworthy. The press also found the blossoming drug culture of the past twenty years a subject worthy of news coverage. Government agents and journalists often crossed paths in their investigations of protests and pot. The police often viewed the press as an unfriendly ally in these situations. Journalists can gain access to information that law enforcement officials cannot. Reporters frequently meet and talk with persons the law defines as fugitives or criminals. The information obtained by a reporter can save police officers hours or even weeks of investigation.

The press of the seventies and eighties is different from the press of earlier eras. True, many "investigative reporters" of this modern era do little more than "reporters" did in the not too distant past. But the glorification of the investigative reporter is not all hype. Many segments of modern journalism have taken on a new aggressive stance and have begun to peer into corners of society which have escaped scrutiny in the past. Journalists are frequently less willing to accept government spokespersons as the only source of news about society's outlaws, political activists, and other persons on the fringe of the community. Reporters feel compelled to talk to the persons who are making the news—radicals, bomb throwers, drug pushers, and so forth. The press has often gained the confidence of these societal "outs" who are valuable sources of information for the public—and for government investigators.

Finally, many people in our society have gained considerable sophistication in how to "use" the press to tell a story without facing the consequences of the publication of the story. During a lawsuit an attorney can often feed a reporter information about the case that she wants published, but which a judge has ordered to be kept confidential. A government employee can expose the failings or follies of his supervisors by acting as a confidential source for a reporter. Usually journalists know that they are being used, but the journalists also know they have an exclusive if not explosive story. For these reasons and others, reporters, who had long enjoyed their imagined role as spectators of the passing scene, suddenly became unwilling participants. As participants they had information which often interested government authorities and others. Tell us what we want to know or face a stay in jail was often the choice which faced the journalist. This is a tough choice; reveal a source and you lose the ability to get the news from other sources who wish to remain anonymous. But a jail cell can be unpleasant too.

The choice for society is not an easy one either. The interests that are involved in this dilemma are very basic to our system of government. Members of the United States Senate studied the issues involved in the reporters' claim to keep the names of news sources confidential. Former Senator Sam Ervin, chairman of the committee which looked into the problem, said he had never dealt with a more difficult problem during his years in Congress.

On the one hand, it is clearly the obligation of every citizen to cooperate with the government and testify before the proper authorities. This concept was so well established by the early eighteenth century that it had become a maxim. Wigmore, in his classic treatise on evidence (*A Treatise on the Anglo-American System of Evidence*), cites the concept thus: "The public has a right to everyman's evidence." The right to have witnesses and to compel them to testify is one of our cherished constitutional guarantees. The Sixth Amendment states, "In all criminal prosecutions, the accused shall enjoy the right to be confronted with the witnesses against him; and have compulsory process for obtaining witnesses in his favor." This is an important guarantee.

Suppose you were arrested for a crime you did not commit and that you had a witness who could prove you were fifty miles away at the time the crime was committed. How would you feel if your witness decided that he really did not have time to go to court and testify? that he was too busy? that he did not want to get involved? Your right to compel his testimony could be crucial to your freedom.

The Supreme Court has said on many occasions that it is a citizen's duty to testify. In 1919 the Court wrote as follows on the duties and rights of witnesses (*Blair* v. *U.S.*):

> [I]t is clearly recognized that the giving of testimony and the attendance upon court or grand jury in order to testify are public duties which everyone within the jurisdiction of the government is bound to perform upon being properly summoned, . . . the personal sacrifice involved is a part of the necessary contribution to the public welfare.

Most journalists do not dispute the immense societal value of the power to compel testimony. But they do argue that, on the other hand, in most cases involving a reporter's sources society will benefit more if the reporter is not compelled to testify. Briefly the argument is this. The press is the eyes and ears of the people. Nothing should interfere with this role. The people must be informed; they must have access to the fullest information possible in order to operate properly as citizens in a democracy. Sometimes the only way a reporter can gain crucial information is to get it from an anonymous source. When a reporter is forced to reveal the name of a source, other potential sources will refuse to cooperate with journalists for fear that their identity will be made public as well. In the end it is society which will lose, as it is deprived of the information which these sources might provide. At least this is the argument made by journalists.

Many reporters insist that news sources have dried up and will continue to dry up so long as there exists the potential that their identity might somehow be revealed. They cite studies by organizations such as the Reporters Committee of Freedom of the Press to support their argument. Other persons inside and outside the press dispute such evidence and note that only a small number of journalists use confidential sources regularly and that an even smaller number are ever called upon to reveal the identity of these sources. While recognizing the existence of a problem, these persons consider it a fairly small problem (Chamberlin, "Protection of Confidential News Sources: An Unresolved Issue").

Big or small, the problem of a reporter's source confidentiality is an issue that the law has had to attempt to resolve. Doctors, lawyers, members of the clergy, and even accountants enjoy privilege which allows them to protect the confidentiality of discussions they have with patients, clients, or parishioners. Reporters seek a similar privilege, and in the past ten years have made some headway in gaining such protection. An analysis of the depth and breadth of the reporter's privilege begins with the 1972 ruling by the Supreme Court of the United States in *Branzburg* v. *Hayes*.

Branzburg v. *Hayes*

The case was really three cases, *Branzburg* v. *Hayes*, in re *Pappas*, and *U.S.* v. *Caldwell*. Today, the Court's decisions are referred to collectively as the *Branzburg* ruling.

Paul Branzburg was a staff reporter for the *Louisville Courier-Journal*. In 1969 and 1971 he wrote two stories about drug use in Jefferson County, Kentucky. In the first story he described in detail his observations of two young men synthesizing hashish. When he was called before a grand jury, he refused to identify the two individuals in his story, citing both the Kentucky reporters' privilege statute, which he claimed exempted him from having to give testimony, and the First Amendment. A Kentucky appellate court rejected his First Amendment argument and ruled that while the state's statute afforded a reporter the privilege of refusing to divulge the identity of a confidential source it did not give the reporter the right to refuse to testify about events he had witnessed personally. The second story was about drug use in Franklin County, Kentucky, and the court rejected Branzburg's arguments a second time when he refused to testify before a Franklin County grand jury. He appealed to the Supreme Court.

Paul Pappas was a reporter for a New Bedford, Massachusetts, television station. In July 1970 he was assigned to cover civil disturbances in an area near the headquarters of the local Black Panther organization. That afternoon he gained access to the Panther's headquarters and recorded and photographed a prepared statement read by one of the Black Panthers. He returned to Panther headquarters that evening and was allowed to spend three hours with members of the black militant organization as they waited for an anticipated police raid upon their headquarters—a raid which failed to materialize. As a condition of entry into Panther headquarters Pappas agreed not to disclose anything he saw or heard there. He was called to testify before a Bristol County grand jury, but he refused to answer questions about what took place inside the Panther headquarters, citing his privilege under the First Amendment. Massachusetts courts rejected his argument.

Earl Caldwell worked for the *New York Times* in 1970, an era in which there was significant public concern about the militancy of the Black Panthers. The press succeeded in fueling this fear by publishing masses of misinformation. Earl Caldwell, who was black, had gained the confidence of Black Panther leaders in Oakland, California, and consistently provided readers of the *Times* with accurate, illuminating accounts of the organization. It was probably natural, then, that when a federal grand jury began investigating the Panthers Earl Caldwell was subpoenaed and told to bring his notes and audiotapes. Caldwell refused, arguing that giving information to the government would destroy his ability to report on the Black Panthers, that none of the leaders would ever again take him into their confidence or even talk with him.

A federal district court partially supported Caldwell's plea. It said that he would not have to answer questions unless in each case the government could demonstrate that "a compelling and overriding national interest" would be served by Caldwell's answer to a question and that no alternative means of getting the information was available. The court based its ruling on the strong First Amendment interests which it said were at the core of the issue.

Caldwell and the *New York Times* were not satisfied, for the ruling still required the reporter to answer some questions. Since the proceedings were secret, the Panthers would never know which questions Caldwell answered and which questions he did not answer. Caldwell appealed to the Ninth Circuit Court of New York and again won. This time the court ruled that when it is shown that the public's First Amendment right to be informed will be jeopardized by requiring a journalist to submit to a secret grand jury interrogation the government must respond by demonstrating a compelling need for even the witness's presence before attendance can be required. The court added that this case was very unusual, since most news sources are not as sensitive as the Black Panther organization and most reporters do not enjoy such unique trust and confidence of news sources. Still, the ruling was a significant First Amendment victory for the press. Such a victory, in fact, that the government appealed the ruling to the Supreme Court.

The Court was badly split in its decision on the three cases. Four justices voted against the constitutional privilege, four voted in favor of the constitutional privilege, and Justice Lewis Powell voted in favor of the constitutional privilege in some circumstances, but not in these cases. Let us look first at the votes against the privilege.

Justice Byron White wrote the opinion of the court to which Chief Justice Warren Burger, Justice William Rehnquist, and Justice Harry Blackmun subscribed. White said that while the Court was sensitive to First Amendment considerations the case did not present any such considerations. There were no prior restraint, no limitations on what the press may publish, and no order for the press to publish information it did not wish to. No penalty for publishing certain content was imposed. White wrote (*Branzburg* v. *Hayes*, 1972):

> The use of confidential sources by the press is not forbidden or restricted. . . .
> The sole issue before us is the obligation of reporters to respond to grand jury subpoenas as other citizens do and answer questions relevant to an investigation into the commission of crime. Citizens generally are not constitutionally

immune from grand jury subpoenas; and neither the First Amendment nor other constitutional provisions protect the average citizen from the disclosing to a grand jury information that he has received in confidence.

Reporters are no better than average citizens, White concluded.

The four dissenters differed sharply with the other justices. Justice Potter Stewart wrote, "The Court's crabbed view of the First Amendment reflects a disturbing insensitivity to the crucial role of an independent press in our society."

Justice Douglas took the view that the First Amendment protection provides the press with an absolute and unqualified privilege. In any circumstance, under any condition, the reporter should be able to shield the identity of a confidential source. Justices Potter Stewart, William Brennan, and Thurgood Marshall were unwilling to go as far as Justice Douglas and instead proposed that reporters should be protected by a privilege that is qualified, not absolute. The three dissenters argued that the reporter should be able to protect the identity of the confidential source unless the government can show the following:

1. That there is a probable cause to believe that the reporter has information that is clearly relevant to a specific violation of the law
2. That the information sought cannot be obtained by alternative means less destructive of First Amendment rights
3. That the state has a compelling and overriding interest in the information

When the government cannot fulfill all three requirements, Justice Stewart wrote for the dissenters, the journalist should not be forced to testify.

With four votes against a constitutional privilege for journalists called to testify before a grand jury and four votes in favor of at least a limited privilege in such a circumstance, the vote of Justice Lewis Powell—the ninth member of the court—became critical. Powell concurred with Justices White, Rehnquist, and Blackmun and Chief Justice Burger in concluding that in the cases presented to the court no First Amendment privilege existed. But Powell refused to accept the notion that the First Amendment might not provide the journalist with a privilege in other instances in which the reporter was asked to reveal the identity of a source. Powell said that no harrassment of news reporters could be allowed. A balance must be struck between freedom of the press and the obligation of all citizens to give relevant testimony. "The Court," Powell added, "does not hold that newsmen, subpoenaed to testify before a grand jury, are without constitutional rights with respect to the gathering of news or in safeguarding their sources." In short, Justice Powell added, "The courts will be available to newsmen under circumstances where legitimate First Amendment interests require protection." Justice Powell noted two years later in a footnote in another case (*Saxbe* v. *Washington Post*, 1974) that the Court's ruling in *Branzburg* had been an extremely narrow one and that news reporters were not without First Amendment rights to protect the identity of their sources.

Lower Court Rulings

The *Branzburg* decision was initially a bitter blow to those persons who believed that the recognition of at least a limited reporter's privilege was essential to the free flow of information in the society. But in the past twelve years the lower courts have chosen to read this Supreme Court ruling in such a way as to sharply minimize its impact upon this problem. Justice Lewis Powell's concurring opinion has become highly important for the lower courts. A lower court judge, faced with a government request that a reporter reveal the names of news sources, can look to the associate justice's concurrence for guidance. If Justice Powell would agree that a legitimate First Amendment interest exists, then Powell, plus Marshall, Douglas, Brennan, and Stewart, made a five-man majority in favor of granting the privilege. If Justice Powell would not recognize the First Amendment privilege, then the majority in the *Branzburg* ruling—Powell, Burger, Rehnquist, Blackmun, and White—would carry the day. On this basis lower courts can make a decision with some assurance that they will not later be overruled by the high Court. In addition, many lower courts have limited the reach of the *Branzburg* ruling to only grand jury investigations. The Third United States Court of Appeals recently noted with regard to *Branzburg (Riley v. Chester,* 1979):

> There, the Supreme Court decided that a journalist does not have an absolute privilege under the First Amendment to refuse to appear and testify before a grand jury to answer questions relevant to an investigation into the commission of a crime. No Supreme Court case since that decision has extended the holding beyond that which was necessary there to vindicate the public interest in law enforcement and ensuing effective grand jury proceedings.

Limiting the impact of the *Branzburg* ruling has given lower courts an opportunity to fashion a more balanced response to the problems posed by the reporter's claim of a privilege to protect the identity of news sources. While we must be wary of painting with too broad a stroke, it is fair to say that in most jurisdictions the judiciary has fashioned a kind of constitutional/common law privilege which in many situations gives the journalist the right to refuse to answer questions about news sources. The successful application of the privilege depends upon several factors. A court will likely respond differently to the assertion of the privilege in a situation involving a grand jury proceeding than it will in a civil lawsuit. Whether the parties seeking the information have sought it first elsewhere is also a consideration. Let us look at some of these factors in our attempt to outline the scope of the reporter's privilege.

The privilege of the reporter to refuse to answer questions about the names of confidential news sources is most often granted in civil lawsuits, especially in those cases where the reporter is not a party to the case. The successful application of the privilege in these instances dates back to 1973, in the virtual shadow of the *Branzburg* ruling, when the Democratic party brought a civil action to win damages for the Watergate break-in. Ten reporters from the *New York Times, Washington Post, Washington Star-News, Time* magazine, and other publications were subpoenaed and told to bring their tapes, notes, letters, documents, and all other materials obtained during their reporting of the Watergate break-in. A United States district court quashed the subpoena, noting that the press is entitled to at least a qualified privilege to refuse to answer such questions under the First Amendment (*Democratic National Committee* v. *McCord*, 1973).

In 1977 the Tenth United States Circuit Court of Appeals refused to force filmmaker Arthur Hirsch to reveal confidential information he had obtained in connection with a civil action by the estate of Karen Silkwood against the Kerr-McGee Corporation. Hirsch was preparing a documentary film on the mysterious death of the young woman when he was subpoenaed by Kerr-McGee. The Tenth Circuit Court ruled that a limited First Amendment privilege protected the filmmaker and that before he could be required to answer questions the trial court was bound to consider whether the party seeking the information had independently attempted to obtain the information elsewhere and had been unsuccessful, whether the information sought from the reporter went to the heart of the matter before the court, and whether the information was of certain relevance in the case. In this case Hirsch did not have to testify (*Silkwood* v. *Kerr-McGee*, 1977). Courts in many jurisdictions have made similar rulings, granting a reporter an exemption from the normal requirement to testify.

Normally a court asks three questions before determining whether the privilege should be granted to the journalist.

1. Has the person seeking the information (normally the plaintiff) shown that the reporter's information is of *certain relevance* in the case?
2. Does the information go to the heart of the matter before the court?
3. Can the person who is seeking the reporter's information demonstrate that there is no other source for this information?

If *all* three questions can be answered yes, the chances are good the reporter will be required to testify. But this is a heavy burden for the plaintiff or the defendant to meet, and in most instances journalists are being excused from testimony (see in re *Consumers Union*, 1978; *Riley* v. *Chester*, 1979; and *McGraw-Hill* v. *Arizona*, 1982).

The privilege is not as readily granted to journalists in civil lawsuits when the reporter is a party in the case. A reporter can end up in a lawsuit either as a plaintiff or a defendant. If the reporter is a plaintiff in a lawsuit and has information which is critical to the case, it is unlikely that a court will permit the reporter to remain silent regarding these issues. When columnist Jack Anderson attempted to sue Richard Nixon and other former government officials for allegedly conspiring to deprive him of his civil rights, he refused to cooperate with the defendants seeking from him the names of confidential sources who gave the columnist information regarding the activities of Nixon and his White House associates. Citing the First Amendment, Anderson refused to reveal the names sought. But a federal district judge ordered him to give the information to the court if he hoped to continue his suit. The judge ruled that Anderson was attempting to use the First Amendment simultaneously "as a sword and a shield. . . . He cannot have it both ways. Plaintiff is not a bystander in the process, but a principal. He cannot ask for justice and deny it to those he accuses." Anderson was forced to withdraw his suit (*Anderson* v. *Nixon* et al., 1978).

A reporter usually ends up as a defendant in a lawsuit when a libel suit is filed because of something the reporter wrote or broadcast. Often the reporter based the libelous news report on confidential information or sources. It is important for the plaintiff in such a libel case to find out where the reporter obtained the information for the story to demonstrate that the journalist was negligent or that the material was published with actual malice (see pages 146–52 to refresh your memory about the meaning of these terms). It is much more difficult to predict how a court will respond to a plaintiff's demand that the reporter reveal confidential information in these kinds of instances. But some patterns have developed. For example, many courts insist that the plaintiff prove that the information which is sought is crucial to the matter of proving either negligence or actual malice. The 1972 ruling in *Cervantes* v. *Time* is a good example. The lawsuit was a $12-million libel action against *Life* magazine for publishing a story which suggested that the mayor of St. Louis, Alfonso Cervantes, had underworld connections. The mayor wanted to know the names of the sources in the Federal Bureau of Investigation and justice department who supplied the information to reporter Denny Walsh. Cervantes said he could not prove malice without these names.

However, the information about the mayor was a small part of the story, which was extremely well documented. The charges against Cervantes comprised only four paragraphs of the eighty-seven-paragraph story. The court of appeals ruled, "To compel a newsman to breach a confidential relationship merely because a libel suit has been filed against him would seem inevitably to lead to an excessive restraint on the scope of legitimate news-gathering activity." The court said that if the plaintiff was able to provide persuasive evidence that this information was crucial to the question of malice the privilege might then have to give way. However, in this case, "The mayor has wholly failed to demonstrate with convincing clarity that either the defendant acted with knowledge of falsity or reckless disregard of the truth." There was just no reasonable probability that the plaintiff would succeed in proving malice.

The same conclusion was reached in *Baker* v. *F & F Investment* (1972). In this case Alfred Balk, a former writer on the *Saturday Evening Post*, had written an article on blockbusting in Chicago. In an action filed in federal court charging a real estate firm with discrimination, Balk was called as a witness and asked to reveal the sources of information for his article. He refused, and the federal court of appeals upheld his refusal. The court said the plaintiff in the civil suit had not exhausted other sources of information, that the disclosure by Balk was not essential to protection of the public interest, and that the material sought did not go to the heart of the matter at issue in the case. Judge Kaufman wrote (*Baker* v. *F & F Investment*, 1972):

> While we recognize that there are cases—few in number to be sure—where First Amendment rights must yield, we are still mindful of the preferred position which the First Amendment occupies in the pantheon of freedoms. Accordingly, though a journalist's right to protect confidential sources may not take precedence over that rare overriding and compelling interest, we are of the view that there are circumstances, at the very least in civil cases, in which the public interest in nondisclosure of a journalist's confidential sources outweighs the public and the private interest in compelled testimony.

In other libel suits when reporters were asked to testify, the courts have ruled that the plaintiff need only show that there is a genuine issue of fact about the truth or falsity of the libelous material. It is not necessary to demonstrate that the reporter might have information which will resolve this issue. In a libel suit against the *Wall Street Journal,* the Massachusetts Supreme Judicial Court ruled that there was no privilege to protect the newspaper from revealing the name of the source of its story so long as questions material to the case remained to be resolved. "The obligation of newsmen, we think, is that of every citizen, *viz.,* to appear when summoned, with relevant written or other material when required, and to answer relevant and reasonable inquiries" (*Dow Jones* v. *Superior Court,* 1973). The New Hampshire Supreme Court ruled that a public-official libel plaintiff must satisfy the trial court that he has evidence to establish that there is a genuine issue of fact regarding the falsity of the publication. Once the plaintiff meets this burden, the privilege to withhold confidential information ceases to exist (*Downing* v. *Monitor Publishing Co.,* 1980). And the United States Supreme Court ruled in 1979 that plaintiffs may explore what the defendant was thinking about while preparing the story for publication or broadcast. The high Court ruled in *Herbert* v. *Lando* that so long as the public-figure libel plaintiff has a special burden of proof in a defamation case denial of "discovery of editorial state of mind would make that burden unduly onerous." What this means is that the plaintiff can ask reporters or producers or editors if they had any doubts about the truth of the material when they published the story: Did they think they should check things a bit more before broadcasting the libelous charges? were there other sources with whom they considered talking? and so forth.

Some courts have reacted rather sharply when journalists refused to reveal the names of news sources or other confidential information in a libel suit. They have said that refusal to name a source supports the inference that no source exists (see *Downing* v. *Monitor Publishing Co.*, 1980, and *Greenberg* v. *CBS*, 1979). A court effectively strips a publication or broadcasting station of its defenses when it rules that there is no source for a libelous story. This is tantamount to saying that the story was fabricated. The defendant is normally going to lose the libel suit when this happens. Perhaps the best-known cases in which this has occurred were tried in Idaho. In *Sierra Life* v. *Magic Valley Newspapers* the trial judge completely struck the newspaper's defenses "as sanctions for their willful refusal" to obey his order to disclose confidential information and awarded $1.9 million to the plaintiff. But the Idaho Supreme Court overturned the ruling in September 1980 and ordered the newspaper's defenses reinstated. The state high court said that at no time during the trial did the plaintiff show that its inability to discover the reporter's confidential sources obstructed its ability to prove the falsity of the story (*Sierra Life* v. *Magic Valley Newspapers,* 1980). In another Idaho case the state high court ruled that reporter Jay Shelledy's refusal to identify a confidential source for a story published in the *Lewiston Tribune* must be treated as an admission by Shelledy that no such source exists. When the case was sent back for trial, Shelledy revealed the name of his source, an individual who had died and whose widow had consented to end the agreement of confidentiality. But the judge still instructed the jury to presume that no source existed. Despite this action, the *Tribune* won the case when the jury ruled ten to two that the article was not even libelous (*Caldero* v. *Tribune Publishing Co.,* 1977, 1980).

Stripping a newspaper's defenses in a lawsuit puts the press in the position of choosing between suffering a libel judgment or disclosing a confidential source.

It is not healthy for society that the journalist must make such a choice. If the reporter is unable to keep the names of sources confidential, such sources will not be used as often—and the public will be denied the information such sources might provide. Costly libel judgments can also reduce the flow of news and information to the public by prompting newspapers and broadcasting stations to be more conservative in their news coverage.

Criminal Cases

Reporters normally have less luck shielding confidential information in criminal cases than in the typical civil suit where the reporter is not a party to the action. In criminal cases the privilege often runs directly into the right of criminal defendants to defend themselves. Courts often again apply variations of a three-part test to determine whether the reporter must reveal the information. The person seeking the information must show the following:

1. That the reporter has information which is relevant and material to the proof of the crime which has been charged or to the defendant's defense
2. That there is a compelling need for the disclosure of the information
3. That the party seeking the information has unsuccessfully attempted to obtain the information from other sources

The first part of the test is usually most important. Often, once it is determined that reporters have information relevant to the case they will be required to testify. The case of *Kansas* v. *Sandstrom* in 1978 provides a good example.

Milda Sandstrom was charged with murder in connection with the death of her husband. Reporter Joe Pennington testified at the trial that a confidential source had revealed to him that at a party shortly before Thad Sandstrom was killed one of the state's witnesses had threatened to kill Sandstrom. Pennington said the informant had heard about the threat from another person who attended the party, but refused to reveal the name of the informant. The Kansas Supreme Court ruled that Pennington did not enjoy a First Amendment privilege in this instance to refuse to identify the confidential informant.

The state's high court noted that lower courts which had applied the *Branzburg* ruling to criminal cases had generally concluded that the proper test for determining the existence of a reporter's privilege in a particular criminal case was to balance *the need of the defendant for a fair trial against the reporter's need for confidentiality* (author emphasis). "As a general rule, disclosure has been required only in those criminal cases where it is shown the information in possession of the news reporter is material to prove an element of the offense, to prove a defense asserted by the defendant, to reduce the classification or gradation of the offense charged, or to mitigate or lessen the sentence imposed," the court noted. In this case the trial court felt that the identity of the confidential informant could lead to information relevant to Mrs. Sandstrom's defense, the high court said. That is a reasonable position to adopt, it was concluded.

In other instances courts have required that all three parts of the test just outlined be satisfied before forcing a journalist to testify. In 1980 the Third United States Court of Appeals ruled that Jan Schaffer, a reporter for the *Philadelphia Inquirer,* had to testify about a conversation she had with a prosecuting attorney before a criminal trial. The defendants in a government Abscam prosecution moved for a dismissal of the charges on the grounds that there had been massive pretrial publicity about the case which would prevent them from getting a fair trial. The defendants charged that the publicity was the result of misconduct by the prosecutor, who they said improperly gave reporters details of the sting operation. The prosecutor admitted talking with reporters about the case, but the defendants sought the reporter's testimony to confirm the prosecutor's statements. The court, applying the three-part test, ruled that Schaffer would have to testify. The reporter obviously had the information—the prosecutor admitted talking with her about the case. There was a compelling need for the information; it was central to the defendant's charges of misconduct by the prosecutor. And the defense had attempted to get the information elsewhere—from the prosecutor himself. The reporter was the only source left (*U.S.* v. *Criden,* 1980). There are numerous other decisions which support these two rulings.

The California court of appeals refused to quash a subpoena against the Columbia Broadcasting System (CBS) for media materials in a criminal prosecution against drug dealers. The material involved clandestine videotapes and audiotapes made by the network (in cooperation with the Santa Clara sheriff's department) of meetings between narcotics officers and the criminal defendants (*CBS* v. *Superior Court,* 1978). Similarly, the First Amendment arguments made by reporter Myron Farber of the *New York Times* when he was called upon to produce material relevant to the defense in a New Jersey murder case were rejected by various state and federal courts (in re *Farber,* 1978). Farber, incidently, was pardoned by Gov. Brendan Byrne in 1982. His dispute with the New Jersey trial court had cost him forty days in jail and had cost the *New York Times* nearly $300,000 in fines.

The application of the three-part test in a criminal case does not always result in the forced disclosure of confidential information. In 1982, for example, authorities called a reporter to testify in a criminal case against a physician who was charged with violating federal drug laws. Reporter Patrick Malone had written a story about the use and misuse of the drug Quaalude. The story included several statements which Malone attributed to the defendant in the drug case. The government wanted Malone to testify, to verify that Dr. Frederick Blanton had made the statements attributed to him in the article. Malone refused and the trial court supported the reporter. Judge Paine ruled that the government had not shown that it had exhausted all efforts to get the information from other sources, or that there was a compelling need to get this information at all (*U.S.* v. *Blanton,* 1982). In Virginia the state supreme court permitted a reporter to refuse to reveal the name of a confidential source of a story he wrote about a murder case. The defendant in this case wanted to use the reporter's source in an attempt to impeach a witness for the state. The supreme court ruled that since the information sought was not at the heart of the issue in the trial the First Amendment took precedence (*Brown* v. *Commonwealth,* 1974). In *Florida* v. *Morel* in 1979 a district court quashed a subpoena issued against a reporter in a criminal trial when the criminal defendant failed to meet the requirements of the three-part test. A similar result was reached in another Florida case, *Florida* v. *Beattie* (1979).

In cases in which journalists have been called to testify before a grand jury, lower courts have generally followed the *Branzburg* ruling very closely. The *Branzburg* case, after all, involved reporters who were asked to testify before a grand jury. It is much harder for lower courts to distinguish this Supreme Court precedent when confronted with a similar circumstance in their own jurisdiction. Brenda Presley and Sherrie Bursey were reporters for the Black Panther newspaper. They wrote a story about a speech by Panther leader David Hilliard in which he either did or did not threaten former President Richard Nixon. They were called to testify before several grand juries. Although the reporters always answered some of the questions, they refused to answer all queries regarding confidential information and information regarding management of the Panther paper. The government presented sufficient evidence to convince the district court that there was a compelling and overriding national interest, and the women were called to testify. They refused to answer fifty-six different questions. On appeal, the United States Ninth Circuit Court of Appeals of California ruled that the two reporters had to answer seventeen of the fifty-six questions (*Bursey* v. *U.S.*, 1972). The court said the women did not have to answer queries about the people who worked at the newspaper or about how the paper was edited, but they did have to answer questions about whether they had seen firearms and explosives at Panther headquarters and about whether the Panther leaders conducted discussions concerning violent activities. The government interests were legitimate and compelling, the court said, and infringement upon the First Amendment was incidental.

In a case related to the disappearance of Patty Hearst, the manager of radio station KPFK in Los Angeles was held in contempt for refusing to surrender to a grand jury investigating the matter the original tapes and letters received from the Symbionese Liberation Army. Will Lewis gave authorities copies of the tapes and letters, but refused to surrender the original tapes. The United States Ninth Circuit Court of Appeals ruled that the grand jury was conducting a legitimate law enforcement investigation and that fact outweighed the First Amendment considerations (in re *Lewis*, 1974).

In 1978 a Vermont court required the appearance and testimony of a reporter before a state inquest judge following the publication of the journalist's story regarding the sale of potentially contaminated marijuana. The court noted that the inquest was similar to a grand jury and that the inquiry was a good faith criminal investigation conducted under judicial supervision (in re *Powers*, 1978).

About the only good news one can find when examining the manner in which courts have responded to reporters' refusal to testify before grand juries is the diminishing number of subpoenas which are being issued today. Journalists are simply not being called to testify as often in the 1980s as in the past.

The lower federal courts and state courts have succeeded in fashioning a qualified First Amendment-common law privilege which protects reporters who have been called upon to reveal confidential information during legal proceedings. The courts have done this by confining the impact of the Supreme Court's opinion in *Branzburg* v. *Hayes* to the facts of that case—grand jury investigations—and by looking to Justice Powell's concurring opinion and Justice Stewart's dissenting opinion for guidance in other cases. By doing so the courts have often effectively thwarted the efforts of the government and other agencies to use reporters as an auxiliary investigative arm.

Telephone Records

The names of confidential news sources, reporters' notes, news film, and photographs are not the only records that have been sought by government agents through the use of a subpoena. The records of toll telephone calls made by reporters have also come under government scrutiny in recent years.

The telephone company maintains subscriber records for toll telephone calls for about six months. For long-distance calls billed to the subscriber's telephone number these records indicate the telephone number called, as well as the date, time, and duration of the call. The records are no secret; a copy of the monthly toll-call record is provided to each subscriber with each month's bill.

In 1974 the American Telephone and Telegraph Company (AT&T) announced that in the future it would not release these records to the government without a subpoena and as a general policy would seek to notify subscribers immediately when their individual records had been subpoenaed by a government agency. However, when records are subpoenaed pursuant to a felony investigation, the telephone company said it will not notify the subscriber of the subpoena so long as the government certifies that an official investigation is being conducted, and that notification to the subscriber can impede the investigation.

The Reporter's Committee for Freedom of the Press challenged the telephone company's policy of releasing *any* records to the government, arguing that the government could use such records to determine reporters' sources. Journalists raised both the Fourth Amendment and the First Amendment as bars to this cooperation between AT&T and the government.

The U.S. Court of Appeals seemed unpersuaded that this cooperation created a real problem and ruled against the Reporter's Committee. The Fourth Amendment claim lacked merit, the court said, because the constitutional prohibition against illegal search and seizure "does not insulate all personal activity from official scrutiny." The First Amendment claim was similarly rejected. The court asserted that the First Amendment offers no additional protections against good faith criminal investigations beyond that afforded by the Fourth and Fifth amendments (*Reporter's Committee* v. *AT&T,* 1978):

> The principle is clear. To the extent individuals desire to excercise their First Amendment rights in private, free from possible good faith law enforcement investigation, they must operate within the zone of privacy secured by the Fourth Amendment. When individuals expose their activities to third parties, they similarly expose these activities to possible government scrutiny.

Summary

In recent years more and more reporters have been called to testify in legal proceedings. Often they are asked to reveal confidential information to aid police in criminal investigations, to assist in the defense of a criminal defendant, or to help a libel plaintiff establish negligence or actual malice. Failure to comply with a court order can result in a citation for contempt of court. The Supreme Court of the United States ruled in 1972 that reporters were like all other citizens; they did not enjoy a First Amendment privilege which permitted them to refuse to testify before a grand jury. Despite this high Court ruling, the lower federal courts and state courts have fashioned a constitutional-common law privilege which often protects a journalist who has been subpoenaed to testify at a legal hearing. The privilege is qualified. In many instances a court will not require a journalist to testify unless the person seeking the information held by the journalist can demonstrate that the reporter has information which is relevant to the hearing, that there is a compelling need for the disclosure of this information, and that there are no alternative sources for this information.

Courts tend to apply this three-part test differently in different types of legal proceedings. Journalists are most likely to escape being forced to testify in a civil suit in which they are not a party to the litigation. Courts are less likely to grant journalists the privilege of refusing to testify if they are defendants in a libel suit and the information they hold is critical to proving the plaintiff's charges. Journalists who hold information relevant to charges against a criminal suspect or to the suspect's defense against those charges will usually be asked to divulge this confidential material. And reporters called to testify before a grand jury must in nearly all circumstances reveal the information that is sought or face a contempt citation. The United States Court of Appeals has also ruled that the records of toll telephone calls made by journalists may also be subpoenaed to further legitimate law enforcement proceedings.

LEGISLATIVE AND EXECUTIVE PROTECTION OF NEWS SOURCES

While the courts have erected limited barriers to protect journalists from subpoenas issued by government agencies, the state legislatures and the United States Department of Justice have attempted to protect reporters as well. Twenty-six states have passed statutes which shield reporters in one way or another from subpoenas which might force them to reveal confidential information, and the Department of Justice has developed an extensive set of guidelines which sharply limit when and how federal agents may use subpoenas against journalists. First, let us look at the state statutes.

Shield Laws

In 1896 Maryland granted journalists a limited privilege to refuse to testify in court proceedings. Since then more than half of the fifty states have passed what the press refers to as **shield laws.** These laws set down in specific terms what the privilege entails, who may use it, and when it may be used. Some laws are nearly absolute. For example, the Alabama Shield Law provides:

> No person engaged in, connected with, or employed on any newspaper (or radio broadcasting station or television station) while engaged in a news gathering capacity shall be compelled to disclose, in any legal proceeding or trial, before any court or before a grand jury of any court, or before the presiding officers of any tribunal or his agent or agents, or before any committee of the legislature, or elsewhere, the sources of any information procured or obtained by him and published in the newspaper (or broadcast by any broadcasting station or televised by any television station) on which he is engaged, connected with, or employed.

The laws in some states are far more qualified and prohibit use of the privilege in libel suits, for example, where the information might be material to the proof of malice. The privilege might also be denied in cases in which it is essential to prevent justice going astray, in which an overriding public interest is at stake, and in which reporters witness a crime. In some states the statutes are so filled with exceptions that at best the protection is of minimal value.

While shield laws can be effective in warding off unwanted and unnecessary subpoenas, they often create problems rather than provide protection. Two recent examples suffice to demonstrate these problems. In New York State an author who was preparing a book on organized crime was subpoenaed to produce the notes and tapes of his conversations with a witness in a murder prosecution. When he raised the state's shield law as a defense, the trial judge ruled that the law was inapplicable because the author of the book was not "a journalist engaged in gathering, preparing, or editing of news for newspapers, magazines, news agencies, press associations or wire service." The decision was later upheld by the state appellate court (*New York* v. *LeGrand*, 1979).

In Montana a reporter for the Associated Press telephoned a home where a gunman was holding two hostages. In a conversation with the reporter which was tape recorded the gunman admitted shooting a policeman. The audiotape was subpoenaed by the state, but the Associated Press refused to surrender it, citing the Montana shield law which stipulates that no person employed by any news service for the purpose of gathering news may be required to disclose information gained through news gathering. A Montana district court ruled that the law protected only the reporter—not the Associated Press, which is an organization. The wire service had to surrender the tape (in re *Investigative File*, 1978).

There is a distinct lack of consistency among the shield laws in the twenty-six states having such laws.

In California, for example, the manager of an FM radio station refused to answer questions before a grand jury concerning the murder of Marcus Foster, Oakland school superintendent. The station became involved in the case when it received a letter from the Symbionese Liberation Army claiming credit for the killing. The California Supreme Court ruled that the state's shield law protected the broadcaster and he did not have to testify (in re *Foster,* 1974). In a similar case in New York City radio station WBAI was forced to give up a letter it had received from a radical group. The New York court said the state's shield law did not protect the station employees (*WBAI-FM* v. *Proskin,* 1973).

Enactment of a federal shield law is one way many people suggest to solve the problem of inconsistency. Congress would pass a law displacing all state laws in order to ensure protection of Fourteenth Amendment rights, that is, freedom of the press. This solution seems unlikely, however, since Congress has been considering a shield law which covers only federal courts and other federal proceedings for several years and has not yet voted on the law.

The problem of inconsistency is especially vexing to news organizations like television networks and major newspapers whose reporters frequently work in many different states on a single assignment. Knowledge of the law is an important dimension of self-protection, and requiring a reporter to understand the subtleties and nuances of two dozen different laws is a significant difficulty.

Shield laws also suffer from definitional problems. That is, what a specific section of a law means depends upon the court interpreting it. Look at the Alabama law, for example. In the first sentence note the reference to newspapers: "No person engaged in, connected with or employed on any newspaper." What is a newspaper? The *New York Times* is a newspaper. A suburban weekly which covers the village government and schools is a newspaper. What about a militant propaganda sheet published by a radical group? Is it a newspaper? In Los Angeles among the requirements to qualify as a newspaper and have reporters get police press passes, according to the police and sheriff's departments, a publication must undertake "regular gathering and distribution of hard-core news generated through police and fire activities." The police say that the coverage of what they call "sociological news—riots, demonstrations, assassinations, news conferences" does not qualify a publication to be a newspaper.

Not all communities define a newspaper so narrowly. Defining a newspaper and its function is a real issue, however. Is the man who mimeographs a four-page newsletter and distributes it on street corners once a week publishing a newspaper? What about pamphlets? Do they qualify as newspapers? Many people say no before they remember the important role of pamphlets in our history, especially during the revolutionary period.

Even the so-called absolute shield laws are rarely absolute. Exceptions that can trap journalists are always present. Most shield laws protect reporters only with regard to information gained while they are engaged in "a news-gathering capacity." If reporters are given information on their day off, or if someone approaches them with a tip after working hours, the law probably would not protect them. Doctors may be on duty twenty-four hours a day, but reporters are generally not believed to be that dedicated.

Frequently reporters are protected by the law only when they receive information secondhand. Reporters who are witness to criminal activity are required by law to testify.

In Maryland, home of the nation's oldest shield law, a reporter wrote a story about being offered a joint of marijuana by a clerk in a store. He was called by the grand jury and asked the name of the clerk and of the store. He refused to give the names and argued that the shield law protected him. The court said no, that in this case he had witnessed a crime and *he* was the source. The story was based on his firsthand account (*Lightman* v. *State,* 1972). Paul Branzburg got into trouble the same way, for Kentucky had a shield law. The courts ruled that Branzburg was a witness to a crime when he watched the hashish being synthesized. There was no other source. Two reporters in New York State found out the same thing. Stewart Dan and Roland Barnes of television station WGR-TV were inside Attica during the prison riots in 1972. They were questioned by a grand jury and asked what they saw. They refused to tell, using the state's shield law as a defense. They lost. The court said the New York law protects news sources, not reporters who witness crimes (*People* v. *Dan,* 1973).

Finally, many courts do not like shield laws and therefore interpret the laws as narrowly as possible to force reporters to comply with subpoenas or with judges' instructions. For example, in New Jersey reporter Peter Bridge was called before a grand jury and ordered to give the unpublished details of his interview with a housing commissioner in Newark, New Jersey, who claimed she had been offered a bribe. Bridge attempted to use the state's shield law, but was unsuccessful. The court said that since the source of the story was already known and since Bridge had already revealed some information about the interview he had waived his right to use the privilege. Bridge spent twenty days in jail (in re *Bridge,* 1972).

One of the most perplexing of all the shield law cases is the case of William Farr. The case is a classic example of how a shield law can sometimes prove to be absolutely worthless. In 1970 Farr, a reporter for the *Los Angeles Herald-Examiner,* was assigned to cover the trial of Charles Manson and his followers. A restrictive order was in effect during the trial prohibiting trial participants from releasing the content or nature of all testimony given at the trial. During the trial a witness gave a member of the prosecution a written statement that one of the defendants in the case, Susan Atkins, had confessed to the crimes for which she and the rest of the Manson clan were being tried. Copies of the statement were prepared and given to each of the attorneys in the trial. One of them gave a copy to Farr who published it as part of a story in the *Herald-Examiner*. At the conclusion of the trial the judge convened a special hearing to determine the source of Farr's story. Called as a witness, Farr refused to identify the attorney who had given him the copy of the statement. Farr argued that he did not have to testify because of the California shield law, but the court ruled that the privilege did not apply to Farr because at the time of the post-trial hearing he had resigned from the *Herald-Examiner* and was working as a press aide to the Los Angeles district attorney. He was no longer a reporter. In addition, the California district court of appeals ruled that even if Farr was a working journalist the shield law was inapplicable because its use would interfere with the right of the trial court to enforce its edicts and control the conduct of participants at the trial: "To construe the statute as granting immunity to petitioner, Farr, in the face of the facts here present would be to countenance an unconstitutional interference by the legislative branch with an inherent and vital power of the court to control its own proceedings and officers" (*Farr* v. *Superior Court,* 1971). In other words, the people of California have no business giving journalists this privilege if it interferes with the work of the courts. Bill Farr spent forty-six days in an eight-by-twelve-foot cell with no windows before the California court of appeals vacated the district court's contempt order. The state shield law was revised to prohibit judges from sentencing reporters to indefinite jail terms and to prevent a court from forcing reporters to reveal their sources after they leave journalism.

The Oregon Supreme Court recently ruled that the state shield law violated the state constitution and the Sixth Amendment to the United States Constitution and found it inapplicable as a protection for a television reporter called to testify as a witness in a criminal case (*Oregon* v. *Knorr,* 1982). And in California a superior court recently ruled that the law does not protect freelance writers who simply have future expectations of marketing their work. The shield will only protect free-lancers who have already entered into a contractural arrangement with a publisher or other organization that is protected under the statute (in re *Van Ness,* 1982). It is plain that often judges go out of their way to construe the shield protection as narrowly as possible.

Many persons argue that shield laws give the reporter an illusion of protection rather than real protection. Yet such laws have been used successfully to thwart official investigations. In addition, the number of subpoenas which were never sent to journalists simply because of the existence of a shield law cannot be calculated. Still, many reporters find it more to their liking to work to develop the limited First Amendment protection than to ask the government—the same government upon which they are expected to report—for a special protection. When push comes to shove, many reporters note, the government can strip away any protection it has given to the press. That cannot happen so easily with a privilege grounded in the First Amendment.

Federal Guidelines   As a kind of corollary to a shield law, the Department of Justice has adopted rules which define when and how a United States attorney can obtain a subpoena against a working reporter. Here is a summary of the guidelines.

1. The Department of Justice must attempt to strike a balance between the public's interest in the free dissemination of ideas and information and the public interest in effective law enforcement when determining whether to seek a subpoena for a journalist's confidential information.

2. All reasonable attempts should be made to obtain the information from alternative sources before considering issuing a subpoena to a member of the news media.

3. Negotiations with the news media to gain the information which is sought shall be pursued in all cases in which a subpoena to a member of the news media is contemplated.

4. If the negotiations fail (if the reporter won't provide the material voluntarily), the attorney general must approve the subpoena based on the following guidelines.

   a. There must be sufficient evidence of a crime from a nonpress source. The department does not approve of using reporters as springboards for investigation.

   b. The information the reporter has must be essential to a successful investigation—not peripheral or speculative.

   c. The government must have unsuccessfully attempted to get the information from an alternative nonpress source.

   d. Great caution must be exercised with respect to subpoenas for unpublished information or where confidentiality is alleged.

   e. Even subpoenas for published information must be treated with care because reporters have encountered harrassment on the grounds that information collected will be available to the government.

   f. The subpoena must be directed to specific information.

Telephone Records   Rules one through three above apply when federal agents seek to subpoena the toll telephone records of members of the media as well. If the negotiations to get the records fail, the agents must seek permission from the attorney general to issue the subpoena. In such a case the following guidelines apply.

1. There should be reasonable grounds to believe that a crime has been committed, and that the information sought is essential to the successful investigation of that crime.

2. The subpoena should be directed at only relevant information regarding a limited subject matter and should cover a limited period of time.

3. The government should have pursued all reasonable alternative means before seeking the subpoena.

4. Reporters must be given timely notice that the government intends to issue a subpoena.
5. Information obtained through the subpoena must be closely guarded so that unauthorized persons cannot gain access to it.

These federal guidelines have worked well. In some federal cases judges have insisted that the government must demonstrate that it has followed these guidelines before it will force a reporter to testify (*U.S.* v. *Blanton,* 1982, for example). Some state and local law enforcement agencies have adopted rules similar to these federal rules. The federal guidelines apply to criminal cases, civil matters, and subpoena of telephone records. It is true that these guidelines do not completely protect the working journalist, but the guidelines often work better than shield laws, and they go a considerable distance in reducing animosity that was mounting between the press, the police, and the courts.

Newsroom Searches

Does a newsroom or a journalist's home enjoy any constitutional protection from a search by the police or federal agents? The Supreme Court of the United States refused to extend the First Amendment in such a manner in 1978 (*Zurcher* v. *Stanford Daily*). Since then, however, the Congress and many state legislatures have provided qualified legislative protection for premises where news and scholarship are produced. The lawsuit which resulted in the Supreme Court ruling stemmed from the political turmoil of the early seventies which generated many of the previously discussed cases regarding reporters' sources.

In April of 1971 police were asked to remove student demonstrators who were occupying the administrative offices of Stanford University Hospital. When police entered the west end of the building, demonstrators poured out of the east end, and during the ensuing melee outside the building several police officers were hurt, two seriously. The battle between the police and the students was photographed by a student, and the following day pictures of the incident were published in the *Stanford Daily* student newspaper. In an effort to discover which students had attacked the injured police officers, law enforcement officials from Santa Clara County secured a warrant for a search of the *Daily*'s newsroom, hoping to find more pictures taken by the student photographer. It was hoped the pictures might provide visual evidence of which students had battered the lawmen. There was no allegation that any member of the *Daily* staff was involved in the attack or other unlawful acts. No evidence was discovered during the thorough search.

This type of search is known as an innocent third-party search, or simply a third-party search. Police search the premises or a room for evidence relating to a crime, even though there is no reason to suspect that the owner of the premises or the occupant of the room is involved in the crime which is being investigated. Such searches are not uncommon, but in the lawsuit that followed the student newspaper argued that this kind of search threatened the freedom of the press and should not be permitted unless police officials first obtain a subpoena—which is more difficult for lawmen to get than is a simple search warrant. The subpoena process would also provide the press with notice prior to the search and allow editors and reporters to challenge the issuance of the subpoena.

The newspaper argued that the unannounced third-party search of a newsroom seriously threatened the ability of the press to gather, analyze, and disseminate news. The searches could be physically disruptive for a craft in which meeting deadlines is essential. Confidential sources—fearful that some evidence which would reveal their identity might surface in such a search— would refuse to cooperate with reporters. Reporters would be deterred from keeping notes and tapes if such material could be seized in a search. All of this and more could have a chilling effect on the press, lawyers for the newspaper argued.

The Supreme Court, in a five-to-three ruling, disagreed with the newspaper. Justice Byron White ruled that the problem was essentially a Fourth Amendment question (i.e., was the search permissible under the Fourth Amendment?), not a First Amendment question, and that under existing law a warrant may be issued to search any property if there is reason to believe that evidence of a crime will be found. "The Fourth Amendment has itself struck the balance between privacy and public need and there is no occasion or justification for a court to revise the Amendment and strike a new balance. . .," White wrote. The associate justice conceded that "where the materials sought to be seized may be protected by the First Amendment, the requirements of the Fourth Amendment must be applied with 'scrupulous exactitude.' " He added, "Where presumptively protected materials are sought to be seized, the warrant requirement should be administered to leave as little as possible to the discretion of the officer in the field." But Justice White rejected the notion that such unannounced searches are a threat to the freedom of the press, arguing that the framers of the constitution were certainly aware of the struggle between the press and the crown in the seventeenth and eighteenth centuries when the general search warrant was a serious problem for the press. Yet the framers did not forbid the use of search warrants where the press was involved, White asserted. They obviously believed the protections of the Fourth Amendment would sufficiently protect the press (*Zurcher* v. *Stanford Daily,* 1978).

The decision by the Supreme Court reinforced existing law on the question and did not represent a dramatic change in policy. But prior to the search of the *Stanford Daily* in 1971, there had been only fifteen police searches of newsrooms in this country, ever, according to Anthony Lewis, columnist for the *New York Times*. The Supreme Court ruling seemed to suggest the value of such searches to law enforcement agencies across the United States, for in the next ten years nearly twenty newsroom searches were conducted. What happened at KBCI-TV in Boise, Idaho, is typical. There was a riot at the Idaho State Penitentiary in July 1980. Inmates invited Bob Loy, managing editor of KBCI-TV, to meet with them to hear their grievances. Loy toured the facility with a cameraman, who shot videotape of the $15 million in damage at the prison. After the riot was quelled, County Prosecutor James Harris and police searched the KBCI newsroom for the videotapes taken at the penitentiary. The prosecutor obtained the search warrant on the grounds that he wanted to use the videotape in his prosecution of inmates for damaging the prison. After ninety minutes of what was described by *TV Guide* as "heavy-handed" searching, the tapes were found and confiscated. KBCI brought suit to have the search declared illegal and to get an injunction against future searches, but the case was dismissed by the Idaho district court which cited the *Zurcher* ruling (*Reiss* v. *Harris,* 1980).

Incidents like these demonstrated the need for some kind of legislative relief, and Congress responded by passing the Privacy Protection Act of 1980. The law prohibits law officers and government agents from searching for or seizing materials that are in the hands of persons working for the mass media or persons who expect to publicly disseminate the material in some other manner (e.g., public speech). The statute designates two categories of material which are protected: work products and documentary materials. The law says a work product "encompasses the material whose very creation arises out of a purpose to convey information to the public." In layman's language work products are reporters' notes, unexposed film, outtakes, and so forth. Documentary materials are described as "materials upon which information is formally recorded" such as government reports, manuscripts, and the like. Congress based the statute on the commerce clause in the United States Constitution in order to extend the reach of the law to include state and local agencies as well as federal law enforcement personnel. To obtain either work products or documentary materials law enforcement agencies must obtain a subpoena; a search warrant will not do. There are, however, exceptions to the rule. A law enforcement agency may conduct a warranted search of a newsroom to find "work products" in either of the following two situations:

1. When there is a probable cause to believe that the person possessing such materials has committed or is committing a criminal offense to which the materials will relate
2. Where there is reason to believe that the immediate seizure of such materials is necessary to prevent the death of or serious harm to a person

A search warrant may be used instead of a subpoena to obtain documentary materials if either of the two conditions listed above are met in either of these two situations:

1. There is reason to believe that the giving of notice pursuant to gaining a subpoena would result in the destruction, alteration, or concealment of such materials
2. That such materials have not been provided in response to a court order directing compliance with a subpoena, all other legal remedies have been exhausted, and there is reason to believe that further delay in gaining the material would threaten the interests of justice

In most instances, then, law enforcement personnel will be forced to seek a subpoena to gain access to information kept in a newsroom or a reporter's home. Many state legislatures have passed similar laws. Hence, the problem of newsroom searches has been significantly reduced.

Government intrusion into news gathering and news processing creates serious difficulties for the press. The sanctity of the newsroom must be preserved if the press is to function properly as a neutral observer in this society. Even the hint of government meddling in the news process could cause a sharp reduction in the flow of information into newsrooms (and ultimately to the public) and could create distrust of the press among many readers and viewers.

Summary

State legislatures and the federal government have adopted statutes and rules which offer some protection to journalists who hold confidential information sought by government agents and other individuals. Twenty-six states have adopted so-called shield laws which provide a qualified privilege for reporters to refuse to testify in legal proceedings. While sometimes these statutes can be helpful, they are not without problems. There is a lack of consistency among the state shield laws, and the Congress has not adopted federal legislation in this area. These laws have definitional problems which permit courts to construe them very narrowly if they choose to. The laws usually protect only what someone tells a reporter, not what a reporter personally sees or hears. Often courts see the statutes as legislative interference with judicial prerogatives and go out of their way to interpret the laws in the least useful manner.

The Department of Justice has adopted rules which govern when and how federal agents may subpoena journalists, records possessed by journalists, and telephone toll records. The rules require federal agents to strike a balance between the public's interest in the free flow of information and effective law enforcement. United States attorneys are instructed to attempt to obtain information from alternative sources or negotiate with the journalist to get the material before seeking a subpoena. The attorney general must approve all subpoenas under guidelines outlined in these rules.

In response to a ruling by the United States Supreme Court that the First Amendment does not ban searches of newsrooms or reporters' homes, Congress passed the Privacy Protection Act of 1980. This act requires federal, state, and local police agencies who seek a journalist's work products or other documentary materials to get a subpoena for these materials rather than seize them under the authority of a search warrant. The statute does provide exceptions to these rules. For example, premises may be searched and materials seized under a search warrant if police believe the reporter has committed a crime, if there is reason to believe someone will be harmed if the materials are not seized, or if police fear the materials might be destroyed if a subpoena is sought.

THE CONTEMPT POWER

We have seen that reporters have been subpoenaed to testify in a wide range of legal proceedings. Television news departments have been ordered to surrender films and videotapes. Broadcast journalists have been required under court order to supply audiotape recordings to police and prosecutors. And, of course, if journalists refuse to cooperate, they face severe penalty under the courts' power to punish for contempt. What is the contempt power? Without a thorough understanding of the contempt power, it is difficult to truly appreciate the predicament journalists can find themselves in when asked to produce the name of a news source or other confidential information.

History of Contempt

In 1631 in England a British subject was convicted of a felony, not a very uncommon event. This particular subject was angered at being found guilty, and after the sentence was read he threw a brickbat at the judge. The brickbat missed the judge, but the man was quickly seized, his right hand was cut off and nailed to the gallows, and he was immediately hanged in the presence of the court (this story is recounted by Ronald Goldfarb in *The Contempt Power*).

While such judicial retribution is an uncommon exercise of the contempt power, it nevertheless is a representative example of the power of judges to control what goes on in their courtrooms. Even as the end of the twentieth century approaches, disobedience or disrespect of the court is normally put down swiftly by exercise of the power of contempt. Any act which interferes with the orderly processes of justice is usually promptly stopped and the offender is quickly punished. While other governmental bodies (legislative bodies, for example) can use the contempt power, its use by judges, which is the subject of this chapter, is far more common today.

Does it not seem odd in what are supposedly representative democracies like the United States and Great Britain, countries in which the guarantee of civil liberties has long been part of the national heritage, that a single individual like a judge can wield such awesome power? The answer to that question is yes. But supporters of the contempt power point out that it is a necessary tool for judges to have to ensure the orderly function of the courts. Courts are an indispensable part of our governmental system. The courts make freedom of the press, freedom of speech, freedom of religion, and other civil liberties meaningful rights by protecting these constitutional guarantees. If the court system is impeded in some way, if judges are waylaid in their trek toward justice, society then suffers.

Even this rationale does not explain why judges and justices retain such extraordinary powers, powers which include summary punishment, when justice is stripped of many of the basic constitutional guarantees which the courts are supposed to protect. Nor does this rationale explain why supposedly intelligent men can believe that our court system, or any court system, can be infallible and should be free from citizen scrutiny and comment. The answers to these questions are, once again, found in the past.

In 1927 British legal scholar John Fox wrote in *The History of Contempt of Court*, "Rules for preserving discipline . . . came into existence with the law itself, and contempt of court has been a recognized phase of English law from the twelfth century to the present time." Order has always been essential to the administration of justice. Courts, after all, are where rational decision making must prevail. Yet the contempt power is peculiar to the common law nations. Judges in France or Holland or Italy do not enjoy such extraordinary latitude in dealing with disturbance, disobedience, and disrespect. The common law judges were able to assume such power because the first common law judge was the king himself. He was the administrator of justice. As Ronald Goldfarb points out in his important study of the contempt power, the people revered the king. Goldfarb writes, "This was but another, though not different, step from the sanctity of the medicine man, the priestly character of primitive royalty, and the Christian concepts of obedience." This legal scholar adds that the contempt power is clearly understandable, then, when viewed from the perspective of the age of its inception, "an age of alleged divinely ordained monarchies, ruled by a king totally invested with all sovereign legal powers and accountable only to God." In some instances resistance to the king was a sin, punishable by damnation. Being jailed or fined or tortured for being contemptuous of the king was really rather unimportant when compared to the fate offenders faced on judgment day in the hereafter.

When the king became too busy to hear all the cases coming before his court, he appointed ministers to sit in judgment throughout the realm. Logically, disrespect toward one of the king's judges should not be a serious offense since the discourtesy was aimed at a mere mortal, not at a person divinely ordained to rule. But that was not the case, because while the king was not physically present in the courtroom, he was assumed to be there spiritually, guiding the hand of justice. Surely this assumption sounds like nonsense, but men will believe almost anything if the belief is important to them. In any case, disrespect or disobedience of the judge were considered to be disrespect or disobedience of the king or of the spiritual presence of the king. Punishment by the judge was as swift and as sure as punishment by the king would have been.

As representative democracy developed in England and royal influence on the government diminished, judges retained the contempt power and it became institutionalized in common law courts in both Great Britain and the United States. Courts today rarely justify the exercise of the contempt power on the grounds that it protects the integrity of the judge. Today, protection of the authority, order, and decorum of the court is the usual reason given for the use of the contempt power, and sometimes it is protection of the rights of the litigants using the court to settle a dispute.

Kinds of Contempt	Historically, legal scholars have tried to classify the various kinds of contempt power judges have at their disposal into either civil or criminal contempt, but contempt seems to defy classification, or at least to defy consistent classification. Goldfarb refers to the "chameleonic characteristic" of contempt: that is, an action considered civil contempt in one court may be viewed as criminal contempt in another. Writing in the *Tennessee Law Review* (1971), Professor Luis Kutner notes the problem:

> The distinction between civil and criminal contempt is not clear-cut. The same act in different situations may be regarded as either civil or criminal. Contempt has been regarded criminal if the purpose is to punish the contemnor for his misconduct in the presence of the court or for conduct out of the court's presence challenging its authority, and the contemnor is fined a fixed amount or imprisoned for a definite term; it is regarded as civil if the primary purpose is to coerce compliance with a court order, usually for the benefit of an injured suitor, and the contemnor is imprisoned only until he complies. Whether the contempt is civil or criminal is determined by the judicial decision maker.

Despite the "chameleonic" nature of the contempt power, scholars frequently use the following method of classification. The classification is based on the purpose of the punishment: (1) punishment exacted to protect the rights of a private party in a legal dispute before the court and (2) punishment exacted to vindicate the law, the authority of the court, or the power of the judge. When the punishment is exacted for the first reason, the contempt is normally called a civil contempt. When the punishment is exacted for the second reason, the contempt is usually considered a criminal contempt. Here is a brief discussion of the types of contempt based on this classification scheme.

Civil Contempt

A **civil contempt** is not an affront to the court itself, but is more likely failure or refusal to obey a court ruling, decision, or order made to protect the rights of one of the litigants in the case. Normally, the punishment in a civil contempt suit is a jail sentence which is terminated when the contemnor agrees either to do something or to stop doing something. For example, if a broadcasting station is sued for libel because it has broadcast a defamatory news story, and the reporter refuses to divulge the source of the story under questioning by the plaintiff, the reporter can be held in civil contempt. She can be put in jail and forced to stay there until she is willing to cooperate with the court. The court is protecting the rights of the libel plaintiff in this case. Civil contempt, then, is charged to obtain obedience to judgment, court orders, and court processes and is designed to protect the rights of the litigants in a case.

Criminal Contempt

Criminal contempt, on the other hand, is charged to protect the court itself, to punish a wrong against the court. Obstruction of court proceedings or court officers, attacks on court personnel, and deliberate acts of bad faith or fraud are all examples of criminal contempt. There are two kinds of criminal contempt, direct contempt and indirect contempt.

A **direct criminal contempt** is an action committed "in the presence of the court," that is, in the courtroom or near the courtroom. Generally two conditions underlie a direct contempt: first, the judge has actual personal knowledge of what occurred, and second, the act or action had a significant impact upon the judicial proceedings. The key seems to be the judge's personal knowledge of the events. In the instance of a direct criminal contempt, the judge is normally empowered to use what is called his **summary contempt power.** When the judge exercises his summary power, he acts as prosecutor, jury, and judge. Suppose that in the midst of the trial the defendant jumps on a table and begins to play an accordian. The judge can use his summary power. "I accuse you of disrupting this trial by playing an accordian [the prosecutor's role], I find you guilty of disrupting the trial [the jury's role], and I fine you $200 [the judge's role]."

Summary punishment is the most onerous aspect of the contempt power, for the citizen is not allowed to exercise some of the basic constitutional guarantees which are normally a part of the criminal process. There is no jury trial. The accuser is also the judge and jury. The accused has no right to call witnesses in his behalf. Many authorities argue that because the summary power can normally be exercised only in a direct criminal contempt, an instance in which the judge has direct personal knowledge of what took place, the summary power is really not a threat to civil liberty. But this argument is questionable. Anytime one person can wield such power, a threat to civil liberties exists.

Any contempt conviction can be appealed. As in any other case the appeal is taken to the next higher court in the state or in the federal system if the contempt stems from the action of a federal district judge. Normally the punishment is held in abeyance until the disposition of the appeal is settled. It is possible, but not likely, that a reporter who has been jailed for a contempt might stay in jail during at least a portion of the appeal process. But usually the journalist is freed pending the results of the appeal. In the appeal process, however, the only record of the facts in the case is prepared by the judge who issued the citation. The appeal is based upon this factual record, the facts as seen by the trial judge.

The press infrequently gets involved in direct criminal contempt. However, if a photographer were to snap a flash picture in the midst of a trial, he would undoubtedly find himself in direct criminal contempt.

Indirect criminal contempt is sometimes called constructive contempt and can be described as misconduct which occurs apart from the trial or apart from the court, but which still interferes with the proceeding.

Another definition of indirect criminal contempt is that it is a contempt about which the court or the judge has no firsthand knowledge, or a contemptuous act that does not occur in the presence of the court. Comments published in a newspaper about the conduct of the court or of the judge in the midst of the trial can be constructive contempt. When during a trial a television station broadcasts the details of the defendant's confession after the judge suppressed the information, the station commits an indirect contempt. Publication of false or grossly inaccurate stories about the proceedings of a court can be considered a constructive contempt. Any action which interferes with the administration of justice, but which occurs away from the courtroom, can be considered an indirect criminal contempt.

Limitations on Contempt Power

Before the limits of the contempt power are discussed, it should be noted at this point that truth is not generally considered a limitation. That is, truthful criticism of the court, publishing truthful comments about a pending case, can be and frequently is regarded as contempt. As one author puts it, any adverse comment by the mass media, no matter how true, can interfere with the administration of justice and can be punished in most courts as contempt. The Supreme Court established this principle in the early years of this century when it upheld a Colorado court decision to punish the editor and publisher of a Denver newspaper for printing articles which questioned both the motives of the state's high court and the manner in which two of the supreme court judges had been seated. The criticism was published as part of a commentary on a case pending before the state high court. Justice Oliver Wendell Holmes, writing for the United States Supreme Court, said the comments were inappropriate because the case was being considered by the court. "When a case is finished," he wrote, "courts are subject to the same criticism as other people, but the propriety and necessity of preventing interference with the course of justice by premature statement, argument or intimidation hardly can be denied" (*Patterson v. Colorado,* 1907). Holmes added that the fact that the criticism is truthful is immaterial in a case of constructive contempt.

The early years of the twentieth century must be regarded as a high-water mark for the contempt power, because since that time the opponents of this power have succeeded in placing rather severe limitations upon its use.

Make no mistake. It is not a sterile power. Judges can and still do use their contempt power. But in the last quarter of the twentieth century, judges throughout the United States have far less freedom in how they use this power than they had in the first quarter of this century.

Legislative Limits

One important limitation upon the power of the court to use contempt comes from legislatures. For example, for more than sixty years the Congress has passed laws which limit use of the summary power by federal judges to dispose of contempt citations. The 1914 Clayton Antitrust Act, for example, requires that judges provide a jury trial in a contempt case when the contemptuous action is also a crime under federal or state law. In 1932 as a part of the Norris-LaGuardia Act, the Congress mandated jury trials for all constructive contempts arising out of labor disputes. The 1957 civil rights law provided for a jury trial for contempt when the sentence imposed exceeds forty-five days in jail. The 1964 civil rights law contains the same provision.

Court-Imposed Limits

The bench itself imposes limitations upon the use of the summary power. The *Federal Rules of Criminal Procedure* requires that in indirect contempt notice be given the contemnor and a hearing be allowed. In addition, there are the right to counsel, the right to cross-examine witnesses, the right to offer testimony, and in many instances the right to a jury trial. If the contempt citation is based upon criticism or disrespect of a judge, that judge is disqualified from the proceeding. Bail is also allowed. The courts and legislatures in many states also deem that a jury trial is a requirement in an indirect contempt.

In the instances just noted, the legislature or the bench itself grants the right to a jury trial. Is there a constitutional right to a jury trial in such cases? The United States Supreme Court has been grappling with this question since the 1960s.

In 1964 the high Court ruled that there is no constitutional right to a jury trial in a contempt case in upholding the contempt conviction of the governor of Mississippi, Ross Barnett, who willfully disobeyed an order of the Fifth Circuit Court of Appeals. As one might expect at that time and in that place, the substantive question involved was civil rights. However, a footnote in the court's opinion states, "Some members of the Court are of the view that, without regard to the seriousness of the offense, punishment by summary trial without a jury would be constitutionally limited to that penalty provided for petty offenses" (*U.S.* v. *Barnett,* 1964).

Petty offenses generally carry a sentence of six months or less. What the court seemed to be hinting at is that a jury trial is required constitutionally if the penalty exceeds more than six months in jail. A few years later in *Cheff* v. *Schnackenberg* (1966) the high Court specifically said what it implied in the *Barnett* case—that sentences exceeding six months cannot be imposed in cases of criminal contempt without giving the accused a jury trial. Then in

1968 in *Bloom* v. *Illinois* the high Court took the last step and ruled that criminal contempt is a crime in the ordinary sense, and that since the United States Constitution guarantees the right to a jury trial in criminal cases, prosecutions by state courts for serious criminal contempts (those with more than a six-month penalty) must be heard by a jury.

One of the most interesting court-imposed limitations upon the power of contempt concerns judicial interpretation of the 1831 federal contempt statute. One of the first acts of the first United States Congress in 1789 was to establish a federal judiciary system. In doing so it gave federal judges the power "to punish by fine or imprisonment, at the discretion of said courts, all contempts of authority in any case or hearing before the same."

This broad authority to use the contempt power remained unchanged until the 1830s when federal Judge James H. Peck arbitrarily punished an attorney who published an article critical of the judge. The judge's action resulted in his own impeachment. He was acquitted by a vote of twenty-two to twenty-one, but the trial prompted Congress to place a limit on the summary power. The 1831 law strictly limited federal judges' use of summary punishment to those contempts committed in the presence of the court, "or so near thereto" as to obstruct the administration of justice. The change in the law, then, was designed to limit the power of federal judges. But by the Civil War this law had been forgotten, and federal judges once again used their summary power to punish a wide variety of contemptuous behavior.

Typical of this attitude was a decision by the Arkansas Supreme Court in 1855 which rejected a state statute limiting use of the contempt power and ruled that the power in courts to punish for contempt springs into existence upon the creation of the courts, that it is a part of the court's inherent power (*State* v. *Morrill*).

In 1918 a question over interpretation of the 1831 law came before the Supreme Court. Toledo, Ohio, was in the throes of a major dispute over a change in the transit fares. While a federal judge deliberated over the constitutionality of the change in the price of a streetcar ride, a local newspaper, the *News-Bee*, published unflattering remarks about him. After the judge ruled that the change in fare was unconstitutional, he found the newspaper in contempt and summarily fined the publisher. The newspaper appealed the action on the grounds that the judge lacked the authority to invoke a summary punishment, that summary punishment could only be used in cases in which the contempt is committed in the presence of the court, or "so near thereto" as to create an obstruction of administration of justice. The *News-Bee* was published miles from the courthouse, not in the presence of the court nor "so near thereto." In other words, the *News-Bee* said that the 1831 law placed a geographic limitation upon the judge's use of the summary punishment. The high Court disagreed. It ruled that the 1831 limitation placed a causal, rather than a geographic, limitation upon the use of the summary power (*Toledo Newspaper Co.* v. *U.S.*, 1918). Chief Justice Edward F. White wrote that *so near thereto* meant that any action that was in "close relationship" to the administration of justice could be punished summarily. In this case, the newspaper articles critical of the judge surely had a relationship to the case at hand.

The matter appeared settled, albeit wrongly. In 1928 Walter Nelles and Alice King, legal researchers, looked into the history of the 1831 law ("Contempt by Publication in the United States"). By their research these writers demonstrated that the 1831 measure was designed to limit the power of federal judges, not to enlarge it, as a majority of the Supreme Court contended in the Toledo newspaper case in 1918.

In 1941 the Supreme Court had the opportunity to apply these research findings (*Nye* v. *U.S.*) in a case that did not involve the press. Instead the case originated in a civil suit filed in federal district court against a patent medicine company. The plaintiff claimed that his son died as a result of drinking the medicine. Agents from the patent medicine maker plied the father with liquor one night and cajoled him into writing a letter to the judge, asking that the suit be dismissed. The judge was suspicious, investigated the request, and discovered the skulduggery by the drug company. He summarily fined the two men for their contemptuous behavior, despite the fact that their meeting with the plaintiff took place more than one hundred miles from the court. In an appeal to the Supreme Court the convictions were overturned. Justice William O. Douglas, citing the legal research published by Nelles and King, noted that "so near thereto" has a geographic meaning, that before the summary power can be used the misbehavior must be in the vicinity of the courtroom, that is, in physical proximity to the proceedings.

Justice Douglas did not indicate how close, but most experts today believe that a federal judge's right to use his summary power probably extends to the hallway outside the courtroom and perhaps even to the lobby of the building when a disturbance occurs. Conceivably a demonstration on the sidewalk outside the building can also be ruled to be in physical proximity if the disturbance is noisy and disturbs proceedings.

Through various means, then, during this century the summary power of judges has been limited, and in turn the limitations have reduced the contempt power. Through statutes which explicitly limit the use of the summary power and through court rulings which limit the severity of punishment which may be applied in the absence of a jury, the absolute power of judges has been trimmed. Nevertheless, the summary power is still a threat. And even six months in jail is a long time!

First Amendment Limitations

The First Amendment was not raised as a barrier to contempt conviction until relatively modern times, in 1941 to be exact. In 1941 and again in 1946 and 1947 the United States Supreme Court ruled that freedom of the press to comment on the judiciary must be protected except in those circumstances in which the commentary presents a serious threat to the proper functioning of the legal process. These three decisions, *Bridges* v. *California* and *Times Mirror Co.* v. *Superior Court, Pennekamp* v. *Florida,* and *Craig* v. *Harney*, stand as the bedrock support for the argument that the First Amendment protects the press in writing about the judiciary.

The first case, *Bridges* v. *California* and *Times Mirror Co.* v. *Superior Court* (1941), actually consisted of two appeals from decisions by California courts, and the cases were decided together as one case. In the first instance a newspaper, the *Los Angeles Times,* was ruled in contempt for publishing a series of anti-labor editorials. The trial court claimed that the editorials were aimed at influencing the disposition of cases before the court concerning labor unionists. In the second case, labor leader Harry Bridges was held in contempt of court when he publicly threatened to take the dockworkers out on strike if the courts attempted to enforce a judicial ruling going against Bridges and his union. While the specter of a militant anti-labor union newspaper and a militant labor leader arguing on the same side of this question is remarkable, it is not as remarkable as the high Court's decision which voided both contempt citations.

In a five-to-four decision the high Court repudiated the idea that the contempt power is valid because it is deeply rooted in English common law. Justice Hugo Black wrote that even if this were the case the idea ignores the generally accepted historical belief that "one of the objects of the Revolution was to get rid of the English law on liberty of speech and press." Black said that before a judge can use his contempt power to close off discussion of a case there must be a "clear and present danger" that the discussion will produce interference with the proper administration of justice. In applying Holmes's famous World War I clear and present danger sedition test to contempt, Black meant that only those threats to justice which are imminent or immediate can be punished. The substantive evil must be extremely serious and the degree of imminence extremely high before utterances can be punished, he wrote.

The government argued in these cases that commentary on a case is clearly proper, but only *after* the case is completed so that the course of justice cannot be influenced. Black rejected this notion, saying that it is while a trial is underway that the public interest about a case is highest. He wrote:

> We cannot start with the assumption that publications actually do threaten to change the nature of legal trials and that to preserve judicial impartiality it is necessary for judges to have a contempt power by which they can close all channels of public expression to matters touching on the pending cases.

It should be noted parenthetically that in using the clear and present danger test to block contempt convictions, Justice Black made better use of those four words than did the high Court in its application of the test in sedition trials. For the clear and present danger test indeed became an effective means of stopping contempt convictions against the press.

This concept was reinforced five years later when in the second case, *Pennekamp* v. *Florida* (1946), the high Court reviewed an appeal from the Florida Supreme Court involving a contempt citation against the *Miami Herald*.

The *Herald* had been highly critical of the trial courts in Dade County, Florida, for many months. In at least two editorials the editors argued that the courts worked harder to protect the criminals than they worked to protect the people. But the editors' evaluation of the courts' performance was founded on serious misstatement of facts. The court found both the editor, John D. Pennekamp, and the newspaper in contempt and levied fines against them both.

The Supreme Court overturned the convictions, noting, "We are not willing to say under the circumstances of this case that these editorials are a clear and present danger to the fair administration of justice in Florida." Justice Stanley Reed wrote that while he could not precisely define clear and present danger, certainly the criticism of a judge's actions in a nonjury trial would not affect the legal process. What about the factual errors in the editorials? Justice Reed said the errors were quite immaterial. Free discussion, Reed said, is a cardinal principle of Americanism. Discussion after a trial ends might be inadequate and can endanger the public welfare. Freedom of discussion should be given the widest range compatible with the essential requirement of the fair and orderly administration of justice. "We conclude," Reed wrote, "that the danger under this record to fair judicial administration has not the clearness and immediacy necessary to close the door of permissible public comment. When that door is closed, it closes all doors behind it."

The following year, the high Court once again reinforced the First Amendment barrier to the use of the contempt power in its decision in *Craig* v. *Harney* (1947), the third case. In this case a Texas newspaper had been highly critical of a judge who directed a jury to return a verdict against a well-liked citizen in a civil suit. The *Corpus Christi Caller-Times* was found in contempt of court, and again the high Court struck down the conviction. Justice William O. Douglas admitted that in the Court's opinion the critical articles were unfair because they contained significant errors about what actually occurred at the trial. "But inaccuracies in reporting," he wrote, "are commonplace. Certainly a reporter could not be laid by the heels for contempt because he missed the essential point in a trial or failed to summarize the issues to accord with the views of the judge who sat on the case."

Douglas wrote that it took more imagination than the court possessed to find "in this sketchy and one-sided report of a case any imminent or serious threat to a judge of reasonable fortitude. . . ." Douglas added, "Where public matters are involved, the doubts should be resolved in favor of freedom of expression rather than against it."

The three cases just discussed, *Bridges, Pennekamp,* and *Craig,* represent three strong statements in favor of a broad discussion of judicial matters, of trials, and of the legal process. To some degree they also represent a limitation upon the contempt power of the courts. The clear and present danger test is a formidable hurdle for any judge to clear before punishing a newspaper or television station with a contempt citation. However, lest we get swept away by the Court's rhetoric, it is important to look at what was involved in each of these cases, or rather what was not involved. In none of the cases did the judge first issue an order banning certain kinds of publicity about the case. In none of the cases could a jury have been influenced by the media publicity. In none of the cases did the press publish or broadcast evidence or statements prohibited at the trial. As a matter of fact, all three cases involved the same question—commentary or criticism directed toward a judge. From these cases it is clear that the Supreme Court expects the nation's judges to be strong, not to bend in the wind of public opinion, not to be influenced by journalistic commentary. But the Court has never indicated that it has the same expectations with regard to juries. It has never said that a judge must allow the press free rein in its comments on a pending case with regard to material evidence or the credibility of witnesses. The caution, then, is not to read more into these decisions than is actually there. *Bridges, Pennekamp,* and *Craig* stand for almost unlimited discussion of pending nonjury cases. That is about as far as we dare go, however.

A few other limitations upon the contempt power also exist. At times judges have been prone to use contempt rather than libel as the means of defending their reputation from press criticism. Appellate courts are sensitive to this tactic and routinely overturn such contempt convictions. Courts are also prohibited from stopping publication of certain material in advance on the grounds that publishing it constitutes a contempt of court. This is another instance in which prior restraint is forbidden. However, a Washington state superior court judge recently found Spokane radio station KHQ in contempt of court for broadcasting an audio tape recording of a conversation (recorded by police) between a criminal defendant and a police undercover agent. The tape was played in open court, and newspapers had published transcripts of the conversation, but the judge barred the broadcast of the tape because he said it might cause psychological harm to the defendant. The radio station violated this order and was held in contempt. The ruling was overturned by Washington State Supreme Court on free speech grounds. (*Washington* v. *Coe,* 1984).

Present Status

The threat of a contempt citation is the judge's most potent weapon to enforce an order issued by the court. Reporters and others must be sensitive to the notion that the violation of a court rule or court order can result in punishment for contempt. And in some jurisdictions the contempt citation will stand even if the court order or court rule that was violated is later declared illegal or unconstitutional by an appellate court. A case which dramatically makes this point is *U.S.* v. *Dickinson* (1972).

In November 1971 a hearing was underway in federal court in Baton Rouge, Louisiana. A VISTA worker had been indicted by the state on charges of conspiring to murder the mayor of Baton Rouge. The defendant complained that the state had no evidence in the case and that prosecution was merely an attempt to harass him. The hearing in federal court was to determine the motives of the state in the prosecution. Since it was possible that the charges would be sustained and that the VISTA worker would be tried later in criminal court, the federal judge ruled that there could be no publicity about what took place during the hearing. The press could report that such a hearing was taking place, but that was all. Reporters Gibbs Adams and Larry Dickinson of the *Baton Rouge Morning Advocate and State Times* ignored the order, published a story about the hearing, and were found in criminal contempt and fined $300 each.

Upon appeal, the United States Court of Appeals for the Fifth Circuit struck down the trial court's no-publicity order, but at the same time upheld the contempt convictions. The court cited a 1967 Supreme Court ruling—*Walker* v. *Birmingham*—as precedent. In that case Martin Luther King and seven other clergymen were arrested and held in contempt for violating a Birmingham, Alabama, court injunction banning all marches, parades, sit-ins, and so forth. The high Court ruled that while the ban on marches and parades was unconstitutional Dr. King and the other defendants should have challenged the ban in court rather than just violate it. The contempt citations stood.

The same logic was applied in the *Dickinson* case. Judge John R. Brown wrote (*U.S.* v. *Dickinson,* 1972):

> The conclusion that the District Court's order was constitutionally invalid does not necessarily end the matter of the validity of the contempt convictions. There remains the very formidable questions of whether a person may with impunity violate an order which turns out to be invalid. We hold that in the circumstances of this case he may not.

This decision perplexes many persons who cannot understand why the press or anyone else for that matter should be punished for not obeying an order that is not legal in the first place. It is probably best to have Judge Brown explain by quoting a lengthy passage from his opinion in the *Dickinson* case:

> We begin with the well-established principle in proceedings for criminal contempt that an injunction duly issuing out of a court having subject matter and personal jurisdiction *must be obeyed*, irrespective of the ultimate validity of the order. Invalidity is no defense to criminal contempt. "People simply cannot have the luxury of knowing that they have a right to contest the correctness of the judge's order in deciding whether to wilfully disobey it. . . . Court orders have to be obeyed until they are reversed or set aside in an orderly fashion. . . ."

The criminal-contempt exception requiring compliance with court orders, while invalid nonjudicial directives may be disregarded, is not the product of self-protection or arrogance of judges. Rather it is born of an experience-proved recognition that this rule is essential for the system to work. Judges, after all, are charged with the final responsibility to adjudicate legal disputes. It is the judiciary which is vested with the duty and power to interpret and apply statutory and constitutional law. Determinations take the form of orders. The problem is unique to the judiciary because of its particular role. Disobedience to a legislative pronouncement in no way interferes with the legislature's ability to discharge its responsibilities [passing laws]. The dispute is simply pursued in the judiciary and the legislature is ordinarily free to continue its function unencumbered by any burdens resulting from the disregard of its directives. Similarly, law enforcement is not prevented by failure to convict those who disregard the unconstitutional commands of a policeman.

On the other hand, the deliberate refusal to obey an order of the court without testing its validity through established processes requires further action by the judiciary, and therefore directly affects the judiciary's ability to discharge its duties and responsibilities. Therefore, "while it is sparingly to be used, yet the power of courts to punish for contempts is a necessary and integral part of the independence of the judiciary, and is absolutely essential to the performance of the duties imposed upon them by law. Without it they are mere boards of arbitration whose judgments and decrees would be only advisory."

While most members of the press accept this logic to a point, they argue that the press presents a special case because time is a crucial factor in news gathering. Had the reporters in the *Dickinson* case, for example, not disobeyed the order, but instead appealed the decision to a higher court, the trial which they were covering would have been over before the restrictive order could have been declared invalid.

Judge Brown said that timeliness is an important aspect of news and that an appellate court should grant a speedy review of such orders. "But newsmen are citizens too," he wrote. "They too may sometimes have to wait. They are not yet wrapped in an immunity or given the absolute right to decide with impunity whether a judge's order is to be obeyed or whether an appellate court is acting promptly enough." Although Judge Brown seemed to see the need for speed, nine months elapsed between the original contempt citation and his ruling in the court of appeals.

The reporters appealed the ruling to the Supreme Court, but the high Court declined to hear the matter. Many authorities interpret the refusal as approval by the Court of the Fifth Circuit Court decision (*U.S.* v. *Dickinson*, 1972).

The implications of *Dickinson* are rather frightening. In a paper entitled "Judicial Restraints on the Press," Professor Donald Gillmor quotes Dickinson's attorney:

> If the heavy burden which must be borne by the government to support any prior restraint can be met merely by the assertion of the possibility of a conflict . . . between constitutional rights, then freedom of the press as we know it would be held hostage to the fertile imagination of judges.

Many experts predicted that the precedent in *Dickinson* would be an open invitation to abuse by trial courts, and such prophecies were quickly realized.

In the summer of 1972 several persons were arrested on charges of conspiring to disrupt the 1972 Republican Convention in Miami. It is normal procedure in many courts to prohibit photography in the courtroom (more about this in a later section). Many newspapers and television stations use artists to make drawings of the proceedings. In the trial of the conspirators the judge told the press that sketching would not be permitted in the courtroom if the sketches were intended for publication. As a way around the court order, an artist for the Columbia Broadcasting System attended the trial (without pad and pencil) and sketched scenes from memory after the court session. Four sketches were broadcast by the network, which was immediately held in contempt for violating the order. The trial court then issued an order that banned sketching both inside and outside the courtroom and forbade publication of any sketch of the courthouse "regardless of the place where the sketch is made." The Columbia Broadcasting System appealed the order and the contempt citation.

The court of appeals struck down the ban on sketching, but upheld the contempt citation. Citing the *Dickinson* ruling, Judge Dyer wrote (*U.S.* v. *CBS*, 1974):

> That case stands for the proposition that before a prior restraint may be imposed by a judge, even in the interest of assuring a fair trial, there must be "an imminent," not merely a likely threat, to the administration of justice. The danger must not be remote or even probable, it must immediately imperil.

Despite the fact that the district court made no showing whatsoever that the sketching was obtrusive or disruptive or an imminent threat to the administration of justice, the court said the order should have been challenged rather than disobeyed.

The rule in the *Dickinson* case—that a contempt citation will stand even if the court order is later ruled invalid—is not accepted in all states or by all courts. For example, in a case similar to *Dickinson*, the Washington State Supreme Court ruled in an opposite fashion. In the Washington case a trial judge ordered the press to refrain from publishing reports about anything that occurred at a public trial when the jury was not in the courtroom. Two reporters from the *Seattle Times* violated the order and were found in contempt. The state's high court said the court order was unconstitutional, that it violated the reporters' right to publish what happened in an open trial. The high court also voided the contempt citation, ruling that the violation of a court order that was patently void on its face could not produce a valid judgment of contempt. "To sustain this judgment of contempt," Justice Walter McGovern wrote, "would be to say that the mere possibility of prejudicial matter reaching a juror outside the courtroom is more important in the eyes of the law than is a constitutionally guaranteed freedom of expression. This we cannot say" (*State* ex rel. *Superior Court* v. *Sperry*, 1971).

Similarly, an Illinois appellate court in 1977 rejected the reasoning in *Dickinson* when it voided a contempt citation issued against a newspaper for the violation of a court order. The paper had been sued for libel, and the trial judge presiding at the defamation suit issued an order prohibiting the newspaper from publishing any editorials in which the lawsuit was discussed. The judge said he was fearful such material might prejudice jurors in the community. The newspaper and its publisher were held in contempt of court when a subsequent editorial was published. The Illinois court of appeals ruled that the court order was an unconstitutional restraint on freedom of the press and threw out the contempt citation as well. Justice Seidenfeld wrote that the *Dickinson* case failed to clearly recognize the strong presumption against the validity of prior restraints on the press and the irremedial nature of the injury inflicted upon the press by the kind of ban on publication issued in the case, the Illinois court was not persuaded by the logic of the Fifth Circuit ruling. "If the case [*Dickinson*] stands for the rule that no order prohibiting pure speech may be disobeyed while in effect, we do not agree," he wrote (*Cooper* v. *Rockford Newspapers*, 1977).

These state cases are important to consider alongside *Dickinson*. It must be remembered that each state can adopt its own rule regarding the viability of a contempt citation issued for the violation of a patently unconstitutional court order. Federal courts outside the Fifth Circuit are also not governed by the **Dickinson rule.** It might also be noted that at the time this chapter was being prepared the Congress was considering a major revision of the federal criminal code. Under revised portions of the code reporters and newspapers can defend themselves against a contempt citation by proving that the court order which was violated was a constitutionally invalid prior restraint upon the freedom of the press. Basically, the revision would overturn the *Dickinson* rule and require federal courts to follow a rule similar to the one applied in the 1971 Washington State case noted earlier.

Reporters who seek to protect the integrity of the news-gathering process from intrusion by the government must be extremely careful. Even the best attorneys have difficulty protecting a journalist from the contempt power of the judge. Myron Farber of the *New York Times* spent forty days in jail for contempt of court. William Farr of the *Los Angeles Times* spent forty-six days in a small cell for contempt of court. Both men worked for powerful news organizations and were ably represented by counsel. Yet each still spent more than a month in jail.

It is difficult for a reporter to raise the shield of the First Amendment in attempting to resist the power of a court to punish for contempt. While freedom of expression is the essence of a democratic state, the contempt power seems out of place in a democracy. Writing in "Contempt Power: The Black Robe—A Proposal for Due Process," Luis Kutner states the issue best:

> The contempt power, which arose as an extension of monarchial power, is incongruous in a nation dedicated to the principles of popular democracy . . . all contempts are examples of unlimited and arbitrary powers remaining as historical accidents and anomalies, inconsistent and incompatible with individual liberties and rights.

Summary

The power of a judge to punish for contempt of court is a remnant of the power of English kings. Today, courts have broad powers to punish persons who offend the court, interfere with legal proceedings, or disobey court orders. Contempt has been roughly divided into the following two categories:

1. Civil contempt: The power of a court to obtain obedience to court orders and judgments to protect the rights of the litigants in a case
2. Criminal contempt: The power to punish a wrong committed against the court itself
   a. Direct criminal contempt: an action taken against the court in the presence of the judge (e.g., shouting obscenities at a judge)
   b. Indirect or constructive contempt: an action taken against a court outside the presence of the judge (e.g., a newspaper editorial criticizing a court ruling)

Some limits have been placed upon the contempt power. Legislatures often restrict the kinds of sentences judges may impose for contempt or require a jury trial before a contempt conviction. The Supreme Court has ruled that before criticism of a court may be punished by contempt it must be shown that the criticism created a clear and present danger of the likelihood of interference with the administration of justice. In some jurisdictions appellate courts have ruled that persons must obey even unconstitutional contempt orders (the *Dickinson* rule).

BIBLIOGRAPHY

Here is a list of some of the sources that have been helpful in the preparation of chapter 6.

Books

Fox, John. *The History of Contempt of Court.* Oxford: Clarendon Press, 1927.
Goldfarb, Ronald. *The Contempt Power.* New York: Columbia University Press, 1963.
Gordon, David. *Newsman's Privilege and the Law.* Columbia, Mo.: Freedom of Information Center, 1974.
Wigmore, John H. *A Treatise on the Anglo-American System of Evidence in Trials at Common Law.* 2d. ed. Boston: Little, Brown & Co., 1934.

Articles

Blasi, Vince. "Press Subpoenas: An Empirical and Legal Analysis." 70 *Michigan Law Review* 229, 1971.

Boyd, J. Kirk. "Legislative Response to *Zurcher* v. *Standford Daily*." 9 *Pepperdine Law Review* 131, 1981.

Chamberlin, Bill. "Protection of Confidential News Sources: An Unresolved Issue." 44 *Popular Government* 18, 1978.

Goodale, James C. "*Branzburg* versus *Hayes* and the Development of a Qualified Privilege for Newsmen." 26 *Hastings Law Review* 709, 1975.

Guest, James, and Stanzler, Alan. "The Constitutional Argument for Newsmen Concealing Their Sources." 64 *Northwestern University Law Review* 18, 1969.

Kutner, Louis. "Contempt Power: The Black Robe—A Proposal for Due Process." 39 *Tennessee Law Review* 27, 1971.

Mullen, Lawrence J. "Developments in the News Media Privilege: The Qualified Constitutional Approach Becoming Common Law." 33 *Maine Law Review* 401, 1981.

Nelles, Walter, and King, C. W. "Contempt by Publication in the United States." 28 *Columbia Law Review* 401, 1928.

Cases

Anderson v. *Nixon* et al., 444 F. Supp. 1195 (1978).
Baker v. *F & F Investment*, 470 F.2d 778 (1972).
Blair v. *U.S.*, 250 U.S. 273 (1919).
Bloom v. *Illinois*, 391 U.S. 194 (1968).
Branzburg v. *Hayes*, 408 U.S. 655 (1972).
in re *Bridge*, 295 A.2d 3 (1972).
Bridges v. *California* and *Times Mirror Co.* v. *Superior Court*, 314 U.S. 252 (1941).
Brown v. *Commonwealth*, 204 S.E.2d 429 (1974).
Bursey v. *U.S.*, 466 F.2d 1059 (1972).
Caldero v. *Tribune Publishing Co.*, 562 P.2d 791 (1977).
CBS v. *Superior Court*, 85 Cal. App.3d 241 (1978).
Cervantes v. *Time*, 446 F.2d 986 (1972).
Cheff v. *Schnackenberg*, 384 U.S. 373 (1966).
in re *Consumers Union*, 4 M.L. Rept. 2119 (1978).
Cooper v. *Rockford Newspapers*, 365 N.E.2d 746 (1977).
Craig v. *Harney*, 331 U.S. 367 (1947).
Democratic National Committee v. *McCord*, 356 F. Supp. 1394 (1973).
Dow Jones v. *Superior Court*, 303 N.E.2d 487 (1973).
Downing v. *Monitor Publishing Co.*, 415 A.2d 683 (1980).
in re *Farber*, 394 A.2d 330 (1978).
in re *Farr*, 111 Cal. Rptr. 649 (1974).
Farr v. *Superior Court*, 99 Cal. Rptr. 342 (1971).
Florida v. *Beattie*, 4 M.L. Rept. 2150 (1979).
Florida v. *Morel*, 4 M.L. Rept. 2304 (1979).
in re *Foster* (Alameda County, California Superior Court, March 28, 1974).
Greenberg v. *CBS*, 69 A.D.2d 693 (1979).
Herbert v. *Lando*, 441 U.S. 153 (1979).
in re *Investigative File*, 4 M.L. Rept. 1865 (1978).
Kansas v. *Sandstrom*, 581 P.2d 812 (1978).
in re *Lewis*, 501 F.2d 418 (1974).
Lightman v. *State*, 294 A.2d 149 (1972).
McGraw-Hill v. *Arizona*, 680 F.2d 5 (1982).

New York v. *LeGrand*, 4 M.L. Rept. 1897 (1979).
Nye v. *U.S.*, 313 U.S. 33 (1941).
Oregon v. *Knorr*, 8 M.L. Rept. 2067 (1982).
in re *Pappas*, 266 N.E.2d 297 (1971).
Patterson v. *Colorado*, 205 U.S. 454 (1907).
Pennekamp v. *Florida*, 328 U.S. 331 (1946).
People v. *Dan*, 41 A.D.2d 687 (1973).
in re *Powers*, 4 M.L. Rept. 1600 (1978).
Reiss v. *Harris*, No. 72454 (Idaho District Court, Ada County, 1980).
Reporter's Committee v. *AT&T*, 593 F.2d 1030 (1978).
Riley v. *Chester*, 612 F.2d 708 (1979).
Sierra Life v. *Magic Valley Newspapers*, 623 P.2d 103 (1980).
Silkwood v. *Kerr-McGee*, 563 F.2d 433 (1977).
State ex rel. *Superior Court* v. *Sperry*, 483 P.2d 608 (1971).
State v. *Morrill*, 16 Ark. 384 (1855).
Toledo Newspaper Co. v. *U.S.*, 247 U.S. 402 (1918).
U.S. v. *Barnett*, 376 U.S. 681 (1964).
U.S. v. *Blanton*, 534 F. Supp. 295 (1982).
U.S. v. *CBS*, 497 F.2d 102 (1974).
U.S. v. *Criden*, 633 F.2d. 346 (1980).
U.S. v. *Dickinson*, 465 F.2d 496 (1972).
in re *Van Ness*, 8 M.L. Rept. 2563 (1982).
Walker v. *Birmingham*, 388 U.S. 307 (1967).
Washington v. *Coe*, 10 M.L. Rept. 1465 (1984).
WBAI v. *Proskin*, 42 A.D.2d 5 (1973).
Zurcher v. *Stanford Daily*, 436 U.S. 547 (1978).

7 FREE PRESS AND FAIR TRIAL

People have complained about the abundance of crime news in American newspapers almost as long as American newspapers have existed, at least since the 1830s and 1840s when the newspaper evolved from being primarily a political journal to being a chronicler of public occurrences. For some as yet untold reason, both the press and the public seem to share a continuing fascination with the troubles and travails of humankind, especially the plight of persons caught up in the web of the law. For better than one hundred fifty years the press has provided Americans with a daily, weekly and/or monthly diet of crime news. Sometimes there was more crime news than at other times. Persons who complain that today reporters spend too much time writing about murder and kidnapping surely cannot remember the four decades between 1890 and 1930 when crime news was a staple of most American newspapers and the police reporter was the most important, envied man in the city room. Ben Hecht's remembrances in his play *Front Page* and his autobiography *A Child of the Century* are far more truthful than most journalists like to admit.

While some persons object to the publication of crime news because they believe it to be in bad taste, because they think such information is not relevant to present-day existence, or because they think the press should spend its time pursuing other news, other persons object to publication of crime news for another reason. Many people believe that the press—newspapers and broadcasting stations—interfere with the judicial process by the publication of such information.

The argument goes something like this: Every person accused of a crime has the right to a fair trial. According to the Sixth Amendment to the United States Constitution, a fair trial includes the right to an "impartial jury." Juries are selected from members of the community who read newspapers and watch television and listen to the radio. The trial process has built-in safeguards that protect accused persons. Certain kinds of information cannot be used as evidence against a suspected criminal. A past criminal record, for example, is immaterial in most trials. So are the results of examinations using the so-called lie detector. The court keeps this kind of information from the jury during the trial. What happens if the jurors read about these circumstances before the trial begins? What if they read, for example, that the defendant has a long record of convictions? What if they read that she refused to take a lie detector test? What if they read that he is an army deserter or that she operates a brothel? Does not the publication of such facts tend to prejudice jurors against the defendant? Many people believe that it does.

What is the solution? To stop the press from publishing such facts? After all, the Sixth Amendment guarantees a fair trial, an impartial jury. This solution is fine—except for one problem: the First Amendment, which guarantees a free press, an unimpeded press, a press at liberty from governmental restrictions.

If this situation strikes you as a dilemma, it is. Justice Felix Frankfurter stated the problem quite succinctly in 1946 in his concurring opinion in the case of *Pennekamp* v. *Florida:*

> A free press is not to be preferred to an independent judiciary, nor an independent judiciary to a free press. Neither has primacy over the other; both are indispensable to a free society. The freedom of the press in itself presupposes an independent judiciary through which that freedom may, if necessary, be vindicated. And one of the potent means for assuring judges their independence is a free press.

The recent history of the free press–fair trial controversy in the United States has been the attempt to discover a way to balance these two very important constitutional rights. The attempt has not been completely successful. In those communities which solved the problem best, courts are forced to take extra care in shielding juries from publicity and in protecting defendants. The press also has to demonstrate its responsibility by exercising caution in publishing and broadcasting material about criminal and civil cases.

In this chapter the dimensions of both the problem and its solutions are sketched. First, the kinds of publicity many persons believe to be harmful to defendants are discussed, along with evaluation of the extent to which the mass media can in fact interfere with the trial process. In the remainder of the chapter the many schemes and ideas either proposed or enacted to solve the problem are outlined. It must again be remembered that in the free press–fair trial controversy fifty-one different judicial systems are involved. That is, while the problem is clearly national, the solutions tend to be local or regional in scope. Consequently, generalizations about such a complex issue can sometimes be misleading. Reporters and broadcasters are urged to investigate the specific rules applicable to their state regarding publication of material about the judicial process. A simple way to do this is to talk to judges, members of bar associations, and veteran court reporters.

PREJUDICIAL CRIME REPORTING

It is quite easy to find examples of the kinds of news stories that many people believe might prejudice potential jurors. For example, the *Los Angeles Times* ran a story a few years ago beginning this way:

> A television sportscaster, Stan Duke, shot and killed a radio commentator, Averill Berman, early Sunday at the Wilshire District home of Duke's estranged wife, police reported. Duke was booked on suspicion of murder.

Readers probably wondered why Duke was arrested for suspicion of murder when it was patently obvious from reading the lead that Duke had committed the crime—or had according to the *Los Angeles Times*. Under the American system of justice a man is presumed innocent until it is proved he is guilty. In other words the state had to prove that Duke shot and killed Berman.

A newspaper in Washington State ran a far less sensational story, but in its own way it could have been even more damaging. The *Yakima Herald-Republic* headlined the story: "Innocent Not Tried, Claims Prosecutor." The first sentence stated, " 'Because of the screening process built into the criminal justice system in this county, innocent men never go to trial,' John Moore, Yakima County Deputy Prosecutor, said Wednesday." The people of that county probably spent a considerable amount of time wondering why they had courts at all if only the guilty went to trial. All that was really needed was an administrator of some kind to hand out sentences and fines.

The first story was written in the flush of journalistic excitement brought on by a sensational murder. The second story was written by a reporter who should have challenged the outrageous statement on the spot. Numerous other specific examples can be cited, but probably a better idea is to summarize the kinds of information many people agree can possibly interfere with the defendant's right to a fair trial. The following list was taken from lists published by the American Bar Association and various state press-bench-bar committees.

1. Confessions or stories about the confession that a defendant is said to have made, including even alluding to the fact that there may be a confession. The Fifth Amendment says that a person does not have to testify against himself. Therefore a confession given to police may be subsequently retracted and usually cannot be used against the defendant at the trial.

2. Stories about the defendant's performance on a test using a polygraph, or lie detector, or similar device, and about the defendant's refusal to take such a test. Most of this information is not permitted at the trial.

3. Stories about the defendant's past criminal record or that state he is a former convict. This information is not permitted at the trial. It may seem entirely logical to some people that when a man has committed ninety-nine robberies and is again arrested for robbery he probably did commit the crime. As a matter of fact, past behavior is immaterial in his current trial for robbery. The state must prove that he committed *this* robbery.

4. Stories which question the credibility of witnesses and which contain the personal feelings of witnesses about prosecutors, police, victims, or even judges. To illustrate: in the Sam Sheppard case, which will be discussed a little later, the judge was quoted as telling a reporter—before the trial started—that he thought Sam Sheppard was "guilty as hell," and the remark was published (*Sheppard* v. *Maxwell,* 1966).

5. Stories about the defendant's character (he hates children and dogs), his associates (he hangs around with known syndicate gunmen), and his personality (he attacks people on the slightest provocation).

6. Stories which tend to inflame the public mood against the defendant. Such stories include editorial campaigns which demand the arrest of a suspect before sufficient evidence has been collected; man-on-the-street interviews

concerning the guilt of the defendant or the kind of punishment he should receive after he is convicted; televised debates about the evidence of the guilt or innocence of the defendant. All these kinds of stories put the jury in the hot seat, as well as circulate vast quantities of misinformation.

This list is not exhaustive. There are other kinds of stories which many people agree can interfere with the judicial process. A study conducted by Professor Fred Siebert in Michigan a few years ago (in *Free Press and Fair Trial,* ed. Chilton R. Bush) reported that judges believed publication of criminal records, performance on tests, and information about confessions were potentially the most damaging kinds of stories. They felt further that publication of such stories was inappropriate in nearly every case.

One positive note should be made at this point. Stories like these are less common today. Professor George Hough (in *Free Press and Fair Trial*, ed. Chilton R. Bush) at the University of Georgia documented a fact that most journalists have long believed: Newspapers today carry less crime news than most critics claim. After studying both court records and newspapers in Detroit for a six-month period, Hough found that of all the felony cases in which warrants were issued only 7 percent were even reported in the newspapers. Hough also found that during a one-year period in which 9,140 felony warrants were issued only 3.4 percent of the cases ever came to jury trial. These statistics seem to argue that the press ignores most cases. Consequently, in most criminal cases there exists no danger of prejudicial publicity affecting the judicial process.

A recent study by Professor J. Edward Gerald reported in *Journalism Quarterly* ("Press-Bar Relationships: Progress Since Sheppard and Reardon") reinforces Hough's findings. A majority of the prosecutors in the two hundred seventy-six urban counties surveyed by Gerald said that newspapers and broadcasting stations have sharply curtailed publication and broadcast of prejudicial news.

Even editors are beginning to realize that readers are really not as interested in crime news as they perhaps once were. One editor commented, "We don't get any calls for the gory stuff anymore. Most people who call in want to know why there isn't more good news."

Impact on Jurors

Despite the fact that there is less crime news in the press today than say, sixty years ago, newspapers and television stations still have a tendency to publish and broadcast "prejudicial" information about defendants in some cases. Usually such cases are the big, sensational ones: Ax Murderer Confesses, Ex-Con Nabbed for Mass Murder, Sex Killer Arrested at Rape Scene. Does this kind of story endanger a defendant's right to a fair trial?

Before that question can be answered, another question must be first considered: Will such stories influence jurors who read this news in their deliberations on the guilt or innocence of defendants? Consensus on the answer to this question is slight.

Attorneys and judges are in disagreement. Many say that this kind of publicity destroys the possibility of impartiality in potential jurors. Others agree with this opinion, but argue that screening processes (which are discussed later) will keep biased persons out of jury boxes. Still others argue that even when jurors are biased they follow the judge's admonition to decide the case on the facts presented in the courtroom, not on information from the press (Pember, Don R., "Pre-Trial Publicity in Criminal Cases: A Case Study").

Social scientists have attempted to systematically examine the question of the impact of prejudicial material on jurors over the past twenty-five years. A major defect in the work has been the inability of researchers to study the behavior and deliberations of real jurors in actual trials. Most researchers have been forced to try to duplicate the trial process and study the behavior of mock juries. The results of this research have been inconclusive. In some instances there is evidence that the prejudicial material had an important impact upon the subjects tested; in other studies the impact is far less clear.

Researchers at the Indiana University School of Journalism recently attempted to draw conclusions from seventeen empirical studies (conducted during the past twenty years) of the potential impact of pretrial publicity on jurors. These seventeen studies indicate that pretrial publicity, even nonsensational pretrial publicity—can lead jurors to prejudge the guilt or innocence of a person accused of a crime. Information about a confession or a prior criminal record is most likely to result in bias against the defendant. However, nonsensational publicity about a crime may also decrease the willingness of a juror to prejudge a defendant if the coverage leads to greater knowledge of correct facts about the case. The results of these seventeen studies indicated, according to the Indiana researchers, that the effect of pretrial publicity is substantially decreased by the trial process itself, especially when attorneys skillfully question the potential jurors about knowledge of the case before the trial is started (the voir dire examination). Finally, researchers said that the studies indicate that willingness to offer an opinion about the guilt or innocence of a defendant before a trial takes place is not by itself evidence of juror prejudice or predictive of how a juror will vote.

There is a tendency today to overestimate the public's ability to consume all the news and information that is offered in the mass media. William J. Bauer, a judge of the Seventh United States Court of Appeals, is one of many jurists who have suggested this notion to the press. Judge Bauer told the delegates to the 1976 convention of the American Society of Newspaper Editors that in trying highly publicized cases where the issues were brought out daily for weeks and months beforehand in the press 94 percent of the prospective jurors could not remember the story when questioned. The other 6 percent remembered vaguely that they had read something about the case, but only one-half of 1 percent remembered what it was they had read, and less than half of these people had made up their minds as a result of what they had read, Bauer said. Judge MacKinnon of the District of Columbia United States Court of Appeals recently echoed Judge Bauer's sentiments when he noted in an opinion that there is a tendency to "frequently overestimate the extent of the public's awareness of news" (in re *Application of NBC,* 1981).

Many persons in both the law and journalism have presumed that publicity about a criminal case which is unfavorable to the defendant can create prejudice in the minds of jurors. This does not mean, however, that the law regards potential jurors as biased because they have seen prejudicial material or admit to having a slight bias. Justice Thurgood Marshall, writing for the majority of the Supreme Court of the United States, noted in 1975: "The constitutional standard of fairness requires that a defendant have 'a panel of impartial, indifferent jurors.' They need not be wholly ignorant of the facts, for this would establish an impossible standard" (*Murphy* v. *Florida,* 1975).

The Law and Prejudicial News

The definition of an impartial juror used by the courts in the United States is over one hundred seventy years old and stems from a ruling by Chief Justice John Marshall in the trial of Aaron Burr. Charges that the jurors were biased were made at the trial. In 1807 Marshall proclaimed that an impartial juror was one free from the dominant influence of knowledge acquired outside the courtroom, free from strong and deep impressions which close the mind. *"Light impressions,"* Marshall wrote, *"which may fairly be supposed to yield to the testimony that may be offered, which leave the mind open to a fair consideration of that testimony, constitute no sufficient objection to a juror . . ."* [author emphasis] (*U.S.* v. *Burr,* 1807).

While this definition is fairly precise, modern courts nevertheless have to cope with the problem of applying the definition to specific situations. It is appellate courts that most often must apply Marshall's definition to cases in which convicted defendants ask for a reversal on the grounds that the jury is not impartial, as guaranteed by the Sixth Amendment. Indeed, reversal is one important, if costly, remedy the judicial system uses to cope with prejudicial publicity, that is, to simply reverse the guilty verdict and require that the defendant be retried.

Appellate courts appear to consider several factors in determining whether the defendant's trial was fair and impartial. Was there publicity about the case? Was the publicity prejudicial? Is there evidence that the jurors saw the prejudicial publicity? What kinds of information were contained in the publicity? It is not a simple task to uncover the answers to many of these questions, and not surprisingly, different courts often reach opposite conclusions in cases which appear to have similar facts. But even small differences in the facts can be important. For example, a United States court of appeals ruled in 1951 that a defendant's right to a fair trial was not damaged simply because a newspaper containing information about the case was found in a jury room. The judge had told the jury to disregard the contents of the news story and there was no evidence presented to the contrary (*Leviton v. U.S.,* 1951). Eight years later, however, the United States Supreme Court overturned a criminal conviction when evidence was presented that jurors had seen stories in newspapers which were found in the courtroom about a defendant's prior criminal record. The jurors told the judge they had read the stories, but vowed they could decide the case solely on the evidence presented in court. The nation's high Court said it was not reasonable to believe that the jurors could be impartial in such a case (*Marshall v. U.S.,* 1959).

Appellate courts also pay attention to what the jurors tell judges in the pretrial questioning (voir dire) when they are asked about their knowledge of the case. Compare how the Supreme Court resolved these two appeals.

Leslie Irvin was arrested in connection with a series of sex murders. Statements that Irvin had confessed to all six killings received widespread publicity. At the trial, of 430 persons called as potential jurors, 375 told the judge that they believed Irvin was guilty. Of the twelve jurors finally selected, eight told the court they thought he was guilty before the trial started. The Supreme Court overturned the conviction, noting that in this case, in which so many persons so many times admitted prejudice, statements of impartiality could be given little weight (*Irvin v. Dowd,* 1961).

Fourteen years later Jack Murphy, the original "Murph the Surf," appealed his conviction for robbery and assault on the grounds that the jury had been prejudiced by extensive publicity about his previous criminal record and other extralegal exploits. The Supreme Court disagreed. Only twenty of the seventy-eight potential jurors who were questioned told the Florida trial judge they believed Murphy was guilty. The high Court said that this was not comparable to the evidence of hostility or overwhelming prejudice toward the defendant that was found in the Irvin case. The Constitution requires that the defendant have a "panel of impartial, indifferent jurors," ruled Justice Thurgood Marshall; "they need not, however, be totally ignorant of the facts and issues involved." It is sufficient that a juror can lay aside his impressions and opinions and render an opinion based on the evidence presented in court. Many people see this 1975 ruling in *Murphy v. Florida* as rejecting the often-asserted principle that publicity about a criminal case automatically results in bias toward the defendant.

In looking at the scores of decisions by appellate courts one is persuaded that judges seem to have greater faith in jurors and the jury system than many social scientists who have studied these issues. Whether this is misplaced faith may never be known. Perhaps the answer is to be found in Professor Walter Wilcox's rhetorical question, "Could it be that the American jury confounds all the subtle nuances of the behavioral sciences and simply does its duty?" (in *Free Press and Fair Trial,* ed. Chilton R. Bush).

Summary

The First Amendment to the United States Constitution guarantees freedom of the press; the Sixth Amendment guarantees every criminal defendant a fair trial. Many people believe these two amendments are in conflict because often publicity about a criminal case can prejudice a community against a defendant and make it impossible to find a fair and impartial jury in the case. The kinds of publicity which can be most damaging to a defendant includes material about confessions or alleged confessions, stories about a past criminal record, statements about the defendant's character, and comments about the defendant's performance on scientific tests or refusal to take such tests.

Social science has not yet proved conclusively that such publicity does in fact create prejudice or that persons cannot set aside their beliefs about a case and render a verdict based on the facts presented at the trial. An impartial juror is not required to be free of all knowledge or impressions about a case; the juror must be free of deep impressions and beliefs that will not yield to the evidence that is presented in court during the trial.

COMPENSATING
FOR PRETRIAL
PUBLICITY

The law has many ways to minimize or even to eliminate the problem of prejudicial publicity in a criminal case. As a last resort a criminal conviction can be reversed by an appellate court if there is evidence that the trial was tainted by publicity.

Retrials cost the taxpayers money; considerable inconvenience results for witnesses, attorneys, and other participants. Defendants face continued hardship from uncertainty or even jail if they have not been released on bail. Most persons concerned with this problem consider reversal a remedy of last resort—something to do if all else fails.

Other remedies are considered far better in attempting to solve the problems which could result from pretrial publicity. These remedies fall into two broad categories:

1. Remedies which can be used by the trial court to compensate for the publication or broadcast of prejudicial publicity.
2. Remedies aimed at controlling the amount and kind of information which might be broadcast or published.

The remedies in the first category have existed for a long time and can be applied by trial judges with little difficulty in most instances. These include delaying the trial, moving the trial, carefully questioning the jurors to determine their bias, and other means. The impact upon both the judicial system and the press tends to be minimal when such remedies are applied.

The remedies in the second category can be more drastic and can cause serious problems, especially for the press. These remedies include issuing orders specifically limiting what can be published or broadcast, issuing orders which forbid participants in the trial process from talking about the case, and even barring public and press attendance at pretrial proceedings. This latter category also includes, however, nonbinding bench-bar-press guidelines which have been adopted in many states and seem to many persons to work the least hardship of any of the remedies in either of the categories on both the press and the judicial system. A close examination of all these remedies follows.

Traditional Judicial Remedies

Trial judges have at their disposal a battery of procedural tools which can be used to alleviate the impact of prejudicial publicity.

Voir Dire

Before prospective jurors finally make it to the jury box, they must pass a series of hurdles erected by both the attorneys in the case and the judge. These hurdles are designed to protect the judicial process from jurors who have already made up their mind about the case or who have a strong bias toward one litigant or the other. In a process called **voir dire** each prospective juror is questioned prior to being impaneled in an effort to discover bias. Pretrial publicity is only one source of juror prejudice. If the prospective juror is the mother of a police officer, she is likely to be biased if the defendant is on trial for shooting a police officer. Perhaps the juror is a business associate of the defendant. Possibly the juror has read extensively about the case in the newspapers and believes the police are trying to frame the defendant.

Both sides in the case question the jurors and both sides can ask the court to excuse a juror. This procedure is called challenging a juror. There are two kinds of challenges: **challenges for cause** and **peremptory challenges.** To challenge a juror for cause, an attorney must convince the court that there is a good reason for this person not to sit on the jury. Deep-seated prejudice is one good reason. Being an acquaintance of one of the parties in the case is also a good reason. Any reason can be used to challenge a potential juror. All the attorney must do is to convince the judge that the reason is proper. There is no limit on the number of challenges for cause that both prosecutor and defense attorney may exercise.

A peremptory challenge is somewhat different. This challenge can be exercised without cause, and the judge has no power to refuse such a challenge. There is a limit, however, on the number of such challenges that may be exercised. Sometimes there are as few as two or three and sometimes as many as ten or twenty, depending upon the case, the kind of crime involved, the state statute, and sometimes the judge. This kind of challenge is reserved for use against persons whom the defense or the prosecution does not want on the jury, but whom the judge refuses to excuse for cause. For example, in the various Watergate trials, attorneys for John Mitchell, H. R. Haldeman, John Erlichman, and other Nixon associates sought jurors who were strong believers in law and order. Potential jurors were asked subtle questions about crime in the streets, the kinds of television programs they liked, the types of movies they enjoyed, and so forth. It was felt that people who thought that criminals were pampered and who liked cop shows on television and John Wayne blood-and-guts movies were "Nixon people" and might react more favorably toward the defendants in the trial. The defense used its peremptory challenges to excuse the opposite kind of persons: typical "bleeding-heart liberals" who looked at crime as a social disease, abhorred violence on television, thought George Patton was an authoritarian kook, and could not stand John Wayne movies. Obviously, this account is an oversimplification, but psychologists did draw up such profiles for the defense. The scheme worked in the first trial in which John Mitchell, Maurice Stans, and a few other defendants were acquitted. At the end of that trial the federal prosecutor said the government had not paid enough attention to selecting the jury.

Is voir dire a good way to screen prejudiced jurors? Seventy-nine percent of a large group of judges surveyed by Professor Emeritus Fred Siebert of Michigan State University said (in *Free Press and Fair Trial,* ed. Chilton R. Bush) that the questioning process was either highly effective or moderately effective in screening biased jurors. Most trial lawyers also agree, to a point. It is difficult, however, to argue with critics who say that voir dire uncovers only the prejudice that the prospective juror is aware of or is not too embarrassed to admit. Biased jurors can lie when questioned about their bias. They may not even know their mind is made up about the defendant's guilt. But these kinds of objections attack the root of the entire jury system. The only way to find jurors who are not biased in even a small way is to lock up babies when they are born and raise them as jurors, isolate them from the rest of the world until they are adults, and then release them to act only as jurors at trials. Nobody wants this kind of system. The faith that most persons have in the effectiveness of voir dire is comparable to their faith in the entire jury system.

Change of Venue

Many judges and legal authorities describe a **change of venue** as an effective means of dealing with massive pretrial publicity. Imagine for a moment that John Smith is arrested for a series of six brutal murders committed in River City over a period of six weeks and highly publicized by the local press. When Smith is arrested, the local news media saturate the community with stories about the killings, about the arrest, and about Smith. Day after day the newspapers and broadcasting stations focus on one new angle after another. Soon most of the people in River City know more about the suspect's past than even the police and his parents know. One means to compensate for such publicity about a defendant in the community in which the crime takes place is to move the trial to another community. This procedure is called a change of venue. While the people in River City may be prejudiced against Smith by virtue of the reports in the news media, the people across the state in Ames have hardly heard of the matter. Therefore, the trial, including the prosecutor, the defendant, the judges, the witnesses, and assorted other trial participants, is moved to Ames for the month or two of the trial. The jury is selected from a panel of people who live in Ames. Seventy-seven percent of the judges surveyed think a change of venue is highly effective or moderately effective in controlling prejudicial publicity (*Free Press and Fair Trial*).

Change of venue is costly. Witnesses, attorneys, and other persons must be transported and housed and fed while the trial takes place in a distant city. The defendant must surrender the constitutional right to a trial in the district in which the crime was committed. Publicity about the case could appear in the media located in the community in which the trial is scheduled to be held, defeating the purpose of the change of venue. Often the effectiveness of the change of venue depends upon how far the trial is moved from the city in which the crime was committed. A trial judge in Washington State who was concerned about newspaper coverage of a local murder case granted a change of venue. But he moved the trial to an adjoining county, the only other county in the state in which the "offending" newspaper had significant circulation. The move accomplished very little, and the judge ultimately was forced to close portions of the proceedings to the press (*Federated Publications* v. *Kurtz,* 1980). Used wisely, a change of venue can be an effective device to protect the defendant's right to a fair trial, especially for crimes committed in rural counties where the number of potential jurors is small, and news often travels faster by word of mouth than through the mass media. But there is normally ample opportunity in an urban area with a large population to find a panel of impartial jurors in even the most sensational criminal trials. A change of venue in such a case is normally a waste of money.

Continuance

A **continuance** is somewhat like a change of venue. But the time of the trial, instead of the location, is changed. That is, the trial is postponed. Back to John Smith for a moment. A delay of six to nine months in his trial might have pushed the slayings to the back of the mind of the community. People rapidly forget information not vital to their lives. It is probably far easier to impanel an unbiased jury after a continuance of six months. But again there are problems. The defendant sacrifices his right to a speedy trial. While the right to a speedy trial is one of the myths we are content to live with in the United States, continuance nevertheless means an even longer delay than normal. If the defendant cannot make bail or if bail is not permitted, he spends the six months of the continuance in jail. Also, this scheme assumes that there will be little or no further publicity about the case. This assumption might be incorrect. The week before the continued trial is scheduled to begin the press may start publicizing the case again. It is hoped, of course, that other news will have pushed the interest in the case to the back of the newspaper by then. A continuance can work very effectively in cases of accidental publicity. A judge told of how just as he was scheduled to begin hearing a malpractice suit on a Monday morning the Sunday paper, quite innocently, carried a long feature story on the skyrocketing costs of physicians' malpractice insurance because of the large judgments handed down in malpractice suits. The article pointed out that physicians passed the additional charges along to patients. The story was widely read. Jurors, who also pay doctors' bills, might hesitate to award a judgment to an injured patient knowing that it would raise insurance rates and ultimately cost patients more. The judge therefore continued the case for two months to let the story fade from the public mind.

Admonition to the Jury

Once a jury is impaneled, its members are instructed by the judge to render their verdict in the case solely on the basis of the evidence presented in the courtroom. Judges believe that most jurors take this **admonition** quite seriously. Jurors are also warned not to read newspaper stories or watch television broadcasts about the case while the trial is being held. Often jurors are excused from the courtroom while the trial judge hears arguments from the attorneys or even testimony from witnesses. In such instances the court usually wants to determine whether certain evidence is admissible in the case before the evidence is presented to the jury. The press may publish or broadcast reports about this evidence whether or not it is admitted in the case. It would accomplish very little to keep such evidence from the jury during the trial if jurors could watch news stories about this evidence during the evening television newscasts.

The following admonition, which is one used by King County, Washington, superior court judges, is typical:

> Do not discuss this case or any criminal case or any criminal matter among yourselves or with anyone else. Do not permit anyone to discuss such subjects with you or in your presence. . . . Do not read, view, or listen to any report in a newspaper, radio, or television on the subject of this trial or any other criminal trial. Do not permit anyone to read about or comment on this trial or any criminal trial to you or in your presence.

There is evidence that jurors follow these instructions closely. In the single major study in which real jury deliberations were examined to determine the impact of mass media publicity on the trial process, researchers found that jurors listen carefully to the cautionary instructions given to them by judges. The coordinator of that research project, Harry Kalven, noted in a letter to the director of the American Law Institute:

> We do . . . have evidence that the jurors take with surprising seriousness the admonition not to read the paper or discuss the case with other people. . . . Our overall impression . . . is that the jury is a pretty stubborn, healthy institution not likely to be overwhelmed either by a remark of counsel or a remark in the press.

Sequestration of Jury

For cases in which a high level of publicity is expected, publicity which might prove hard for a jury to avoid, the court has another device: **sequestration of the jury,** which means that once it is impaneled, the jury is locked up. Jurors eat together, are housed at state expense at a hotel or motel, and are not permitted to visit with friends and relatives. Phone calls are screened, as is contact with the mass media. Jurors are allowed to read newspapers only after court officials delete stories which could be objectionable.

Sequestration is a costly process for both the state and the jurors. Sequestration for three or four days might be a lark, but the trials in which juries are normally sequestered are long trials sometimes lasting as long as six months. Life can be seriously disrupted. The number of people who can afford the loss of income involved in such a situation is limited.

Although sequestered jurors are free from prejudicial publicity, attorneys fear the long quarantine produces a different kind of prejudice—prejudice against one or the other of the two sides in the case—wrought from keeping jurors away from friends and family for so long. Defense attorneys express this fear most often, feeling that jurors will tend to hold the defendant responsible for the inconvenience and therefore vote for conviction.

Summary

Trial courts have many ways to compensate for the prejudicial pretrial publicity in a criminal case. Each citizen is questioned by the attorneys and the judge before being accepted as a juror. During this voir dire examination questions can be asked of the potential jurors about the kinds of information they already know about the case. Persons who have already made up their minds about the defendant's guilt or innocence can be excluded from the jury.

Courts have the power to move a trial to a distant county to find a jury which has not been exposed to the publicity about the case which has been generated by local mass media. While such a change of venue can be costly, it can also be an effective means of compensating for sensational publicity about a case.

A trial can be delayed until the publicity about the case dies down. The defendant must waive the right to a speedy trial, but except in highly sensational cases, granting a continuance in a trial can thwart the impact of the massive publicity often generated in the wake of a serious crime.

Jurors are always admonished by the judge to base their decision on the facts presented in court and not to read or view any news stories about the case while they are on the jury. There is evidence that they take these warnings quite seriously.

In important cases it is always possible to lock up or sequester the jury after it is chosen to shield it from publicity about the trial.

The remedies just outlined have been used by trial judges for decades to reduce or eliminate the impact of prejudicial publicity. These remedies do not stop the publication of information about a criminal or civil case. They are used to compensate for the publication of prejudicial material. Such remedies are favored by the press because they have no direct impact upon the mass media.

However, many persons in the legal profession believe that compensating for publicity is a rather costly and sloppy way to solve the free press–fair trial dilemma. These compensatory remedies often create headaches for judges (extensive voir dire) or for trial participants (continuance, change of venue). They invariably cost all parties—especially the state—extra money, and they do not always completely compensate for massive publicity about a case, especially a sensational criminal case. Would it not be better if the press did not publish prejudicial information in the first place?

Agreements have been reached in many states between the press and the courts which attempt to limit certain kinds of publicity about criminal cases. These bench-bar-press guidelines are an effort to amicably resolve the free press-fair trial problem (these guidelines are discussed on pages 363–65).

But courts have also attempted other, more coercive means to limit publicity about criminal cases. Some trial judges have prohibited the press from publishing certain information about criminal cases. Violation of these orders, called restrictive orders by lawyers and judges and **gag orders** by journalists, can result in a citation for contempt of court. Other judges have barred journalists and other persons from attending pretrial hearings and even trials, to keep information which might prejudice a jury out of the hands of reporters. No other aspect of mass media law has sparked more controversy in the past ten years than the restrictive-order–closed-courtroom issue. Since 1976 the Supreme Court of the United States has focused upon one or another aspect of this issue no less than six times. Yet there is still no final resolution of the problems involved. This section of the text outlines these attempts to control the publication of information about criminal and civil matters. Restrictive orders are examined first; then the matter of closed courtrooms is discussed. Finally, we will outline the dimensions of bench-bar-press guidelines.

RESTRICTIVE
ORDERS TO
CONTROL
PUBLICITY

Can a trial judge constitutionally forbid the press from publishing information about a criminal case which it has obtained legally? The answer is yes, a judge can issue an order restricting the news media from publishing prejudicial pretrial information. But such a **restrictive order** can be issued only when there is evidence that publication of the material will create a clear and present danger of interfering with the defendant's right to a trial by an impartial jury. The Supreme Court has ruled that such a restriction is permissible only if the judge has determined that "the gravity of the evil, discounted by its improbability, justifies such an invasion of free speech as is necessary to avoid the danger" (*Nebraska Press Association* v. *Stuart,* 1976). In order for such an order to be issued, there must be sufficient evidence to reasonably conclude that the following conditions prevail:

1. Intense and pervasive publicity concerning the case is certain.
2. No other alternative measure—such as a change of venue or continuance or extensive voir dire process—is likely to mitigate the effects of the pretrial publicity.
3. The restrictive order will in fact effectively prevent prejudicial material from reaching potential jurors.

If all three elements can be established, a restrictive order which applies prior restraint against the press may be constitutionally issued by a trial judge. The history of such restraints is important and needs to be discussed before this drastic judicial remedy to stop pretrial publicity is explored more fully.

While judges have probably always had the power to issue such orders, they were not commonly used until ten to fifteen years ago. One Supreme Court ruling more than any other can be said to be responsible for the growth in use of this remedy. This was the United States Supreme Court ruling in the case of *Samuel Sheppard* v. *Maxwell*.

The *Sheppard* Case

Sam Sheppard, a prominent Ohio osteopath, was arrested for the bludgeoning death of his wife Marilyn. The doctor professed his innocence in the case, claiming that an intruder had entered their home at night, knocked him unconscious, and killed his wife. The Sheppard story broke during the slow-news Fourth of July weekend in 1954 and immediately caught the fancy of the nation's press. The publicity in the case was massive, far more extensive than the simple slaying merited. The coroner's inquest was held in a school gymnasium and broadcast live to the community. Debates were held about Sheppard's guilt or innocence. At the trial the press—much of it national rather than local press—dominated the courtroom. Participants in the case—police, prosecutors, defense attorneys, and witnesses—appeared to try to outdo themselves in offering extraneous, often outrageous statements to reporters, who dutifully published these comments. One appellate court later described the trial as a Roman holiday for the press, an orgy of sensation. Sheppard was convicted.

The United States Supreme Court rejected Sam Sheppard's first appeal that his trial was prejudiced by the massive publicity. But years later, in 1966, the high Court agreed to hear the doctor's plea. In a stinging rebuke of trial judge Blythin, the high Court reversed Sam Sheppard's conviction for murder.*

*The state of Ohio chose to reprosecute Sheppard twelve years after the crime, but this time the middle-aged doctor was acquitted. Sheppard, who failed to reestablish his osteopathic career, died several years later.

Justice Tom Clark wrote the high Court's opinion in the *Sheppard* case. The Supreme Court came down hard on the press, noting that bedlam reigned during the trial and that "newsmen took over practically the entire courtroom, hounding most of the participants in the trial, especially Sheppard. . . ." Justice Clark saved his sharpest criticism for Judge Blythin, who conducted the trial, and the other officers of the court for allowing the publicity about the case and the coverage of the trial to get out of hand. Here are some excerpts from Clark's opinion (*Sheppard* v. *Maxwell,* 1966):

> Bearing in mind the massive pretrial publicity, the judge should have adopted stricter rules governing the use of the courtroom by newsmen . . . the court should have insulated witnesses [from the media]. . . . The court should have made some effort to control the release of leads, information and gossip to the press by police officers, witnesses and the counsel for both sides. . . . And it is obvious that the judge should have further sought to alleviate this problem by imposing control over the statements made to the news media by counsel, witnesses, and especially the coroner and police officers. . . . The court might well have proscribed extrajudicial statements by any lawyer, party, witness or court official which divulged prejudicial matters . . . the court could also have requested the appropriate city and county officials to promulgate a regulation with respect to dissemination of information about the case by their employees. In addition, reporters who wrote or broadcast prejudicial stories could have been warned as to the impropriety of publishing material not introduced in the proceedings.

The Supreme Court made it quite clear in the *Sheppard* decision that it holds the trial judge responsible for ensuring that the defendant's rights are not jeopardized by prejudicial press publicity. While the court was critical of the press's behavior, no suggestion was made that the judicial system launch an attack on the press. Nevertheless, at a meeting following the decision, a professor of law, in explaining the high Court's opinion in *Sheppard,* suggested that the Court proposed that judges use the contempt power to control the press. Justice Clark, who was at the same meeting, told the assembled trial lawyers that the professor misinterpreted the court's ruling (Friendly and Goldfarb, *Crime and Publicity*):

> The Court never held up contempt and it may well be that it will never hold up contempt because the restraint is too stringent. . . . The Court's opinion never mentioned any guidelines for the press. . . . I am not proposing that you jerk a newspaper reporter into the courtroom and hold him in contempt. We do not have to jeopardize freedom of the press.

As we will see shortly, the remarks by Justice Clark were soon forgotten.

The Supreme Court's ruling that trial judges are responsible for controlling the publicity surrounding a criminal trial received an important boost from the American Bar Association (ABA) in the years following the *Sheppard* ruling. The ABA *Standards Relating to Fair Trial and Free Press* recommended that trial judges use court orders to control comments about a criminal case which might be made by participants in the trial such as prosecutors, witnesses, and defense attorneys. The report, which was adopted in 1968, recommended that judges use the contempt power against persons who knowingly violate a valid judicial order not to disseminate information about the case. This report, nicknamed the Reardon Report because it was drafted by a committee headed by Chief Justice Paul Reardon of the Massachusetts Supreme Judicial Court, was approved by the ABA House of Delegates, but never adopted by the judiciary in a single state. Still, it made an impression. In the *Sheppard* ruling the Supreme Court told trial judges they must control publicity about a case. The Reardon Report told them how to do it: with restrictive orders designed to silence the participants in the trial.

Use of Restrictive Orders

Starting in the mid-to-late sixties, courts throughout the United States began to hand down an increasing number of restrictive orders at the opening of many newsworthy trials. Some of these orders were aimed directly at the press—forbidding the media from publicizing certain aspects of a case. Other orders were aimed at trial participants. One observer has estimated that between 1966 and 1976 courts issued 174 such orders, thirty-nine of which were aimed directly at the press. In addition, nearly all of the federal courts adopted standing orders regarding publicity in criminal cases.

There is no such thing as a typical restrictive order. Such an order can limit the publicity about many different aspects of a trial. That is one reason judges favor such orders; they can be tailored to meet the needs of individual cases. Generally these orders tend to be quite comprehensive, as can be seen from the order issued by Judge William B. Keene for the Charles Manson murder trial (pages 346–47). Most try to limit the publicity surrounding the most critical elements of the case: a defendant's confession or prior criminal record, statements from witnesses or credibility of witnesses, the defendant's performance on tests such as the polygraph or the defendant's refusal to take such tests, and information about other scientific evidence, such as the results of ballistics tests. At times, however, judges have gone farther. In Minnesota the press was ordered not to print a word about the sentencing of young car thieves. The judge passed sentence in open court on December 7, but the press was barred from reporting the matter until December 9. Why? A brother of one of the defendants was getting married on December 8, and the family wanted the news kept out of the newspapers until after the wedding.

<u>Superior Court of the State of California</u>
<u>for the County of Los Angeles</u>

People of the State of California
Plaintiffs,

vs.

Charles Manson, et al.,
Defendants

No. A 253156

ORDER RE PUBLICITY

It is apparent, and this Court is going to take judicial notice of the fact, that this case has received extensive news media coverage as a direct result of its apparent public interest; further, it is equally apparent to this Court by reading various newspapers and weekly periodicals that this news media coverage is not limited to the County of Los Angeles, but has been extensive not only in the entire State of California but in the Nation as well, and of this fact the Court now takes judicial notice. This Court is of the firm conviction that the impossible task of attempting to choose between the constitutional guarantees of a free press and fair trial need not be made, but that they are compatible with some reasonable restrictions imposed upon pretrial publicity. It further appears to the Court that the dissemination by any means of public communication of any out-of-court statements relating to this case may interfere with the constitutional right of the defendants to a fair trial and disrupt the proper administration of justice. Some of the defendants now being for the first time before this Court, this Court now exercises its jurisdiction and assumes its duty to do everything within its constitutional powers to make certain that each defendant does receive a fair trial, and now issues the following orders, a violation of which will be considered as a contempt of this Court and will result in appropriate action to punish for such contempt.

It is the order of this Court that no party to this action, nor any attorney connected with this case as defense counsel or as prosecutor, nor any other attorney associated with this case, nor any judicial attache or employee, nor any public official now holding office, including but not limited to any chief of police or any sheriff, who has obtained information related to this action, which information has not previously been disseminated to the public, nor any agent, deputy, or employee of any such persons, nor any grand juror, nor any witness having appeared before the Grand Jury in this matter, nor any person subpoenaed to testify at the trial of this matter, shall release or authorize the release for public dissemination of any purported extrajudicial statement of the defendant relating to this case, nor shall any such persons release or authorize the release of any documents, exhibits, or any evidence, the admissibility of which may have to be determined by the Court, nor shall any such person make any statement for public dissemination as to the existence or possible existence of any document, exhibit, or any other evidence, the admissibility of which may have to be determined by the Court. Nor shall any such persons express outside of court an opinion or make any comment for public dissemination as to the weight, value, or effect of any evidence as tending to establish guilt or innocence. Nor shall any such persons make any statement outside of court for public dissemination as to the weight, value, or effect of any testimony that has been given. Nor shall any such persons issue any statement for public dissemination as to the identity of any prospective witness, or his probable testimony, or the effect thereof. Nor shall any such person make any out-of-court statement for public dissemination as to the weight, value, source, or effect of any purported evidence alleged to have been accumulated as a result of the investigation of this matter. Nor shall any such persons make any statement for public dissemination as to the content, nature, substance, or effect of any testimony which may be given in any proceeding related to this matter, except that a witness may discuss any matter with any attorney of record or agent thereof.

This order does not include any of the following:

1. Factual statements of the accused person's name, age, residence, occupation, and family status.

2. The circumstances of the arrest, namely, the time and place of the arrest, the identity of the arresting and investigation officers and agencies, and the length of the investigation.

3. The nature, substance, and text of the charge, including a brief description of the offenses charged.

4. Quotations from, or any reference without comment to, public records of the Court in the case, or to other public records or communications heretofore disseminated to the public.

5. The scheduling and result of any stage of the judicial proceeding held in open court in an open or public session.

6. A request for assistance in obtaining evidence.

7. Any information as to any person not in custody who is sought as a possible suspect or witness, nor any statement aimed at warning the public of any possible danger as to such person not in custody.

8. A request for assistance in the obtaining of evidence or the names of possible witnesses.

Further, this order is not intended to preclude any witness from discussing any matter in connection with the case with any of the attorneys representing the defendant or the People, or any representative of such attorneys.

It is further the order of the Court that the Grand Jury transcripts in this case not be disclosed to any person (other than those specifically mentioned in Penal Code Section 928.1) until 10 days after a copy thereof has been delivered by this Court to each defendant named in the indictment; provided, however, that if any defendant during such time, shall move the Court that such transcript, or any portion thereof, not be available for public inspection pending trial, such time shall be extended subject to the Court's ruling on such motion.

It is further ordered that a copy of this order be attached to any subpoena served on any witness in this matter, and that the return of service of the subpoena shall also include the fact of service of a copy of this order.

This order shall be in force until this matter has been disposed of or until further order of Court.

Dated: December 10, 1969

William B. Keene
Judge of the Superior Court

Restrictive Orders and the First Amendment

The issue of restrictive orders came to a head in 1976 when Judge Hugh Stuart of North Platte, Nebraska, barred the press from reporting information which had been publicly aired during the preliminary examination of Erwin Simants for the charge of murder. Simants was arrested in 1975 and charged with killing all six members of the Henry Kellie family. The case immediately attracted widespread press attention, and Judge Stuart issued a restrictive order barring the publication of certain kinds of prejudicial information. The order was ultimately modified by the Nebraska Supreme Court to prohibit only the reporting of the existence and nature of any confessions or admissions made by Simants to police, any confessions or admissions Simants made to third parties, and other facts "strongly implicative" of the accused. The order was to stand in effect until the jury was impaneled.

The press in the state appealed the publication ban to the United States Supreme Court, and in June 1976 the high Court ruled that Judge Stuart's order was an unconstitutional prior restraint upon the press (*Nebraska Press Association* v. *Stuart,* 1976). While all nine members of the high Court agreed that the restrictive order in this case was a violation of the First Amendment, five members of the Court suggested that under the guidelines outlined at the beginning of this section (page 343) such an order might be proper. Chief Justice Burger wrote the opinion for the Court, in which he stressed that prior restraint was the exception, not the rule. There must be a clear and present danger to the defendant's rights before such a restrictive order might be constitutionally permitted, he said. But the Chief Justice did suggest that if the judge could demonstrate that the publicity about the case was intense and pervasive, that no other means could be used to compensate for such publicity, and that the restrictive order would be effective in keeping the prejudicial information out of the hands of prospective jurors such an order might stand. In Simants's case, Burger said, while there was heavy publicity about the matter, there was no evidence that Judge Stuart had considered the efficacy of other remedies to compensate for this publicity. Also, the small community was filled with rumors about Simants and what he had told the police. Burger expressed serious doubts whether the restrictive order would have in fact kept prejudicial information out of public hands.

Of the remaining four members of the high Court, Justices Stewart, Brennan, and Marshall stated that such prior restraints against the press would not be constitutional under any circumstance. Justice White implied that he agreed with that notion, but since he was not compelled to answer that question in the case before the Court, he would wait until another day to face the issue.

Please note, the Supreme Court did not declare restrictive orders aimed only at *trial participants* to be unconstitutional. This issue was not raised in the trial, but it is assumed that courts have much broader power to limit what attorneys, police, and other trial participants can say about a case out of court.

The *Guidelines on Fair Trial/Free Press* issued by the United States Judicial Conference, for example, recommends that federal courts adopt rules which limit public discussion of criminal cases by attorneys and court personnel and suggests that courts issue special rules in sensational criminal cases to bar extrajudicial comments by all trial participants. But, in light of the ruling in *Nebraska Press Association* v. *Stuart,* the conference *Guidelines* specifically state:

> No rule of court or judicial order should be promulgated by a United States district court which would prohibit representatives of the news media from broadcasting or publishing any information in their possession relating to a criminal case.

In both 1978 and 1979 the Supreme Court issued opinions in cases which had the effect of reinforcing the rule from the *Nebraska Press Association* decision that restrictions upon what the press may publish are to be tolerated only in very rare circumstances. In 1978 the high Court prohibited the state of Virginia from punishing the *Virginian Pilot* newspaper for publishing an accurate story regarding the confidential proceedings of a state judicial review commission (*Landmark Communications* v. *Virginia,* 1978). A Virginia State statute authorized the commission to hear complaints of a judge's disability or misconduct, and because of the sensitive nature of such hearings, the Virginia law closed the proceedings to the public and the press. The state argued that confidentiality was necessary to encourage the filing of complaints and the testimony of witnesses, to protect the judge from the injury that might result from the publication of unwarranted or unexamined charges, and to maintain confidence in the judiciary that might be undermined by the publication of groundless charges. While acknowledging the desirability of confidentiality, the Supreme Court nevertheless ruled against the state. Chief Justice Burger, writing for a unanimous Court, stated that the "publication Virginia seeks to punish under its statute lies near the core of the First Amendment, and the Commonwealth's interests advanced by the imposition of criminal sanctions are insufficient to justify the actual and potential encroachments on freedom of speech and of the press. . . ." The court did acknowledge that the state commission could certainly meet in secret, and that its reports and materials could be kept confidential. But while the press has no right to gain access to such information, once it possesses the information, it cannot be punished for its publication. In this sense the Court followed the *Nebraska Press Association* rule limiting restraints placed upon the press's right to publish.

In 1979 the high Court declared unconstitutional a West Virginia statute that made it a crime for a newspaper to publish the name of a youth charged as a juvenile offender without the written approval of the juvenile court (*Smith* v. *Daily Mail Publishing Company,* 1979). Again Chief Justice Burger wrote the opinion for the Court and stressed the fact that once the press has legally obtained truthful information it cannot be stopped from its publication. In this case two Charleston, West Virginia, newspapers published the name of a fourteen-year-old boy who was arrested for the shooting death of a fifteen-year-old student. Reporters for the newspapers got the name from persons who had witnessed the shooting. "If the information is lawfully obtained," the Chief Justice wrote, "the state may not punish its publication except when necessary to further an interest more substantial than is present here."

The Rhode Island Supreme Court ruled recently that a juvenile court acted improperly when it barred a reporter from attending a juvenile court hearing simply because the reporter's newspaper had published the name of the juvenile suspect in violation of an agreement between the press and the juvenile court. Other reporters were allowed to attend the hearing. The newspaper had legally obtained the name of the juvenile suspect in the murder case. The court said that a judge cannot condition future attendance at juvenile hearings upon the newspaper's agreement in advance not to publish the names of juvenile suspects. If the newspaper obtained the name improperly from judicial sources, or as the result of attending a nonpublic juvenile hearing, the court could order that the name not be published. But if the newspaper learned the name through its own investigation, the trial judge cannot stop the publication of this information and cannot bar reporters from the newspaper from future juvenile hearings (*Sherman Publishing* v. *Goldberg,* 1982).

Restrictive orders which bar the press from publishing information about a criminal case have ceased to be a serious problem for journalists. Orders which limit what trial participants can say remain a nuisance, however, and probably do not serve the judicial system as well as many observers might imagine. Rumors tend to thrive in an atmosphere where the release of accurate information is stifled. Research has suggested that the publication of even massive amounts of factual information about a trial may reduce the likelihood of juror prejudice (see page 333). It would be better perhaps to provide journalists bound to publish something about a case with accurate and truthful statements rather than push them to report what is ground out by a rumor mill.

Summary

In some instances trial courts have attempted to limit the publication of prejudicial information about a case by issuing court orders restricting what the press may publish or what the trial participants may publicly say about a case. These restrictive orders grew out of a famous United States Supreme Court decision in the mid-1960s which ruled that a trial judge is responsible for controlling the publicity about a case.

In 1976 the Supreme Court ruled that the press may not be prohibited from publishing information it has legally obtained about a criminal case unless these conditions are met:

1. Intense and pervasive publicity about the case is certain.
2. No other reasonable alternative is likely to mitigate the effects of the pretrial publicity.
3. The restrictive order will prevent prejudicial material from reaching the jurors (*Nebraska Press Association* v. *Stuart*).

Judges may, however, limit what trial participants say publicly about a case.

In two subsequent rulings the high Court reaffirmed its 1976 decision that confidential information legally obtained by the press may be published. These cases involved the name of a juvenile suspect in a murder case (*Smith* v. *Daily Mail*) and the names of judges whose conduct had been reviewed by a confidential state judicial commission (*Landmark Communications* v. *Virginia*).

CLOSED COURTROOMS

Inherent, if not implicit, in both the *Landmark* ruling and the *Daily Mail* decision, however, is the notion that government has the power to keep confidential material out of the hands of the press in the first place. Chief Justice Burger noted in his opinion in the *Daily Mail* case that the Supreme Court's holding was a narrow one. "There is no issue before us of unlawful press access to confidential judicial proceedings." The Chief Justice made a similar point in a less obvious way in the *Nebraska Press Association* ruling. In footnote eight in the ruling Burger noted, "Closing of pretrial proceedings with the consent of the defendant when required is also recommended in guidelines that have emerged from various studies. . . . We are not now confronted with such issues."

Whether motivated by the suggestion in the footnote or the inability to restrain the press following the *Nebraska Press Association* ruling, trial judges began closing trials and pretrial hearings in the late seventies to an extent never before seen in the United States. They did so ostensibly to protect the Sixth Amendment fair-trial rights of the defendant. In doing so, however, judges ran squarely into confrontation with the press, which claimed that long-standing First Amendment rights were being sacrificed. Ultimately these issues were joined before the high Court. Closure of pretrial hearings will be considered first.

Much information which might be prejudicial to a defendant and which might never be disclosed during a trial is discussed at a **pretrial hearing.** For example, a defendant might have confessed to the crime shortly after being arrested. Later, he asserts the confession was wrested from him by unlawful police interrogation and argues that the confession should not be admitted as evidence against him during the trial. The argument would be made at the pretrial hearing, normally an open proceeding which may be attended by the press and the public. Assume, for a moment, that the judge agrees with the defendant and rules the confession inadmissible as evidence. The thrust of the recent rulings by the Supreme Court makes it impossible for the judge to stop the press from reporting what took place at the pretrial hearing. Stories may be published and broadcast that a defendant had confessed, but that the confession could not be introduced as evidence. But if potential jurors can read about a confession, a defendant's right to a trial by an impartial jury could be seriously jeopardized. Or so the argument goes. The solution? Close the pretrial proceeding to the press and the public. If the information can be kept out of the hands of the press in the first place, the court can rest assured it cannot be published. The need for the restrictive order vanishes. At the end of the seventies, closure of pretrial hearings became a popular judicial remedy to stop the circulation of potentially prejudicial material.

Pretrial Hearings

Can a trial judge, with the agreement of the defendant and the state, legally and constitutionally close a pretrial hearing to the public and the press? In 1979 a majority of the United States Supreme Court said a judge can bar the public and the press from attending such a hearing.

Two constitutional amendments appear to suggest the opposite conclusion; that the closure of such a hearing would not be constitutional. The First Amendment guarantees freedom of speech and of the press. In the past two hundred years it has been presumed by many authorities that this guarantee is included among the first ten amendments to the constitution as a means of ensuring that the press can report upon the activities of the government without interference. Closing the door to an important part of the judicial process seems hardly consistent with this constitutional mandate. The Sixth Amendment guarantees that "in all criminal prosecutions, the accused shall enjoy the right to a speedy and *public* [author emphasis] trial. . . ." A public trial implies an open trial, one in which the people can make certain that the courts are administering justice properly and fairly. But in the case of *Gannett* v. *DePasquale* (1979), a majority of the high Court rejected both constitutional arguments and placed its imprimatur upon a closed pretrial hearing as a means of controlling prejudicial publicity in criminal trials.

Gannett v. *DePasquale*

In 1976 the state of New York brought charges of second-degree murder and burglary against Kyle Greathouse and David Jones in connection with the slaying of a former Seneca County police officer. Considerable publicity surrounded the death of Wayne Clapp and the capture in Michigan of the two defendants. Before the trial began, both defendants sought to suppress statements they had given to police on the grounds that the statements had been given involuntarily. They also sought to suppress evidence that the police had uncovered as a result of those statements. Because of the intensive publicity surrounding the case, defense lawyers sought to close the pretrial hearings where arguments would be made to suppress the prejudicial evidence. The state agreed to this closure, and Judge DePasquale prohibited the press and public from attending the sessions. Gannett, which publishes both Rochester newspapers, appealed the judge's ruling. But the New York courts refused to overturn Judge DePasquale's order. The United States Supreme Court agreed to hear the case and in July 1979 sustained the trial judge's closure order.

The Court decision was fractured, and five separate opinions were written. Justice Potter Stewart's opinion for the Court drew support from only one other member of the tribunal, Justice John Paul Stevens. Chief Justice Burger, Justice Lewis Powell, and Justice Rehnquist each wrote a separate concurring opinion, and Justices Marshall, White, and Brennan concurred in a strong dissent by Justice Blackmun.

Justice Stewart said that if the defendant, the prosecutor, and the trial judge agree, a pretrial hearing can be closed to the public. Stewart suggested that a trial might be closed as well under the same circumstances. Stewart said that the right to a public trial guaranteed by the Sixth Amendment is a right belonging to a defendant alone. The defendant could choose to waive that right at any time and seek to have a closed hearing. Justice Stewart acknowledged that there is a legitimate public concern that the criminal justice system work properly. But he said that "in an adversary system of criminal justice, the public interest in the administration of justice is protected by the participants in the litigation." If the state and the trial judge agree with the defendant, the hearing can be closed. Stewart rejected the notion that the First Amendment was even material in this case and ruled that the Court would not decide in the abstract whether the press enjoyed a constitutional right to attend a pretrial hearing or a trial. Assuming for the sake of argument that the First Amendment does provide a limited right of access to pretrial hearings, the trial judge had given careful consideration in this case to the press's First Amendment rights, Justice Stewart said. Because of the intensive publicity surrounding the trial, the First Amendment interests had to be abrogated to protect the defendants' right to a fair trial. Also, Stewart noted that the denial of access in this case was only temporary, since the transcript of the pretrial suppression hearing was made available to the press and public once the trial was under way. It is important to note, however, that Justice Stewart based his decision almost exclusively upon the Sixth Amendment. He did not decide whether under different circumstances (a case in which there is much less publicity surrounding the trial, for example) the First Amendment might not prohibit a judge from closing a hearing. Justice Rehnquist, who wrote a separate opinion, also based his support of the closure of the hearing upon the defendants' Sixth Amendment rights.

Chief Justice Burger agreed with Stewart that the Sixth Amendment's guarantee of a public trial did not guarantee the right of the people or the press to attend pretrial hearings. But Burger stressed that the same rationale did not necessarily apply to trials, as Stewart suggested. When the Sixth

Amendment was drafted, suppression hearings were not a part of American jurisprudence, the Chief Justice noted. Similarly the common law rule which mandated an open trial did not envision the exclusionary rule and pretrial motions to suppress evidence. Hence, it is impossible to argue that the Sixth Amendment's guarantee of a public trial includes the guarantee of a public pretrial hearing.

The fifth member of the majority was Justice Lewis Powell. He was the only member of the high Court who, in his opinion, gave serious consideration to the guarantees of freedom of expression. Powell said there is a right under the First Amendment for the press and the public to attend pretrial hearings—but it is not an absolute right. The right of the press and the public must be balanced against the right of the defendant to a fair trial. When a closed hearing is requested, Powell wrote, the judge should consider whether there are other ways of protecting the defendant's right less damaging to the press than to close the hearing. The press must be allowed to make arguments opposing the closure of the courtroom before the order is issued, Powell said. The press can argue that a defendant's right can be protected in ways other than by closing a hearing. If in the end the trial judge is convinced by the evidence that closing the hearing is the only way to protect the defendant's right to a fair trial, the First Amendment right to attend the proceeding must then be sacrificed. Powell was the only one of the nine members of the Court to focus exclusively on the First Amendment, and the only justice who argued that there is even a limited right for the public and the press to attend such hearings. In this case, however, he said he was convinced that Judge De-Pasquale had determined that the only way to protect the rights of the defendants was to close the hearing. And Justice Powell accepted this determination by the trial judge.

The dissenters, led by a long and forceful opinion by Justice Blackmun, argued that the right to a public trial was put in the constitution to protect the people as much as to protect the defendant. Blackmun wrote that the Sixth Amendment guarantee of a public trial "embodies our belief that secret judicial proceedings would be a menace to liberty. The public trial is rooted in the principle that justice cannot survive behind walls of silence." He added (*Gannett* v. *DePasquale*):

> The public trial guarantee, moreover, ensures that not only judges but all participants in the criminal justice system are subjected to public scrutiny as they conduct the public's business of prosecuting crime. This publicity guards against the miscarriage of justice by subjecting the police, prosecutors, and judicial processes to extensive public scrutiny and criticism.

Blackmun argued that the public interest in both trial and pretrial proceedings cannot adequately be protected by the prosecutor and the judge, as suggested by Justice Stewart. "The specter of a trial or suppression hearing where a defendant of the same political party as the prosecutor and judge—both of whom are elected officials perhaps beholden to the very defendant they are to try—obtains closure of the proceeding without any consideration for the substantial public interest at stake is sufficiently real to cause me to reject the Court's suggestion that the parties be given complete discretion to dispose of the public's interest as they see fit," the justice wrote. The dissenters said that the Sixth Amendment does not impose an absolute requirement that all courts be open at all times. But before closing a hearing the judge surely must find that an open pretrial will cause irreparable damage to the defendant's right to a fair trial, that alternatives to closing the hearing will not protect the defendant, but that the closed hearing will ensure a trial by an impartial jury for the defendant.

But Justice Blackmun's strong opinions did not carry the day. According to the Supreme Court's opinion in *Gannett* v. *DePasquale,* there is no firm constitutional right for any member of the press or public to attend a pretrial hearing. Judges need not even give a reason for closure, according to Justice Stewart's opinion.

Developments since 1979 have had an impact upon the rule enunciated by Justice Stewart in the *Gannett* v. *DePasquale* case. Guidelines have been adopted by many agencies, such as the American Bar Association and the United States Judicial Conference, which judges and attorneys may use when faced with requests for closure of pretrial hearings. A few lower courts have interpreted the Supreme Court rules rather strictly and have permitted the closure of pretrial hearings. But some courts appear to be repeating a pattern which developed in the wake of the Supreme Court's *Branzburg* v. *Hayes* ruling (see pages 288–91). In that case a badly split Supreme Court ruled that there was no constitutional privilege which permitted reporters to refuse to reveal the names of confidential news sources when subpoenaed to testify before a grand jury. But the lower federal and state courts, relying on Justice Powell's concurrence and a dissent by four other members of the Court, nevertheless fashioned a qualified privilege to protect journalists. The Third United States Court of Appeals and other courts have followed the same path regarding closed pretrial hearings (*U.S.* v. *Criden,* 1982). Let us look at each of these developments briefly.

Guidelines

The Department of Justice issued *Guidelines on Open Judicial Proceedings* in 1980. United States attorneys were instructed to ordinarily oppose any motions for the closure of any judicial proceeding. The *Guidelines* state that before seeking closure or consenting to closure the United States attorney must be satisified that these conditions are met:

1. No other alternative exists to protect the defendant's rights.
2. Closure will succeed in preventing harm to the defendant.
3. The degree of closure is minimized to the greatest extent possible.

4. The public is given adequate notice of the proposed closure.
5. Failure to close the proceedings will produce any one of the following effects:
    a. Substantial likelihood of the denial of the right of fair trial to the defendant.
    b. Substantial likelihood of danger to the safety of participants in the trial.
    c. Substantial likelihood that ongoing investigations will be seriously jeopardized.

A United States attorney must get authorization from the deputy United States attorney general before seeking to close a hearing or consenting to a motion to close the hearing made by another party in the case. Of course these rules apply only to litigation in which the Department of Justice is involved.

The American Bar Association added a section on the closure of pretrial proceedings to its *Standards Relating to the Administration of Justice, Free Press and Fair Trial.* The ABA guidelines state that pretrial proceedings should generally be open. In cases where evidence revealed at the hearing might threaten the defendant's right to a fair trial, the judge should first seek voluntary cooperation from the news media to delay dissemination of the material. If the media refuse to cooperate, the judge can close the hearing, but only if dissemination of the information from such a proceeding would create a clear and present danger of interfering with a fair trial for the defendant, and if the prejudicial effects cannot be avoided by any reasonable alternative means. The rules adopted by the United States Judicial Conference are somewhat less favorable to open hearings than those of the ABA. In its *Fair Trial–Free Press Guidelines,* the conference recommends that pretrial proceedings should be open, but may be closed by a judge if these conditions are met:

1. There is a reasonable likelihood that the dissemination of information disclosed at such proceedings would impair the defendant's right to a fair trial.
2. Reasonable alternatives to closure will not adequately protect the defendant's right to a fair trial.

While these guidelines sound somewhat like the ABA guidelines, the requirement that the motion for closure be accompanied by a showing of a "reasonable likelihood" of harm to the defendant rather than a "clear and present danger" of harm to the defendant is substantially different. It is far easier to demonstrate a "reasonable likelihood" than a "clear and present danger." It will be easier to close a pretrial if a judge follows the Judicial Conference *Guidelines* rather than the ABA recommendations.

None of these guidelines overcomes the Supreme Court ruling that trial judges may close any pretrial hearing if they choose to do so. But the guidelines do represent an attempt to accommodate the interests of the public and the press somewhat better than the majority of the high Court did in *Gannett v. DePasquale*. As such, they are important developments in the press's effort to keep pretrial hearings open. Many local and state court organizations have adopted similar rules as well. Investigate the guidelines used by the state and county judges in your jurisdiction.

Lower Court Rulings

The Supreme Court's ruling in *Gannett v. DePasquale* permits a trial judge to close a pretrial hearing with often little cause. Many trial judges reject motions for closure or apply guidelines like those just outlined. But the closure of pretrial hearings is a relatively common occurrence in most states today. The Reporter's Committee on Freedom of the Press reports that during the period from July 1979 through May 1981 the closure of 246 pretrial hearings was requested. Courts closed these hearings in 141 cases. Typical of the kinds of cases in which closure has been granted are *Kansas City Star* v. *Fossey* and *Federated Publications* v. *Kurtz*.

The *Kansas City Star* sought access to a pretrial suppression hearing in which a trial judge was to determine the nature of two incriminating statements made by the defendant. The jury had already been impaneled in the sensational murder case, but was excused for the day so that the hearing could be held in the courtroom. The Kansas State Supreme Court upheld Judge Fossey's closure order. The court said there were no facilities to sequester the jury, and it was reasonable for Judge Fossey to conclude that the highly prejudicial information might reach the jury if it was published or broadcast as a result of being discussed in an open hearing (*Kansas City Star* v. *Fossey*, 1981).

A Whatcom County, Washington Superior Court judge closed a pretrial hearing in a murder case to prevent a local newspaper from covering the proceeding. The newspaper had published prejudicial information about the case in the past, the trial judge determined, and so could not be trusted to behave differently in the future. The Washington State Supreme Court upheld the closure, noting that these were reasonable grounds for Judge Kurtz to close the hearing (*Federated Publications* v. *Kurtz*, 1980). In neither of these cases did the trial court ever make a finding that the citizens in the community were so prejudiced against the defendant that it would be impossible or even difficult to find a dozen citizens for an impartial jury. In most cases when the closure of a pretrial hearing is sought, it is the defense attorney who initiates the process. He or she will ask the judge to close the hearing on the grounds that there has been considerable publicity in the case, and that the release of further information at an open pretrial hearing would seriously harm the defendant's right to a fair trial. Of course, this is all speculation. The trial judge will normally make several important assumptions to justify closing the hearing. First, there is the assumption that information prejudicial to the defendant will be discussed at the pretrial hearing. Next, it must be assumed that the press will report this information, and that the public will read it or watch it on television. If in fact the people do read it, it must be assumed that this will create prejudice against the defendant. Finally, it must be assumed that enough people will learn this information to make it impossible to find a jury of twelve citizens to render a fair verdict in the case. Many authorities consider this string of assumptions a frail foundation upon which to base the closure of a normally open and important public hearing. And pretrial hearings are important in the criminal justice system.

Such hearings have become an essential part of the criminal justice system today, whereas even fifty years ago they were rare. The growth and almost institutionalization of "plea bargaining" in the criminal justice system is one reason for the importance of the hearings. If the defendant is quite certain to be convicted of the crime as charged, it is advantageous for both the accused and the prosecutor to bargain. Defendants will agree to plead guilty to a lesser crime, robbery rather than armed robbery, for example. They will usually get a softer penalty for the lesser crime, and the state will not have to pay the expense of a jury trial. As a matter of fact, more than 85 percent of all criminal defendants plead guilty. The pretrial hearing is often crucial to the state's case, and it is frequently the only real judicial hearing held. As Justice Blackmun noted in his dissent in *Gannett v. DePasquale:*

> The pretrial suppression hearing often is critical and it may be decisive in the prosecution of a criminal case. If the defendant prevails, he will have dealt the prosecution's case a serious, perhaps fatal, blow; the proceeding often then will be dismissed or negotiated on terms favorable to the defense. If the prosecution successfully resists the motion to suppress, the defendant may have little hope of success at trial . . . with the result that the likelihood of a guilty plea is substantially increased. The suppression hearing often is the only judicial proceeding of substantial importance that takes place during a criminal prosecution.

In addition, the pretrial hearing may be the only point in the trial process at which the conduct of the law enforcement officers is at issue. Because such conduct frequently occurs outside the public view, beneficial public scrutiny may never take place if not at the hearing itself.

For these reasons and many others, many persons in journalism and in the law believe that public attendance at pretrial hearings is a very important part of our democratic system of government. To those people two recent U.S. Court of Appeals rulings were like a breath of fresh air.

A federal trial judge in Philadelphia held an unannounced, closed evidentiary hearing in the trial of four defendants nabbed in one of the FBI's infamous Abscam investigations. The closure was justified on the grounds that if information discussed at the hearing was brought out and publicized it would impair the defendants' right to a fair trial. The defendants in the case were three Philadelphia city councilmen and a private attorney.

The Third United States Court of Appeals ruled that the closure order was improper (*U.S.* v. *Criden*, 1982). The public has the First Amendment right of access to pretrial hearings, the court ruled. Who will protect the interests of the public and the press in these hearings if access is denied? Chief Judge Seitz asked. "The defendant's interests will obviously not coincide with that of the press," he said. The government has the duty to ensure a fair trial, but is also interested in securing a conviction that will withstand appeal. The reversal of a conviction because of prejudicial publicity poses a risk to a successful prosecution. "We, therefore, cannot expect the government to vindicate the public's first amendement rights." Judge Seitz said that the trial judge could not be expected to be the "sole guardian of First Amendment interests even against the express wishes of both parties." No one has an interest to protect the rights of public and press in a closed hearing. "The public has some First Amendment right of access to information about how one of these great branches of our government conducts its business," he concluded.

In *Gannett* v. *DePasquale* the Supreme Court ruled there was no Sixth Amendment right of access to pretrial hearings. "The majority assumed, without deciding, that the First Amendment provides for such a right to attend pretrial hearings, but found that it had not been abridged," Judge Seitz noted. But the right is not absolute, Judge Seitz ruled. A judge may close a pretrial hearing if the proper procedures are followed. Motions for closure must be posted on the court docket to give notice to the public. The district court must at least consider alternatives to closure and explicitly state its reasons for rejecting such alternatives. There must be evidence to support the conclusion of the trial judge that other means will be insufficient to preserve the defendant's rights, and that closure is necessary to protect effectively against perceived harm. Among the alternatives Judge Seitz suggested that trial judges consider holding the pretrial hearing after the jury has been selected. By admonishing the jury not to read about the case or through sequestration, information revealed at the pretrial can be kept from jurors (*U.S.* v. *Criden*, 1982).

In *U.S.* v. *Brooklier* (1982) a federal trial court barred the press and public from the suppression hearing and other evidentiary hearings in a case in which several persons were charged with violating federal racketeering laws. The court also partially closed the voir dire proceedings where potential jurors were questioned by attorneys before being chosen to serve on the jury panel. The Ninth United States Court of Appeals ruled the closures improper in this case, stating that Justice Blackmun's test from his dissenting opinion in *Gannett* v. *DePasquale* must be met before such a closure is proper. The accused must demonstrate that closure is "strictly and inescapably necessary in order to protect the right to a fair trial guarantee." To do this it is necessary to demonstrate the substantial probability of irreparable damage to the fair trial guarantee from conducting the hearings in public and a substantial probability that alternatives to closure will not adequately protect the right to a fair trial, and that the closure will be effective in protecting the rights of the accused. Chief Judge Browning noted that "Justice Blackmun's opinion in *Gannett* on behalf of himself and Justices Brennan, White, and Marshall concluded that the public had the right of access to pretrial suppression hearings under the Sixth Amendment for essentially the same reasons as led the Court in *Richmond Newspapers* and *Globe Newspapers* [see pages 360–63 for an explanation of these cases] to hold that the public had a right of access to criminal trials under the First Amendment." This was a broad affirmation of the right of the public and the press to attend all manner of judicial hearings. Both the Georgia and Florida supreme courts have also ruled that the public has access to pretrial hearings in most instances (see *Page Corp.* v. *Lumpkin,* 1982 and *Miami Herald* v. *Lewis,* 1982).

These rulings have given many observers hope that the lower federal courts and state courts will develop rules which offer more protection to the public interest than was provided by the Supreme Court in *Gannett* v. *DePasquale.* Make no mistake, the *Gannett* ruling is still the law. A judge may close a pretrial hearing for little or no cause. But the development of case law which limits the rights of trial judges in this regard is seen as a hopeful sign by persons in journalism.

Clearly, closure of pretrial proceedings is a remedy against the press as drastic as the now uncommon gag order. Perhaps closure does not do as much direct violence to the First Amendment as does the prior restraint inherent in a restrictive order, but the result for the public is about the same—a blackout of information about crucial aspects of the criminal justice system.

Closed Trials

The United States Supreme Court has spoken far more clearly on the matter of open trials than it has regarding the closure of pretrial hearings. Chief Justice Burger and six members of the high Court ruled in 1980 that the right of the public and the press to attend a criminal trial is guaranteed by both the common law and the United States Constitution (*Richmond Newspapers* v. *Virginia,* 1980). Only Justice Rehnquist dissented from this ruling. (Justice Powell took no part in the case since he had represented the Richmond Newspapers before he was appointed to the Supreme Court.)

In March 1976 John Stevenson was indicted for murder. He was tried and convicted of second degree murder, but his conviction was reversed. A second trial ended in a mistrial when a juror asked to be excused in the midst of the hearing. A third trial also resulted in a mistrial because a prospective juror told other prospective jurors about Stevenson's earlier conviction on the same charges. This was not revealed until after the trial had started. As proceedings were about to begin for the fourth time in late 1978, the defense asked that the trial be closed. The prosecution did not object and the court closed the trial. Richmond Newspapers protested the closure to no avail. An appeal came before the United States Supreme Court in February 1980.

Chief Justice Burger wrote the Court's opinion. He noted at the outset that the *DePasquale* decision a year earlier had applied only to pretrial hearings. But much to the disappointment of many persons the majority did not reverse the earlier ruling on pretrial hearings. Burger wrote that "through its evolution the trial has been open to all who cared to observe." A presumption of open hearings is the very nature of a criminal trial under our system of justice, the Chief Justice added. While there is no specific provision in the Bill of Rights or the Constitution to support the open trial, the expressly guaranteed freedoms in the First Amendment "share a common core purpose of assuring freedom of communication on matters relating to the functioning of government," Burger wrote. "In guaranteeing freedoms such as those of speech and press the First Amendment can be read as protecting the right of everyone to attend trials so as to give meaning to those explicit guarantees," he added. The First Amendment, then, the Chief Justice noted, prohibits the government from summarily closing courtroom doors, which had been open to the public at the time that amendment was adopted.

But the Chief Justice refused to see the First Amendment as an absolute bar to closed trials. He noted that in some circumstances, which he explicitly declined to define at this time, a trial judge could bar the public and the press from a trial in the interest of the fair administration of justice. But, while the Court did not outline such circumstances, it was clear from both the tone and the language of the Chief Justice's opinion that in his mind such circumstances would indeed be unusual.

Justices White, Stevens, Brennan, Marshall, Stewart, and Blackmun all concurred with the Chief Justice in five separate opinions. All but Stewart seemingly went farther in guaranteeing access to trials than did Chief Justice Burger. Justice Rehnquist dissented.

But as the Chief Justice said, the right of access to a trial is not absolute. In two instances since 1980, courts have had to consider exceptions to the general rule of open trials. The Vermont Supreme Court ruled in December 1981 that the ruling in the *Richmond Newspapers* case did not extend to juvenile proceedings. That is, the state may continue to hold such hearings—which are like trials—behind closed doors. The *Burlington Free Press* sought access to a juvenile proceeding where a judge was to consider the status (adult or juvenile) of a fifteen-year-old boy who had murdered one young girl and assaulted another. Juvenile proceedings were supposed to be kept confidential under Vermont state law. The Vermont Supreme Court noted that there was no tradition of openness in these proceedings which mirrored the American tradition of public trials. In a juvenile proceeding there is no criminal conviction, often no punishment. "A juvenile proceeding is so unlike a criminal prosecution that the limited right of access described in *Richmond Newspapers* does not govern," the court ruled. In addition, there were many good reasons to keep such hearings closed, the court said. Publication of the name could impair the young person's opportunity for rehabilitation; confidentiality will protect the juvenile from carrying a stigma in the future. Publicity is often seen as a reward for a hard-core juvenile delinquent, the high court added (in re *J.S.*, 1981).

Access to juvenile proceedings is governed in most states by statute. Often reporters can gain access to such proceedings by promising not to reveal the names of the participants. Reporters who cover juvenile courts should know their statutory rights to attend such hearings.

Juvenile hearings are one common exception to the general rule of opening trials. Many states have laws which also close criminal trials when the juvenile victims of a sexual offense testify. In 1982 the Supreme Court ruled that a Massachusetts law which *required* a trial judge to exclude the press and the public from the courtroom during such testimony was unconstitutional (*Globe Newspapers* v. *Superior Court,* 1982). The state argued that the law had two purposes: to encourage young victims to come forward to testify in such cases and to protect these young people from psychological harm once they come forward. The state law required the judge to close the trial when the victim testified; other portions of the trial could be closed at the judge's discretion. The flaw in the law, according to Justice William Brennan who wrote the Court's opinion, was that the trial judge was *required* to close the trial during the victim's testimony. Brennan agreed that protecting the physical and psychological well-being of a minor is a compelling interest:

> But as compelling as that interest is, it does not justify a mandatory-closure rule, for it is clear that the circumstances of the particular case may affect the significance of the interest. A trial court can determine on a case-by-case basis whether the closure is necessary to protect the welfare of a minor victim.

Under the statute the trial judge is not permitted to allow testimony in open court even if the victim desires it, Brennan said.

Justice Brennan rejected the argument that a mandatory closure law is more likely to prompt young victims of sexual assault to come forward to testify. He said there was no empirical support for this claim; in addition the argument was not logical. Reporters are permitted to attend the remainder of the trial, and can get the victim's name and details of the testimony from the transcript of the trial. The statute really does not do what the state thinks it should do, while it runs squarely against the presumption of open trials enunciated in the *Richmond Newspapers* case. Dissenters Burger and Rehnquist disagreed, arguing that the state has a long-standing right to protect juveniles as well as a long tradition of excluding the public from trials involving victims of sexual assault. Justice Stevens also dissented because he believed the Supreme Court was rendering an improper advisory opinion in the case (*Globe Newspapers* v. *Superior Court,* 1982). While the right of the public and the press to attend a criminal trial is not yet completely defined, this appears to be an expansive right, especially when dealing with trials of adults.

Summary

The closure of pretrial hearings and even of trials is another method used by some trial courts to control the flow of information about a case to the public. In a controversial 1979 decision the Supreme Court ruled that neither the public nor the press enjoyed the constitutional right to attend pretrial hearings in criminal cases (*Gannett* v. *DePasquale*). Some lower courts have followed the Supreme Court ruling rather strictly. But some legal groups, such as the American Bar Association, and some lower courts have taken the position that the closure of a pretrial hearing is the last, not the first, option a judge should exercise to control the effects of prejudicial publicity. These persons argue that before the pretrial is closed the judge should determine that the release of information will in fact do serious harm to the defendant's chances for a fair trial, and should also determine that there is no other way to compensate for the prejudice the release of this information might create.

The Supreme Court ruled in 1980 that criminal trials are presumptively open; that citizens enjoy the common law and the constitutional right to attend these hearings (*Richmond Newspapers* v. *Virginia*). Exceptions exist to this general presumption of openness, but they are rare. The Vermont Supreme Court noted one exception when it ruled that juvenile proceedings did not fall under the Supreme Court mandate for open trials (in re *J.S.*, 1981).

BENCH-BAR-PRESS GUIDELINES

Both restrictive orders and the closure of court proceedings are admittedly effective ways of stopping publicity from reaching the hands of potential jurors, but they are equally dangerous in a representative democracy where information about how well government is operating is fundamental to the success of the political system. The bench, the bar, and the press in many states have found that cooperation, restraint, and mutual trust can be equally effective in protecting the rights of a defendant, while at the same time far less damaging to rights of the people.

In twenty-eight states the members of the bench, the bar, and the press have tried to reach a common understanding of the problems of pretrial news coverage and have offered suggestions on how most of these problems might be resolved. These suggestions are usually offered in the form of guidelines or recommendations to the press and to participants in the criminal justice system. **Bench-bar-press guidelines** normally suggest to law enforcement officers that certain kinds of information about a criminal suspect and a crime can be released and published with little danger of harm to the trial process. The guidelines also suggest to journalists that the publication of certain kinds of information about a case (see the list of damaging kinds of statements on pages 331–32) can be harmful to the defendant's chances for a fair trial without providing the public with useful or important information. The guidelines are often presented in a very brief form; at other times they encompass several pages of text.

Bench-bar-press guidelines have existed in some states for more than twenty years. In some communities these guidelines work very well in managing the problems surrounding the free press–fair trial dilemma. A spirit of cooperation exists between press, courts, attorneys, and law enforcement personnel. In such communities it is rare to find a restrictive order or a closed courtroom. But most communities and states have found it takes considerable effort to make the guidelines work. Drafting the guidelines is only the first step. If after agreement is reached upon the recommendations, the bench, the bar, and the press go their separate ways, the guidelines usually fail as a means to resolve the free press–fair trial problems.

For many years the state of Washington had one of the most successful bench-bar-press agreements in the nation. Recent events (which will be noted shortly) undercut the guidelines and today the relationship between the press and the courts in Washington is not as healthy as it once was. But it is instructive to note what the people in Washington did that helped make the guidelines work for so many years. The Bench-Bar-Press Committee in Washington has been meeting regularly since 1966. In addition, the committee periodically sponsors day-long seminars around the state to educate attorneys, reporters, and judges in application of the guidelines. The Washington Supreme Court is very active in its support of the committee, and the chief justice sits as chairman of the committee. This has the distinct effect of getting both trial lawyers and other judges to attend the seminars.

Support by the state's leading newspapers is also helpful in getting reporters to attend. Discussion of libel and related press-law problems is also a device used to lure the press to meetings, so that a dose of free press–fair trial guidelines can be administered as well.

Also a subcommittee—called the liaison committee—of the state's bench-bar-press committee composed of a judge, an attorney, and a journalist acts as a special education group. The job of the committee is to respond quickly to immediate free press–fair trial problems. For example, a Seattle judge informed the press at the beginning of a trial that reporters would be excluded from certain portions of the trial. The reporters became angry, and the managing editor of one of the daily papers in Seattle immediately called the chairman of the bench-bar-press committee who in turn activated the liaison committee. The entire chain of events took about four hours. The judge who sat on the liaison committee called his colleague on the bench who had announced the trial closure. The committee member asked the judge whether he realized that by closing the trial he violated provisions of the bench-bar-press agreement. He then informed the judge that it was his experience that the press can be trusted in situations like these and need not be excluded from a trial. The peer pressure worked. The trial judge called reporters into his chambers and told them he had changed his mind, and the trial would be open. But he asked the press to refrain from reporting certain sensational details of the testimony. The reporters honored his request. In other instances judges complained about newsmen, and the journalist on the liaison committee successfully applied the same kind of educational pressure to his colleagues.

The issuance of restrictive orders and the closure of pretrial hearings and trials has seriously deteriorated the goodwill that existed between the press and the courts in this nation. Washington is not immune from these problems, despite the existence of the bench-bar-press guidelines. A pretrial was closed in 1980 and the closure was upheld by the state supreme court (*Federated Publications* v. *Kurtz*, 1980). The following year a trial judge refused a defense motion to close a pretrial suppression hearing, but told reporters they could not attend the hearing unless they signed an agreement to abide by the provisions of the voluntary bench-bar-press guidelines. The public was permitted to attend the hearing without signing anything. Many reporters refused to sign the agreement, deeming the judge's order a prior restraint. An appeal of the order followed, but the state supreme court upheld the trial judge. The high court disagreed that the judge's order amounted to a prior restraint, especially since there was no penalty attached to violating the agreement. That is, reporters would not have been punished had they signed the agreement and then wrote stories which violated the provisions of the voluntary bench-bar-press guidelines (*Federated Publications* v. *Swedberg,* 1981). The United States Supreme Court refused to review the ruling.

The five-to-four decision threw the Washington bench-bar-press committee into a tizzy. All the state press associations represented on the committee (weeklies, dailies, broadcasters, etc.) formally withdrew their support from the guidelines. The impact of the Swedberg ruling was felt nationwide as the press in many states began to reevaluate their support of voluntary bench-bar-press agreements. The Arizona Newspaper Association pulled its support from the Arizona guidelines. The association's bulletin probably reflected the feelings of journalists across America when it said that the Swedberg decision "has left many newspaper groups in the country with the feeling that they created a 'monster' when the papers agreed to the 'voluntary' guidelines." There must be much healing of the open sores that now exist upon the relationship between the courts and the press before bench-bar-press guidelines can be as effective as they once were in many states. Even in the state of Washington, where a new version of the bench-bar-press principles that stresses the voluntary nature of the relationship has been adopted, there is still considerable suspicion between the bench and the press.

Summary   In some states the press, attorneys, and judges have agreed to try to solve the problems surrounding the free press–fair trial controversy through voluntary bench-bar-press agreements. Such agreements usually contain suggestions to all parties on what information should and should not be publicized about criminal cases. When the guidelines work, there is usually a cooperative, rather than a combative, spirit among the members of the press, the judiciary, and the bar. These guidelines often reduce or eliminate the need for restrictive orders or closed hearings. But a ruling by the Washington State Supreme Court which upheld a trial judge's order requiring reporters to agree to follow the voluntary bench-bar-press guidelines in order to attend a pretrial hearing has seriously undercut the effectiveness of these voluntary agreements. Press groups consider such a requirement a prior restraint, and are withdrawing their support from the voluntary agreements in some states.

CAMERAS IN THE COURTROOM

Journalists in but a handful of states were prohibited from bringing cameras and tape recorders into courtrooms in the mid-1960s. Today such news gathering equipment is permitted in the state courts in nearly thirty-five states. And the Supreme Court of the United States has ruled that the use of recorders and cameras by journalists during a trial does not by itself deprive the defendant of the constitutionally guaranteed right to a fair trail (*Chandler* v. *Florida,* 1981).

This swift reversal of the rules regarding the use of cameras in the courtroom climaxed a forty-year struggle by the press for relaxation of prohibitions which were instituted in the 1930s. At that time the press had conducted itself in an outrageous fashion in covering the trial of Bruno Hauptmann, who was charged with kidnapping the baby of Charles and Anne Lindberg. The trial judge, who had great difficulty in controlling the press, ordered that no pictures be taken during the court sessions. But photographers equipped with large, bulky, flash-equipped cameras moved freely about the courtroom, ignoring the judge's orders and taking pictures almost at will. As a result of this travesty, the American Bar Association adopted rules prohibiting the use of cameras and other electronic equipment in courtrooms. The rules, known as Canon 35, were adopted in most states and were followed in practice in those states that did not adopt the rules (see Frank M. White, "Cameras in the Courtroom: A U.S. Survey").

After World War II when the photographic equipment became smaller and less obtrusive and faster film permitted photography indoors without flash equipment, the press began to agitate for changes in the rules. The television industry especially chafed under the proscriptions (the ABA rules had been amended in 1952 to include television), as they put broadcast reporters who depended upon film to tell a story at a distinct disadvantage in the competition with wordsmiths of the printed press. In the mid-1960s the United States Supreme Court had a chance to consider the constitutionality of the ban on cameras in the courtroom in a case which began in Texas, one of a handful of states that occasionally allowed photography and recording in the courtroom.

The defendant was Billie Sol Estes who was accused of a salad oil swindle. The story was important in the Lone Star State, television was therefore permitted at the initial pretrial hearing, and still photographers were permitted throughout the trial. But the disruption of the trial was considerable. Twelve cameramen crowded into the tiny courtroom, cables and wires snaked across the floor, microphones were everywhere, and the distraction caused by this media invasion was significant. The situation improved during the trial when television and recording equipment was housed in a booth at the back of the courtroom. Estes appealed his conviction to the United States Supreme Court on the grounds that he had been denied a fair trial because of the presence of the cameras and recorders. The court agreed with the salad oil magnate. "While maximum freedom must be allowed the press in carrying out this important function [informing the public] in a democratic society, its exercise must necessarily be subject to the maintenance of absolute fairness in the judicial process," wrote Justice Tom Clark for the majority (*Estes* v. *Texas,* 1965). The photography and broadcasting equipment simply created too many impediments to a fair trial.

However, experimentation with cameras in the courtroom continued. Telecasting equipment improved. Journalists demonstrated to judges that they could act responsibly if they were permitted access to courtrooms with their cameras and recorders. More and more states began to permit telecasts and broadcasts of criminal and civil trials, as well as of the oral arguments at appellate hearings. In the early eighties two former Miami police officers challenged the new rules in Florida that permitted cameras in the courtroom. They argued that television coverage of their trial in and of itself had deprived them of a fair trial. The Florida Supreme Court rejected their contention, and the United States Supreme Court agreed to hear the case. In a unanimous decision the high Court ruled that the mere presence of cameras in the courtroom or simply televising or broadcasting portions of a trial does not in and of itself cause prejudice to the defendant or interfere with the right to a fair trial. Chief Justice Burger wrote that at present "no one has been able to present empirical data sufficient to establish that the mere presence of the broadcast media inherently has an adverse effect on that [trial] process." It is true the presence of such equipment in the courtroom or the broadcast of a trial could endanger the defendant's right to a fair trial. But, Burger said, "an absolute constitutional ban on broadcast coverage of trials cannot be justified simply because there is a danger that, in some cases, prejudicial broadcast accounts of pretrial and trial events may impair the ability of jurors to decide the issue of guilt or innocence uninfluenced by extraneous matter." The Chief Justice said that in order to block the use of cameras and recorders at a trial a defendant is going to have to demonstrate to the court how the trial will be adversely affected by the presence of this equipment. To overturn a conviction at a trial that has been televised, the defendant will need to show that the recording and photography equipment actually made a substantial difference in some material aspect of the trial. Proof that the jurors were aware of the cameras or that the presence of television cameras "told" jurors this was a big trial will not be sufficient to demonsrate prejudice, Burger wrote (*Chandler* v. *Florida,* 1981).

State courts have started to develop standards to assess complaints of prejudice from defendants who do not want their trials televised. In Florida, for example, the state supreme court has ruled that the trial court must hold an evidentiary hearing if a defendant or other participant in the trial protests the television coverage. There must be a finding that electronic coverage of the trial would have important "qualitatively different effect" on the trial than would other types of coverage before the cameras and recorders may be excluded (*Florida* v. *Palm Beach Newspapers,* 1981). Another Florida case demonstrates how such a difference might be shown. The defendant in the case had previously been found incompetent to stand trial. Treatment subsequently rendered her competent to proceed with the case. Her attorneys, armed with testimony from psychiatrists, asserted that television cameras in the courtroom would adversely affect the defendant's ability to communicate with her counsel and she might lapse into psychosis. The Florida Supreme Court ruled that this kind of evidence satisfied the standard for excluding television cameras (*Florida* v. *Green,* 1981).

Cameras are not allowed in federal courtrooms, and federal judges have resisted all efforts to televise court hearings, even when the defendant sought to have cameras in the courtroom (see *U.S.* v. *Hastings,* 1983). The *Chandler* case stands for the principle that if the state decides to let cameras into the courtroom their presence does not violate the constitutional guarantee of a fair trial. But nothing in the Court's opinion in *Chandler* suggests that states or the federal courts *must* permit cameras in the courtroom (see *Combined Communications* v. *Finesilver,* 1982).

State rules on the use of cameras in the courtroom are generally flexible. They often permit the trial judge final authority in determining whether cameras can come into a courtroom. In some states if a witness or other participant objects to being photographed or recorded, the press must honor these wishes and exclude these persons from its coverage. Most states have adopted guidelines which establish the number of still and motion picture cameras permitted in the courtroom at any one time. Rules often specify where the cameras may be placed, require that all pictures be taken with available light, and even set standards of dress for photographers and technicians. The press must often be willing to share the fruits of the photography through pooling agreements, since most states have guidelines limiting movement and placement of cameras to only when the court is in recess.

How have the rules worked? Seemingly quite well. After the rules in Washington had been in effect for two years, a King County Superior Court judge surveyed trial judges in the state and found them overwhelmingly satisfied with the performance of the press and the success of the new rules. Experience in other states has been similar.

Summary

Until recently cameras and recorders were banned from courtrooms in nearly all states. But today such equipment may be used during a trial in nearly two-thirds of the states. The Supreme Court has ruled that the mere presence of cameras or recorders in the courtroom does not prejudice the defendant's right to a fair trial (*Chandler* v. *Florida*). To block the use of the cameras or to seek the reversal of a conviction at a trial which has been televised or recorded, a defendant will have to offer specific proof that the use of the electronic news-gathering equipment will or did interfere with the right to a fair trial.

A good deal of space has been devoted to the free press–fair trial problem because it is an important problem and because it continues to be a problem. Within both the press and the law sharp divisions regarding solution of the problem remain. Many years ago during a battle over a free press–fair trial issue in one Southern state, the national office of the American Civil Liberties Union filed an amicus curiae (friend of the court) brief supporting a free and unfettered press, while the state chapter of the same civil liberties group filed a brief in favor of the court's position supporting a fair trial.

Most journalists probably agree that we need more, not less, reporting on the justice system in the United States. In *Crime and Publicity* Alfred Friendly and Ronald Goldfarb write:

> To shackle the press is to curtail the public watch over the administration of criminal justice. . . . The press serves at the gate house of justice. Additionally, it serves in the manorhouse itself, and all along the complicated route to it from the police station and the streets, to the purlieus of the prosecutor's office, to the courtroom corridors where the pressures mount and the deals are made.

The two authors also point out that we do not want a press that is free, more or less, just as we should not tolerate trials that are almost fair. "And to complicate the issue," they note, "it is evident that a free press is one of society's principal guarantors of fair trials, while fair trials provide a major assurance of the press's freedom."

Reporters dealing with the courts and the court system must be extremely sensitive to these issues. They should not be blinded as they clamor for news to the sensitive mechanisms which operate in the courts to provide justice and fairness. At the same time they should not let the authoritarian aspects of the judicial system block their effort to provide the information essential to the functioning of the democracy.

BIBLIOGRAPHY

Here is a list of some of the sources that have been helpful in the preparation of chapter 7.

Books

Advisory Committee on Fair Trial and Free Press. *Approved Draft Standards Relating to Fair Trial and Free Press.* New York: American Bar Association, 1968.

Barron, Jerome, and Dienes, C. Thomas. *Handbook of Free Speech and Free Press.* Boston: Little, Brown & Co., 1979.

Buddenbaum, Judith M., et al. *Pretrial Publicity and Juries: A Review of Research.* Research Report No. 11, School of Journalism, Indiana University, 1981.

Bush, Chilton R., ed. *Free Press and Fair Trial: Some Dimensions of the Problem.* Athens: University of Georgia Press, 1971.

Friendly, Alfred, and Goldfarb, Ronald. *Crime and Publicity.* New York: Random House, Vintage Books, 1968.

Gillmor, Donald M. *Judicial Restraints on the Press.* Columbia: Freedom of Information Center, University of Missouri, 1974.

Judicial Administration Division. *Courts and Community.* Salt Lake City: American Bar Association, 1973.

Pember, Don R. *Pre-Trial Publicity in Criminal Proceedings: A Case Study.* Unpublished Master's Thesis, Michigan State University, 1966.

White, Frank W. *Cameras in the Courtroom: A U.S. Survey.* 60 *Journalism Monographs,* 1979.

Articles

Gerald, J. Edward. "Press-Bar Relationships: Progress Since Sheppard and Reardon." 47 *Journalism Quarterly* 223, 1970.

Kline, Gerald, and Jess, Paul. "Prejudicial Publicity: Its Effect on Law School Mock Juries." 43 *Journalism Quarterly* 113, 1966.

Landau, Jack C. "The Challenge of the Communications Media." 62 *American Bar Association Journal* 55, January, 1976.

Riley, Sam. "Pre-Trial Publicity: A Field Study." 50 *Journalism Quarterly* 17, 1973.

Simon, Rita. "Murders, Juries and the Press." May-June *Transaction* 40, 1966.

Trager, Robert, and Stonecipher, Harry W. "Gag Orders: An Unresolved Dilemma." 55 *Journalism Quarterly* 231, 1978.

Warren, Robert S., and Abell, Jeffrey M. "Free Press–Fair Trial, the Gag Order: A California Aberration." 45 *Southern California Law Review* 51, 1972.

Cases

in re *Application of NBC*, 653 F.2d 609 (1981).
Branzburg, v. Hayes, 408 U.S. 655 (1972).
Chandler v. Florida, 101 S.Ct. 802 (1981).
Combined Communications v. Finesilver, 8 M.L. Rept. 1233 (1982).
Estes v. Texas, 381 U.S. 532 (1965).
Federated Publications v. Kurtz, 94 Wn.2d 51 (1980).
Federated Publications v. Swedberg, 96 Wn.2d 13 (1981).
Florida v. Green, 7 M.L. Rept. 1025 (1981).
Florida v. Palm Beach Newspapers, 7 M.L. Rept. 1021 (1981).
Gannett v. DePasquale, 99 S.Ct. 2898 (1979).
Globe Newspapers v. Superior Court, 102 S.Ct. 2613 (1982).
Irvin v. Dowd, 366 U.S. 717 (1961).
in re *J.S.*, 438 A.2d 1125 (1981).
Kansas City Star v. Fossey, 630 P.2d 1176 (1981).
Landmark Communication v. Virginia, 435 U.S. 829 (1978).
Leviton v. U.S., 193 F.2d 848 (1951).
Marshall v. U.S., 360 U.S. 310 (1959).
Miami Herald v. Lewis, 8 M.L. Rept. 2281 (1982).
Murphy v. Florida, 95 S.Ct. 2031 (1975).
Nebraska Press Association v. Stuart, 96 S.Ct. 2791 (1976).
Page Corp. v. Lumpkin, 8 M.L. Rept. 1824 (1982).
Pennekamp v. Florida, 328 U.S. 331 (1946).
Richmond Newspapers, v. Virginia, 448 U.S. 555 (1980).
Shepherd v. Florida, 341 U.S. 50 (1951).
Sheppard v. Maxwell, 384 U.S. 333 (1966).
Sherman Publishing v. Goldberg, 443 N.E.2d 1252 (1982).
Smith v. Daily Mail Publishing Company, 99 S.Ct. 2667 (1979).
U.S. v. Brooklier, 685 F.2d 1162 (1982).
U.S. v. Burr, 24 Fed. Cas. 49 No. 14692g (1807).
U.S. v. Criden, 675 F.2d 550 (1982).
U.S. v. Hastings, 695 F.2d 1278 (1983).

8 OBSCENITY

The contemporary journalist rarely takes on a censor over a question of obscenity. Erotic material is just not a large part of the mainstream mass media in the United States today. About the sexiest things in most newspapers are the movie advertisements, and such display advertisements are frequently liberally doctored by newspaper artists who are adept at painting clothing on naked females and by rewrite men who clumsily revise film titles to excise naughty words or double entendres. At some newspapers, however, even these ads are disappearing. The *Seattle Times* is one of many newspapers which refuse to publish advertisements for X-rated films, and the *New York Times* is one of several newspapers which limit the size, content, and format of advertisements for such motion pictures. Occasionally, however, a journalist, usually a loner, the publisher of an underground newspaper or a counterculture magazine, runs afoul of obscenity laws. Sometimes in such cases "professional journalists" have little sympathy for the plight of their "less respectable" colleagues: "After all, if he hadn't published that junk in the first place, he wouldn't be in trouble. And what does that have to do with news anyway." To those journalists and to other persons who think that journalists shouldn't be worried about obscenity convictions, the words uttered by Judge Cuthbert Pound sixty years ago are appropriate, "Although the defendant may be the worst of men . . . the rights of the best men are secure only as the rights of the vilest and most abhorrent are protected" (*People* v. *Gitlow,* 1921).

Perhaps more salient is Harry Clor's question concerning obscenity and pornography in *Obscenity and Public Morality.* "Why," Clor asks, "in an age which is not lacking in life-and-death issues must we continue to wrestle with this one?" The author goes on to answer his own question by arguing that vital issues lurk beneath the surface of this seemingly nonsensical dilemma. And, he noted, the problem of obscenity "manifests a strange capacity to arouse the interest, engage the passions, and enlist the efforts of large numbers of Americans." How right Clor is, for even today in the so-called age of reason it is very difficult to engage in a discussion of obscenity and pornography without the conversation quickly descending to a level of emotionalism and witless jabber.

The problem of obscenity is truly interesting, at least for a while. We do not intend to present an exhaustive report on the subject in these few pages. Instead, a brief introduction to the issue is provided, the history of the law of obscenity in the United States is highlighted, and the ways in which the Supreme Court has defined obscenity are discussed. Then we will consider how the law operates in real life at the local level and briefly note some aspects of both postal censorship and film censorship.

The broadcast of obscene or indecent speech over radio and television is a separate problem and is outlined in chapter 11 on broadcast regulation (pages 524–29).

There is great disagreement about what is and what is not obscene. Some people who paper their walls with photographs of nude couples in various states of recline might consider war and violence obscene. To a man who thinks that shooting at kids who try to steal melons from his patch is big sport and who likes his killing in slow motion at the drive-in movie, any nudity at all is degenerate. While the university student might think the profits made by oil companies are "obscene," a stockholder in an oil company might think it obscene for a student to live in a commune with six other men and women. And so it goes.

Definitions for obscenity can be found in many places. In reputable dictionaries among the meanings for the word *obscene* is "indecent, lewd, or licentious." In turn, we will find *licentious* to mean "lewd or lascivious." Further research shows that *lascivious* means "inclined to be lewd or lustful." *Lustful* proves to mean "having lewd desires." Finally, *lewd* turns out to mean "indecent or obscene." We have come full circle.

The courts themselves have been in a constant state of confusion over the matter of obscenity. In 1948 the Ohio Court of Common Pleas wrote (*State* v. *Lerner*):

> Obscenity is not a legal term. It cannot be defined so that it will mean the same to all people, all the time everywhere. Obscenity is very much a figment of the imagination—an indefinable something in the minds of some and not in the minds of others, and it is not the same in the minds of the people of every clime and country, nor the same today that it was yesterday and will be tomorrow.

Former justice of the United States Supreme Court John Marshall Harlan expressed a similar kind of frustration when he warned, "Anyone who undertakes to examine the Supreme Court's decisions since *Roth* which have held particular material obscene or not obscene would find himself in utter bewilderment" (*Ginsberg* v. *New York,* 1968). Harlan referred at least partially to the fact that between the *Roth* case in 1957 and 1968 when he wrote that comment the high Court had published signed opinions in thirteen obscenity cases. Fifty-four separate opinions were published in those thirteen cases!

Social scientists have also entered the definitional fray. Probably the most well-known definition of pornography is that of Eberhard and Phyllis Kronhausen in their study *Pornography and the Law.* The researchers said that the main purpose of pornography is to stimulate an erotic response. They also listed several characteristics of pornography, among which were heavy emphasis on the physiological reponses of participants, heavy emphasis on aberrant or forbidden forms of sexuality, heavy sadism and passive submission, and unrealistic presentation of both sexual activities and sexual capacities. Anthropologist Margaret Mead defined pornography as "words or acts or representations that are calculated to stimulate sex feelings independent of the presence of another loved and chosen human being." But even these kinds of definitions contain little precision and little agreement. Sexual aberrations which stimulate some persons nauseate others. The clothed body is far more erotic to some people than is naked flesh.

The general governmental response to obscenity and pornography (whatever these words mean, they are used interchangeably in this chapter) has been to pass laws against it. There are federal laws, state laws, city laws, county laws, township laws, and so forth. There are laws against importing obscenity, transporting it in interstate commerce, mailing it, or broadcasting it over the radio and television. There are laws against publishing it, distributing it, selling it, displaying it, circulating it, and even possessing it if you plan to distribute it, sell it, display it, or circulate it.

The fact that obscenity is such an elusive concept to define makes prosecution extremely difficult sometimes. An obscenity case is not like a bank robbery or like most other crime for that matter, where everyone agrees that a criminal act has occurred (e.g., a bank robbery), and the legal debate is about whether the defendant is the robber. In an obscenity case there is usually agreement that the defendant did commit the act (e.g., sold a book or showed a movie). The debate is over whether what the defendant did was a criminal act, whether the book was obscene or not.

The ambiguities in the law also make life less than certain for booksellers and theater operators. They really can never be certain whether a local jury will rule that the books in the morning mail are obscene and whether selling a copy of such books is a criminal act.

Professor Paul Freund neatly summarized many of the problems of obscenity in a speech before the Twenty-Ninth Annual Judicial Conference in 1966 (Federal Rules Decisions, 1966):

> The problem is rendered difficult, I think, because we are working with old statutes, based on outmoded, or at least unexamined assumptions, with poorly defined conceptions of the subject matter, directed at the protection of persons who don't want to be protected, without a very clear idea of why they need protection and from what.

Why is obscenity banned? For many persons this is the sixty-four-dollar question. Many police believe that pornography is somehow tied to sexual crimes, although there is very little evidence to support the notion. Many persons argue, as we will note later in this chapter, that dissemination of pornography and obscenity has a deleterious impact upon communities. This argument also has really little scientific evidence to support it. At the same time there is little evidence to support the argument of persons who oppose obscenity laws that distribution of the material has no impact at all. Probably the best reason to explain why obscenity is banned is that it has been banned for more than one hundred years, and once a good suppression is started, it is hard to stop. Once an obscenity law goes on the books, it usually stays there, often virtually unenforced. Nevertheless, legislators rarely vote for repeal of an obscenity law. To many constituents a vote for repeal is a vote for obscenity. That could be a heavy cross to bear during an election.

EARLY OBSCENITY LAW

The Puritans were not the first to pass laws against obscene books and pictures. There is some confusion about obscenity laws during the colonial period, because many persons argue that pre-Revolutionary laws against blasphemy also prohibited obscenity. However, the best evidence available does not support this argument.

Some of the other facts we know, or do not know, about pornography in the eighteenth and early nineteenth centuries are these.

Substantial amounts of pornography were in circulation at that time, some of it homegrown, much of it imported. As busy as he was, Benjamin Franklin still had time to write erotic literature.

We do not know whether the drafters of the Bill of Rights intended to include obscenity within the mantle of protection offered by the First Amendment. Various justices of the Supreme Court, including Justice Brennan in his opinion in 1957 in the famous case of *Roth* v. *U.S.,* have argued that the framers of the First Amendment never meant to protect obscene materials through the guarantees of free speech and press. But such assertions are made without evidence and should be accorded little historical merit. Court records are devoid of evidence of obscenity prosecutions until 1815 when a man named Jesse Sharpless was fined for exhibiting a picture of a man "in an imprudent posture with a woman." Earlier, other persons were tried for offenses tied to obscenity, but they were tried under the common law for theological crimes against God, not for merely displaying erotic pictures. In 1821 Peter Holmes was convicted for publishing an edition of John Cleland's *Memoirs of a Woman of Pleasure,* better known to us as *Fanny Hill.* Although the book was first published in 1740, the prosecution in Massachusetts was based not on the original version, but on an edition in which Holmes added both more explicit text and pictures.

In the late 1820s and 1830s the nation experienced the first strong attack on obscenity when several states passed laws limiting the distribution and sale of such material. Why should obscenity laws be passed at that particular period in our history? No one knows for certain, but numerous contemporary events and conditions may have been factors. This was a period of popular reform movements such as abolition, prohibition, and women's rights. It was also a time in which universal free education made great strides and more people were able to read, thereby increasing the market for erotic literature. The changes in printing technology which made publishing of books and magazines less expensive could also have resulted in wider distribution and visibility of erotic material. The more visible and widespread such material became, the better target it also became for reformers. Laws were the result.

The first of dozens of federal laws was passed in 1842. It was a customs law and prohibited importation of obscene paintings, lithographs, engravings, and so forth. The law was amended many times to prohibit more and more kinds of materials. The first postal law was passed in 1865, but it was an ineffective measure, because the government had no authority to exclude material from the mails, only to bring a prosecution after the shipment was delivered. In 1873 a more effective law was adopted. This was largely the handiwork of Anthony Comstock, whom some authorities have described as a zealous reformer who got a thrill from suppressing what other people liked. First it was liquor that Comstock sought to snuff out. Then he attacked prostitution. To him there was no such thing as erotic art, only pornography. With the help of the Protestant leaders in New York and the Young Men's Christian Association, Comstock succeeded in gaining passage, first, of a New York law against obscenity and, then, in 1873 of a federal law, the so-called Comstock Law. After passage of the bill Comstock was named a special agent for the Post Office Department, and he worked with his Committee for the Suppression of Vice for more than forty years to stamp out smut. As a kind of incentive the government gave Comstock a percentage of all the fines collected on successful prosecutions based on his work. It has been suggested that he may be the first man to have made a million dollars from pornography.

The 1873 law was simple: All obscene books, pamphlets, pictures, and so forth, were declared to be nonmailable. Violation of the law could result in a fine of $5,000 and five years in jail for the first offense and $10,000 and ten years for each offense thereafter. The Congress did not define obscenity, however, but left that to the courts.

After passage of this spate of laws in the late nineteenth century, the country underwent a terrible seventy-year period of censorship of erotic material. The censors tended to lump all erotic work into one huge pile of prohibited material. They made no attempt to distinguish art from smut— Boccacio's *Decameron* from *The Dance with the Dominant Whip* or other junk literature. The Post Office Department banned books on sex education as well as medical journals which dealt with sexual problems. The *American Journal of Eugenics* (the study of hereditary improvement) was declared nonmailable at one point because it carried an advertisement for a book entitled *The History of Prostitution*. The *Journal* was not obscene, but the book advertised in its pages was considered offensive. The *Journal* therefore was not allowed to be sent through the mails.

In the 1930s the Post Office Department banned, among other books, John O'Hara's *Appointment in Samara,* Hemingway's *For Whom the Bell Tolls,* and nearly everything that Erskine Caldwell wrote. In the forties the list included *From Here to Eternity, Butterfield Eight,* and *Memoirs of Hecate County.* Lots of girlie magazines, humor magazines, scandal magazines (e.g., *Confidential*), and even a skin diver's manual (because it contained pictures of several female divers with breasts exposed) were barred from the mails, and the publishers were often prosecuted.

The postal service used various devices in addition to prosecution as means of controlling pornography. It attempted to strip some publications of their second-class mailing subsidy because they failed to publish work that was for the public good. Obscenity was not for the public good, postal officials claimed. This ploy failed after a time (see *Hannegan* v. *Esquire,* 1946). The Post Office Department also used the mail block against publishers whose magazines contained solicitations for erotic materials. For example, if a magazine advertised that a reader could order an erotic book by sending $2 to the publisher, the postal service stopped delivering mail to the publisher in order to deprive him of those book orders. He received no mail at all! Not his electric bill, not his bank statement, nothing. The courts declared this action illegal, but the post office continued the practice for several years (*Walker* v. *Popenoe,* 1945). According to Patricia Robertus in her study of the Post Office Department ("Postal Control of Obscene Literature 1942–1957"), postal regulations were so restrictive that in the early 1940s a magazine with the power of *Esquire* took advance copies of both stories and layouts to postal authorities to see whether they met postal standards of mailability. In some instances postal officials asked for changes and got them. This is informal prior censorship at its boldest.

Laws against importation were also prosecuted vigorously, and customs agents, until the 1930s at least, rarely discriminated between works that were art and works that were trash. Consequently, there are scores of horror stories of customs officials destroying art works, art catalogs, religious works, and other materials which they believed to be obscene.

This can only be described as an awful period in the cultural history of the United States. Closely parallel is the struggle for freedom of the press that radicals and labor leaders endured (recounted earlier in this book), with one exception: whereas the courts grew more tolerant of aberrant political and economic philosophy, they showed little tolerance for erotic materials. Except for striking down some of the Post Office Department's most outrageous censorship techniques, the Supreme Court stayed out of the fray, leaving the lower courts to work out the definition of obscenity and construct constitutional guidelines. That is, the Supreme Court stayed out until 1957 when it entered the controversy wholeheartedly (*Roth* v. *U.S.*) and has been there ever since, attempting to explain to judges, lawyers, censors, writers, artists, filmmakers, and other people what the term *obscenity* means when used by the Court. As you will no doubt conclude after reading the next section, the efforts of the Court in this endeavor have not been terribly effective.

Since 1957 when the United States Supreme Court ruled in *Roth* v. *United States* (pages 381–82) that obscenity falls outside the general protection granted to speech and press under the First Amendment, courts have been forced to attempt to define what is and what is not obscene. The ultimate responsibility has fallen to the Supreme Court as the final arbiter of the meaning of the Constitution. In the twenty years between 1957 and 1977 the high Court heard arguments in almost ninety obscenity cases and wrote opinions in nearly forty of the cases. The remainder of the cases were decided by **per curiam** rulings (this term is explained on page 25). Yet most observers agree that the Court has failed in the task of defining obscenity in a comprehensive and unambiguous fashion.

The Supreme Court borrowed and devised various tests in the past century in its frequent attempts to describe obscenity definitively. None of the tests have been satisfactory, but some were worse than others. The fatal defect in each test is that it is made up of words, words which have different meanings for different people. For example, the test in use today declares that if a work has serious literary value it is not obscene. What does "serious literary value" mean? A comic book may have serious literary value for some people. At the other end of the spectrum, even professors of literature haggle among themselves about whether some of the classics really have serious literary value. What we are faced with, therefore, is a dispute over not only the kinds of works which are obscene, but also the meaning of the words which the courts use to define obscenity.

Three important legal tests of obscenity were developed during the past one hundred years or so. The *Hicklin* rule of the late nineteenth century was used by judges to define obscenity for more than seventy-five years. This rule was abandoned in the late fifties and sixties in favor of what was called the *Roth-Memoirs* test. Then in the early seventies the United States Supreme Court fashioned still another test, the *Miller-Hamling* test, which supplanted the *Roth-Memoirs* definition of obscenity. We will examine the *Hicklin* rule and the *Roth-Memoirs* test to help explain the *Miller-Hamling* test, which is currently the law in the United States. We will also look at some other obscenity problems faced by the Supreme Court as well as at a report issued by the Presidential Commission on Obscenity and Pornography.

The *Hicklin* Rule

The first widely used American test of obscenity was the *Hicklin* rule. The United States Supreme Court borrowed the *Hicklin* rule from British law when it was called upon to undertake an early interpretation of the 1873 postal statute on obscenity. Benjamin Hicklin was the recorder of London who presided over an obscenity trial in that city in the 1860s. He ruled that the pamphlet in question was not obscene, but on appeal by the government, a higher court reversed the decision. Lord Chief Justice Alexander Cockburn handed down a ruling which included a definition of obscenity, a definition to which poor Benjamin Hicklin's name has been attached ever since (*Regina* v. *Hicklin,* 1868).

The *Hicklin* rule says that a work is obscene if it has a tendency to deprave and corrupt those whose minds are open to such immoral influences and into whose hands it might happen to fall.

Look at the elements of this test for a moment. First, a work is obscene if it has a tendency to deprave and corrupt. It does not have to deprave and corrupt, but only a tendency to deprave and corrupt is required; that is, it might deprave and corrupt. You can decide for yourself what *deprave* and *corrupt* mean. The second aspect of the test was even deadlier for authors and painters. Whom must the work have a tendency to deprave and corrupt? Those whose minds are open to such influences, in other words, anyone who runs across the book or drawing. Children's minds are obviously open to depravation and corruption from obscenity. Children might also run across such works in a library or at a bookstore. Therefore, the *Hicklin* rule comes down to this: If a book might have an impact upon a child or an extremely sensitive person, it is obscene and no one can read it. The *Hicklin* rule reduced the population of the nation to reading what was fit only for children.

In adopting the *Hicklin* rule American courts also decided that if any part of a book or play or magazine or whatever was obscene the entire work was then obscene. Selected passages which might be harmful to children could result in an entire book or magazine being banned. While the tests that the Supreme Court developed in the past twenty-five years cannot be called extremely liberal, compared to the *Hicklin* rule they provide virtually absolute freedom. The *Hicklin* rule was an extremely onerous test which was used for about seventy-five years. This test was what made prosecution of obscenity so easy in the twenties, thirties, and forties, and success in prosecution made government censors even more aggressive in rooting out "filth" and "smut."

In 1957 the Supreme Court wrote the obituary for the *Hicklin* rule when it declared that condemning the adult population to read only what children might safely read was unconstitutional (*Butler* v. *Michigan,* 1957). Various lower courts had tentatively reached this conclusion in the preceding fifty years, but the *Hicklin* rule remained law in most jurisdictions.

Summary

Prosecutions for obscenity did not occur in this nation until the early nineteenth century. In the 1820s and 1830s many states adopted their first obscenity laws. The first federal law was passed in 1842. The government actively prosecuted obscenity in the wake of the Civil War, and in 1873 the Congress adopted a strict new obscenity law. Obscenity was defined by the Supreme Court as being anything which has a tendency to deprave and corrupt those whose minds might be open to such immoral influences and into whose hands it might happen to fall. This was called the *Hicklin rule*. The rule meant that if any part of a book or other work had the tendency to deprave or corrupt any person (such as a child or overly sensitive individual) who might happen to see the work the material was obscene and no person could buy it or see it.

ROTH-MEMOIRS TEST

The 1957 decision in *Butler* was the first of a long series of high Court rulings which by 1966 had fashioned a new test for determining obscenity. Although it was not apparent in the beginning, the key cases, *Roth* v. *U.S.* in 1957 and *A Book Named John Cleland's Memoirs of a Woman of Pleasure* v. *Massachusetts* in 1966 (and a dozen or so lesser decisions in between), resulted in liberalizing the law with regard to obscenity (see, for example, *Manuel Enterprises* v. *Day,* 1962 and *Jacobellis* v. *Ohio,* 1964).

In 1957 the high Court announced definitively that obscenity is not protected by the First Amendment. Justice William Brennan, who was to be the chief architect of the high Court's new obscenity standards during the next nine years, wrote that while all ideas which have even the slightest redeeming social importance are entitled to the full protection of the First Amendment, obscenity and pornography were not included within this protection. In the *Roth* decision Brennan wrote, ". . . implicit in the history of the First Amendment is the rejection of obscenity as utterly without redeeming social importance."

By placing obscenity beyond the pale of First Amendment protection, the Court silenced those persons who believed the clear and present danger test should be used for determining obscenity as well as for determining dangerous political speech. Since obscenity is not guaranteed the protection of freedom of the press, the clear and present danger test does not apply. What is obscene then? In the *Roth* case Brennan said that a work is obscene if, to the average person, applying contemporary community standards, the dominant theme of the material taken as a whole appeals to prurient interest. The Court continued to reshape this test slightly until 1966 when in the *Memoirs* case the test evolved into the three-part definition which was used for nearly seven years. Under the *Roth-Memoirs* test, before a court can rule that a work is obscene, three requirements must be met.

First, the dominant theme of the material taken as a whole must appeal to prurient interest in sex. Implicit in this part of the test is the concept that the prurient (erotic) appeal of a book or film is determined by its impact upon the average man or woman, not upon a child or an extremely sensitive person. Also, the dominant theme of the work, not just selected passages or a few pages, must have this prurient appeal.

Second, a court must find that the material is patently offensive because it affronts contemporary community standards relating to the description or representation of sexual matters. Something that is patently offensive is something that is clearly indecent, and while we are hesitant to use this term, some people have argued that *patently offensive* means hard-core pornography. By contemporary standards the Court meant current standards, but the Court did not define what it meant by community: Were the standards local, state, or national?

Third, before something can be found to be obscene it must be utterly without redeeming social value. That means to have no social value at all.

Two aspects of this test should be noted: First, all three of these elements had to be present before something was obscene. Something that was patently offensive and had a prurient appeal was still not legally obscene if it had redeeming social value. All three elements must coalesce. Second, it was not a balancing test. Social value was not weighed against prurient appeal. If there was any social value at all, the material was then not obscene. And this fact, probably more than any other, made prosecution of obscenity cases very difficult. Utterly without redeeming social value is a difficult standard to prove. Some appellate court judges believed that if even only one or two persons found some value in a book or movie it was not *utterly* without redeeming social value. Consequently, the typical tack taken by defense attorneys was to bring in expert witnesses—psychiatrists, English professors, art critics, and the like— to testify that the work had some value as sexual therapy or as an example of a certain type of literature or art.

As liberal as the *Roth-Memoirs* standard was, it was not liberal enough for some civil libertarians. Absolutists argued that because of the First Amendment the government had no business telling people what they could read or watch. The First Amendment prohibition which says there is to be no law abridging freedom of speech and press means no law. Judge Jerome Frank, who heard the *Roth* case in the court of appeals, argued that restrictions against obscenity were extremely dangerous (*U.S. v. Roth,* 1956):

> If the government possesses the power to censor publications which arouse sexual thoughts, regardless of whether those thoughts tend probably to transform themselves into anti-social behavior, why may not the government censor political and religious publications regardless of any causal relation to probably dangerous deeds?

Justice Brennan, who constructed the *Roth-Memoirs* test, dismissed such criticism. There is no social value to obscenity, he said, and therefore society loses little if it is banned.*

*Of interest is the fact that Brennan turned his back on his own ruling some sixteen years later in his dissent in *Miller* v. *California* (1973) and in the *Paris Theatre* (1973) case when the aging justice wrote:

> Our experience since *Roth* requires us not only to abandon the effort to pick out obscene materials on a case by case basis, but also to reconsider a fundamental postulate of *Roth*: that there exists a definable class of sexually oriented expression that may be totally suppressed by the Federal and State governments. Assuming that such a class of expression does in fact exist, I am forced to conclude that the concept of "obscenity" cannot be defined with sufficient specificity and clarity to provide fair notice to persons who create and distribute sexually oriented materials, to prevent substantial erosion of protected speech as a by-product of the attempt to suppress unprotected speech. . . .

Summary

In the 1950s and early 1960s the Supreme Court adopted a new definition or test for obscenity, the *Roth-Memoirs* test. The test had three main parts.

1. The dominant theme of the material, taken as a whole, appeals to an average person's prurient interest in sex. This modified the *Hicklin* rule in two ways.
   a. Material that was offensive to children or overly sensitive persons was no longer declared obscene for all.
   b. The entire work, not just a part of a book or film, must be considered when determining whether it is obscene.
2. The material is patently offensive because it affronts contemporary community standards relating to sexual matters. It was assumed that there was a single, national standard which was applicable to all parts of the country.
3. The material is utterly without redeeming social value. It has no value at all.

CONTEMPORARY OBSCENITY LAW

In 1967 the Commission on Obscenity and Pornography was established, at least in part, because of the judicial and scientific uncertainty regarding the effects of obscenity on persons who consume it. The commission, which was made up of social scientists, religious leaders, and government officials, spent two million dollars and two years studying what some observers called the "puzzle of pornography." At the end of the study a majority of the commission—twelve of the seventeen members—concluded that there is no evidence that viewing obscenity produces harmful effects and recommended that all laws restricting the consumption of such materials by consenting adults be repealed. Three members of the commission fielded a vigorous dissent and two others said they believed the evidence, but didn't think it was sufficient to warrant the repeal of all laws.

The study was roundly criticized by persons who disagreed with its conclusions—rightly so in some cases. There were no long-range studies on the effects of exposure to pornography, for example, and no in-depth clinical studies. In some of the surveys people were asked blatantly foolish questions. For example, one survey asked people if they had experienced a breakdown in morals or had gone "sex crazy" from viewing explicit sexual material. Who would say yes to those questions? Patients at mental hospitals were questioned regarding the influence of pornography on sex crimes they had committed.

The single survey which received the widest publicity was the one which discovered that 60 percent of the persons questioned believed that adults should be able to read and watch whatever they want. However, to another question in the same survey, 73 percent of the respondents said that sex scenes in movies that merely titillate should be censored. Moreover, in 1969 both the Harris and Gallup polls found that about 80 percent of the people wanted stiffer controls on obscenity and pornography.

Regardless of what the commission found or of the flaws in its research, its recommendations were never adopted. The Senate rejected the report out of hand, and Richard Nixon, who was president at that time, vowed that so long as he was in the White House there would be no relaxation of the national effort to control and eliminate smut from our national life. Nixon noted that despite the commission's scientific evidence to the contrary, "Centuries of civilization and ten minutes of common sense tell us otherwise." Adding a phrase that would come back to haunt him in a different context four years later, Nixon said, "American morality is not to be trifled with."

The *Miller* Test

In 1973 and 1974, in apparent agreement with the president, the Supreme Court handed down a series of rulings which reshaped the legal test for obscenity. The central case in this group of decisions was *Miller* v. *California* (1973), a suit which emanated from California. Marvin Miller was convicted of violating the California Penal Code for sending five unsolicited brochures to a restaurant in Newport Beach. The brochures, which advertised four erotic books and one film, contained pictures and drawings of men and women engaging in a variety of sexual activities. The recipient of the mailing complained to police, and Miller was prosecuted by state authorities.

In *Miller*, for the first time since 1957, a majority of the Supreme Court reached agreement on a definition of obscenity. Chief Justice Warren Burger and four other members of the high Court agreed that material is obscene if the following standards are met.

1. An average person, applying contemporary local community standards, finds that the work, taken as a whole, appeals to prurient interest.
2. The work depicts in a patently offensive way sexual conduct specifically defined by applicable state law.
3. The work in question lacks serious literary, artistic, political, or scientific value.

As in the *Roth-Memoirs* test, the implications and ambiguities in these three elements create the need for fuller explanation. As a result of the *Miller* ruling and subsequent obscenity decisions handed down by the Burger Court since 1973, some guidelines have emerged. Before the guidelines are examined in detail, it is instructive to look at the rationale presented by Chief Justice Burger for his movement away from the *Roth-Memoirs* test to more conservative standards.

Justification

As noted previously, until 1973 the high Court had justified regulation of obscenity by arguing that because such material lacks social value it is not intended to be protected by the First Amendment. But in the *Miller* and subsequent decisions Chief Justice Burger took a less neutral approach and asserted that not only did such material lack social value, but it was also harmful to society.

In *Paris Adult Theatre I* v. *Slaton* (1973), a ruling handed down at the same time the *Miller* decision was announced, the Chief Justice said that there is a clear justification for banning adults-only theaters, even if they do not intrude upon the privacy of others and even if patrons are properly warned of the kind of film they will see. The justification is, he said, "the interest of the public in the quality of life and the total community environment, the tone of commerce in the great city centers and, possibly, the public safety itself."

Ignoring the majority report from the President's Commission on Obscenity and Pornography, Burger noted that the minority report states that there is an arguable correlation between obscene material and crime. Even if there were no scientific evidence, the Chief Justice wrote, "We do not demand of legislatures 'scientifically certain criteria of legislation,' for unprovable assumptions underlie much lawful state regulation of commercial and business affairs." There need not be conclusive proof of a connection between antisocial behavior and obscene material for a state legislature to reasonably conclude that such a connection exists or might exist, Burger said.

The basic thrust of the Burger argument is a kind of quality-of-life argument which many thoughtful scholars have made for several years. In the *Paris Theatre* opinion Burger in fact quoted Professor Alexander Bickel, who represented the *New York Times* in the *Pentagon Papers* case. In 1971 in *The Public Interest* concerning justification for regulation of obscenity Bickel writes:

> It concerns the tone of the society, the mode, or to use terms that have perhaps greater currency, the style and quality of life, now and in the future. A man may be entitled to read an obscene book in his room, or expose himself indecently there. . . . We should protect his privacy. But if he demands a right to obtain the books and pictures he wants in the market, and to foregather in public places—discreet, if you will, but accessible to all—with others who share his tastes, then to grant him his right is to affect the world about the rest of us, and to impinge on other privacies. Even supposing that each of us can, if he wishes, effectively avert the eye and stop the ear (which in truth we cannot) what is commonly read and seen and heard and done intrudes upon us all, want it or not.

Perhaps the most literate spokesman for this point of view is Harry M. Clor in his book *Obscenity and Public Morality* (1969). The book came out at a time when the Warren Court was pushing the limits of permissibility farther and farther, and Clor was chided for even thinking about a change of direction by the Supreme Court. Now it appears that the Court has adopted his logic, if not his standards.

Clor argues that some kind of common ethos is needed in order to have a community and that the agencies which formerly provided this ethos—schools, churches, families—do not do it any longer. The law should set the example, he says. "It must be a task of modern government and law to support and promote the public morality upon which a good social life depends."

To enforce his argument Clor quotes Aristotle (in *Politics*):

> The education of a citizen in the spirit of his constitution does not consist in his doing the actions in which the partisans of oligarchy or the adherents of democracy delight. It consists in his doing the actions by which an oligarchy or a democracy will be enabled to survive.

Clor also cites Walter Berns (in *Freedom, Virtue, and the First Amendment*):

> Since the way of the community depends upon citizens of a certain character, it must be the business of the law to promote that character. Thus, the formation of the character is the principal duty of government.

Clor concludes his argument:

> It is generally understood that, whatever other purposes such laws may have, they are also designed to implement community ethical standards.

This is a thoughtful argument, and while many authorities may disagree, it seems to make some sense in the chaotic 1980s. There is another side to the coin, however, and perhaps Justice Brennan expresses it best in his dissent in the *Paris Theatre* (1973) ruling:

> I am now inclined to argue that the Constitution protects the right to receive information and ideas, and that this right to receive information and ideas, regardless of their social worth . . . is fundamental to our free society. . . . This right is closely tied . . . to the right to be free, except in very limited circumstances, from unwarranted governmental intrusions into one's privacy. . . . It is similarly related to the right of the individual, married or single, to be free from unwarranted governmental intrusion into matters so fundamentally affecting a person as the decision whether to bear or beget a child . . . and the right to exercise autonomous control over the development and expression of one's intellect, interests, tastes, and personality.

The Meaning of *Miller*   The three-part obscenity test laid down by Chief Justice Burger in the *Miller* case has proved to be as elusive and unsatisfying as previous tests devised by the judiciary. It is best understood when reduced to its essential elements.

Community Standards   The first element of the test concerns community standards: To an average person, applying contemporary local community standards, the work, taken as a whole, appeals to prurient interest. While this standard resembles the *Roth-Memoirs* test, the Supreme Court emphasized that local rather than national standards are to be applied, which represents a departure from the earlier rulings. The Supreme Court had previously been silent on this question. In 1964 in *Jacobellis* v. *Ohio,* Justice Brennan subscribed to the notion that the applicable community standard was a national one. Only one other justice joined Brennan in this opinion, but as the only word on the subject it led many observers to believe that the community standards applicable under the *Roth-Memoirs* test were national standards. The Chief Justice rejected this in *Miller,* arguing that it was silly to suggest that persons in a small town in Utah shared the same standards as persons living in Los Angeles.

The application of local standards has placed significant emphasis upon the trier of fact in the case. This can be the trial judge, but more often it is the jury. The Supreme Court expects the trier of fact to rely upon his own knowledge of the standards in the community to determine the applicable standards in an obscenity case. In 1974 in *Hamling* v. *United States* Justice Rehnquist wrote:

> This Court has emphasized on more than one occasion that a principal concern in requiring that a judgment be made on the basis of contemporary community standards is to assure that the material is judged neither on the basis of each juror's personal opinion nor by its effect on a particular sensitive or insensitive person or group.

The matter of instructing jurors in the question of determining community standards surfaced quickly as a problem. Jurors are not supposed to rely on their own subjective preference; the jury is not a distillation of the standards of the community. The jurors are supposed to apply standards that they believe to be the prevailing ones in the community, standards that can be more conservative or more liberal than their own. Justice Rehnquist noted in his *Hamling* opinion that the jury should not judge the material on the basis of how it might affect a particularly sensitive person. Yet there are sensitive persons in every community. Do not their tastes matter, too?

In California a trial judge in giving jurors instructions in an obscenity trial told them to consider the effect of the material upon members of the community as a whole including children and sensitive persons. In 1978 in *Pinkus* v. *U.S.* the Supreme Court ruled that the instructions to the jury had been faulty. In considering community standards, "Children are not to be included for these purposes as part of the 'community' . . . ," wrote Chief Justice Burger. However, instructing the jury to consider the impact of the material upon sensitive or insensitive persons is permissible, so long as these persons are looked at as a part of the entire community. Burger wrote:

> In the narrow and limited context of this case, the community includes all adults who comprise it, and a jury can consider them all in determining relevant community standards. The vice is in focusing upon the most susceptible or sensitive members when judging the obscenity of the materials, not in including them along with all others in the community.

In summary, then, the jury is most often the fact finder of community standards. The jurors are supposed to rely upon their knowledge of the standards of the adult members of the entire community to determine whether the material appeals to prurient interest or is patently offensive. The jurors are not supposed to apply their own standards. One commentator notes that this new approach, which places such heavy emphasis on the jury, assumes that jurors know the prevailing standards in the community as well as have the needed exposure to "all manner of descriptions or representations of sexual matters, whether spoken, written or performed." This assumption is largely untested.

Which community is meant? Chief Justice Burger ruled in *Miller* that local community standards must prevail. Does this mean state, county, city, or neighborhood? In many instances state standards are the ones which apply. In some instances state high courts have even ruled that cities and counties have no right to pass obscenity laws, since the states, through state statutes, have preempted the field of criminalizing obscenity (see *Spokane* v. *Portch,* 1979, for example). Yet for all practical purposes, since jurors are most normally drawn from county or city voting lists, and jurors are expected to rely upon their knowledge of community standards, local standards are applied in determining the obscenity of the material.

In 1977 the Supreme Court was forced to consider an unusual case from Iowa which focused upon the role of the state in determining community standards. Between 1974 and 1978 Iowa state law prohibited only the distribution of obscene materials to minors. During this period Jerry Lee Smith used the United States postal service to distribute within Iowa several erotic magazines to adult recipients. His distribution did not violate state law, but he was charged with violating federal obscenity laws which prohibit the mailing of obscene material. At his trial Smith argued that since the state did not prohibit the distribution of such material to adults, his mailings had not offended the prevailing community standards. The federal trial judge nevertheless instructed jurors to draw upon their knowledge of the views of the people in the community to determine community standards. As part of their determination jurors could consider the state law, but the absence of statutes prohibiting the distribution of obscene material among adults was not a controlling factor in determining community standards. The Supreme Court, by a five-to-four vote, supported this position. The jury's discretion to determine community standards was not circumscribed by state law or the absence of state law (*Smith* v. *U.S.,* 1977). Justice Blackmun wrote that it would be inappropriate for a state legislature to attempt to freeze a jury to one definition of contemporary community standards. The state legislature can define within a statute the kinds of conduct that will be regulated by the state. It can adopt a geographic limit in the determination of community standards by defining the area from which the jury can be selected in an obscenity case. But it must leave to the jury the question of community standards. Blackmun also pointed out that this was a federal case. "The community standards aspects of the federal law present issues of federal law upon which a state statute such as Iowa's cannot have a conclusive effect," he added (*Smith* v. *U.S.*, 1977).

The question of applicable community standards is also an important factor in cases which involve the shipment of erotic material over long distances and its importation from abroad. Consider these hypothetical situations. A woman in New York mails obscene materials to another woman in Nebraska. She is arrested and tried. At her trial, do the community standards of New York or the standards of Nebraska apply? Here is another case. A man in Florida orders erotic material from Sweden. The material enters this country in Boston and is seized, and the United States customs service calls for a determination of whether the material is obscene. What community standards should apply? Those of Boston or of Florida?

The answers to these questions are tentative, but case law suggests the following guidelines.

In cases involving violation of postal laws, the government may choose to try the case in the community in which the material was sent or received or in any district through which the material passed (see section on postal censorship, pages 403–5). Consequently, the applicable standards are the standards existing in the community in which the trial is held. In the hypothetical cases just given, if the government chose to prosecute the defendant in New York, the standards of that community would apply. If the government chose to prosecute in Nebraska, those community standards would apply. Recently a postmaster in Oregon asked a postmaster in Wyoming to use a false name and solicit by mail erotic material distributed by an Oregon man. The defendant sent the material to Wyoming, was arrested and tried, and Wyoming community standards were applied. The record showed that the defendant had never resided in, traveled through, or had any previous business contact in Wyoming—prior to the time he sent the erotic matter through the mails to the Wyoming postmaster. Still, the Tenth Circuit Court of Appeals concluded (*U.S.* v. *Blucher,* 1978):

> So long as *Hamling* is the law, publishers and distributors everywhere who are willing to fill subscriptions nationwide are subject to the creative zeal of federal enforcement officers who are free to shop for venue from which juries with the most restrictive views are likely to be impanelled. . . .

A similar decision was reached in *U.S.* v. *McManus* (1976).

In cases involving import laws and customs regulations, the community standards of the district in which the material was seized—not of the district in which the addressee lives—are normally the applicable standards. In the hypothetical case just cited, Boston standards rather than Florida standards would be applied. When customs officials seized hundreds of printed articles in New York, they sent notices to all 573 intended recipients advising them that the material would be destroyed within 20 days because it was obscene unless the recipients made a claim challenging the government determination that importation of the material was illegal. Fourteen persons made such claims and sought hearings. None of these persons lived in New York, yet the Second Circuit Court of Appeals ruled that since the material was seized in New York, and since the obscenity hearing would be held in New York, New York community standards should be applied (*U.S.* v. *Various Articles of Obscene Merchandise,* 1977).

If the first element of the *Miller* obscenity test appears to give the trier of fact (judge or jury) almost total power in determining what is and is not obscene, the second element, as interpreted by the Supreme Court, limits that power.

Patent Offensiveness

The second element of the *Miller* test says that a work is obscene if it depicts in a patently offensive way sexual conduct specifically defined by applicable state law. There are two basic parts to the test: (1) patent offensiveness as determined by community standards and (2) sexual conduct specifically defined by applicable state law. Each of the two elements are important.

Patent offensiveness is to be determined by the trier of the fact, the judge or the jury, using contemporary community standards. But that phrase is deceptive, because the courts have ruled that the discretion of juror or judge in determining patent offensiveness is not unlimited. The kinds of conduct that may be labeled "patently offensive" in a prosecution for obscenity are hardcore types of conduct. A 1974 Supreme Court ruling illustrates this seeming contradiction. In 1974 in *Jenkins* v. *Georgia* the Supreme Court was faced with the decision by a Georgia jury that the movie *Carnal Knowledge* was obscene. The film was an R-rated movie, and while it had scenes which included partial nudity, it contained no scenes of the explicit sexual conduct usually associated wih X-rated films. Nevertheless, because in the *Miller* ruling the United States Supreme Court had given communities the power to determine community standards, and because this jury found that *Carnal Knowledge* violated those standards, the Georgia Supreme Court upheld the conviction.

The United States Supreme Court reversed the ruling, saying that the Georgia courts obviously misunderstood the *Miller* decision. The jury did have the right to determine local standards, but only those descriptions or depictions of sexual conduct that are patently offensive can be censored, regardless of local standards. Justice Rehnquist noted that in the *Miller* case Chief Justice Burger gave two examples of the kind of patently offensive material he was talking about. These examples included "representations or descriptions of ultimate sexual acts, normal or perverted, actual or simulated," and "representations or descriptions of masturbation, excretory functions, and lewd exhibition of the genitals." Rehnquist said that while this catalog of descriptions was not exhaustive, it was "intended to fix substantive constitutional limitations . . . on the type of material . . . subject to a determination of obscenity" (*Jenkins* v. *Georgia,* 1974). Therefore, under the second part of the *Miller* test, a jury is limited in what it can find to be obscene to what commentators call hard-core pornography.

The second aspect of the test to be noted is this: Chief Justice Burger said the descriptions or depictions of sexual conduct which are banned have to be specifically defined by the applicable state law as written or authoritatively construed. This sounds as though before a state can prohibit a description of a certain kind of sexual conduct the state must pass a specific law defining that kind of material.

How specific does the applicable state statute have to be? Not very. The high Court approved an Ohio statute which defined material as being obscene if it contained a display or description of nudity, sexual excitement, sexual conduct, bestiality, extreme or bizarre violence, cruelty, brutality, or human bodily functions or eliminations.

What if a state law does not define obscenity? What if it merely prohibits "obscene materials"? This is really not a problem, according to Justice Burger, who ruled that it is sufficient in such states if the state supreme court rules that the term *obscene materials* in the law means specific descriptions of sexual conduct. For example, the Supreme Court in 1977 upheld the conviction of an individual who had been found guilty of selling two sadomasochistic publications. The defendant argued that the state law did not specifically prohibit the sale of such material. But Justice White and four members of the high Court ruled that such an argument had no merit, that such material had been held to violate Illinois state law long before the *Miller* ruling, and that such authoritative construction of the statute was sufficient to meet the test outlined under *Miller*. The examples cited by Justice Burger in the *Miller* ruling, according to Justice White, were not exhaustive, but simply illustrative of the kinds of materials which could be considered patently offensive (*Ward* v. *Illinois,* 1977). Since 1973 most state obscenity statutes have been found to comply with the *Miller* standards, because of either specific descriptive language in the statute or authoritative construction by the state's high court.

Serious Value

To be obscene a work must lack serious literary, artistic, political, or scientific value. This is the third element of the *Miller* test. This element is designed to be a kind of check on the first two parts of the test, an effort to protect important works from obscenity prosecution. "The judicial role is more pronounced in the determination of the 'serious value' of the material, which is *not* [author emphasis] to be judged by the tastes of the average person or measured by community standards" (*Penthouse* v. *Mcauliffe,* 1981).

This standard is obviously considerably narrower than the "utterly without redeeming social value" standard of the *Roth-Memoirs* test. Both prosecutors and defendants often introduce "expert" testimony to persuade a judge that a film or book has some kind of serious value. Courts often have difficulty sorting out the conflicting statements from these witnesses because the Supreme Court has never defined "serious value" for the lower courts. In *Miller* v. *California* Chief Justice Burger warned lower courts to "always remain sensitive to any infringement on genuinely serious literary, artistic, political, or scientific value," but such an admonition does not help define the concept. Many courts have ruled that mere entertainment value in a film or book, or the existence of a tenuous story line, or the inclusion of an isolated idea are usually insufficient to redeem an otherwise obscene work (see *Penthouse* v. *Mcauliffe,* 1981, for example).

A United States district judge in Georgia defined serious value in this way when he was asked to determine whether the film *Caligula* was obscene (*Penthouse* v. *Mcauliffe,* 1981):

> We believe that by the phrase "serious value" the Supreme Court meant to extend constitutional protection to material which advocates ideas and in which the ideas are not used merely as a disguise or a sham for presenting obscenity. The ideas must be a substantial part of the material and treated in a nonfrivolous manner. . . . We do not believe that the "serious value" test of *Miller* was meant to extend protection only to works which are artistic successes or which include textual political commentary. All political views and ideas, including historical narrative and social criticism, are protected, as are all serious artistic and intellectual efforts, whether they appeal to the average person or not.

The judge ruled that the film, which portrays violence and explicit sex in telling the story of the life of Roman Emperor Caligula during his reign from 37 A.D. to 41 A.D., had serious political and artistic value.

The Supreme Court has also instructed lower appellate courts not to hesitate to closely scrutinize trial court judgments regarding "serious value." Justice Blackmun in *Smith* v. *U.S.* noted that the determination of whether a book or magazine or film lacks value "is particularly amenable to appellate review." Hence, while an appellate court should be reluctant to second guess a jury on a determination of contemporary community standards, it should not be hesitant in making an independent determination that a work either has or has not literary, artistic, political, or scientific value (*Smith* v. *U.S.,* 1977).

The Impact
of *Miller*

In an article in the *Seton Hall Law Review* in 1978 Rodney Grunes argued that obscenity might be the only policy area where the Burger Court significantly reversed the policies developed by the Warren Court. Conventional wisdom suggests then that the impact of the *Miller* ruling on freedom of expression, upon prosecution for obscenity, and upon other related areas would be great. This does not seem to be the case, however. In 1977 researchers attempted to evaluate the impact of the *Miller* test upon the law by questioning attorneys, police, judges, legislators, and persons who sell or distribute erotic materials. On the basis of nearly five hundred fifty completed questionnaires and nearly one hundred personal interviews, the researchers found that even though most observers agreed that the *Miller* test made it easier for the state to prosecute for obscenity there was actually a decrease in the number of obscenity prosecutions in the years following the *Miller* ruling. Similarly there was no evidence of a significant shift to nonprosecutory techniques such as zoning laws (page 401), nuisance actions, or licensing regulations. Researchers also found that "*Miller* has had little, if any, inhibiting effect on the content of sexually explicit material." Researchers could find little difference in the amount or kind of erotica available before and after the *Miller* decision, despite dire predictions regarding its impact upon creativity and art. Finally, though *Miller* has made the prosecution of all hard-core pornography permissible, most large jurisdictions move only against a narrow range of the most explicit materials, materials that likely could have been and were prosecuted under the old *Roth-Memoirs* standards, according to the research data (*New York University Law Review,* 1977).

These results immediately prompt the question why. Three answers come to mind. First, conventional wisdom might be wrong. In fact, not all authorities agree that the *Miller* test, on its face less liberal than the *Roth-Memoirs* test, actually makes it easier to prosecute obscenity. Of the great many prosecutors questioned and interviewed for the survey just noted, less than thirty percent said they believed the *Miller* test made it easier to win an obscenity case. Fifty-four percent could see no change; seventeen percent said the *Miller* test made it more difficult. The latter argument—that *Miller* has actually made it more difficult to win a case—was echoed in an article by Kenneth Mott and Christine Kellett in the 1979 volume of the *Suffolk University Law Review.* These writers asserted that by defining community standards as local standards the Supreme Court has seriously complicated obscenity prosecutions. They noted:

> The uniqueness of each smaller community makes it necessary for the state to move against a distributor or his agent in a separate action in each locality. Ironically, the desire of the Burger Court to give each community the privilege of setting its own standards has been defeated by the correlative duty of the community to prove the obscene nature of the material without relying on judgments of obscenity from other communities.

The result of this phenomenon has raised the cost of obscenity prosecutions and made them less attractive to budget-conscious public officials. The Los Angeles city attorney told researchers in 1977 that the average contested obscenity prosecution cost the city between $10,000 and $25,000.

The increase in cost of prosecutions, the corresponding decrease in revenues at most levels of government, and the rise in numbers of other more serious crimes have forced prosecutors to be highly selective in moving against pornographers. This set of circumstances is another reason many observers believe that *Miller* has not wrought the anticipated change in the law. In the mid-1970s *New York Times* reporter James Sterba wrote, "The police say they have more important crimes to fight. Many local prosecutors comment that they have neither the time nor the money to spend cracking down on smut dealers." In 1977 prosecutors told New York University Law School researchers the same thing, and this circumstance leads to the conclusion that "despite the rising tide of sexually explicit materials, prosecutors have not committed more time and money to the battle against obscenity."

Finally, because of a legal-political phenomenon identified by political scientists as "compliance," there is some question whether the fine tuning that Chief Justice Burger did to the definition of obscenity really makes much difference on the streets, where pornography is sold and pornographers are arrested and tried.

Political scientists have proved "scientifically" a fact that good lawyers and judges have known for some time: simply because the United States Supreme Court says something is "the law" does not mean that it is "the law" at local levels, at least not right after a decision. Local noncompliance with Supreme Court rulings is not a new phenomenon, but it has become more apparent during the last quarter century. It is a function of the fact that a lawsuit is a dispute between two parties, and the resolution of that dispute by the courts technically affects only those two parties, not everyone else in a similar situation. If the Supreme Court rules that it is unconstitutional for the state of Maine to print a prayer on its license plates, the other forty-nine states would undoubtedly follow that ruling without being forced to, because it is really not a very important issue. However, if the Supreme Court tells Maine it cannot ban certain kinds of hard-core pornography, many other jurisdictions would probably be reluctant to follow that ruling until a court stops them from doing the same thing. Why? Because this issue is important. Technically, the states do not have to comply unless they are forced to by a court.

In a study of compliance with obscenity rulings in Oregon, Stephen L. Wasby wrote recently that one of the reasons for lack of compliance is the lack of agreement on what the Court intends by its opinion on the subject. "The development of Oregon obscenity policy," Wasby added, "gives evidence that the impact nationwide of a Supreme Court decision is by no means uniform. If there is as much variance in interpretation *within* one state as occurred in Oregon, certainly considerable variation must exist across the nation as a whole" ("The Pure and the Prurient: The Supreme Court, Obscenity and Oregon Policy").

What are the factors involved in compliance and noncompliance? Wasby identified several: role of the lawyers, legitimacy ascribed to the decision, direction of the decision, sentiment of the public, precision or ambiguity of the decision, decisiveness of the ruling, number of relevant opinions, and so forth.

What does compliance have to do with the impact of *Miller* on obscenity law? It has been suggested that local communities act largely unto themselves in prosecuting obscenity. The *Roth-Memoirs* test gave general guidelines for obscenity which were followed as closely as possible. The changes in these guidelines wrought by the Burger opinion in *Miller* are too subtle to be reflected locally, where judges are forced to instruct juries in common language as to what is and what is not obscene. So sexually oriented materials that were protected by the First Amendment under the *Roth-Memoirs* test remain protected under the *Miller* test in most communities. And what was legally obscene under *Roth-Memoirs* remains obscene under *Miller*. While the changes in the law appear to be dramatic, except for the very few cases which are appealed and can be examined closely by high appellate courts, the changes in the law have had little impact for police, prosecutors, pornographers, and trial judges. The best definition of obscenity in any local community still remains what a local jury says is obscene and has changed little in the past fifteen years.

Selective Standards

Two other dimensions of the definition of obscenity which developd in the years prior to *Miller* seem to retain vitality today.

In 1966 in *Ginzburg* v. *U.S.,* the Supreme Court ruled that the manner in which material is marketed, advertised, and displayed can be a factor in determining whether a work is obscene or not. This case was the result of publisher Ralph Ginzburg's efforts to sell three different publications. In marketing these publications, Justice Brennan said, Ginzburg emphasized their erotic nature and thus was engaged in "**pandering**"—that is, in "the business of purveying textual or graphic matter openly advertised to appeal to the erotic interest of customers." This action can be a key factor in determining whether a publication or a film is obscene or not, Brennan said. Ginzburg's conviction was affirmed.

Richard Kuh, in *Foolish Figleaves,* cites as examples of pandering such schemes as using a provocative cover, using advertisements that list the previous bannings of the work, displaying the work along with other borderline items, and in various other ways promoting the erotic, deviant, or scatological appeal of the material. In 1977 in *Splawn* v. *California* four members of the Supreme Court agreed with Justice Rehnquist's majority opinion that "evidence of pandering to prurient interests in the creation, promotion, or dissemination of material is relevant in determining whether the material was obscene." One year later, in writing for a seven-man majority, Chief Justice

Burger noted, "We have held, and reaffirmed, that to aid a jury in its determination of whether materials are obscene, the methods of their creation, promotion, or dissemination are relevant. . ." (*Pinkus* v. *U.S.,* 1978). Hence it seems assured that if proof of pandering is introduced by the prosecution, the jury may consider it evidence in determining the obscenity of the books or films or magazines.

The Supreme Court has also ruled that states may adopt **variable obscenity standards** of obscenity for juveniles and for adults. That is, material acceptable for sale to adults may not be acceptable for sale to children. A bookseller or a theater owner can be prosecuted for providing obscene material to young people. This is a standard that emerged in 1968 in *Ginsberg* v. *New York* and was upheld as recently as 1975 in *Erznoznik* v. *City of Jacksonville.* In the latter case the city forbade drive-in theaters to show movies in which female buttocks and bare breasts were shown if the theater screen was visible from the street. The ordinance, which was justified in part as a means of protecting the city's youth from exposure to such material, was defective according to the Supreme Court. The high Court said that laws aimed at setting variable standards of obscenity for adults and for children were permissible, but must be carefully constructed. "Only in relatively narrow and well-defined circumstances may government bar public dissemination of protected materials to children," Justice Powell wrote. Banning the showing of nudity is simply not narrow enough; only materials which have significant erotic appeal to juveniles may be suppressed under such a statute, he added. A simple ban on all nudity, regardless of context, justification, or other factors violates the First Amendment.

For example, a Georgia state law aimed at shielding juveniles from obscenity was recently ruled unconstitutional because it infringed upon the rights of adults. The law made it illegal to display obscenity in public or in any establishment frequented by minors or where minors may be invited as part of the general public. But the definition of obscenity in the statute was not based upon the *Miller* test; it included a wider range of material than would be defined as obscene under that three-part standard. Surely the state may go farther in protecting children from obscenity, the court ruled. But in this case the ban on the public display of material that would not be obscene under the *Miller* test limits the availability of that material to adults as well as to children (*American Booksellers Association* v. *Mcauliffe,* 1981).

Child Pornography

In 1982 the United States Supreme Court unanimously upheld a New York statute aimed at limiting the distribution of child pornography. The state law prohibits any person from knowingly promoting a sexual performance by a child under the age of sixteen years by distributing material which photographically depicts such a performance. The statute explicitly defines sexual performance as sexual conduct and lists the kind of conduct which is not permitted to be shown. Justice Byron White wrote that child pornography defined in the statute is unprotected speech and can be subject to content-based regulation. The state has a strong state interest in protecting the well-being of children. To help prevent the abuse of children who are made to engage in sexual conduct for commercial purposes, the state can prohibit the distribution of material which shows children engaged in such conduct, even if this material might not be obscene under the three-part *Miller* test. White said that when a judge considers photographic depictions of live sexual performances by children the *Miller* formulation should be adjusted in the following respects: "A trier of fact need not find that the material appeals to the prurient interest of the average person; it is not required that sexual conduct portrayed be done so in a patently offensive manner; and the material at issue need not be considered as a whole." The value of permitting live performances and photographic reproductions of children engaged in lewd sexual conduct is exceedingly modest, the Justice said. The law is aimed at stopping the sexual exploitation of children. One sure way to stop or at least reduce this exploitation is to ban the distribution of films in which children are depicted in sexual conduct. Distribution of written descriptions or other kinds of depictions (drawings) of children engaged in sexual conduct which are not otherwise obscene and which do not involve live performances are still protected by the First Amendment, White said (*New York* v. *Ferber,* 1982).

Summary

The *Miller-Hamling* test is used today by American courts to determine whether something is obscene. It has three parts. Material is legally obscene under the following conditions.

1. An average person, applying contemporary local community standards, finds that the work, taken as a whole, appeals to prurient interest. This test requires the fact finder to apply local (usually state or county) standards rather than a national standard. The judge or jury determines the standard, based upon their knowledge of what is acceptable in the community.

2. The work depicts in a patently offensive way sexual conduct specifically defined by applicable state law. Again, the fact finder in the case determines patent offensiveness based upon local community standards. But the Supreme Court has ruled that only so-called hard-core pornography can be found to be patently offensive. Also, either the legislature or the state supreme court must specifically define the kind of offensive material which may be declared to be obscene.

3. The material lacks serious literary, artistic, political, or scientific value. This is a question of law, not of fact, to be decided by the judge.

The three-part *Miller-Hamling* test is the test that courts must use in defining obscenity in all cases except those involving juveniles. The Supreme Court has ruled that states may use a broader definition of obscenity when they attempt to block the sale or distribution of erotic material to children, or when they attempt to stop the exploitation of children who are forced to engage in sexual conduct by pornographic filmmakers.

STATE AND FEDERAL CONTROLS ON OBSCENITY

Various means can be used to regulate the dissemination of obscene materials including criminal prosecution, passing nuisance and zoning laws, and regulating the types of films that can be shown. The federal government can also use postal censorship to prevent obscene materials from being disseminated. Let us look more closely at these measures for controlling obscene materials.

The Obscenity Case

Prosecutions for obscenity are complicated criminal matters. To be successful in such cases prosecutors must follow carefully prescribed paths in deciding whether material is obscene, collecting and seizing evidence, and making arrests. Often persons charged with exhibiting or selling obscene materials seek to plea bargain with the state to reduce the charge. Booksellers, theater owners, and other merchants who deal in pornographic materials often do not want to fight the government in an obscenity prosecution. They are not in the business to crusade for the First Amendment. Their goal is to stay out of jail and to return to selling books or showing movies. If the state can be convinced to reduce the obscenity charge in exchange for a guilty plea, the defendant can often get by with paying a fine instead of going to jail, and be back in business within a few days of the arrest. Prosecutors seem amenable to such plea bargaining because, as one noted, "Our business is to stop public distribution of certain obscene materials, not put people in jail."

If a case goes to trial, the judge and the jury are the ones who must determine whether the material sold or exhibited is obscene. The fact finder in the trial—the jury or the judge if there is not a jury—determines parts one and two of the *Miller* test, prurient appeal and patent offensiveness. The judge normally rules on the serious value of the work as a matter of law. The instructions given to the jury by the judge are usually vitally important to the outcome of an obscenity case. The instructions, of course, tell the jury what the law is—in other words, how to determine whether the material is obscene. A trial judge generally bases his instructions both on his personal reading of the law and on personal experience. Judge David Soukup of the Washington State Superior Court, who has tried numerous obscenity cases, told researcher Kirk Anderson this about jury instructions:

> Basically the matter of deciding what to include in a set of instructions depends on what the judge himself feels is necessary such that the jury can make a knowledgeable and legally sound determination, a judgment that is predicated upon his own interpretation of the law and what it requires, in combination with

what his practical experience tells him jurors need in order to best understand the criteria they must apply to the facts at hand. The result of this highly individualized process, which is also influenced by the judge's philosophy of his role under the law and his feeling about pornography in general, is that some judges will stick pretty close to the *Miller* test and the definitions of it provided by the Supreme Court, while others will attempt to embellish them by adding varying degrees of explanation arising from their own interpretations of the law. . . .

In addition to determining whether the material is obscene, jurors are also called upon to answer the question of whether the defendant was knowledgeable about the contents of what he was selling or distributing or publishing. This is called scienter, or guilty knowledge. In a 1959 case, *Smith* v. *California,* the United States Supreme Court ruled that before a person can be convicted for selling obscene books the state has to prove that the seller was aware of the contents of the books, that he knew what they were about. The reason for this ruling is quite simple. As Justice William Brennan wrote more than twenty years ago, "If the bookseller is criminally liable without knowledge of the contents, . . . he will tend to restrict the books he sells to those he has inspected; and thus the state will have imposed a restriction upon the distribution of constitutionally protected as well as obscene literature . . ." (*Smith* v. *California,* 1959).

There has always been some confusion about exactly what a state or other jurisdiction must prove. For example, does the bookseller have to know the books are obscene? In the *Hamling* decision the Supreme Court tried to clarify this point by repeating that scienter merely means proving that the defendant has a general knowledge of the material in question, that it is a book about homosexuals, for example, or that the movie contains sadistic scenes. It is not necessary that the bookseller or the theater operator know that the material is legally obscene. Normally a prosecutor can demonstrate scienter without much trouble, but it is another question which the jury must decide.

What this process suggests is that, like other street crimes, the prosecution of obscenity in any community depends largely upon how the law is administered and interpreted *locally*. And within certain parameters, a community can read the books it wants to read, see the movies it wants to see, and buy the kinds of magazines it wants to buy. What the United States Supreme Court says about obscenity is relevant to most communities in only an indirect way. These practical realities regarding obscenity prosecutions suggest that the nation's appellate courts—especially the Supreme Court of the United States—probably spend far too much time contemplating this matter.

Nuisance Laws

Some communities have attempted to block the sale or exhibition of obscene material through the use of nuisance laws. Under such statutes a city, for example, can ask a court to declare an adult-oriented business to be a public nuisance because it sells obscene materials. If, in the civil trial that follows, the court rules that the business is a public nuisance, the owner can be blocked by an injunction from selling or exhibiting similar merchandise in the future. North Carolina, for example, passed a nuisance statute aimed at theaters regularly showing pornographic films and adult bookstores which had coin-operated film projectors (peep shows) showing explicit sexual activity or sold pictorial magazines or photographs showing similar activity. The statute defined obscenity using the three-part *Miller* test. The state is obliged to prove that a bookstore owner or theater operator which it takes to court deals predominantly and in the regular course of business with such obscene material. If the court agrees that the material is obscene and that it is a principal or substantial part of the defendant's stock in trade, an injunction will be issued barring the future sale or exhibition of comparable material. If this injunction is violated, the individual can be held in contempt of court and fined or jailed. The Fourth United States Court of Appeals upheld the North Carolina law despite protests by the defendant that it was a prior restraint (*Fehlhaber* v. *North Carolina*, 1982).

In 1981 the United States Supreme Court struck down a similar law. But this Texas statute had the fatal defect of allowing a court to issue a temporary restraining order against a theater owner barring as a nuisance the exhibition of a film even *before* a court determined that the film was obscene. In other words, the Texas law permitted courts to perpetually block the showing of films at a theater before a judge ever determined that the theater had shown an obscene film. A theater owner who continued to show a film in violation of the injunction could be held in contempt, even if it turned out at a future trial that the film was not obscene. The Supreme Court ruled this to be an unconstitutional prior restraint (*Vance* v. *Universal Amusement*, 1980).

The North Carolina law does not have this defect. The injunction is not issued by a judge until a judicial determination has been made that the material which has been seized is obscene. Then all future sales or exhibitions of *comparable* material are barred. But that is what troubles some persons about such statutes. Circuit Judge Phillips dissented in the Fourth United States Court of Appeals ruling approving the North Carolina law. He noted (*Fehlhaber* v. *North Carolina*, 1982):

> The key feature of this civil nuisance statute remains . . . the power it gives the state courts to enjoin, under the peril of a contempt sanction, the sale and exhibition of materials that no judicial tribunal has yet determined to be obscene. This is a violation of the principles enunciated by the Supreme Court in *Near* v. *Minnesota*.

There has been little appellate litigation over these nuisance statutes. One suspects that sooner or later the United States Supreme Court will be forced to resolve the seeming difference between the logic of *Near* v. *Minnesota* (see pages 70–71) which outlaws most prior censorship and the prior restraints in these public nuisance statutes.

Zoning Laws

Much erotic material which is not legally obscene is still offensive to many persons in a community. Attempts to prosecute the purveyors of this so-called adult material often end in acquittals for the defendants. In many communities zoning regulations have been used instead to regulate adult bookstores, theaters, and news racks. Seattle passed a law in 1977 which requires all adult theaters to be located within a small area downtown. City officials said that the character and quality of Seattle neighborhoods could be preserved and protected by isolating this adult activity in a small area downtown. Detroit took just the opposite approach. A city law passed in 1972 prohibits adult theaters from being located within 1,000 feet of other adult theaters, adult bookstores, cabarets, bars, taxi dance halls, hotels, pawnshops, pool halls, secondhand stores, and shoeshine parlors or within 500 feet of areas zoned residential. The city did not want such businesses clustered together or near other types of "problem" businesses in the community. Both these statutes were upheld by the courts (*Northend Cinema* v. *Seattle,* 1978; *Young* v. *American-Mini Theaters, Inc.,* 1976).

The owners of these adult establishments have found that zoning, while perhaps inconvenient, provides them with a kind of safe haven from police harassment. They are normally permitted to operate their businesses without trouble unless they attempt to sell or exhibit material which is legally obscene (i.e., meets the definition of obscenity in the *Miller* test), or unless other criminal laws are violated as a result of the traffic into the adult establishments.

But there are clearly limits to such zoning regulations, as there are with any time, place, and manner regulations. In 1981 the United States Supreme Court struck down a Mount Ephraim, New Jersey, zoning regulation because it was unreasonable. An adult bookstore in the community installed a device which permitted customers who paid a fee to watch live nude dancers perform behind a glass panel. The borough charged the bookstore with violating its zoning laws which banned all live entertainment in parts of the city zoned commercial. Justice Byron White wrote for the seven-person majority (*Schad* v. *Mount Ephraim,* 1981):

> By excluding live entertainment throughout the borough, the Mount Ephraim ordinance prohibits a wide range of expression that has long been held to be within the protections of the First and Fourteenth Amendments. Entertainment, as well as political and ideological speech is protected: motion pictures, programs broadcast by radio and television, and live entertainment such as musical and dramatic works, fall within the First Amendment guarantee.

Nudity does not in itself place otherwise protected material outside the mantle of the First Amendment, White said. Live entertainment may be banned in the community only if the borough can sufficiently justify its exclusion, he added. Zoning power is broad, but it is "not infinite and unchallengeable; it must be exercised within constitutional limits." Zoning ordinances which infringe upon expression protected by the First Amendment must be both clearly justified by the community and narrowly drawn to impinge upon only the barest minimum of protected speech.

Attorneys for Mount Ephraim attempted to justify the rules by citing the high Court's approval of zoning laws in Detroit (*Young* v. *American Mini-Theaters*). Justice White said that the city of Detroit ordinance had been thoroughly justified by many studies of land-use policy, impact statements, and the like. Also, the Detroit ordinance did not ban speech, but merely dispersed it throughout the city. Mount Ephraim had presented no justification for its law, which had the impact of totally excluding live entertainment from the community (*Schad* v. *Mount Ephraim,* 1981).

In other cases other courts have thrown out zoning ordinances. The Sixth United States Court of Appeals voided a Keego Harbor, Michigan, zoning law which prohibited adult theaters within 500 feet of a bar or tavern, a church, or a school. There was no place in the small community (which had 20 bars or taverns) that was not within 500 feet of a tavern or bar, a church, or a school. "When a city effectively zones protected activity out of the political entity, the justification required is more substantial than when the First Amendment burden is merely incidental as it was in *Young* v. *American Mini-Theaters,*" the court ruled. Keego Harbor had supplied very little justification for the zoning rule. Its attorneys argued that adult theaters create traffic problems on narrow city streets. But the community failed to demonstrate why adult theaters, which were not permitted, create more traffic problems than normal theaters, which were permitted (*Keego Harbor Company* v. *Keego Harbor,* 1981). The New Mexico Supreme Court invalidated a Santa Fe zoning law which prohibited adult bookstores and adult theaters within 1,000 feet of a "residential area." The law did not define "residential area." The Detroit statute which had much the same language prohibited adult establishments within 500 feet of an area *zoned residential*. This difference in language in the Santa Fe law made it constitutionally vague and invalid (*Harris Book* v. *Santa Fe,* 1982).

It is clear that while cities and towns can use zoning laws to regulate the sale and exhibition of adult material these laws must meet several requirements.

1. The laws must be sufficiently justified. In other words, the community must prove that the sale or exhibition of adult materials will have a serious deleterious impact upon the community if not regulated by zoning. It must also be demonstrated that the zoning laws will significantly relieve or ease this impact.
2. The laws normally must not totally exclude such activity from the community.

3. The laws must be narrowly drawn so as to inhibit the narrowest possible range of protected speech.
4. The laws must be precise, unambiguous, and clearly drawn so there is no confusion over the meaning of the statute.

If laws meet these tests, it seems certain the appellate courts will continue to permit communities to use zoning regulations to regulate the sale and exhibition of adult materials.

Postal Censorship

Use of the postal service to censor obscenity has a long tradition in the United States. In fact, it is largely through the postal system that the federal government becomes involved in the regulation of obscenity. The Post Office Department has long been an insensitive and moralistic censor of all sorts of material. Armed with congressional authority as well as a nineteenth-century Supreme Court ruling which designated use of the mails a privilege and not a right (ex parte *Jackson,* 1878), the postal service has worked hard to keep the mails free of "smut," even smut in plain brown wrappers. While the government cannot tamper with first-class mail legally, publishers of magazines of all kinds—girly, nudist, art, anthropological, crime, true confessions—have long been plagued by postal inspectors. While the loss of much of this material would not be a severe blow to the nation's cultural heritage, it is still highly frustrating to publishers who must depend upon the postal service to deliver their wares. For most publications the Post Office Department runs the only game in town.

The Post Office Department has traditionally been plagued with administrative slovenliness which causes it to run afoul of the law. Federal courts have for years been telling the postal service that it cannot do this or that: institute a mail block, for example, or deny due process of law in obscenity hearings, ban publications which do not contribute to "the public good," or force patrons to come to the post office to pick up mail from Communist countries. In 1968 the postal service took a new tack in regulating certain kinds of obscene material, a tack designed to take the service off the legal hot seat. What is known as the Anti-Pandering Law or Section 3008 of Title 39 of the United States Code was put into effect by Congress. It was designed to stop the delivery of unwanted obscene solicitations to mail patrons' homes. This had been a problem for years, a real problem in many cases. Mailers were indiscriminate in sending out such material, and it was not uncommon for youngsters to receive lurid solicitations from magazines, books, and pictures.

Section 3008 allows postal patrons to remain free from such solicitations, but only after they have received such an advertisement. It works this way. Imagine that John Smith finds an advertisement for La Femme French postcards in his mailbox and is properly shocked. Under Section 3008 John can fill out a postal form which is sent by the post office to the La Femme company advising the mailer that Mr. Smith does not want to receive such solicitations in the future. If La Femme were to send John a subsequent mailing, the company could be subject to prosecution.

The interesting aspect of this law concerns the definition of obscenity—there is none. Postal patrons decide for themselves what is obscene. If they do not like the material, the dislike then is all that is needed. Once the notice is sent to the mailer, *any* subsequent mailing is a violation of the law. John might decide that a *Time* magazine solicitation or an advertisement for seat covers or a record club is obscene. There must be solicitation, but that is the only requirement.

The distributors of erotic material challenged this law, since to remove a name from a mailing list is quite costly. Also they argued that the law violated their First Amendment rights, and because the law did not define obscenity, it was too vague and therefore a violation of Fifth Amendment rights. But the Supreme Court unanimously supported the law. The Court said that Congress intended to give the postal patron the right to decide on the obscenity of an advertisement, and this right eliminates the Post Office Department from a censorship role.

As far as the First Amendment right to communicate (if there is such a right) is concerned, the high Court ruled that the right of privacy is also guaranteed by the Constitution. This law does impede the flow of ideas, information, and so forth. However, Chief Justice Burger wrote (*Rowan* v. *Post Office,* 1970):

> . . . today everyman's mail is made up overwhelmingly of material he did not seek from persons he does not know. And all too often it is matter he finds offensive. It seems to us that a mailer's right to communicate must stop at the mailbox of an unreceptive addressee. . . . We categorically reject the argument that a vendor has a right under the Constitution or otherwise to send unwanted material into the home of another.

A more recent addition to the postal laws operates on somewhat the same principle, and has caused the pornography distributors even more headaches. Section 3010 of Title 39, United States Code, called the Goldwater Amendment to the Postal Reorganization Bill, allows mail patrons the opportunity to get off a pornographer's mailing list even before they receive the first solicitation. Under this law John Smith can fill out a form at his local post office which asserts that he does not want to receive any sexually oriented advertising. The postal service periodically publishes computerized lists of the names and addresses of persons who have signed this form. After a person's name has been on the list for thirty days, it is illegal to send that individual sexually oriented advertising matter. Mailers who ignore this are subject to both criminal and civil penalties.

Where do the mailers get the lists of names? They have to buy the lists from the government. When the law went into effect a few years ago, the cost of a master list was more than $5,000. Of course supplements are published periodically, and they must be purchased as well.

Section 3010 is different from Section 3008 in that it defines sexually oriented material, whereas the Anti-Pandering Law lets postal patrons decide on their own.

Here is how the statute defines sexually oriented material:

> . . . any advertisement that depicts in actual or simulated form, or explicitly describes, in a predominantly sexual context, human genitalia, any act of natural or unnatural sexual intercourse, or any act of sadism or masochism, or any other erotic subject directly related to the foregoing.

The law does not pertain to materials in which the sexually oriented advertisement comprises only a small and insignificant part of a larger catalog, book, or periodical. This statute was also upheld by the federal courts (*Pent-R-Books* v. *U.S. Postal Service,* 1971). This law also provides that any envelope containing an advertisement which falls within the definition just given must carry a warning on the outside as to the nature of the contents.

Both of these statutes have been widely used and have solved one of the most serious problems relating to pornography—its shipment to people who do not want it. However, neither of these laws precludes the possibility of criminal obscenity prosecution against advertisers for sending out such material, even to people who want it. The 1974 *Hamling* case was based on just such an advertisement.

Regulating Films

Courts have always treated movies differently than they treat books, magazines, and artwork. Films have been censored for a great many reasons, including obscenity. Initially the Supreme Court refused to include films under the protection of the First Amendment. In 1915 in the case of *Mutual Film Corp.* v. *Industrial Commission of Ohio,* Justice Joseph McKenna wrote for the Court that while, indeed, movies may be mediums of thought, so are many other things such as circuses and the theaters. "It cannot be put out of view," the justice wrote, "that the exhibition of moving pictures is a business, pure and simple, originated and conducted for profit, like other spectacles, not to be regarded . . . as part of the press of the country or as organs of public opinion."

This was the law until the 1950s when the high Court ruled that film is a medium protected by the First Amendment and cannot be censored by a state, except in cases of obscenity (*Burstyn* v. *Wilson,* 1952). This seemed to put moviemakers on the same footing as magazine publishers, with one exception. The courts permitted prior censorship with regard to motion pictures; that is, a theater owner or film distributor could constitutionally be required to present the film to a board of censors for approval before showing it in the theater. In 1961 a film distributor challenged this practice and lost. In a five-to-four ruling the high Court said that there is no complete and absolute freedom to exhibit, even once, any and every kind of motion picture (*Times Film Corp. v. Chicago*).

While approving prior censorship for motion pictures, the high Court also demands procedures within the censorship system which protect the rights of theater owners. Concerning such, the high Court struck down several film censorship systems (for example, in Maryland and Dallas) which took too long to reach a decision, placed the burden of proof on the theater owner rather than on the government, and so forth (*Freedman* v. *Maryland,* 1965 and *Interstate Circuit v. Dallas,* 1968). In 1965 when the Court struck down the Maryland censorship law in *Freedman* v. *Maryland* it outlined the constitutional requirements of a permissible film ordinance. But the Court was unable to find an ordinance that passed muster until 1974 when it summarily affirmed the judgment of a three-judge panel which approved the revamped Maryland law.

The Maryland law which was approved in *Star* v. *Preller* (1974) had these provisions.

1. Every film, including those in coin-operated loop machines, must have a license from the state board of censors before it can be shown. Showing a film without a license is a crime, regardless of whether it is obscene.
2. Once a film is submitted to the censorship board, the board must either issue a license or initiate an action in court against the film within eight days.
3. In a court action to determine whether the film is obscene, the censorship board must prove the film is obscene. The film distributor does not have to prove that it is not obscene.
4. Hearing must be held in court within five days after the action is filed.
5. The court must issue a ruling within two days after the hearing is over. There is also a provision for expedited appeals.
6. The film cannot be shown until the hearing is completed.

Given the fact that prior restraint is allowed, the benefit of this ordinance is that a film must be licensed or declared obscene in a maximum of fifteen days. Moreover, the state bears the burden of proof in any hearing that results. Perhaps this seems like crumbs for a starving man, but this system is nevertheless far superior to those of yesterday in which motion pictures were often tied up for months with the censors, and the theater owner or film distributor was forced to go into court and try to prove a negative: that a movie was not obscene.

Many communities no longer operate film censorship boards. They are costly, and because the censors frequently abuse the system, these boards have a bad name. In Chicago, for example, the censorship board, which was comprised of police officers and the proverbial little old ladies in tennis shoes, once cut a scene showing the birth of a deer from a Walt Disney nature movie. Most communities proceed against obscene movies much as they do against obscene books—case-by-case prosecution.

Film prosecutions also present problems. In the case of an obscene book, an undercover officer can buy a copy of the suspect edition, and it can be scrutinized and later used as evidence if a criminal action results. But the price of a movie ticket includes only the right to look, not to take. So the police and the courts experienced many years of pushing and shoving over what was and was not legal. For a while the police merely seized all copies of the film. But the courts did not approve of that, because whether the film was obscene was for the courts to decide. If the jury decided the film was not obscene, seizure then constituted a clear case of prior restraint. So the police were forced to use other means. In some cities the police videotaped portions of the movie for use as evidence in a trial. But the quality of the tape was poor, and often theater owners who were arguing about the high technical quality of a film complained that the police copy made the picture look worse than it actually was.

In 1973 in *Heller* v. *New York,* the Supreme Court handed down rules which clarified the matter, even though the new policies did not satisfy many people on either side. Under the *Heller* rules a film cannot be seized by police as evidence until a warrant is issued by a neutral judge or magistrate who has viewed the film and has ruled that it is obscene. The hearing in which the judge issues the warrant is not an adversary hearing, because the theater owner is not represented. This warrant is called an ex parte warrant. Only the state is represented, and all that the warrant says is that one judge has seen the film and thinks it is obscene.

The Fifth United States Court of Appeals modified these rules in 1979 when it decided that a judge or magistrate can also issue a warrant for seizure of the film on the basis of a government agent's *detailed* affidavit describing the film's content. The judge or magistrate does not actually have to see the film in order to issue the warrant (*U.S.* v. *Middleton,* 1979). Whether the United States Supreme Court will agree with this ruling has not been tested. The high Court will not permit so-called open-ended warrants. A police officer in New York bought two films at an adult bookstore and permitted a judge to view them. The judge declared the films to be obscene and gave the police officer a warrant to seize all copies of the two films and other obscene materials at the store. Police raided the store and seized eight hundred different items. The names and descriptions of these items were filled in on the warrant *after* they were seized. The Supreme Court unanimously ruled that such a procedure was a violation of the Fourth Amendment. "Our society is better able to tolerate the admittedly pornographic business of petitioner [the store owner] than a return to the general warrant era," Chief Justice Burger wrote (*Lo-Ji Sales* v. *New York,* 1979).

Following seizure of a film, an adversary hearing—a trial—is held to determine whether the film is in fact obscene. During the period between seizure and final judicial determination of obscenity, the theater owner can continue to show the motion picture if he has a second copy. If no second copy is available, the state must then permit the exhibitor to make a copy of the film that was seized so that exhibition of the movie can go on. Therefore, the police get their evidence and the theater owner can keep showing the movie until the trial is over. The only serious problem is that it is expensive for the theater owner to make a second copy of the movie.

Summary

Criminal prosecution is not the only way in which communities have attempted to regulate the sale or exhibition of obscene or adult materials. Laws have been passed which permit a court to declare a business that deals in legally obscene materials to be a public nuisance. Continued sale or exhibition of obscene materials by a business deemed to be a public nuisance can result in a contempt-of-court citation. Many communities have attempted to use zoning regulations to control the sale and exhibition of nonobscene adult materials. These laws are permissible as long as they are well justified, do not totally exclude such material from the community, and are written to inhibit only the narrowest possible range of speech or otherwise protect speech.

Federal regulations make it possible for postal patrons to block the delivery of solicitations for adult materials and other obscene publications. Communities may also censor films before they are shown so long as they follow strict procedures laid down by the United States Supreme Court.

In the end, one question seems to always pop up: Why is there so much ado about nothing? Of course there are persons who argue that obscenity is not "nothing"; it is something, something very important. The morality of the community is at stake. And maybe it is.

The First Amendment has not worked very well with regard to obscenity. The eloquent vagueness of the drafters of the Bill of Rights has not served us at all well in this issue. Both sides use the silence of the First Amendment with regard to obscenity to bolster their opposite arguments.

One does not get a great deal of satisfaction from studying the obscenity problem for any length of time. Often it appears that in this dispute no one is right. The trash that is normally peddled as erotic art seems not much worse than nonerotic trash, but it costs much more. Society wastes an immense amount of money, and police, prosecutors, and courts waste an immense amount of time trying to control "the obscenity problem." In one recent term 10 percent of the case load of the United States Supreme Court were obscenity cases. The debate on both sides is rarely lofty; the principles at stake are often obscure. It is troublesome that in an age which is rife with problems we spend so much time on this controversy.

BIBLIOGRAPHY

Here is a list of some of the sources that have been helpful in the preparation of chapter 8.

Books

Berns, Walter. *Freedom, Virtue, and the First Amendment.* Chicago: Henry Regnery Co., Gateway Editions, 1965.

Clor, Harry M. *Obscenity and Public Morality.* Chicago: University of Chicago Press, 1969.

Kennedy, Michael, and Lefcourt, Gerald. "Trial Strategy in an Obscenity Case." In *Obscenity and the Law.* New York: Practicing Law Institute, 1974.

Kronhausen, Eberhard, and Kronhausen, Phyllis. *Pornography and the Law.* Rev. ed. New York: Ballantine Books, 1964.

Paul, James C. N., and Schwartz, Murray L. *Federal Censorship: Obscenity in the Mail.* Glencoe, Ill.: Free Press, 1961.

Robertus, Patricia. *Postal Control of Obscene Literature 1942–1957.* Ph.D. Dissertation, University of Washington, 1974.

Sunderland, Lane. *Obscenity, The Court, The Congress and the President's Commission.* Washington, D.C.: American Institute for Public Policy Research, 1974.

Wasby, Stephen L. "The Pure and the Prurient: The Supreme Court, Obscenity and Oregon Policy." In *The Supreme Court as Policy Maker*, edited by David Everson. Carbondale, Ill.: Public Affairs Research Bureau, Southern Illinois University, 1968.

Articles

Bickel, Alexander. "On Pornography: Concurring and Dissenting Opinions." 22, *The Public Interest* 25, 1971.

"An Empirical Inquiry Into the Effects of *Miller* v. *California* on the Control of Obscenity." 52 *New York University Law Review* 810, 1977.

Grunes, Rodney. "Obscenity Law and the Justices: Reversing Policy on the Supreme Court." 9 *Seton Hall Law Review* 403, 1978.

Leventhal, Harold. "1973 Round of Obscenity-Pornography Decisions." *American Bar Association Journal* 59, 1974.

Mott, Kenneth, and Kellett, Christine. "Obscenity, Community Standards, and the Burger Court: From Deterrence to Disarray." 13 *Suffolk University Law Review* 14, 1979.

Shogue, Richard. "An Atlas for Obscenity: Exploring Community Standard." 7 *Creighton Law Review* 157, 1974.

Teeter, Dwight L., and Pember, Don R. "Obscenity, 1971: The Rejuvenation of State Power and the Return to Roth." 17 *Villanova Law Review* 211, 1971.

Teeter, Dwight L., and Pember, Don R. "The Retreat from Obscenity: *Redrup* v. *New York*." 21 *Hastings Law Journal* 175, 1969.

Cases

American Booksellers Association v. Mcauliffe, 533 F. Supp. 50 (1981).
Burstyn v. Wilson, 343, U.S. 495 (1952).
Butler v. Michigan, 352 U.S. 380 (1957).
Erznoznik v. City of Jacksonville, 95 S.Ct. 2268 (1975).
ex parte Jackson, 96 U.S. 727 (1878).
Fehlhaber v. North Carolina, 675 F.2d. 1365 (1982).
Freedman v. Maryland, 380 U.S. 51 (1965).
Ginsberg v. New York, 390 U.S. 629 (1968).
Ginzburg v. U.S., 383 U.S. 463 (1966).
Hamling v. U.S., 418 U.S. 87 (1974).
Hannegan v. Esquire, 327 U.S. 146 (1946).
Harris Book v. Santa Fe, 647 P.2d 868 (1982).
Heller v. New York, 413 U.S. 483 (1973).
Interstate Circuit v. Dallas, 390 U.S. 676 (1968).
Jacobellis v. Ohio, 378 U.S. 184 (1964).
Jenkins v. Georgia, 418 U.S. 153 (1974).
Keego Harbor Company v. Keego Harbor, 657 F.2d 94 (1981).
Lo-Ji Sales v. New York, 99 S.Ct. 2319 (1979).
Manuel Enterprises v. Day, 370 U.S. 478 (1962).
Memoirs v. Massachusetts, 383 U.S. 413 (1966).
Miller v. California, 413 U.S. 15 (1973).
Mutual Film Corp. v. Industrial Commission of Ohio, 236 U.S. 230 (1915).
New York v. Ferber, 102 S.Ct. 3348 (1982).
Northend Cinema v. Seattle, 585 P.2d 1153 (1978).
Paris Adult Theatre I v. Slaton, 413 U.S. 49 (1973).
Penthouse v. Mcauliffe, 610 F.2d 1353 (1981).
Pent-R-Books v. U.S. Postal Service, 328 F. Supp. 297 (1971).
People v. Gitlow, 195 A. D. 773 (1921).
Pinkus v. U.S., 98 S.Ct. 1808 (1978).
Regina v. Hicklin, L.R. 3 Q.B. 360 (1868).
Roth v. U.S., 354 U.S. 476 (1957).
Rowan v. Post Office, 397 U.S. 728 (1970).
Schad v. Mount Ephraim, 101 S.Ct. 2176 (1981).
Smith v. California, 361 U.S. 147 (1959).
Smith v. U.S., 97 S.Ct. 1756 (1977).
Splawn v. California, 431 U.S. 595 (1977).
Spokane v. Portch, 92 Wn.2d 342 (1979).
Star v. Preller, 95 S.Ct. 217 (1974).
State v. Lerner, 81 N.E.2d 282 (1948).
Times Film Corp. v. Chicago, 365 U.S. 43 (1961).
U.S. v. Blucher, 581 F.2d 244 (1978).
U.S. v. McManus, 535 F.2d 460 (1976).
U.S. v. Middleton, 599 F.2d 1349 (1979).
U.S. v. Roth, 237 F.2d 796 (1956).
U.S. v. Various Articles of Obscene Merchandise, 62 F.2d 185 (1977).
Vance v. Universal Amusement, 445 U.S. 308 (1980).
Walker v. Popenoe, 149 F.2d 511 (1945).
Ward v. Illinois, 431 U.S. 767 (1977).
Young v. American Mini-Theaters, Inc., 96 S.Ct. 2440 (1976).

9 <u>COPYRIGHT</u>

Pac-Man is a yellow, pie-shaped creature which inhabits millions of video games in arcades and homes. The ravenous gobbler has spent its entire technological life consuming pink dots, power capsules, and ghosts on electronic screens across the United States. In 1982 the feisty little creation of Midway Games overcame its biggest challenge when it vanquished K. C. Munchkin, a Pac-Man clone manufactured by North American Phillips. But it was not Pac-Man's metered mouth that devoured Munchkin; it was Midway's attorneys armed with the law of copyright who did the deed. A United States court of appeals ruled that the similarities between the two games far outweighed the differences, that Munchkin "captures the total feel and substance of Pac-Man," and this was an infringement upon the Midway copyright on the popular game. A preliminary injunction was issued which blocked the sale of the North American Phillips game (*Advertising Age,* 17 May 1982).

Copyright is an area of the law which deals with immaterial property, property that a man cannot put his hands on, that cannot be felt or touched or locked in a safe. Some examples of this kind of property are inventions, ideas, writing, painting, music, and drama. In this chapter the rights of authors, composers, artists, inventors, and playwrights are discussed. This area of the law seems at first glance to be terribly complicated, but when the facts are sorted out, copyright law is really not too difficult to understand.

People who work in the mass media do not need to become copyright and patent attorneys in order to avoid lawsuits in the 1980s. But writers and broadcasters should know both how to protect their own work from theft and how to avoid illegally taking the work of someone else.

Until 1976, when the Congress passed a major revision of the copyright law, this nation suffered under a statute that had been adopted in 1909 and became out of date soon afterward. Beginning in the mid-fifties, the Congress began work on revision of the 1909 law. It seemed as though each time the revision was completed new technology such as cable television and photocopying made the proposal obsolete. In addition, special interest groups lobbied long and hard to have the law framed in a way favorable to them. Publishing groups, librarians, jukebox operators, and cable television operators are just some of the kinds of interest groups which put pressure on the Congress.

Copyright law covers a great many subjects which fall outside the scope of this book, which is law affecting the mass media. Hence, we will focus on a narrow range of subjects within the broader measure. First, the conditions creating the need for copyright laws and development of the law are discussed. Second, the kinds of works that may be copyrighted and the kinds that may not are considered. Third, how authors may protect their own work is discussed. Finally, the precautions which should be taken to avoid stealing the work of other persons, either inadvertently or advertently, are outlined. Also considered briefly are free-lance and cable television copyright and damages assessed in copyright suits.

PROTECTING LITERARY PROPERTY

Law professor Paul Goldstein writes in the *Columbia Law Review* (1970), "Copyright is the uniquely legitimate offspring of censorship." British history from the late fifteenth century through the early eighteenth century partially substantiates this assertion. It is naive, however, to think of copyright as solely a limiting force on the production of written works. Protection of the rights of an author, after all, can give impetus to authors to write and publish more. There were really few legal problems in protecting literary property prior to the development of mechanical printing. Each hand-copied manuscript was the result of the labor of a copyist. It was an individual entity, a specific creation. As such, it was protected by the law of personal property. But the printing press, which permitted mass production of exact copies of a written work, changed the situation. The press produced both a piece of physical property—the book itself—and an immaterial property—the arrangement and organization of the words or ideas. The immaterial property was called literary property and was not protected by British law.

Roots of the Law

As noted in chapter 2, printing created many problems for the king. The Crown was fearful of the power of the press to rouse the passions of the people against the government. Therefore, in the sixteenth century the government sanctioned and supported the grant of printing privileges to certain master printers in exchange for loyalty and assistance in ferreting out antigovernment writers and publishers. In *The First Copyright Statute* Harry Ransom writes:

> The privilege had its origins in the Crown's patronage of specific printers. Warrants granting rights to print books or a specific book, usually for a certain term—two years, ten years, or the lifetime of the printer—were a natural outgrowth of the system of appointing King's printers. The grant was a recognition of confidence in his printing and a protective guarantee of his right in copy. It was a means of extending royal control of the press through official choice of printers to be encouraged by patronage.

The first recorded privilege or royal grant was given in 1518 according to Professor Ransom. About forty years later the Stationers' Company was founded for much the same purpose. This was an organization of master printers chartered by the government to control, regulate, and protect printing. The company had sufficient power to regulate who did the printing and what was printed. The Crown cooperated with this guild, because it served as a useful tool for censorship. Some of the basic rudiments of copyright law were developed by the Stationers' Company. The company required printers to record the publication of their works in a registration book. While this device was used originally to keep track of what printers published, the registration book later became evidence in lawsuits over printing privileges. Registration of a book prior to publication of a pirated version substantiated a claim of ownership. It was in 1586 that a court first accepted the registration book as evidence of ownership.

What about the rights of authors, the persons who wrote the books published by the printers? In the sixteenth century authors had few rights. Generally when an author sold his manuscript to a printer or a bookseller, he sold all rights with it for a single fee. If the book sold well, the bookseller might further compensate the author, but the additional compensation stemmed from generosity, not from legal obligation. Ransom reports that many sixteenth-century authors were jailed for nonpayment of debt, others went hungry, and most had to undertake some kind of additional labor to keep body and soul together. If the author printed the work himself, he retained rights which would provide him a royalty, or he might make an agreement with a printer or bookseller to gain part of the proceeds of sales. Such arrangements were uncommon, and there was no organized royalty system.

In the seventeenth century litigation over the ownership of books increased, and with the increased litigation certain common law principles developed. A decree by the Star Chamber in 1637 asserted that all books which were published had to be registered in the Stationers' registration book, that the name of the printer or bookseller must appear in the published book, and that there was to be no infringement on the publishing rights of persons who held the printing privilege, that is, no theft of another person's work. In 1649 the government passed a law which provided a penalty—a fine—for anyone found guilty of reprinting works entered in the register.

More laws were passed and more cases tried in the second half of the seventeenth century. It soon became obvious, however, that problems of authors—who were becoming quite angry—and of booksellers and printers as well could not be solved by any measure short of a comprehensive law. Petitions began to appear at Parliament urging legislation to protect the rights of authors. In 1710 Parliament passed the first British copyright law: "An Act for the Encouragement of Learning, by Vesting the Copies of Printed Books in the Authors or Purchasers of Such Copies, during the Times therein mentioned." The law was passed in the eighth year of the reign of Queen Anne and hence became known as the Statute of Eight Anne.

The law gave the legal claim of ownership of a piece of literary property to the person who created the work or to a person who acquired the rights to the work from the author. The claim of ownership lasted for only fourteen years. The copyright could be renewed for fourteen more years, but after twenty-eight years the work fell into the public domain and could be copied by anyone. The copyright owner had to give nine copies to the government for use in libraries and had to register the book with the Stationers' Company.

The most important aspect of this law was not the specific legal provisions, but the recognition by the British government that writers or authors should enjoy the right of ownership in their creations. This concept is very important, for without it we might find ourselves with far less to read today. While most authors are motivated by a desire to inform and entertain, they must also subsist. By providing them the right of ownership in their work, authors are compensated in such a way as to encourage them to continue to write.

Clearly any law giving authors the right of ownership automatically limits copying and use of the literary property. This limitation is what Professor Goldstein means when he talks of censorship. A copyright law does in fact act as censorship since it restricts the right to republish or copy books, articles, photographs, and any work that is copyrighted.

The Statute of Eight Anne did not go unchallenged. Booksellers were angered by the limit on ownership. (The law provided that the ownership in any work created before the statute was adopted would terminate in twenty-one years.) Publishers rushed into print with works the law ruled were in the public domain, but which booksellers still claimed as literary property. The booksellers sought injunctions to stop what they called pirating. They argued that under the common law their ownership of a book was perpetual—it lasted forever. The Parliament could not take this away from them, they said. This dispute finally came before Britain's highest court, the House of Lords, in 1774. The House of Lords ruled that it was true that at common law the right of first printing and publishing lasted forever, but that the statute superseded the common law, revoked the common law copyright in perpetuity for published works. The common law no longer applied. Twenty-eight years were the maximum for ownership of published literary property.

This case, *Donaldson* v. *Beckett,* established a very important point in copyright law: that the law treated an unpublished work differently from a published work. Eight Anne specifically applied to works which had been published. The House of Lords ruled that limited ownership applied to such works. However, the law did not embrace unpublished works, and hence the common law rule of ownership in perpetuity remained in force.

While our copyright laws are direct descendants of the British law, the British law had little impact in the colonies. The colonies had no separate copyright statute, but printing and publishing original books and pamphlets was not an active business prior to the Revolution. After the Revolution, of course, the British law did not apply.

Our first constitution, the Articles of Confederation, made no mention of the protection of literary property. Congress did, however, recommend that the states adopt legislation to protect the rights of authors. Several states did before our present Constitution was adopted in 1789. In Article I, Section 8, of that document lies the basic authority for modern United States copyright law:

> The Congress shall have the power . . . To promote the Progress of Science and useful Arts, by securing for limited Times to Authors and Inventors the exclusive Right to their respective Writings and Discoveries.

This provision gives the Congress the power to legislate on both copyright and patent. The Congress did in 1790 by adopting a statute similar to that of Eight Anne. The law gave authors who were United States citizens the right to protect their books, maps, and charts for a total of twenty-eight years—a fourteen-year original grant plus a fourteen-year renewal. In 1802 the law was amended to include prints as well as books, maps, and charts. In 1831 the period of protection was expanded by fourteen years. The original grant became twenty-eight years with a fourteen-year renewal. Also, musical compositions were granted protection. Photography was given protection in 1865, and works of fine art were included five years later. Translation rights were added in 1870.

A major revision of the law was enacted in 1909, and as was previously noted, our current law was adopted in 1976.

What May Be Copyrighted

The law of copyright gives to the author, or the owner of the copyright, the sole and exclusive right to reproduce the copyrighted work in any form for any reason. Before a copyrighted work may be printed, broadcast, dramatized, translated, or whatever, the consent of the copyright owner must first be obtained. The law grants this individual exclusive monopoly over the use of that material.

What kinds of works are protected? The federal statute lists a wide range of items which can be copyrighted:

1. Literary works
2. Musical works, including any accompanying words
3. Dramatic works, including any accompanying music
4. Pantomimes and choreographic works
5. Pictorial, graphic, and sculptural works
6. Motion pictures and other audiovisual works
7. Sound recordings

To quote the statute specifically, copyright extends to "original works of authorship fixed in any tangible medium of expression." The Congress has defined *fixed in a tangible medium* as that work which is "sufficiently permanent or stable to permit it to be perceived, reproduced, or otherwise communicated for a period of more than a transitory duration." Under these standards such things as newspaper stories or entire newspapers, magazine articles, advertisements, and almost anything else created for the mass media can be copyrighted. Performances, extemporaneous speeches, and improvised sketches are examples of materials that are not fixed in a tangible medium and are not protected by the federal copyright statute. But this does not mean that someone can film or record a performer's act, for example, without the performer's permission. This would be forbidden by other laws such as the right to publicity (see pages 199–203) and common law copyright.*

Copyright law is equally specific about what cannot be copyrighted.

1. Trivial materials cannot be copyrighted. Such things as titles, slogans, and minor variations on works in the public domain are not protected by the law of literary property. (But these items might be protected by other laws, such as unfair competition, for example.)

2. Ideas are not copyrightable. The law protects the literary or dramatic expression of an author's idea—such as a script—but does not protect the ideas themselves.

3. Utilitarian goods—things whose purpose of existence is to produce other things—are not protected by copyright law, according to William Strong in *The Copyright Book*. A lamp is a utilitarian object whose sole purpose is to produce light. One cannot copyright the basic design of a lamp. But the design of any element which can be identified separately from the useful article can be copyrighted, according to Strong. The design of a Tiffany lamp can be copyrighted. The unique aspects of a Tiffany lamp have nothing to do with the utilitarian purpose of producing light; these aspects are purely decorative.

4. Methods, systems, and mathematical principles, formulas, and equations cannot be copyrighted. But a description, an explanation, or an illustration of an idea or system can be copyrighted. In such an instance the law is protecting the particular literary or pictorial form in which an author chooses to express himself, not the idea or plan or method itself. Imagine, for example, that an individual develops a new method to teach people to type, the "X-System." The X-System is an idea, and as such cannot be copyrighted. But the developer of the system can copyright instruction booklets, audiovisual materials, charts, drawings, and anything else used to describe or explain the X-System. These materials are considered "expressions of an idea" and are protected by the law.

*Under the 1909 law the United States had two kinds of copyright protection: common law copyright and statutory copyright. Much as it did in eighteenth-century England, the common law protected any work which had not been published. Common law protection was automatic; that is, the work was protected from the point of its creation. And it lasted forever—or until the work was published. In order to protect published works, the author, photographer, or composer had to register the book or picture or song with the United States government and place a copyright notice on the work. The 1976 statute does away with common law copyright for all practical purposes. The only kinds of works protected by the common law are works like extemporaneous speeches and sketches which have not been fixed in a tangible medium. They are still protected from the point of their creation by common law copyright. Once they are written down, recorded, filmed, or fixed in a tangible medium in any way, they come under the protection of the new law.

There is a limit, however, to how far the law will go in protecting such materials. You cannot protect the expression of an idea (through instruction books, charts, etc.) to the point where it prevents other persons from using the idea (the X-System of typing) at all.

Original Works

Can all books and motion pictures be copyrighted? Not really. The law specifically says that only "original" works can be copyrighted. What is an original work? In interpreting this term in the 1909 law, courts ruled that the word *original* means that the work must owe its origin to the author. In 1973 a court reporter, an employee of the court who transcribes the proceedings, attempted to claim copyright over a transcript he made of some of the proceedings during the investigation of the death of Mary Jo Kopechne. This young woman drowned when a car driven by Senator Edward Kennedy went off a bridge and into a creek near Chappaquiddick, Massachusetts. In *Lipman* v. *Commonwealth* (1973), a federal judge ruled that the transcript could not be copyrighted. "Since transcription is by very definition a verbatim recording of other persons' statements, there can be no originality in the reporter's product."

The work must be original. Must it be of high quality or be new or novel? The answer to both questions is no. Even common and mundane works are copyrightable. Courts have consistently ruled that it is not the function of the legal system to act as literary or art critic when applying copyright law. In 1903 Justice Oliver Wendell Holmes wrote in *Bleistein* v. *Donaldson Lithographing Co.,* "It would be a dangerous undertaking for persons trained only to the law to constitute themselves final judges of the worth of pictorial illustrations, outside of the narrowest and most obvious limits." Even the least pretentious picture can be an original, Holmes noted in reference to the posters involved in this case. Likewise, novelty is not important to copyright: the author does not have to be the first person to say something in order to copyright it. "All that is needed to satisfy both the Constitution and the statute is that the 'author' contributed something more than a merely trivial variation, something recognizably his own," one court ruled (*Amsterdam* v. *Triangle Publishing Co.,* 1951).

The key is how much of the author's own work is invested. In 1946 the *Philadelphia Inquirer* printed a copy of a map in connection with publication of a historical article. The map had been copyrighted by the Franklin Survey Company, which promptly sued for copyright infringement. The survey company created the map by studying other maps; the company did no surveying itself. It obtained road numbers from the highway department and road names almost exclusively from other maps. There was no question that the Franklin Survey Company had spent a good deal of time assembling this material, but the fact was that the company did not create much of the material by its own labor. The court ruled that the survey company's copyright was invalid because the creative work by the plaintiff was not sufficient to make the map original (*Amsterdam* v. *Triangle Publishing Co., 1951*). There must be at least a modicum of creative work in the map, the court said. Had Franklin not assembled this information in an original or unique fashion? This fact was immaterial, the court ruled. A map is protected only when the publisher gets some of the material "by the sweat of his brow." Originality is therefore the key; whether the work is novel or of artistic quality is not important.

News Events

Can an event be copyrighted? Suppose a reporter is standing next to a building which suddenly and violently collapses, killing scores of people trapped inside. Suppose the reporter is the only one who saw the building collapse. Can she write a news story about this disaster, copyright it, and then prohibit others from writing about the event as well? The answer is no.

This point was established in an interesting case. In 1917 the *New York Tribune* published a copyrighted story about the first large-scale use of submarine warfare by the Germans in World War I. The New York paper sold the republication rights for the story to the *Chicago Daily News*. Before the *Daily News* could print the story, the *Chicago Record-Herald* printed its own version of the story. The initial paragraph of the *Herald* version began, "The *Tribune* this morning in a copyrighted article of Louis Durant Edwards, a correspondent in Germany, says that Germany to make the final effort against Great Britain has plunged 300 or more submersibles into the North Sea."

The remainder of the *Herald* story was comprised of five additional paragraphs, each of which was almost an exact duplication of a paragraph from the much longer *Tribune* story. The *Tribune* sued for infringement of copyright. The *Herald* answered by saying that a newspaper cannot copyright the news. Lawyers for the defendant argued that all the newspaper did was made use of facts which were in the public domain.

The circuit court of appeals agreed that as such news is not copyrightable. If the *Herald* story had been merely a summary or statement of the *Tribune* story, the *Tribune* would then have no case. However, the *Herald* did not stick to just a summary of the facts, but used parts of the article including the literary style and quality. The article itself, the way the words were organized, the style—the creative aspects of the report—can be (and in this case were) protected by copyright. The court said (*Chicago Record-Herald* v. *Tribune Association,* 1921):

> This is plainly more than a mere chronicle of facts or news. It reveals a peculiar power of portrayal and a felicity of wording and phrasing, well calculated to seize and hold the interest of the reader, which is quite beyond and apart from the mere setting forth of facts. But if the whole of it were considered as stating news or facts, yet, the arrangement and manner of statement plainly discloses a distinct literary flavor and individuality of expression peculiar to the authorship, bringing the article clearly within the purview and protection of the copyright law.

The court ruled that the fact that the *Herald* gave the *Tribune* credit did not alleviate the theft. On the contrary, the court said, it might have conveyed to the public the incorrect idea that the *Herald* had got permission from the *Tribune* to use the story.

News cannot be copyrighted. But the style or manner of presentation can be protected. Consider the imaginary building-disaster story again. If reporter Jane Adams is the only one to witness the building collapse and publishes a copyrighted story about it, no one else can publish that story without permission. Other news media can report that Jane Adams reported in a copyrighted story that a building collapsed, killing many people. These news media can also summarize—note, summarize—the facts given by Adams in her story. This summary is not an infringement of copyright.

A case in Florida recently raised an interesting question about the difference between facts and expression of facts. Gene Miller, a Pulitizer-Prize-winning reporter for the *Miami Herald,* wrote a book entitled *83 Hours Till Dawn,* an account of the kidnapping of Barbara Mackle. Miller said he had spent more than 2,500 hours on the book, and many aspects of the kidnapping case were uncovered by the journalist and reported only in his book.

Universal Studios wanted to film a dramatization of the 1971 incident, but was unable to come to terms with Miller on payment for the rights. Through a series of errors and bad judgments, the studio produced the so-called docu-drama anyway, and Miller sued for infringement of copyright. The similarities between Miller's book and the Universal script were striking—even some of the errors Miller had made in preparing the book were found in the film. But Universal argued that it was simply telling a story of a news event, and as such the research that Miller had done in digging out the facts regarding the story was not protected by copyright law. A United States district court agreed with Miller's contention. "The court views the labor and expense of the research involved in the obtaining of those uncopyrightable facts to be intellectually distinct from those facts, and more similar to the expression of the facts than the facts themselves," the court said. The judge ruled that it was necessary to reward the effort and ingenuity involved in giving expression to a fact (*Miller* v. *Universal Studios,* 1978). But the Fifth United States Court of Appeals reversed the lower court ruling. "The valuable distinction in copyright law between facts and the expression of facts cannot be maintained if research is held to be copyrightable. There is no rational basis for distinguishing between facts and the research involved in obtaining the facts," the court said. To hold research copyrightable, the court said, is no more or less than to hold that the facts discovered as a result of research are entitled to copyright protection (*Miller* v. *Universal City Studios,* 1981).

The path followed by the Fifth United States Court of Appeals in the *Miller* case had been forged a year earlier by the Second United States Court of Appeals in a similar ruling. In March 1980 that court ruled that Universal Studios did not infringe upon the copyright of author A. A. Hoehling, who wrote *Who Destroyed the Hindenberg?* when it produced a film on the 1937 airship disaster. In writing his opinion Chief Judge Irving Kaufman noted that the Second Circuit Court had in the past refused "to subscribe to the view that an author is absolutely precluded from saving time and effort by referring to and relying upon prior published material. . . . It is just such wasted effort that the proscription against the copyright of ideas and facts . . . are designed to prevent"(*Hoehling* v. *Universal Studios,* 1980).

Misappropriation

While this chapter focuses upon copyright, an ancillary area of the law needs to be briefly mentioned as it too guards against the theft of immaterial property. **Misappropriation** or unfair competition is sometimes invoked as an additional legal remedy in suits for copyright infringement. Unlike copyright, which springs largely from federal statute today, misappropriation or unfair competition remains a creature of the common law. One of the most important media-oriented misappropriation cases was decided by the Supreme Court more than sixty years ago and stemmed from a dispute between the Associated Press (AP) and the International News Service (INS), a rival press association owned by William Randolph Hearst. (INS merged with the United Press in 1958 and today represents the *I* in *UPI.*)

The Associated Press charged that the International News Service pirated its news, saying that INS bribed AP employees to gain access to news before it was sent to AP member newspapers. The press agency also charged that the Hearst wire service copied news from bulletin boards and early editions of newspapers which carried AP dispatches. Sometimes INS editors rewrote the news, and other times they sent the news as written by AP. Copyright was not the question, because AP did not copyright its material. The agency said it could not copyright all its dispatches because there were too many and they had to be transmitted too fast. The International News Service argued that because the material was not copyrighted it was in the public domain and could be used by anyone.

Justice Mahlon Pitney wrote the opinion in the seven-to-one decision. He said there can be no property right in the news itself, the events, the happenings, which are publici juris, the common property of all, the history of the day. However, the jurist went on to say (*Associated Press* v. *International News Service,* 1918):

> Although we may and do assume that neither party [AP or INS] has any remaining property interest as against the public in uncopyrighted matter after the moment of its first publication, it by no means follows that there is no remaining property interest in it as between themselves.

Pitney said there was a distinct difference between taking the news collected by AP and publishing it for use by readers and taking the news and transmitting that news for commercial use, in competition with the plaintiff. This action is unfair competition, he said—interference with the business of the AP precisely at the point where profit is to be reaped.

In 1963 a Pennsylvania broadcasting station was found guilty of pirating the news from a local newspaper and reading it over the air as if it were the fruits of its own news-gathering efforts (*Pottstown Daily News Publishing* v. *Pottstown Broadcasting,* 1963).

The decision in both these cases was based on the doctrine of unfair competition, or misappropriation. Courts have applied the doctrine in various instances of fraudulent or dishonest competitive business practices, but particularly in those instances where one seller attempts to substitute his own products for those of a well-known competitor by counterfeiting a trade name, package design, or trademark. For example, the owner of the Acme Motel remodels his building in the guise of a Holiday Inn, calls his remodeled creation Holiday Inn, and attempts to lure weary travelers into his establishment on the basis of the reputation of the real Holiday Inn. This practice is considered unfair competition. In *Associated Press* v. *International News Service* the Hearst wire service attempted to pass off Associated Press news as its own, and the court said the deception was unfair.

Another more recent case explores a different dimension of the problem. Orion Pictures bought the film rights to a French novel entitled $E = MC^2$ and prepared to make a film of the story entitled *A Little Romance*. Dell Publishing Company bought the translation rights to the same book and attempted to negotiate with Orion for a tie-in publicity campaign heralding the release of both the movie and the book. But Orion refused, claiming that the story had been changed so much in the film that it no longer resembled the book. Dell pushed on anyway and published the book using the movie title—*A Little Romance*—and the cover of book stated "Now A Major Motion Picture." The promotional material for the book emphasized the tie in with the film and was an attempt to boost sales of the book. Orion sued for unfair competition, arguing that the sale of the book could hurt the film. A federal judge agreed, noting that after he had read the book and seen the film he considered the motion picture to be substantially better than the novel. "It is the Court's belief that if one were to read the book first, the entertaining achievement of the film would not be anticipated." The court said that the Dell book, through its title and cover promotion, gives the impression that it is the "official novel" version of the film and therefore has similar content. This misleads the public and constitutes unfair competition (*Orion Pictures* v. *Dell Publishing,* 1979). The book company was attempting to trade on the name of the picture in promoting the book. This practice is illegal, even though the title of a film cannot be copyrighted.

Duration of Copyright Protection

Any work created after January 1, 1978, will be protected for the life of the creator, plus fifty years. This allows creators to enjoy the fruits of their labor until death and then allows the heirs to profit from the work of their fathers, mothers, sisters, or brothers for an additional one-half century. After fifty years the work goes into what is called public domain. At that point it may be copied by any person for any reason without the payment of royalty to the original owner. The copyright on a work created by two or more authors extends through the life of the last author to die plus fifty years. A work for hire (i.e., where an author is paid to create a book for a corporation which then holds the copyright) is protected for seventy-five years after publication or for one hundred years after creation.

Prior to 1978 works could be copyrighted for a term of twenty-eight years and then renewed for twenty-eight more years for a total of fifty-six years. The 1976 copyright revision prolongs the protection of works copyrighted before 1978 for a total of seventy-five years.

If the work is in its initial term of copyright, it is protected for the remainder of that term plus forty-seven years. That is, the owner of the copyright on a book which expires in 1987 can retain ownership of that book from the present time until 1987 plus forty-seven years. However, in order to gain this additional forty-seven years of protection, copyright holders must seek renewal as was required under the previous statute. Without renewal, copyright owners forfeit their ownership of the work, which will move into the public domain.

If the copyrighted work is in its renewal term—the second twenty-eight years under the old law—the work is protected for a total of seventy-five years. For example, a book which is in the fifteenth year of its second, or renewal, term has already been protected for one full term, twenty-eight years, and for fifteen years of the renewal term—a total of forty-three years. That book is protected for thirty-two more years from today, or a total of seventy-five years. No renewal request is needed.*

Owners of a copyright are granted almost exclusive monopoly over the use of their creations. The word "almost" must be used, for there are really four limitations upon this monopoly. Three of the limitations have been discussed already. First, the work must be something that can be copyrighted. There can be no legal monopoly on the use of something that cannot be protected by the law. Second, the monopoly only protects original authorship or creation. If the creation is not original, it cannot be protected. Third, copyright protection does not last forever. At some point the protection ceases and the work falls into the public domain.

*Additional information concerning duration of copyright is available in circulars *R15A* and *R15T,* which are published by The Copyright Office, Library of Congress, Washington, D.C., 20559.

Summary

American copyright law derives from rules and regulations established by the British government in the sixteenth and seventeenth centuries. The contemporary basis for the protection of immaterial property is contained in the United States Constitution, and since 1789 the nation has had numerous federal copyright statutes. The current law, adopted in 1976, gives to the author or owner of a work the sole and exclusive right to reproduce the copyrighted work in any form for any reason. The statute protects all original works of authorship fixed in any tangible medium. Included are such things as literary works, newspaper stories, magazine articles, television programs, films, and even advertisements. Trivial items, utilitarian goods, ideas, and methods or systems cannot be copyrighted.

News events cannot be copyrighted, but stories or broadcasts which endeavor to describe or explain these events can be copyrighted. What is being protected is the author's style or manner of presentation of the news. Similarly, facts cannot be copyrighted, but works which relate these facts can be protected as expression. While news and facts cannot be copyrighted, anyone who attempts to present news or facts gathered by someone else as his or her own work may be guilty of breaking other laws, such as misappropriation or unfair competition. In most cases copyrighted works are protected for the life of the author or creator plus fifty years. Different rules apply for works created before 1978 and for works made for hire.

FAIR USE

The fourth limitation upon exclusive monopoly is broader than the other three and certainly more controversial and is concerned with limited copying of copyrighted material. This is the doctrine of fair use, which has been defined by one court as (*Triangle* v. *Knight-Ridder,* 1980):

> A rule of reason . . . to balance the author's right to compensation for his work, on the one hand, against the public's interest in the widest possible dissemination of ideas and information on the other.

This doctrine, then, permits limited copying of an original creation that has been properly copyrighted and has not yet fallen into the public domain.

Under previous copyright laws all copying of a copyrighted work was against the law. This absolute prohibition on copying constituted a hardship for scholars, critics, and teachers seeking to use small parts of copyrighted materials in their work. A judicial remedy for this problem was sought. It was argued that since the purpose of the original copyright statute was to promote art and science the copyright law should not be administered in such a way as to frustrate artists and scientists who publish scholarly materials. In 1879 the United States Supreme Court ruled in *Baker* v. *Selden:*

> The very object of publishing a book on science or the useful arts is to communicate to the world the useful knowledge which it contains. But this object would be frustrated if the useful knowledge could not be used without incurring the guilt of piracy of the book.

The doctrine of **fair use** emerged from the courts, and under this judicial doctrine small amounts of copying were permitted so long as the publication of the material advanced science, the arts, criticism, and so forth.

The 1976 copyright law contains the common law doctrine of fair use. Section 107 of the new measure declares, "the fair use of a copyrighted work . . . for purposes such as criticism, comment, news reporting, teaching (including multiple copies for classroom use), scholarship or research is not an infringement of copyright."

In determining whether the use of a particular work is a fair use, the statute says that courts should consider the following factors:

1. The purpose and character of the use, including whether such use is of a commercial nature or is for nonprofit educational purposes
2. The nature of the copyrighted work
3. The amount and substantiality of the portion used in relation to the copyrighted work as a whole
4. The effect of the use upon the potential market for or value of the copyrighted work

These, then, are the factors that judges will take into account in determining whether a use is an infringement or a fair use. Fair use is perhaps the most confusing and complex part of the law, and the section of the law dealing with fair use became a major battleground for disputes between librarians and publishers. The librarians and other persons interested in photocopying of published works sought liberal rules under fair use. Publishers and copyright holders wanted tight rules against photocopying. The law seems to be a compromise, allowing for the photocopying of a single copy of a work for library use, but with several qualifications of the general rule.

Purpose and Character of Use

Interestingly, the fair use criteria included in the statute and just listed (1 through 4) above are very close to the criteria that courts used under the old common law fair use doctrine. This is no accident. In a report issued by committees in the House and the Senate on Section 107, the legislators said that the new law "endorses the purpose and general scope of the judicial doctrine of fair use," but did not intend that the law be frozen as it existed in 1976. "The courts must be free to adapt the doctrine to particular situations on a case-by-case basis. Section 107 is intended to restate the present judicial doctrine of fair use, not to change, narrow, or enlarge it in any way."

Fair use is easiest to understand by looking at each of the four elements individually, as a judge would do in determining whether a particular use is a fair use. It is dangerous to assign relative weight to each of these elements, as in any given case a court may place more weight upon one than upon another because of the facts in the case, biases of the court, or any number of other reasons.

The purpose and charcter of the use—how the copyrighted material will be used—is very important. Courts look far more favorably upon noncommercial or nonprofit uses. The law specifically lists several categories of use which normally fall under fair use: criticism, comment, news reports, teaching, scholarship, and research. A book reviewer, for example, is clearly protected when quoting even long passages from a work being evaluated. A journalist could undoubtedly publish one or two stanzas from a poem by a poet named winner of a Pulitzer Prize. Yet if a poster publisher took the same two stanzas of poetry, printed them in large type on eleven-by-fourteen stock, and tried to sell them for $2.50 each, the publisher would be guilty of an infringement of copyright. The purpose of the use in the case of the journalist was to give readers an example of the poet's work, but the poster publisher simply wanted to make a few bucks.

Another dimension of purpose or character focuses upon the material itself and the public interest. In 1966 the Second Circuit Court of Appeals erected the public interest dimension of fair use in a complex copyright suit involving America's best-known recluse, the late Howard Hughes. Random House planned to publish a biography of Hughes in which a series of articles about Hughes in *Look* magazine were quoted rather extensively. When he learned of the Random House project, Hughes, who manifested almost a compulsion about his privacy, formed a corporation called Rosemont which bought the rights to the *Look* magazine story. Rosemont then sued Random House for using material from the series. All these events took place even before the book was published.

Judge Lumbard ruled in favor of Random House, noting that the purpose of the copyright laws was not to stop dissemination of information about publicity-shy public figures. It would be contrary to the public interest, he said, to allow a man to buy up the rights to anything written about him to stop authors from using the material. Lumbard said that at least the spirit of the First Amendment applied to the copyright laws, and that the courts should not tolerate the use of the copyright laws to interfere with the public's right to be informed regarding matters of general interest. Rosemont (Hughes) protested that such copying might be appropriate if the work in question were a scholarly biography of Hughes, but that the Random House venture was commercial. Judge Lumbard said this fact was immaterial (*Rosemont* v. *Random House,* 1966):

> Whether an author or publisher reaps economic benefits from the sale of a biographical work, or whether its publication is motivated in part by desire for commercial gain, or whether it is designed for the popular market, i.e., the average citizen rather than the college professor, has no bearing on whether a public benefit may be derived from such a work. . . . Thus, we conclude that whether an author or publisher has a commercial motive or writes in a popular style is irrelevant to a determination of whether a particular use of copyrighted material in a work which offers some benefit to the public constitutes a fair use.

The decision in *Rosemont* represented a bold new step forward in copyright law, a step which many authorities felt was long overdue. On its face the case could not have been equitably decided any other way. Hughes's attempt to buy up his own life story was so patently obvious that the entire suit was really a farce—a mild diversion for the idle rich. Many persons asked, Will the public interest ruling stand?

Two years later a federal district court in New York used the standard to allow the copying of several frames of very famous motion-picture film. An amateur photographer named Abraham Zapruder happened to be filming President John F. Kennedy when he was shot by an assassin in Dallas in 1963. The film is crude, but is the only film available. *Life* magazine bought the rights to the film from Zapruder for $15,000 with the stipulation that the magazine would allow government agencies to use it in connection with investigation of the president's death. *Life* had a tendency to buy the rights to important events, for example, signing contracts with all the astronauts for exclusive stories. The Zapruder film became (and remains) a central piece of evidence in the death of John Kennedy, and many persons who believe that the Warren Commission was wrong, that there was a conspiracy, that there was more than one gunman, use the Zapruder film to attempt to prove their thesis. In this case the defendant wanted to publish several frames of the film in his book proposing a multi-assassin theory. When *Life* refused permission to use the film, the author used the frames anyway. Was this fair use?

Life said no, but the court disagreed. The judge said that there was little damage to the magazine as a result of publication of the pictures, that customers purchased the book because of its thesis, not because of its pictures, and that without the photographs the author's thesis was at best difficult to explain. "There is a public interest in having the fullest information available on the murder of President Kennedy. Thompson [the author] did serious work on the subject and had a theory entitled to public consideration." The public interest won out over the magazine's property rights (*Time, Inc.* v. *Bernard Geis Associates,* 1968).

But the public interest standard enunciated in *Rosemont* and *Zapruder* is not without boundaries. Copyright law cannot be ignored or abandoned simply because there is great public interest in the reporting of an event or a story about an important person. Both the American Broadcasting System (ABC) and the Columbia Broadcasting System (CBS) discovered recently that the fair use doctrine has limits.

While James Doran was a student at Iowa States University he produced a twenty-eight minute biography of wrestler Dan Gable. The film was financed by Iowa State and the Gable family, and the university held the copyright. Doran worked for ABC as a videotape operator during the 1972 Olympic Games during which Gable won a gold medal in wrestling. Doran told ABC about his film while network reporters were scrambling for some biographical film about Gable. ABC broadcast long segments of the film during its telecast of the Olympic Games, without first obtaining permission from Iowa State University. The network claimed that these broadcasts were fair use in the copyright infringement suit that followed. The network said it was engaged in the laudable pursuit of disseminating the life story of an important public figure involved in an event of intense public interest. But the Second United States Court of Appeals rejected this argument. The network could have used other, noncopyrighted material for its film biography of the gold-medal-winning wrestler. The film was used at least in part for commercial exploitation by the network, the court ruled. No fair use (*Iowa State* v. *ABC*, 1980).

CBS found itself in a similar mess in 1982 after it had broadcast a copyrighted compilation of Charlie Chaplin films on the occasion of the great comedian's death. Roy Export Company owned the rights to the motion pictures excerpted in the thirteen-minute montage. This compilation of segments from six of Chaplin's greatest films had been put together by Roy Export for a one-time telecast on NBC during the 1972 Academy Award presentations, which featured a special segment on Charlie Chaplin. CBS had tried to buy the rights to the compilation from Roy Export, but the company refused the offer. When Chaplin died, CBS nevertheless obtained a copy of the film compilation from NBC, which had kept a videotape of the Academy Awards ceremony, and broadcast it as a memorial biography of the great comedian.

When the network was sued for copyright infringement, it claimed its telecast of the material was fair use. Chaplin's death was newsworthy, and a biography of the comedian's life would be incomplete without showing excerpts from some of his greatest films, the network argued. But the Second United States Court of Appeals disagreed. "The showing of copyrighted films was not essential to CBS's news report of Charlie Chaplin's death or to its assessment of his place in history," the court ruled. Other films which were in the public domain were available, the court said. Also, the public is generally familiar with Chaplin's work.

CBS also argued that the 1972 Academy Award ceremony was a very important news event since it marked the return of Charlie Chaplin to Hollywood after a twenty-year exile in Europe after the Communist witch-hunts in the film industry in the early 1950s. Again the court rejected the network's ideas. "The audiovisual news event, if there was one, was Chaplin's appearance, not the showing of his work," the judge ruled. The showing of the copyrighted compilation of Chaplin's film exceeded fair use (*Roy Export Co.* v. *CBS*, 1982).

It is important to note the difference between these latter two cases and the earlier decision on the Zapruder film, for this difference is a key to understanding what are perhaps one set of limits to the public interest standard in fair use. Assume for a moment that comparable public interest exists in all three events—the Kennedy assassination, Dan Gable winning an Olympic Gold Medal, and the death of Charlie Chaplin. There was considerable noncopyrighted material available for the networks to use in reporting the latter two events. The broadcast of the copyrighted films was not essential to telling an important news story. In the case of the Zapruder film, however, much of the book's argument about the Kennedy assassination was based upon the film taken by Zapruder. No suitable substitute existed. Courts in the future may use this criterion as an element in deciding whether the use of copyrighted material is fair use. The question will be, Was other noncopyrighted material available which could have been used to tell the story and thus serve the public interest?

Nature of Copyrighted Work

When the nature of the copyrighted work is considered, at least two important considerations of the protected work must be made. First, is the work still available? If a copyrighted book is out of print, unavailable for purchase, the user may have more justification for copying a portion of it than if it is readily available. The lack of the availability of the work cannot be used as an excuse for copying a work which has never been formally published. Second, what kind of work is it? Copying consumable materials like workbooks, exercise books, standardized tests, and so forth, is rarely if ever a fair use. If such materials could be copied freely, only a single workbook, for example, would ever have to be purchased. Copies could be made continuously, and the author would be deprived of justly earned royalties. The use of materials from publications like newspapers, news magazines, and reference books is less likely to be an infringement. Use of materials from these sorts of works is rarely harmful to the publisher—unless the copying is a persistent occurrence.

Amount of a Work Used

The amount and the substantiality of the portion used in relation to the copyrighted work as a whole—as stated—is a relative standard. Word counts, for example, do not mean very much. The use of 500 words from a 450-page book is far less damaging than the use of 3 lines from a 5-line poem. The question is always how much was used in comparison to the total size of the work. A court of appeals ruled that a novelist who copied 24 passages from a biography of the life of Hans Christian Andersen exceeded fair use. The passages were translations of Danish documents, and while the documents were in the public domain, the biographer had translated them into English. While 24 passages does not sound like very much, the court ruled that the defendant, who used the material in a novel based upon the life of Andersen, appropriated too much material to be considered a fair use. By using the fruits of the biographer's work, the translation of the Danish documents, the novelist was able to finish her work in far less time. She got much value from the plaintiff's work (*Toksvig* v. *Bruce Publishing Co.,* 1950).

It was the massive appropriation of copyrighted films that resulted in a successful suit for infringement against an educational services board in Erie County, New York. The educational board was sued by three corporations, including the Encyclopaedia Britannica, which made, acquired, and leased educational films. The defendant in the case rented films from various companies and then made videotapes of them for future use by the schools. Films broadcast on television were also videotaped for classroom use. Despite the nonprofit nature of the use of these materials, the court ruled that such activity was not a fair use. An important factor in the court's decision was that the educational services board used from five to eight full-time employees to do the copying and had made as many as ten thousand tapes per year since 1966. This was high-volume copying, and the court ruled it was not a fair use (*Encyclopaedia Britannica* v. *Crooks,* 1978). The issue of the amount of copying that can be done in the name of education arose again recently when nine book publishers sued New York University, nine of its professors, and an off-campus copy center for copyright infringement. The suit charges that the faculty members repeatedly copied major amounts from many popular works such as Truman Capote's *In Cold Blood* and *The Final Days* by Bob Woodward and Carl Bernstein. The publishers argued that such copying was done semester after semester. The publishers dropped their suit in April 1983 in return for a pledge from the defendant school and faculty to adhere to copying guidelines.

One of the toughest tasks a judge must face is measuring fair use when someone presents a parody of a copyrighted work. To be successful a parody must conjure up in the viewers' or listeners' minds the original work; hence, it must use some aspects of the original work. But how much of the original can be used? "Saturday Night Live," a National Broadcasting Company television program, presented a parody of a New York City public relations campaign. The city had even commissioned the writing of a song—"I Love New York"—as a theme for the campaign. The NBC "Saturday Night Live" parody ended with the singing of "I Love Sodom" to the tune of "I Love New York." The city claimed this was a copyright infringement, but the court disagreed. "A parody is entitled to conjure up the original. Even more extensive use would still be fair use, provided the parody builds upon the original, using the original as a known element of modern culture and contributing something new for humorous effect or commentary," the Second United States Court of Appeals ruled (*Elsmere Music* v. *NBC,* 1980). (See *MGM* v. *Showcase Atlanta,* 1981, for an example of a parody that went too far.) What is added to the copyrighted material is almost as important as how much of the original is used when determining whether a parody is a fair use.

It is important to remember that the amount of material which may be fairly copied is not an absolute, but is always relative to the size of the total work from which the material is taken.

Effect of Use on Market

The effect of the use upon the potential market for or value of the copyrighted work is the fourth criterion. While a cautionary note has been sounded against assigning relative weight to the four criteria, this final one—harm to the plaintiff—is probably given greater weight by most courts than any of the other three. In a Congressional Committee report on the 1976 law, the legislators noted that "with certain special exceptions . . . a use that supplants any part of the normal market for a copyrighted work would ordinarily be considered an infringement." There is a considerable amount of both pre-1976 and post-1976 case law which focuses upon this point.

A group of song writers once sued *Mad* magazine for publishing parody song lyrics of their compositions. The publication appeared in the special bonus to the *Fourth Annual Edition of Mad* and was described by the magazine as "a collection of parody lyrics to fifty-seven old standards which reflect the idiotic world in which we live." The parody lyrics were written in the meter of the original songs and were to be sung to the melody of the standard versions. The parody lyrics to the song "The Last Time I Saw Paris" concerned a sports hero turned television pitchman, and the song was called "The First Time I Saw Maris." A song about a woman hypochondriac was sung to the tune of "A Pretty Girl is Like a Melody" and was called "Louella Schwartz Describes her Malady."

The judge asked, "How were the songwriters hurt?" In a negligible way, the court concluded. The parody of lyrics was not a theft. They were not about the same topic and did not have the same rhyme scheme. The parody lyrics were in the same meter as the original lyrics, which was necessary if the original songs were to be recognized and the lyrics were to fit the melodies. "We doubt," the court added, "that even so eminent a composer as plaintiff Irving Berlin should be permitted to claim a property interest in the iambic pentameter." The use by *Mad* of the song titles and references to their melodies was fair use, the court ruled (*Berlin* v. *E. C. Publications, Inc.,* 1964).

In 1977 a federal district court refused to grant a temporary order enjoining the publication of a cumulative 111-year name index of the 111 annually issued volumes of the *New York Times Index*. The *Times* index is organized alphabetically within each annual volume. The *Roxbury Index* of the annual *New York Times Indexes* was to be organized alphabetically over the 111 years from 1863 to 1974. The index of the *Times* index would be of great benefit to researchers. For example, using only the *New York Times Index* for material on Charles Evans Hughes, a researcher would have to look in more than 40 annual volumes spanning the late Chief Justice's life. But with the *Roxbury Index,* a researcher would need only to look in a single volume under Hughes's name for all the references during the 45-year period. While this would be a great boon to researchers, there was no question that by its very nature the *Roxbury Index* included much material copied from the copyrighted *New York Times Index*. The court ruled, however, that the effect of the personal-name index on the market for the *New York Times Index* appeared "slight or nonexistent." As a matter of fact, persons could not use the *Roxbury Index* without also using the *New York Times Index,* so rather than being in competition with the annual index, the cumulative name index enhanced the value of the *New York Times* publication (*New York Times* v. *Roxbury Data Interface,* 1977).

The Fifth United States Court of Appeals ruled that it was fair use when the *Miami Herald* displayed copyrighted covers of *TV Guide* magazine in advertising for the newspaper's new television magazine. *TV Guide* had argued that such use was an infringement upon its copyright, since the advertisement for the *Herald* magazine was a blatantly commercial use of the *TV Guide* covers. The court conceded it was indeed a commercial use, but noted that the use of the covers had absolutely no effect upon the potential market or value of the copyrighted *TV Guide* magazine covers. True, the advertisements for the *Herald* television magazine might hurt *TV Guide* sales. But the *advertising* did this, not the use of the covers of old editions of *TV Guide* (*Triangle Publications* v. *Knight-Ridder Newspapers, Inc.* 1980). In this case the court said that the fourth factor, the effect of the use on the market for the copyrighted work, "is widely accepted to be the most important factor."

Finally, the *Nation* magazine was found guilty of copyright infringement after publishing a 2,000-word excerpt from the 200,000-word copyrighted memoirs of former President Gerald Ford. The magazine somehow got its hands on a copy of a draft of the Ford memoirs. The editor of *Nation* said he knew that the memoirs were soon to be published as a book by Harper and Row and the Reader's Digest Association. He said he also knew that *Time* magazine had purchased the right to publish excerpts from the memoirs before the publication of the book. *Nation* nevertheless, without permission, published a section of the memoirs, including portions in which Ford tried to explain why he pardoned former President Richard M. Nixon for his Watergate crimes. Harper and Row sued. *Nation* said the material it published was news and should be protected by the fair use doctrine. But the U.S. District Court disagreed. The court looked at each of the four fair use criteria and made these judgments: *Nation* published the article for profit. The revelations about Ford's pardoning Nixon were not really news; the former president had given these facts in testimony before the Congress in 1974 and the story was widely reported then. The Ford memoirs were just about to be published by Harper and Row, and this was the point at which the publisher might be harmed the most by the infringement. The excerpts published by *Nation* constituted only 2,000 words of a much larger work, but they also constituted the heart of the Ford memoirs. Finally, and very importantly, the publication by *Nation* seriously harmed Harper and Row. *Time* magazine aborted its agreement to publish excerpts. This cost the plaintiffs the substantial fee that *Time* had agreed to pay Harper and Row for the pre-publication rights. (*Harper and Row* v. *Nation,* 1983). *Nation* has appealed the ruling.

The doctrine of fair use presented the nation in the 1980s with one of the most interesting copyright problems in decades. Is it fair use when the owner of a home videotape recorder copies television programs and motion pictures broadcast by television networks and local stations and then replays them for strictly personal use? Universal City Studios, Walt Disney Productions, and other program production companies brought suit in 1979 to stop such home recording. Named as defendants in the case were Sony Corporation of America and several distributors and sellers of the home video-recording equipment. Universal charged that the home copying of programs amounted to massive infringement of their copyrights on these programs. Sony and the other defendants argued that this was fair use of the material. The trial court ruled in favor of the defendants, noting that the copying was not undertaken for commercial purposes, and that the harm to the plaintiffs in the case was purely speculative (*Universal City Studios* v. *Sony,* 1979). But the Ninth United States Court of Appeals reversed this decision and ruled against Sony. The court said such home recording was not fair use. The law states that *nonprofit educational* use may be fair use, but this is not the same as *noncommerical* use, the court said. The recording of entire programs was something certainly never contemplated when the fair use standards were written, the court added. Finally, such copying could have a severe impact upon the plaintiffs. In the imminent future a large percentage of the nation's seventy-five million television households will have a videotape recorder, and massive amounts of copying will take place, the court predicted. Viewers would watch the playback of programs they had copied, rather than new programs; commercials would be deleted in the playback; and the audience for rerun programming would be significantly reduced, the court concluded (*Universal City Studios* v. *Sony,* 1981). The Supreme Court quickly agreed to hear an appeal of the ruling, which had made several million videotape recorder owners outlaws in the eyes of the law. In June 1983 the high Court postponed its decision in the case and asked that the matter be reargued in the fall of 1983.

Many observers believed the high Court was hoping a legislative solution might be reached before it had to decide the matter. Several bills were introduced in the Congress to revise the law in such a way as to permit home copying. Some proposals would simply exempt such copying from copyright liability (see S. 1758 and H.R. 4792). Others would exempt such copying from liability, but call for a royalty fee attached to the price of blank videotape cartridges, to be paid to the entertainment industry (H.R. 5705 and S. 1333).

Summary

While the copyright statute gives the author or owner of a copyrighted work an exclusive monopoly over the use of that work, there has been recognition that it is important in some instances for other persons to be able to copy portions of a protected work. No liability will attach to such copying if the use is what the law calls a "fair use."

A court will consider four factors when determining whether a specific use is fair use.

1. What is the purpose of the use? Why was the material copied? Was it a commercial use or for nonprofit educational purpose? Was the use intended to further the public interest in some way?

2. What is the nature of the copyrighted work? Is it a consumable item such as a workbook, or is it a work that might more likely be borrowed from such as a newspaper or magazine article? Is the copyrighted work in print and available for sale?

3. How much of the copyrighted work was used in relation to the entire copyrighted work? Was it a small amount of a large work? or was it a large portion of a small work?

4. What impact does the use have on the potential market or value of the copyrighted work? Has the use of the material diminished the chances for sale of the original work? or is the use unrelated to the value or sale of the copyrighted material?

While a court considers each of these items closely, most courts tend to give extra weight to item four. In a close ruling the impact on the market or value of the copyrighted work often becomes the most crucial question.

COPYRIGHT NOTICE AND INFRINGEMENT

In order for a work to be protected under the copyright law, it must contain what is called a **copyright notice.** The new law specifically prescribes the kind of notice required and states that it consists of three parts.

Proper Notice

The first part of the notice contains the word *Copyright,* or the abbreviation *Copr.,* and the symbol © (the letter *C* within a circle). (The symbol ℗ is used on phonorecords.) The second part gives the year of publication. For periodicals the date supplied is the date of publication. For books the date is the year in which the book is first offered for sale (e.g., a book printed in November or December 1981 to go on sale January 1982 should carry a 1982 copyright). The third part gives the name of the copyright holder or owner. Most authorities recommend that both the word *Copyright* and the symbol © be used, since the use of the symbol is required to meet the standards of the international copyright agreements. The symbol © protects the work from piracy in most foreign countries. A copyright notice should look something like this:

Copyright © 1985 by Jane Adams

The courts will be very strict with regard to the composition of the notice. Any old notice will not do. For example, a notice saying "This book was written by Jane Adams and is her property until 2005" will not qualify as proper notice. The new statute is virtually identical with previous statutes in prescribing the composition of the notice. In 1903 the Supreme Court ruled that since the statute states a specific way to give the reader proper notice that is what the courts will demand. "In determining whether a notice of copyright is misleading, we are not bound to look beyond the face of the notice, and inquire whether under the facts of the particular case it is reasonable to suppose an intelligent person could actually have been misled" (*Mifflin* v. *H. H. White,* 1903).

The copyright notice can be placed anywhere that it "can be visually perceived" on all publicly distributed copies. (The rules are different for sound recordings which by law cannot be visually perceived.) The Copyright Office of the Library of Congress has issued rules which implement the statutory description that the notice be visually perceptible. For example, the rules list eight different places where copyright notice might be put in a book, including the title page, the page immediately following the title page, either side of the front cover, and so forth. For photographs, a copyright notice label can be affixed to the back or front of a picture or on any mounting or framing to which the photographs are *permanently* attached.*

The 1976 copyright law also provides that omission of the proper notice does not destroy copyright protection for the work if the notice is omitted from only a relatively small number of copies, if an effort is made within five years to correct the omission, or if the notice is omitted in violation of the copyright holder's express requirement that as a condition of publication the work carry a copyright notice.

At the same time the law protects persons who copy a work on which the copyright notice was inadvertently omitted. Such an innocent infringer incurs no liability—cannot be sued—unless this infringement continues beyond the time notice is received that the work has been copyrighted.

---

*Additional information is available in the bulletin *Methods of Affixation and Position of The Copyright,* published by The Copyright Office, and in the *Federal Register,* vol. 42, no. 247, for 23 December 1977, pp. 64374–78.

Proper notice is the only requirement that an author must fulfill to copyright a work. The work is then protected from the moment of creation for the life of the author plus fifty years. However, before a copyright holder can sue for infringement under the law, the copyrighted work must be registered with the federal government. To register a work the author or owner must do three things.

1. Fill out the proper registration form. The type of form varies, depending upon the kind of work being registered. The forms are available from the Information and Publications Section, Copyright Office, Library of Congress, Washington, D.C. 20559.
2. Pay a ten-dollar fee.
3. Deposit two complete copies of the work with the Copyright Office.

The statute gives an author or owner ninety days to get a work registered. What happens if the work is still not registered after ninety days and an infringement takes place? The owner can still register the work and bring suit. But a successful plaintiff in such a suit cannot win statutory damages (see pages 445–46) or win compensation for attorney's fees. It is best to get into the habit of registering a work as soon as it is published or broadcast.

The requirement of notice is a very important one. It allows all the works which no one wants to copyright to fall into the public domain immediately. It also tells the reader whether a work is copyrighted, was ever copyrighted, or is still copyrighted. It also identifies the owner of the work and the date of publication. The change in the law which protects authors who accidently forget to include a copyright notice on their works is healthy and worthwhile. But writers and broadcasters should get into the habit of putting the notice on all material which they believe to be valuable, whether it is published or not.

It is important for authors to know how to protect their own work. It is equally important to know how to avoid being sued for stealing someone else's copyrighted material. Such theft does not always result in a successful suit or even in a suit at all. Many times the owner of the copyrighted matter is unaware of the theft. Other times the harm to the copyright holder is insignificant. In copyright, as in other areas of mass media law, who you are is often more important than what you stole. For example, if the *East Ames Morning Dispatch and World Advertiser* publishes in its entertainment section, without permission, one complete act of a Neil Simon play, the newspaper might get a nasty letter from Simon's attorney, but probably not much more. But if the American Broadcasting Company presents the same act on one of its shows, it will surely get slapped with a copyright suit. Publication of the play in a small newspaper has not harmed the playwright significantly, and in addition the paper probably does not have much money. But presentation of even a single act of the play on ABC can diminish Simon's future royalties since it would probably lessen the number of future stage productions of the play.

The United States copyright statute does not really define infringement. The law states that anyone who violates any of the "exclusive rights" of the copyright holder is an infringer of the copyright. That statement is of little help to courts attempting to determine whether an infringement has taken place. Consequently, it is expected that the courts will continue to rely upon the definition of infringement forged during the past one hundred fifty years. Courts look to a variety of criteria to determine whether an infringement has taken place. We will focus upon three of these criteria which seem to be the most important: originality, access, and copying and substantial similarity. The burden of proof falls on the plaintiff in a copyright suit, but of course the defendant will do everything possible to prove that no copyright infringement has occurred. So both sides normally present evidence.

Originality

One of the first questions the court asks in an infringement suit is whether the *plaintiff's* work is original. In other words, is the copyright on the plaintiff's book or article or film valid? If the copyright is not valid because the plaintiff's work is not original, no suit for infringement can be maintained. Many persons copyright material which is noncopyrightable. History, for example, exists for all to use in a book or story. Margaret Alexander brought a copyright suit against Alex Haley claiming that he had copied portions of her novel *Jubilee* and her pamphlet *How I Wrote Jubilee* when writing his successful novel *Roots*. The court ruled in Haley's favor, noting that much of what the plaintiff claimed Haley had copied was material based on history—the westward movement in the United States, for example—and material that was in the public domain, such as folk customs which are an embodiment of black culture. "Where common sources exist for the alleged similarities, or the material that is similar is not original with the plaintiff, there is no infringement," the court ruled. Similarly, the court rejected the argument that Haley had copied Alexander's work when he used cliché language. "Words and metaphors are not subject to copyright protection; nor are phrases and expressions conveying an idea that can be, or is typically, expressed in a limited number of stereotyped fashions," noted the judge, citing the phrase "poor white trash" as an example of such an expression. In its ruling the court said that while certain conventional material appeared in both books the material was not original with Alexander's works, but belonged more generally to the nation's history or its idiomatic expressions. As such, illegal "copying" from the plaintiff had not occurred (*Alexander* v. *Haley,* 1978).

Access

The second dimension of an infringement suit is access: the plaintiff must convince the court that the defendant had access to the copyrighted work. An opportunity to copy has to exist. If plaintiffs cannot prove that the so-called literary pirate had a chance to see and read the work, they are hard pressed to prove piracy. As Judge Learned Hand once wrote (*Sheldon* v. *Metro-Gold-wyn-Mayer Pictures,* 1939):

> . . . if by some magic a man who had never known it were to compose anew Keats's, "Ode on a Grecian Urn," he would be an 'author' and if he copyrighted it, others might not copy that poem, though they might of course copy Keats's.

Here in contemporary terms is what Judge Hand said. If through some incredible coincidence a young composer were to write and publish a song called "Alfie" which was an exact duplicate of the song by Burt Bacharach and Hal David, it would not be an infringement of copyright. Publishing a song exactly like a copyrighted song is not infringement; copying a copyrighted song is infringement. Moreover, if the young composer could prove that he had lived in a cave since birth, had never listened to the radio or records, and had never watched television or gone to the movies, and if Bacharach and David could not prove that the defendant had had access to "Alfie," they would lose their suit. It must be obvious that such a coincidence can never occur, but this illustration nevertheless makes the point. The *plaintiff* must prove access to the stolen work. The smaller the circulation of the copyrighted matter, the harder it is to prove access.

Failure to prove the defendant had access to a copyrighted book was fatal to a lawsuit brought by Sonya Jason against the writers and producers of the film *Coming Home.* Defendants Jane Fonda and others stated that their film was conceived in the late 1960s, that a first draft of the screenplay was completed by late 1973 and was revised in 1977. Jason's book, *Concomitant Soldier,* was first printed in April 1974. Only 1,100 copies were printed. About 500 copies were sold in New Jersey, 100 were sold through the plaintiff's church, 200 copies were returned to the printer because they were defective, and the remaining copies were sold in southern California. Jason claimed that a copy of the book might have been given to Nancy Dowd, a screenwriter for the film, but there was no evidence that Dowd or anyone else connected with the film saw the book. Jason was only able to prove that several hundred copies of *Concomitant Soldier* were sold in southern California where Fonda, Dowd, and others associated with the film lived and worked. "That level of availability creates no more than a 'bare possibility' that defendants may have had access to plaintiff's book," the court said. "In and of itself, such a bare possibility is insufficient to create a genuine issue of whether defendants copied plaintiff's book" (*Jason* v. *Fonda,* et al., 1981). It might be noted parenthetically that such copyright or plagarism suits against successful films and television productions are becoming commonplace today. Most studios do not even open envelopes containing unsolicited manuscripts, to diminish the possibility of a plaintiff later showing access to a copyrighted story.

Copying and substantial similarity are normally the final criteria examined
by the court in an infringement suit. The court will first seek direct evidence
that the defendant did in fact copy the plaintiff's work. If the defendant's work
is a word-for-word replica of the plaintiff's work, copying is highly probable.
Such cases are rare. More typical are cases like one which occurred in the
1940s when the publication *Racing News* sued a New England newspaper for
stealing its handicapping information. The *Racing News* is the bible of the
fans of thoroughbred racing and publishes daily comprehensive data on horses
running at tracks around the nation. Newspapers usually publish smaller
amounts of information on horses running in a few well-known races or at
local tracks. The *Racing News* contended that the defendant newspaper took
its published material on the past performances of horses, rewrote it, and published the information as its own. The newspaper argued that while it did use
material from the *Racing News* it used other information as well and that it
rewrote all material that it published. Does paraphrasing a copyrighted work
protect one from an infringement suit? Not at all, the court said. District Judge
Wyzanski ruled that copying need not be ipsissma verba, that material stated
in equivalent words is also infringement. "*Soule's Dictionary of English Syn-
onyms* is not a licensed sanctuary for literary pirates," he added (*Triangle
Publishing Co.* v. *New England Newspaper Publishing,* 1942).

In a more recent case a group aptly named Air Pirates copied Walt Disney characters for posters and T-shirts. Instead of portraying Mickey and
Donald and Pluto and the gang as their lovable Disney selves, the company
translated the characters into what the court called "awful characters."
Changing the nature of the character did not excuse the infringement, the
court said (*Walt Disney Productions* v. *Air Pirates,* 1972). Disney still owned
the characters. Changing the medium does not work either. A toy manufacturer cannot make a plastic doll in the likeness of a comic strip character without first getting permission of the copyright owner of the comic character.

More than likely there will be no direct evidence of copying. In such a
case the courts then must determine whether the works in question are substantially similar. If they are similar, and if the defendant had access to plaintiff's work, a court will normally presume that copying took place and an
infringement occurred. More than just minor similarities must be present: the
two works must be substantially alike. In *Folsom* v. *Marsh,* a very old copyright case involving the letters and documents of President George Washington, Justice Story wrote, "If enough is taken to diminish the value of the original
or the labors of the original author are substantially appropriated," piracy
occurs (*Folsom* v. *Marsh,* 1841). In a more recent statement of the same theme,
the United States Ninth Court of Appeals said that the evaluation was "not
an analytic or other comparison" of the works, but rather "whether defendant
took from plaintiff's works so much of what is pleasing to the audience that

the defendant wrongfully appropriated something which belongs to the plaintiff" (*Sid and Marty Krofft Television Productions* v. *McDonald's Corp.,* 1977).

Courts usually ask two questions in attempting to determine the substantial similarity of two works.

1. Is there substantial similarity in the *idea* between the two works? If there is not, the lawsuit ends. If the answer is yes, then the second question is applied.
2. Is there substantial similarity in the expression of this idea?

In seeking these similarities, courts rely upon what is called the "ordinary observer" test. A judge asks whether an average lay observer, rather than an expert, would recognize the alleged copy as having been appropriated from the copyrighted work. Let us look at some recent cases to see how substantial similarity is actually measured.

Artist Albert Gilbert painted a picture of two cardinals on an apple tree branch for the National Wildlife Art Exchange. Three years later he painted a picture of two cardinals on an apple tree branch for the Franklin Mint. National Wildlife Art Exchange, which held copyright to the first drawing, sued Franklin Mint for infringement. The United States Court of Appeals for the Third Circuit found similarities in the two pictures. Both contained two cardinals, one male and one female, in profile on apple tree branches in blossom. But there were differences as well. The male bird was on the top in one picture and on the bottom in the other; in one the male was calm; in the other, he appeared aggressive. There was a large yellow butterfly in one; there was no butterfly in the other. The idea in both pictures was similar, the court ruled. But copyright does not protect thematic concepts. The expression of this concept—two cardinals on the branches of an apple tree—was different. "A pattern of differences is sufficient to establish a diversity of expression rather than only an echo . . . ," the court noted. The fact that the same subject matter may be present in two paintings—or in stories or plays for that matter—does not prove similarity and infringement of copyright (*Franklin Mint* v. *National Wildlife Art Exchange,* 1978).

The producers of two popular motion pictures sued for copyright infringement when programs with similar themes appeared on network television. Twentieth Century-Fox sued the producers of *Battlestar Galactica,* which Fox said was a copy of their successful film *Star Wars.* The trial court ruled that the basic idea in the two productions—a battle between good and evil in outer space—was indeed similar. But almost everything else about the two productions, including the story line and the main characters, was different. There was no copyright infringement, the trial court ruled (*Twentieth Century-Fox* v. *MCA,* 1980), but the Ninth United States Court of Appeals reversed the lower court ruling and ordered a trial in the case. "After viewing the *Star Wars* and *Battlestar* motion pictures, we conclude that the films in fact raise genuine issues of material face as to whether only the *Star Wars* idea or the expression of that idea was copied. At a minimum, it is a close enough question that it should be resolved by way of a trial," the court ruled.

Warner Brothers, the producers of the recent Superman movies, took ABC to court when the network broadcast "The Greatest American Hero." In both stories a character with superhuman powers battles the forces of evil. But the court ruled that Warner Brothers could not "claim a protected interest in the theme of a man dressed in a cape and tights who has the power to fly, resist bullets, crash through walls, break handcuffs, etc." The plaintiff must show that the concrete expression of the *Superman* idea has been appropriated. Warner Brothers could not do this. The characters in *Superman* and "The Greatest American Hero" are quite different. The hero of the ABC program is Ralph Hinckley, an ordinary man who reluctantly takes on abnormal abilities through a magic costume and is comically inept. Superman is naturally endowed with these powers, which he wields with grace and confidence. As a person Hinckley is the antithesis of the strong Superman character, the court said. In some ways the ABC show is a parody of Superman. "As a comedy that parodies American superheroes," Judge Motley wrote, " 'The Greatest American Hero' has a very different appeal from Superman, a real superhero, and plaintiffs have not sufficiently proven that it will reduce demand for movies and programs about Superman, and products bearing the Superman image" (*Warner Bros.* v. *ABC*, 1981).

It is not impossible to demonstrate substantial similarity between two works. Universal City Studios successfully sued Film Ventures for copyright infringement when the company released a film called *Great White* which was very similar to the movie *Jaws*. In this case the idea of both films was the same, the major characters were the same, the sequence of incidents was the same, the development and interplay of the major characters was the same, and even minor story points were the same. The court said the films were not identical, but that "defendants have captured the total concept and feel of plaintiff's motion picture."

The court pointed to the following similarities in the films. In both films a local politician plays down the news of a great white shark in the interest of local tourism. Both films featured a salty English sea captain and a shark expert who go out to hunt the shark. The opening scenes of both films show innocent teenagers swimming on a beach who become the first victims of the shark. In both films a local fisherman's empty boat is found. In both films the shark approaches a small boat, bumps it hard, and causes a child to fall into the water. Finally, in both films the shark devours the English sea captain during the hunt, but is finally killed when it swallows something which explodes in its stomach. "In light of the great similarity in expression, it would seem fair to conclude that the creators of *Great White* [which was titled *The*

Last Jaws when it was released overseas] wished to be as closely connected with plaintiff's motion picture *Jaws* as possible." The court issued an injunction to stop the exhibition of *Great White* and set a hearing to consider the award of damages (*Universal City Studios* v. *Film Ventures*, 1982).

It is not easy to prove infringement of copyright; yet surprisingly, a large number of suits are settled each year in favor of plaintiffs. In such instances the obvious theft of the material would generally appall an honest person. An individual who works to be creative in fashioning a story or a play or a piece of art usually has little to fear. The best and simplest way to avoid a suit for infringement is simply to do your own work, to be original.

Summary

To protect the copyright of a work the author or owner must give proper notice and register the work with the government. A proper copyright notice looks like this:

Copyright © 1985 by Jane Adams (use the letter ℗ for phonorecords)

Notice must be placed anywhere it may be visually perceived. Once notice is given, the work is protected. However, to gain the full benefits of the law a work must be registered with the Copyright Office in the Library of Congress. The proper registration form along with ten dollars and two complete copies of the work must be sent to the Register of Copyrights.

When a plaintiff sues for infringement of copyright, the court will consider three important criteria. First, is the plaintiff's work original? If the plaintiff has attempted to copyright material that legitimately belongs in the public domain, the plaintiff cannot sue for infringement of copyright. Second, did the defendant have access to the plaintiff's work? There must be some evidence that the defendant viewed or heard the copyrighted work before the alleged infringement took place. Finally, is there evidence that the defendant actually copied the plaintiff's work? If no such evidence exists, are the two works substantially similar? In examining this latter issue the court seeks to determine whether the ideas in the two works are similar. If they are, is the expression of these ideas similar as well?

FREE-LANCING AND COPYRIGHT

What rights does a free-lance journalist or author or photographer hold in regard to stories or pictures that are sold to publishers? The writer or photographer is the creator of the work; he or she owns the story or the photograph. Consequently, as many rights as such free-lancers choose to relinquish can be sold or given to a publisher. Beginning writers and photographers often do not have much choice but to follow the policy of the book or magazine publisher. Authors whose works are in demand, however, can retain most rights to the material for their future benefit. Most publishers have established policies on exactly what rights they purchase when they decide to buy a story or photograph or drawing. *The Writer's Market* is the best reference guide for the free-lancer. Here are some of the rights that publishers might buy:

1. All rights: The creator sells complete ownership of the story or photograph.
2. First serial rights: The buyer has the right to use the piece of writing or picture for the first time in a periodical published anywhere in the world. But the publisher can use it only once, and then the creator can sell it to someone else.
3. First North American serial rights: The rights are the same as provided in number 2, except the publisher buys the right to publish the material first in North America, not anywhere in the world.
4. Simultaneous rights: The publisher buys the right to print the material at the same time other periodicals print the material. All the publishers, however, must be aware that simultaneous publication will occur.
5. One-time rights: The publisher purchases the right to use a piece just one time, and there is no guarantee that it has not been published elsewhere first.

It is a common practice for publishers to buy all rights to a story or photograph, but agree to reassign the rights to the creator after publication. In such cases the burden of initiating the reassignment rests with the writer or photographer, who must request reassignment immediately following publication. The publisher signs a transfer of rights to the creator, and the creator should record this transfer of rights with the Copyright Office within two or three weeks. When this transaction has taken place, the creator can then resell the material. A ten-dollar fee must accompany either the original form or a certified copy of the transfer form when it is sent to the Register of Copyrights.

What if no agreement between the publisher and the writer or photographer is made? Neither the publisher nor the creator of the work should really be this careless, but if they are, it is generally presumed the publisher has purchased the following rights:

1. The right to use the material in that particular publication (an issue of *Sports Illustrated*, for example)
2. The use of the material in a collection of works from the publication (a book entitled *The Best Stories from Sports Illustrated*, for example)
3. Any revisions of the collection of works noted above (a second or third or fourth revision of *The Best Stories from Sports Illustrated*, for example)
4. The right to run the material again in a later issue of the same magazine or periodical

It is obvious that the creator gives away a considerable amount by not taking the time to ensure that his or her rights are protected. It is best for the writer or photographer to specifically stipulate what rights are being offered in the query letter to the publisher regarding the story or photograph. For example, the author might tell the publisher that "one-time North American rights" are being offered. In the absence of a subsequent formal or specific agreement, the existence of such an offer in the query letter could materially aid the writer or photographer in establishing the future ownership of the story or photograph. Free-lancers are also urged to beware of endorsements on payment checks from publishers. It is not uncommon for a publisher to include a statement on a royalty check to the effect that "the endorsement of this check constitutes a grant of reprint rights to the publisher." In order to cash the check, the writer must agree to grant the reprint rights. In such cases writers should quickly notify the publisher that such an agreement is unacceptable and demand immediate payment for the single use of the story. Other pitfalls too numerous to mention await the inexperienced free-lancer. The best advice is to understand exactly what you are doing at all times during the negotiation of rights. Take nothing for granted; just because you are honest and ethical does not mean everyone else is. And if questions come up, consult a qualified attorney. Legal advice is costly, but it can save a writer or photographer money in the long run.

COPYRIGHT AND CABLE TELEVISION

The growth of cable television in the past decade provoked one of the most serious copyright problems of the century. A television station which broadcasts a film or a syndicated television program must pay copyright royalties to the owner of the film or syndicated program. A cable television company, however, can pick up that broadcast signal and relay it into thousands of additional homes. And for years cable companies did not pay royalties to anyone for the right to transmit these programs. In both 1968 and 1974 the Supreme Court ruled that cable companies were not required to pay such royalties because they were simply relaying existing signals, not broadcasting or "performing" these copyrighted works.

The 1976 revision of the copyright act changed these rules. Today a cable company must apply for a license to transmit many of these films or television shows and pay royalties to the producers of such programs or motion pictures. The cable company must obtain a license and pay royalties when any one of the following conditions exists:

1. Any change is made in the program containing the copyrighted work
2. Any change is made in the advertisements that immediately precede or follow the program or are interspersed in the program
3. If the relay of the program by the cable company is not simultaneous with the over-the-air broadcast of the program

4. If the transmission is made available only to a limited group, such as a group of pay-television customers

These rules apply only to the transmission of non-network television programs and only to transmissions made to areas outside the area covered by the over-the-air broadcast of the program or film.

The licensing rules are limited, therefore. If a small cable company simply relays over-the-air programming to households in a local broadcast area, no license is required, and no royalties must be paid. But if the cable company changes the non-network programming, changes the commercials, delays the relay of a program, or attempts to transmit a program to a limited audience, royalties must be paid on those transmissions which extend beyond the normal over-the-air broadcast area.

A federal Copyright Royalty Tribunal sets the royalty fees and disperses the monies which are collected each year. In 1982 program syndicators and motion-picture producers got the lion's share of the royalties, 75 percent. Sports leagues received 12 percent, television broadcasters received about 3 percent, and public television and the copyright holders on music received the remainder. The National Association of Broadcasters protested that this distribution is inequitable, but a federal court disagreed (*NAB* v. *Copyright Royalty Tribunal,* 1982).

DAMAGES

Plaintiffs in a copyright suit can ask the court to assess the defendant for any damage they have suffered, plus the profits made by the infringer from pirating the protected work. Damages can be a little bit or a lot. In each case the plaintiff must prove to the court the amount of the loss or of the defendant's profit. But, rather than prove actual damage, the plaintiff can ask the court to assess what are called statutory damages, or damage amounts prescribed by the statute. The smallest statutory award is $250, although in the case of an innocent infringement the court may use its discretion and lower the damage amount to $100. The highest statutory award is $10,000. However, if the plaintiff can prove that the infringement was committed willfully, the maximum damage award can be as much as $50,000.

In addition the courts have other powers in a copyright suit. A judge can restrain a defendant from continued infringement, can impound the material which contains the infringement, and can order the destruction of these works. Impoundment and destruction are rare today.

A defendant might also be charged with a criminal offense in a copyright infringement case. If the defendant infringed upon a copyright "willfully and for purposes of commercial advantage or private financial gain," he could be fined up to $10,000 and jailed for not more than one year. The fines for pirating phonograph records and motion pictures are much higher: $25,000 and one year in jail for the first offense and $50,000 and up to two years in jail for subsequent offenses. Criminal actions for copyright infringement are rare today.

The law of copyright is not difficult to understand and should not be a threat to most creative persons in the mass media. The law simply says to do your own work and not to steal from the work of other persons. Some authorities argue that copyright is an infringement upon freedom of the press. In a small way it probably is. Nevertheless most writers, most authors, and most newsmen—persons who most often take advantage of freedom of the press—support copyright laws which protect their rights to property which they create. Judge Jerome Frank once attempted to explain this apparent contradiction by arguing that we are adept at concealing from ourselves the fact that we maintain and support "side by side as it were, beliefs which are inherently incompatible." Frank suggested that we keep these separate antagonistic beliefs in separate "logic-tight compartments."

The courts have recognized the needs of society as well as the needs of authors and have hence allowed considerable latitude for copying material which serves some public function. Because of this attitude, copyright law has little, or should have little, impact upon the information-oriented mass media. No new law changes this situation.

BIBLIOGRAPHY

Here is a list of some of the sources that have been helpful in the preparation of chapter 9.

Books

Ball, Horace. *The Law of Copyright and Literary Property.* New York: Banks & Co., 1944.

Cambridge Research Institute. *Omnibus Copyright Revision.* Washington, D.C.: American Society for Information Science, 1973.

Kaplan, Benjamin, and Brown, Ralph S., Jr. *Cases on Copyright.* 2d ed. Mineola, N.Y.: Foundation Press, 1974.

Nimmer, Melville B. *Nimmer on Copyright.* New York: Mathew Bender & Co., 1963.

Pilpel, Harriet F., and Goldberg, Morton D. *A Copyright Guide,* 4th ed. New York: R. R. Bowker Co., 1969.

Ransom, Harry. *The First Copyright Statute: An Essay on An Act for the Encouragement of Learning, 1710.* Austin: University of Texas Press, 1956.

Strong, William. *The Copyright Book.* Cambridge, Mass.: The M.I.T. Press, 1981.

Articles

"Copyright: Hollywood Versus Substantial Similarity." 32 *Oklahoma Law Review* 177, 1979.

"Copyright Infringement and the First Amendment." 70 *Columbia Law Review* 320, 1979.

Goldstein, Paul. "Copyright and the First Amendment." 70 *Columbia Law Review* 983, 1970.

Holbrook, Lanny R. "Copyright Infringement and Fair Use." 40 *University of Cincinnati Law Review* 534, 1971.

Nimmer, Melville B. "Does Copyright Abridge the First Amendment Guarantees of Free Speech and Press?" 17 *UCLA Law Review* 1180, 1970.

Schulman, John. "Fair Use and the Revision of the Copyright Act." 53 *Iowa Law Review* 832, 1968.

Yankwich, Leon R. "What Is Fair Use?" 22 *University of Chicago Law Review* 203, 1954.

Cases

Alexander v. *Haley*, 460 F. Supp. 40 (1978).

Amsterdam v. *Triangle Publishing Co.*, 189 F.2d 104 (1951).

Associated Press v. *International News Service*, 248 U.S. 215 (1918).

Baker v. *Selden*, 101 U.S. 99 (1879).

Berlin v. *E. C. Publications, Inc.*, 329 F.2d 541 (1964).

Bleistein v. *Donaldson Lithographing Co.*, 188 U.S. 239 (1903).

Chicago Record-Herald v. *Tribune Association*, 275 F.2d 797 (1921).

Donaldson v. *Beckett, 4 Burr.* 2408 (1774).

Elsmere Music v. *NBC*, 623 F.2d 252 (1980).

Encyclopaedia Britannica v. *Crooks*, 447 F. Supp. 243 (1978).

Folsom v. *Marsh*, 2 Fed. Cas. 342, No. 4901 (C.C.D. Mass. 1841).

Franklin Mint v. *National Wildlife Art Exchange.* 575 F.2d 62 (1978).

Hoehling v. *Universal Studios*, 618 F.2d 972 (1980).

Iowa State v. *ABC*, 621 F.2d 57 (1980).

Jason v. *Fonda*, et al., 526 F. Supp. 774 (1981).

Lipman v. *Commonwealth*, 475 F.2d 565 (1973).

MGM v. *Showcase Atlanta*, 7 M.L. Rept. 2190 (1981).

Mifflin v. *H. R. White*, 190 U.S. 260 (1903).

Miller v. *Universal City Studios*, 650 F.2d 1365 (1981).

NAB v. *Copyright Royalty Tribunal*, 675 F.2d 367 (1982).

New York Times v. *Roxbury Data Interface*, 434 F. Supp. 217 (1977).

Orion Pictures v. *Dell Publishing*, 471 F. Supp. 392 (1979).

Pottstown Daily News v. *Pottstown Broadcasting*, 192 A.2d 657 (1963).

Rosemont v. *Random House*, 366 F.2d 303 (1966).

Roy Export Co. v. *CBS*, 672 F.2d 1095 (1982).

Sheldon v. *Metro-Goldwyn-Mayer Pictures*, 81 F.2d 49 (1939).

Sid and Marty Krofft Television Productions v. *McDonald's Corp.*, 562 F.2d 1157 (1977).

Time, Inc. v. *Bernard Geis Associates*, 293 F. Supp. 130 (1968).

Toksvig v. *Bruce Publishing Co.*, 181 F.2d 664 (1950).

Triangle Publications v. *Knight-Ridder Newspapers, Inc.*, 445 F. Supp. 875 (1978); affd. 6 M.L. Rept. 1734 (1980).

Triangle Publishing Co. v. *New England Newspaper Publishing*, 46 F. Supp. 198 (1942).

Twentieth Century-Fox v. *MCA*, 6 M.L. Rept. 2016 (1980).

Universal City Studios v. *Film Ventures*, 543 F. Supp. 1134 (1982).

Universal City Studios v. *Sony*, 480 F. Supp. 429 (1979); revd. 659 F.2d 963 (1981).

Walt Disney Productions v. *Air Pirates*, 345 F. Supp. 180 (1972).

Warner Bros. v. *ABC*, 523 F. Supp. 611 (1981).

10 REGULATION OF ADVERTISING

Americans are treated to scores of advertisements daily. Someone has estimated that each of us is exposed to at least one hundred ten advertisements per day, and at least seventy-six of them register in our consciousness. People in the business tell us that advertising is the cornerstone of our capitalistic economic system. Low prices for consumers are dependent upon mass production, mass production is dependent upon volume sales, and volume sales are dependent upon advertising. Many economists support this theory. Critics of advertising argue that while people probably would pay more for some products without the savings wrought by mass production and advertising, they would pay less for many more products such as cosmetics and patent medicines, for which about half the purchase price of the product pays for large advertising expenditures. Critics also argue (not without challenge) that people buy more than they really need because of advertising. Regardless of who is right, it is a fact that scores of billions of dollars are spent each year on advertising. About four cents of every dollar spent by every man, woman, and child for goods and services goes to pay for advertising costs. Some companies in this country spend one dollar for every three dollars they earn in sales on advertisements for their products. Far more money is spent for advertising than for many social needs, a fact which makes advertising controversial.

Regulation of advertising is also controversial. Many persons argue that advertising deserves the same measure of First Amendment protection as other kinds of speech, and that government interference with advertising is a serious violation of at least the spirit of freedom of expression. They say that our capitalistic system is based upon a laissez-faire economic theory in which consumers must compete in the marketplace like everyone else. Within bare limits (such as laws against selling dangerous medicines or tainted meat), the consumer must learn to shop carefully, read advertising closely, be skeptical about any claim: caveat emptor—let the buyer beware.

On the other hand, there are persons who consider purely commercial messages, those designed to convince consumers to purchase products, undeserving of First Amendment protection. Freedom of the press is designed to protect ideas, not the trivialities of advertising. Consumer information is the basis of our capitalistic system, they argue, and only those advertisements which inform truthfully and accurately should be published or aired. Each time they make a purchase, consumers should not have to worry that they are being lied to or deceived by the manufacturer. The government should police unfair and deceptive advertising just as it polices other fraudulent conduct such as extortion and phony land sales. Caveat venditor—let the seller beware.

In the last quarter of the twentieth century, advertisers find themselves somewhere between the two positions. A measure of regulation has been built into the law, as this chapter will show. We will take a brief look at the history of advertising regulation in the United States and consider some of the conditions making regulation necessary. Then we will consider the protection the First Amendment affords advertising claims and get a brief perspective of the means available to regulate unfair and deceptive advertising including industry and governmental regulation. We will examine the Federal Trade Commission, the primary watchdog of advertising in this country. Its jurisdiction, its standards, its remedies to correct bad advertising, and its procedures are discussed. Finally, the various kinds of deceptive advertising are identified and discussed briefly, and the defenses an advertiser can use in a false-advertising suit are outlined.

THE LAW, THE ADVERTISER, AND THE FIRST AMENDMENT

From a historical standpoint, the regulation of advertising is a fairly recent phenomenon in this country because advertising as we know it today is a relatively modern practice. True, the first American newspaper published more than two hundred seventy-five years ago contained advertisements, but these were really announcements by merchants that goods had arrived or that certain merchandise was now in stock. The announcements were embellished somewhat, of course, but the modern advertising pitch did not become a common affair until the last part of the nineteenth century. Advertising depended upon the mass marketing of goods, which depended upon the so-called industrial revolution and modern modes of transportation.

In the past one hundred years or so the nation has moved gradually from having no regulations upon advertising to having hundreds of different kinds of laws whose purpose is to regulate advertising. While in this chapter we are primarily concerned with how untrue and deceptive advertising is policed, it must also be noted that today there are scores of other laws applicable to commercial messages of which advertisers and advertising agencies must be aware.

In the wake of the civil rights movement of the past two decades, a whole range of regulations whose purpose is to make advertisements comply with equal rights provisions have been adopted. In employment and housing advertisements, for example, it is illegal under federal as well as under many state laws to discriminate against persons because of sex, race, national origin, or marital status. The publication, as well as the advertiser, can be held liable for the violation of such laws. The Truth in Lending Law placed various credit disclosure requirements upon advertisers. There are numerous laws at both federal and state levels which prescribe certain rules for political advertising. The rates for political advertising are frequently limited. In many states newspapers and broadcasting stations must file the names of political advertisers with public disclosure commissions. In most states the name of the sponsor of a political advertisement must be included in the advertisement. Political party labels must also be conspicuous.

Other laws dictate what can and cannot be said in specific kinds of advertisements. For example, strict regulations apply to liquor advertising. The law requires the publication in a conspicuous type size of alcoholic content (86 proof) and kind (bourbon) of whiskey.

The provisions just given are but a few examples of how advertising laws have evolved to meet changing political and social conditions in the United States. It is sufficient to say that the advertiser must be both cautious and knowledgeable when preparing advertisements.

Need for Regulation

The first fact an advertiser must remember is that he must obey the laws which specifically regulate advertising messages *in addition* to all the other laws which regulate the mass media. In other words, an advertisement can be libelous and the advertiser can be sued for defamation. An advertisement can be obscene and can invade the privacy of a person. It can violate copyright law or violate the Federal Communications Act. It can violate a federal, state, or local advertising regulation.

The basic thrust of advertising regulation at all levels is to outlaw deceptive advertisements, advertisements which are dishonest or untruthful. Here is where the first—perhaps the biggest—problem arises. Whose standard of truth do we use? While this question is considered in greater detail later in the chapter, it is important to note at this point that there are persons who think that most advertising is dishonest, that the concepts of truth and advertising are antithetical in most instances. To demand advertising to be truthful, some argue, would be to stop most advertising. This argument is worth exploring for a moment.

Were a man to invent a truly unique product—such as an automobile which can be powered by tap water—advertising for such a product could simply be informative and tell consumers that this product is available. But if there were such a product, advertisements would not really be needed for long. Changes in the product might require advertising, but consumers rarely have to be convinced to buy a product with such obvious advantages. However, if you watch television closely and read the advertisements in newspapers and magazines, you will find that most advertising is not about products like the water-powered car. Most advertising dollars are spent on products which are not unique—headache remedies, toothpastes, automobiles, cosmetics, detergents, soda pop, and so forth. Because the differences between various brands of these products are usually marginal, the consumer must be given reasons to buy Bufferin rather than Bayer Aspirin or Anacin, Seven-Up rather than Pepsi-Cola. Those who argue that there is little truth in advertising point to such advertisements and say that these advertisements manufacture differences that do not exist or are not important. They ask, who cares about such differences? and say that to promote them is dishonest.

There is considerable truth in such an argument, but not enough to halt a fifty billion dollar per year industry. The regulators of advertising in the United States find it fairly easy to rationalize that such advertisements really do not hurt anybody, because consumers are smart enough to realize that their only purpose is to catch the attention, not to inform. What harm is done when one cigarette advertises that it is milder, another that it is longer, another that it is cooler, another that it is more masculine, and another that it is more feminine? No one believes these advertisements anyway. But can we be sure that consumers are skeptical of advertisements? As we will see, the law does not require that advertising actually inform, only that it does not deceive.

Advertising and the First Amendment

Commercial advertising enjoys a qualified First Amendment protection. It was less than ten years ago that the Supreme Court ruled that some advertising—what lawyers call commercial speech—is immune from government regulation. The extent of the constitutional protection of advertising is ill defined at present. The courts have not had sufficient time to fully develop the boundaries of this First Amendment shield. But we can outline a few basic rules.

1. The First Amendment does not protect advertising for unlawful activities.
2. The First Amendment does not protect false, deceptive, or misleading advertising.

In addition the government may regulate a truthful advertisement for a lawful activity only if it can prove the following conditions:

1. That the regulation of the advertising directly advances a substantial governmental interest
2. That the regulation is no more extensive than necessary to serve the interest asserted by the state

If the state can demonstrate that the regulation advances an important state interest, and that the regulation is narrowly drawn to restrict a limited range of communication, the courts will normally permit the advertising in question to be limited or completely prohibited. But if the state interest advanced by the regulation is of little importance, or the government fails to assert a substantial state interest at all, or if the ban on advertising is too broad (if it prohibits a wider range of commercial speech than is necessary to protect the important state interest), then the regulation will be stricken as a violation of the First Amendment. This all may sound a bit complicated at first, but if we look at the history of the development of what lawyers now call the **commercial speech doctrine,** you will get a better idea of how the Supreme Court applies this four-part evaluation.

In 1942 the Supreme Court of the United States ruled that "the Constitution imposes no . . . restraint on government as respects purely commercial advertising." The decision came in an unusual case in which a man attempted to circulate handbills on a city street urging citizens to make a paid visit to a submarine he had moored at a nearby wharf (*Valentine* v. *Chrestensen,* 1942). Most authorities believed, despite the unusual nature of the case, that this decision settled the matter: advertising was not protected by the First Amendment. In 1964 the Supreme Court ruled that *political* or *editorial* advertising is protected by the First Amendment (*New York Times* v. *Sullivan*). But most authorities rationalized that the First Amendment is designed to protect political speech, and political advertising is certainly political speech. Hence, this was hardly a revolutionary decision.

It was not until the mid-seventies that the high Court ruled that *commercial* advertising enjoys the benefits of the First Amendment as well. In a truly landmark decision the high Court reversed the conviction of a Virginia newspaper editor who had been found guilty of publishing an advertisement which offered assistance to women seeking an abortion. Abortion was illegal in Virginia in 1971 when the advertisement was published. The Woman's Pavilion, a New York group, urged women who wanted an abortion to come to New York. Justice Blackmun wrote for the Court that speech does not lose the protection of the First Amendment merely because it appears in the form of a commercial advertisement. Blackmun distinguished this ruling from the high Court's ruling in *Chrestensen* by arguing that in that instance the Supreme Court merely upheld the New York ordinance as a reasonable regulation *of the manner in which commercial advertising can be distributed* [author emphasis]. Blackmun refused to open the door completely or to state explicitly how far this ruling opened the door. "We need not decide in this case," he wrote, "the precise extent to which the First Amendment permits regulation of advertising that is related to activities the state may legitimately regulate or even prohibit" (*Bigelow* v. *Virginia,*1975).

In 1976 the Supreme Court clarified the extent to which advertising is protected by the First Amendment in the case of *Virginia State Board of Pharmacy* v. *Virginia Citizens' Consumer Council, Inc.* The high Court ruled that a Virginia statute which had the effect of prohibiting pharmacies from advertising the price of prescription drugs violated the guarantee of freedom of expression in the First Amendment. Justice Harry Blackmun wrote:

> Advertising, however tasteless and excessive it sometimes may seem, is nonetheless dissemination of information as to who is producing and selling what product, for what reason, and at what price. So long as we preserve a predominantly free enterprise economy, the allocation of our resources in large measure will be made through numerous private economic decisions. It is a matter of public interest that those decisions in the aggregate be intelligent and well informed. To this end, the free flow of commercial information is indispensable.

The high Court made it equally clear, however, that the government was completely free to continue to regulate commercial speech which is false, misleading, or deceptive or which proposes illegal transactions.

Perhaps the ruling which most enriched the commercial speech doctrine was handed down in 1977. The township of Willingboro, New Jersey, banned the display of For Sale and Sold signs on homes and lawns in the community. The motivation for the ban was the fear that such signs contributed to panic selling by white homeowners who feared that the township was becoming populated predominantly by black families, and that property values would decline. The black population had increased in the community, while white homeowners moved elsewhere. Persons testified before the township council that "the reason 80 percent of the sellers gave for their decision to sell was that 'the whole town was for sale and they didn't want to be caught in any bind.' " Community leaders reasoned that banning For Sale signs might diminish the fear that "everyone is selling" and might also stabilize the population.

When the ban was challenged on First Amendment grounds, Willingboro attempted to justify the policy on two grounds: first, that homeowners had other means of communicating that their property was for sale, including newspaper advertising and, second, that the goal of the ban was to provide stable, racially integrated housing, two factors which the community and the region considered important. But Justice Thurgood Marshall and a majority of the high Court rejected both arguments. Marshall wrote that advertising in the newspaper was not a satisfactory alternative because it was a costly and less-effective medium for communicating the specific message that a home was for sale. He added that while the goal of racial integration was important so too were the goals asserted by the government in *Bigelow* and *Virginia Pharmacy*. Marshall asserted that the constitutional defect of the Willingboro for-sale-sign ban was basic (*Linmark Associates* v. *Township of Willingboro*, 1977):

> The Township Council . . . acted to prevent its residents from obtaining certain information. That information . . . is of vital interest to Willingboro residents, since it may bear on one of the most important decisions they have a right to make: where to live and raise their families. . . . If the dissemination of this information can be restricted, then every locality in the country can suppress any facts that reflect poorly on the locality. . . . *Virginia Pharmacy* denies government such sweeping powers.

A decision two years later demonstrated that there are limits to the high Court's protection of commercial speech. The Court ruled that it was permissible for the State of Texas to constitutionally prohibit the practice of optometry under a trade name. Customers could be misled or deceived through the use of such trade names, Justice Powell wrote for the majority of the high

Court. "The trade name of an optometrical practice can remain unchanged despite changes in the staff of optometrists upon whose skill and care the public depends when it patronizes its practice," Powell noted. The jurist added that the use of an optometric trade name is strictly a business use; it does not provide consumers with information or knowledge useful in making an economic decision (*Friedman* v. *Rogers,* 1979).

In 1980 the Supreme Court handed down its most definitive ruling on commercial speech, establishing clearly for the first time the guidelines outlined at the beginning of this section (see page 452). Central Hudson Gas and Electric Corporation asked the Supreme Court to invalidate a New York Public Service Commission rule that forbade utilities to publish or broadcast any advertising that promoted the use of electricity. The commission justified the rule as a means of promoting energy conservation. The high Court struck down the ban in an eight-to-one ruling. Justice Powell noted that the utility's advertising did not promote an unlawful activity. Also, the state ban was aimed at all such advertising, not merely deceptive or misleading advertising. When advertising is truthful and does not promote an illegal activity, Powell said, the Court must examine the regulation itself more closely. What are the substantial state interests which are asserted in this case? New York argued that advertising which promoted electrical service interfered with the state's effort to convince citizens to conserve energy. The advertising also fostered inequities in the utility's rate structures, the state said. Powell agreed that the ban on advertising did further the state's interest in energy conservation, and that this was a substantial interest. But he said the link between advertising and inequitable rate structures was tenuous at best.

Was the rule no more extensive than necessary to serve the state interest in energy conservation? Justice Powell said the rule was too broad. It prohibited Central Hudson Gas and Electric from advertising more efficient electrical energy devices such as heat pumps and electric power as a backup for solar energy. The energy conservation rationale, as important as it is, cannot justify suppressing all promotional advertisements, including those that would cause no net increase in total energy use, Powell wrote for the majority. The state failed to show that a more limited restriction on content would not adequately serve the same state interests (*Central Hudson* v. *Public Service Commission,* 1980; see also *Consolidated Edison* v. *Public Service Commission,* 1980, discussed on page 95).

Finally, the high Court ruled in June 1983 that a federal statute which barred the mailing of unsolicited advertisements for contraceptives was unconstitutional when applied to a contraceptive manufacturer's mailing of informational pamphlets that promoted its products but also discussed important public issues such as family planning and venereal disease. Justice Thurgood Marshall, writing for the court, ruled that the government's interests asserted in support of the statute were insufficient to warrant the "sweeping prohibition" against mailing the advertisements. The government's interest in shielding persons from receiving mail which they are likely to find offensive "carries little weight," Marshall wrote. The government's second interest, aiding parents in directing the manner in which their children become informed about birth control, is substantial, Marshall conceded. But the statute goes too far, offering a "marginal degree of protection" only by "purging all mailboxes of unsolicited material that is entirely suitable for adults." (*Bolger* v. *Young Drug Products Corporation*, 1983)

By the late seventies and early eighties lower courts were also handing down rulings that helped shape the boundaries of the commercial speech doctrine. The federal District Court for Northern California struck down a state law which prohibited clinical laboratories from advertising to the general public (*Metpath* v. *Myers*, 1978). In Rhode Island a district court ruled that a statute which prohibited the broadcast of advertisements by persons who prepare income tax returns was unconstitutional (*Rhode Island Broadcasters* v. *Michaelson*, 1978). In Pennsylvania the state's supreme court invalidated the state law which prohibited "situation or job wanted" advertisements from listing the advertiser's race, color, religious creed, ancestry, age, sex, or national origin. The law was initiated as a good-faith effort to enforce the state's policy of fostering nondiscrimination in employment. While such a ban on persons seeking to hire workers was permissible, the ban on persons seeking work violated the First Amendment. Citing *Linmark*, the court ruled that "it is clear that commercial speech cannot be banned because of an unsubstantial belief that its impact is detrimental" (*Pennsylvania* v. *Pittsburgh Press*, 1979).

And in 1983 a United States District Court in Minnesota ruled unconstitutional a Minnesota statute that prohibited the publication of any advertisement concerning the inducement of miscarriages or abortions, including the publication of truthful, non-deceptive advertisements for lawful abortion services (*Medowbrook Women's Clinic* v. *Minnesota*, 1983).

As 1983 closed, two U.S. courts of appeal were in conflict concerning the permissibility of a state law banning advertisements for alcoholic beverages. The Tenth U.S. Court of Appeals ruled that Oklahoma could ban the advertising of liquor, beer, and wine to further its interest in discouraging the consumption of alcoholic beverages. (*Oklahoma Telecasters Association* v. *Crisp*, 1983). But the Fifth U.S. Court of Appeals struck down a similar rule in Mississippi. The court said the ban on such advertising was not shown to directly advance the state's substantial interest in promoting temperance in the use of alcoholic beverages, and it thus violated the First Amendment (*Lamar Outdoor Advertising* v. *Mississippi Tax Commission*, 1983). The Fifth Court of Appeals did announce that it would rehear the case en banc in lieu of the Oklahoma decision, which was handed down at about the same time. If the two courts remain in conflict, the Supreme Court will likely be asked to resolve the dispute.

Advertising Professional Services

The qualified constitutional protection for advertising just outlined is also applicable to advertising for professional services by doctors, dentists, lawyers, and other specialists. Yet the Supreme Court has demonstrated far greater concern for the potential deceptive nature of advertisements for such professional services. For example, while the high Court will clearly tolerate claims of quality service by plumbers, electricians, and piano teachers, lawyers and physicians may not make such claims in their advertisements. Such claims would be considered deceptive. Let us look briefly at the development of the rules regarding advertising by professionals.

In 1977 the high Court struck down rules which prohibited lawyers from advertising and ruled that price advertising for routine legal services is protected by the First Amendment as long as it is not false or misleading. The high Court would not tolerate advertisements regarding the quality of legal services, Justice Blackmun wrote for the Court's majority. Such advertisements (Jones and Jones Lawyers win more acquittals in drunk driving cases than any other lawyers in town) are not susceptible to verification and "might well be deceptive or misleading to the public, or even false" (*Bates and Van O'Steen* v. *Arizona,* 1977).

The *Bates* decision left confusion in the minds of many attorneys about just how far a lawyer could go in advertising services, and just how far state bar associations could go in limiting such advertising. Personal solicitation by attorneys has always been banned, and in 1978 the high Court ruled that such rules did not run afoul of the First Amendment. Such advertising is distinctly different from price advertising, wrote Justice Blackmun for a majority of the Court (*Ohralik* v. *Ohio State Bar Association,* 1978).

But four years later the high Court ruled that the Missouri Bar Association had read the *Bates* ruling too narrowly and adopted rules which were far too restrictive. State bar rules in Missouri permitted lawyers to advertise only the following information:

1. Name, address, and telephone number
2. Date and place of birth, schools attended, and foreign-language specialty
3. Office hours, fee for initial consultation, availability of fee schedule, credit arrangements, and fixed fees for certain specific routine legal services
4. Areas of practice

Under areas of practice the bar association listed twenty-three specialties which could be listed.

The association reprimanded an attorney who included in his advertisement the statements that he was licensed to practice in both Missouri and Illinois, that he was admitted to practice law before the Supreme Court of the United States, and that he also carried two legal specialties not listed among the twenty-three approved for advertising by the bar association. Justice Powell, writing for a unanimous Supreme Court, ruled that the Missouri bar regulations prohibited far more than was necessary to prevent misleading advertisements. Regulation of such advertisements is permissible "only where particular advertising is inherently likely to deceive or where the record indicates that a particular form or method of advertising has in fact been deceptive," Powell wrote. The state can regulate truthful advertisements only if a substantial state interest is asserted and the interference with speech and press is in proportion to the state interest served by the regulation. In this case the advertisements were not misleading, and no substantial state interest was asserted, Powell wrote (in re *R. M. J.,* 1982).

The commercial speech doctrine is still being shaped by the courts, but changes in the law in the past decade represent a remarkable growth of First Amendment protection for an area of speech and press heretofore thought to be unprotected. Is such a change a wise one? The growth of the commercial speech doctrine has not received universal approval from all traditional free-speech advocates. They argue that the First Amendment is somehow tarnished when its protection is extended to such trivial material as advertising. But other observers argue that advertising often contains valuable information for consumers, and in an era in which economic concerns tend to dominate domestic life, any information about prices or the availability of goods and services merits protection so that it may flow freely in the marketplace.

Summary

American advertising is regulated by scores of laws adopted by all levels of government. Persons in advertising must be aware of such rules, as well as of all other regulations (libel, invasion of privacy, obscenity, etc.) which restrict the content and flow of printed and broadcast material. Since the mid-1970s commercial advertising has been given the qualified protection of the First Amendment because much advertising contains information which is valuable to consumers. The government may regulate or prohibit advertising (1) which promotes an unlawful activity or (2) which is misleading or untruthful. The state may also regulate truthful advertising for lawful activities and goods if it can prove (1) that such regulation is needed to advance a substantial governmental interest and (2) that the regulation is no more extensive than needed to serve that important governmental interest. Advertising by professionals such as attorneys and physicians may be regulated in a somewhat more restrictive fashion.

The regulation of unfair and deceptive advertising is a most difficult task, for as previously noted disagreement about what is and what is not unfair and deceptive is frequent. Society uses various means to control this kind of advertising. The industry—the advertisers, the advertising agencies, and the mass media—polices itself. Both competitors (of errant advertisers) and consumers use the courts to seek redress for false or unfair advertising. Cities and states also have laws which prohibit untrue and deceptive advertising. Regardless of all these efforts, the federal government is the primary agent in regulation of advertising. To understand why this is so, we must first examine the controls just mentioned.

Self-Regulation

The advertising industry takes self-regulation quite seriously in the 1980s. The industry has various codes which proscribe certain unfair and deceptive advertising practices. Since 1971 the **National Advertising Division** (NAD) of the Council of Better Business Bureaus and the National Advertising Review Board, both industry-sponsored groups, have been active in resolving complaints against advertisers. According to one estimate the NAD has handled more than 2,000 cases since July 1971. The mass media, the newspapers and broadcasting stations, usually have policies on the kinds of advertising they will and will not accept. The television networks, for example, all have commercial editors who screen advertisements before they are permitted on the air. ABC has fifteen such editors, CBS has eight, and NBC has six. Advertisements are scrutinized to determine whether they meet network standards for taste and in the case of specific claims about a product truthfulness. These rules are quite tough. ABC, for example, rejects four out of every ten commercials it is asked to air, according to reporter Bill Abrams in an article in the *Wall Street Journal*. Also, legal counsel for the advertisers and the advertising agencies scrutinize every national advertisement published or broadcast.

Is self-regulation effective? The answer to this question depends upon whom you ask. Most people in the industry regard it as an effective tool to regulate deceptive or untruthful advertising. Consumer advocates often do not regard it quite as highly. Louis Engman, former chairman of the Federal Trade Commission (FTC), said in a speech to the American Bar Association in 1974, "The voluntary approach [to regulation] yields far more satisfactory progress in the development of compliance mechanisms than it does in the development of substantive standards." In other words, the industry sets up codes and panels and boards, but has not been successful in establishing hard rules on what is and what is not deceptive advertising. Staff consultants to the Federal Trade Commission were even more critical in 1973 in the *Staff Report to the Federal Trade Commission:*

> . . . from the advertiser's perspective the purpose of marketing communications is ultimately to sell the product or the service. Thus, to the extent that the provision . . . [information which educates the consumer] conflicts with the ability

of the advertiser to sell the product it is unlikely that he will indulge voluntarily in such "informational" communication.

At the very basis of self-regulation is the assumption that the advertiser and the consumer agree upon standards of deception and honesty, that they share a value system regarding the sale of consumer goods. Such agreement is perhaps beyond human facility at this point in its evolution. While newspapers and broadcasting stations do not necessarily share the advertisers' point of view, they tend to be more sympathetic to advertisers since they are after all the ones paying the bills.

Even those persons who do argue that self-regulation is an effective policing mechanism usually concede it is a tool which is more helpful to competing advertisers than to consumers. Remember, distinct groups of persons are concerned about the truthfulness of an advertisement. Consumers fear being cheated by deceptive advertisements which promise more than products or services can deliver. Competing business persons fear the loss of sales because of a competitor's deceptive advertising campaign. The interests of consumers and competitors surely overlap to some extent, but not completely. The consumer is concerned that all advertising is completely truthful and honest. Business persons are frequently concerned only that a competitor's advertising is as truthful as their own advertising. For example, consumers are undoubtedly concerned that the manufacturers of expensive brand-name pain relievers not be permitted to make the untruthful claim that their products are more effective than the cheaper, generic pain relievers. But the manufacturer of Bayer Aspirin is concerned only that the maker of Anacin not be permitted to claim that that analgesic is more effective than Bayer Aspirin.

Competing advertisers themselves have found agencies such as the National Advertising Division (NAD) of the Council of Better Business Bureaus to be effective in controlling deceptive competitor claims. This is especially true in an era of advertising in which almost 25 percent of all advertisements compare one product to a specific competitor's product. At one time a kind of unwritten code of ethics within the industry would have prevented an advertiser from mentioning a competing brand. Television networks were also reluctant to broadcast such comparative advertisements. But the Federal Trade Commission (FTC) has actually encouraged such head-to-head comparative advertising in recent years on the theory that out of such conflicts the consumer will learn more about the weaknesses and strengths of the products advertised.

A tremendous growth in the number of complaints filed with the NAD is one direct result of the increase in comparative advertising. Coca-Cola, which manufactures Minute Maid products, complained to the NAD about advertisements by Country Time Lemonade Flavored Drink Mix which stressed that the peel of a lemon contains the richest flavor, and that is what makes

Country Time taste like "good old-fashioned lemonade." Country Time contains lemon oil but no lemon juice. The NAD ruled the advertisements were not deceptive. Country Time then complained about an advertisement which said that Minute Maid Lemonade Crystals contain the juice of twenty lemons, but that Country Time contains no lemon juice. After Country Time raised the issue, Minute Maid discontinued the advertisement. Next came an advertisement which proclaimed that Country Time tastes better than Minute Maid. Minute Maid complained; the NAD asked for proof. Country Time provided the results of a blind taste test which showed its drink was preferred by 55 percent of the drinkers. Issue ended.

Sometimes the NAD rules that an advertisement is in fact deceptive. During the great laxative wars of the early eighties, Nature's Remedy ran an advertisement that said that a competitor, Ex-Lax, contains an artificial chemical, whereas Nature's Remedy has "natural active ingredients." The advertisement was accurate enough, but the NAD said it was misleading in our health-conscious society where words like "artificial" and "chemical" have taken on health-threatening connotations. Both laxatives had been certified by the federal Food and Drug Administration (FDA) as safe and effective.

When a complaint is made to the NAD, the agency reviews the allegations and normally asks the advertiser to submit evidence to support the claims. If the advertising claim is not supported by the data, the agency can ask that the advertisement copy be altered or the advertisement be withdrawn. While the NAD cannot punish an advertiser who refuses to comply, broadcasters and publishers normally refuse to run an advertisement declared deceptive by the NAD. If the NAD fails to resolve the controversy, an appeal can be made to a five-member panel of the National Advertising Review Board (NARD). This panel is drawn from fifty men and women representing national advertisers, advertising agencies, and the public sector. Advertisers can also make their initial complaint about a competitor's advertisement to the NARB.

Sometimes a competing advertiser does not believe a complaint to the NAD is sufficient to stop an advertisement or advertising campaign. Instead, a complaint is filed in court. That is another level of advertising self-regulation.

Civil Suits and Consumer Action

It is very difficult for a private party to bring a successful lawsuit against an advertiser in court. Consumers have almost no chance of winning such an action (see page 463), and even competing advertisers have problems. Consequently only very large advertisers go to court, and they only do so in usually the most grievous circumstances.

The law itself is the major impediment to a successful suit against an advertiser. There is no deceptive advertising tort at common law. Only business torts such as unfair competition apply. It is difficult, if not impossible, for a competitor to sue for unfair competition on the basis of simply a false advertisement. Both courts and legislatures have been hostile to the development of competitor suits. The courts have enough work without being burdened by hundreds of false-advertising suits.

A competitor can sue for disparagement of property, which is sometimes known as trade libel (see chapter 3). But this action applies only to advertisements making false and harmful statements about a competitor's product, and the burden of proof upon the plaintiff is heavy since proof of falsity, malice, and damages must be presented.

The American Home Products Company, the makers of Anacin, and Johnson & Johnson, manufacturers of Tylenol, tried another tack in the mid-1970s when they sued each other during the so-called aspirin wars over competing claims concerning their respective products' effectiveness. The suits were based on Section 1125 of the Lanham Trademark Act which prohibits firms from making false claims which have an adverse effect on a competitor's business. In what to many persons appeared to be a gross waste of time for the judiciary, a federal district judge plowed through masses of data purporting to prove one product was superior to the other. In the end, Johnson & Johnson won an injunction which stopped the makers of Anacin from claiming its product was superior to Tylenol for conditions "associated with inflammation or inflammation components" (*American Home Products* v. *Johnson & Johnson*, 1977).

Since 1977 more and more advertisers have been going to court to stop competitors from bad-mouthing their products in comparative advertisements. In early 1981 Budget Rent-A-Car filed a ten-million-dollar suit against Hertz, accusing the competing rental car company of falsely claiming Hertz had lowered its rates to meet Budget's rates. Cuisinarts Inc., a manufacturer of home food processors, sued rival Robot-Coupé, claiming false advertising and misappropriation of Cuisinart's reputation. The suit succeeded in blocking some Robot-Coupé advertisements. Twinoaks Products, the maker of a toilet bowl cleaner, also went to court in 1981 to stop Vanish commercials that claimed that long-lasting toilet bowl cleaners, like Twinoaks' 120 Automatic Bowl Cleaner, are harmful to plumbing while Vanish is not.

The most publicized suit of the early eighties stemmed from the multibillion dollar "burger wars" between McDonalds Restaurants and a host of competitors. Wendy's International and McDonalds both went to court to block Burger King television advertisements which claimed that people preferred the taste of Burger King burgers to those made by the other two fast-food franchisers.

Court suits brought by one company against another can be an effective if expensive way to rid the airwaves or the printed page of a few deceptive advertisements. But such suits surely do not have an impact upon most advertising claims, and as noted earlier, they usually seek to eliminate only those false or deceptive claims which outrage or harm competitors, not consumers.

Consumers are left in the lurch when it comes to policing false advertising. They too can report false and deceptive advertising to the authorities, but as individuals they have virtually no remedy at law for a deceptive advertisement. As George and Peter Rosden point out in their massive compendium, *The Law of Advertising,* historically common law courts have not been receptive to protecting consumers. "During the most formative period of common law," they write, "only a few goods in the marketplace were manufactured products so that the buyer was in an excellent position to judge for himself goods offered to him." Dairy products could be judged by their smell and texture; vegetables, meat, and fruit, by their looks. Judgments about wine, beer, and cloth were also easy to make. Protection was really necessary only in case of fraud such as watered beer. The basic slogan in those days was caveat emptor—buyer beware.

While today consumers are far better protected—they must be because of the thousands of consumer products about which they know little or nothing—there is little consumers can do themselves to attack the dishonest advertiser short of reporting the advertisement to the proper authorities. Even if the law allowed a suit to redress an injury wrought by a false advertisement, where can a consumer find a lawyer to handle the case? Let us say you buy a certain toothpaste because the advertisements claim it will brighten your teeth and stop formation of cavities. If your teeth do not get brighter and you sue, your damages are for 94 cents. On a contingency fee the lawyer gets 40 percent or about 38 cents. Even suit over a $150 dental bill does not give an attorney-at-law much to work for, especially when a malpractice victim who wants to sue for $200,000 may lurk around the next corner.

The Rosdens point out that it is possible for a consumer to sue under product liability laws, but in such cases the advertisement must contain a commitment about the product which is not fulfilled after purchase by the consumer. For example, an advertisement for a carpet cleaning product states that it will not damage carpets, but after a consumer uses the product, a large hole appears in the rug. The consumer would be able to sue (if she could find a lawyer) for a new carpet. Products rarely make such claims today. Hedging is much more common. That is, the advertisement states that in normal use the cleaner will not harm a carpet, but also suggests that the cleaner be tested first in an inconspicuous area of the carpet. Then, if the cleaner makes a hole in the carpet, the only problem for the manufacturer is a small hole in a carpet, which is not very serious. At least that may be the court's opinion in awarding the consumer only $15 in damages.

Consumers and competitors are marvelous snitches for attorneys general and the Federal Trade Commission. Unhappily our legal system is just not designed to allow individual attack on a false advertisement. A new law makes it possible for the Federal Trade Commission to sue on behalf of consumers to get back money wasted because of false promises. How often the FTC sues under this law and how well the law works remain to be seen.

State and Local Laws State regulation of advertising predates federal regulation by several years. This fact is not surprising when you consider that at the time the public became interested in advertising regulation—around the turn of the century— the federal government was a minuscule creature relative to its present size. Harry Nims, a New York lawyer, drafted a model law called the *Printers' Ink* Statute (it was *Printers' Ink* magazine that urged passage of the law) in 1911. All but three states (Arkansas, Delaware, and New Mexico) have adopted one version or another of this law. Here is the text of the original law:

> Any person, firm, corporation or association who, with intent to sell or in any way dispose of merchandise, securities, service, or anything offered by such person, firm, corporation or association, directly or indirectly, to the public for sale, or distribution, or with intent to increase the consumption thereof, or to induce the public in any manner to enter into any obligation relating thereto, or to acquire title thereto, or an interest therein, makes, publishes, disseminates, circulates, or places before the public, or causes, directly or indirectly, to be made, published, disseminated, circulated, or placed before the public, in this State, in a newspaper or other publication, or in the form of a book, notice, handbill, poster, bill circular, pamphlet, or letter, or in any other way, an advertisement of any sort regarding merchandise, securities, service, or anything so offered to the public, which advertisement contains any assertion, representation or statement of fact which is untrue, deceptive or misleading, shall be guilty of a misdemeanor.

The general verdict is that these statutes have been fairly ineffective in dealing with false advertising. Enforcement, which is in the hands of attorneys general or local prosecutors, has been weak because these legal officers have many other statutes to enforce. When people are being murdered or robbed or maimed or kidnapped, the fact that you or I have been deceived by an advertisement from a local furniture store seems relatively unimportant.

However, because of the consumer revolution of the last twenty years, cities, counties, and states have all strengthened their laws and their enforcement of false and deceptive advertising. In some areas prosecution is quite vigorous; in others, it is not. The laws vary from state to state, even from city to city. It is advised that persons involved in advertising obtain copies of all relevant laws regarding statutes in the area in which publication is made.

Most states do not do very well in policing false advertising statutes. There are exceptions like Washington and Wisconsin. Prosecuting false advertising is a rigorous, time-consuming chore. Big companies can afford good legal counsel to defend their advertising practices. The suits are complicated. In the time needed to begin a prosecution, the offensive advertising campaign has usually long since ended. Victory really brings little satisfaction. Outright fraud—used cars being sold as new—is usually promptly policed. However, it is costly, time-consuming, and of not much interest to the general public to take an automobile dealer to court for claiming that a used car gets 22 miles to a gallon of gasoline when it actually gets only 15 miles.

It is probably unfair to dismiss state and local regulation of deceptive advertising as handily as is done here. In some areas, cities and state attorneys general really do a superior job of protecting consumers. But this is not the norm. Unfortunately, the consumer's best friend when it comes to stopping false and misleading advertisements is also a distant friend, the federal government.

The Federal Trade Commission

Here is the advertiser, surrounded by industry codes, media regulations, and state and city laws, and confused at best. But the worst is yet to come. The primary agent of the federal government for regulation of advertising is, of course, the Federal Trade Commission, which has a general mandate to police unfair and deceptive advertising. In addition to the Federal Trade Commission Act, federal regulations on advertising can be found in at least thirty-two other statutes. To name a few: the Communication Act, Federal Drug and Cosmetics Act, Consumer Credit Protection Act, Copyright Acts, Consumer Products Safety Act, Federal Cigarette Labeling and Advertising Act, Wool Products Labeling Act of 1939, and Plant Variety Protection Act. In addition, regulations can be found in the Age Discrimination Employment Act, Federal Seed Act, National Stamping Act, Savings and Loan Act of 1952, Securities Act, and Aid to Blind and Handicapped Act. Also postal regulations contain numerous provisions regarding the mailability of advertising matter.

Then there are specific statutes which limit such practices as using the United States flag for advertising purposes and using the name of the Federal Bureau of Investigation or its acronym FBI in an advertisement without the permission of the bureau. Rules exist that regulate the use of likenesses of United States currencies and securities in advertisements. Good books which give students a broad, comprehensive picture of this multitude of laws and regulations are available (the Bibliography at the end of this chapter has some suggestions). In the remainder of this chapter our discussion is mainly about the agency having primary responsibility for the creation and enforcement of advertising rules and regulations—the Federal Trade Commission—and also includes consideration of deceptive advertising.

The Federal Trade Commission was created in 1914 to police unfair methods of competition. As Congress conceived the agency, the FTC was to make certain that Company A did not engage in practices which gave it an unfair advantage over its competitive rival Company B. One method of unfair competition is deceptive advertising. If Company A advertises that its widgets are four times quieter than any other widgets and they aren't, this claim gives Company A an unfair competitive advantage. What about the consumers, the people who buy widgets? As originally conceived, the FTC was not to worry about the effect of advertising on buyers, only on competitors. (This is the role played most prominently by the NAD today.)

In the 1920s the agency began to flex its muscles illegally and cracked down on all kinds of deceptive advertising: advertising that endangered competition and advertising that merely cheated customers. Until 1931, that is. At that time the Supreme Court ruled in *FTC* v. *Raladam* that the FTC could not stop a false advertisement unless there was proof that the advertisement had unfairly affected the advertiser's competitors. While the ruling did not totally destroy the efficacy of the agency, it did slow it down and made action against false and deceptive advertising more difficult.

In 1938 Congress bolstered the power of the FTC when it passed the Wheeler-Lea Amendment to the Trade Commission Act giving the agency the authority to proceed against all unfair and deceptive acts or practices in commerce, regardless of whether they affected competition. This amendment gave the commission the power it had been seeking.

Today the FTC is one of the largest of the independent regulatory agencies. In addition to policing false advertising the agency is charged with enforcing the nation's antitrust laws, the Flammable Fabrics Act, the Truth in Lending Law, the Fair Credit Reporting Act, and various labeling laws. The five members of the commission are appointed by the president and confirmed by the Senate for a term of seven years. No more than three of the commissioners can be from the same political party. The chairman, one of the five members of the commission, is named by the president. While the agency is located in Washington, D.C., it has regional offices in Atlanta, Boston, Chicago, Cleveland, Dallas, Kansas City, Los Angeles, New Orleans, New York, San Francisco, and Seattle.

The history of the regulation of advertising by the FTC is a mirror of recent political times. When conservatism swept the nation (in the fifties and early eighties), the agency did little to regulate American business. This inaction during the early fifties earned the FTC the nickname "Little Gray Lady of Pennsylvania Avenue." But during eras of liberalism and reform (most notably the late sixties and seventies), the agency has been aggressive in its posture against advertising and business in general. It is useful to briefly recount the recent history of the FTC and advertising regulation.

Under the leadership of two aggressive chairmen in the early seventies (Casper Weinberger and Miles Kirkpatrick), the Federal Trade Commission actively sought to regulate advertising, pulling some of the nation's largest advertisers (Coca-Cola, ITT Continental Baking, etc.) on the carpet for allegedly deceiving consumers. In the early seventies the agencies developed several new regulatory methods including advertisement substantiation, under which an advertiser must substantiate its claims, and corrective advertising, a scheme where advertisers must tell consumers previous advertisements were misleading (these powers are described fully on pages 476–80). In 1975 Congress greatly enhanced the agency's power by giving it the authority to issue trade regulation rules which could be used to curb deceptive advertising practices by an entire industry, not just by a single advertiser.

The FTC quickly sought to use these powers. Led by Michael Pertschuk, an industrious consumer advocate, the commission proposed rules that angered American business, and in the end, the Congress of the United States. Included were regulations that would have forced funeral homes to furnish the bereaved with a complete price listing of all services and that required used car dealers to put stickers on car windows spelling out just what might be wrong with used cars they hoped to sell. The FTC instituted antitrust actions against the giant citrus cooperative Sunkist Growers and tried to take away trademark protection for words such as *Formica* from the firms which developed these products. Perhaps the most controversial set of rules proposed were those which would have banned all television advertising aimed at young children, prohibited television advertising of sweetened foods aimed at older children, and forced advertisers of sugared products to broadcast a nutritional message to balance other statements in the advertisements for their products. The FTC contended that all advertising aimed at children is unfair because the youngsters are unable to intelligently evaluate product claims. Agency attorneys argued that since the advertisements were unfair, they could be stopped under the law.

By the early eighties the consumer spirit of the sixties and seventies had waned considerably, and what spirit remained was seemingly overwhelmed by the conservative spirit of the nation's political leadership. "Let's get government off the back of business" became an operational philosophy in Washington, D.C. The FTC, still flush from its successes of the earlier decade, ran into a congressional buzz saw. The national legislature adopted the Federal Trade Commission Improvements Act of 1980, a law which bore little resemblance to the suggestion in its title. Congress gave itself the power under the law to kill any FTC trade regulation rule if, within ninety days of the date the rule becomes effective, both the Senate and the House adopt resolutions disapproving it. This new veto power was used for the first time in early 1982 when Congress killed the FTC's attempt to force used-car dealers to inform customers of defects in the cars they offered for sale. But in October 1982 the United States Court of Appeals in Washington, D.C., struck down the congressional power to veto FTC rules on grounds that it violated the separation of powers established in the United States Constitution. Two other federal appellate courts had stricken other congressional attempts to veto federal regulatory agency rules. In mid-1983, the Supreme Court, in a case involving the legislative veto of Immigration and Naturalization Service deportation rulings, struck down the use of such a congressional veto as a violation of the separation of powers outlined in the U.S. Constitution. This ruling appeared to give the FTC the go-ahead for its used-car rule on the disclosure of vehicle defects to customers. But the agency had not yet ruled on implementing the requirement when this chapter was written.

The FTC Improvements Act also undercut the agency's rule-making proposals regarding advertising on television programs for children. Congress adopted a temporary rule that prohibited the FTC from issuing a trade regulation rule aimed at advertising that was merely "unfair." Advertising must be "deceptive" as well as "unfair" before the commission may adopt a rule prohibiting it. This struck at the heart of the commission's case against advertising aimed at children, and in October 1981 the commission voted to abandon its attempt to regulate such commercial messages. Shortly thereafter the agency also voted to end its five-year proceeding on a proposed rule governing the advertising of over-the-counter drugs.

Many philosophical conservatives were appointed to important government regulatory posts as a result of the election of Ronald Reagan as president. James C. Miller, a conservative economist who worked for the White House Office of Management and Budget, was named to head the FTC. Miller's critical statement during his confirmation hearing that the FTC's Bureau of Consumer Protection had "an overly adversarial posture" left little doubt about his position on regulation of business. The new FTC chairman radiates the Reagan attitude of the fewer regulations the better. He has asked Congress to extend the temporary ban on rule making against "unfair" advertising practices. He asked Congress to more clearly define the term *deceptive,* and outlined his own proposals at legislative hearings. Miller said he believes that the FTC should not have the authority to challenge an advertisement under the deception clause of the FTC Act "unless we can first prove that the advertisement was so false that a reasonable consumer was actually harmed." He suggested Congress adopt a definition of *deceptive* that would require the FTC to prove these three elements before it could issue a complaint.

1. The consumer injury is substantial and involves objective forms of harm.
2. The injury from the allegedly deceptive advertisement outweighs the benefits of the advertisement. (The cost and effectiveness of possible remedies must also be considered.)
3. The harm caused by the deceptive advertisement must be one which the consumer could not have reasonably avoided.

Should Congress adopt a definition of "deceptive advertising" modeled on Chairman Miller's suggestions, the power of the FTC to regulate advertising would be severely limited to those occasional grievous examples of serious fraud in the marketplace. Such a definition could do more to hamstring the agency than all previous Congressional actions.

True to beliefs he outlined during his confirmation hearings, Chairman Miller has sought to slow down the work of the FTC's Bureau of Consumer Protection. Upon gaining power as chairman he quickly consolidated forty-two ongoing cases against advertisers into twenty-two proceedings.

No one knows how deep the spirit of conservatism that now seemingly permeates official Washington, D.C., will cut into the regulation of advertising. In outlining the remainder of this section on the FTC we can only describe the law as it now exists. And what will be described are *potential* FTC powers to regulate advertising. If Chairman Miller and other officials choose not to use these powers, there will be a considerable reduction in the scrutiny given to advertising by the federal government. Only time will tell.

Summary

Self-regulation by the advertising industry has increased in recent years, especially because of the growth of so-called comparative advertising in which one product is measured against a specific competing product. The National Advertising Division of the Council of Better Business Bureaus and the National Advertising Review Board both provide the means for competitors and consumers to register complaints against advertising practices. Such self-regulation, however, is most often geared to the needs of competing advertisers. Court suits by one advertiser against another have become more common in recent years. Consumers have almost no chance of winning such suits against advertisers. The law is also stacked against a successful suit by one advertiser against another.

Government regulation of advertising exists at all government levels, but the primary agent against false and misleading advertising is the Federal Trade Commission. After aggressively pursuing many national advertisers in the 1970s, this federal regulatory agency has been somewhat handcuffed both by Congressional action as well as by the conservative, pro-business mood which washed over the nation in the early eighties. Several important rule-making proceedings have been terminated by the agency and the new commission chairman, James C. Miller, has asked Congress to significantly limit the FTC's power by defining the term *deceptive* advertising in a very limited fashion.

FEDERAL TRADE COMMISSION POWERS

The **Federal Trade Commission,** through practice and legal custom, has defined advertising as any action, method, or device intended to draw the attention of the public to merchandise, to services, to persons, and to organizations (see, for example, *Rast* v. *van Deman & Lewis Co.,* 1916, and *State* v. *Cusick,* 1957). Trading stamps, contests, freebies, premiums, and even product labels are included in this definition, in addition to more common product and service advertising.

Does the FTC regulate all advertising? Legally, no, it cannot. Practically, it can regulate almost all advertising. Because the agency was created under the authority of Congress to regulate interstate commerce, products or services must be sold in interstate commerce or the advertising medium must be somehow affected by interstate commerce before the FTC can intervene. While many products and services are sold locally only, nearly every conceivable advertising medium is somehow affected by or affects interstate commerce. All broadcasting stations are considered to affect interstate commerce. Most newspapers ship at least a few copies across state lines. Even when a newspaper is not mailed across state lines, it is very likely that some of the news in the newspaper comes across state lines, or that the paper on which the news is printed, the ink and type used to print the news, or parts of the printing machinery travel across state lines. The federal government became quite adept at demonstrating that businesses affect interstate commerce or are affected by interstate commerce as it learned to enforce laws like the Public Accommodations Act. The motel owner who declared that he did not have to abide by the federal law because his business was a local operation soon discovered that if the chickens or apples he served in his restaurant were shipped in from out of state the courts were willing to say that his motel operation was a part of interstate commerce.

There are some other requirements which must be met before the FTC can act. It must be shown that the agency is acting in the public interest, which is really not too difficult since false advertising generally has an impact upon the public. If the FTC says it is acting in the public interest, courts usually take its word for it.

The advertisement must be untruthful or deceptive before the FTC can act. Although deceptive advertising is discussed more fully later in the chapter and specific words and types of advertisements are considered, a few general facts about deceptive advertising must be given at this point. (Remember, if Chairman Miller gets his way, the legal definition of "deceptive" will be dramatically changed.) An advertisement is deceptive if it has a tendency to deceive (see *FTC* v. *Raladam,* 1942). The FTC does not have to show that any person has been deceived. In fact, the commission can rule that an advertisement is deceptive even if the advertiser presents as witnesses consumers who testify that the advertisement is not deceptive.

Deceptive Advertising

There are really four aspects of the determination that an advertisement is deceptive. First, the meaning of the advertisement must be determined—that is, what promise is made. Second, the truth of the message must be determined. Is the promise kept? Third, when only part of the advertisement is false, it must be determined whether the false part is a material aspect of the advertisement, that is, capable of affecting the purchasing decision of consumers (*Moretrench Corp.* v. *FTC,* 1942). The Chevron F-310 gasoline additive advertisements of the early seventies illustrate this point very well. A spokesman for the company claimed he was standing in front of the Standard Oil research laboratories when in fact he was standing in front of a county courthouse. This was a false statement. But was the statement a material aspect of the advertisement as a whole? A hearing examiner said no, that the location of a spokesman is irrelevant to a consumer making a purchasing decision.

The fourth dimension of deception concerns the level of understanding and experience of the audience to which the advertisement is directed. This aspect, in turn, has several dimensions.

If the advertisement is directed toward a special group—children—it is judged by the ordinary perception of that group. In 1974 when the FTC announced that advertising directed at children which focused on premium offers (such as advertisements for breakfast cereals) was banned, Chairman Louis Engman said:

> The child who makes or participates in a purchasing decision faces an already taxing and complex task. Even so simple a decision as the rational selection of a breakfast cereal involves the weighing of price, taste, nutritional value, convenience and promotional devices designed to create distinctiveness. The injection of a premium offer cannot help but multiply the difficulties of choice. When that factor is irrelevant to the merits of the product, it can only increase the likelihood of confusion.

The same special consideration is given advertisements directed at specialists. An advertisement prepared for publication in a technical magazine read by engineers need not be meaningful to average consumers. However, the FTC might consider an advertisement written for a special audience but published in a magazine for the general public to be deceptive.

How does the FTC evaluate the intelligence of that great mass audience to which you and I belong? For years the commission took the approach of the lowest common denominator. The FTC really did not think we were very bright or cautious. In a 1942 case, *Aronberg* v. *FTC,* a federal judge outlined the prevailing standard:

> The law is not made for experts but to protect the public—the vast multitude of which includes the ignorant, the unthinking, and the credulous who are making purchases, do not stop to analyze but too often are governed by appearances and general impressions.

This was, perhaps still is, the standard the FTC uses in judging advertising. However, experts in this area recently noted a swing away from this standard to a standard based on "the average man." The first clue cited in the change of attitude is a ruling by the FTC in 1963. Commissioner Elman, speaking for the agency, said (*Heinz* v. *Kirchner*):

> Perhaps a few misguided souls believe, for example, that all "Danish pastry" is made in Denmark. Is it therefore an actionable deception to advertise "Danish pastry" when it is made in this country?

The commission said no. An advertisement is not false and deceptive merely because it is "unreasonably misunderstood by an insignificant and unrepresentative segment" of buyers.

Ten years later the FTC rejected the argument of its staff that advertisements for Hi-C fruit drinks implied that the beverages (which contain about 10 percent fruit juice) were as good as or better than fresh orange juice. The FTC ruling implied (it did not specifically say) that the average consumer is smart enough to tell the difference between Hi-C and real fruit juice (in re *Coca-Cola Co.,* 1973). Commissioners dissenting from this point of view argued that the agency was changing its definition of consumers, that it was beginning to assume they were discriminating, knowledgeable, skeptical, and incredulous. One dissenter said, "This consumer knows that fruit drinks are not the same as citrus juices despite what Hi-C ads say." Whether the FTC has adopted a new standard remains to be seen.

When it comes down to the bottom line, most lawyers who represent advertisers before the FTC have a simple, if cynical, definition of deceptiveness. An advertisement is deceptive, they say, if the FTC says it is. This assertion seems to contain substantial truth. A finding of deceptiveness by the FTC does bind courts which must often hear appeals from commission decisions, as will become obvious in the discussion of commission procedures.

Remedies

In 1973 a law professor named Richard Posner concluded a study of the FTC with the observation that the cardinal weakness in the agency was its lack of remedies to control false and misleading advertising. "To be sure," Posner wrote in his study for the American Institute for Public Policy Research, "it is possible that even though the commission's constructive activity is very small in any given year the very existence of the commission serves to deter a great deal of unlawful conduct. But it is unlikely that the FTC's power to deter is very great, given the limitations of its sanctions" *(Regulation of Advertising by the Federal Trade Commission).* But things changed dramatically in the ten years following Posner's study. New and potent remedies were added to the FTC arsenal. The agency became a power to be reckoned with by even the strongest business corporation. Indeed, it was the use of these powers that brought the wrath of Congress and the White House down upon the commission in the past four years. But even with its often immense powers, certain factors work against any agency which wishes to regulate advertising.

The commission's greatest enemy in dealing with false advertising is time, the time needed to bring an action against the advertiser. Advertising campaigns are ephemeral—here today, gone tomorrow. The average campaign does not last more than six or eight months. It normally takes the commission much longer than that to catch up with the advertiser, to comply with all the due-process requirements involved in a hearing, and to ultimately decide whether there has been a violation of the law. By that time everybody has forgotten about the advertisement, and the advertiser is promising people a new pot of gold at rainbow's end.

Media historian and critic Erik Barnouw argues that contemporary regulation of advertising has another serious weakness as well—it is word oriented. Barnouw points out that by the time the FTC had won its campaign against the makers of Geritol (see page 475) the firm had switched to a more effective advertising strategy. The advertisements that got Geritol into trouble were word-oriented messages—promises that Geritol would be helpful to persons who felt tired and run-down. The new messages made no claims at all. The television spots showed radiantly healthy young women who urged viewers to "take care of yourself, be the best you can." Then the actresses told the viewers that they took Geritol every day. Barnouw says, "The success of the campaign suggests the increasing irrelevance of most FTC review, which tends to be word oriented. In the new commercial dramaturgy, verbal promise is a secondary matter, vague and understated, while situation and imagery work on a more visceral level."

Less subtle examples of what Barnouw refers to can be seen in the advertisements for Sanka coffee and American Express. Sanka hired actor Robert Young for its slice-of-life messages. For years Young was popular on television as Doctor Marcus Welby. In these commercials actor Young (or is that Dr. Welby talking?) tells viewers that Sanka contains no caffeine and will not make them as nervous or jumpy as regular coffee. The message can have the ring of *medical* advice for many stalwart television viewers. And while Young was starring in the Welby television series, nearly a quarter of a million viewers wrote him asking for medical advice. Similarly, when Karl Malden suggests that carrying an American Express credit card is safer than carrying cash, who do viewers see giving them the advice? Karl Malden, actor, or police Lt. Mike Stone, a character Malden played on the successful television show "Streets of San Francisco"? Malden even wears a hat during the ad, a trademark of his performance as Mike Stone. Again, no verbal connection is made between the actor and the police officer during the advertisement. At this time, as Barnouw points out, the law cannot cope with such subtleties, since viewers make the crucial (and misleading) connection in their heads.

What remedies are available to the FTC to control false and misleading advertising? There is a wide range of remedies that begin with simple guidelines and end with the strong, industry-wide, rule-making power which got the agency into trouble with the Congress.

Guides

At the top of the list of remedies is the power of the commission to issue industry guides, which are really policy statements by the commission about potential problems. For example, if a cigar company wants to know whether it can legally advertise its cigars as "the coolest-burning cigar in town," it can ask the FTC for an opinion before launching the campaign. Normally the FTC will advise companies about the legality of proposed claims. In some cases the FTC issues an industry guide, which is merely an advisory interpretation of what the FTC believes the law to be on the subject. For example, the FTC has issued a guide on the use of the word *free* and similar representations in advertising. It has issued a guide for advertising private vocational schools and home study courses. It has issued a guide for the decorative wall paneling industry. There are many, many other guides. In a guide the commission tells the advertiser that statement X can be made, statement Y cannot be made, statement Z cannot be made without substantiation, and so forth. The purpose of the guides is to help advertisers stay within the law. What happens when an advertiser fails to comply with the provisions of a guide? The FTC must proceed against the advertisement as it would against any other advertisement. The guides do not have the force of law. They are merely FTC opinions about what the law says. Deceptiveness still has to be proved in an FTC hearing.

Voluntary Compliance

Industry guides and advisory opinions apply only to prospective advertising campaigns, events that have not yet occurred. The next remedy on the ladder is voluntary compliance and is used for advertising campaigns that are over or nearly over. Imagine that the cigar company is nearing the end of its coolest-burning-cigar-in-town campaign. The FTC believes that the claim is deceptive. If the advertiser has had a good record in the past and if the offense is not too great, the company can voluntarily agree to terminate the advertisement and never use the claim again. In doing this, the advertiser makes no admission and the agency no determination that the claim is deceptive. There is just an agreement not to repeat that particular claim in future advertising campaigns. Such an agreement saves the advertiser considerable legal hassle, publicity, and money, all especially desirable since the advertising campaign is over or almost over.

Consent Orders

The next remedy seems to be similar to voluntary compliance, but is more complicated and more binding. The remedy is called a **consent order** and is a written agreement between the commission and the advertiser in which the advertiser again makes promises concerning future advertising. The advertiser is asked to agree not to do certain things and may also be asked to do certain other things. If the advertiser signs the agreement, the FTC takes no further action.

The Ford Motor Company agreed to stop claiming that its LTD cars ran quieter than a glider in flight. Why was this claim a problem? Apparently a glider is really quite noisy in flight, and the FTC believed that the advertisement in which the announcer said "Nobody has to convince you how quiet a glider is" was misleading. The Morton Salt Company agreed to stop advertising its product Lite Salt in such a way as to lead buyers to believe that it was more healthful than ordinary salt. The company also agreed that all future advertising of Lite Salt would contain the statement "Not to be used by persons on sodium- or potassium-restricted diets unless approved by a physician." The company which makes Gaines Burgers dog food agreed recently to stop claiming that Gaines Burgers contain nutrient ingredients unless the ingredients are present in a nutritionally significant amount. The firm also agreed to stop advertising that pets have a need for a nutrient that in fact they do not need and to stop making representation about the nutritional quality of its dog food unless it has evidence to support the claim.

General Foods Corporation also agreed to stop its advertisements for Post Grape Nuts which depicted the late Euell Gibbons picking and eating, or pointing to, wild plants and bushes and stating that this vegetation was edible and tasty. The FTC said that the advertisements could influence children to eat plants and shrubs most of which are not edible and may be poisonous.

As will be noted in the discussion of FTC procedures, there is considerable pressure on the advertiser to agree to a consent order. The chance of winning a case before the FTC is usually slim. The litigation is also costly. Finally, the publicity that results from such litigation often does the product more harm than any FTC sanction.

If after accepting the consent order the advertiser then violates the agreement, the company is subject to a severe fine, up to $10,000 a day while the violation continues (i.e., while the advertising campaign continues).

Cease and Desist Orders What happens if the cigar company really believes that its cigar is "the coolest-burning cigar in town" and does not want to sign a consent order? The commission issues a **cease and desist order.** The advertisements must stop or the advertiser faces severe civil penalty: again, a fine of up to $10,000 a day. In the long-running (eleven years) Geritol case, for example, the commission issued an order in 1965 prohibiting the J. B. Williams Company from implying in its advertising for Geritol that its product can be helpful to persons who are tired and run-down (in re *J. B. Williams Co.,* 1965; in re *J. B. Williams Co.* v. *FTC,* 1967). The commission contended that medical evidence demonstrates that Geritol, a vitamin-and-iron tonic, helps only a small percentage of persons who are tired and that in most persons tiredness is a symptom of ailments for which Geritol has no therapeutic value. The J. B. Williams Company violated the cease and desist order (at least, that is what the commission alleged) and in 1973 was fined more than $800,000. A court of appeals threw out the fine in 1974 and sent the case back to district court for a jury trial, which the advertisers had been denied the first time around (*U.S.* v. *J. B. Williams Co.,* 1974). The jury was to decide whether the Geritol advertisements did in fact violate the cease and desist order. At a second hearing in 1976 the FTC won a $280,000 judgment against the patent medicine manufacturer.

In 1976 the manufacturer of STP was ordered to stop making false claims regarding the effectiveness of its oil treatment. In 1978 a court found that the advertisement violated the order, and a $500,000 fine was levied.

Standard Oil of California was ordered to stop claiming that its Chevron gasolines with F-310 produce pollution-free exhaust. The commission banned television and print advertisements in which the company claimed that just six tankfuls of Chevron will clean up a car's exhaust to the point that it is almost free of exhaust-emission pollutants.

In 1983 the FTC ordered the manufacturers of Bufferin, Excedrin, Bayer Aspirin, Cope, Vanquish, and Midol to stop claiming that these products were superior to or safer than similar products. The agency said that Sterling Drugs and Bristol-Myers Co., the patent medicine manufacturers, could only make such claims if they had well-controlled clinical tests to prove the claims. Such studies do not exist, the FTC said. The commission said that Bristol-Myers had wrongly claimed that doctors recommend Bufferin more than other nonprescription pain relievers. This claim was false, FTC Commissioner David A. Clanton said. The commission said that claims made by Sterling Drugs that Bayer Aspirin had greater purity, stability, freshness, and disintegration speed were also unproven. The order issued by the agency states that advertising claims must be proven by two well-controlled clinical studies, although other forms of proof may be acceptable on a case-by-case basis. This kind of substantiation is noted in the next section.

Few advertisers are willing to carry a case as far as the cease and desist order, and those that go that far frequently go beyond to a court of appeals to challenge the FTC's ruling. The appeal process is explored in the discussion of FTC procedures (pages 483–85).

The pressure is heavy upon advertisers to voluntarily comply or to sign a consent order, especially since in neither case is there admission of wrong-doing and in both instances the legal processes will take so long that the offensive advertising campaign will probably be finished before the case is heard. Many people feel that the FTC does its job if it gains compliance voluntarily, for the mission of the agency is, after all, to stop deceptive advertising, not to punish advertisers. Other observers disagree, however, and argue that without stronger sanctions the advertiser is not motivated to refrain from future illegal acts. This kind of argument prompted the FTC to undertake new regulatory schemes, which we will now examine.

Substantiation

Substantiation of an advertisement at first glance hardly seems like an important regulatory scheme, but it is a very important one. The program began in 1971 and had only limited success. Since then it has been modified and reportedly now works better. The basis of the program is simple: the FTC asks advertisers to substantiate all claims in their advertisements. There is no assertion that a claim is false or misleading. The government merely tells advertisers to prove what they say.

At first the FTC chose an entire industry—like the soap and detergent makers—and gave all companies in the industry sixty days to provide documentation for all their claims: claims that Ivory Soap is pure, that Clorox is able to do what detergents alone cannot do, and that Pine-Sol kills household germs, and so forth.

The firms then supplied the FTC with support for their claims if they could, and most of the companies could. If they could not, through a consent order the FTC usually asked them to stop making the claim. All kinds of industries were included in substantiation orders: the automobile industry; the air-conditioning manufacturers; the makers of shampoos, electric shavers, cough and cold remedies, and antiperspirants; and so forth. However, problems arose. About 90 percent of the material submitted as documentation was too technical for a layman to understand, and since one of the goals of the project was to allow consumers to study the proof offered by the advertisers, this aspect of the program was a failure. In 1974 the FTC ordered that when documentation is in technical or scientific language it must be accompanied by a summary in lay language.

Another problem was the amount of information submitted. When an entire industry, or industries, had to submit documentation, there was just too much material. Now the FTC uses a committee of experts to screen advertising claims and target those advertisements which seem the most suspect for substantiation. Also, the time the advertiser has to submit material was cut from sixty to thirty days.

Finally, the FTC changed its policy concerning publicity about substantiation. In the past the agency publicly announced that all automakers, for example, had been asked to document their claims. Advertisers complained that many consumers incorrectly presumed that the claims were somehow deceptive. Why else would the government seek documentation? Now, no announcement is made until after the commission receives the material and places it on the public record.

There are still other complaints about substantiation. The Brown & Williamson Tobacco Company, for example, has complained that the FTC has required it to submit documents concerning its advertising practices over the past fourteen years. Senator Wendell Ford of Kentucky told *Newsweek* that it cost the company $800,000 to comply with the requests, but the FTC never did tell the firm why the material was needed. "The only reason I've ever been able to get out of them is that it was their curiosity," Ford said, citing this incident as an example of the agency's sometime arbitrary, if not irresponsible, behavior.

On its face substantiation seems a fairly innocent little process. Nevertheless from a legal standpoint it has had a major impact on regulation, because it shifted the burden of proof in a great many advertising cases from the commission, which in the past had to prove that an advertisement was deceptive, to the advertiser who must now prove that it is true. If the case goes to litigation and a hearing, the FTC must still prove that the advertising claim is deceptive. Since most problems are solved short of this stage by consent agreement, substantiation has reduced considerably the work load of the FTC. The FTC no longer has to convince advertisers prior to getting their assent to an agreement that it can prove the advertisement is deceptive. By not being able to substantiate its claim, the advertiser accomplishes the proof himself.

Corrective Advertising

Corrective advertising is a highly controversial scheme which the FTC first used in 1971 against the ITT Continental Baking Company. The scheme is based on the premise that to merely stop an advertisement is in some instances insufficient. If the advertising campaign is successful and long running, a residue of misleading information remains in the mind of the public after the offensive advertisements have been removed. Under the corrective advertising scheme the FTC forces the advertiser to inform the public that in the past it has not been honest or has been misleading. One commentator called the scheme "commercial hara-kiri."

Under what circumstances will the FTC ask for corrective advertising sanctions? The commission has resisted issuing a specific policy regarding this question. For example, in 1979 it responded to a request for such a policy from the Institute for Public Representation in Washington, D.C., by saying it would continue to deal with corrective advertising problems on a case-by-case basis. In the past, however, the agency has adopted this rather vague standard for the imposition of corrective advertising:

> If a deceptive advertisement has played a substantial role in creating or reinforcing in the public's mind a false and material belief which lives on after the false advertising ceases, there is clear and continuing injury to competition and to the consuming public as consumers continue to make purchasing decisions based on the false belief.

In such a case, corrective advertising is appropriate, according to the FTC.

The FTC first attempted to force what it calls affirmative or corrective disclosures in 1950, but a court of appeals ruled that it lacked the power to do so under the Federal Trade Commission Act. The court ruled in *Alberty* v. *FTC* (1950) that the agency lacked the authority to encourage or require informative advertising. Ten years later, however, in *Feil* v. *FTC* (1960), the courts reversed the *Alberty* decision. The FTC threatened to use the remedy against the Campbell Soup Company to correct the misperception created when the company put clear marbles in the bottom of a bowl of vegetable soup to force the vegetables to the top (*Campbell Soup Co.,* 1970). The first corrective advertisement did not appear until 1971. As mentioned earlier, it was the result of a consent order signed by the ITT Continental Baking Company with regard to its advertising for Profile Bread. The television version of the advertisement was this:

> I'm Julia Meade for Profile Bread. And like all mothers I'm concerned about nutrition and balanced meals. So I'd like to clear up any misunderstanding you may have about Profile Bread from its advertising or even its name. Does Profile

have fewer calories than other breads? No, Profile has about the same per ounce as other breads. To be exact Profile has seven fewer calories per slice. But that's because it's sliced thinner. But eating Profile Bread will not cause you to lose weight. A reduction of seven calories is insignificant. It's total calories and balanced nutrition that counts. And Profile can help you achieve a balanced meal, because it provides protein and B vitamins as well as other nutrients.

This corrective advertisement was in response to a Profile campaign that led some people to believe that one could lose weight by eating Profile Bread.

The commission required that corrective advertisements like this one constitute 25 percent of the advertising for Profile Bread during the year following the agreement. This is the typical percentage in a corrective-advertising agreement, although at times the FTC has agreed to allow advertisers to allot only 15 percent of their advertising budget for corrective advertisements.

Only a few other manufacturers of well-known nationally advertised products have been forced to make corrective disclosures. One was the company making Ocean Spray Cranberry Juice which for years advertised that its cranberry juice had more food energy than other juices. Since food energy is really only another way of saying caloric value, the FTC ordered the juice maker to tell people that fact in a corrective ad (*Ocean Spray Cranberries, Inc.,* 1972). Neither the Profile advertisement nor the cranberry juice advertisement pleased all consumer advocates. Many thought the advertisements were too weak. In fact, studies showed that sales of Profile Bread were not hurt by the corrective campaign.

The FTC has been both tougher and more prepared to use the corrective-advertising device against small advertisers. Some corrective advertisements even have to include what lawyers dub "the Scarlet Letter," a statement by advertisers that the FTC found previous advertising to be deceptive. An example of such an order is the one agreed to by Wasem's Drug Store in Clarkston, Washington. The store marketed vitamin pills under its own name in advertising which the FTC deemed to be false and misleading. In the consent order the firm agreed to devote 25 percent of its advertising for one year to corrective advertising, to refrain from using the word *super* in the trade name of the vitamins, and to broadcast seven 60-second corrective advertisements on seven consecutive days on local television stations. This is the corrective ad, including the Scarlet Letter:

> This advertisement is run pursuant to an order of the Federal Trade Commission. I have previously been advertising Wasem's Super B Vitamins and have made various claims which are erroneous or misleading. Contrary to what I told you previously, Super B will not make you feel better nor make you better to live with nor work with on the job. There is no need for most people to supplement their diet with vitamins and minerals. Excess dosages over the recommended daily adult requirement of most vitamins will be flushed through the body and be of no benefit whatsoever. Contrary to my previous ads, neither the Food and Drug Administration nor the Federal Trade Commission nor anyone

else has recommended Super B or approved our prior claims. Super B Vitamins are sold on a money-back guarantee, so if you are not fully satisfied, then return them to me at Wasem's Rexall Drug Store in Clarkston for a refund.

But in an important ruling by the United States Court of Appeals in 1977, the future of the so-called Scarlet Letter was clouded. Warner-Lambert, the maker of Listerine Mouthwash, was ordered by the FTC to stop claiming that its product prevents, cures, or alleviates the common cold. The agency also ordered the firm to include the following statement in its future advertisements: "Contrary to prior advertising, Listerine will not help prevent colds or sore throats or lessen their severity." Warner-Lambert challenged the entire order, arguing that the FTC had no power to force corrective advertising. United States Court of Appeals (D.C.) Judge Skelly Wright wrote on behalf of the two-to-one majority that the FTC does have the power to force corrective advertising statements in appropriate cases, but ruled that the phrase "contrary to prior advertising" was superfluous and was intended to humiliate the company. Wright said that while humiliation might be appropriate for an "egregious case of deliberate deception" it was not appropriate here. The FTC has only the power to correct the problem, not to be punitive in its actions. The firm was ordered to publish and broadcast the corrective claims in the next ten million dollars of its advertising for the mouthwash, which was the average annual sum spent on advertising between 1962 and 1972 when the complaint against Warner-Lambert was first issued. (The Supreme Court later refused to hear an appeal by the drug company.) While the ruling strongly upheld corrective advertising, the Court of Appeals nevertheless cast doubts on the propriety of the use of the so-called Scarlet Letter.

Nobody really knows whether these kinds of corrective advertisements are effective in ridding the consumer's mind of the falsity. Probably many buyers retain an unfavorable impression of the advertiser. Corrective advertising has been used only infrequently as a remedy in the past few years.

Injunctions

When Congress passed the Trans-Alaska Pipeline Authorization Act in 1973, attached to that piece of legislation was a bill which authorized the FTC to seek an injunction to stop advertisements which it believed violated the law. Attorneys for the FTC can seek these restraining orders in federal court. An injunction is clearly a drastic remedy and one which the agency has said it will not use often. Spokesmen for the FTC have said that the agency will use the power only in those instances in which the advertising can cause harm, in those cases where there is a clear law violation, and in those cases where there is no prospect that the advertising practice will end soon.

The first time the FTC used its new power was in 1973 when it sought and got a restraining order against several West Coast travel agents who promoted trips to the Philippines for "psychic surgery." The FTC said that many

Americans were being fleeced by so-called psychic surgeons who supposedly performed bloodless operations on patients by using their minds rather than scalpels. The agency won its case.

Trade Regulation Rules

In January 1975 President Ford signed the Magnuson-Moss Warranty—Federal Trade Commission Improvement Act, the most significant piece of trade regulation legislation since the Wheeler-Lea Amendment in 1938. The new law did many things, but basically it greatly enlarged both the power and the jurisdiction of the FTC. Until the bill was signed, the FTC was limited to dealing with unfair and deceptive practices which were "in commerce." The new law expanded the jurisdiction to practices "affecting commerce." The change of a single word gave the FTC broad new areas to regulate. The law also gave the agency important new power. It is the vigorous use of this new power that caused the problems (discussed earlier) that the agency now has with the Congress.

Three sections of the act expanded the remedies the FTC can use against deceptive advertising. First, the agency was given the power to issue trade regulation rules defining and outlawing unfair and deceptive acts or practices. The importance of this power alone cannot be overestimated. In the past the agency had to pursue deceptive advertisements one at a time. Imagine, for example, that four or five different breakfast cereals all advertise that they are good for children because they contain nine times the recommended daily allowance of vitamins and minerals. Medical experts argue that any vitamins in excess of 100 percent of the recommended daily allowance are useless; therefore these advertisements are probably deceptive or misleading. In the past the FTC would have had to issue a complaint against each advertiser and in each case prove that the statement was a violation of the law. Under the new rules the agency can issue a trade regulation rule—as it had done for nutritional claims—which declares that claims of product superiority based on excessive dosage of vitamins and minerals are false and misleading. If advertisers make such claims, they are in violation of the law. All the commission must prove is that the advertiser had actual knowledge of the trade regulation rule, or "knowledge fairly implied from the objective circumstances."

The advantages of the **trade regulation rules,** or TRRs as they are called, are numerous. They speed up and simplify the process of enforcement. Advertisers can still litigate the question, challenge the trade regulation rule, seek an appeal in court, and so forth. In most cases they probably will not go to that expense. Trade regulation rules should have a great deterrent effect, as they comprehensively delimit what constitutes an illegal practice. In the past after the commission issued a cease and desist order, businesses frequently attempted to undertake practices which fell just outside the narrow boundaries of the order. The TRRs are much broader and make it much harder for advertisers to skirt the limitations. Finally, via TRRs the FTC is able to deal with problems most evenhandedly. An entire industry can be treated similarly, and just one or two businesses are not picked out for complaint.

While the FTC has issued TRRs since 1962, it has done so sparingly, since it was unsure of its power to take this action. In 1974 a court of appeals upheld the right of the agency to promulgate such rules (*National Petroleum Refiners Association* v. *FTC,* 1974). This court decision was made law by Congress in the FTC Improvement Act. Since that time, according to one FTC representative, the commission has been busy promulgating rules, so that this aspect of regulation is more visible now.

The two other aspects of the new law which improved FTC remedies are these. The FTC may seek civil penalties against anyone who knowingly violates the provisions of a cease and desist order, even if that person was not originally the subject of the order. To wit: A Chemical Company sells a spray paint which is toxic if used in a closed area, but the product is advertised as being completely harmless. The FTC moves against the company and issues a cease and desist order that states that in the future the firm must not advertise the product as being completely harmless. B Chemical Company also sells a spray paint which has the same toxicity and is advertised the same way. If it can be shown that B Company was aware of the provisions of the order against A Company and continued to advertise its product as being completely safe, B can be fined up to $10,000 per day for violating the order, even though the order is not directed against B.

Finally, the new law gave the FTC the right to sue in federal court on behalf of consumers who have been victimized by practices that are in violation of a cease and desist order or by practices that are in violation of a TRR.

As you can see, the FTC has a potent array of remedies to use against the errant advertiser. But the agency must aggressively pursue deceptive and misleading advertising if these remedies are to act as deterrents. The commission did far more to police advertising in the early 1970s when it had fewer remedies than it does today, when it has many more sanctions. In a sense Professor Posner was wrong when he said that lack of remedies was the cardinal weakness in the FTC (see page 472). The will to use these remedies must exist before the FTC becomes an effective agent against misleading and deceptive advertising. For better or worse, such will seems to be lacking in the current era.

Summary

The Federal Trade Commission has the power to regulate virtually all advertising which is deceptive or misleading. The agency attempts to determine whether the material aspects of the advertisement are truthful and can be understood by the audience to which the advertisement is aimed. The FTC has many remedies which may be applied to attempt to regulate deceptive or untruthful advertising:

1. Guides or advisory opinions which attempt to outline in advance what advertisers may say about a product
2. Voluntary agreements by advertisers to terminate a deceptive advertisement
3. Consent orders or written agreements signed by advertisers promising to terminate a deceptive advertisement
4. Cease and desist orders to advertisers to terminate a particular advertising claim, for which failure to comply can result in severe penalty
5. Substantiation of advertisements in which the advertiser must prove all claims made in an advertisement
6. Corrective advertising in which an advertiser must admit in future advertisements that past advertisements have been incorrect
7. Injunctive power to immediately halt advertising campaigns which could cause harm to consumers
8. Trade regulation rules which can be issued to regulate advertising throughout an entire industry

---

THE REGULATORY PROCESS

To understand the importance of the regulatory process, students should be familiar with procedures followed in a deceptive advertising case, be aware of the kinds of advertising that can be considered deceptive, and be familiar with the defenses to a charge of deceptive advertising.

Procedures

Most cases come to the attention of the FTC from letters written either by consumers or by competitors of the offending advertiser. The legal staff of the agency then does a preliminary investigation. If the complaint counsel, an FTC staff attorney, feels there is no substance to the charge, the case ends. But if he believes there is a provable violation, he writes a memorandum to the commission. A proposed complaint and a proposed consent order accompany the memorandum. Chairman James Miller has recently established an evaluation committee at the FTC to review prospective cases and weed out the weak cases that consume staff resources and time. He said that he wants to be certain that the FTC will prevail in those cases that are intitated by the agency.

After the proposed complaint has been prepared by the staff and reviewed, the commissioners vote on it. If they agree with staff lawyers—and they normally do—the advertiser is notified that a complaint is about to be issued. The advertiser is given the opportunity to sign the consent order or to negotiate a more favorable consent order. At this point there can be three results. First, the advertiser can agree to the consent order and the commission can vote to accept the consent order. Second, the commission can vote not to accept the order. Third, the advertiser can reject the consent order. If the first happens, the order is published and sixty days later is made final.

If either the commission or the advertiser rejects the consent order, a complaint is issued, and a hearing is scheduled before an administrative law judge, who works within the FTC and officiates at commission hearings. At the hearing that follows—which is a lot like an informal trial—the burden of proof rests upon the FTC staff lawyers—complaint counsels—to show a violation of the law. In a criminal trial for robbery or murder, the evidence must show "beyond a reasonable doubt" that the defendant is guilty. In a civil case, liability must be established by "preponderance of evidence." In a hearing before an administrative law judge all the complaint counsel must show is that there is "substantial evidence" of a violation of the law. While what substantial evidence is, is hard to define, it is less evidence than is required in either a criminal suit or a civil suit. After the hearing the judge either orders the case dismissed or issues a cease and desist order. The decision is final unless either the complaint counsel or the advertiser appeals. If that happens, the entire commission decides the matter. Overruling an administrative law judge is not uncommon. For example, after the hearing on Chevron F-310 the commission overruled the judge's decision to dismiss the charges. More recently the commission overruled a judge's cease and desist order against several television advertisements for Dry Ban spray deodorant. The judge agreed with complaint counsel that the advertisements implied that the spray "went on dry," but in fact was wet when it hit the skin. The FTC disagreed and said that all the advertisement implied was that Ban went on the skin drier than other antiperspirant sprays. A court of appeals must finalize either a consent order or a cease and desist order, but this is a routine matter.

If the FTC dismisses the cease and desist order, the matter ends there. If it supports the order, the advertiser can still appeal to the courts for relief. This is not a common practice, however. It is difficult for courts to reverse an FTC ruling. There are only a handful of reasons which a judge can use to overturn the commission decision. The case goes to the court of appeals and there is no new finding of fact: what the FTC says is fact, is fact. The following are all instances in which a court can overturn a FTC ruling (1) "convincing evidence" that the agency made an error in the proceedings, (2) no evidence to support the commission's findings, (3) violation of the Constitution, for example, the agency did not provide due process of law, (4) the action goes beyond the agency's powers, (5) facts relied upon in making the ruling are not supported by sufficient evidence, and (6) arbitrary or capricious acts by the commission. Such an event is an extreme rarity. An appeal of an adverse ruling by a circuit court can be taken to the Supreme Court, but only if certiorari is granted.

The enforcement powers of the FTC are limited, but can be nevertheless effective. Violation of either a cease and desist order or a consent order can result in a penalty of $10,000 per violation per day. A fine such as this can add up fast! As a result of the *Geritol* case the agency can be forced into district court to prove to a jury that in fact the orders were violated. This action impedes the enforcement procedure, for a jury trial is time-consuming and costly. As an alternative the agency can go back to the court of appeals which finalized the consent order or the cease and desist order and seek a civil contempt citation against the advertiser. The penalty is then up to the judge and will probably be much smaller, since civil contempt damages are considered remedial and are not intended as a deterrent.

Enforcement is a complex and sometimes confusing process. This fact at least partially explains why FTC procedures often move so slowly. It also explains why the agency works so hard to gain compliance with consent orders, since voluntary compliance alleviates many bureaucratic hassles.

Aspects of Deception

It must be obvious that advertising regulations are fairly clear on one point: deceptive, misleading, untruthful advertising is not permitted. But what is deceptive, misleading, untruthful advertising? It is the same kind of question we confronted when defining what is obscene and what is libelous. There is no great scroll in the sky providing a complete and comprehensive list of advertisements that are permitted and those that are not permissible. An advertiser is expected to use common sense to some extent and to supplement common sense by examining what the various regulatory agencies in the past have deemed to be deceptive. In this section we will talk about the regulatory guidelines, but you are cautioned that this discussion is by no means exhaustive or complete. Scores of deceptions which have been prohibited are not included here, and scores and scores are yet to be created. So be forewarned.

Just because an advertisement is untruthful does not mean that it is deceptive or illegal. When a supermarket advertises that the Easter Bunny left lots of good grocery buys in the produce section or a gasoline company advertises that you can put a tiger in your tank, most people realize that they are being kidded. These kinds of fanciful nonmaterial untruths are generally acceptable so long as the advertiser does not get carried away. All other kinds of untruths including explicit untruths (big lies), half-truths, and more subtle deceptions are problems.

If you advertise a watch as being waterproof and it is not, that is a lie and is a violation of the law. An advertiser cannot qualify a lie appearing in one part of an advertisement by providing a sneaky list of exceptions elsewhere in the advertisement (*Giant Food, Inc.*, v. *FTC*, 1963). For example, it is deceptive to claim in a prominent headline that your brand of watch is waterproof and then in a footnote in small type at the bottom of the advertisement indicate that the watch is waterproof except when immersed in water for more than 14 seconds.

Not telling the whole truth is also deceptive. To claim that 93 percent of all your watches sold since 1952 still keep perfect time is a half-truth unless you also state that the watches have only been on the market for the last three years. Deceptive mock-ups and demonstrations are also considered illegal if the mock-up is used as proof of an advertising claim (*FTC* v. *Colgate-Palmolive Co.,* 1965). More explanation is needed. For many years a shaving cream company claimed that its product was so good that it could be used to shave sandpaper. In a television commercial an actor put Rapid Shave on sandpaper and a few minutes later was shown shaving off the sand. While the claim was apparently true (if the shaving cream was left on the sandpaper long enough, that is), the demonstration was phony. What the actor shaved was not sandpaper, but loose sand sprinkled on glass. The government said this was deceptive advertising, and the courts—including the United States Supreme Court—agreed, despite advertiser pleas that it had tried to shave real sandpaper in the commercial, but because the sand and the paper were the same color, and because the advertisements were in black and white, viewers could not see that the sand really came off. In other words, as one author wrote, a mock-up cannot overcome the shortcomings of the medium, even were the claims true.

In its decision the Supreme Court did not rule that all fake demonstrations or mock-ups are illegal, only those in which the faked portion is supposed to prove a product claim (*FTC* v. *Colgate-Palmolive Co.,* 1965). For example, let us say that in a television commercial packaged ice cubes are the product being sold. The film must be shot under hot lights. Since the ice cubes would melt in the heat, plastic cubes are used. A pile of the plastic cubes are put on a table, and while the cameras grind away, an announcer extolls the virtues of these marvelous, uniform-size, crystal-clear ice cubes. This device is illegal because the plastic cubes are used to prove the advertising claims. Let us now say that soda pop instead of ice cubes is being sold, and the actor drops three or four plastic cubes into a glass before he pours in "the mouth-watering, cool, and refreshing" soda. It is permissible to use the plastic cubes in this situation because they are not being used to demonstrate a product claim.

What about advertisements that have a double meaning, a truthful meaning and one that is not? Here is a classic example. "We will put a new motor in your old car for $350." What does this statement mean? It can be read to mean that the advertiser will sell you a new motor and install it in your car for $350. That is a good deal. However, the statement can also mean that if you have a new motor for your old car the advertiser will install it for $350, which is not such a good deal. In such situations the government presumes that people believe the misleading meaning, and such advertising is deceptive (*FTC* v. *Sterling Drug Co.,* 1963).

The entire problem of half-truths, partial truths, double meanings, and so forth, is one of the most serious problems the government faces. Complaints against such advertisements are common. More than twenty years ago the FTC challenged an advertisement for Old Gold cigarettes which quoted an independent survey finding Old Golds to be low in nicotine and tar (*P. Lorillard Co.,* 1950). This claim was true, but the group which did the research also concluded that none of the cigarettes tested—including Old Gold—had sufficiently low nicotine-and-tar content to be safe. The cigarette maker did not disclose this fact, making the advertisement deceptive. More recently the government has pressured the company that makes Wonder Bread for advertising that its product contains vitamins and minerals which will help young people grow up to be big and strong. The government says that nearly all commercially baked bread is fortified with vitamins and minerals and will help young people grow up to be big and strong. The FTC argues that by not disclosing that Wonder Bread is no different from any other bread the company tells only half the story (in re *ITT Continental Baking Co.,* 1971). The makers of Geritol, by not saying that Geritol does not help most people who are tired, and the Ford Motor Company, by comparing the quietness of their car to that of a glider and not saying that a glider is noisy in flight, were guilty of the same kind of deception. This kind of deceptive advertising is probably the most common problem today.

Testimonials

Testimonials ranging from Joe Namath advertising panty hose to "the average man" promoting a pain reliever, are a large part of the advertising business. Before 1932, when a company paid for a testimonial—any testimonial—that fact had to be revealed in the advertisement. This has not been the law for more than forty years, however (*Northam Warren Corp.* v. *FTC,* 1932). Today, within certain limits, paid testimonials are allowed. The testifier must have in fact endorsed the product (*Eastern Railroad Presidents' Conference* v. *Noerr Motor Freight, Inc.,* 1961). It is deceptive, as well as an invasion of privacy, for an advertiser to assert that astronaut Neil Armstrong eats X brand of breakfast cereal if Armstrong does not, in fact, endorse the product. A testimonial cannot be altered to change the meaning (see *FTC* v. *Standard Education Society,* 1937). Suppose this is a movie review: "This is the worst movie of the year. You can see it—but only if you want to make yourself ill." Now here is an advertisement for the movie citing the review: "The critics loved it. '. . . the movie of the year. See it. . . .' " The quotation is used out of context and this use is deceptive. An advertisement can note that a testimonial is unsolicited, but only if it is unsolicited (*FTC* v. *Inecto, Inc.,* 1934).

The FTC adopted a new set of rules for testimonial advertising in 1975. Experts who endorse products must now have the expertise to evaluate the products. The law is quite rigid concerning products which relate to health and safety. The FTC ruled that an "expert" endorsement by former astronaut Gordon Cooper of a product that supposedly increased automobile performance, reduced smog emission, and cleaned an engine was improper. Cooper's skill related to space missions; he did not have the education or training to qualify as an "expert" in the field of automobile engineering (in re *Leroy Gordon Cooper,* 1979).

A celebrity or expert endorser must be a bona fide user of a product at the time of the endorsement. This means the individual must use the product more than "now and then," or "once in a while." And endorsers must use a product because they like it and approve of it. The advertiser can continue to use the endorsement only so long as there is good reason to believe that the endorser still uses the product.

When an organization—like the National Football League—endorses a product there must be evidence that the endorsement represents the collective judgment of the members of the organizations, not just the judgment of the executive director or the management council of the group.

Payment made to an expert or celebrity endorser does not have to be revealed as long as there is no representation made in the advertisement that the endorsement was given without compensation. Payment made to a non-famous endorser (the typical man on the street) need be revealed only if the endorser knows that a favorable review of a product might result in the use of the endorsement as an advertisement. Here is an example. An advertiser announces that it is looking for man-on-the-street endorsements for Snappy Soda and invites persons to taste it and give their reactions to the drink. The fact that the tasters know in advance that a favorable review might get them a lucrative television commercial could color their reaction to the drink. But if the advertiser secretly records an individual's reactions to Snappy Soda and has not told this person such reactions might be used as a television endorsement, no disclosure of subsequent payment need be made.

Celebrity endorsements must also reveal a material connection between endorsers and products if one exists. Pat Boone was fined by the FTC for failing to meet this rule in his endorsements of Acne-Statin, a skin-blemish medication. Cooga Mooga Corporation, owned and operated by Boone for the purpose of promoting the performer's business interests, was one of several companies marketing and promoting the skin medication. Boone received twenty-five cents for each nine-dollar bottle sold. In this case Boone also implied that his four daughters had used the preparation successfully, which was not completely true, and that Acne-Statin was superior to other similar products, an expert evaluation he was not qualified to make (in re *Cooga Mooga, Inc. and Charles E. Boone,* 1978). This was the first time a celebrity had been held directly responsible for deceptive endorsement. The singer paid a large fine and was ordered to pay partial restitution to persons who had bought the product. The link between a product and a celebrity endorser does not have to be as direct as the connection between Boone and Acne-Statin to require disclosure. Former astronaut Gordon Cooper was paid for his endorsement of the previously noted automotive product on the basis of the number of devices sold. The more products sold, the more money he received. The FTC ruled that this was a material connection between the product and the endorser and should have been revealed in the endorsements (in re *Leroy Gordon Cooper,* 1979).

An endorser cannot make any statement that an advertiser cannot make; that is, the endorser also must have support for his conclusions. The makers of a cough syrup cannot honestly say that their product cures a cough. A housewife who endorses the cough syrup cannot make that statement either. If an endorser changes his view and decides the product is no good, the advertiser must stop using his testimonial.

Endorsements which claim to be from typical consumers must be made by consumers, not by actors playing the part of consumers. Laymen cannot endorse the effectiveness of drug products. If an endorser says she removes facial hair safely with a depilatory, her experience must be typical of most consumers. She cannot be the exception to the fact that the product damages the skin of most women who use it.

Puffery

Under the common law a distinction between an advertiser's assertions of factual claims and his assertion of opinion developed. Dean William Prosser in *Handbook of the Law of Torts* writes that it is a seller's privilege to "lie his head off" so long as nothing specific is said about the product. A reasonable man knows that these generalities are merely subjective **puffery** or hyperbole about the product. Therefore under the common law, statements claiming that a sport coat is all wool, is made in England, and is the lowest-priced coat in town have to be true because they give specific facts about the product. However, it is all right to say that the coat is the best-looking sport coat in town, or that it is the best buy today, or that girls will really notice men when they wear the coat. These claims are puffery which reasonable people do not tend to believe. Objective statements must be true. Opinion or subjective statements can be exaggerated.

Today there is very little common law adjudication of false advertising claims. The FTC and state and local agencies which police advertising are not as receptive to puffery as is the common law. In a ruling in 1957 the commission noted, "*Puffing* . . . is a term frequently used to denote exaggerations reasonably to be expected of a seller as to the degree of quality of his product, the truth or falsity of which cannot be precisely determined" (in re *The Matter of Better Living,* 1957). Since that time the agency has shown little inclination to allow puffery. In the 1974 *Staff Report to the Federal Trade Commission* prepared by John Howard and James Hulbert, the two researchers write, "The traditional common law distinction between misrepresentation of fact and of opinion—the latter not being considered actionable—has to a large extent been rejected under the FTC Act." In *The Law of Advertising* Rosden and Rosden argue, "Advertisers who do not want to risk a proceeding before the Commission will have to be exceedingly careful in using hyperbole in their advertising." The Rosdens note that the test must be whether ordinary consumers of the advertised goods or service can recognize hyperbole for what it is or will be deceived by it (*Western Radio Corp.* v. *FTC,* 1965).

<table>
<tr><td>*Bait-and-Switch Advertising*</td><td>One of the classic false advertising games is what is called **bait-and-switch advertising.** Here is the general idea. An appliance store advertises in the newspaper that it is selling a brand-new washing machine for $57. The advertisement is the bait, to get customers into the store. When customers come to the store to grab up this bargain, the salespeople are very honest about the advertised washer and say that it is a pile of junk (and it probably is!): it has no dials, it tears fine fabrics, it tends to leak, its motor is loud, and so forth. However, over in a corner is a really good buy, a snappy model for only $395, for only a few days. This high-pressure selling is the switch. If customers insist on buying the bait, chances are they will be told the machines have all been sold. The merchant had never intended to sell that model. The whole idea is to use the bait to lure into the store people who are in the market for washing machines, and then skillful, if not honest, salespersons switch customers to a more costly model via high-pressure selling—convenient monthly payments, and so forth.</td></tr>
</table>

Bait-and-switch advertising is illegal. Technically the law says that it is deceptive to advertise goods or services with the intent not to sell them as advertised or to advertise goods and services with the intent not to supply reasonably expected public demand, unless limitation on the quantity is noted in the advertisement (see Title 16 *Code of Federal Regulations,* 238).

Bait-and-switch advertising is not the same as loss-leader advertising, legal in many places, in which a merchant offers to sell one item at below cost (the leader) in order to get customers into the store who in turn then buy (he hopes) additional merchandise at regular cost. Supermarkets use this scheme and so do other retail outlets. Those states which outlawed this practice did so because of pressure from small merchants who cannot afford to sell anything at a loss and do not want to be put at a marketing disadvantage with high-volume sellers.

<table>
<tr><td>*Other Deceptions*</td><td>Advertising can be deceptive in any number of ways. Let us look at a few more examples.</td></tr>
</table>

It is deceptive to be untruthful about matters of cost and price; to say that the price of an item is reduced when it is not; to advertise a factory discount price when it is not; to advertise a special introductory price when it is not. The use of the word *free* causes many problems. If a merchant gives a free toothbrush to all persons who come into the store, he can advertise that he is giving away free toothbrushes. The word *free* may be used in connection with mail-order giveaways, even if the customer is charged a small fee for postage and handling, fifteen or twenty-five cents. However, to advertise a free set of drinking glasses and then require people to pay three dollars postage and handling is illegal.

The word *free* can be used even when the customers are required to buy another item before getting the free item so long as this fact is made clear in the advertisement: a free toothbrush with every purchase of a tube of toothpaste. However, this rule applies only so long as the price of the toothpaste is not inflated to cover even partial cost of the toothbrush. The toothpaste must be sold at the regular price. The same limitation applies to two-for-one sales: the first item must be sold at regular price, not at an inflated price.

A seller cannot falsely advertise the origin of merchandise, that is, say it is imported when it is not or claim cheese is Wisconsin cheese when it is really Vermont cheese. A seller cannot exaggerate about the quantity, that is, advertise a bushel of apples that is really only a peck or label a small can of coffee giant economy size when in fact the price per ounce of the coffee is higher than the regular-size can.

Deceptions about the quality of merchandise are also prohibited. A merchant cannot advertise a chair as an antique unless it meets strict government definition of what is and what is not an antique. Under the 1931 Tariff Act only furniture made before 1830 is considered antique. The same is true for porcelain and silver. A rug made after 1701 is not an antique. A violin made before 1801 is. And so on. Unless the item meets these standards, it cannot be advertised as antique. The word *cure* implies that a permanent solution to a problem is offered. Most medicines give temporary relief, and then only for the symptoms of a specific medical problem. The word *permanent* means just that—permanent. Hair dye cannot be advertised as *permanent* because hair continues to grow, and new undyed roots will always appear. The word *remedy* also implies a permanent cure: there is no such thing as a *headache remedy* since these words imply that users will have no more headaches. There are products, however, which temporarily relieve headaches.

At times—but not consistently—the FTC has said that advertising which invokes an irrelevant factor to win sales is deceptive. Health products are especially vulnerable to this interpretation. What is an irrelevancy? For example, an advertisement based on sex appeal. The FTC recently issued a complaint against Vivarin, a patent medicine which contains both an analgesic and a stimulant, for advertising which implies that use of the product makes persons more exciting and attractive, improves their personality, marriage, and sex life, and solves mental and personal problems. These benefits are irrelevant (as well as exaggerated) to the primary purpose of the product, to relieve a headache (in re *J. B. Williams,* 1972).

Defenses   The basic defense in any false advertising suit is truth, that is, proving that a product does what the advertiser claims it does, that it is made where he says it is made or that it is as beneficial as it is advertised to be. While the burden is upon the government to disprove the advertiser's claim, it is always helpful for an advertiser to offer proof to substantiate advertising copy.

Another angle which advertisers can pursue is to attack a different aspect of the government's case rather than try to prove the statement true. For example, an advertiser can argue that the deceptive statement is not material to the advertisement as a whole, that is, it will not influence the purchasing decision, or that the advertisement does not imply what the government thinks it implies. For example, to say that a deodorant "goes on dry" does not mean that it is dry when it is applied, merely that its application is drier than that of other antiperspirants.

The success rate in defending false-advertising cases is not high. As for most legal problems, it is best to consult legal counsel before a problem arises and not after a complaint has been issued.

Advertising law is complicated, involved, and constantly changing. Even advertisers who set out to honestly follow the straight and narrow run into difficulty once in a while. The best way to cope with these problems is thorough understanding of both the law and the way the law operates.

Summary   Complaints against advertisers are prepared by the FTC staff and approved by a vote of the commission. Administrative law judges can hold hearings which are somewhat like trials to determine whether the FTC charges are valid. A United States court of appeals can review all commission orders.

Many kinds of advertising have been found to be deceptive. Deliberately lying in an advertisement is normally considered deceptive. Failure to tell the complete truth in an advertisement can also be deceptive. Testimonial advertising is scrutinized very closely by the FTC. Rules require that expert endorsers have the qualifications needed to make an expert endorsement, that celebrity endorsers actually use and like the products they endorse, and that material connections between endorsers and products they promote be revealed in the advertisement. While the common law has traditionally permitted a certain amount of exaggeration about product quality (puffery), the FTC has looked unfavorably upon such hyperbole. The law also outlaws bait-and-switch advertising in which customers are lured to a store with promises of low prices, but are pushed to buy more expensive products by salespersons. The FTC also prohibits untruthful statements about the cost of a product, the quality of a product, or the quantity of a product. The best and only real defense to a charge of false advertising is to prove the truth of the claim.

BIBLIOGRAPHY

Here is a list of some of the sources that have been helpful in the preparation of chapter 10.

Books

Alexander, George. *Honesty and Competition.* Syracuse: Syracuse University Press, 1967.

Howard, John A., and Hulbert, James. *A Staff Report to the Federal Trade Commission.* Washington, D.C.: Federal Trade Commission, 1974.

Posner, Richard A. *Regulation of Advertising by the Federal Trade Commission.* Washington, D.C.: American Enterprise Institute for Public Policy Research, 1973.

Prosser, William L. *Handbook of the Law of Torts.* St. Paul: West Publishing Co., 1964.

Rohrer, Daniel M., ed. *Mass Media, Freedom of Speech, and Advertising.* Dubuque: Kendall/Hunt, 1979.

Rosden, George E., and Rosden, Peter. *The Law of Advertising.* New York: Matthew Bender & Co., 1975.

Articles

Devore, Cameron, and Nelson, Marshall. "Commercial Speech and Paid Access to the Press." 26 *Hastings Law Journal* 745, 1975.

Jones, Michael E. "Celebrity Endorsements: A Cause for Alarm and Concern for the Future." 15 *New England Law Review* 521, 1980.

"Note: Corrective Advertising and the FTC." 70 *Michigan Law Review* 374, 1971.

Townley, Rod. "No Hitting Below the (Money) Belt." August 7 *TV Guide*, p. 18, 1982.

Zanot, Eric. "The National Advertising Review Board 1971–1976." 59 *Journalism Monograph* 1, 1979.

Cases

Alberty v. *FTC*, 182 F.2d 36 (1950).

American Home Products v. *Johnson & Johnson*, 436 F. Supp. 785 (1977).

Aronberg v. *FTC*, 132 F.2d 165 (1942).

Bates and Van O'Steen v. *Arizona*, 97 S.Ct. 2691 (1977).

Bigelow v. *Virginia*, 95 S.Ct. 2222 (1975).

Bolger v. *Young Drug Products Corp.* (citation pending).

Campbell Soup Co., 77 FTC 664 (1970).

Central Hudson v. *Public Service Commission*, 100 S.Ct. 2343 (1980).

in re *Coca-Cola Co.*, Docket No. 8839 (1973).

in re *Cooga Mooga, Inc. and Charles E. Boone*, 92 FTC 310 (1978).

in re *LeRoy Gordon Cooper*, 94 FTC 674 (1979).

Eastern Railroad Presidents' Conference v. *Noerr Motor Freight, Inc.*, 365 U.S. 127 (1961).

Feil v. *FTC*, 285 F.2d 879 (1960).

Friedman v. *Rogers*, 99 S.Ct. 887 (1979).

FTC v. *Colgate-Palmolive Co.*, 380 U.S. 374 (1965).

FTC v. *Inecto, Inc.*, 70 F.2d 370 (1934).

FTC v. *Raladam*, 283 U.S. 643 (1931).

FTC v. *Raladam*, 316 U.S. 149 (1942).

FTC v. *Standard Education Society*, 302 U.S. 112 (1937).

FTC v. *Sterling Drug Co.*, 317 F.2d 669 (1963).

Giant Food, Inc., v. *FTC*, 322 F.2d 977 (1963).

Heinz v. *Kirchner*, 63 FTC 1282 (1963); affd. sub. nom. *Kirchner* v. *FTC*, 337 F.2d 751 (1964).

in re *ITT Continental Baking Co.*, 79 FTC 248 (1971).

Lamar Outdoor Advertising v. *Mississippi Tax Commission*, 9 M.L. Rept. 1419 (1983).

Linmark Associates v. *Township of Willingboro*, 97 S.Ct. 1614 (1977).

in re *The Matter of Better Living*, 54 FTC 648 (1957).

Medowbrook Women's Clinic v. *Minnesota*, 9 M.L. Rept. 1325 (1983).

Metpath v. *Myers*, 462 F. Supp. 1104 (1978).

Moretrench Corp. v. *FTC*, 127 F.2d 792 (1942).

National Petroleum Refiner's Association v. *FTC*, 340 F. Supp. 1343 (1972); revd. 482 F.2d 672 (1974).

Northam Warren Corp. v. *FTC*, 59 F.2d 196 (1932).

Ocean Spray Cranberries, Inc., 70 FTC 975 (1972).

Ohralik v. *Ohio State Bar Association*, 98 S.Ct. 1912 (1978).

Oklahoma Telecasters Association v. *Crisp*, 9 M.L. Rept. 1089 (1983).

Pennsylvania v. *Pittsburgh Press*, 396 A.2d 1187 (1979).

Pittsburgh Press Co. v. *Pittsburgh Commission on Human Rights*, 413 U.S. 476 (1973).

Rast v. *van Deman & Lewis Co.*, 240 U.S. 342 (1916).

Rhode Island Broadcasters v. *Michaelson*, 4 M.L. Rept. 2224 (1978).

in re *R. M. J.*, 102 S.Ct. 929 (1982).

State v. *Cusick*, 84 N.W.2d 544 (1957).

U.S. v. *J. B. Williams Co.*, 498 F.2d 414 (1974).

Valentine v. *Chrestensen*, 316 U.S. 52 (1942).

Virginia State Board of Pharmacy v. *Virginia Citizens' Consumer Council, Inc.*, 96 S.Ct. 1817 (1976).

Warner-Lambert v. *FTC*, 562 F.2d 749 (1977).

Western Radio Corp. v. *FTC*, 339 F.2d 937 (1965).

in re *J. B. Williams Co.*, 68 FTC 481 (1965); 79 FTC 410 (1971); 81 FTC 238 (1972).

in re *J. B. Williams* v. *FTC*, 381 F.2d 884 (1967).

11 BROADCAST REGULATION

The world is in the midst of a revolution in both communication technology and communication. Nowhere is this more evident than in what is called the broadcasting industry; radio, television, cable television, and so forth. Each day stories in the popular press inform us of new broadcasting hardware, new transmission systems, and new software packages such as laser video discs. Most persons will soon have access to scores of television and radio channels, free and pay, local and distant, oriented toward both entertainment and information. The recent distinctions between over-the-air television and cable television are fast disappearing. People in the broadcast industry talk of "products" (programming) and "delivery systems," not telecasting or cablecasting. Many believe we stand on the threshhold of a great new age of information.

The world of broadcast regulation is also in the midst of a kind of revolution. Both the Congress and the Federal Communications Commission (FCC), the regulatory agency assigned the task of regulating the electronic media, realized late in the 1970s that regulatory policies cannot continue to reflect now passé over-the-air media versus cable mentality of the 1960s. Congress has attempted (unsuccessfully) to adopt more comprehensive legislation for the electronic communications industry. The Federal Communications Commission in September 1982 combined its Broadcast Bureau and its Cable Television Bureau into the single Mass Media Bureau.

A revolution of another sort is also under way in broadcast regulation. Persons in the industry call it "deregulation." After more than fifty years of rather strict government control of broadcasting, there is a strong push for granting broadcasters considerably more freedom than ever before. Some persons in the broadcast industry—especially broadcast journalists—have vocally protested government regulation for decades. But while the industry as a whole often groused about its regulated status, no serious effort was made to break this yoke of government control. Even today, the industry supports deregulation, but often in a most diffident manner. Many broadcasters watched what happened to other controlled industries when deregulation occurred (the airline industry, for example) and remain somewhat concerned about their future.

The strongest impetus for deregulation today comes from government itself—from both the Federal Communications Commission and the Congress. It is time to free the broadcaster from government control, proponents argue. It is time to change the law. Changes in the broadcast law were proposed in earlier times, but such proposals amounted to tinkering with the law when compared with the wholesale modifications proposed in Congress today. The supporters of deregulation—including FCC Chairman Mark Fowler—challenge the very theoretical basis upon which broadcasting has been regulated since the first quarter of this century.

REGULATION HISTORY AND RATIONALE

The individuals who created our system of regulation of broadcasting adopted what some call a trusteeship model for a pattern. The model suggests that the broadcaster should act as a public trustee, using the valuable broadcast airwaves for the benefit of the public. It was no accident that this model was adopted. It was dictated in no small part by the early history of radio. Let us examine that history briefly. Then we can attempt to outline the basic rationale which supports this trusteeship model.

Development of Radio

Radio is not the invention of a single individual. Rather, it represents an accumulation of many ideas that emerged during the last years of the nineteenth century. At first only simple radio signals were transmitted. But gradually transmission of more complicated voice signals became possible. The basic hardware of radio had been developed by 1910, but the medium grew far differently than did the print medium. Remember, printing came at a time when people were groping for a means of spreading propaganda, and the printing press became a major weapon in the battle for religious freedom in England. The press was used as a means of spreading information and ideas. Radio has never really been dedicated to those ends. Initially it was a gadget which tinkerers built as a plaything for talking with friends and neighbors and for listening to strangers in distant places. The military was first to see the practical value of radio. The navy used radio as a means of keeping track of its ships out of port and for transmitting messages to captains on the high seas. The army too saw radio as an effective device for improving military communications. After World War I the armed forces made one concerted push to have the government take control of all radio communication, but the effort failed.

Aside from the military, few persons could see the practical side of radio, especially of radio broadcasting. The giant radio manufacturers were the first to reason that if they used radio to broadcast entertainment people would want to buy radio sets. Commercialism took a big step forward in the early twenties when the concept of broadcasters selling broadcast time to sponsors developed.

Radio Act of 1912

The regulation of broadcasting in the United States dates from 1910 when Congress ruled that all United States passenger ships must carry a radio. Two years later the lawmakers passed the **Radio Act of 1912** in response to considerable pressure from the army and navy which asserted that increasing numbers of amateur broadcasters interfered with military transmissions. The 1912 law required that all radio transmitters be licensed by the federal government and that operators of the transmitters be required to have a license. The secretary of labor and commerce, who was delegated the job of administering the law, was given authority to assign specific broadcast wavelengths to specific kinds of broadcasting (military wavelength, ship-to-shore wavelength, etc.). The secretary also had the power to determine the time periods when broadcasts could be carried, but he had no discretionary power to license. Anyone walking in the door and filling out an application could get a license.

Part of the problem in the early 1920s was the proliferation of licenses. Too many people wanted a license and too many radio stations wanted to transmit at the same time. In 1923 Secretary of Commerce Herbert Hoover decided to take things into his own hands when he refused to grant a license to an applicant, claiming that this discretion was inherent in the 1912 law. A federal court disagreed with the secretary, however. "The duty of issuing licenses to persons or corporations coming within the classification designated in the act reposes no discretion whatever in the Secretary of Commerce. The duty is mandatory," Judge Van Orsdel wrote (*Hoover* v. *Intercity Radio Co., Inc.,* 1923).

While Hoover was defeated in the courts, conscientious broadcasters and other persons concerned with the future of radio continued to urge the secretary to set up regulations to control broadcasting. At the Fourth National Radio Conference in 1925 (Hoover called yearly meetings to draft broadcasting regulations which Congress annually rejected), the secretary of commerce outlined his philosophy with regard to broadcast regulation. This philosophy remains today the basic foundation for the regulatory scheme:

> We hear a great deal about freedom of the air, but there are two parties to freedom of the air, and to freedom of speech for that matter. Certainly in radio I believe in freedom for the listener. . . . Freedom cannot mean a license to every person or corporation who wishes to broadcast his name or his wares, and thus monopolize the listener's set. We do not get much freedom of speech if one hundred fifty people speak at the same time at the same place. The airwaves are a public medium, and their use must be for the public benefit. The main consideration in the radio field is, and always will be, the great body of the listening public, millions in number, countrywide in distribution. There is no proper line of conflict between the broadcaster and the listener. Their interests are mutual, for without the one the other could not exist.

Under pressure from elements in the broadcasting industry and somewhat flush with the consensus which the annual radio conferences seemed to indicate, Hoover continued to act beyond his legal authority in regulating broadcasting. In 1926 his actions were again challenged, this time by Eugene F. McDonald who operated station WJAZ in Chicago on an unauthorized wavelength and at times not authorized by his license. His challenge to Hoover was joined in federal district court and Hoover lost. Judge Wilkerson ruled, "There is no express grant of power in the [1912] Act to the Secretary of Commerce to establish regulations" (*U.S.* v. *Zenith Radio Corp.,* 1926).

Hoover insisted that the attorney general appeal the ruling, but in a lengthy opinion Acting Attorney General William J. Donovan stated that he agreed with Wilkerson's interpretation of the law. Donovan wrote that, while stations were required to have licenses to operate, the secretary of commerce had no authority to assign specific stations to specific wavelengths, to limit hours of operation, or to place limitations on the amount of broadcast power used by a station. Donovan added:

> It is apparent from the answers contained in this opinion that the present legislation is inadequate to cover the art of broadcasting, which has been almost entirely developed since the passage of the 1912 Act. If the present situation requires control, I can only suggest that it be sought in new legislation, carefully adopted to meet the needs of both the present and the future.

Hoover capitulated, and the chaos which the secretary's illegal regulations had somewhat abated returned to the airwaves. Finally, Congress could no longer ignore the mounting pressure and adopted federal legislation by passing the comprehensive **Radio Act of 1927.**

Radio Act of 1927

The nation had operated without substantial regulation of broadcasting for about twenty years, but nonregulation did not seem to work. A traffic cop was obviously necessary to make certain that broadcasters transmitted on assigned wavelengths, that they operated during assigned hours, and that they operated at assigned levels of power. Only with this kind of regulation could listeners use the medium. The Radio Act of 1927 created much more than a traffic cop however. As former FCC Commissioner Glen Robinson notes in *The Administrative Process,* "Even a cursory examination of the Act, however, indicates that the regulatory powers granted to the Federal Radio Commission (and later to the FCC) exceeded those minimally required to avoid electronic interference." The new law governed programming, licensing and renewal, and many other aspects of radio not associated with broadcast signals and electronic interference.

The years immediately following the passage of the new law brought order to broadcasting. The courts upheld the power of the federal government to regulate the broadcast media, and the system of regulations which exist today began to take shape. The 1927 act also provided the basic philosophical foundation for broadcasting regulation. The law asserted that the radio spectrum, the airwaves, belongs to the public and that broadcasters merely use this public resource while they operate a licensed station. The law established that the broadcaster must operate in "the public interest, convenience or necessity" at all times. This was the standard of conduct which would be used to evaluate licensees at renewal time. An independent agency, the Federal Radio Commission, was also established to supervise the regulation of broadcasting.

While the 1927 legislation was satisfactory in dealing with the problems of broadcasting, it became evident following a study initiated by President Franklin D. Roosevelt in 1933 that the radio industry and the telephone and telegraph industries were interdependent. In 1934 Roosevelt urged Congress to adopt a new law which would be broad enough in scope to govern all these media. After extensive hearings and debates the Federal Communications Act of 1934 was approved. This law has been amended frequently since 1934, but it stands as the basic regulation of the broadcast industry today (47 *United States Code*, Section 151, 1970).

Justification of Regulation

If we study this history closely we can see that regulation of American broadcasting was really justified on three grounds: scarcity, public benefit, and fear. Let us examine each of these three justifications a bit more closely.

Scarcity

There is a real and absolute limit on the number of persons who can broadcast over the airwaves at any given time. What engineers call the broadcast spectrum—the roadways in the atmosphere on which broadcast signals travel—is finite. When the roads are filled, no one else can drive. When the full spectrum is being used, no one else can broadcast. This fact of nature became painfully obvious in the early days of radio when anyone who wanted to tried to broadcast over the airwaves. The result was cacophony and chaos. Space on the broadcast spectrum was (and is) a scarce item. Not everyone who wants to operate a radio or television station can do so. Someone must decide who shall be permitted to use this scarce resource. This need for an arbiter proved to be an important impetus to government licensing of broadcast stations.

Public Benefit

It is thought by many people that when a broadcaster uses the airwaves to transmit radio and television signals the broadcaster is using a public resource that belongs to all persons in the nation. Some agency must administer this valuable public resource in behalf of the public. Someone must make certain that those individuals who do use the "public airwaves" serve the best interests of the people when they use this public resource. There must be some means to assure that the public gets some kind of value for permitting persons to make a profit by using a public resource.

Fear

The broadcast media are thought by many persons to be powerful and even potentially dangerous mass media. We can bring the electronic media into our homes with little or no effort by the mere flick of a switch. Once we buy a receiver, we do not even have to pay for what we receive. The broadcast media can be used to spread dangerous ideas to large numbers of persons almost instantaneously. They can harm a community or a nation by spreading false information about important issues. They can offend or even foster serious social problems; for example, violence on television and its possible influence on violence in our society. Vulnerable children have easy access to the content of broadcasting. Finally, broadcasters can use the electronic media solely for private gain and flood the airwaves with advertising and commercial promotions. This valuable communications device could be turned into a giant selling machine.

Under the trusteeship model, the government is assigned the responsibility of controlling broadcasting. Because of the scarcity of broadcast frequencies, the government must assign those frequencies to those persons who can best serve the nation. Because these frequencies are a public resource, the government must act to ensure that those broadcasters who use the scarce frequencies serve the public interest—the greatest good for the greatest number. And because broadcasting is powerful and could cause harm, the government must ensure that the electronic media are not used in an improper manner. Under the trusteeship model the government will maintain ownership of the public airwaves in behalf of the people and temporarily assign broadcast frequencies to private individuals who are expected to act as trustees for the public in the use of this valuable resource. The public interest will be served through government regulation of these trustees.

Challenge to the Trusteeship Model

The trusteeship theory is being challenged today by what FCC Chairman Mark Fowler describes as the "marketplace theory" or "marketplace approach." This theory suggests that the marketplace should regulate broadcasting and that government should play a very minimal role. Fowler suggests that the marketplace approach will come to replace the trusteeship theory for three reasons:

1. "There is a growing national consensus that market-oriented solutions, in which consumers interact with market players unimpeded by the filters of government, are preferable to a system where the government attempts to regulate the marketplace," according to the chairman. This solution has been applied in many industries—such as the airlines industry—with varying success. But the spirit of deregulation, the philosophy of "getting government off the back of business" is strong today.

There is also some evidence that the marketplace can successfully "regulate" broadcasting in some ways. In 1970 virtually every radio station in the United States entertained its audience by playing phonograph records throughout the broadcast day. Today, there is a great diversity in radio programming, including a growing segment of stations which program large blocks of news and information. Some stations broadcast all news. For fifty years the FCC fought vainly to convince broadcasters to carry more news and public affairs programs as a service to the public. The agency failed. But the marketplace—the radio listeners—seems to have succeeded. It is success in the ratings with demographically attractive listeners that has spurred the growth of the news- and information-oriented radio stations.

2. "A second distinct reason for this shift from trusteeship to market theory arises out of the failure of traditional rationales to justify imposition of program content-related regulation. The long-standing explanation for why government got into broadcast regulation—the so-called scarcity of spectrum rationale—is logically suspect and factually threadbare," Fowler wrote in *Television/Radio Age* in 1982. When one looks at a community and sees three television stations and fifteen radio stations one hardly sees scarcity. But look further. There are also newspapers, magazines, books, and other written materials. A single cable television system can carry scores of channels through a single wire. Direct broadcast satellites and multiple distribution services can beam an almost limitless number of video channels into a home through a dish-shaped antenna. True, not everyone who wants to can operate a broadcast station, but this fact should no longer be a material consideration, the deregulators argue. High costs make it impossible for everyone who wants to operate a viable newspaper or magazine, yet these media are not regulated. Proponents of deregulation turn the matter of scarcity on its head and look not at the potential for ownership, but at the amount of mass media in the marketplace. Surely there is no scarcity today, they argue.

3. "My third impetus for a marketplace approach to broadcast regulation," wrote Commissioner Fowler, "stems from the First Amendment to the Constitution. The concept of a free and uninhibited press is undermined by a regulatory structure that has a federal commission conducting periodic oversight of the programming content of broadcasters." Justifying government regulation of broadcasting in the face of the First Amendment has always been difficult. But in the past fifty years several important developments have taken place that make it more difficult than ever to accept simultaneously the commands of the First Amendment and the restrictions of broadcast regulation.

Comprehensive broadcast regulation was first adopted in 1927. Recall what was written about the history of the First Amendment in chapter 2. Serious judicial development of the meaning of the First Amendment did not take place in this nation until the 1930s. Hence, broadcast regulation was conceived, was adopted, and took hold in an era when the scope of the First Amendment was largely undefined. The growth of news- and public-affairs programs in broadcasting did not take on serious proportions until the 1930s as well. The First Amendment undoubtedly appeared in 1927 to be a limited impediment to the regulation of what was largely entertainment-oriented radio. By the time radio news took its proper place in the spectrum of programming, regulation of broadcasting was an established fact of life. Since the thirties the public has come to rely upon broadcasting for news and information to a far greater extent. The First Amendment has also come to mean a great deal more today than it did in 1927. (Indeed, the First Amendment has already been used to strike down one control on broadcasting, the congressional mandate that prohibited public broadcasting stations which receive government funds from editorializing (*League of Women Voters* v. *FCC,* 1982.) This alone could prompt one to reexamine broadcast regulation in light of the constitutional guarantees of freedom of speech and press. But there is more.

In the recent past one could easily distinguish newspapers, which were not licensed or regulated by the government, from broadcast media, which were. Information carried by newspapers was printed with black ink on cheap paper made from wood pulp. Each edition of the newspaper contained many pages which opened from right to left and folded in the middle. Broadcast news and information were relayed to the viewer or listener via the airwaves or cable. Spoken words or visual images were used to transmit the stories. Today it is not so easy to make these distinctions. Some newspapers transmit news stories from their computer through the airwaves or through a wire to a home television set which displays the words in the story on the screen. This is called teletext. When this occurs, is the newspaper acting as a broadcast or a print medium? Some television stations transmit stories from their computers through the airwaves or a wire to a home television set which displays the words in the story on a screen. More teletext. Is the television station acting as a print or broadcast medium when it does this? In both cases outlined what rules apply? Can the government control it as if it were broadcast? or is it print media out of the reach of government control? Imagine this. Station KJHG carries a story about abortion on the 6 P.M. newscast. The news story is subject to the provisions of the Fairness Doctrine, a government rule which states that when a broadcaster carries material on controversial public issues all sides of that controversy must be aired (see pages 539–51). The station then transmits a textual version of the same story to its teletext customers. Does the Fairness Doctrine apply to the teletext version also?

Questions like these have forced government regulators to look anew at the relationship between broadcast regulation and the First Amendment. Also, as more and more newspapers get involved in electronic information transmission, they have become more and more sympathetic to the plight of the broadcaster who operates only with the permission of the government. Newspaper publishers do not want to find themselves in the same boat in a few years. This situation has spurred the movement to reduce if not eliminate broadcast regulation.

There is one additional reason why the FCC seems ready to abandon the trusteeship model, and why large segments of the public seem to support the commission in this action.

The fourth reason given in support of deregulation is that regulation of broadcasting does not seem to work very well, according to many persons. The FCC and the Congress have done little in the regulation of broadcasting to protect the public interest during the past six decades, critics argue. The system of broadcasting nurtured by government regulation is rife with commercialism. The public interest normally runs a distant second to profit making in the eyes of the broadcaster, critics say. Some of the regulations imposed upon broadcasting to protect the public interest are actually used by broadcasters to avoid meeting public responsibilities. For example, the refusal by some stations to cover controversial public issues is sometimes justified by the broadcaster's fear of government intrusion into its news department via the Fairness Doctrine. The song is a familiar one: "If we carry a broadcast on one side of an issue, we will have to carry additional programs explaining other sides of the same issue. We have neither the time nor the money to do that. Hence, we won't carry anything at all." The government's equal time rule is often raised as a bar by a station which does not wish to allow a political candidate to use its broadcasting facilities to talk to the community. "If we let one candidate use the station, all the candidates have the right to use the station. It is better to bar them all."

But while broadcasting regulation does not appear to have been effective enough to serve the public interest in many cases, it has been effective enough to intimidate some broadcasters. President Richard Nixon and Vice-President Spiro Agnew discovered that requests by the FCC for copies of station commentary about a presidential speech resulted in many stations canceling such commentary. Surely the use of the law in this way does not serve the needs of the nation. Consequently, many persons—even some who strongly believe that the broadcast system must be operated for the public benefit—see the current regulatory system as being more harmful than beneficial. And they are willing to at least try a marketplace approach in hope that the people can exercise more responsible control of broadcasting than the government has exercised since 1927.

It should be noted that many persons and groups who find the current system of broadcast regulation less than satisfactory do not believe deregulation is the best solution. They believe that more intensive regulation, better regulation, is the correct answer to the problem. But these groups find it harder to be heard today than in the late sixties or early seventies. Proponents of deregulation have dominated the public forum lately, and the choice appears to be deregulation or more of the same kind of regulation. Enhanced regulation does not seem to be a viable option at this point.

The current movement for deregulation of the broadcast industry does not mean that the FCC will be abolished, that the Communications Act will be repealed. It simply means that some of the more onerous (in the eyes of broadcasters) rules may be dropped. In the past twelve months FCC Chairman Mark Fowler has led the government movement toward deregulation. The FCC sent a legislative package to the Congress which contains the following proposals:

1. Repeal of the Fairness Doctrine, the thirty-five-year-old rule which requires that broadcasters give radio and television coverage to controversial issues and mandates that this coverage be fair, not one-sided

2. Repeal of the equal time rule which stipulates that when a television or radio station allows one candidate for public office to use the station's broadcasting facilities all candidates for the same office must be given a similar opportunity

3. Repeal of the twelve-year-old reasonable access rule which requires broadcasters to give candidates for federal office a reasonable opportunity to purchase broadcast time during an election campaign

4. Repeal of laws authorizing the FCC to revoke or refuse broadcast licenses to applicants who have previously violated United States antitrust laws

5. Change in the comparative license renewal law so that any licensee, whose past performance is void of any serious deficiencies in statutory terms, would automatically have its license renewed, regardless of whether another applicant for the license promised to give the community better service

In addition to these suggestions made to the Congress, the FCC has reexamined its own rules. The agency recently repealed a forty-year-old rule which forced broadcasters to file complex annual financial reports with the commission. Chairman Fowler has proposed that the commission also abandon rules which bar local television stations from owning cable television systems in the same market in which they broadcast, rules which bar networks from owning cable systems anywhere, and rules which forbid a single company or individual from owning more than seven television stations, seven amplitude modulation (AM) radio stations, and seven frequency modulation (FM) radio stations. In 1982 the FCC granted a waiver to its ban on network ownership of cable television companies, giving CBS permission to acquire a cable system or cable systems serving no more than 90,000 subscribers, or 0.5 percent of all United States cable subscribers, whichever is less. The agency said it would grant the same waiver to the other networks as well.

This current move toward deregulation follows a substantial deregulation of the radio industry in 1981. The FCC removed rules that required radio stations to devote a certain amount of airtime to news or public affairs. The FCC also set aside rules which limited the number of commercial minutes which can be carried each hour. The agency also freed radio stations from many tedious record-keeping practices and lifted some rules which forced the radio broadcaster to formally measure the needs and interests of persons in the community in order to provide proper programming. These latter regulations are called ascertainment rules. This deregulation of radio was generally upheld in May 1983 by the U.S. Court of Appeals in Washington, D.C. (*Office of Communication of the United Church of Christ* v. *FCC,* 1983). On the heels of this judicial approval, the FCC voted unanimously in late July 1983 to propose a similar deregulation for television. Testimony was to be taken on the proposal during the winter of 1983–84, and a final decision on elimination of these rules for commercial television was expected in the spring of 1984.

How far will Chairman Fowler and other authorities get in their movement toward deregulation of the broadcast industry? That is difficult to tell. Earlier congressional attempts at substantially changing broadcast regulations were not successful. In 1977, the House Subcommittee on Communications attempted to entirely rewrite the Communications Act of 1934. Almost 100 days of public hearings were held on the new proposal sponsored by Representative Lionel Van Deerlin. More than 1,200 witnesses testified regarding the proposed measure. But the entire effort was abandoned in August 1979 when, according to one Washington broadcast lobbyist quoted in *TV Guide,* it became clear to members of the subcommittee that "no one really liked H.R. 3333 [the proposed measure]." The Van Deerlin bill would have removed most federal rules governing radio, relaxed many controls on television, taxed broadcasters fairly heavily for their use of the airwaves, totally reshaped public television, lengthened the term of broadcast licenses, and allowed the telephone company (American Telephone & Telegraph) to get into cable television—to name just a few aspects of the proposed measure. However, in writing such a comprehensive measure, Van Deerlin found that his bill alienated a wide range of persons. Public interest groups opposed deregulation of broadcasting—they believed that the government should force radio and television to do more to serve the public, not less. Broadcasters favored deregulation, but did not like the heavy new taxes. Cable operators opposed allowing the telephone company to get involved in cablecasting. Ron Miller of the Knight News Service said that in the end Van Deerlin had "all of broadcasting, most citizen media reform groups and a host of academics lined up against him. It was something like trying to unify the Armed Forces. With the Army, Navy, Air Force and Marines against you, the outcome might be somewhat predictable."

Whatever the success of the current effort toward deregulation, broadcast regulation is still a fact of life today. In the remainder of this chapter we will outline the law as it exists as this book is written. Those sections of the law that might be changed or abandoned will be noted.

Summary

American broadcasting has been regulated almost from its inception. Regulation is based on what some call a trusteeship theory. This theory is based upon three pillars:

1. There is a scarcity of broadcast frequencies, and someone must decide who can best use these frequencies.
2. The broadcast spectrum is a valuable public resource. Users must be regulated to ensure that society gets the greatest benefit possible from radio and television.
3. Broadcasting is a powerful medium. Radio and television must be regulated so that they will not be used in a manner which could harm the public or be used solely for the profit of the users.

The trusteeship theory is being challenged today by persons who argue that a marketplace approach can better serve the people by creating a broadcast system more responsive to public needs. Four reasons have been cited for abandoning the trusteeship approach:

1. The marketplace is a more efficient regulator of broadcasting than is the government.
2. There is no real scarcity; there is a great availability of diverse kinds of mass media.
3. The regulation of broadcasting flies in the face of the freedom of expression guarantees contained in the First Amendment.
4. Government regulation does not work well and has not produced a broadcast system sensitive to public needs.

Currently the Congress is considering important changes in broadcast regulation which, if adopted, would abolish many content rules such as the Fairness Doctrine and the equal time rule, as well as change many regulations which relate to licensing.

REGULATION THROUGH LICENSING

Federal Communications Commission

The broadcasting industry is regulated by the Federal Communications Commission, which accomplishes this primarily by the granting of licenses to broadcast and the renewing of those licenses.

The 1934 Federal Communications Act provided that a seven-member **Federal Communications Commission** regulate the broadcast industry. In 1982 Congress reduced the size of the commission to five members as an economy measure. Members of the FCC are appointed by the president, with the approval of the Senate, to serve a seven-year term. One member is selected by the president to be chairman. No more than a simple majority of the commission (three members) can be from the same political party.

Like all administrative agencies, the FCC is guided by broad congressional mandate—in this case the federal Communications Act. The agency has the power to make rules and regulations within the broad framework of the Communications Act, and these regulations carry the force of the law. With regard to some matters the 1934 law is very specific. For example, Section 315—the equal opportunity provision (or equal time rule)—details regulations concerning the use of the broadcast media by political candidates. But in other areas Congress was eloquently vague. The mandate that broadcasters operate their stations in "the public interest, convenience or necessity" can mean almost anything a person wants it to mean. Consequently, the FCC developed rules like the Fairness Doctrine and the ascertainment rules (we will talk about these rules in detail later) in its effort to implement the public interest requirement.

Procedures

The commission employs a large staff and is divided into various divisions. The Mass Media Bureau, for example, deals exclusively with broadcasting and cable television problems. Other divisions work with telephone and telegraph problems and with safety and special services. Administrative law judges, who are assigned to the FCC by the Civil Service Commission, are independent of control and direction by the agency. The administrative law judges are responsible for conducting inquiries for the agency and have powers which are normally incident to conducting trials and hearings. Their decisions on matters, such as controversy involving alleged violation of the Fairness Doctrine and license revocation, are final unless an exception is filed by any of the parties in a case. If there is an exception, the FCC commissioners themselves normally hear the dispute and render a decision. Here is an example of this procedure.

Imagine that the National Rifle Association accuses television station KLOP of violating the Fairness Doctrine in presentation of material on gun control. The Fairness Doctrine requires that when a broadcaster presents a discussion of a controversial public issue all sides of the issue be fairly presented. The National Rifle Association files a complaint with the FCC which the Mass Media Bureau then investigates. Assume that after its investigation the Mass Media Bureau concludes that the station did violate the Fairness Doctrine. It then files a complaint with KLOP. The administrative law judge then conducts the hearing in the dispute. The Mass Media Bureau argues that the Fairness Doctrine was violated, and the station argues that it was not. Imagine that the judge decides that the station did not act fairly and rules against KLOP. This decision is final unless the station files an exception within thirty days. If the judge rules that the station did not violate the doctrine, the Mass Media Bureau can file an exception. The issue of whether KLOP violated the Fairness Doctrine then goes before the five commissioners where oral argument is held and a decision is reached.

What happens if the FCC rules against KLOP? Is the matter finished? No. The station can ask a United States court of appeals (not the district court since the FCC has already conducted its fact finding) to review the decision.

An appellate court cannot substitute its own judgment for that of the Federal Communications Commission. The judges do not review the factual record to see whether they reach the same conclusion. FCC decisions, like the decisions of all administrative agencies, cannot be overruled except for quite specific reasons. The court can check to see whether the petitioner (the party who brings the appeal) has been afforded due process of law. It can investigate various other issues. Were there procedural irregularities? Did the FCC make an adequate finding of the facts? Did the commission state the reasons for its decision? Are the findings of the agency supported by the evidence in the record? Did the action by the FCC conform to its congressional mandate or did it go beyond the authority granted in the Communications Act?

While theoretically these are the only kinds of issues a court can examine, courts on occasion have gone beyond these limits to examine the factual questions. Some judges have been reluctant to refrain from examining the substantive issues involved and sometimes have even reached conclusions different from those reached by the FCC. The United States Supreme Court is available for the final appeal.

We have briefly reviewed how the FCC operates. Other aspects of FCC procedures are considered when licensing and programming controls are discussed in detail. Let us next take a quick look at FCC powers as invested by the Communications Act of 1934.

Powers

An important aspect of the 1934 law is the affirmation of the philosophy in the 1927 measure which established a privately owned broadcasting system operating over the public airwaves. This was a kind of compromise between establishing complete government control of broadcasting, as in most nations, and allowing the broadcasting industry to operate like most other industries, that is, with no government regulation.

The Congress approved the 1934 law under the authority of the commerce clause of the United States Constitution which gives the federal legislature the exclusive power to regulate interstate commerce. Under the 1927 act the question had arisen of whether this clause meant that the federal government lacked power to regulate broadcasters whose signals did not cross state lines, stations that were not engaged in interstate commerce. In 1933 in *FRC* v. *Nelson Brothers* the United States Supreme Court ruled that state lines did not divide radio waves and that national regulation of broadcasting was not only appropriate, but also essential to the efficient use of radio facilities. However, laws must be based on the Constitution, not just on efficiency. What legal logic did the Court use to back up its opinion? Simply this: While a radio station's signal may not cross state lines, it can interfere with the signal from a radio station which does cross state lines. Consequently, regulation of intrastate broadcasting is "ancillary" to the regulation of interstate broadcasting. In order to properly regulate the vast majority of broadcasting which falls within interstate commerce, the federal government must have the power to regulate all broadcasting. Later in this chapter we will see that this is the same rationale used to justify federal regulation of cable television.

While the Communications Act branded telephone and telegraph companies common carriers (because they are monopolies, they have to be common carriers; that is, they must accept business from anyone who wishes to use their services), broadcasting stations were not so designated. Because broadcasters are not common carriers, they may refuse to do business with anyone or any company. Broadcasters do not have to make their facilities available to all members of the public. In addition the commission lacks the power to set rates for the sale of broadcasting time. Broadcasting is founded on the basis of free competition among holders of broadcast licenses.

The Communications Act makes it clear that while broadcasters may freely compete they in no way assume ownership of a frequency or wavelength by virtue of using it for three years or for three hundred years. When a license is granted, the broadcaster must sign a form in which is waived any claim to the perpetual use of a particular frequency.

While the FCC has direct control over all broadcasting stations, there is nothing in the Communications Act which gives the agency authority to control the broadcast networks. The National Broadcasting Company (NBC), the broadcast network, does not really broadcast anything itself. The network transmits programs to its affiliate stations which in turn do the broadcasting. Technically, therefore, the FCC has no power over the networks because they do not "broadcast."

But the FCC has exerted its authority over the broadcast networks, and the courts have upheld this authority. The agency ruled, for example, that networks can no longer syndicate old television programs, but have to sell them to someone else for syndication. This was a direct regulation and was challenged in court. But the United States Court of Appeals for the District of Columbia upheld the right of the FCC to take such actions. In *Mt. Mansfield Television* v. *FCC* (1971) the court ruled that the fact that the Communications Act vested no explicit authority in the FCC to regulate the networks is not conclusive. The court said the rules passed by the agency, though they are direct regulation of the networks, are within the commission's statutory power if they are "reasonably ancillary to the effective performance of the Commission's various responsibilities for the regulation of television broadcasting."

The commission can also regulate networks in two other ways. Each network owns many radio and television stations. Rules levied against these stations indirectly affect the network. Also, rules can be adopted that limit how stations affiliated with networks can operate, and these rules indirectly affect the networks too. In 1975 the FCC ruled that network-affiliated television stations in the nation's top fifty markets normally could not broadcast more than three hours of network programming during the prime evening viewing hours, 7 P.M. to 11 P.M. By limiting what the local stations could broadcast, the FCC indirectly limited what the networks could transmit.

Technically the FCC lacks the power to censor broadcasters. Section 326 of the Communications Act states:

> Nothing in this act shall be understood or construed to give the commission the power of censorship over radio communications or signals transmitted by any radio station, or condition shall be promulgated or fixed by the commission which shall interfere with the right of free speech by means of radio communication.

No censorship, then. At least that is what Section 326 states. But that is not the way this section has been interpreted. The FCC has chosen to interpret Section 326 (with the approval of the courts) to mean that it may not censor specific programs, that is, forbid a broadcaster to carry programs on radical politicians or programs which picture members of a minority group in a derogatory fashion. However, at license renewal time the agency can consider the kind of programming the licensee broadcasts, and if the agency finds the programming objectionable, this fact can be held against the licensee. The U.S. Supreme Court adopted this understanding of Section 326 in its 1978 ruling in *FCC* v. *Pacifica Foundation* when the Court sustained the agency's censure of WBAI-FM for broadcasting George Carlin's monologue "Seven Dirty Words" (see pages 525–26). Most people would call this censorship. Section 326, then, has limited meaning and is of limited value to broadcasters.

The commission has broad-ranging powers in dealing with American broadcasters. Section 303 of the Communications Act outlines some of the basic responsibilities of the agency which include classification of stations, determination of the power and technical facilities licensees must use, and specification of hours during the day and night stations can broadcast. The FCC also regulates the location of stations, the area each station can serve, the assignment of frequency or wavelength, and even the designation of call letters. There are not many things that broadcasters can do without first seeking the approval or consent of the Federal Communications Commission.

The key powers held by the FCC, however, focus on licensing and renewal of licenses and the authority to regulate programming and program content. It is toward these powers that primary consideration is directed in the remainder of this chapter.

Licensing

Issuing and renewing broadcast licenses are perhaps the most important functions of the FCC. These functions are very important to broadcasters as well, for without a license there can be no broadcasting. Virtually everything the broadcaster does is tied in some way to having the license renewed. In addition to getting a license for a new station, the broadcaster must also seek FCC approval for most operational changes such as increasing power, changing the antenna height or location, selling the station, transferring ownership, and so forth. Broadcasting licenses are granted to radio stations for seven years; a license to operate a television station lasts only five years. Until late 1981 only three-year licenses were granted to radio and television stations.

The **licensing process** is very complex and loaded with small but important details. An applicant for a new broadcast license must complete an incredible amount of paperwork in order to be considered by the FCC. A person who is seeking a new broadcast license must first obtain a construction permit, permission to start building the station. Obtaining this permit is actually the biggest hurdle. If the permit is granted, if construction of the station conforms to technical requirements, and if the work is completed within the time specified in the permit, the license is routinely issued.

What kinds of qualifications must the prospective licensee meet? The applicant must be a United States citizen, must be capable of building and operating the station for one year without taking in any revenue, and must possess (or be able to hire people who possess) the technical competence to construct and operate a broadcasting station. The applicant must also be honest and open in dealing with the commission and must have generally good character. The applicant must meet the qualifications under the multiple-ownership rules which prohibit one individual from owning more than seven television stations, two of which must be ultrahigh frequency (UHF) stations, seven amplitude modulation (AM) radio stations, and seven frequency modulation (FM) radio stations. There are additional rules which limit ownership of multiple broadcasting properties and newspapers and broadcasting stations within a city or market area (these regulations are discussed in more detail in chapter 12). The applicant has to endeavor to ascertain the needs and interests of the people in the community to be served by the station and then prepare a programming scheme which will serve those needs and interests (ascertainment is discussed further on page 516). If the applicant shows the commission that he is in compliance with these requirements, and if there is no competing applicant or community protest against granting the permit, the permit to construct the station will be granted. The license then follows when construction is completed.

Competing Applicants

What happens when more than one person wants the same broadcast license? The government must decide who shall get it. The qualifications of both candidates are studied (a list of the kinds of criteria used by the FCC is given on page 518) and the most deserving gets the license. If the candidates are substantially equal, the license may be awarded through a lottery system that was established in 1982.

An applicant for a new license might also be challenged by someone who already holds a broadcast license in the same area and believes that the local market cannot absorb another broadcasting station. The existing license holder can argue in one of two ways to try to convince the FCC not to grant the new license:

1. The addition of another broadcast signal will damage the quality of the owner's existing broadcast signal.
2. The addition of a new station will cause economic harm to the owner of the existing station. There is not enough advertising revenue in the community to support an additional station without harming the existing station.

The FCC can accept the second argument only if the station operator can show that the reduced revenues will *adversely affect program service.* Demonstrating a potential loss in profits is not sufficient. The United States Court of Appeals for the District of Columbia noted in 1958 that "to license two stations where there is revenue for only one may result in no good service at all" (*Carroll Broadcasting Co.* v. *FCC,* 1958).

Renewal of Licenses

Broadcast licenses are granted for limited periods of time. Television stations are licensed for five years; radio stations are licensed for seven years. These broadcast licenses must be renewed by the FCC before the broadcaster can continue to operate. Most broadcasters consider the renewal process to be one of the most odious aspects of regulation. Public interest groups which seek to improve or change broadcasting, however, find renewal to be a valuable process during which they can challenge what they consider to be weak or harmful broadcasting practices.

To gain renewal of a license the broadcaster must provide the FCC with volumes of data about the broadcast operation. This points out an important fact about renewal: the FCC does not conduct an independent investigation of the licensee. Rather, the broadcaster (and sometimes other interested parties such as the aforementioned public interest groups) provides the commission with nearly all material relevant to the renewal. The data provided to the

FCC focus upon technical matters, business matters, and programming matters.

The FCC establishes what is called a composite week, taking a Monday from one month, a Tuesday from another month, perhaps a Wednesday from the following month, and so forth. The licensee must report what programs were broadcast on those days. Licensees must break down other program data into categories such as news and public affairs, religion, and so forth, and must also show that they have provided programs on local needs and interests, all of which will be discussed in some detail further on. If the FCC is not satisfied with what it sees, it can schedule a formal hearing on the renewal application. A formal hearing is prerequisite to both nonrenewal and revocation of a license before expiration.

Renewal of a broadcast license could involve a vigorous examination of a licensee's policies and practices. But this is not the case. The FCC simply has too few employees to conduct such a thorough examination of each licensee. And the agency's budget has recently become smaller, not larger. This lack of staff has resulted in a renewal process which is largely a ritual. If all the paperwork is completely and properly filled out, renewal is normally automatic.

If a problem does arise during renewal, it often takes years for the FCC to resolve the matter. In 1975, for example, the FCC voted to strip the licenses from all the public television stations in Alabama because they had discriminated against blacks in the 1960s. By 1975, when the FCC took its action, these public broadcasting stations had solved the problems of the 1960s, served the minority community with high-quality programming, and were considered a model broadcasting operation with regard to the employment of minority persons. In 1976 the FCC voted to deny renewal to station WHBI in Newark, New Jersey, for failing to adequately supervise its programming. The action had started seven years earlier in 1969 when the station sought renewal of its license (*Cosmopolitan Broadcasting Corp.,* 59 FCC 2d, 558, 1976).

The commission may refuse to renew a broadcast license if the licensee has violated any important provision of the Federal Communications Act or FCC rules. Stations which broadcast fraudulent advertising have been denied the renewal of their licenses (*May Seed and Nursery Co.,* 1936). The renewal of a license for a station which was used solely to promote the causes of its owner was denied (*Young People's Association for the Propagation of the Gospel,* 1938). If a station does not adequately supervise the programming it carries, its license may not be renewed (*Cosmopolitan Broadcasting Corp.,* 1976). Federal courts have ruled that denial of a license renewal does not violate the First Amendment. Acknowledging that a First Amendment issue might arise when a licensee is stripped of the power to broadcast, the United

States Court of Appeals for the District of Columbia nevertheless ruled more than a half-century ago (*Trinity Methodist Church, South* v. *FRC,* 1932):

> This does not mean that the government, through agencies established by Congress, may not refuse a renewal of license to one who has abused it to broadcast defamatory or untrue matter. In that case there is not a denial of freedom of speech, but merely the application of the regulatory power of Congress in a field within the scope of its legislative authority.

The previous year another United States court of appeals judge had ruled that the commission had a perfect right to look to past programming practices of a renewal applicant to determine whether the license should be renewed. Invoking the Biblical injunction "by their fruits ye shall know them," the court affirmed that past programming is a central issue in consideration of service in the public interest (*KFKB Broadcasting Association* v. *FRC,* 1931).

When a license renewal is denied, the broadcaster can appeal the FCC ruling to a United States court of appeals, and sometimes the court will reverse the decision by the agency. In one of the most widely publicized license renewal disputes of recent times the United States Court of Appeals for the District of Columbia partially overturned a commission ruling which stripped RKO General, one of the nation's largest broadcasting chains, of television licenses in New York, Boston, and Los Angeles. The FCC had ruled in 1980 that the broadcaster and its parent company, General Tire and Rubber Company, had engaged in "extensive and serious" misconduct and could no longer be trusted as broadcasters. The agency upheld several charges which had been first levied against RKO General in 1974. The commission ruled that the renewal of licenses for stations WOR-TV in New York and KHJ-TV in Los Angeles were conditioned on the outcome of a hearing that was held to determine whether the license for WNAC-TV in Boston should be renewed. At the conclusion of the hearings on WNAC-TV the FCC found misconduct in four areas and refused to renew any of the valuable licenses. RKO General appealed this decision. The Court of Appeals ruled that three of the four reasons given by the FCC for denial of the license renewal applications were invalid. The fourth reason—that RKO General had failed to be candid with the FCC during the Boston hearing about problems its parent company (General Tire) was having with the Securities and Exchange Commission—was sufficient to deny the renewal of the license for WNAC-TV, but not the television licenses for WOR and KHJ (*RKO* v. *FCC,* 1981). RKO-General remained unsatisfied and sought to win back its Boston license through an appeal to the United States Supreme Court. But the high Court declined to hear the case. The FCC action against RKO General both angered and frightened radio and television station owners and spurred the broadcast industry in its efforts to win deregulation.

Ascertainment   Persons who seek to gain a new television license or renew an old one must conduct what the FCC calls ascertainment proceedings. Until 1981 all radio stations had to undertake formal **ascertainment** as well, but the FCC lifted this burden from the shoulders of commercial radio broadcasters in 1981. Noncommercial radio stations, however, must continue to follow these policies. If the deregulation for commercial television proposed by the FCC in July 1983 becomes a reality, television stations will also be relieved of most of the burdens of ascertainment.

Ascertainment is a formal method by which broadcasters are expected to survey the needs and problems in their community. There are three parts to ascertainment, as outlined in the 1973 *FCC Primer on Ascertainment of Community Problems by Broadcast Applicants* which was qualified and expanded by additional guidelines in 1975.

A broadcaster must first determine the demographic profile of the community: the number of men, women, and children and the social, racial, ethnic, educational, and economic characteristics of the persons in the broadcast area. This determination can be done using census data. Next the broadcaster must interview community leaders in labor, business, agriculture, religious, education, government, and other areas. Minority persons must also be included in such interviews. The station owner or management-level personnel must conduct at least half of the interviews. Finally, the broadcaster must conduct a survey of the general public. Usually a random sample of persons is drawn and interviewed by a professional polling agency.

The entire ascertainment process must be undertaken six months before the application for license renewal is filed with the commission. However, it is FCC policy that at least some community leaders should be contacted annually.

Ascertainment is not designed to elicit program suggestions from the people. Rather, it is to discover community problems which broadcasters must attempt to explore in their programming. Not all problems must be treated in programming. The broadcaster is expected to make a good-faith effort to determine which problems merit treatment, and then "propose what programs it will broadcast to deal with those problems, giving a description of the program or program series, its anticipated time segment, duration and frequency of broadcast." Programming can take the form of public service announcements, editorials, segments of newscasts, or special programs. The FCC has also recognized that not all media must treat all problems to the same extent. A small television station, for example, is not expected to respond to the same extent as a larger television station in dealing with problems uncovered during the ascertainment process.

Despite the fact that the FCC has lifted the formal ascertainment procedures from commercial radio broadcasters, the agency still insists that radio station management be responsive to the needs of the community. The radio broadcasters are free to use any means possible to elicit these needs.

Renewal Challenges   Ninety-nine percent of the time the license renewal process remains a matter between the broadcaster and the FCC. In some instances, however, other persons enter the process in an effort to block the renewal of the license. In some instances members of the public attempt to convince the FCC to deny renewal; other times persons who seek the same broadcast license hope to block renewal and win the license themselves.

Public challenges to license renewals are a recent phenomenon. It was less than twenty years ago that the United States Court of Appeals (D.C.) ruled that private citizens have the right to take part in the renewal process. A group of persons from Mississippi were blocked by the FCC in their attempt to stop the renewal of a television license for a station in Jackson, Mississippi, which citizens accused of racist policies. The FCC said the group lacked "standing" to take part in the hearing. "Standing" is a legal word which means a direct and substantial interest in the outcome of the hearing. Judge Warren Burger (who is now the nation's Chief Justice) wrote in *Office of Communication, United Church of Christ* v. *FCC* (1966) that the action of the FCC:

> . . . denies standing to spokesmen for the listeners, who are often most directly concerned with and intimately affected by the performance of the licensee. . . . The theory that the commission can always effectively represent the listener interests in a renewal proceeding without the aid and participation of legitimate listener representatives . . . is one of the assumptions we collectively try to work with so long as they are reasonable and adequate. When it becomes clear, as it does to us now, that it is no longer a valid assumption which stands up under the realities of actual experience, neither we nor the commission can continue to rely upon it.

Citizens' groups have taken advantage of this ruling to make a mark on the license renewal process. It is rare that a citizens' group will actually convince the commission to reject an application for renewal. But participation by citizens' groups in renewal processes can often force the commission to hold a hearing on a license renewal. This will force the broadcaster to devote considerably more time, energy, and money in getting the license renewed. Often the citizens' group uses the threat of a license challenge to force a broadcaster to make changes in station policy. For example, a citizens' group which believes a station needs more minority staffers, needs better children's programming, and needs to pay more attention to senior citizen concerns might petition the FCC to deny the station's renewal application. The group will then seek to negotiate solutions to these problems with station management. If the station can satisfy the critics, the citizens' group will withdraw its petition to deny the renewal of the license. While this process effectively involves more people in the renewal process, many persons consider such citizen pressure "blackmail" and question its legitimacy.

A broadcaster's application for license renewal might also be challenged by another broadcaster who seeks to have the license. Since only one person can broadcast on the same frequency in the same community at the same time, the FCC must choose which of these two individuals should have the right to use the broadcast license.

Under current law the FCC must hold what is called a **comparative license hearing** whenever there are two or more applicants for the same license. In the hearing the FCC attempts to determine which of the two license applicants will best serve the public interest. In 1965 the FCC outlined a list of seven items it said it would consider in looking at the applications from competing applicants.

1. Diversification of control of the media: Persons holding existing media (like a newspaper or a second broadcasting station) in the area or having significant media holdings elsewhere will not be considered as favorably as those without or with fewer media holdings.

2. Full-time participation in station operation by the owners: The FCC will favor working owners over absentee owners.

3. Proposed program service: What does the applicant propose to do with the frequency? Supposedly, applicants who plan to devote more time to programs on public affairs and education and information will be favored over those who plan to program heavily with entertainment.

4. The past broadcast record of the current license holder as well as the record of other broadcasters who seek the license: If the past record is average, it is disregarded. If it is exceptional with unusual attention to public needs and interests, or if it is especially poor with regard to serving the public interest, the past record then becomes a factor.

5. Efficient use of the frequency: This is a technical question and has to do with judicious use of the spectrum.

6. Character of applicant: Does the applicant have a record free of criminal prosecution? Is he considered honest and trustworthy? and so forth.

7. Other factors: The report did not outline these additional factors.

Theoretically, based on these criteria, the best applicant in a comparative broadcast license hearing will be given the license. But theory does not always rule in such hearings, and the actions of the FCC with regard to competing applicants often have been erratic during the past two decades. It sounds quite simple to say that the FCC should score each applicant on seven criteria and announce a winner. But is it fair to compare the real programming records of an existing broadcaster with the promises of a challenger? Is it not possible that an individual who holds several broadcast properties might be better qualified—by virtue of this experience—to operate another station than someone without other broadcast holdings? Why should applicants' activities outside the broadcast industry be used against them in a comparative hearing? All of these questions and many more we could list raise difficult issues. And taking away a broadcast license is not a simple matter. The license holder has millions of dollars tied up in property and equipment that would be unusable without the license. Rulings by the FCC in comparative hearings reflect the problems inherent in these proceedings. And time and again the federal courts have overturned FCC decisions, adding to the confusion in this area. A recent ruling regarding a Florida broadcasting station is a good case in point.

Cowles Communication, Inc., held the license for a Daytona Beach television station, WESH-TV. In 1969 Cowles was challenged when it sought renewal of that license by a group entitled Central Florida Enterprises, Inc. Despite findings that the Cowles company had violated an FCC rule by moving a production studio without first getting permission, that some principals in the Cowles organization had pleaded no contest to charges of mail fraud for a *Look* magazine subscription scheme, and that Central Florida was rated more highly on the diversification and integration of ownership and management criteria, the FCC returned the license to Cowles after the comparative hearings. The commission concluded that Cowles had provided substantial service in the past which should provide the owners with a "renewal expectancy." In 1978, nine years after the renewal application was filed, the United States Court of Appeals (D.C.) called the decision unreasonable and overturned it. The court said it was simply unfair to place so much weight upon past performance when the challenger was superior on other criteria (*Central Florida Enterprises, Inc.* v. *FCC*, 1978). "The fly in the analysis is that the Commission judges incumbents largely on the basis of their broadcast records," wrote Judge Wilkey, "to which there will be nothing comparable on the side of the challenger in any case." Four months later in an unusual statement, Judge Wilkey tried to clarify his earlier ruling in denying the FCC's petition to rehear the case:

> Our principal reason [for setting aside the renewal]. . . . was that the Commission's manner of balancing its findings was wholly unintelligible, based as it was said, on "administrative feel." Admittedly, licensing in the public interest entails a good many discretionary choices, but even if some of them rest inescapably on agency intuition . . . , we may at least insist that they do not contradict whatever rules for choosing do exist.

To the assertion by the FCC that the decision by the court had created great apprehension among licensees, the Court replied, "The only legitimate fear which should move licensees is the fear of their own substandard performance, and that would be all to the public good."

The uncertainty created by both FCC decisions and court rulings has prompted broadcast lobbyists to seek a change in the law. In 1970 the FCC announced that it would give preference to license holders over challengers when there were competing applicants for the same license, and if license holders could demonstrate that there were no serious deficiencies in their record and that they had been substantially attuned to the needs and interests of the community, licenses would be renewed without a hearing. But this policy was overturned a year later by the United States Court of Appeals (D.C.) which declared that the FCC could not change the federal Communications Act, which called for comparative hearings when there was more than one applicant for a license (*Citizens Communication Center* v. *FCC,* 1971).

Today the FCC is seeking to have Congress change the law. The commission has proposed a two-tiered plan for renewal. Under the proposal a broadcast license would be renewed automatically if the licensee's past performance is void of any serious deficiencies. If the renewal applicant's record does contain serious deficiencies, the FCC will declare the channel vacant and entertain new applicants for the license. A lottery system might be used to award the license in this case.

If such a rule is adopted, it will reduce the uncertainty among broadcasters concerning renewal. But critics say it will also lower the quality of broadcasting by permitting licensees who meet only minimum standards to hold their broadcast licenses.

Summary

The five-member Federal Communications Commission has been established by law to regulate the broadcasting industry. The agency has the responsibility to supervise all over-the-air broadcasting as well as any other electronic communication which has an impact upon over-the-air communications. While the FCC is forbidden by law from censoring the content of broadcast programming, the agency nevertheless has considerable control over what is broadcast by radio and television. By licensing and relicensing broadcasting stations, the FCC can ensure that broadcasters meet certain standards, including programming standards.

Television stations are licensed for five years; radio stations are licensed for seven years. To gain a license to broadcast an applicant must meet several important criteria which have been established by the Congress and by the FCC. When two or more persons seek the same license, the FCC must decide which applicant would best serve the public interest. When candidates appear equally qualified, a lottery may be used to award the franchise.

Renewal of broadcast licenses is one of the most time-consuming tasks undertaken by the FCC. Because there are so many licenses to renew each year and because the FCC is not a large agency, renewal of broadcast licenses does not involve an intensive examination of station practices; in fact, it is largely a ritual. Adverse FCC decisions regarding renewal can be appealed to the United States Court of Appeals (D.C.).

Ascertaining the needs of the community is a requirement before an applicant can either get a new broadcast license or have an old license renewed. The FCC has established formal procedures which must be followed by the licensees who own or operate television stations and noncommercial radio stations. Commercial radio station owners can use any means they deem fit to elicit community needs.

When a licensee seeks to renew a broadcast license, other interested persons may challenge the license holder. Often citizen watchdog groups ask the FCC to deny the renewal of a license in order to force the broadcaster to change what group members believe to be onerous policies. Other persons who seek to use the broadcast license may also challenge the license holder at renewal time. Under current law the FCC must hold what is called a comparative hearing when such a challenge is made. Congress, however, is considering changing the law to protect license holders. Under a proposed new law a hearing would only be needed if the record of the current license holder contains serious deficiencies.

REGULATION OF PROGRAM CONTENT

The regulation of program content is not directly tied to license renewal, but the failure of a broadcaster to observe FCC rules regarding programming can certainly be considered at renewal time. Despite the rule against censorship in the Communications Act (see page 511), the commission has extensive control over a wide range of programming matters. Content controls range from specific federal statutes (the laws which prohibit the broadcast of obscenity) to rather vague commission guidelines (such as the policy statement regarding broadcasters' responsibility for phonograph records played over the air). Many programming rules are contained in the Federal Communications Act; others have been generated by the FCC under the agency mandate to regulate broadcasting in the public interest, convenience, and necessity.

The FCC has a wide range of sanctions with which to enforce these rules. These include in order of magnitude the following:

1. A letter of reprimand that is put in a licensee's file and may be material at renewal time
2. Cease and desist order which is rarely issued, but can be used to stop a broadcaster from doing something the commission does not believe should be done
3. Forfeiture or fine which can range up to $20,000 for a serious violation (the FCC has asked the Congress to give it the authority to raise the limits on forfeitures to $100,000 for serious violations)
4. Short-term renewal from six months to two years while the FCC studies the broadcaster's record to determine whether the license should be renewed at all
5. Nonrenewal or revocation of the license, the nuclear bomb of broadcast regulation (rarely used as a sanction)

Sometimes the commission will simply write a letter to a broadcaster inquiring about a programming practice. This letter alerts station management that the FCC is aware of the practice or even concerned about the practice. Often the letter of inquiry results in the station changing the programming practice. Some people call this "regulation by raised eyebrow."

Broadcasters have many programming responsibilities which are supervised by the FCC. In the broadest sense the radio or television station owner must carry programming which serves the needs of the community as they have been determined through ascertainment or other means. There was a time when the FCC required each and every broadcaster to carry a wide variety of programming: religious, educational, agricultural, news, sports, weather, and many other kinds. At renewal time a checklist was prepared to be certain the broadcaster fulfilled the station's responsibilities in all these areas. This is not done any longer, but a broadcaster is still expected to meet these kinds of needs if they exist in the community.

In a narrower sense, there are many simple little program rules which have been promulgated by both the Congress and the commission. Stations, for example, are required to identify themselves periodically. Broadcasters must announce when the station or program receives a gratuity in return for an advertising plug on the air. A station may not knowingly broadcast fraudulent advertisements. It is illegal for a station to broadcast a lottery (a lottery is a contest in which a person trades something of value for the chance to win a prize). The license for station WWBZ in Vineland, New Jersey, was not renewed in 1955 at least partially because it had broadcast information on lotteries—in this case horse races. Giving the race results from the local track as a part of the evening news is one thing, but broadcasting up-to-the-minute race results from racetracks around the country is something else altogether. At least the FCC thought so and ruled that such information is useful primarily to persons involved in illegal gambling (in re *Community Broadcasting Service, Inc.,* WWBZ, 1955). The broadcast or telecast of information about state lotteries, including live coverage of prize drawings, is considered news coverage as well.

At one time the FCC tried to ban two nationally broadcast game shows which were constructed around participation by viewers and listeners at home. A band played a melody and the emcee called randomly selected listeners. If the listeners could "name that tune" or tell the band to "stop the music," they won a prize. The commission said that the games were lotteries and were illegal for broadcast purposes. The Supreme Court disagreed, ruling that while the FCC may indeed regulate the broadcast of lotteries, these games were not lotteries (*FCC* v. *American Broadcasting Co.* et. al., 1954). To qualify as a lottery a contest must have three elements. First, there must be a prize for the winner. Second, the prize must be awarded to a person chosen wholly or partly by chance. Finally, winners must be required to furnish something of value—called consideration—in order to participate in the game. When participants must buy a product before they are allowed to play the game, have to ante up money, or have to send in a box top, they are furnishing consideration. The third element was missing from the musical game shows and is missing from nearly all televised game shows today. (Tickets to shows to get a chance to play the games are always free.)

Can the FCC control a broadcast station's format as part of its regulation of programming content? For many years the FCC resisted efforts by citizens' groups to force the agency to get involved when a radio station dropped one kind of music format, classical, for example, and adopted another format, let us say rock. But listeners went to federal court, and the FCC was ordered in 1970 to *review* a format change by a station when the abandonment of a unique format produced community protests (*Citizens Committee to Preserve the Voice of the Arts in Atlanta* v. *FCC,* 1970). The United States Court of Appeals in Washington, D.C., went one step further in 1974 and ordered the FCC to *hold a hearing* whenever a unique format was being abandoned by a radio station and persons in the community objected (*Citizens' Committee to Save WEFM* v. *FCC,* 1974). A unique format would be one which no other station in the market used. The loss of this format would deny the citizens in the community access to a particular kind of music or programming. Normally it has been supporters of classical music who have protested when a local station drops the classical format. But in Seattle in 1981 New Wave rock fans mounted a protest when the community's only (at that time) New Wave station abandoned that format. Despite the earlier court rulings, the FCC continued to argue through the late seventies that the marketplace should determine the broadcaster's format; the government should not get involved. And in 1981 the Supreme Court of the United States supported the agency and overturned a lower federal court decision calling for a hearing on a format change. Justice Byron White, writing for the seven-person majority, stated, "We decline to overturn the commission's Policy Statement which prefers reliance on market forces to its own attempt to oversee format changes at the behest of disaffected listeners." Justice White warned the agency, however, to be alert to the consequences of its policies and stand ready to change its rules if necessary to serve the public interest more fully (*FCC* v. *WNCN Listeners Guild,* 1981).

Station breaks, lotteries, and format changes are all important content regulations. But it is in three other areas that the FCC exercises what many believe to be its heaviest hand in content regulation. Let us look at each of these areas—obscene material, political broadcasting, and public affairs broadcasting—separately and in some depth.

Obscene or Indecent Material

Broadcasters have a special set of problems concerning pornography. Section 1464, Title 18, of the *United States Code* gives the Federal Communications Commission the power to revoke any broadcast license if the licensee transmits obscene or indecent material over the airwaves. No station, however, has ever had its license revoked for broadcasting obscenity. Nor has the FCC denied renewal of a license solely on the grounds that the licensee broadcast pornographic or indecent material. The commission is quite hesitant to use its big guns in this area because of the immense constitutional questions involved. It is clearly a free-speech issue. Yet stations have been put on short-term renewal and have been fined, as will be noted momentarily.

Normally, when the FCC receives a complaint from a listener or viewer about a broadcast believed to contain obscene language or pictures, the agency responds with a form letter which includes the following statement:

> The broadcast of obscene, indecent or profane language is prohibited by a federal criminal statute. Although the Department of Justice is responsible for prosecution of federal law violations, the commission is authorized to impose sanctions on broadcast licensees for violation of this statute, including revocation of the license or the imposition of a monetary forfeiture. However, both the commission and the Department of Justice are governed by past decisions of the courts as to what constitutes obscenity, and the broadcast of material which may be offensive to many persons would not necessarily be held by the courts to violate the statute.

Although the FCC approaches the problem of obscenity cautiously, the mere fact that it sends out even a form letter has an impact upon conservative broadcasters.

In 1975, the National Association of Broadcasters (NAB), following suggestions made by CBS president Arthur Taylor and at least condoned by the other networks, instituted what it called "the family hour." Stations which subscribe to the NAB Code of Good Practices were told that the hours from seven to nine each evening were to be set aside for family viewing, and that programs with sexual overtones and excessive violence were taboo in this period. The censorship undertaken by the networks was heavy-handed. The word *virgin* was cut from one program (*innocent* was substituted). Censors began to look anew at Cher's navel and a braless guest on the "Phyllis" show was redressed before filming began. Programs which had been broadcast in the 8 P.M. time slot for several years were either moved or toned down to meet the new family-hour standards. But the rule was challenged by the creators of television programs. Writers and directors in Hollywood, where most television programs are produced, went to court, and in 1976 federal Judge Warren J. Ferguson of the District Court for Southern California ruled that the "adoption of the Family Viewing Policy by each of the three networks constituted a violation of the First Amendment." The judge ruled that the policy had been motivated by informal statements from the Federal Communications Commission which threatened government action against the industry should not the family hour or something like it be adopted (*Writers Guild* v. *FCC*, 1976). The judge's conclusion is more than substantiated in Geoffrey Cowan's fascinating book *See No Evil*, the story of the genesis of the family hour.

A United States court of appeals later overturned the lower court ruling on the grounds that the federal district court had no jurisdiction in the case, that the Federal Communications Commission should have heard the issue (*Writers Guild*, v. *ABC*, 1979). The networks, however, made no effort to reestablish the policy.

Law professor Harry Kalven wrote more than ten years ago in the *Michigan Law Review* that while a regulation may not directly interfere with free speech "in operation it may trigger a set of behavioral consequences which amount in effect to people censoring themselves in order to avoid trouble with the law." Or what people believe will be trouble with the law. Such is the case with the regulation of obscenity in broadcasting. The family hour is a good example of this tendency.

In the past twenty years the FCC has considered several instances in which charges were made that obscene or indecent material was broadcast. In 1962 the commission refused to renew the license of radio station WDKD at least partially because a disc jockey at the station habitually told "off-color" or "indecent" jokes on the air (in re *Palmetto Broadcasting Co.*, 1962). A college radio station was fined $100 for broadcasting "indecent" four-letter words over the air in 1970 (in re *WUHY-FM, Eastern Educational Radio*, 1970). A $2,000 fine was levied against an Illinois radio station in 1973 for broadcasting a discussion between an announcer and a listener about oral sexual practices (*Sonderling Broadcasting Corp.*, 1973). The discussion stemmed from the station's call-in "topless radio" format. A federal court of appeals upheld the judgment two years later (*Illinois Citizens Committee for Broadcasting* v. *FCC*, 1975).

Undoubtedly the most significant decision on broadcast indecency came in 1978 when the Supreme Court upheld an FCC ruling that station WBAI in New York City had violated the federal law when it presented a recorded monologue on the English language by George Carlin. The recording, which was played in midafternoon after the announcer warned listeners that it might be offensive to some, contained seven four-letter words which were used many times. The record was played as part of a program on society's attitude toward language. The FCC got one complaint, and as a result took action against the station on the grounds that it had broadcast indecent language. The agency defined indecent language as "language that describes in terms patently offensive as measured by contemporary community standards for the broadcast medium, sexual or excretory activities and organs, at times of the day when there is a reasonable risk children may be in the audience." The FCC said the WBAI broadcast met this definition.

Pacifica Foundation, which owns and operates the station, challenged the ruling, and in March 1977 the United States Court of Appeals (D.C.) overturned the FCC action, ruling that the commission's order was overbroad and vague. Two years later, however, the Supreme Court reversed the court of appeals and sustained the FCC ruling. Justice John Paul Stevens wrote the opinion for the Court, noting that because of its unique characteristics broadcasting had traditionally received the least First Amendment protection of all media. Stevens said broadcast was uniquely pervasive, that it can have an impact upon persons not only in public, but also in the privacy of their own home. Prior warning cannot completely protect the listener or viewer, he added. Also, "The ease with which children may obtain access to broadcast material . . . amply justifies special treatment of indecent broadcasting," Stevens wrote. The majority denied that the order was vague or overbroad. Stevens said that the ruling would deter only the broadcast of offensive references to excretory and sexual organs and activities. "While some of these references may be protected, they surely lie at the periphery of First Amendment concern," he said. The associate justice added that the Court's ruling did not involve Elizabethan comedy or even citizens band transmission. "We have not decided that an occasional expletive in either setting would justify any sanction . . .," Stevens noted, adding that the FCC decision rested on a nuisance rationale—"putting the right thing in a wrong place." Stevens added, "Like a pig in a parlor" (*FCC* v. *Pacifica Foundation*, 1978).

Many observers were sharply critical of the Court ruling, noting that if broadcast standards were to be determined by what was fit for children to listen to, the court was then turning its back on its 1957 ruling in *Butler* v. *Michigan.* In that case the Supreme Court invalidated a Michigan statute that forbade the sale of erotic material to anyone if the material would be offensive to children (see page 380). Critics also argued that the high Court left too many loose ends in its ruling. Children can be present in the radio audience at any time of day or night. Does this mean such material can never be broadcast? Or can it be broadcast late at night when children are not expected to be listening? Who is a child? Many feared that given the timidity of the broadcast industry the ruling would have a serious, chilling effect on radio stations, causing them to overreact and censor too much material. Only time will determine whether this prediction has merit.

In practical terms there is little government censorship of broadcast obscenity. The broadcasters censor themselves too well for obscenity to be much of a problem. The cases that do pop up tend to be from stations which are not in the mainstream of broadcasting—little educational stations, offbeat FM stations, and the like. The managers of these kinds of stations tend to believe the First Amendment means what it says and are not afraid to rock the boat. The vast majority of station owners and managers, however, are reluctant to even get into the boat. To see how shock waves can reverberate through the industry let us look briefly at the controversy over drugs and song lyrics.

In the early 1970s as the United States tried to put its finger on the reason why so many young people were turning to drugs to find salvation and happiness, someone, somewhere, suggested that popular music was probably a factor. The reasoning was that all those musicians and singers used dope and talked about dope and drugs in all their songs. There were undoubtedly Pied Pipers leading little Billy and Sally astray. Peter G. Hammond, the executive director of the National Coordinating Council on Drug Abuse and Education, as well as numerous other experts on drug use and drug abuse, testified that he found no evidence whatsoever of a cause-and-effect relationship between song lyrics and drug abuse. Nevertheless in March 1971 the FCC issued Public Notice 71–205 regarding *Licensee Responsibilities to Review Records Before Their Broadcast*. On its face it was a harmless enough document: it merely reminded licensees that they were responsible for material broadcast over their station—including songs whose lyrics promoted the use of drugs. When it hit the rock stations, the notice literally caused an explosion. Most broadcasters saw it as an effort by the FCC to exclude certain kinds of songs from air play, but they complied with what they believed to be the wishes of the commission. One station owner confiscated the entire record library and then eliminated all Bob Dylan songs because he could not understand the lyrics.

The disc jockeys were told not to play any songs which mentioned drugs and were threatened that if they violated this rule the station would change from a rock station to an easy-listening format. Do Not Play Lists, common at all radio stations even before the public notice, suddenly expanded from listing a few records to listing often hundreds. Some of the records put off limits included "With a Little Help from My Friends" by the Beatles, "White Rabbit" by the Jefferson Airplane, the Beatles' "I Am the Walrus" and "Lucy in the Sky with Diamonds," "One Toke Over the Line" by Brewer and Shipley, and "Mr. Tambourine Man" by Bob Dylan and the Byrds. Even "Puff the Magic Dragon" by Peter, Paul, and Mary was banned at many stations. Some station owners read the notice to mean that all drug-related songs, not just songs which glorified or suggested the use of drugs, were banned. Songs like "The Pusher" and "Snowblind Friend" by Steppenwolf, both of which had strong antidrug lyrics, were also banned by many stations.

Because of the vast number of songs issued each week, and because the lyrics of many rock songs are unintelligible or subject to various interpretations, many songs were banned from the airwaves because there was not time to give them a careful screening or because the screeners found it impossible to understand either the words or the meaning of the lyrics. Some songs were banned at one station, but not at another station in the same community. Record companies began to distribute copies of the lyrics with the records and sometimes tossed in an explanation of what the words meant if it was needed. One record company fired most of its artists—those who would admit they used drugs or those who were suspected of using drugs—and promoted its new "clean" image to radio stations and record buyers. All these events took place within the span of about one month.

Five weeks after the initial notice, the situation was so bad that the FCC had to publish an explanation of its original notice. In the explanation the agency said that it was not suggesting that radio stations ban certain records, but were merely pointing out that licensees' responsibility for the material broadcast over their facilities extends to phonograph records. The agency added that broadcasters must make the judgment. At renewal time, the explanation continued, the commission will look at the broadcaster's overall programming record, not at whether this song or that song was broadcast. Serving the public interest is the key, the memorandum noted. The constitutionality of the notice was upheld by the United States Court of Appeals for the District of Columbia (*Yale Broadcasting Co.* v. *FCC,* 1973).

The explanation lowered the blood pressure in the industry by thirty or forty points, and since then things have cooled off. But this incident remains an interesting case study of the sensitivity of the broadcast industry to any little twitch by the regulatory agency.

It should be noted parenthetically that while the spirit of deregulation has descended full-blown upon the FCC and the Congress, no one in a position of authority has suggested that regulations concerning the broadcast of obscene or indecent material be abandoned. Just the opposite is true. The success of the pay cable channels which broadcast adult movies has prompted many persons to attempt to close the loopholes in the law which permit these cable operators to transmit (not broadcast) R-rated films which often include nudity. Utah, for example, adopted a criminal statute in 1981 to punish any person who distributed by wire or cable any pornographic or indecent material to subscribers. The United States District Court ruled that such a statute could only prohibit the distribution of hard-core pornography as defined in *Miller* v. *California* (see pages 384–85). The Utah statute was too broad because it defined indecent material to include nudity, which has not been ruled to be legally obscene by the Supreme Court. The state argued it sought to protect children from such adult fare. The court urged the legislators to read the rulings in *Butler* v. *Michigan* (see page 380) and *Erznoznik* v. *City of Jacksonville* (page 396) where the Supreme Court said that a state could not regulate materials for adults on the basis of what is fit for children. The judge added (*Home Box Office* v. *Wilkinson,* 1982):

> That's one of the nice things about TV—not just cable TV, but also regular broadcast channels that are allocated, licensed and regulated by the government. There is no law that says you have to watch. There is no law that says you have to purchase a television set. There is no law that says you have to subscribe to a cable TV service any more than you have to subscribe to the *Salt Lake Tribune.*

Legislation was also introduced in Congress in early 1982 (Senate bill 2136) which would ban obscene, indecent, or profane language or materials from cable television. It did not pass during the 1982 session. Should the cable operator, who technically does not use the airwaves, be treated differently than the over-the-air broadcaster with respect to the transmission of obscene or indecent material? It seems likely the Supreme Court of the United States will soon be asked to resolve this question.

Summary

The FCC has broad control over the content of broadcast programming. To enforce this control the agency has a wide variety of sanctions which include letters of reprimand, fine or forfeiture, and nonrenewal or revocation of broadcast licenses. Content regulations involve a wide range of broadcast programming. In the broadest sense the broadcaster must program to meet the needs of the community as determined through the previously discussed ascertainment procedures. But programming rules also involve simple regulations such as the requirement to present station identification at various times of the broadcast day. Broadcasters are also prevented from broadcasting or promoting contests which are legal lotteries.

The FCC has chosen not to attempt to control the selection of format by a broadcaster. Citizens' groups have urged the FCC to hold hearings when a radio station drops one program format and adopts a new one. In the early seventies federal courts supported these citizen protests, but in 1981 the United States Supreme Court ruled that the government need not get involved when a broadcaster decides to switch from one format to another.

Federal law prohibits the broadcast of any obscene or indecent material. In 1979 the Supreme Court ruled that a radio or television station can be punished for broadcasting material which is not legally obscene, but is merely indecent. The court based its ruling on the fact that children might be present during the broadcast.

Several states have attempted to adopt laws which limit the transmission of adult R-rated films over pay cable television. Federal courts have struck down these laws on the basis that only hard-core pornography can be legally barred from such nonbroadcast television transmission.

REGULATION OF POLITICAL BROADCASTS

The guarantees of freedom of speech and freedom of the press were added to the Constitution in large measure to protect the political debate in this nation from interference by the government. Yet the Federal Communications Commission substantially regulates political broadcasting in this nation. How can we permit the government to have any control whatsoever over a kind of expression which is so important to the democratic system? Supporters of the federal regulation of political broadcasting argue that it is because political speech is so important that the government must ensure that broadcasters serve the public interest and not their own political interests in this area. Opponents of the political broadcast rules refer to this argument as Orwellian logic worthy of Big Brother in the frightening novel *1984*. Let us examine what controls the FCC exercises over political broadcasting.

Candidate Access Rule

Broadcasters cannot completely block candidates for federal office from buying airtime on the station to promote their candidacies because of the existence of the **candidate access rule.** Section 312 (a) (7) of the Federal Communications Act, adopted in 1971 by the Congress, states that a broadcast license can be revoked for willful and repeated failure "to allow reasonable access to or to permit the purchase of reasonable amounts of time for the use of a broadcasting station by a legally qualified candidate for federal elective office on behalf of his candidacy." This statute only applies to candidates for federal office: presidents and vice-presidents and United States senators and representatives. The FCC has asked the Congress to repeal this law in its effort to deregulate broadcasting.

Federal courts have provided two important interpretations of this statute. Both cases stemmed from the 1980 presidential election campaign. The Carter-Mondale Presidential Committee sought to buy thirty minutes of time on all three networks in early December 1979 for President Jimmy Carter to announce that he would be a candidate for reelection, and to present a film outlining Carter's record as president. The request was made in October 1979. NBC refused. ABC said it could not reach a decision on the question. CBS offered two, five-minute segments, one at 10:55 P.M. and one during the day. Privately, all three networks were fearful of breaking into their prime time entertainment schedules for a political broadcast. But publicly the broadcasters argued that the political campaign had not yet started; it was too early (the election was scheduled for November 1980) to begin to carry political programming.

The FCC ruled against the networks, the United States Court of Appeals (D.C.) ruled against the networks, and the Supreme Court of the United States ruled against the networks. The high Court ruled in its six-to-three decision that a broadcaster could not institute an across-the-board policy rejecting all requests from federal candidates for airtime. Chief Justice Burger wrote that once a political campaign begins a broadcaster must give reasonable and good faith attention to access requests from legally qualified candidates (*CBS* v. *FCC,* 1981):

> Such requests must be considered on an individualized basis, and broadcasters are required to tailor their responses to accommodate, as much as reasonably possible, a candidate's stated purpose in seeking airtime. In responding to access requests, however, broadcasters may also give weight to such factors as the amount

of time previously sold to the candidate, the disruptive impact on regular programming, and the likelihood of requests for time by rival candidates under the equal opportunities provision of Section 315 (a). These considerations may not be invoked as pretexts for denying access; to justify a negative response, broadcasters must cite a realistic danger of substantial program disruption—perhaps caused by insufficient notice to allow adjustments in the schedule—or of an excessive number of equal time requests.

Burger added that broadcasters must explain their reasons for refusing airtime or making limited counteroffers so the FCC can review these decisions if needed. Each of the networks had argued, however, that the 1980 presidential campaign had not really started. After all, the time period sought by Carter was eleven months prior to the election. In this case the networks should not be bound by Section 312, they asserted. The majority of the Supreme Court rejected this argument, noting the following evidence that the campaign had started:

1. Ten Republican candidates and two Democratic candidates had announced they were running for president.
2. The selection of delegates to the national political conventions had started in many states.
3. Many candidates were making speeches in an effort to raise money.
4. The Iowa caucuses to select convention delegates were scheduled for January, one month after the broadcast time sought by Carter.
5. Newspapers had been covering the national political campaign for at least two months.

Burger rejected the notion that Section 312 created a right of access to the media. None is created by this decision, he added. But a licensed broadcaster is "granted the free and exclusive use of a limited and valuable part of the public domain; when he accepts that franchise it is burdened by enforceable public obligations" (*CBS* v. *FCC,* 1981).

The Supreme Court's ruling means that a broadcaster cannot adopt an across-the-board policy of rejecting all requests for airtime. Each request must be considered individually, and can be rejected only if the broadcaster can demonstrate a good cause.

Section 312 implies that the candidate can seek to buy time on a station or ask for free time. Does this mean a broadcast station must *give* a candidate for federal office free time if fulfilling such a request would not interfere substantially with the broadcast schedule or would not prompt requests for equal time from other candidates? The United States Court of Appeals for the District of Columbia answered no when that question was asked. On March 14, 1980, then President Carter delivered a thirty-minute speech on the economic condition of the nation which was carried on all three networks. This was four days before the presidential primary in Illinois. Senator Ted Kennedy, who was also seeking the Democratic nomination for president, requested that the networks *give* him thirty minutes of airtime to respond to the president's speech. The networks said they would sell Kennedy the time, but would not give it to him. Kennedy argued that they were obliged to provide him thirty minutes at no cost because of Section 312. The United States Court of Appeals (D.C.) supported the FCC's denial of Kennedy's request. The law does not confer upon a candidate the privilege of using a broadcaster's facilities without charge. Broadcasters may meet the demands of Section 312 by either giving the candidate free time or making time available for purchase, the court said. The networks had already given Kennedy's campaign considerable free time through its news coverage of the candidate (*Kennedy for President Committee* v. *FCC,* 1980).

Supporters of Section 312 see it as a means to permit candidates for federal office to use the important broadcast communication channels in this nation to talk to prospective voters. Opponents say it is government interference in broadcasters' operation of their business, and it can cause severe financial hardship if programming schedules are disrupted to facilitate political broadcasts. The FCC has asked Congress to abandon this law, but most observers do not believe Congress will repeal this statute.

When Congress adopted Section 312 in 1971 it also specified the highest rates which a broadcaster can charge a candidate for federal office for using station facilities. The general rule is: Forty-five days before a primary election and sixty days before a general election, the charge to a candidate cannot exceed the lowest rate the station charges its local advertisers for that particular time slot. At other times the rate must be "comparable" to what the station charges other advertisers. There are considerable details in these rules which are important, but which are too involved to outline here. Students who intend to enter broadcast sales should closely study Section 312 of 47 *United States Code.*

One final note. Section 312 only applies to candidates for federal office. However, a broadcast station has an obligation to serve the public interest. In light of federal legislation on this question, the FCC could surely find that a broadcaster who consistently refuses to provide access to candidates for state or local office was not properly serving the public interest.

Equal Time Rule

Section 315 contains the equal opportunities or **equal time rule.** It has been a part of the Federal Communications Act since the law was passed in 1934. It was significantly changed by the Congress in 1959. Section 315 is not really difficult to understand. If a broadcasting station permits one legally qualified candidate for public office to use its facilities, it must afford equal opportunity to all other such legally qualified candidates for the same office. Section 315 also specifically prohibits the station from censoring material in broadcasts by political candidates. The FCC recently fined a Stamford, Connecticut, radio station $10,000 for censoring the paid political broadcasts of two mayoralty candidates (see *Kuczo* v. *Western Connecticut Broadcasting Company,* 1973).

What does equal opportunity mean? It means equal time, equal facilities, and comparable costs. If John Smith buys one-half hour of television time on station KLOP to campaign for the office of mayor, other legally qualified candidates for that office must be allowed to purchase one-half hour of time as well. If Smith is able to use the station's equipment to prerecord his talk, other candidates must have the same opportunity. If the station charges Smith one hundred dollars for the one-half hour of time, the station must charge his opponents one hundred dollars.

The station does not have to solicit appearance by the other candidates; it merely must give them the opportunity to use the facilities if they request such use within one week of Smith's appearance. Finally, Section 315 clearly states that broadcasters do not have to allow any political candidates the use of their facilities if they so choose. However, if they allow one candidate to use the facilities, they must allow the same use to all seeking the same office. Of course the provisions of Section 312 of the Communications Act are relevant to use of a station's facilities by a candidate.

Use of the Airwaves

Section 315 states that "use" by one candidate of a broadcast facility entitles all opponents to "use" the facility as well. A key question then is, What does the word *use* mean? What constitutes an appearance by a candidate in the eyes of the law? It is easiest to begin by listing those things which do not constitute a "use."

1. The appearance by a candidate in a bona-fide or legitimate newscast does not constitute use of the facility in the eyes of the law. Section 315 will not be triggered. The FCC has ruled that appearances by political candidates on ABC's "Good Morning America," NBC's "Today" and the "CBS Morning News" are exempt from provisions of Section 315. The agency considers all three programs bona fide newscasts.

2. The appearance of a candidate in a bona fide news interview program does not constitute a use. The key words are *bona fide*. An appearance on "Meet the Press," which is a bona fide news interview show, is not use of a broadcasting facility. But an appearance on "Meet the Candidates," a public-affairs show created by a television station for the express purpose of interviewing candidates prior to an election is use because it is not a bona fide news interview show. The show was created especially for the election campaign by the station and is not broadcast when electioneering is not in progress.

3. The appearance of a candidate in the spot news coverage of a bona fide news event is not use. When candidate Smith is interviewed at the scene of a bad fire about the problems of arson in the city, this is not "use" in terms of Section 315. Political conventions are considered bona fide news events; therefore an appearance by a candidate at the convention can be broadcast without invoking Section 315.

4. The appearance of a candidate in a news documentary is not a use if the appearance is incidental to the presentation of the subject of the program. Example: During the spring months of the 1968 political campaign, CBS broadcast a documentary on reform of the federal income tax laws. An interview with Senator Robert Kennedy, who was leading a fight in the United States Senate for tax reform, was included in the program. At that time Kennedy was a candidate for the presidency, but his appearance in the documentary did not activate the equal opportunity rule because the program was about tax laws. Kennedy's appearance was incidental to that subject. A news documentary about Kennedy would have been a different story and would have triggered the Section 315 sanction. In the documentary the network was merely talking to Kennedy about a national problem on which he was an expert.

Debates between political candidates are considered bona fide news events, and the broadcast of these events will not initiate use of Section 315, according to an FCC ruling in 1975. The only qualification for a debate to be exempt is that the debate be sponsored by and under the control of someone other than either the broadcaster or the political candidates. In federal elections the FCC has ruled that only tax-exempt organizations can sponsor or control the debates. The 1980 Carter-Reagan debate was sponsored by the League of Women Voters and was covered by the television networks as a bona fide news event. This interpretation of the law has been upheld by the courts. The equal opportunity rule was not triggered by these telecasts (see in re *Aspen Institute and CBS, Inc.,* 1975 and *Chisholm* v. *FCC,* 1976).

Press conferences held by political candidates are also normally considered bona-fide news events and are exempt from the provisions of Section 315. A press conference held by President Jimmy Carter in February 1980, several months after he announced he was a candidate for reelection, was broadcast live by all the television networks. Carter's opponent for the Democratic nomination, Ted Kennedy, sought time from the television networks under the equal opportunity rule. The networks said no. The FCC agreed with the broadcasters; the press conference was a bona-fide news event. The agency had ruled in 1975 that all press conferences featuring political candidates were exempt from Section 315 as news events. Kennedy appealed the ruling to the United States Court of Appeals (D.C.) and lost. The court said that to determine whether the coverage of a news conference can be considered spot coverage of a bona-fide news event three criteria must be examined:

1. Was the press conference broadcast live? Coverage of spot news should be live coverage.
2. Was there any evidence of favoritism on the part of the broadcaster? Did the station just carry Carter's press conferences and ignore his opponent's conferences?
3. Finally, did the broadcaster make a good-faith judgment that the news conference was a bona-fide news event?

In this case the press conference was carried live, the networks had covered Kennedy press conferences, and it was obvious that a determination had been made by the broadcasters that this was an important news event (*Kennedy for President Committee* v. *FCC,* 1980).

With these exceptions, all other appearances by a candidate are considered use in the meaning of Section 315. A paid political broadcast, a spot announcement, and even a five-minute interview on the "Tonight Show" are all appearances that will invoke Section 315. Opposing candidates would have the right to ask for equal opportunity. During Ronald Reagan's campaign for the presidency, stations had to refrain from showing his old movies and segments of "Death Valley Days" in which he appeared as the host (see *Adrian Weiss,* 1976). Pat Paulsen's quadrennial run for the White House forced television stations and networks to pull movies in which he appeared out of their libraries until the election was over. Once, Johnny Carson entertained the mayor of Burbank, California, on his program in recognition of the fame that town gained by being the butt of a joke on Rowan and Martin's "Laugh-In." But Carson's staff had not done their homework, for the mayor was in the midst of a campaign for reelection. The National Broadcasting Company affiliate in Los Angeles was forced to give each of the mayor's dozen or so opponents equal time.

Legally Qualified Candidates

One of the most confusing aspects of Section 315 regards the FCC's definition of a legally qualified candidate. It is a long definition filled with lots of *ands* and *ors* and needs clarification.

A legally qualified candidate is any person (1) who publicly announces that he or she is a candidate for nomination or election to any local, county, state, or national office, *and* (2) who meets the qualifications prescribed by law for that office, *and* (3) who qualifies for a place on the ballot or is eligible to be voted for by sticker or write-in methods, *and* (4) who was duly nominated by a political party which is commonly known and regarded as such or makes a substantial showing that he or she is a bona fide candidate.

There should be no question about number one in the definition: the candidate must be an announced candidate. Number two merely states that the person must be eligible to hold the office to which he or she aspires. Henry Kissinger, for example, is not eligible to be president since he is not a natural-born citizen. Despite the fact that he may be an announced candidate for that office, he is not a legally qualified candidate. Number three is self-explanatory: the person's name must appear on the ballot or he or she must be an eligible write-in or sticker candidate. Number four is the confusing qualification. Who knows what a substantial showing really is? What is a political party "commonly known and regarded as such"? Answers to these questions are judgment calls, and broadcasters with questions can solicit answers from the FCC. In fact, it is through the solicitation of such questions that the agency makes most of its Section 315 rulings.

Equal opportunity cases are rare. Normally the broadcaster asks the agency for guidance and then follows the recommendations of the commission. If there is a valid Section 315 complaint, the FCC usually just informs the licensee that candidate Adams is entitled to equal opportunity time and the station provides the time.

Many critics charge that a smart politician can refrain from announcing his candidacy for reelection, for example, and just make many television appearances and not be in violation of Section 315. That is true. But stations should be able to see what the candidate is doing and can refuse to allow appearances by an unannounced candidate, especially appearances which are clearly political in nature. A station which is not careful in this regard can be subject to problems at renewal time.

The FCC has granted two qualifications for the application of the equal opportunity doctrine, one of which appears much more important than it really is. The first qualification is broad: In primary elections, Section 315 applies to intraparty contests rather than to interparty contests. In a primary election, the situation is not Republicans versus Democrats, it is Republican versus Republican and Democrat versus Democrat. Only opponents can get equal opportunity. Imagine Jane Adams is a Republican candidate for governor. She is one of four Republicans seeking to win the primary. Six Democrats are also seeking to win the primary election and gain the nomination for the governorship in their party. Ms. Adams appears on KLOP for fifteen minutes. What are the station's obligations? The station is obliged to give equal opportunity to the other three Republican candidates, since they are the ones against whom Jane is running. The Democrats are not running against Ms. Adams at this time. While this qualification is broad, it makes a good deal of sense.

The second qualification turns out to be not much of a qualification at all, although it appears to be on its face. The only appearance that can trigger use of Section 315 is an appearance by the candidate. Under Section 315 appearances by friends, relatives, supporters, and so forth, do not require the station to give equal opportunity to opponents. However (this is an important however), the FCC has decided that such noncandidate appearances do require the station to provide an opportunity for appearances by supporters of the other legally qualified candidates.

This is known as the **Zapple rule** and was formulated a few years ago in response to a letter from Nicholas Zapple, formerly a staff member of the Senate Subcommittee on Communications. It was restated in the FCC's 1972 *Report Regarding the Handling of Political Broadcasts*. This is what the FCC said:

> The commission held in "Zapple" that when a licensee sells time to supporters or spokesmen of a candidate during an election campaign who urge the candidate's election, discuss the campaign issues, or criticize an opponent then the licensee must afford comparable time to the spokesmen for an opponent. Known as the quasi-equal opportunity or political party corollary to the fairness

doctrine, the "Zapple" doctrine is based on the equal opportunity requirement of Section 315 of the Communications Act; accordingly, free reply time need not be afforded to respond to a paid program.

The Zapple rule is a fairly specific formulation of one part of what had been vague FCC policy for some time, that is, that during political campaigns programs that do not invoke Section 315 fall under the ambit of the Fairness Doctrine. This means that licensees are required to play fair with all candidates. Broadcasters are therefore obliged to scrutinize even those programs which are exempt from Section 315 such as newscasts to ensure that a balance of some sort is maintained.

Two last points need to be made about Section 315. First, since broadcasters are not permitted to censor the remarks of a political candidate, they are immune from libel suits based on those remarks. In 1959 the Supreme Court ruled that since stations cannot control what candidates say over the air they should not be held responsible for the remarks. The candidate, however, can still be sued (*Farmers Educational and Cooperative Union of America* v. *WDAY*, 1959). Second, ballot issues like school bond levies, initiatives, and referendums do not fall under Section 315, but are treated as controversial issues under the Fairness Doctrine. The FCC has asked the Congress to repeal Section 315 as a part of its plan to deregulate broadcasting. It is not likely that the Congress will take this action.

Summary

Several rules govern political broadcasts carried by radio and television broadcasters. Section 312 of the Communications Act states that broadcasters cannot have an across-the-board policy rejecting all paid and nonpaid appearances by candidates for federal office. A candidate's request must be evaluated and can be rejected only if it could cause serious disruption of program schedules or might prompt an excessive number of equal time requests. While this rule applies only to requests from candidates for federal office, the government's mandate that broadcasters operate their stations in the public interest may very well include similar standards for the treatment by broadcasters of requests for access to airtime from state and local candidates.

Section 315 states that if a broadcaster provides one candidate for office with the opportunity to use a station's broadcast facilities all other legally qualified candidates for the same office must be given the same opportunity. The use of the station's facilities includes all appearances on the station with the exception of the following:

1. Bona-fide newscasts
2. Bona-fide news interview programs
3. Spot news coverage
4. Incidental appearance in a news documentary

Candidate press conferences and many debates between candidates are considered spot news events. During primary elections Section 315 applies only to candidates from the same political party running against each other to win the party's nomination to run in the general election.

PUBLIC AFFAIRS PROGRAMMING AND THE FAIRNESS DOCTRINE

The FCC treads a bit softer when it comes to dealing with news programming. The commission normally gets involved in news programming through its enforcement of the Fairness Doctrine, which we shall consider shortly. There have been instances in which charges were made that stations and networks falsified the news. Congress also gets into such debates as it did in the controversy over the CBS broadcast "The Selling of the Pentagon," but usually takes no action. The FCC is also reluctant to act in such cases. The only difference is that the FCC astutely seeks to avoid confronting the issues involved in the charge of news falsification, whereas inaction by Congress results from both sensitivity to the First Amendment and inertia.

Complaints were made to the commission about such programs as "The Selling of the Pentagon" and "Hunger in America." The Columbia Broadcasting System was accused of careless editing in the program on the Pentagon, editing which took quotations from various parts of a speech and made it appear that these separate statements were actually one statement. There were other questionable editing practices as well. In "Hunger in America" the same network showed viewers a baby which it claimed had died of malnutrition. While many babies do die each week of malnutrition, the one photographed by the network had, in fact, died of other causes. The response of the FCC in "The Selling of the Pentagon" case is typical of how that agency handles such complaints. "Lacking evidence or documents that on their face reflect deliberate distortion, we believe that this government licensing agency cannot properly intervene," the commission ruled. "As we stated in the 'Hunger in America' ruling, the commission is not the national arbiter of truth." While taking a hands-off action itself, the agency reminded broadcasters, "The licensee must have a policy of requiring honesty of its news staff and must take reasonable precautions to see that news is fairly handled. The licensee's investigation of substantial complaints . . . must be a thorough, conscientious one, resulting in remedial action where appropriate." From this statement one can presume that obvious and blatant staging of news will be considered a disservice to the public interest, but that the FCC is not capable of evaluating or monitoring the editing techniques of thousands of news departments. Errors will have to be fairly serious and well documented before the commission will intervene.

The Fairness Doctrine　　　There is no aspect of broadcast regulation that is more controversial than the **Fairness Doctrine.** Some authorities consider it a flagrant affront to the First Amendment's guarantee of freedom of expression; others argue that the Fairness Doctrine is the only thing which makes freedom of expression a reality in broadcasting. In addition to being controversial, the doctrine is confusing.

The Fairness Doctrine is a broad doctrine, affecting some advertising (as will be noted later in this chapter), political campaigns, and political candidates, as was just noted briefly. Its primary thrust, however, is aimed at public-affairs programming and controversial public issues. In barest essentials the Fairness Doctrine involves a two-fold duty for broadcasters. First, broadcasters must devote a reasonable percentage of their broadcast time to the coverage of public issues. Second, the coverage of these issues must be fair in the sense that an opportunity for presentation of contrasting points of view is provided. What is so hard about that? Well, little words like *reasonable* and *public issues* and *fair* and *contrasting* are the troublemakers. These are the words that need to be clarified.

A quick look at the origin of the Fairness Doctrine is in order first. In 1927 and again in 1933 members of Congress tried to include a kind of Fairness Doctrine in federal legislation regulating broadcasting. All attempts failed, stopped either by the Congress itself or by presidential veto. In 1947 another attempt was made when a Senate bill to adopt a legislative Fairness Doctrine was introduced, but again the effort failed.

With or without a law, however, first the Federal Radio Commission (FRC) and later the Federal Communications Commission (FCC) ruled that balance and fairness were requirements of broadcasting which serves the public interest, convenience, or necessity. In 1929 in the *Great Lakes Broadcasting* case the FRC ruled, "insofar as a program consists of discussion of public questions, public interest requires ample play for the free and fair competition of opposing views and the commission believes that the principle applies not only to addresses by political candidates but to all discussion of issues of importance to the public" (in re *Great Lakes Broadcasting Co.,* 1929). Sixteen years later in the *United Broadcasting* case the FCC echoed the FRC. The commission agreed with the broadcaster's contention that a radio station is not a common carrier, but noted also (in re *United Broadcasting Co.,* 1945):

> These facts, however, in no way impinge upon the duty of each station licensee to be sensitive to the problems of public concern in the community and to make sufficient time available, on a non-discriminatory basis, for a full discussion thereof. . . .

The first "official" announcement of what we know as the Fairness Doctrine was made in 1949 when the FCC issued the long report *In the Matter of Editorializating by Broadcast Licensees.* The report was the result of an extensive study that the commission undertook after broadcasters and other persons protested a 1941 ruling by the agency that licensees could not editorialize on their stations (in re *Mayflower Broadcasting Corp., WAAB,* 1941). The editorialization report stated that broadcasters had an affirmative responsibility to provide a reasonable amount of time for the presentation of programs devoted to the discussion and consideration of public issues. The report added that it was the licensee's responsibility to afford a reasonable opportunity for the presentation of all responsible positions on the matters discussed. The commission said that licensees would not be meeting their Fairness Doctrine responsibility if they refused to broadcast all controversial matter. The FCC also noted:

> . . . it is clear that any approximation of fairness in the presentation of any controversy will be difficult if not impossible of achievement unless the licensee plays a conscious and positive role in bringing about balanced presentation of the opposing viewpoints.

To the question that would surely be raised about the commission's role as censor in applying the Fairness Doctrine, the agency noted, "The duty to operate in the public interest is no esoteric mystery, but essentially a duty to operate a radio station with good judgment and good faith guided by a reasonable regard for the interests of the community to be served."

In 1959 when Congress amended Section 315 of the Communications Act to exclude news programming from the ambit of the equal opportunity rule, the legislators approved language in the measure which said that nothing in the amendment should be construed to relieve broadcasters "from the obligation imposed upon them under this Act to operate in the public interest and to afford reasonable opportunity for the discussion of conflicting views on issues of public importance." Many legal authorities, including the United States Supreme Court, consider this to be congressional sanction of the Fairness Doctrine which, as we have seen, was created by the FCC. Other observers note that if this be the case the 1959 congressional action was at best tenuous authority for such broad legal powers as the Fairness Doctrine gives the FCC.

Before the application of the doctrine is discussed, one point needs to be further emphasized. Broadcasters have an affirmative responsibility to make certain that all sides of a public question are presented. That is, broadcasters must either find spokes persons or make the presentation themselves. Merely allowing persons who have a different viewpoint to use the station is not sufficient. Broadcasters are obliged to seek out spokes persons for divergent viewpoints.

What the Doctrine Means

In 1971 the FCC decided to review the Fairness Doctrine. Did it work? Should it be replaced? be modified? be abandoned? In 1974 the commission issued its findings in a report entitled *The Fairness Report*. To sum up what the agency said in a single sentence is quite simple: The Fairness Doctrine is needed and it works just fine. The scarcity of broadcast frequencies was used by the commission to justify the doctrine. The 1974 report dismissed changing technology as a means of alleviating the scarcity problem:

> The effective development of an electronic medium with an abundance of channels (through the use of cable, or otherwise) is still very much a thing of the future. For the present we do not believe that it would be appropriate—or even permissible—for a government agency charged with the allocation of the channels now available to ignore the legitimate First Amendment interests of the general public.

The commission went on to assert that the net effect of the Fairness Doctrine has been to enhance the volume and quality of the coverage of issues of public importance, which is important in the complex era in which we live. Quoting from an earlier opinion it had issued, the commission alerted broadcasters, "We regard strict adherence to the Fairness Doctrine—including the affirmative obligation to provide coverage of issues of public importance—as the single most important requirement of operation in the public interest, the *sine qua non* ["the indispensable requisite"], for grant of a renewal of license." Of course, by 1983 the FCC had changed its mind and sought the repeal of the Fairness Doctrine by Congress.

In addition to defending the Fairness Doctrine in the 1974 report, the FCC outlined and provided an interpretation of the doctrine. If this interpretation is used as a guide, it is possible to gain a good understanding of what the Fairness Doctrine means today.

Question one: What is adequate time for the discussion of public issues? This determination is up to the broadcaster, according to the FCC. Some persons—even some members of the FCC—have suggested that the agency set a minimum standard for public affairs programming. For example, former Commissioner Nicholas Johnson proposed that at least 5 percent of a station's programming be devoted to the discussion of public issues. However the FCC has resisted adopting such a scheme. "It is the individual broadcaster who, after evaluating the needs of his particular community, must determine what percentage of the limited broadcast day should be devoted to news and discussion or consideration of public issues," the FCC said.

An FCC ruling in 1976 helped clarify what is adequate time for the discussion of public issues. Representative Patsy Mink, the sponsor of an anti-strip-mining bill in Congress, asked a West Virginia radio station to broadcast an eleven-minute audiotaped discussion of her bill. The station refused, noting that it had not carried any pro-strip-mining broadcasts and consequently was not required to carry an anti-strip-mining program. Representative Mink complained to the FCC that the station had not fulfilled its obligations under the Fairness Doctrine to provide an adequate amount of time for a discussion of public issues. The station argued that it had covered the issue by presenting Associated Press news reports on the issue during its regular newscasts.

The FCC ruled against the station, reaffirming that "the Fairness Doctrine imposes two affirmative responsibilities on the broadcaster: coverage of issues of public importance must be adequate and must fairly reflect differing viewpoints." The commission noted that the requirement to present contrasting viewpoints would not make much sense without a corresponding obligation to cover issues of public importance. But what about the station's contention that the issue was covered via newscasts? Doesn't the broadcaster enjoy the discretion to fulfill Fairness Doctrine obligations in this manner? While acknowledging that the licensee was not obligated to address each and every issue which may be important to the public, the commission ruled (*Patsy Mink,* 1976):

> Where, as in the present case, an issue has significant and possibly unique impact on the licensee's service area, it will not be sufficient for the licensee as an indication of compliance with the Fairness Doctrine to show that it may have broadcast an unknown amount of news touching on a general topic related to the issue cited in a complaint. Rather it must be shown that there has been some attempt to inform the public of the nature of the controversy, not only that such a controversy exists.

The ruling should not be taken as standard policy for the FCC. The agency was specific in noting that the principle of the *Mink* case would be reserved for issues that are "critical and of great public importance." Still, the *Mink* ruling was the first time the FCC had taken such a strong stand on this issue and may mark a distinct change in the direction of the application of this aspect of the Fairness Doctrine.

Question two: What is a reasonable opportunity for opposing viewpoints? The Fairness Doctrine does not require—as does Section 315—one-to-one precision in granting time for opposing viewpoints. So long as all sides of the issue are reasonably aired (this is terribly vague), the strictures of the Fairness Doctrine will have been met. Do all viewpoints have to be aired? What about the fellow in the valley whose ideas are different from those of everyone else? No, that would be unreasonable. The commission requires an airing only of viewpoints which have a significant measure of support or viewpoints which reflect the ideas of a significant segment of the community. But remember, it is the duty of broadcasters to make certain that these views are publicly aired. They have an affirmative duty to find someone to raise these points or have someone at the station present these ideas.

Question three: What is a controversial issue of public importance? In actual practice the broadcaster decides what is controversial and what is not.

Some of the factors which the FCC suggests that the licensee take into consideration when determining whether an issue is controversial include the following:

1. The degree of media coverage of the issue
2. The degree of attention the issue receives from government officials and other community leaders
3. The impact the issue is likely to have on the community at large

A recent ruling by the FCC, supported by the Court of Appeals (D.C.), indicates that a controversial issue is expected to be rather specific and narrow. A conservative political-action group calling itself American Security Council Foundation (ASCF) undertook a content analysis of CBS television news broadcasts in 1975 and 1976 and concluded that the network's coverage of the national security issue was not balanced. The group called the coverage "too dovish." The FCC rejected the complaint, noting among other things that ASCF had not defined a controversial issue with sufficient specificity in its complaint. The United States Court of Appeals upheld this ruling in 1979, arguing that the items included under the umbrella of "national security" were simply too diverse to be bunched together under a single national security heading. The ASCF looked at such items as NATO, detente with China and Russia, SALT treaties, amnesty for persons prosecuted during the Vietnam War for a wide range of offenses, Vietnam War itself, Middle East issues, and others. "The issues analyzed by ASCF arose independently in time and were largely discussed and acted upon on an independent basis," the court ruled. "Consideration of the issues together, rather than individually, would not provide a basis for determining whether the broadcaster presented a reasonable balance of conflicting views, because views on any one issue do not support or contradict views on the others," the six-person majority noted. What does NATO have to do with detente in China? or what does amnesty have to do with SALT? the court asked. An issue is not a "particular, well-defined" issue for Fairness Doctrine purposes if the separate issues comprising it are so indirectly related that a view on one does not, in a way that would be apparent to an average viewer, support or contradict a view on any other (*American Security Council Foundation* v. *FCC,* 1979).

In 1980 the FCC dismissed a complaint made against all three networks by the National Committee for Responsive Philanthropy. The committee alleged that the networks had failed to balance the issue raised by broadcast of spot announcements urging persons to support the United Way fund drives ("Thanks to you, it's working:"). The United States Court of Appeals for the District of Columbia upheld the commission action, noting that the committee's complaint failed to show that such announcements meaningfully addressed a controversial issue of public importance. The Fairness Doctrine only applies, the court said, when a broadcast statement amounts to advocacy of a position on one side of an ongoing public debate and obviously and substantially addresses that issue in a meaningful way (*National Committee for Responsive Philanthropy* v. *FCC,* 1981).

By and large it comes down to whether the broadcaster believes that an issue is important, is controversial, and does stimulate debate within the community.

How the Doctrine Works

The FCC does no monitoring for violations of the Fairness Doctrine itself, but depends instead upon viewer and listener complaints. Organizations like Accuracy in Media (AIM) which take the pose of "professional media monitors" are popping up across the nation. Usually these groups have an axe to grind of one sort or another. Nevertheless, they do make complaints, and have created problems for broadcasters.

The FCC requires that a Fairness Doctrine complaint contain the following items:

1. The name of the particular station involved
2. The particular issue of a controversial nature discussed over the air
3. The date and time when the program was carried
4. The basis for the claim that the station presented only one side of the question
5. Whether the station afforded or has plans to afford an opportunity for presentation of contrasting viewpoints

Numbers one and three are simple to accomplish. Number two can be a problem, however, for the station may define the issue aired during the program somewhat differently than does the complainant, as we shall soon see. Number five requires that the complainant talk to the station before making a complaint, which is the only way the question can be answered. It is number four, however, that is the primary problem for unhappy viewers. The Fairness Doctrine does not require that a station present all sides of an issue within the context of a single program. What is required is that in its *overall programming* it make a balanced presentation of the issues. This month the station might present a program which is against abortion, and next month it may present one which is for abortion. Overall, the station has been fair. Therefore, in alleging that the station has presented only one side of an issue, the complainant has to have a pretty good idea of the station's overall programming—what has gone on in the past as well as what is going to happen in the future. This is a heavy burden for persons who seek to complain. Imagine seeing a one-sided gun-control program on television tonight. How certain are you that somewhere along the line in the past few months the station did not present the other side of the issue? maybe in a documentary? maybe during the news? maybe on a Sunday afternoon while you were watching a football game on another channel? While complaints are not foreclosed, they are difficult to make. More than 10,300 complaints and inquiries were submitted by the public to the FCC in 1980. Approximately 99 percent of the complaints were rejected outright because the complainant had not followed the proper procedure or had misunderstood the role of the Fairness Doctrine. Of the 1 percent of the complaints that were initially accepted, only about 15 percent were eventually resolved against the station. This amounted to less than twenty complaints, according to the National Citizens Committee for Broadcasting.

If the complaint is forwarded to the station, the FCC letter asks the broadcaster these two questions:

1. Is the issue of controversial public importance in your viewing area?
2. Have you fulfilled your Fairness Doctrine obligations by presenting balanced programming on that issue?

If the broadcaster says that the issue is not controversial or not of public importance, the FCC must accept the answer unless there is evidence that the broadcaster is arbitrary or capricious in making the determination. So long as the broadcaster makes a good-faith judgment that the issue is not controversial, there is nothing the FCC can do. The broadcaster has the discretion to decide what is and what is not controversial. Furthermore the FCC cannot substitute its judgment for that of the broadcaster. Clearly if the broadcaster ignores overwhelming evidence that the people are interested, if he ignores the fact that a vigorous public debate is underway, the FCC can then rule that the determination is not made in good faith. But this is a very rare kind of ruling. Generally the agency takes the licensee's word.

In 1972 NBC broadcast a program entitled "The Broken Promise," a documentary about private pension plans. It was very critical of certain private pension plans and graphically showed how millions of Americans had been ripped off and cheated. Narrator Edwin Newman told viewers *that most private pension plans are good,* that they provide a real benefit to the workers. Most of the NBC program, however, dealt *with bad pension plans.*

A Fairness Doctrine complaint was lodged against the network by AIM. The FCC asked NBC whether the program dealt with a controversial issue. The network said no, and this was its reasoning. The program talked about bad private pension plans. There were no allegations that all pension plans were bad. In fact, quite the opposite: it was stated that most plans are good. NBC focused on the bad plans. Everybody agrees that some plans are bad. There is no controversy about that. Since the program focused only on the bad plans, it did not deal with a controversial issue.

The FCC did not accept this logic. But when the decision was appealed to a court of appeals, the agency had its hand slapped. The court said that so long as the network had made a good-faith judgment, NBC was to exercise discretion as to whether the issue was controversial (*NBC* v. *FCC,* 1974). The

FCC could not come to a different conclusion on the basis of the same evidence. That was not permitted. What the agency must ask is this: Was there any evidence that could lead the network to decide that the issue was not controversial? And if there was, then NBC's determination was made in good faith.

Because the case took so long to get through the courts, the rulings by both the FCC and the court of appeals were in the end moot. The controversy disappeared when Congress passed its pension-reform bill. So the "Broken Promise" case is not a precedent. However, the rules have not changed. The case was cited to show how the rules work. If another case were to come along tomorrow, the same kinds of restrictions upon the FCC would exist. It is basically the broadcaster's decision whether the issue at hand is controversial and important.

If the licensee says the issue is controversial, the station must then tell the commission how it has fulfilled the Fairness Doctrine requirements, or how it plans to fulfill its responsibilities. Here the FCC has a bit more discretion. However the key is still whether broadcasters *make a good-faith effort to provide balanced programming,* rather than whether they *provide balanced programming.* Unless the licensee is really out in left field, the commissioners are usually satisfied. It is only in outrageous cases that the FCC demands a hearing or demands that the broadcaster provide time for opposing viewpoints. Remember also that the initial burden of proof is upon the complainant to convince the FCC that a violation of the doctrine did indeed occur. Before the FCC even sends out a letter to the station, the complainant must provide "a reasonable basis for the conclusion that the licensee has failed in its overall programming to present a reasonable opportunity for contrasting views."

What happens if the FCC finds there has been a violation? A request may be made that the station provide time for airing opposing viewpoints, or a fine may be levied against the broadcaster. In extreme cases the broadcast license may not be renewed (see *Brandywine-Main Line Radio, Inc.,* v. *FCC,* 1972). Denial of renewal generally results only when a pattern of flagrant abuses of the Fairness Doctrine can be shown. Few fairness complaints result in action of any kind against the station. Still, the time and trouble involved in answering such a complaint, especially one which evolves into a hearing and a court case like the NBC case just discussed, are quite onerous. Typical complaints may cost from $500 to $1,000 to answer. When a hearing is involved, expenses can easily reach into the tens of thousands of dollars. A West Coast television station won a Fairness Doctrine hearing which cost the broadcaster $20,000 to defend.

Advertising

The Fairness Doctrine has been applied to advertising as well as to other subjects. In 1967 in response to a petition from a young attorney named John Banzhaf, the commission ruled that stations which carry advertisements for cigarettes must carry free public service messages showing the dangers of smoking as well (*WCBS-TV: Applicability of the Fairness Doctrine to Cigarette Advertising,* 1967). The United States Court of Appeals (D.C.) sustained the ruling in *Banzhaf* v. *FCC* (1969). Cigarette smoking was a controversial subject. Later, of course, Congress passed a law which banned cigarette advertisements from the airwaves completely.

Following the *Banzhaf* ruling other public interest groups sought to have broadcasters balance advertisements for gasoline and automobiles with messages about environmental protection. But the FCC did not agree to these proposals. The commission argued that the smoking decision was unusual, that smoking is a habit that can disappear, that the government urged the discontinuance of cigarette smoking, that government studies showed the danger of smoking, and so forth. In other words the problem of smoking is different from the problem of pollution. So the Friends of the Earth went to court, and in 1971 the Court of Appeals (D.C.) reversed the FCC ruling. The court said it could not see the distinction between the cigarette case and that case (in re *Wilderness Society and Friends of the Earth,* 1971):

> Commercials which continue to insinuate that the human personality finds greater fulfillment in the larger car with the quick getaway do, it seems to us, ventilate a point of view which not only has become controversial but involves an issue of public importance. Where there is undisputed evidence, as there is here, that the hazards to health implicit in air pollution are enlarged and aggravated by such products, then the parallel with cigarette advertising is exact and the relevance of *Banzhaf* inescapable.

The court said, however, that stations do not have to broadcast anti–big-car advertising, as in the cigarette advertisements case. The key is overall programming. If the licensees carry programming which discusses the environmental dangers of pollution and the diminution of resources, the Fairness Doctrine will be satisfied.

In its 1974 report the FCC discussed the application of the Fairness Doctrine to advertising. The commission said that it would apply the doctrine to editorial advertising—commercials which consist of direct and substantial commentary on important public issues—but not to product advertising, not even to controversial products. It said that the cigarette decision was a mistake; if it had to decide the case today, it would not make the same decision. "We believe that standard product commercials," the commissioners wrote, "make no meaningful contribution toward informing the public on any side of any issue." The courts have upheld this decision by the FCC, most recently in 1977 (*National Citizens Committee for Broadcasting* v. *FCC,* 1977). The commission also rejected a proposal by the Federal Trade Commission that the FCC require stations to offer rebuttal time to public interest groups to answer commercials which raise controversial issues, commercials which make claims which are based on disputed scientific premises, and commercials which are silent about the negative aspects of the advertised products (like too many aspirin can be harmful). The FCC said that almost all commercials raise controversial issues for some people, that such a "counteradvertising proposal" could have an adverse economic effect on broadcasting, and that it did not believe that the Fairness Doctrine was an appropriate vehicle with which to correct false and misleading advertising.

The case of *Public Media Center* v. *FCC* (1978) is an example of the kind of advertising to which the FCC will apply the Fairness Doctrine. In this case, in which eight California television stations were charged with violating the Fairness Doctrine for broadcasting commercials for the Pacific Gas and Electric Company advocating development of nuclear power without presenting the views of opponents of such development, the United States Court of Appeals (D.C.) upheld the commission ruling. The court also remanded the case to the FCC to clarify why it had not made the same ruling regarding four other stations which had also broadcast the same television commercials.

One additional note: the FCC has not applied the Fairness Doctrine to entertainment programs, even to controversial shows such as the two-part "Maude" episode concerning abortion (*Diocesan Union of Holy Name Societies of Rockville Centre and Long Island Coalition for Life,* 1973).

Personal Attacks and Political Editorials

While the Fairness Doctrine remains a nebulous policy which has been outlined almost on a case-by-case basis, the commission has drafted specific rules with regard to one portion of the doctrine—what are known as the **personal attack rules.** The agency has also enunciated specific rules governing political editorials. These rules are subsections of the Fairness Doctrine. (see 32 Fed. Reg. 10303; 11531; and 33 Fed. Reg. 5362; 1967) and deal with a specific kind of one-sided presentation. Here are the rules:

Personal attacks
  (a) When, during the presentation of views on a controversial issue of public importance, an attack is made upon the honesty, character, integrity or like personal qualities of an identified person or group, the licensee shall, within a reasonable time and in no event later than one week after the attack, transmit to the person or group attacked (1) notification of the date, time and identification of the broadcast; (2) a script or tape (or an accurate summary if a script or tape is not available) of the attack; and (3) an offer of a reasonable opportunity to respond over the licensee's facilities.
  (b) The provisions of paragraph (a) of this section shall not be applicable (1) to attacks on foreign groups or foreign public figures; (2) to personal attacks which are made by legally qualified candidates, their authorized spokesmen, or those associated with them in the campaign, or other such candidates, their authorized spokesmen, or persons associated with the candidates in the campaign; and (3) to bona fide newscasts, bona fide news interviews, and on-the-spot coverage of a bona fide news event (including commentary or analysis contained in the foregoing programs, but the provisions of paragraph (a) of this section shall be applicable to editorials of the licensee).
  NOTE: The Fairness Doctrine is applicable to situations coming within [(3)], above, and, in a specific factual situation, may be applicable in the general area of political broadcasts [(2)], above.

Political editorials

(c) Where a licensee, in an editorial, (i) endorses or (ii) opposes a legally qualified candidate or candidates, the licensee shall, within 24 hours after the editorial, transmit to respectively (i) the other qualified candidate or candidates for the same office or (i) the candidate opposed in the editorial (1) notification of the date and time of the editorial; (2) a script or tape of the editorial; and (3) an offer of a reasonable opportunity for a candidate or a spokesman of the candidate to respond over the licensee's facilities: *Provided, however,* that where such editorials are broadcast within 72 hours prior to the day of the election, the licensee shall comply with the provisions of this paragraph sufficiently far in advance of the broadcast to enable the candidate or candidates to have a reasonable opportunity to prepare a response and to present it in a timely fashion.

The personal attack rules stem from FCC rulings in 1962 stating that when licensees broadcast what amounts to a personal attack upon an individual or group within the community they have an affirmative obligation to notify the target of the attack of the broadcast and offer the target an opportunity to respond. In 1967 these earlier decisions were clarified and made more specific with the publication of the personal attack rules.

As you can see from the rules, the licensee's obligations are quite specific. It is important to remember that just naming someone in an editorial or commentary does not necessarily constitute a personal attack. On the other hand the rules apply to attacks made by everyone, not just by the station itself.

Paragraph (b) of the rules exempts attacks made by candidates and their followers upon other candidates and their followers. Newscasts, news interviews, and on-the-spot news coverage are also exempted from the personal attack rules, but not from the more general provisions of the Fairness Doctrine. Paragraph (c) outlines licensee obligations with regard to editorial endorsements of candidates.

Soon after the personal attack rules were published, they were challenged in court. A small radio station in Pennsylvania challenged an FCC ruling requiring it to provide free time to Fred Cook, an author, who had been attacked by right-wing evangelist Billy James Hargis. The United States Court of Appeals for the District of Columbia upheld the constitutionality of both the personal attack rules and the Fairness Doctrine (*Red Lion Broadcasting Co.* v. *FCC,* 1967). While this case was being litigated, the Radio and Television News Directors Association and other broadcasting organizations petitioned the United States Court of Appeals for the Seventh District in Chicago to review the constitutionality of the Fairness Doctrine. In this case the court of appeals struck down both the personal attack rules and the Fairness Doctrine as being in violation of the First Amendment (*Radio and Television News Directors' Association* v. *U.S.,* 1968). With two circuit courts at odds on the question, the Supreme Court had to decide the issue.

The argument made by opponents of the Fairness Doctrine, more specifically of the personal attack rules, was two pronged. First, it was asserted that by forcing broadcasters to carry material, that is, the reply by the target of the attack, the government interfered with the First Amendment rights of broadcasters. Second, it was claimed that the Fairness Doctrine amounts to prior restraint as well. Here is the argument. A station has a public affairs budget of $5,000, just enough to produce and air a documentary opposing mandatory busing of children. The Fairness Doctrine requires the licensee to present both sides of the issue; therefore the station has to produce a second documentary which outlines the favorable aspects of busing. But the station has no money for that and therefore cannot air the first documentary opposing busing. This government interference amounts to restraining the broadcast of the documentary opposed to busing. Hence, there is a violation of the First Amendment, there is prior restraint.

Whatever merit you may find in these arguments, the Supreme Court found little to recommend them. In a unanimous decision in 1969 the high Court upheld the constitutionality of both the personal attack rules and the Fairness Doctrine with the argument that the First Amendment operates as a command to the government to protect the public from one-sided presentations of public issues. Going back to the original congressional mandate that the broadcaster operate in the public interest, the Court said the public interest is served only when the community receives exposure to all sides of controversial matters. As far as the First Amendment is concerned, wrote Justice Byron White, the licensed broadcaster stands no better off than those to whom the licenses are refused (*Red Lion Broadcasting Co.* v. *FCC,* 1969):

> A license permits broadcasting, but the licensee has no constitutional right to be the one who holds the license or to monopolize a radio frequency to the exclusion of his fellow citizens. There is nothing in the First Amendment which prevents the government from requiring a licensee to share his frequency with others and to conduct himself as a proxy or fiduciary with obligations to present those views and voices which are representative of his community and which would otherwise, by necessity, be barred from the air waves.

Later in the opinion Justice White asserted, "It is the right of the public to receive suitable access to social, political, esthetic, moral and other ideas and experiences, which is crucial here. That right may not constitutionally be abridged either by the Congress or by the FCC."

This case, *Red Lion Broadcasting* v. *FCC,* stands as the leading declaration that the First Amendment is for the people, not for the media, that the purpose of the First Amendment is to ensure that the public obtain the information needed to act as knowledgeable voters and citizens. The Court is willing to stand behind this philosophy with regard to broadcasting, but rejects these ideas with regard to the printed press in the *Tornillo* case discussed earlier in the book. How strong the high Court will stand behind the Fairness Doctrine today as it is battered from all sides is an important question. In 1973 at least some of the nine justices hinted that perhaps they were pulling back somewhat from their earlier unanimous declaration in a case involving the obligation of a broadcaster to sell, note the word *sell,* time to persons seeking to air controversial public issues.

The First Amendment

Broadcasting stations are not common carriers. That is, they have the right to refuse to do business with anyone they choose. During 1969 and 1970 two groups, the Democratic National Committee and a Washington, D.C., organization known as Business Executives Movement for Peace sought to buy time from television stations and networks to solicit funds for their protest of the Vietnam War and to voice their objections to the way the war was being prosecuted by the government. Broadcasters rebuffed these groups on the grounds that airing such controversial advertisements and programming would evoke the Fairness Doctrine, and they would then be obligated to ensure that all sides of the controversy were aired. Such action was a nuisance and could be costly. The broadcasters told the Democratic committee and the businessmen that one of their basic policies was not to sell time to any individual or group seeking to set forth views on controversial issues.

When this policy was challenged before the FCC, the commission sided with the broadcasters, noting that it was up to each individual licensee to determine how best to fulfill Fairness Doctrine obligations. But the United States Court of Appeals for the District of Columbia reversed the FCC ruling, citing the *Red Lion* decision that the right of the public to receive information is deeply rooted in the First Amendment. A ban on editorial advertising, the court ruled, "leaves a paternalistic structure in which licensees and bureaucrats decide what issues are important, whether to fully cover them, and the format, time and style of coverage. . . ." This kind of system, the court ruled, is inimical to the First Amendment (in re *Business Executives Movement for Peace* v. *FCC,* 1971):

> It may unsettle some of us to see an antiwar message or a political party message in the accustomed place of a soap or beer commercial. . . . We must not equate what is habitual with what is right or what is constitutional. A society already so saturated with commercialism can well afford another outlet for speech on public issues. All that we may lose is some of our apathy.

The victory of the businessmen and Democrats was short-lived, for by a seven-to-two vote, the United States Supreme Court overturned the appellate court ruling (*CBS* v. *Democratic National Committee,* 1973). Stations have an absolute right to refuse to sell time for advertising dealing with political campaigns and controversial issues. To give the FCC the power over such advertising runs the risk of enlarging government control over the content of broadcast discussion of public issues.

In response to the argument that by permitting broadcasters to refuse such advertising we place in their hands the power to decide what the people shall see or hear on important public issues Justice Burger wrote:

> For better or worse, editing is what editors are for; and editing is the selection and choice of material. That editors—newspaper or broadcast—can and do abuse this power is beyond doubt, but that is no reason to deny the discretion Congress provided. Calculated risks of abuse are taken in order to preserve high values.

The Court was badly fractured on this case and Justices Brennan and Marshall dissented. Only two other justices—Stewart and Rehnquist—joined the chief justice in his opinion. The remainder joined in overturning the court of appeals ruling, but for their own reasons. It could be said that the issue is not completely resolved, yet in light of the unanimous *Tornillo* decision the following year the matter probably is settled (*Miami Herald Co.* v. *Tornillo*, 1974). Broadcasters are required to present programming on public issues and to do so in such a manner as to ensure that all sides get a fair hearing. How this is to be accomplished is the business of the broadcaster. The Fairness Doctrine does not provide right of access to television or radio.

The FCC has asked the Congress to repeal all aspects of the Fairness Doctrine, including the personal attack rules, as a part of the deregulation of broadcasting.

One final note about both the regulations on political broadcasts (Section 312 and Section 315) and the Fairness Doctrine. The FCC proposed in June 1983 to modify or eliminate all Fairness Doctrine and Section 312 and Section 315 requirements as applied to *cable television*. The commission accepted public comments on this matter and is expected to issue a final rule soon.

Summary

The government may also exercise control over the content of public affairs programs. While the FCC has thus far rejected complaints that television news coverage was slanted or staged, the agency does attempt to enforce the Fairness Doctrine. This rule states that a broadcaster must devote adequate amounts of time for the discussion of important public issues, and that the coverage of these issues must reflect contrasting community viewpoints on the issues. The Fairness Doctrine puts an affirmative responsibility upon the broadcaster to ensure that coverage is fair; it is insufficient for a radio or television station operator to present one side of an issue and then invite persons with opposing viewpoints to appear as a means of fulfilling Fairness Doctrine responsibilities.

The FCC has refused to define "adequate time" for the dicussion of public issues. Affording a reasonable opportunity for opposing viewpoints means making certain that those views which reflect the ideas of significant segments of the community are aired. The broadcaster can decide what is a controversial issue of public importance. An examination of the media coverage of the issue, the impact the issue may have on the community, and the degree of attention the issue has received from community leaders may be used to guide the broadcaster in making this judgement.

It is difficult for a citizen to make an effective complaint against a broadcaster for violating the Fairness Doctrine. So long as the licensee has made a good-faith effort to present balanced coverage of important community issues, the FCC is reluctant to take action against the broadcaster. The Fairness Doctrine applies to editorial advertising (trying to sell an idea), but not to product advertising. A specific section of the Fairness Doctrine called the personal attack rules requires a broadcaster to notify a person or group that it plans to attack on the air and provide free time for the individual or group to respond to the attack.

The Supreme Court has ruled that the Fairness Doctrine does not violate the First Amendment. But the high Court has also ruled that broadcasters do not have to sell time to persons who wish to broadcast messages about controversial public issues.

REGULATION AND NEW TECHNOLOGY

A bewildering array of new electronic-information transmitting technology has seemingly burst upon the scene in recent years. Cable television, low-power television, direct-broadcast satellite, and other transmission systems open the door to a new information age for the American people. Should the government regulate these new systems as broadcasting is regulated? or should they be treated like newspapers with no licensing or other formal regulation? Because these systems are transmitted electronically and tend to bring traditional broadcast fare into homes, the government has presumed a regulatory function. As in broadcast regulation, the FCC is the principal agent of federal regulation. But unlike in traditional broadcast regulation, local government is also given a role. There is no way a comprehensive outline of the regulation of these new technologies can be presented in a few pages. The problems are bewilderingly complex; the regulation almost tentative at this point. But we can sketch the broad designs. Interested readers can pursue the subject in sources that can more accurately reflect the almost monthly changes in these laws.

Cable Regulation

Cable television is the oldest of the new technologies. Community antenna television, the forerunner of what we now call cable television, began in the late 1940s. The FCC first asserted jurisdiction over cable television in 1962. Initial regulatory moves by the agency were tentative. Rules were issued only for cable systems that transmitted the television signals via microwave relays (over-the-airwaves transmission) as well as by wire. These actions were sustained by the courts (in re *Carter Mountain Transmission Corp.,* 1962, 1963). In 1966 the agency issued rules which affected all cable systems, those that used the microwave relays and those that did not. Cable operators argued that the agency had no power to regulate cable transmission which did not use the broadcast spectrum, which was transmitted exclusively by wire. But the Supreme Court supported the FCC in a 1968 ruling. Justice Harlan wrote for the Court (*U.S.* v. *Southwestern Cable Co.,* 1968):

> The commission has been charged with broad responsibilities for the orderly development of an appropriate system of local television broadcasting. . . . The commission has reasonably found that the successful performance of these duties demands prompt and efficacious regulation of community antenna television systems [cable systems]. We have elsewhere held that we may not, "in the absence of compelling evidence that such was Congress' intention . . . prohibit administration action imperative for the achievement of an agency's ultimate purpose. . . ." There is no such evidence here, and we therefore hold that the commission's authority over "all interstate . . . communication by wire or radio" permits the regulation of CATV systems.

Justice Harlan added that the FCC can regulate cable television at least to the extent "reasonably ancillary to the effective performance of the commission's various responsibilities for the regulation of television broadcasting."

Given a green light by the Supreme Court, the FCC began in the late 1960s and early 1970s to issue more and more wide-ranging regulations. The agency imposed equal time rules, sponsor identification rules, and the Fairness Doctrine upon all programming originated by cable casters. In addition, the FCC ruled that all cable systems having more than 3,500 subscribers would have to operate "to a significant extent as a local outlet by originating cable casting." In other words, the cable operators could no longer merely scoop the signals of other broadcasting stations out of the air and send them into a home via wire. They had to create programs themselves, which required programming facilities far beyond the needs of the simple automated services thus far originated by cable operators.

The Midwest Video Corp. challenged this rule. Again the Supreme Court upheld the authority of the FCC. In a five-to-four decision the Court ruled (*U.S.* v. *Midwest Video Corp.,* 1972):

> The effect of the regulation, after all, is to assure that in the retransmission of broadcast signals viewers are provided suitably diversified programming. . . .
> In sum, the regulation preserves and enhances the integrity of broadcast signals and therefore is "reasonably ancillary" to the effective performance of the commission's various responsibilities for the regulation of television broadcasting.

Cable television operators argued, as did Justice Douglas in a strong dissent, that the FCC was forcing them into the broadcasting business when they did not want to be licensed for that business. A majority of the Court disagreed, however, noting that the cable operators voluntarily engaged themselves in providing that service and that "the commission seeks only to ensure that it satisfactorily meets community needs within the context of their undertaking." Given this broad, sweeping power, the FCC issued a comprehensive set of cable regulations in 1972, the *Fourth Report and Order on Cable Television Service.*

In 1976 the FCC refined these rules to the extent that all cable systems with more than 3,500 subscribers carrying over-the-air broadcast signals had to develop a minimum 20-channel capacity by 1986, had to make certain channels available for access by third parties, and had to furnish equipment and facilities for the creation and broadcast of this "access" programming. Again Midwest Video challenged the commission's ruling. This time the cable company won when the Supreme Court in April 1979 struck down the FCC order, saying that the commission was going beyond its authority. Justice Byron White, writing for the six-person majority, said that these rules were not reasonably ancillary to the effective performance of the commission's responsibility to regulate over-the-air television. White said the access rules transferred control of cable television from the cable operator to the public seeking to use the medium. "Effectively," White wrote, "the commission has regulated cable systems . . . to common carrier status," something which Congress has always rejected for broadcasting in the past (*FCC* v. *Midwest Video Corp.,* 1979). Earlier, the Eighth Circuit Court of Appeals had been even more critical of the commission when it struck down the cable access rules in 1978. The court said the FCC had no jurisdiction to promulgate such rules (*Midwest Video Corp.* v. *FCC,* 1978):

> Jurisdiction is not acquired through visions of Valhalla. An agency can neither create nor lawfully expand its jurisdiction by merely deciding what it thinks the future should be like, finding a private industry that can be restructured to make that future at least possible, and then forcing that restructuring in the mere hope that if it's there it will be used.

But neither the Supreme Court nor the court of appeals said in their decisions that local governments which franchise cable television systems cannot make these access rules a part of the franchising agreement, and many observers believe that this will occur at local levels. Many viewed the *Midwest II* ruling as the beginning of the end of comprehensive FCC control over cable television. The agency itself gave credence to this notion in July 1980 when it announced that it was eliminating two major regulations that limited the programs that cable television could offer its viewers. By a narrow vote the commission said that it would now allow cable operations to import as many distant television signals into their area as they chose to import. Distant signals are broadcast signals coming from more than thirty-five miles away from a cable system in a large market, or more than fifty-five miles away from a cable system in a smaller market. In the past, the FCC sharply limited the number of such signals which might be imported, to protect the local over-the-air broadcasters from too much competition. In addition, the agency announced in July 1980 that it was abandoning rules that stopped cable systems from televising programs carried by stations outside the area if the same programs were carried by local stations. Cable operators will now be able to show, for example, *Star Trek*, when it is carried on a station outside the area even though the same show is being broadcast by a local station. Previously the cable operator could have been forced to black out that portion of his programming. (see *Cable TV Syndicated Program,* 71 FCC 2d 951, 1979, and *Inquiry into the Economic Relationship Between TV Broadcasting and Cable Television,* 71 FCC 632, 1979).

The National Association of Broadcasters, which strongly supports the deregulation of broadcast communications, challenged this deregulation of cable television. But the Second United States Court of Appeals supported the commission's decision, saying the policy represented a "rational weighing of competing policies" (*Malrite TV* v. *FCC,* 1981).

In relaxing its rules on cable television the FCC has worked to strengthen local regulation of cable systems. Cable systems are not licensed by the federal government, but because they are monopolies (a neighborhood or community is served by a single cable system), they must be franchised by local governments. In the late 1970s the FCC issued recommendations to local governments to guide them in issuing cable franchises. The recommendations include the following four items:

1. There should be a full public proceeding before a franchise is awarded.
2. Neither the initial franchise period nor the renewal period should exceed fifteen years.
3. The franchise should specify that the cable operator and franchiser have adopted local procedures for investigating and resolving complaints.
4. Complaint procedures should be spelled out in the franchise agreement, and the cable operator should identify a local person to handle complaints and specify how complaints can be reported and resolved.

Local governments which seek to regulate cable normally adopt a cable television ordinance. These ordinances outline such items as length of the franchise, channel capacity, required reservation of some channels for public or educational use, user fees, and guidelines for cable service coverage. Cable service coverage refers to requirements that the cable operator must wire all areas in a community which have at least a specified density of homes (perhaps fifty) per street mile.

By 1982 cable regulation had become primarily the domain of local governments, but some members of Congress wanted the FCC to reassert its role in cable regulation. Several bills were introduced in an effort to establish national cable policy. A bill introduced by Senators Barry Goldwater and Robert Kasten was approved by the Senate in mid-1983. This measure, if it becomes law, will transfer much of the regulatory authority over cable from municipal governments back to the FCC. If adopted, the law would accomplish the following:

1. Give the FCC clear jurisdiction over cable television.
2. Prohibit localities from charging a franchising fee of more than 5 percent of a system's gross revenues.
3. Require localities to renew an operator's franchise unless the operator has violated an existing agreement, been convicted of a felony, or made "unreasonable" renewal demands.
4. Forbid localities to buy back a cable system from the franchise owner unless the operator has seriously violated the original agreement.
5. Allow system operators to increase rates annually by five percent or by the regional consumer price index, whichever is greater.
6. Prohibit rate regulation of basic cable service in areas served by even the weakest signals of four over-the-air television stations.
7. Permit cable operators and cities to renegotiate existing operating agreements.
8. Require cable systems with more than twenty channels to set aside 10 percent of those channels for use by the public, the government, or the schools, and 10 percent of those channels for other persons who wish to put out programs on the system.

Many observers believe Congress will adopt this legislation sometime during 1984.

Large cable companies which serve many communities find such planned congressional legislation welcome, since it would provide some nationwide consistency to the current patchwork-quilt approach of state and local regulations. Other persons believe that local regulation is best because a community can regulate cable in such a way as to best serve the particular interests of that community.

Other Regulation

In 1982 the FCC gave approval to the development of what is called low-power television (LPTV). LPTV stations broadcast no more than ten miles in one direction, and many supporters argue that they can provide community or neighborhood television service that is not provided by very high frequency and ultrahigh frequency stations with much stronger signals. In granting approval for the development of LPTV the FCC announced its tentative regulatory scheme for the new television stations.

There will be no limits on ownership. Persons who have other broadcast properties can own a LPTV station, and one person or company can own many LPTV stations. Rules such as the Fairness Doctrine and section 315 will be applied in a limited fashion to provide as much freedom as possible for the station owners.

The FCC is currently working toward the development of a policy on direct-broadcast satellites (DBS). With DBS, programs are beamed from transmitters on earth to a geosynchronous satellite overhead and then back to receiving stations in homes or offices. This kind of transmission system will be regulated by the FCC, but the scope of such regulation is not yet clear.

The Federal Communications Act does have sections which permit government to regulate such satellite broadcasts. It is one of these provisions, Section 605 of the act, which makes it possible for pay television programmers to block the interception of their satellite-transmitted signals by persons who have not paid for them. A federal court has ruled that when a subscription television service like Home Box Office or Showtime transmits programs via satellite to cable or multipoint distribution services for use by paying subscribers it is not broadcasting for the use of the general public. The unauthorized interception of such communications is a violation of federal law (*National Subscription Television* v. *S & H TV*, 1981). As this chapter was being prepared, many of the subscription services were undertaking vigorous prosecution of persons who were pirating these transmissions. Some services also announced plans to scramble these signals before transmission to block unauthorized interception.

Regulation of these exotic new technologies is just beginning. As time goes by there will doubtless be extensive new rules to govern the operation of these media systems.

Summary

The federal government has already asserted regulatory authority over the new electronic communication technology which is beginning to develop. Cable television has been regulated for nearly twenty years. The FCC at first eschewed control of the cable television industry, but gradually changed its mind and promulgated more and more rules. In 1978 the Supreme Court voided a set of FCC cable rules, and from that point on the agency sought to transfer regulatory power away from the federal government to local governments. By 1982 cable television was largely regulated by municipal and state governments which adopted licensing ordinances that spelled out specific franchise policies. Legislation before Congress, however, seeks to return some control of cable television to the FCC.

The FCC is also developing policies in the early eighties for the regulation of low-power television stations and direct-broadcast satellites. Changes in technology, however, make attempts at regulation much like shooting at a rapidly moving target.

BIBLIOGRAPHY

Here is a list of some of the sources that have been helpful in the preparation of chapter 11.

Books

Cowan, Geoffrey. *See No Evil.* New York: Simon & Schuster, 1979.
The First Amendment and Broadcasting: Press Freedoms and Broadcast Journalism. Transcript of the 1978 Edward R. Murrow Symposium. Washington State University, April 23–25, 1978.
Geller, Henry. *The Fairness Doctrine in Broadcasting.* Santa Monica: Rand Corp., 1973.
Ginsberg, Douglas. *Regulation of Broadcasting: Law and Policy Towards Radio, Television and Cable Communications.* St. Paul: West Publishing Co., 1979.
Media and the First Amendment in a Free Society. Amherst: University of Massachusetts Press, 1973.
Pember, Don R. *Mass Media in America.* 4th ed. Chicago: Science Research Associates, 1983.
Robinson, Glen O., and Gelhorn, Ernest. *The Administrative Process.* St. Paul: West Publishing Co., 1974.

Articles

Botein, Michael, "Access to Cable Television." 57 *Cornell Law Review* 419, 1972.
"CATV Regulation: A Jumble of Jurisdictions." 45 *New York University Law Review* 816, 1970.
Chamberlin, Bill F. "The FCC and the First Principle of the Fairness Doctrine: A History of Neglect and Distortion." 31 *Federal Communications Law Journal* 361, 1979.
Houser, Thomas J. "The Fairness Doctrine: An Historical Perspective." 47 *Notre Dame Lawyer* 550, 1972.
Johnson, Timothy P. "Regulating CATV: Local Government and the Franchising Process," 19 *South Dakota Law Review* 143, 1974.
Marks, Richard D. "Broadcasting and Censorship: First Amendment Theory After *Red Lion*." 38 *George Washington Law Review* 974, 1970.
Robinson, Glen O. "The FCC and the First Amendment: Observations on 40 Years of Radio and Television Regulation." 52 *Minnesota Law Review* 67, 1967.
Simon, Jules F. "The Collapse of Consensus: Effects of the Deregulation of Cable Television." 81 *Columbia Law Review* 612, 1981.

Cases and Reports

Adrian Weiss, 58 FCC2d 342 (1976).
American Security Council Foundation v. *FCC,* 607 F.2d 438 (1979).
in re *Aspen Institute and CBS, Inc.,* 55 FCC2d 697 (1975).
Brandywine-Main Line Radio, Inc. v. *FCC,* 24 FCC2d 2218 (1970); 473 F.2d 16 (1972).
in re *Business Executives Movement* v. *FCC,* 450 F.2d 642 (1971).
Cable TV Syndicated Programs, 71 FCC2d 951 (1979).
Carroll Broadcasting Co. v. *FCC,* 258 F.2d 440 (1958).

in re *Carter Mountain Transmission Corp.*, 32 FCC 459 (1962); affd. 321 F.2d 359 (1963); 375 U.S. 951 (1963).

CBS v. *Democratic National Committee*, 412 U.S. 94 (1973).

CBS v. *FCC*, 101 S.Ct. 2813 (1981).

Central Florida Enterprises, Inc. v. *FCC*, 598 F.2d 37 (1978).

Chisholm v. *FCC*, 538 F.2d 349 (1976).

Citizens Committee to Preserve the Voice of the Arts in Atlanta v. *FCC*, 436 F.2d 263 (1970).

Citizens' Committee to Save WEFM v. *FCC*, 506 F.2d 246 (1974).

Citizens Communication Center v. *FCC*, 447 F.2d 2101 (1971).

Citizens Communication Center v. *FCC*, 463 F.2d 822 (1972).

Commission en Banc Programming Inquiry, 20 P & F Rad. Regs. 1901 (1960).

in re *Community Broadcasting Service, Inc., WWBZ*, 20 FCC 168 (1955).

Cosmopolitan Broadcasting Corp., 59 FCC2d 558 (1976).

Diocesan Union of Holy Name Societies of Rockville Centre and Long Island Coalition for Life, 41 FCC2d 497 (1973).

In the Matter of Editorializing by Broadcast Licensees, 13 FCC 1246 (1949).

The Fairness Report, 39 Fed.Regs. 26372 (1974).

Farmers Educational and Cooperative Union of American v. *WDAY*, 360 U.S. 525 (1959).

FCC v. *American Broadcasting Co.* et al., 347 U.S. 284 (1954).

FCC v. *Midwest Video Corp.*, 99 S.Ct. 1435 (1979).

FCC v. *Pacifica Foundation*, 98 S.Ct. 3026 (1978).

FCC v. *WNCN Listeners Guild*, 101 S.Ct. 1266 (1981).

First Report and Order on Microwave Served CATV, 38 FCC 683 (1965).

Fourth Report and Order on Cable Television Service, 37 Fed.Regs. 3251 (1972).

FRC v. *Nelson Brothers*, 289 U.S. 266 (1933).

in re *Great Lakes Broadcasting* v. *FRC*, 3 FRC Ann. Rept. 32 (1929); 37 F.2d 993 (1930).

Home Box Office v. *Wilkinson*, 531 F. Supp.987 (1982).

Hoover v. *Intercity Radio Co., Inc.*, 286 F. 1003 (1923).

Illinois Citizens Committee for Broadcasting v. *FCC*, 515 F.2d 397 (1975).

Inquiry into the Economic Relationship Between Broadcasting and Cable Television, 71 FCC2d 632 (1979).

Kennedy for President Committee v. *FCC*, 636 F.2d 417 (1980).

Kennedy for President Committee v. *FCC*, 636 F.2d 432 (1980).

KFKB Broadcasting Association v. *FRC*, 47 F.2d 670 (1931).

Kuczo v. *Western Connecticut Broadcasting*, 424 F. Supp. 1324 (1977).

League of Women Voters v. *FCC*, 547 F. Supp. 379 (1982).

Malrite TV v. *FCC*, 652 F.2d 1140 (1981).

in re *Mayflower Broadcasting Corp., WAAB*, 8 FCC 333 (1941).

May Seed and Nursery Co., 2 FCC 559 (1936).

Miami Herald v. *Tornillo*, 94 S.Ct. 2831 (1974).

Midwest Video Corp. v. *FCC*, 571 F.2d 1025 (1978).

Mt. Mansfield Television v. *FCC*, 442 F.2d 470 (1971).

National Citizens Committee for Broadcasting v. *FCC*, 567 F.2d 1095 (1977).

National Committee for Responsive Philanthropy v. *FCC*, 652 F.2d 589 (1981).

National Subscription Television v. *S & H TV*, 644 F.2d 820 (1981).

NBC v. *FCC*, 516 F.2d 1101 (1974).

Office of Communication, United Church of Christ v. *FCC*, 359 F.2d 994 (1966).

in re *Palmetto Broadcasting Co.*, 33 FCC 250 (1962).

Patsy Mink, 59 FCC2d 984 (1976).

Policy Statement on Comparative Broadcast Hearings, 1 FCC2d 393 (1965).

Policy Statement on Comparative Hearings Involving Regular Renewal Applications, 22 FCC2d 424 (1970).

Primer on Ascertainment of Community Needs, 27 FCC2d 650 (1971).

Primer on Ascertainment of Community Problems by Broadcast Applicants, 27 FCC2d 650 (1973); rev. 53 FCC2d 3 (1975).

Public Media Center v. FCC, 587 F.2d 1322 (1978).

Public Service Responsibility of Broadcast Licensees, (1946).

Radio and Television News Directors' Association v. U.S., 400 F.2d 1002 (1968).

Red Lion Broadcasting Co. v. FCC, 381 F.2d 908 (1967); affd. 395 U.S. 367 (1969).

RKO v. FCC, 670 F.2d 215 (1981).

Second Annual Report of the Federal Radio Commission (1928).

Second Report and Order on Microwave Served CATV, 2 FCC2d 725 (1966).

Sonderling Broadcasting Corp., 27 P & F Rad. Regs. 285 (1973).

Trinity Methodist Church, South v. FRC, 62 F.2d 650 (1932).

in re *United Broadcasting Co.*, 10 FCC 515 (1945).

U.S. v. Midwest Video Corp., 406 U.S. 649 (1972).

U.S. v. Southwestern Cable Co., 392 U.S. 157 (1968).

U.S. v. Zenith Radio Corp., 12 F.2d 616 (1926); 35 Op. Attys. Gen. 126 (1926).

WCBS-TV, 8 FCC2d 381 (1967); affd. Applicability of the Fairness Doctrine to Cigarette Advertising, 9 FCC2d 921 (1967); affd. *Banzhaf v. FCC*, 405 F.2d 1164 (1969).

in re *Wilderness Society and Friends of the Earth*, 30 FCC2d 643 (1971); revd. *Friends of the Earth v. FCC*, 449 F.2d 1164 (1971).

Writers Guild v. ABC, 609 F.2d 355 (1979).

Writers Guild v. FCC, 423 F. Supp. 1064 (1976).

in re *WUHY-FM, Eastern Educational Radio*, 24 FCC2d 408 (1970).

Yale Broadcasting Co. v. FCC, 478 F.2d 594 (1973).

Young People's Association for the Propagation of the Gospel, 6 FCC 178 (1938).

12 REGULATION OF THE MEDIA AS A BUSINESS

The primary purpose of this book is to focus upon the censorship and regulation of what is printed in the press or broadcast over radio and television—the content of mass media communication. Yet mass media face other regulation as well, regulation based not on content, but on other criteria. In the United States newspapers, broadcasting stations, film companies, and magazines are usually private businesses, and as such these media businesses face the myriad rules and regulations confronting other businesses in this nation. Rules regarding minimum wages, maximum working hours, safety, health, taxation, and many other areas apply to the mass media as well as to automobile manufacturers, furniture companies, and beauty salons.

Two factors stand out regarding these rules. First, they are applied to the media regardless of the content of a press. Magazines that aim to contribute to the essential political debate in this country have to meet the same minimum wage rules as do true romance magazines which appeal to the emotions. The makers of serious films must meet the same safety standards at their studios as do the makers of sleazy sex-oriented films. The point is this: Whereas in some areas the law is applied variably to businesses thought to serve the public interest than to those which do not, no such variable application occurs when the media are looked at as businesses.

Second, while the First Amendment has been at the center of our discussion of press regulation to this point in the book, the guarantees of freedom of expression mean very little when the media are regulated as businesses. The First Amendment might protect a newspaper which erroneously labels a politician a crook or a magazine which publishes the intimate secrets of the life of a public official, but it will not protect the publisher who fails to meet fire code regulations or the broadcaster who refuses to pay legitimate taxes. More than forty years ago the Supreme Court made this abundantly clear when it upheld the constitutionality of the National Labor Relations Act which, at the time, was under a First Amendment challenge launched by the Associated Press (AP). "The business of the Associated Press is not immune from regulation because it is an agency of the press," wrote Justice Owen Roberts for the five-man majority. "The publisher of a newspaper has no special immunity from the application of general laws" (*AP* v. *NLRB,* 1937). Broadcasting station operators and publishers often have to be reminded of this. In 1981 a United States district court in Massachusetts ruled that a newspaper has no First Amendment right to decline to participate in the quarterly financial report program of the Federal Trade Commission (FTC). The court said the FTC only sought financial data and did not intrude upon the exercise of editorial judgment (*U.S.* v. *Nanlo,* 1981). The press must meet all its legal responsibilities as a business regardless of the First Amendment.

GOVERNMENT AND THE MASS COMMUNICATION BUSINESS

No attempt will be made in this chapter to outline all the broad areas of regulation affecting the media as a business. Consideration of such rules more properly resides in a class in business law. But two areas of commercial regulation are considered, since both have implications beyond simple business regulation. The regulation of the ownership and operation of the media through antitrust laws and FCC policies is significant, because it can have an important impact on who can own the press and, in some instances, the content of media communication. Taxation of the press will be noted briefly also, since on at least some occasions taxation has been used as a means to indirectly censor the press. These are the broad subjects to be covered in this short chapter.

| Antitrust Laws and Newspapers | The government's primary weapon against economic concentration and restraint of trade in industry are the antitrust laws. The Sherman Act of 1890 and the Clayton Act of 1914 provide the legal bases for the Department of Justice to bring both criminal and civil suits against businesses which use monopolistic tactics to endanger free competition. The press is not immune from such legal pressure, yet surprisingly it has been an infrequent target of government antitrust action. One author notes that between 1945, when the Supreme Court ruled that the First Amendment did not shield the press from action by the government to stop monopolistic practices, and 1969, only twelve antitrust suits were initiated against the press. In 1976, when seventy-two different newspapers changed hands (most were bought up by newspaper chains), there were no antitrust actions against newspaper interests. Why? Catherine B. Roach offered one opinion in an article in the *Memphis State University Law Review:* |

> Because of the structure of the communications industry—basically a collection of local circulation and advertising markets—anti-trust enforcers have encountered difficult problems of proof as to anticompetitive effects in relevant markets.

In an effort to explain some of the anticompetitive problems the federal government has sought to control in the press, here is a summary of some of the litigation in the past forty years.

| *Restrictive Membership Rules* | As noted previously, it was in 1945 that the Supreme Court first gave approval to the prosecution of antitrust action against members of the press. The occasion was a suit by the government against the Associated Press, the giant news cooperative and wire service. Marshall Field had founded the morning *Chicago Sun* and sought an AP membership for his newspaper. But under AP bylaws the owners of the rival *Chicago Tribune* were given the opportunity to approve or disapprove Field's application for membership. Without this approval, the applicant needed the consent of a majority of all AP members for the membership application to be accepted. These rules effectively kept newspapers which competed with AP members from getting the highly desirable membership and access to the AP wire service. |

The federal government brought an antitrust action against the AP, charging that its membership laws resulted in an illegal monopoly in restraint of trade—a violation of the Sherman Act. Among the AP responses to the suit was the vigorous assertion that the Department of Justice lawsuit against the news cooperative represented a serious infringement upon the constitutionally guaranteed freedom of the press. But the high Court ruled that the Associated Press membership provisions were in fact a violation of the Sherman Act. And Justice Hugo Black, writing for the majority, dismissed the argument that the AP was shielded from such legal action by the First Amendment. "Member publishers of the AP are engaged in business for profit exactly as are other businessmen who sell food, steel, aluminum or anything else people need or want," Black wrote. He said that the inability to buy news from the news agency could have serious effects upon a publication and actually endanger its ability to continue to operate successfully. And then Black penned one of his most memorable passages regarding freedom of the press (*AP* v. *U.S.*, 1945):

> The [First] Amendment rests on the assumption that the widest possible dissemination of information from diverse and antagonistic sources is essential to the welfare of the public, that a free press is a condition of a free society. Surely a command that the government itself shall not impede the free flow of ideas does not afford non-governmental combinations a refuge if they impose restraints upon that constitutionally guaranteed freedom. Freedom to publish means freedom for all and not for some. Freedom to publish is guaranteed by the Constitution, but freedom to keep others from publishing is not.

The First Amendment, then, provides no safe house for the business person who violates laws or rules designed to foster free competition. And as we have noted earlier, this generalization rings as true with regard to other commercial regulations as it does with antitrust laws.

Local Monopolies

Six years after the *AP* case the Supreme Court heard arguments in another antitrust action involving the press. This case focused upon what was essentially a monopoly newspaper business in a medium-sized town. The newspaper refused to accept advertising from businesses which also used other community advertising media.

The *Lorain* (Ohio) *Journal* and the *Times Herald* were owned by the same publisher. The combined daily circulation of the two papers reached nearly 100 percent of the families in the community. The only print competition came from the weekly *Sunday News*. In 1948 a radio station began operation in the community. Shortly thereafter the publisher of the two daily papers announced that the newspapers would no longer accept advertising from businesses and industries in the community which also broadcast advertisements over the radio station. The Department of Justice brought an antitrust action against the Lorain Journal Company, charging that the publishing firm was attempting to monopolize interstate commerce and attempting to force advertisers to boycott the radio station. Justice Harold Burton, writing for a unanimous Supreme Court, ruled that the newspaper's policy violated the Sherman Act, "A single newspaper, already enjoying a substantial monopoly in its area, violates the 'attempt to monopolize' clause [of the Sherman Act] . . . when it uses its monopoly to destroy threatened competition." A publisher has the right to refuse to publish any advertisement, but he cannot use this right as "a purposeful means of monopolizing interstate commerce." The First Amendment afforded the paper no special protection: "The injunction applies to a publisher what the law applies to others," Burton wrote (*Lorain Journal Co.* v. *U.S.*, 1951).

Two years later the Supreme Court was forced to scrutinize a tie-in or combination advertising rate scheme used by a New Orleans publisher. The Times-Picayune Company published both the morning *Times-Picayune* and the evening *States*. There was also a competing afternoon paper published in the city, the *Item*. Advertisers who wanted to purchase an advertisement in either the *Times-Picayune* or the *States* had to purchase an advertisement in both. The government brought a civil action against the Times-Picayune Company, charging that its forced combination advertising policy was an unreasonable restraint of trade.

The Supreme Court ruled in a five-to-four decision that the combination advertising rate was not a violation of the law. Justice Tom Clark admitted in his opinion for the majority that such an advertising scheme could hurt competition. Clark cited statistics which showed that of the 598 daily papers that had begun publication between 1929 and 1950, more than 225 of them survived at the end of that period. Of these 598, 46 dailies had encountered combination advertising rate schemes like the one in New Orleans. Of those 46 papers, only 5 survived in 1950.

According to the Supreme Court, however, such an advertising-rate combination or "tying" arrangement was illegal only if a business with a dominant position in the market coerced its customers into buying an unwanted inferior product along with the desired product. The government argued that the *Times-Picayune* was the dominant, desired product and the afternoon *States* was the unwanted, inferior product which advertisers were forced to buy. The crucial questions in the case, according to Clark, were whether the *Times-Picayune* held a dominant market position, and whether the *States* was really an inferior product. The five-man majority answered both questions negatively. The *Times-Picayune* had the greatest circulation, published the most pages, and had the highest amount of advertising, but it was not dominant in the relevant market—the advertising market. The morning paper carried about 40 percent of the classified and display advertising published by the three papers. If all papers had an equal share, the *Times-Picayune* would have still had about 33 percent. The circulation for the *Times-Picayune* was 190,000; for the *States*, 105,000; and for the *Item*, 115,000. The third paper, the *Item*, was flourishing, Clark wrote. He added, "The record in this case thus does not disclose evidence from which demonstrably deleterious effects on competition may be inferred." A majority of the high Court rejected the argument that the *Times-Picayune* was the desired product and the *States* was the inferior product. The products were identical, Clark added (*Times-Picayune* v. *U.S.*, 1953):

> Here . . . two newspapers under single ownership at the same place, time and terms sell indistinguishable products to advertisers; no dominant "tying" product exists . . . no leverage in one market excludes sellers in the second, because for present purposes the products are identical and the market the same.

Five years after the ruling, the Times-Picayune Company purchased the *Item* and created the *State-Item*, making it the only afternoon paper in the city.

Despite the loss in the *Times-Picayune* case, the Department of Justice pushed on with a similar antitrust action in Kansas City against a rate-combination or tie-in advertising policy. This time the government was successful in proving the market dominance of the Kansas City Star Company, something it could not prove with regard to the Times-Picayune Company.

The defendant owned the morning *Kansas City Times* and the afternoon *Kansas City Star*. The two papers were circulated to 96 percent of the homes in the area. In addition, the Kansas City Star Company published the *Sunday Star* and owned WDAF radio and WDAF-TV stations. Through all its holdings, the company received 94 percent of all advertising revenue spent in the area. The only competition in the print media field were weekly and suburban papers.

In order to subscribe to any one of the three Star Company–owned newspapers, a resident had to subscribe to all three: both dailies and the Sunday edition. Advertisers were also required to run advertising in all three newspapers. The Star Company used this monopoly power ruthlessly. Examples documented by the government included threats by the newspaper to stop the news coverage of a professional baseball player who bought space in a competing paper to advertise his florist shop. Also, it was reported that advertisers who failed to buy space in the defendant's newspapers received less favorable treatment in getting advertising on WDAF-AM and WDAF-TV. The United States Eighth Circuit Court of Appeals ruled that such circulation and advertising tie-ins violated the Sherman Act in light of the market dominance by the Star Company. With regard to the First Amendment the court said, "To use the freedom of the press guaranteed by the First Amendment to destroy competition would defeat its own ends, for freedom to print news and express opinions as one chooses is not tantamount to having freedom to monopolize" (*U.S.* v. *Kansas City Star,* 1957).

The conviction in this criminal antitrust action was just the beginning for the Star Company. A subsequent civil suit was settled by the firm through a consent order (this legal device is described on pages 474–75), under which the Star Company agreed to sell its broadcasting properties and to stop the tie-in policies with regard to advertising and circulation. Additional civil suits were generated by media competitors in the Kansas City area, and it is estimated that in the end the Star Company paid out several hundred thousand dollars in damages.

Chain Ownership

Ten years elapsed before a federal court again ruled in an important media antitrust action. And for the first time the government action against the press was initiated because of something other than newspaper policy regarding advertisers or subscribers. In this case the target of the federal suit had merely purchased a nearby newspaper.

Serious concern was generated by many thoughtful students of the media during the sixties with regard to the shrinking number of independently owned newspapers in the United States. Similarly, competition between papers in major cities shrunk rapidly to the point where communities with competing daily newspapers were considered unusual. The statistics tell the story graphically. In 1923 daily newspapers were published in nearly 1,300 American cities. Of that total, 502 cities had two or more competing daily papers. Forty years later in 1963 daily newspapers were published in 1,476 cities, but only 51 communities had competing papers. (By 1982 there were dailies in 1,536 cities, but in only 27 was there competition between daily newspapers.) Many feared the demise of the independent newspaper in the United States. The dearth of competition between papers in communities augured a less vital press and fewer outlets for the publication of ideas and protests. The first real government response to these fears came in southern California when the Department of Justice brought a civil antitrust action against the Times-Mirror Corporation for purchasing a large newspaper company in an adjoining county.

Since 1948 the morning *Los Angeles Times* had had the largest circulation in California. It was an important force in southern California. In the mid-1960s the firm bought the Sun Company which published the morning *Sun,* the afternoon *Telegram,* and the *Sunday Sun-Telegram*, in San Bernardino County, which adjoins Los Angeles County on the east. Until its purchase by the Times-Mirror Corporation, the Sun Company had been the largest independent publisher in southern California. The government argued that the purchase of these newspapers by the Times-Mirror Corporation resulted in a restraint of interstate commerce, in violation of the Sherman Act, and had the impact of lessening competition in the area, which is a violation of the Clayton Act.

In ruling in favor of the government, Judge Warren Ferguson noted that the purchase of the Sun Company newspapers by Times-Mirror was only the latest of a series of actions which had reduced the number of independently owned California newspapers from 59 percent in 1952 to 24 percent in 1966. "The acquisition of the *Sun* by the *Times* was particularly anticompetitive," Judge Ferguson wrote, "because it eliminated one of the few independent papers that had been able to operate successfully in the morning and Sunday fields." Since the purchase of the Sun Company newspapers by the Times-Mirror Corporation, Ferguson noted, two daily newspapers had been closed and two more newspaper mergers in San Bernardino County had occurred. The federal district judge ruled that the acquisition of the Sun Company newspapers by the Times-Mirror Corporation "has raised a barrier to entry of newspapers in the San Bernardino County market that is almost impossible to overcome." Ferguson said that the market for new papers was effectively closed, and "no publisher will risk the expense of unilaterally starting a new daily newspaper there." The judge pointed to the fact that even the prestigious

New York Times failed to break into the market with a West Coast edition of its successful newspaper. Divestiture was ordered by the court, and the Supreme Court affirmed this ruling one year later (*U.S.* v. *Times-Mirror Corporation,* 1968).

Following divestiture the Sun Company newspapers were purchased by the Gannett newspaper chain, the largest chain in the nation. Many persons questioned whether the people in San Bernardino County gained or lost as a result of the government lawsuit and the subsequent purchase of the paper by Gannett. Gannett ownership of the *Sun* and the *Telegram* did create a "second owner" in the community, but was the owner a better owner or as good an owner? Both the Times-Mirror Corporation and Gannett are absentee owners not living in the community in which the newspapers are published. But the Times-Mirror Corporation resided just over the county line and certainly was familiar with the problems and people in the area. Gannett has corporate offices in New York State, completely across the nation. The *Los Angeles Times* is one of the most prestigious newspapers in the United States. It remains speculative whether Gannett has fused this quality into the Sun Company newspapers. The opportunity did exist. However, few Gannett newspapers have risen above a mediocre or adequate level. Chances of producing a superior paper for the people of San Bernardino County seem significantly lower with the Gannett ownership. Finally, while the Times-Mirror Corporation is a large media corporation in its own right, its newspaper holdings remain miniscule compared with the growing Gannett chain which by 1983 owned eighty-five daily newspapers in the nation. What was accomplished, many persons asked, by taking the Sun Company newspapers away from a small newspaper chain and giving it to a large one? The answers to these questions reflect directly on government antitrust policy which appears to focus on the competition among economic units—advertisers and competing newspapers—rather than on the impact upon the reading public.

Joint-Operating Agreements

A year later the justice department's next major newspaper antitrust suit reached the Supreme Court. In this action the Department of Justice sought to break up the **joint-operating agreement** between the Citizen Publishing Company and the Star Publishing Company in Tucson, Arizona. The joint-operating arrangement had been in effect for nearly thirty years in Tucson, and similar agreements existed between newspapers in more than twenty other American cities. The arrangement was simple. Two independent newspapers merged their advertising, printing, and circulation operations to form a third company. The news departments of the two papers remained separate and independent. The third company, Tucson Newspapers Incorporated, handled all advertising and circulation and printing for the evening *Citizen* and the morning and Sunday *Star*. Profits were pooled and shared.

The joint-operating agreement had two clear impacts in the community. First, it provided lower costs for both papers and made it possible for two newspapers to be published in situations where one might only survive in pure head-to-head competition. At the same point, however, the lowered costs for the two newspapers made it difficult if not impossible for a third newspaper to compete. The government attacked several provisions of the arrangement as being violations of the Sherman Act. Specifically the lawyers for the Department of Justice argued that the setting of advertising and subscription prices by Tucson Newspapers was price fixing. They also objected to profit pooling and to the fact that both the Star Publishing Company and the Citizen Publishing Company agreed not to engage in other media business in the area.

After considerable time in the lower courts, the Supreme Court in 1969 declared the arrangement to be a violation of the law (*U.S.* v. *Citizen Publishing Company,* 1969). Justice Douglas wrote that through a joint-operating agreement the two publishers had gained market control over the newspapers in Tucson. The Court did allow the *Star* and the *Citizen* to share some of the same facilities, but struck down policies on profit pooling, establishment of joint advertising and subscription rates, and other similar agreements.

In the months immediately following the ruling in the *Citizen Publishing Company* case, scores of bills were introduced in Congress to salvage the joint-operating agreement. If such policies were against the law, as the Supreme Court ruled, then the law would have to be changed, the publishers argued. And it was. In 1970, after an intensive lobbying effort by the publishing industry, the Congress adopted the Newspaper Preservation Act. Taking a clue from Justice Douglas's opinion in the *Citizen Publishing Company* case, Congress enacted legislation which permitted newspapers to continue to function under joint-operating agreement so long as at the time at which the agreement is made one of the two papers is in "probable danger of failing." Papers seeking to enter into joint-operating agreements in the future have to first gain permission from the Attorney General if they expect to be exempted from the antitrust rules provided for by the law. The measure had the impact of legalizing the twenty-two agreements in effect in 1970, including the one which the Supreme Court had declared illegal in Tucson. The merits of the law have been hotly debated along lines similar to the debate over the joint-operating agreements themselves. While legalizing these agreements has ensured that in twenty-two cities at least newspaper news and editorial competition will survive, the law at the same time makes it practically impossible for other publishers to compete with the two monopoly papers which boast lower operating costs.

After several years of trying to compete with the *San Francisco Examiner* and the *Chronicle,* which have operated under a joint agreement since 1965, Bay Area publisher Bruce Brugman went to court in July 1971 and charged that the Newspaper Preservation Act violated his freedom of the press by encouraging journalistic monopoly. Brugman, who published the monthly *Bay Guardian,* told the court that his small paper had difficulty getting advertisers because of the lower joint advertising rates set by the two newspapers. Many advertisers could not afford to or chose not to advertise beyond the two large San Francisco dailies. Federal district judge Oliver Carter showed little sympathy for Brugman's arguments, however, and in 1972 ruled that the congressional measure did not authorize a monopoly (*Bay Guardian Publishing Company* v. *Chronicle Publishing Company,* 1972). Carter wrote:

> Here the Act was designed to preserve independent editorial voices. Regardless of the economic or social wisdom of such a course, it does not violate the freedom of the press. Rather, it is merely a selective repeal of the antitrust laws. It merely looses the same shady market forces which existed before the passage of the Sherman, Clayton and other antitrust laws. Such a repeal, even when applicable only to the newspaper industry, does not violate the First Amendment.

The law regarding joint-operating agreements has changed little in the past ten years, although some litigation has ensued. In 1979 the E. W. Scripps Company sought Department of Justice approval of a joint-operating agreement between its *Cincinnati Post* and Gannett's *Cincinnati Enquirer.* For the first time a public hearing was held on the question. While the government ultimately agreed that the Scripps's publication met the requirements of a failing newspaper, attorneys for the Department of Justice raised the interesting question of whether a newspaper could truly be termed "failing" when the parent company (Scripps) might be benefitting financially from the tax write-offs accorded by the *Post*'s losses. The matter was not pressed at that time by the government, and the application for the joint-operating agreement was approved.

A hearing was also held before the Department of Justice gave its approval to a joint-operating agreement between the *Seattle Times* and the *Seattle Post-Intelligencer.* Persons protesting the agreement argued that the Hearst Corporation, owner of the *Post-Intelligencer,* was not in danger of failing. They argued that Hearst had taken money out of the newspaper in order to put it in the position of a failing newspaper. They also argued that the corporation had made no effort to try to sell the newspaper so that another owner might keep it independent; in fact Hearst had rejected all offers to purchase the paper. The hearing judge rejected all contentions and approved the joint-operating plan. Attorney William French Smith also approved of the pact, despite arguments from the antitrust division of the Department of Justice that the *Post-Intelligencer* was not legally a "failing newspaper." A court challenge to Attorney General Smith's approval of the agreement was mounted, and in late August 1982 a United States District Court ruled that Smith had acted improperly when he approved the joint-operating proposal. Judge Barbara Rothstein rejected plaintiff's contentions that the Newspaper Preservation Act was a violation of the First Amendment. But she did agree that before the *Post-Intelligencer* could qualify as a failing newspaper there must be a showing by those persons seeking the approval of the agreement that no other viable alternatives exist for maintaining the newspaper's independent editorial voice. Hearst did not have an obligation under the law to try to seek out buyers for the paper. But in this case there was evidence that buyers were interested in the newspaper. Hearst must demonstrate that because of existing economic conditions and other factors a new owner of the newspaper could not make the *Post-Intelligencer* succeed (*Committee* v. *Smith,* 1982). But less than one year later the Ninth U.S. Court of Appeals reversed the district court ruling and held that the Hearst Corporation had met its burden of showing that the alleged alternative owners did not offer a solution to the financial difficulties experienced by the *Post-Intelligencer.* Six people did inquire into the possibility of buying the newspaper, but these were not offers. And these inquiries did not show that the *Post-Intelligencer* could in all probability be sold to a buyer who would continue its operation as an independent newspaper. The critical question in the case, the court of appeals opinion noted, was whether the newspaper was suffering losses that more than likely could not be reversed. There was no evidence that any new owner might be successful in reversing the *Post-Intelligencer's* financial difficulties. In fact, the court said, there was sufficient evidence in the record supporting a negative answer (*Committee for an Independent P–I* v. *Hearst,* 1983).

What most people regard to be the most serious anticompetitive newspaper phenomenon of the 1980s is the rapid growth of newspaper chains and the concurrent demise of the independent newspapers. But the Department of Justice seems unwilling to move against such acquisitions. The antitrust division of the department did investigate the merger of the Gannett newspaper chain with Combined Communications, a large broadcasting chain which also owned two newspapers. But following the investigation *Editor and Publisher* quoted the Assistant Attorney General for Antitrust, John H. Shenefield, as saying:

> The antitrust laws do not flatly prohibit media conglomerates anymore than they prohibit other kinds of conglomerates. Under present law, some measurable impact on competition in some market must be proven before a merger or acquisition will be held to violate the antitrust laws. Indeed, the courts have been generally reluctant to condemn conglomerate mergers where such an impact has not been shown, regardless of the social or other objections that have been asserted.

In an effort to enhance the government's ability to attack the growth of the giant conglomerates, Senator Edward Kennedy introduced a bill in 1979 which, if enacted, would have prohibited companies with more than $2.5 billion in annual sales or more than $2 billion in assets from merging. In addition, under the Kennedy proposal companies with $350 million in annual sales or $200 million in assets could merge only if they could convince the government that such a merger would enhance competition or produce efficiencies of benefit to consumers. The Kennedy proposal would have had little impact upon media conglomerates, as most are not as large as the companies the Kennedy proposal sought to regulate. The Kennedy plan has not yet been adopted by the Congress.

Broadcasting Monopolies

The Department of Justice has carried the largest burden in attempting to control the competitive practices of the newspaper industry. But in broadcasting the Federal Communications Commission (FCC) has taken the lead in regulating the ownership of radio and television stations, and only recently has the Department of Justice moved against members of the industry.

FCC Controls

The Federal Communications Commission has closely regulated the business practices of broadcasters by means of the license renewal procedures and other commission policies. Congress has passed statutes with regard to some matters such as the rates a broadcaster may charge a candidate for public office. The FCC itself has issued scores of rules regarding business and advertising practices. It has also been the FCC which has attempted to control both the growth of broadcast chains and other ownership practices of the members of the industry.

The commission's first rules on ownership were issued in 1940 when it declared that no single individual or company could own more than three television stations and six frequency modulation (FM) radio stations. Amplitude modulation (AM) radio ownership is not limited. These numbers were revised continually until 1954 when rules were adopted which stand today. A single individual or company cannot own more than seven AM stations, seven FM stations, and seven television stations, but only five of the television stations can be the more desirable variety, very high frequency (VHF) stations.

In 1968 the FCC adopted what is called its "one to a customer rule," which was modified in 1971 and is the rule that exists today. The commission will not permit any broadcasting company to own more than a single VHF television station in a given market or one AM-FM radio combination. The 1971 rule was applied prospectively, that is, the agency did not force the owners of existing very high frequency TV–AM-FM combinations to sell one of their properties. It simply announced it would no longer approve the formation of such combinations in the future. The agency took a more flexible position on the ultrahigh frequency TV–AM-FM combinations, announcing that it would rule upon requests for such combinations on a case-by-case basis in the future.

In 1975 the agency attempted to thwart what it saw as another problem: the ownership of broadcast properties by newspaper companies in the same city. The rules promulgated by the commission were rather simple, but provoked a serious court battle. The commission said that in the future it would bar the ownership of a broadcast license by a newspaper operating in the same city. All but a handful of the existing newspaper-broadcast combinations were allowed to remain intact. However the FCC did seek divestiture in communities in which there was common ownership of the only daily newspaper and the only broadcasting station. Similarly, in communities where there was more than one broadcasting station, the agency sought to break up the common ownership of the only daily newspaper and the only television station. Sixteen such forbidden combinations existed, and the license holders were given five years to divest themselves of either the broadcasting property or the newspaper.

The National Citizens Committee for Broadcasting challenged the FCC rules, arguing that while it supported the prospective cross-ownership ban, the FCC should have forced *all* existing combinations to sell either their newspapers or broadcasting properties. In other words, the public interest groups opposed the grandfather clause in the FCC rules. The United States Court of Appeals (D.C.) agreed and ruled that the FCC must order divestiture of all the jointly owned newspaper-broadcast combinations except in "those cases where the evidence clearly discloses that cross-ownership is in the public interest" (*National Citizens Committee for Broadcasting v. FCC,* 1977). Judge McGowan wrote that "although we do not disturb the commission's prospective rules, we conclude that the divestiture order is inconsistent with its longstanding policy that 'nothing can be more important than insuring that there is a free flow of information from as many divergent sources as possible.' "

The FCC appealed the ruling by the court, and in 1978 the Supreme Court reversed the lower court decision. Justice Thurgood Marshall, writing for the unanimous Court, said the court of appeals was mistaken in ruling that the FCC could have no rational reason for not ordering divestiture of the existing combinations. The agency's arguments that it would disrupt the industry, that it would deny to many meritorious broadcast station owners the opportunity to continue service to the public, and that it would likely result in an increase in the growth of broadcast chains as locally owned broadcast properties were sold under the divestiture orders were substantial, Marshall argued. "We believe that the limited divestiture requirement reflects a rational weighing of competing policies," the justice concluded for the court (*FCC v. National Citizens Committee for Broadcasting,* 1978).

It is important to note that FCC Chairman Mark Fowler has asked the commission to consider abandoning some of these ownership rules including the **seven-seven-seven rule** and the one-to-a-customer rule. It is hard to predict how the other four commission members will respond to the chairman's suggestions. Also, any abandonment of these rules would surely be challenged in court. So for the time being, at least, the ownership of broadcast properties is still closely regulated by the FCC.

Another important action aimed at broadcasters in the 1970s was a Department of Justice antitrust suit against the three major television networks, ABC, CBS, and NBC. The Department of Justice filed the actions in 1972, but the complaints were dismissed without prejudice. In 1974 the justice department refiled the actions, which asserted that the networks had violated the Sherman Act by trying to monopolize the programs shown in prime-time evening hours. The government originally sought a court order that would have accomplished the following:

1. Prohibited the networks from obtaining any interest (other than showing the program for the first time) in any entertainment television program, including feature films, made by others
2. Prohibited the networks from the syndication of such programs
3. Prohibited the networks from offering over a network any such programming produced by the network itself or any other network commercial television network
4. Prohibited the network from offering any other commercial network programs it produced

The thrust of what the government sought was to take the television networks out of the program production business. Three years after the litigation began, NBC surprisingly agreed to sign a consent decree which was considerably more limited than the original order sought by the government. In the decree the network agreed to specific restrictions in bargaining with independent program producers, agreed not to acquire syndication rights or other distribution or profit shares in programs produced by others, agreed not to enter into reciprocal arrangements with either CBS or ABC in the purchase or sale of programming rights, and agreed to limit the broadcast of programs it had produced. Under the terms of the settlement, the network agreed that for the next ten years it would limit the broadcast of programs it produced itself to two-and-one-half hours per week during prime time, eight hours per week during daytime hours, and eleven hours per week during fringe hours. However, this programming limitation would only apply if both CBS and ABC either agreed to similar limitations or similar limitations were forced upon them through court order. CBS and ABC came to similar terms with the justice department.

The justice department also attacked television trade association rules which it believed too monopolistic. A majority of television stations belong to the National Association of Broadcasters. The association promulgated an advertising code, which member stations were expected to follow. Rules included a limit on the number of commercials which could be broadcast each hour, the number of commercial interruptions in a particular program, and the number of different products which could be advertised in a commercial lasting less than one full minute. The latter rule, known as the multiple-product rule, prohibited a sponsor from advertising more than one product in a thirty-second commercial, the unit of time which has become the industry standard. The justice department said the rule had the effect of compelling some advertisers to purchase more commercial time than they need or want, and this prohibition artificially increased the demand for commercial time. Since all three networks and most television stations subscribed to the association code, the justice department said these rules violated the Sherman Act, that they were a restraint of trade.

A United States district court agreed in 1982 (*U.S.* v. *NAB*). The court noted that:

> . . . a relatively small business which is able to promote one successful product in a series of thirty-second commercials is precluded by that standard from using any portion of that thirty seconds to launch a second product, the sale of which will not, or not yet, support a commercial of its own.

The court noted that association member stations were monitored and code violations could result in discipline. The association argued that it was promoting the public interest in preventing over commercialization of television. The court disagreed: "Congress has determined where the public interest lies when antitrust liability is at issue: it lies in fair and free competition" (*U.S.* v. *NAB,* 1982).

When the multiple-product standard was struck down, the association was forced to reexamine all its advertising rules. It apparently determined it was vulnerable to antitrust prosecution on other grounds as well, for it abandoned all enforcement of its advertising code. The association had dropped enforcement of its programming standards after the 1976 ruling which voided the family viewing hour. Consequently the National Association of Broadcasters completely closed its doors on such code enforcements in late 1982.

While these events were taking place in the broadcasting industry, the film industry was also under scrutiny by the government for anticompetitive practices that were first banned more than twenty-five years ago.

Antitrust Laws and the Movies

The movie industry has faced government scrutiny for possible antitrust violations since the late 1930s. A succession of officials within the Department of Justice including Thurman Arnold, Francis Biddle, and Tom Clark attacked the Hollywood studios for a variety of commercial practices deemed to be anticompetitive. Particularly onerous was the fact that in the 1930s and 1940s most of the major studios owned vast chains of theaters. By controlling the film industry from the initial creative stages through to the sale of popcorn during the exhibition of a film, the studios exercised powerful dominance in the media. Independent theaters found it extremely difficult to obtain good motion pictures to exhibit—the studios kept those for their own theaters. And independent filmmakers, of which there were few, found it difficult to compete with the large studios. A film made by a major studio was bound to be shown in a good theater—one owned by the film company—and generally costs at least were made. Independent producers had no guarantee that their films would be exhibited at all, let alone at a "good house."

Independent distributors and theater owners also faced a second problem: the block-booking policies of the major studios. Under **block booking** a distributor or theater owner was forced to "buy" a package of movies to exhibit. Generally this package included the popular and quality films the studio produced, but the package was also laced with a great many poorer films, often the lower grade B pictures which the Hollywood studios produced to keep their vast number of salaried technical employees busy and to develop new creative talent within the studio. Theater owners would often lose a considerable amount of money by exhibiting these second-rate films, but had to take them as part of the package containing the good films that would be profitable to exhibit.

By the end of the 1940s, through a series of protracted antitrust litigations, the Department of Justice had succeeded in forcing the major studios to revise many of their policies. In 1948 the courts declared the block-booking practices to be a violation of the Sherman Act (*U.S.* v. *Paramount Pictures,* 1948). The studio policy of forcing independent theaters to charge minimum admission prices (so the independent owners could not undercut the admission prices at the studios' own theaters) was also declared illegal. Henceforth independent theaters were allowed to competitively bid for the right to show any of the films made by the major studios, and there could be no requirement that a theater had to take a bad picture to get a good one. The following year the studios agreed to sell their chains of theaters, a move which broke the back of some of the weaker studios. By 1950 most of the serious anticompetitive practices the industry had developed in its fifty-year history had ended. But while this was a positive step for those in competition with the major studios, some students of film found that the government action hurt the creative end of the motion picture industry. Charles Higham in his book *Hollywood at Sunset* notes:

> . . . in practical terms the victory of the Department of Justice and the independents over wicked Hollywood had incalculably disastrous effects on the film industry and the very character of film entertainment itself. For confidence in a product, the feeling that it could flow out along guaranteed lines of distribution, was what gave many Hollywood films before 1948 their superb attack and vigor. Also, the block-booking custom, evil though it may have been, ensured that many obscure, personal, and fascinating movies could be made and released, featherbedded by the system and underwritten by more conventional ventures.

Higham concluded that the successful antitrust action was a victory for justice, but a defeat for entertainment.

But the illegal practices by the major studios did not altogether cease after 1950. In 1962 the Department of Justice brought an action against

Loew's, Inc., Screen Gems, and other film distributors for using the block-booking techniques in selling movies to television. In Washington WTOP-TV had complained that in order to get quality films such as *Casablanca, Sergeant York,* and *Treasure of Sierra Madre,* the station had to accept a large number of weak, less popular films. The Supreme Court followed its earlier precedents and declared the practice to be illegal under the Sherman Act (*U.S. v. Loew's, Inc.,* 1962). Even as late as 1978 the practice of block booking was found to exist in the film industry. Twentieth Century-Fox pleaded no contest to the charge of forcing theaters to exhibit *The Other Side of Midnight* in order to get the opportunity to book the studio's enormously popular *Star Wars.* The studio was fined $25,000 and assessed court costs of nearly $20,000.

The configuration of the film industry in the 1980s makes such illegal practices almost unnecessary, as the business is dominated by seven major studios which control the distribution of more than 80 percent of the films exhibited in the United States. The 1978 Task Force on the Motion Picture Industry reported that "major producers/distributors are effectively limiting competition by maintaining tight control over the distribution of films, both by their failure to produce more films and by their failure to distribute more films produced by others." As of today, this practice has not been investigated and probably is legal under our current interpretation of antitrust laws. The task force noted that there was no evidence of criminal intent on the part of the film companies, but they have nevertheless agreed to "tacitly limit production among themselves and . . . create sufficient barriers to entry to effectively squash new competition." Independent Hollywood producers are attempting themselves to beat this system by forming their own distribution systems, but it is a difficult and expensive task. Time will tell whether such schemes loosen the rein the major studios have over competition.

If the First Amendment has failed as a defense against antitrust action by the government, it has fared somewhat better as a means for blocking government taxes aimed at harrassing or hurting the press. And that is the next subject of this chapter.

Taxation and the Press   The First Amendment guarantees that the press shall be free from unfair and discriminatory taxes which have an impact upon circulation or distribution. In this area the classic case concerns a United States senator from a southern state and the daily press of that state (*Grosjean* v. *American Press Co.,* 1936).

During the late 1920s and early 1930s the political leader of Louisiana was Huey P. Long. Long was a demagogue by most accounts and in 1934 held his state in virtual dictatorship. He controlled the legislature and the state house and had a deep impact upon the judicial branch as well. Long started his career by attacking big business—Standard Oil of California, to be exact. He became a folk hero among the rural people of Louisiana and was elected governor in 1928. In 1931 he was elected to the United States Senate, and many people believe that he would have attempted to win the presidency had he not been assassinated in 1935.

In 1934 the Long political machine, which the majority of the big-city residents had never favored, became annoyed at the frequent attacks by the state's daily newspapers against the senator and his political machine. The legislature enacted a special 2 percent tax on the gross advertising income of newspapers with a circulation of more than 20,000. Of the 163 newspapers in the state, only 13 had more than 20,000 subscribers, and of the 13, 12 were outspoken in their opposition to Long. The newspapers went to court and argued that the tax violated the First Amendment as well as other constitutional guarantees. The press won at the circuit court level on other grounds, but the state appealed. Then in 1936 the Supreme Court ruled in favor of the newspapers squarely on First Amendment grounds.

The state of Louisiana argued that the English common law, which it claimed the American courts had adopted after the Revolution, conferred the right to tax newspapers and license them if need be upon the government. Justice George Sutherland, who wrote the opinion in this unanimous Supreme Court decision, said however that such taxes upon newspapers were the direct cause of much civil unrest in England and were one of the chief objections Americans had to British policy—objections which ultimately forced independence.

The justice wrote:

> It is impossible to concede that by the words "freedom of the press" the framers of the amendment intended to adopt merely the narrow view then reflected by the law of England that such freedom consisted in immunity from previous censorship. . . . It is equally impossible to believe that it was not intended to bring within the reach of these words such modes of restraint as were embodied in . . . taxation."

Sutherland asserted that the tax not only restricted the amount of revenue the paper earned, but also restrained circulation. Newspapers with less than 20,000 readers would be reluctant to seek new subscribers for fear of increasing circulation to the point where they would have to pay the tax as well. The justice added that any action by the government which prevents free and general discussion of public matters is a kind of censorship. Sutherland said that in this case even the form in which the tax was imposed—levied against a distinct group of newspapers—was suspicious. He then wrote:

> The tax here involved is bad not because it takes money from the pockets of the appellees [the newspapers]. If that were all, a wholly different question would be presented. It is bad because, in the light of its history and of its present setting, it is seen to be a deliberate and calculated device in the guise of a tax to limit

the circulation of information to which the public is entitled in virtue of the constitutional guaranties. A free press stands as one of the great interpreters between the government and the people. To allow it to be fettered is to fetter ourselves.

Therefore in *Grosjean* v. *American Press Co.,* the Supreme Court struck down a discriminatory tax against the press. An interesting footnote to the case concerns the opinion. Justice Sutherland's opinion is one of the most eloquent ever penned in defense of free expression. The justice was not normally such an articulate spokesman. What happened in this case? Speculation is that Sutherland's opinion incorporates a concurring opinion by Justice Benjamin Cardozo, perhaps the greatest writer to ever serve on the Court, and the eloquence of the *Grosjean* opinion is really Cardozo's, not Sutherland's.

Despite the fact that Justice Sutherland specifically noted in his opinion that the ruling in *Grosjean* did not mean that newspapers are immune from ordinary taxes, some newspaper publishers apparently did not read the opinion that way, but saw it instead as a means of escaping other kinds of taxes. After *Grosjean,* for example, unsuccessful attempts were made to have a sales tax in Arizona declared inapplicable to newspapers because it was a restriction on freedom of the press (*Arizona Publishing Co.* v. *O'Neil,* 1938). Since 1953 when the United States Supreme Court refused to hear an appeal from a California decision affirming the constitutionality of a general business tax on newspapers, the matter has been fairly well settled. The California case involved the *Corona Daily Independent* which challenged a business tax imposed by the city of Corona. A license tax of thirty-two dollars had been levied for many years against all businesses. In 1953 the newspaper refused to pay the levy on the grounds that the tax violated its First Amendment rights to freedom of expression. The *Grosjean* case prohibited such taxation, lawyers for the publication argued. The trial court ruled in favor of the newspaper, but the California Appellate Court disagreed and reversed the ruling (*City of Corona* v. *Corona Daily Independent,* 1953). Justice Griffin wrote that there is ample authority to the effect that newspapers are not made exempt from ordinary forms of taxation. Justice Griffin said that the newspaper had not shown that the amount of the tax was harsh or arbitrary, that the tax was oppressive or confiscatory, or that the tax in any way curtailed or abridged the newspaper's right to disseminate news and comment:

> We conclude that a nondiscriminatory tax, levied upon the doing of business, for the sole purpose of maintaining the municipal government, without whose municipal services and protection the press could neither exist nor function, must be sustained as being within the purview and necessary implications of the Constitution and its amendments.

The United States Supreme Court refused to review the ruling in *City of Corona* v. *Corona Daily Independent,* and most people believed the refusal signaled concurrence with the opinion of the California court.

But in 1983 the U.S. Supreme Court did review an unusual tax placed on a handful of Minnesota newspapers. Since 1971 Minnesota had imposed a use tax on the cost of the paper and ink products consumed in the production of a publication. The law was amended in 1974 to exempt the first $100,000 worth of paper and ink used from the tax. After the exemption was adopted, only about fifteen newspapers in the state were forced to pay the tax. And the Minneapolis Star and Tribune Company ended up paying about two-thirds of all the revenues collected under the tax. The Star and Tribune Company challenged the tax, and in March 1983 the high Court ruled that the levy against the newspapers was invalid.

Justice Sandra O'Connor described the tax as a "special tax that applies only to certain publications protected by the First Amendment." She added: "A power to tax differentially, as opposed to a power to tax generally, gives a government a powerful weapon against the taxpayer selected." Such a tax could be used to censor the press, a clear violation of the First Amendment. The tax law is also deficient because it ends up hitting only a few of the newspapers in the state. "Whatever the motive of the legislature in this case," Justice O'Connor wrote for court's majority, "we think that recognizing a power in the State not only to single out the press but also to tailor the tax so it singles out a few members of the press presents such a potential for abuse that no interest suggested by Minnesota can justify the scheme" (*Minneapolis Star* v. *Minnesota Commissioner of Revenue,* 1983).

The basic rule of First Amendment law regarding taxes on the press is this: Newspapers, broadcasting stations, and other mass media must pay the same taxes as any other business. Taxes which are levied only against the press and tend to inhibit circulation or impose other kinds of prior restraints (such as very high taxes which keep all but very wealthy people from publishing newspapers) are unconstitutional.

Regulation of the commercial aspects of the mass media is not new. Yet surely as the media continue to grow as giant businesses and more and more take on the configuration of modern American industry, commercial regulation will increase. The Chief Justice of the United States suggested as much in 1978 in a concurring opinion in the case of *First National Bank of Boston* v. *Bellotti*. The case involved a Massachusetts state law which forbade banks and corporations from making contributions or expenditures for the purpose of "influencing or affecting the vote on any question submitted to the voters." The Court struck down the statute as running afoul of the First Amendment. Chief Justice Burger noted in his concurrence:

> A disquieting aspect of Massachusetts's position is that it may carry the risk of impinging on the First Amendment rights of those who employ the corporate form—as most do—to carry on the business of mass communications, particularly large media conglomerates. This is so because of the difficulty, and

perhaps impossibility, of distinguishing, either as a matter of fact or constitutional law, media corporations from corporations such as the appellants [a bank] in this case.

John Oakes, editorial page editor of the *New York Times,* noted that Burger's opinion "may lead to a questioning of the need for special protection of the press as such, under a First Amendment that was in fact designed to insure the free flow of information and opinion, and not the accretion of corporate power." Oakes added, during a speech at the 1978 Conference on Media and the Public at the Washington Journalism Center, that the growth of concentration of the ownership of the media into fewer hands could lead to a grave dislocation between the press and the public:

> The quality of the product turned out by the conglomerates' publishing and broadcasting arms may be less important in the long run than the loss of public confidence in the press engendered by fears of "the sinister effect of riches" upon the institution of the press.

Oakes added that he feared that public disillusionment with the press could even adversely influence the judiciary's normal strong adherence to the guarantees of a free press.

Summary

Mass media businesses are regulated by the government just like any other businesses, and the First Amendment offers no special protection from such regulation.

The government has brought many antitrust actions against mass media companies. Action by the justice department against newspapers has focused upon industry rules which limit the profitable entry into the newspaper business (the *AP* case) and upon discriminatory newspaper advertising and circulation rules. Antitrust law has been found to be largely ineffective to block the growth of vast chains of newspapers, but has been used to stop concentration of ownership of newspapers in specific local areas. Congress adopted the Newspaper Preservation Act in 1970 which permits monopolistic joint-operating agreements between newspapers in situations where one of the two papers is in danger of failing without such a cost-saving agreement. The law has been ruled to be constitutional by the federal courts.

The government has not used antitrust laws against the concentration of ownership in broadcast because the Federal Communications Commission has adopted ownership rules which limit such concentration, but many of these rules are currently under examination at the FCC and may be abandoned. The government has, however, forced the television networks to stop monopolizing the programs shown in prime time. It has also forced abandonment of industry codes which artificially increased the demand for advertising time on television.

Antitrust actions against the film industry in the late forties forced the major film production studios to sell off their chains of motion-picture theaters and prohibited them from such discriminatory practices as block booking the films they distributed.

While the courts have ruled that newspapers cannot be subject to discriminatory taxes which have the tendency to restrain circulation, publishers and broadcasters are expected to pay normal business taxes. The First Amendment cannot be raised as a bar to such levys.

BIBLIOGRAPHY

Here is a list of some of the sources that have been helpful in the preparation of chapter 12.

Books

Compaine, Benjamin M., ed. *Who Owns the Media?* White Plains, N. Y.: Knowledge Industry Publications, 1979.

Gerald, J. Edward. *The Press and the Constitution.* Minneapolis: University of Minnesota Press, 1948.

Higham, Charles. *Hollywood at Sunset.* New York: Saturday Review Press, 1972.

Oppenheim, S. Chesterfield, and Shields, Carrington. *Newspapers and Antitrust Laws.* Charlottesville, Va.: Michie Company, 1981.

Articles

Roach, Catherine B. "Media Conglomerates, Anti-Trust Law, and the Marketplace of Ideas." 9 *Memphis State University Law Review* 257, 1979.

Cases

AP v. *NLRB*, 301 U.S. 130 (1937).

AP v. *U.S.*, 326 U.S. 1 (1945).

Arizona Publishing Co. v. *O'Neil*, 22 F. Supp. 117, affd. 304 U.S. 543 (1938).

Bay Guardian Publishing Company v. *Chronicle Publishing Company*, 344 F. Supp. 1155 (1972).

City of Corona v. *Corona Daily Independent*, 252 P.2d 56 (1953).

Committee for an Independent P–I v. *Hearst*, 9 M. L. Rept. 1489 (1983).

Committee v. *Smith*, 549 F. Supp. 985 (1982).

FCC v. *National Citizens Committee for Broadcasting*, 436 U.S. 775 (1978).

First National Bank of Boston v. *Bellotti*, 98 S.Ct. 1407 (1978).

Grosjean v. *American Press Co.*, 297 U.S. 233 (1936).

Lorain Journal Co. v. *U.S.*, 342 U.S. 143 (1951).

Minneapolis Star v. *Minnesota Commissioner of Revenue*, 9 M. L. Rept. 1369 (1983).

National Citizens Committee for Broadcasting v. *FCC*, 555 F.2d 938 (1977).

Times-Picayune v. *U.S.*, 345 U.S. 594 (1953).

U.S. v. *Citizen Publishing Co.*, 394 U.S. 131 (1969).

U.S. v. *City* Star, 240 F.2d 643 (1957).

U.S. v. *Loew's, Inc.*, 371 U.S. 38 (1962).

U.S. v. *NAB*, 536 F. Supp. 149 (1982).

U.S. v. *Nanlo*, 7 M. L. Rept. 1950 (1981).

U.S. v. *Paramount Pictures*, 334 U.S. 131 (1948).

U.S. v. *Times-Mirror Corp.*, 274 F. Supp. 607 (1967); affd. 390 U.S. 712 (1968).

GLOSSARY

absolute privilege An immunity from libel suits granted to government officials and others based on remarks uttered or written as part of their official duties.

absolutist theory The proposition that the First Amendment is an absolute, and that government may adopt no laws whatsoever which abridge freedom of expression.

actual damages Damages awarded to a plaintiff in a lawsuit based upon proof of actual harm to the plaintiff.

actual malice A fault standard in libel law: knowledge before publication that the libelous material was false, or reckless disregard of the truth or falsity of the libelous matter.

administrative agency An agency created and funded by the Congress, whose members are appointed by the president, and whose function it is to administer specific legislation such as law regulating broadcasting and advertising.

admonition to a jury Instructions from a judge to a trial jury to avoid talking to other persons about the trial they are hearing, and to avoid news broadcasts and newspaper or magazine stories that discuss the case or issues in the case.

Alien and Sedition Laws of 1798 Laws adopted by the Federalist Congress aimed at stopping criticism of the national government by Republican or Jeffersonian editors and politicians.

amici curiae "Friends of the court"; persons who have no legal right to take part in a lawsuit, but are allowed to appear on behalf of one of the parties in a case.

appellant The party who initiates or takes the appeal of a case from one court to another.

appellate court(s) A court which has both original and appellate jurisdiction; a court to which cases are removed for an appeal.

appellee The person in a case against whom the appeal is taken; that is, the party in the suit who is not making the appeal.

appropriation In the law of privacy, use of a person's name or likeness without consent for advertising or trade purposes.

arraignment The first official court appearance made by a criminal defendant at which he is formally charged with an offense and called upon to plead guilty or not guilty to the charges contained in the state's indictment or information.

ascertainment A procedure established by the Federal Communications Commission which instructs broadcast licensees in the manner in which they are to determine important problems and issues in a community.

bait-and-switch advertising An illegal advertising strategy in which the seller baits an advertisement with a low-priced model of a product, but then switches customers who seek to buy the product to a much higher-priced model by telling them that the cheaper model does not work well or is no longer in stock.

bench-bar-press guidelines Informal agreements among lawyers, judges, police officials, and journalists about what should and should not be published or broadcast about a criminal suspect or criminal case before a trial is held.

block booking An illegal scheme in which a motion-picture distributor requires a theater owner to book a poor film in order to book a popular film.

bond; bonding A large sum of money given by a publisher to a government to be held to ensure good behavior. Should the publisher violate a government rule, the bond is forfeited to the government, and the newspaper or magazine cannot be published again until a new bond is posted.

candidate access rule Section 312 of the Federal Communications Act which forbids a broadcaster from instituting an across-the-board policy which denies all candidates for federal office the opportunity to use the station to further a political campaign.

case reporter(s) A book (or books) which contains a chronological collection of the opinions rendered by a particular court for cases which were decided by the court.

cease and desist order An order issued by a court requiring the cessation of a particular behavior or practice.

challenge for cause The request by a litigant in a criminal or civil case that a juror be dismissed for a specific reason.

change of venue Moving a trial to a distant community in order to find jurors who have not read or viewed prejudicial publicity about the defendant.

citation The reference to a legal opinion contained in a case reporter which gives the name, volume number, and page number where the opinion can be found. The year the opinion was rendered is also included in the citation.

civil complaint A written statement of the plaintiff's legal grievance which normally initiates a civil suit.

civil contempt That variety of contempt of court in which the act of disrespect or disobedience is aimed at one of the parties in the lawsuit, rather than at the court itself.

commercial speech doctrine The legal doctrine which states that truthful advertising for products and services which are not illegal is normally protected by the First Amendment to the United States Constitution.

common law Principles and rules of law which derive their authority not from legislation but from community usage and custom.

comparative license hearing A hearing to evaluate potential licensees when two or more persons seek the same broadcast license, as required by a Federal Communications Commission rule.

concurring opinion A written opinion by an appellate judge or justice in which the author agrees with the decision of the court, but normally states reasons different from those in the court opinion as the basis for his or her decision.

consent A defense in both libel and invasion of privacy cases which provides that individuals who agree to the publication of a libelous story or the appropriation of their name cannot then maintain a lawsuit based upon the libel or the appropriation.

consent order or decree A document in which an individual agrees to terminate a specific behavior such as an advertising campaign or to refrain from a specific action such as making a certain advertising claim.

constitution A written outline of the organization of a government which provides for both the rights and responsibilities of various branches of the government and the limits of the power of the government.

contempt of court An act of disobedience or disrespect to a judge which may be punished by a fine or jail sentence.

continuance The delay of a trial or hearing, that is, the trial is postponed.

copyright That body of law which protects the works created by writers, painters, photographers, performing artists, inventors, and other persons who create immaterial property.

copyright notice The words "© Copyright, 1985, by Don R. Pember" which indicate to a user that a work is copyrighted by the author or creator.

corrective advertising scheme Rules established by the Federal Trade Commission that require an advertiser to correct the false impressions left by deceptive advertising in a certain percentage of future advertisements.

court of chancery A specific court maintained in some jurisdictions that administers only the law of equity.

court's opinion The official opinion of an appellate court that states the reasons or rationale for a decision.

criminal contempt That variety of contempt of court in which the act of disrespect or disobedience is aimed directly at the court.

criminal history privacy laws State laws which limit the access of non-law enforcement personnel to criminal records maintained by states.

criminal libel A libel against the state, or against the dead, or against a large, ill-defined group (such as a race) in which the state prosecutes the libel on behalf of the injured parties.

criminal suit A legal action brought by the state against an individual or group of individuals for violating state criminal laws.

criminal syndicalism laws Laws which outlaw advocacy, planning, or processes aimed at establishing the control over industry by workers or trade unions.

damages Money awarded to the winning party in a civil lawsuit.

defamation Any communication which holds a person up to contempt, hatred, ridicule, or scorn and lowers the reputation of the individual defamed.

defendant The person against whom relief or recovery is sought in a civil lawsuit; the individual against whom a state criminal action is brought.

demurrer An allegation made by the defendant in a lawsuit that even if the facts as stated by the plaintiff are true they do not state a sufficient cause for action.

devisable right A right which may be passed on to an heir.

Dickinson Rule A rule eminating from a decision by the Fifth United States Court of Appeals which states that even a patently unconstitutional court order must be obeyed until it is overturned by an appellate court.

dicta Remarks in a court opinion which do not speak directly to the legal point in question.

direct appeal The statutorily granted right of an aggrieved party to carry the appeal of a case to the Supreme Court of the United States. The high Court can deny this right if the appeal lacks a substantial federal question.

direct criminal contempt A criminal contempt that is committed in the presence of the court, that is, in the courtroom or near the courtroom.

dissenting opinion A written opinion by a judge or justice who disagrees with the appellate court's decision in a case.

en banc; sitting en banc A French term to describe all the justices or judges of an appellate court sitting together to hear a case. This situation is the opposite of the more typical situation in which a small group (called a panel) of judges or justices in a particular court hears a case.

Equal Time Rule Section 315 of the Federal Communications Act which states that when broadcasters permit a legally qualified candidate for elective office to use their broadcasting facilities all other legally qualified candidates for the same elective office must be given the similar opportunity.

equity A system of jurisprudence, distinct from the common law, in which courts are empowered to decide cases upon the basis of equity or fairness and are not bound by the rigid precedents which often exist in the common law.

Espionage Act A law adopted by the Congress in 1917 which outlawed criticism of the United States government and its participation in World War I in Europe.

executive privilege An asserted common law privilege of the president and other executives to keep presidential papers, records, and other documents secret, even from the Congress.

executive session a popular euphemism for a closed meeting held by a government body such as a city council or school board.

fair comment A libel defense which protects the publication of libelous opinion which focuses upon the public activities of a person acting in a public sphere.

Fairness Doctrine A Federal Communications Commission rule which requires that broadcasters devote a reasonable portion of broadcast time to the discussion of important public issues, and that the coverage of these issues be fair in the sense that all important contrasting views on the issues are presented.

fair use A provision of the copyright law which permits a limited amount of copying of material that has been properly copyrighted.

false light That portion of privacy law which prohibits all publication or broadcast which falsely portrays an individual in an offensive manner.

FCC See Federal Communications Commission.

Federal Communications Act The law, adopted in 1934, which is the foundation for the regulation of broadcasting in the United States.

Federal Communications Commission A five-member body appointed by the president whose function is to administer the federal broadcasting and communications laws.

Federal Open Meetings Law (Government in Sunshine Act) A federal law that requires approximately fifty federal agencies and bureaus to hold all their meetings in public, unless a subject under discussion is included within one of the ten exemptions contained in the statute.

Federal Trade Commission A five-member body appointed by the president whose function it is to administer the federal laws relating to advertising, antitrust, and many other business matters.

Fighting Words Doctrine A legal doctrine which permits prior censorship of words which create a clear and present danger of inciting an audience to disorder or violence.

FOIA See Freedom of Information Act.

Freedom of Information Act A federal law which mandates that all the records created and kept by federal agencies in the executive branch of government must be open for public inspection and copying, except those records which fall into one of nine exempted categories listed in the statute.

FTC See Federal Trade Commission.

gag order(s) A restrictive court order which prohibits all or some participants in a trial from speaking about a case, or which stops publications and broadcasting stations from reporting on certain aspects of a case.

Government in Sunshine Act See Federal Open Meetings Law.

grand jury A jury whose function it is to determine whether sufficient evidence exists to issue an indictment or true bill charging an individual or individuals with a crime and to take such persons to trial. It is called a grand jury because it has more members than a petit or trial jury.

identification As used in a libel suit, the requirement that the plaintiff prove that at least one person believes that the subject of the libelous remarks is the plaintiff and not some other person.

impeachment A criminal proceeding against a public officer which is started by written "articles of impeachment" and followed by a trial. The House of Representatives, for example, can issue articles of impeachment against the president, who is then tried by the Senate.

indictment A written accusation issued by a grand jury charging that an individual, or individuals, has committed a specific crime and should be taken to trial.

indirect criminal contempt A criminal contempt committed outside the presence of the court, that is, not in the courtroom or near the courtroom.

information A written accusation issued by a public officer rather than by a grand jury charging that an individual, or individuals, has committed a specific crime and should be taken to trial.

innocent construction rule A state libel rule which requires a judge or jury to read allegedly defamatory material in a nondefamatory way if possible.

intrusion An invasion of privacy committed when one individual intrudes upon or invades the solitude of another individual.

invasion of privacy A civil tort which emerged in the early twentieth century and contains four distinct categories of legal wrongs: appropriation, intrusion, publication of private facts, and false light.

joint-operating agreement An exemption to the federal antitrust law which permits two newspapers in a community to merge advertising, circulation, and printing functions, but maintain separate editorial departments.

judgment of the court The final ruling of a court which determines the outcome of a lawsuit. It is different from the verdict, which is the decision of the jury in a trial.

judicial decree A judgment of a court of equity; a declaration of the court announcing the legal consequences of the facts found to be true by the court.

judicial instructions A statement (often written) made by a judge to the members of a jury informing them about the law (as distinguished from the facts) in a case.

judicial review The power of a court to declare void and unenforceable any statute, rule, or executive order that conflicts with an appropriate state constitution or the federal constitution.

jury A group of men and women called together in a trial court to determine the facts in a civil or criminal lawsuit. It is sometimes called a petit jury to distinguish it from a grand jury.

legal brief(s) (brief) Written legal argument presented to the court by one or both parties in a lawsuit.

libel Published or broadcast communication which lowers the reputation of an individual by holding him or her up to contempt, ridicule, or scorn.

licensing process The process by which a government gives a publisher or a broadcaster prior permission to print a newspaper or operate a broadcasting station. Revocation of a license can be used as punishment for failing to comply with the law or the wishes of the government. Licensing of the printed press in the United States ended in the 1720s.

litigant A party in a lawsuit; a participant in litigation.

memorandum order The announcement by an appellate court of a decision in a case that does not include a written opinion containing the rationale or reasons for the ruling.

misappropriation Taking what belongs to someone else and using it unfairly for one's own gain; for example, attempting to pass off a novel as part of a popular series of novels written and published by someone else. It is often called unfair competition.

Missouri Plan A system used in some states by which judges are appointed to the bench initially and then must stand for reelection on a ballot that permits citizens to vote to retain or not retain the judge.

NAD See next entry.

National Advertising Division (NAD) of the Council of Better Business Bureaus. An industry organization which evaluates and rules upon the truthfulness of advertising claims. Complaints are normally brought to the NAD by competing advertisers.

negligence A fault standard in libel and other tort law. Negligent behavior is normally described as an act or action that a reasonably prudent person or a reasonable individual would not have committed. In libel law courts often measure negligence by asking whether the allegedly libelous material was the work of a person who exercised reasonable care in preparation of the story.

neutral reportage An emerging libel defense or privilege which states that it is permissible to publish or broadcast an accurate account of information about a public figure from a reliable source even when the reporter doubts the truth of the libelous assertion. The defense is not widely accepted.

nonjusticiable matter An issue that is inappropriate for a court to decide because the jurists lack the knowledge to make the ruling, or because another branch of government has the responsibility to answer such questions, or because a court order in the matter would not likely be enforceable or enforced.

open meetings laws State and federal statutes that require that certain meetings of public agencies—normally in the executive branch of government—be open to the public and the press.

open records laws State and federal statutes that require that certain records of public agencies—normally in the executive branch of government—be open for inspection and copying by the public and the press.

opinion The written statement issued by a court that explains the reasons for a judgment and states the rule of law in the case.

oral argument An oral presentation made to a judge or justices in which the litigants argue the merits of their case.

original jurisdiction Jurisdiction in the first instance, as distinguished from appellate jurisdiction. A court exercising original jurisdiction determines both the facts and the law in the case; courts exercising appellate jurisdiction may only rule upon the law and the sufficiency of the facts as determined by a trial court.

pandering The business of purveying textual or graphic material openly advertised to appeal to the erotic interest of customers. This criterion is sometimes used in obscenity prosecution to determine whether the material in question is obscene.

per curiam opinion An unsigned court opinion. The author of the opinion is not known outside the court.

peremptory challenge A challenge without stated cause to remove a juror from a panel. Litigants are given a small number of such challenges in a lawsuit.

personal attack rules Specific rules issued by the Federal Communications Commission which outline the responsibilities of a broadcast licensee if and when an attack upon an individual or identifiable group is made during a radio or television broadcast. The licensee must inform the individual or group of the attack and provide an opportunity for a reply, among other requirements.

petitioner One who petitions a court to take an action; someone who starts a lawsuit, or carries an appeal to a higher court (appellant). This person is the opposite of a respondent, one who responds to a petition.

plaintiff An individual who initiates a civil lawsuit.

pleadings The written statements of the parties in a lawsuit which contain their allegations, denials, and defenses.

precedent An established rule of law set by a previous case. Courts should follow precedent when it is advisable and possible.

preferred position theory A theory on how the First Amendment should be interpreted which states that when the guarantees of freedom of speech and freedom of the press are balanced against other important rights the rights of freedom of expression are to be given extra weight, to be preferred. Legally this proposition requires that persons who would restrict freedom of expression bear the burden of proving that such restrictions are justified and not a violation of the First Amendment.

pretrial hearing A meeting prior to a criminal trial at which attorneys for the state and for the defense make arguments before a judge on evidentiary questions, that is, whether a confession made by the defendant should be admitted as evidence at the trial. This type of hearing is sometimes called a suppression hearing.

Printers' ink statute A model law drafted in 1911 to control false or misleading advertising. Most states adopted some version of this model in the early twentieth century. Such laws are largely ineffective because they are not normally enforced.

prior restraint Prepublication censorship that forbids publication or broadcast or certain objectionable material, as opposed to punishment of a perpetrator after the material was published or broadcast.

Privacy Act A federal statute which forbids the disclosure of specific material held by federal agencies on the grounds that its release could invade the privacy of the subject of the report or document.

publication In libel law, exposing an allegedly libelous statement to one person in addition to the subject of the libel.

publication of private information In privacy law, publicizing embarrassing private information about an individual which is not of legitimate public concern.

puffery Often expansive hyperbole about a product which does not contain factual claims of merit. Normally puffery is permitted by the law (e.g., this is the best-looking automobile on the market today).

punitive damages Money damages awarded to a plaintiff in a lawsuit aimed not to compensate for harm to the injured party, but to punish the defendant or his or her illegal conduct.

qualified privilege In libel law, the privilege of the reporter (or any person) to publish a fair and accurate report of the proceedings of a public meeting or public document and be immune from lawsuit for the publication of libel uttered at the meeting or contained in the document.

Radio Act of 1912 The first federal broadcast law which imposed only minimal regulation on the fledgling broadcast industry. Radio operators were required to have a license under this statute.

Radio Act of 1927 The first comprehensive national broadcast law which provided the basic framework for the regulation of broadcast which was later adopted in the Communications Act of 1934.

reasonable access rule See Candidate Access Rule.

reporter-source privilege The privilege asserted by a reporter to shield the identity of the source of confidential information used in a news story.

respondent The person who responds to a petition placed before a court by another person; the opposite of the petitioner. At the appellate level, the respondent is often called the appellee.

restrictive order A court order limiting the discussion of the facts in a criminal case by both participants in the case and by the press. See also Gag Order.

retraction In libel law, a statement published or broadcast which attempts to retract or correct previously published or broadcast libelous matter. A timely retraction will usually mitigate damages, and in some states which have retraction laws, plaintiffs must seek a retraction before beginning a lawsuit or they lose the ability to collect anything but special damages.

right of publicity An offshoot of privacy law which protects the right of persons to capitalize upon their fame or notoriety for commercial or advertising purposes.

right of reply A little used libel defense which declares as immune from a lawsuit a libelous remark made against an individual in reply to a previously published libelous remark made by that individual.

Section 312 See candidate access rule.

Section 315 See equal time rule.

Sedition Act of 1918 An amendment to the Espionage Act adopted in the midst of World War I which severely limited criticism of the government and criticism of United States participation in the European war.

seditious libel Libeling the government; criticizing the government or government officers. It is sometimes called sedition.

sequestration of the jury Separating the jury from the community during a trial. Usually a jury is lodged at a hotel and members are required to eat together. In general, sequestration means to keep jurors away from other persons. The exposure of the jury to news reports is also screened to shield jurors from news reports about the trial.

Seven-Seven-Seven Rule A federal regulation which forbids any single individual or corporation from owning more than seven FM-radio stations, seven AM-radio stations, and seven television stations.

shield laws State statutes which permit reporters in some circumstances to shield the name of a confidential news source when questioned by a grand jury or in another legal forum.

single mistake rule In libel law, a rule which states that it is not libelous to accuse a professional person or business person of making a single mistake (e.g., Dr. Alan Jones incorrectly diagnosed the patient's illness).

slander Oral defamation.

Smith Act A federal law adopted in 1940 which makes it illegal to advocate the violent overthrow of the government.

special damages Damages which can be awarded to a plaintiff in a lawsuit upon proof of specific monetary loss.

stare decisis "Let the decision stand." This concept is the operating principal in the common law system and requires that judges follow precedent case law when making judgments.

statute of limitations A law which requires that a legal action must begin within a specified period of time (usually one to three years for a civil case) after the legal wrong was committed.

statutes Laws adopted by legislative bodies.

statutory construction The process undertaken by courts to interpret or construe the meaning of statutes.

strict liability A doctrine in tort law which declares that a defendant is liable for even an unintentional and nonnegligent act that causes harm to a plaintiff. Libel law was formerly governed by the doctrine of strict liability.

subpoena A court document that requires a witness to appear and testify or to produce documents or papers pertinent to a pending controversy.

substantiation A Federal Trade Commission rule which requires an advertiser to prove the truth of advertising claims made about a product or service.

summary contempt power The power of a judge to find an individual guilty of a contempt of court and impose a sentence without giving the individual the benefit of a jury trial.

summary judgment A judgment granted to a party in a lawsuit when the pleadings and other materials in the case disclose no material issue of fact between the parties, making it possible for the case to be decided on the basis of the law by the court. A summary judgment avoids a costly jury trial.

time, place, and manner restrictions or rules Rules, when justified by a substantial government interest, that can regulate the time, place, and manner of speaking or publishing and distribution of printed material.

trade libel Product disparagement, and not considered true libel; disparaging a product as opposed to the manufacturer or maker of the product.

trade regulation rules Rules adopted by the Federal Trade Commission which prohibit specific advertising claims about an entire class of products. For example, makers of fruit drinks which contains less than 10 percent fruit juice cannot advertise these products as fruit juice.

trespass Unlawful entry upon another person's land or property.

trial court(s) Normally the first court to hear a lawsuit. This court is the forum in which the facts are determined and the law is initially applied, as opposed to an appellate court, to which decisions are appealed.

unfair competition See Misappropriation.

variable obscenity standards A Supreme Court doctrine which permits states to prohibit the sale or distribution or exhibition of certain kinds of nonobscene matter to children, so long as these laws do not interfere with the accessibility of this material to adults.

verdict The decision of a trial jury based upon the instructions given to it by the judge.

voir dire A preliminary examination the court makes of persons chosen to serve as jurors in a trial. Inappropriate persons can be challenged for cause or on the basis of a peremptory challenge by either side in the legal dispute.

writ of certiorari A writ by which an appellant seeks the review of a case by the Supreme Court of the United States. When the writ is granted, the Court will order the lower court to send up the record of the case for review.

Zapple Rule A corollary to the equal time rule which states that when the supporters of a legally qualified candidate are given time on a radio or television broadcast the supporters of all other legally qualified candidates for the same office must also be given equal opportunity.

TABLE OF CASES

INDEX